Shared Stories, Rival Tellings

Shared Stories, Rival Tellings

Early Encounters of Jews, Christians, and Muslims

Robert C. Gregg

OXFORD

UNIVERSITY PRESS

OXFORD
UNIVERSITY PRESS

Oxford University Press is a department of the University of
Oxford. It furthers the University's objective of excellence in research,
scholarship, and education by publishing worldwide.

Oxford   New York
Auckland   Cape Town   Dar es Salaam   Hong Kong   Karachi
Kuala Lumpur   Madrid   Melbourne   Mexico City   Nairobi
New Delhi   Shanghai   Taipei   Toronto

With offices in
Argentina   Austria   Brazil   Chile   Czech Republic   France   Greece
Guatemala   Hungary   Italy   Japan   Poland   Portugal   Singapore
South Korea   Switzerland   Thailand   Turkey   Ukraine   Vietnam

Oxford is a registered trademark of Oxford University Press
in the UK and certain other countries.

Published in the United States of America by
Oxford University Press
198 Madison Avenue, New York, NY 10016

Library of Congress Cataloging-in-Publication Data
Gregg, Robert C.
Shared stories, rival tellings : early encounters of Jews, Christians, and Muslims /
Robert C. Gregg.
pages cm
Includes bibliographical references and index.
ISBN 978-0-19-023149-1 (cloth : alk. paper)   1. Bible—Criticism, Narrative.
2. Bible stories.   3. Qur'an—Criticism, interpretation, etc.   4. Bible. Old Testament—
Criticism, interpretation, etc.—Jewish.   5. Bible. New Testament—Criticism, interpretation,
etc.—Jewish.   6. Bible—Islamic interpretations.   7. Bible. Old Testament—Comparative
studies.   8. Bible. New Testament—Comparative studies.   9. Qur'an—Comparative studies.
I. Title.
BS521.7.G74 2015
220.609—dc23
2014047882

1 3 5 7 9 8 6 4 2
Printed in the United States of America
on acid-free paper

To Mary Layne,
in thanks for your
greatness of soul

CONTENTS

ACKNOWLEDGMENTS

More years ago than I want to count, Mary Layne suggested that for an audience associated with Stanford's Hopkins Marine Station laboratory I might put together a talk about Jonah; in doing so, she sparked an incentive for this comparative study of sacred stories in the two Bibles and the Qur'an.

Throughout a decade of seminars on sacred stories told three ways, students at Stanford surfaced fascinating things large and small in the texts we pondered. To my benefit, they developed strong skills in detecting, as they put it, "what drives the story."

I am wonderfully fortunate in having scholarly friends who were willing to do close, critical readings of all or parts of this book: Shahzad Bashir, Charlotte Fonrobert, Dennis Groh, Bruce Lawrence, Rebecca Lyman-Bridges, Behnam Sadeghi, Will Sherman, and Steven Weitzman. At critical junctures Ahmad Dallal, Robin Margaret Jensen, Jane Dammen McAuliffe, miriam cooke, Emine Fetvaci, Ebrahim Moosa, Azim Nanji, Gülru Necipoğlu, and Bissera Pentcheva were expert consultants—explaining particular issues and pointing me toward new queries and additional sources.

Particular help with translation challenges came from Kavous Barghi, Patricia Karlin-Neumann, Hesaam Esfandyarpour, and Stephen Hinton, in addition to several of those mentioned above. I received masterful guidance from people in Stanford's Green Library—Rodrigo Muñoz, James Jacobs, Christopher Matson, and Ronnie Fields, and from my colleague Burcak Keskin-Kozat of the Sohaib and Sara Abbasi Program in Islamic Studies.

I am grateful to several volunteer reader-critics of parts of the manuscript—in particular Philip Getchell, Reb and Marilyn Gregg, Dennis Phillips, and Jeff and Carson Howard, who proved to be properly candid.

Cynthia Read and Marcela Maxfield of Oxford University Press ably managed the editing and preparation of the manuscript for publication.

The larger Gregg clan—our children and their families—and a number of close friends who knew about the book only that it was greatly occupying me gave genuine and happy sustenance along the way. They and all named above will, I hope, count themselves contributors to this volume.

NOTE ON CITATIONS

Titles of Jewish, Christian and Muslim primary sources are given in English, with accompanying references to English translations given in the notes. Exceptions to this practice are few. Biblical writings are cited by their books' titles, followed by chapter and verse notations (e.g., *Genesis* 21:1–7) Surah numbers identify passages in the Qur'an, often followed by the Surah's name in English (e.g., Surah 19 (Maryam)). References to the Talmudic passages—for example, *Talmud Tractate Sanhedrin* 106—are (except when otherwise noted) to the Babylonian Talmud.

PROLOGUE

How are we to picture the early encounters of Jews, Christians, and Muslims—the character of their culture contacts? In pursuit of this question, I soon came to wonder how significant were discussions and debates over the meanings of shared scriptural narratives in the interactions among the three religious communities, and in the development of differences between them.

Judaism, Christianity, and Islam arose as book-centered religions, their holy writings consisting in revelations from and about the deity of their experience. However, a more integral and often overlooked connection exists. Narrated in the Hebrew Bible, the Christian Bible, and the Qur'an were over two dozen sacred stories featuring the same cast of characters (for instance, Adam and Eve, Noah, Abraham, Lot, Moses, Samuel, kings David and Solomon, Job, and such prophets as Elijah, Elisha, and Jonah). The two scriptures of the Christians and Muslims shared additional holy narratives—most notably the stories of the prophet John the baptist, and of Jesus and Mary.

Conceiving this study as a comparison of the three religions' scriptural interpretations, I chose five (from the available twenty-seven) narratives: Cain's murder of Abel, his brother; the clash between Abraham's two women, Sarah and Hagar; Joseph the young Hebrew slave in Egypt, tormented by the sexual advances of the wife of his master; the disobedient prophet Jonah and the whale; and the saga of Mary, Jesus's mother (though it appears only in the Christian New Testament and the Qur'an). My intent was to observe carefully the overlap of traditions and to focus especially on how Jews, Christians, and Muslims differently heard, read, and used these sacred stories. How did the interpreters retell them, using story expansions and noticeable twists in order to advance their own communal interests—that is, their distinguishing doctrines, ethics, ritual practices, and modes of spirituality?

Within each of these three book religions were to be found specialists in scripture interpretation: scholar-teachers trained to make line-by-line explanatory comment on their respective holy writings, as well as moralists, preachers, and storytellers. Artists, too, were story interpreters, their ideas and insights coming to expression through imagery in paintings, mosaics, tapestries, and sculpted stones and ivories.

Throughout the book's chapters and in the epilogue I shall advance a thesis about the role of scripture interpreters. These exegetes and commentators participated in each religion's development of its own distinctiveness in belief, worship, and thought, and, at the same time, contributed strongly to the differentiation and distance between the three faith communities.

My attraction to this period of religious and cultural history followed naturally upon a long-time concentration on religious competition in the ancient Mediterranean—namely, the subject of Jews, Christians, and Greco-Roman polytheists (pagans) in their social, political, and intellectual interactions during the opening centuries of the Common Era. Drawn to the "new" multireligious dynamics that occurred when Islam arose in the 620s CE, I shifted my focus from the late Roman era, leaving the pagans behind, and began gathering information about initial relations between the three self-declared monotheistic peoples. What would be involved, I soon realized, was a history in two phases. From the first century on, Jews and Christians were in continuous dialogue over scriptures. This became a trialogue when, in the seventh century, the Muslims arrived on the scene with their Qur'an. The rich range of literature and art presented in this book—all of it concerned with the ongoing interpretation and debate of the five stories—will span the first through the sixteenth centuries.

The three religions' scripture interpreters shared two dominant objectives: maintaining their religious society's sense of uniqueness ("*We are God's elect people!*"), and inspiring that community to stand firm in any altercations with its competitors (the two other "peoples of the book").

An example of the first goal is found in varied Jewish interpretations of the captivating tale of Jonah the prophet. For his resistance to God's command that he go to Nineveh to call its people to repentance, some rabbis faulted Jonah for a jealous nationalism: he was angry that Israel's God might attend to—and possibly forgive—a Gentile population. The theme of Jonah's deficiency required some kind of softening, since he was, after all, a prophet of the Lord. One rabbinic text therefore repaired his honor by adding a new chapter to his life. Confronting in the deep the dreaded sea monster Leviathan, Jonah made a prophetic pledge to capture him and serve his meat as food on the feast day of the messiah's coming. By this added interpretation the prophet was recast as an agent in God's rescue and salvation of the Jews on Judgment Day. Another community-centered use of Jonah's adventures was institutionalized, for reasons worth pondering, in the reading of the *Book of Jonah* at Yom Kippur.

The second objective of interpreters—boundary-drawing and defense of each group's authority—was well-exercised. A prime example suggests itself. Both Jews and Christians believed themselves to be God's elect people by virtue of being children of Abraham—that is, by belonging to the lineage of Abraham through Isaac, Sarah's son. How could the Christians prove that they had superseded the Jews as God's preferred people, and how could Jews refute their arguments? Muslims also called Abraham/Ibrahim their patriarch, but celebrated the heritage stemming from Ishmael, the son of Hagar. Jews and Christians objected: "Your Hagar and Ishmael were disapproved, and sent away!" There was need for three separate family histories, each elaborating upon divine promises received and upon ancestors' marvelous acts. These accounts were not only community-binding but also provided materials for apologetics, for defenses of their claims against competitors' criticisms. This duty, too, fell to each religion's scriptural commentators, storytellers, and artists.

All stories that persist, continuing to be cherished, reread and recited, undergo change. This axiom applies fully to narratives within Muslim, Jewish, and Christian scriptures. Each religious community was aware of its simultaneous tasks of safeguarding its sacred stories *and* of sustaining their vitality through the necessary art of revising and updating their meanings.

Retelling involved a great deal more than minor editorial repairs of gaps or unclear phrases within a biblical or qur'anic text—important though those corrections were. Jewish, Christian, and Muslim artists and commentators sought to discover and expose these narratives' multiple layers of meaning. Their expertise consisted in discerning different types of understanding—from historical to moral to spiritual, or as some Muslims put it, from literal to inner. Fundamental to their labors as interpreters was the shared conviction that their scriptures, inexhaustibly rich and profound, summoned them to ever deeper consciousness of God and of themselves.

The star performers in the chapters that follow are writers, writings, and works of art devoted to interpreting these five stories. These include Jews like the writers Josephus and Philo, compilations of rabbinic traditions in the *Talmud, Midrash Rabbah, Pirke de Rabbi Eliezer*, and treatments of the stories that appear in earliest Jewish art that emerged by the third century. We meet Christian authors Justin Martyr, Origen, John Chrysostom, Ambrose, Augustine, Ephrem the Syrian, and significant pieces of Christian art from the second to the twelfth centuries. Muslim commentators and poets ranging in date from the eighth to the fifteenth century—Ibn Ishaq, al-Tabari, al-Tha`labi, al-Kisa'i, Rumi, and Jami—figure prominently in the chapters that follow, as do important figural paintings found in historians' chronicles and in popular texts telling the *Qisas al-Anbiya*, or Stories of the Prophets.

Scriptural translations used in these pages (unless otherwise noted) are from the Jewish Publication Society's *Tanakh: A New Translation of the Holy Scriptures According to the Traditional Hebrew Text* (1985), *The New Oxford Annotated Bible with Apocrypha: New Revised Standard Version* for the New Testament, and various apocryphal and deuterocanonical writings, and Thomas Cleary's *The Qur'an: A New Translation*, published by Starlatch Press in 2004.

Though lengthy (and in some cases, unresolved) discussions surround the dating of the three communities' scriptures, we may point to conclusions reached by a majority of scholars of the two Bibles and the Qur'an. The Hebrew Bible contains writings that date from ca. 600 BCE (the middle of the First Temple period in Jewish history) to the second century BCE (the *Book of Daniel* refers to events in the 170s). For our purposes—since three of the five scriptural stories are present in their earliest forms in *Genesis*—it is the dating of the Tanakh's initial five books between 600–400 BCE that is most germane. This section of the Bible, understood traditionally to be the five books written by Moses, was referred to as Torah; the same term was later given a much broader sense—the law. The *Book of Jonah*, to which we'll turn our attention in chapter 10, was composed between 500 and 400 BCE.

Another version of the Bible of the Jews was a translation into Greek called the Septuagint. The translation's name and its shorthand signifier, LXX, reflect a pious tradition about the work's miraculous production: seventy translators, isolated from one another, arrived at exactly the same Greek rendering of the Hebrew. Similar lore about the origins of the LXX tells of its production in the third century BCE to serve Greek-speaking Jews in Alexandria. We shall see that Jewish authors writing in Greek, like Philo in the first century CE, were dependent in their writings upon the Septuagint or a related Greek translation of the Hebrew scriptures. The same is shown to be true in Paul's letters and other New Testament books, not to mention subsequent works by Greek fathers of the church. Other translations of the Hebrew scriptures into Aramaic, Latin, and Syriac will be noted at various points within this book.

In strict historical terms, it is misleading to speak of Jews' first contacts with Christians. The initial group of Jesus-followers, not immediately called Christians, emerged as a messianic sect within Judaism. By the end of the first century, however, opposition existed between the great majority of

Jews and those (by this time both Jews and Gentiles) who honored Jesus as their Lord. The twenty-seven writings of what became the Christians' New Testament date from the mid-first century CE to the early years of the second century. Paul's early letters were composed in the 50s CE, and opinions vary concerning the lateness of some of the Gospels, *Revelation*, and certain letters like *2 Peter*. We shall be intrigued—maybe surprised—at the earliest Christian writings' value as interpretations of scripture—that is, of the Bible of the Jews, or what the churches deemed the Old Testament. That is, we find within the New Testament pieces of commentary on the meanings of the stories of Adam's sons, Abraham and his family, Joseph and Potiphar's wife, and Jonah. The case of Mary is of course different, since the narrative about her originates in two of the Gospels.

Early Muslims understood themselves to be distinct from Jews and Christians, whose beliefs and practices were given specific attention in their Holy Book. The Qur'an presents itself as revelations to Muhammad which God commands him to read or recite. These messages, communicated through the angel Gabriel from 610 CE until the time of the Prophet's death in 632 CE, were in time organized in one hundred fourteen surahs (chapters) varying in length from three to two hundred eighty-six ayat (verses). Both ancient and modern discussions take up the question of when the Holy Qur'an assumed written form and how it was collected and codified as Islam's authoritative text. In the time of and under the aegis of Uthman, who was the third caliph (644–655), approved written copies of the Qur'an existed, but the earliest extant evidence of a qur'anic text stands in inscriptions at Jerusalem's Dome of the Rock (completed in 692).[1]

Commencing in the mid-seventh century, then, Muslim scripture interpreters wrote *tafsir* (interpretation of qur'anic verses), histories, and collections of the stories of the prophets. Interpretations of this book's stories by artists whose illuminations appeared in Arabic and Persian manuscripts of the fifteenth to seventeenth centuries are crucial ingredients in our study, even though these works of art portraying human and divine creatures were relatively late, were relatively late in being produced within Islamic societies.

My approach to the art and writings in this book is that of an historian—one whose task is to discover, decipher, and describe the pertinent evidence of Jewish, Christian, and Muslim interactions surrounding shared scriptural narratives. While I consistently examine and seek to clarify particular viewpoints, values, theological emphases, and even biases found within the three religions, I write in an expository way, aiming to present these—not to argue for the superiority (or inferiority) of any one religious tradition. What has motivated me in this and others of my books is a steady desire to understand and appreciate the multiple and varied ways in which communities of religious people think, believe, behave, and relate to others. This perspective and method is, I believe, essential in a comparative historical study of this sort—one that pays attention to three vital religio-cultural movements and to changes within and between them over a span of centuries.

On full display in the following pages is the creativity of numerous Jewish, Christian, and Muslim meaning-seekers—historians, exegetes, storytellers, teachers, preachers, and artists. You, the reader, will spend most of your time observing how they worked, how they gauged their audiences, how they attempted to encourage the faith of their fellow believers, and how they counterpoised their arguments—verbally and visually—to those of their rivals. My hope is that in the course of reading these chapters you come to appreciate the imaginative genius in the three religions' craftings of their distinctive understandings of these five sacred stories, gain insight into the deeper causes and objectives of their interpretations, and ponder the enduring cultural force of the labors of biblical and qur'anic commentators, several of whom may win a place among your favored intellectual and spiritual companions from the past.

A good teaching of Ephrem the Syrian is the right conclusion for this preview. Aware that some people of his era worried that so many and various interpretations of holy texts were possible, even necessary, he offered reassurance:

> If there were [only] one meaning for the words [of Scripture], the first interpreter would find it, and all other listeners would have neither the toil of seeking nor the pleasure of finding.[2]

Shared Stories, Rival Tellings

PART I

Cain and Abel/Qabil and Habil

Preview, Chapters 1–3

The First Murder

Brotherly love—marked by bonds of affection and loyalty—was much prized in the ancient cultures of Israel, Greece, and Rome, but, as scholar Jan Brenner noted, it was also recognized by these peoples that solidarity between and among brothers was strained by issues like inheritance rights, a father's preference for one of his sons, or political ambitions: "in some cases, rivalry could end in fratricide."[1] While a Roman tradition preserves the tale of Romulus's murder of Remus, his twin, the Hebrew Bible's Cain and Abel story captured this tragedy of brotherhood for Jews—and Christians and Muslims had that story too.

What happened between the world's first brothers? What grievances sparked the anger and led to the murder? The narrative describes the origin of human violence. How much more does it tell?

Surprises are to be found in the following three chapters. Qabil (as the Qur'an names Cain) does not know what to do with Habil's (Abel's) body after he has murdered him. How was this first human corpse to be treated? Was the strife between Adam's sons about women—about their competition for a potential mate? What female candidates were available to them? Muslim and Jewish interpreters raise and pursue the question.

Where a break in the text of the Hebrew Bible's account of Cain and Abel kept the reader or hearer from knowing what the brothers said to each other prior to the killing, that gap would be filled in, differently, by the story's varied interpreters. And about the terrible event itself, some asked why God did not intervene, saving the good son of Adam from the bad son's assault. For them the question was about theodicy—the justice of God.

Meeting the saga of the first murder in the biblical account in *Genesis* 4:1–16 or the qur'anic narrative in Surah 5:27–31, moderns find their minds turning to the collapse of trust between fellow beings, to the causes of discord and conflict. We ponder the forces, ideas, strivings, and emotions that affect dealings between human beings, whether as individuals face-to-face or as peoples gathered into their families, groups, religions, races, and nations. How did Jews, Christians, and Muslims in the early and formative periods of their faith communities hear, tell, and picture the story of the first murder?

The making of humankind, part of God's work on the sixth day of creation that was, according to *Genesis* 1:31, "very good," is followed two chapters later by the terrible story of Cain's killing of Abel (*Genesis* 4:1ff). In between, tellingly, falls the account of Adam's and Eve's disobedience and their expulsion from the Garden of Eden. From the biblical point of view, the fall from innocent goodness and peace enjoyed in Paradise has been drastic, resulting in the degradation of human existence, and a life-environment subject to violence.

Islam also registers this crisis on its own terms. When in the Qur'an God commands Muhammad to recite "the story of the two sons of Adam" (Surah 5:27), the narrative ends with words weighing the extreme gravity of a single murder—it is tantamount to killing all of humanity.

It is possible to approach the Cain and Abel story as an etiological tale, conforming to a pattern set in *Genesis* 3, where it is written that *because* of the sin committed in the Garden of Eden, Adam was to spend the rest of his days laboriously tilling the earth, Eve would suffer pangs in childbirth, and the Serpent, once able to stand, was doomed forever to slithering. Read in this light, the tale of Cain and Abel explains how murder entered human existence.

The intrinsic drama of the clash between the world's first brothers immediately demanded, however, that various other questions be posed—about motivations, about decisions to act, about the tensions in relationships, and even about God's reactions to the result of the brothers' conflict. What in Cain's circumstances or personality led him to commit fratricide? For what reason was Abel's offering to God acceptable, and Cain's not? How were Adam and Eve affected by this tragedy? Was Cain adequately punished?

Rabbinic discussions of *Genesis* 4 circle around the contrast between Cain's evil and Abel's righteousness, with most attention falling upon a range of possible causes and motivations for Cain's evil. Was Satan at work in Cain's thoughts and deeds—and if so, does the blame for his act of murder fall only upon him? When God asked Cain, "Where is your brother, Abel?" why did Cain play the innocent? (A rabbi likens Cain to a man raiding a mulberry garden who, when confronted, denied he was stealing, even though his hands were stained.)

Treatments of Abel's innocence are also popular, but special discussion centers on the fact that after his death, Abel's "bloods" (plural) still cry out, audible to God. What does this mean, the rabbis ask, about the state of Abel—does he live still? If so, in what condition? (Again, this is the first mortality; curiosity abounds.)

Philo Judaeus's *Questions and Answers about Genesis* show this philosophical scripture interpreter making the brothers examples of two ways: one path leading to virtue, the other to vice. Cain and Abel also represent two contrasting kinds of love—of the self, and of God—a theme that continues into the theology of St. Augustine's *City of God* five centuries later. Philo's portrait of Abel as sacrificed and triumphant (his continuing voice a sign of his immortality) allows him to speak of the victim as the first of God's martyrs: an innocent who in suffering, was true to his God.

Early Christian artists and writers also wrestle with Cain's murderous act, and like their Jewish counterparts speculate about the influence of Satan, the tempter, in this momentous crime. The appearance of the serpent in a fourth-century catacomb painting of Abel and Cain reveals the artist's investment in this explanatory theme. But more than on any other aspect in the biblical story, interpreters focus upon Abel's death, which they Christianize in striking ways. One author presents Abel's death as a predictive prototype of what would befall Christ—the execution and resurrection, upon which Christians' belief and trust in God depended. In the context of competition between Christians and Jews, this line of reasoning also enabled a harsh anti-Jewish polemic: Cain, it was argued, stood at the beginning of Israel's history of killing God's favored and chosen ones, the prophets—most notably Jesus, God's messiah.

Chapter 2 concludes with the work of three Christian writers who shared a singular interest in the troubled family relations within the household of Adam and Eve. In their pursuit of deeper psychological insight into the tragedy of Cain's fratricide, these authors/preachers gave additional words and emotions to the members of the first family, exposing more fully Cain's criminality, Abel's victimhood, and the impact of this tragedy upon their parents.

Muslim perspectives on the story of Qabil and Habil were both like and unlike those called in the Qur'an "the people of the Book": the Jews and Christians. With their Jewish counterparts, Muslim commentators shared a number of strong interests—the first murder's implications for legal judgments on subsequent killings (i.e., capital crimes), the important theological question of whether Cain's act was "free" or whether it was predetermined by God, and that set of speculations mentioned earlier about the role of their preferences for mates in the clash between Qabil and Habil.

Especially important in Islam's understanding of the story of Adam's sons is a piece of the qur'anic narrative that is not found in the biblical account: Qabil, burdened with the corpse of his brother, receives a sign from God and comes to a realization about himself. This final episode gave grounds for some interpreters' reassessments of Qabil's character.

In tracing trajectories of each community's interpretations of the first murder, we look for evidence of their interactions—and for the element of competition in their ways of framing and maintaining the story's meanings. To discern where and why Jewish, Christian, and Muslim interpretations of Adam's two sons part company—that is, become particular to their own religion, and conflict with the views of their rivals—is to begin to gather significant clues about the historical relations of the religions which counted Abraham their father.

CHAPTER 1

⌇

Cain's Fratricide

Rabbis and Other Early Jewish Writers Judge the Case

Our earliest written account of Cain and Abel, *Genesis* 4, belongs to a body of tradition concerning "the early history of humanity and the story of Israel's ancestors" that was in formation beginning at least in the eighth century BCE, and becoming—sometime in the sixth to fifth centuries—the five book collection attributed to Moses: the Torah, or the Pentateuch.[1] The written legend of Cain and Abel is itself the result of preceding versions and discussions, and we seem to have it in a condensed or compressed form. Nonetheless, the storyline of the dealings between the two brothers can be followed easily enough:

> 4:1 Now the man knew his wife Eve, and she conceived and bore
> Cain, saying, "I have gained a male child with the help of the
> Lord." 2 She then bore his brother Abel. Abel became a keeper of
> sheep, and Cain became a tiller of the soil. 3 In the course of time,
> Cain brought an offering to the Lord from the fruit of the soil; 4 and
> Abel, for his part, brought the choicest of the firstlings of his flock.
> The Lord paid heed to Abel and his offering, 5 but to Cain and his
> offering He paid no heed. Cain was much distressed and his face
> fell. 6 And the Lord said to Cain
> "Why are you distressed,
> And why is your face fallen?
> 7 Surely, if you do right,

> There is uplift.
> But if you do not do right
> Sin couches at the door;
> Its urge is toward you,
> Yet you can be its master."
> 8 Cain said to his brother Abel . . . and when they were in the field,
> Cain set upon his brother Abel and killed him. 9 The Lord said to
> Cain, "Where is your brother Abel?" And he said, "I do not know.
> Am I my brother's keeper?" 10 Then He said, "What have you
> done? Hark, your brother's blood cries out to me from the ground!
> 11 Therefore, you shall be more cursed than the ground [see *Genesis*
> 3.17], which opened its mouth to receive your brother's blood from
> your hand. 12 If you till the soil, it shall no longer yield its strength
> to you. You shall become a ceaseless wanderer on earth."
> 13 Cain said to the Lord, "My punishment is too great to bear!
> 14 Since You have banished me this day from the soil, and I must
> avoid Your presence and become a restless wanderer on earth—
> anyone who meets me may kill me!" 15 The Lord said to him, "I
> promise, if anyone kills Cain, sevenfold vengeance shall be taken
> on him." And the Lord put a mark on Cain, lest anyone who met
> him should kill him. 16 Cain left the presence of the Lord and
> settled in the land of Nod, east of Eden.

A combination of Hebrew prose and verse, *Genesis* 4:1–16 tells of the births and separate vocations of the two sons, their two offered sacrifices with opposite outcomes, of Cain's chagrin and the divine instruction that follows, of the homicide, and of the Lord's subsequent encounter with Cain, resulting in Cain's exile from God's presence. Upon a second and a third reading or hearing, however, the narrative's *untold* things begin to surface. Inquiries naturally arise about other (unmentioned) differences between the brothers, the reason for God's responses to their offerings, and how the brothers came to know God's approval or disapproval. Curiosity also circles around the nature and cause of Cain's "distress" in v. 5, the manner of the killing, the blood that calls out, Cain's responses to God's words to him, and Cain's fate—the promise of protection from those who would kill him, and the "mark" placed upon him. More must be known . . . or, to adapt a remark from Daniel Boyarin to which we shall return shortly, "this [text] cries out, 'interpret me!' "[2]

Modern scholars of the Bible have found in *Genesis* 4 a number of issues to pursue—for example, the theme of conflict between the cultures of crop production and cattle-owning, or between settled and nomadic peoples;

Cain as ancestor and representative of the Kenites (Cainites), his wrath serving as an explanation-in-a-tale of this nomadic tribe's troublesome hostility in relation to the land of Israel; the question of crime and punishment in chapter 4 as it follows the story of the fall of Eve and Adam and points ahead to the saga of the destruction of all but a few creatures and humans by a great flood in chapters 6–7; the ancient cultural and cultic contexts which best illuminate this passage's concerns with earth (its capacity and incapacity to yield) and with bloods (in sacrifices and in murder).

Here, then, in this first of three chapters concerning the saga of Cain and Abel, our objective is to discover how, and how variously, Jews from the first to seventh centuries CE interpreted the first murder.

THE KILLING OF ABEL: A CHRISTIAN PAINTING WITH JEWISH INFLUENCES

The placement of a painting from a Christian book at the beginning of a chapter devoted to Jewish interpretations of the Cain and Abel story needs explanation (see Figure 1.1). The Latin manuscript known as the Ashburnham Pentateuch portrays on a single illustrated page the story of *Genesis* 3:21–4:9. Because it is a piece of art that renders almost the entire narrative, rather than a selected scene, it gives opportunity for comparison with the biblical text itself. More importantly, however, scholars have long claimed that Jewish influences—via a now-lost illuminated Jewish Pentateuch which served as a pictorial model, or through ideas and themes from rabbinic writings—stand behind and inform the work of the Christian artist whose beautiful, brightly colored folios grace this manuscript.[3]

To identify and to put in sequence the painting's ten or eleven elements, and then to reach conclusions about its themes and lessons, we should pass through the painting's scenes twice. The largest of these, the depiction of the murder itself, left the ancient viewer in no doubt concerning the painting's subject. Nearby within this purple background are the juxtaposed images of the two brothers, distinguished (as in *Genesis*) by their vocations; the simple Latin inscriptions read, "This is Abel, where he tends his flock" and "Here Cain cultivates his land." We take note of the two rams charging toward each other at the top border of this panel, their colors matching the color of the garments of Abel (white, except for the one image in which he is posed, sitting, as a shepherd) and Cain (tan or light brown). By virtue both of its conspicuous place on the page and its strong action, this (nonbiblical) image of the rams seems evocative.

Figure 1.1 Cain and Abel. Ashburnham Pentateuch. Sixth–seventh century CE. Painting: 39.5 x 33.5 cm. © Bibliothèque nationale de France, Paris. B.N.F. nouv. acq. lat. 2334, fol. 6r.

If, after identifying the major scenes in the band of purple, we proceed upward into the green band, we see pictured at the right what the inscription describes: "Here Cain is questioned by the Lord concerning Abel." What is represented is the dialogue, after Cain's act of homicide, that runs from *Genesis* 4:9–15, within which falls this portion of the divine punishment: "you shall be more cursed than the ground, which opened its mouth to receive your brother's blood from your hand. If you till the soil, it shall no longer yield its strength to you." We note the messages of hands.

Divine presence and power are signified by God's gesture from the cloud (*J'accuse!*), and its effects are seen upon Cain, whose arms and hands are thrown upward and back as he recoils.

Bypassing for a moment the remaining two scenes to Cain's left, if our eyes move to the two scenes directly above, in the right half of the red panel we recognize Abel carrying a sheep (and some other object—a vessel, perhaps—in his right hand), and beside or behind him, Cain with his offering of bread, in a round loaf. Despite the damaged corner of the page, God's hand remains visible, pointing to Abel. Here it indicates favor, while in the scene below, it condemns. Just to the left we find the next occurrence—the response of God to the gifts. The earliest Jewish composers of *targums* (translations) and extensive commentaries, as we shall see, wrestled with the silence in *Genesis* about how the two brothers learned of the Lord's responses to their sacrifices. Here this question is handled by the body language of the two sons of Adam and Eve. Cain's posture, with hands dropping downward, registers his reaction to having his offering rebuffed, while Abel's hands are turned upward in a prayerful position, a gesture seen regularly in Roman, early Jewish, and Christian art. Abel's head, at least in comparison with Cain's, is also turned Godward.

Adam and Eve appear in the upper left scene; the inscription tells us that we are seeing Adam and his wife in the "garments of skins" God had made for them in the garden of Eden (*Genesis* 3:21). Neither the shelter under which the foreparents stand nor their posture of grieving, in which they seize up their clothing, is related in *Genesis*. Yet a tradition known to us from the *Life of Adam and Eve* (a text dated to the first century CE) informs this portrayal of Adam and Eve: "When they were driven out of Paradise they made for themselves a tent and mourned for seven days, weeping in great sorrow."[4] (We shall meet this motif again in the fresco painting of Adam, Eve, Cain, and Abel found in a Roman catacomb.) In the contiguous scene Eve sits, apparently with both of her sons in her arms, under the same or another shelter.

At this point we return to the two scenes not considered earlier, which are positioned on the left half of the green band of the folio. Eve appears ("Here is Ava at home holding Cain, her son"), and then we find a sizeable picture of Adam driving the oxen who pull the plow, with the inscription, "Here Adam cultivates his land." God's sentence upon Adam for his disobedience in the Garden includes the words of *Genesis* 3:18b–19a: "your food shall be the grasses of the field; by the sweat of your brow shall you get bread to eat, until you return to the ground."

Now, having identified those things within *Genesis* 3:21–4:16 that the painter chose to portray, we can return to the images, starting from the top, with this question in mind: what were the artist's particular interests in retelling the saga of Cain and Abel? The assumption behind the question is that in representing the first murder in this medium, the artist, just as much as any writer addressing the story's meanings, interprets.

At the upper left of the painting, in the second panel, we see Eve holding both sons (the image is damaged, but another child was pictured next to one whose form can be discerned), and we are safe in supposing that this portrait of mother and children relates to the two other scenes in this red zone: the two sons shown in their transactions with God, to whom they bear their offerings. The two appearances of the hand of God indicate judgments—an endorsement of Abel's sacrificial animal, in the right-hand picture, and a refusal of Cain's grain/bread offering in the right-center scene. In the swath of green, again starting at the left, we find Eve with just Cain in her arms, and it is his accusation and condemnation by God that is dramatized at the right. Abel's blood crying from the earth (even trumpeting his continued existence, a theme met in both Jewish and Christian commentaries) *may* be implied, but it cannot be thought to be this panel's chief theme, nor the point of this individual scene. The artist's image is more evidently concentrated upon Cain's evil deed and its consequences—the exposure of Cain's deed and the ensuing reprimand is reminiscent of God's dialogue with frightened and guilty Adam in the garden in *Gen.* 3:9ff. The association of Adam and Cain, both understood to have committed evil, also explains the inclusion of Adam's plowing in this panel of the painting. The painter makes it easy to recall the continuation from father to this son of the burden of toil earned by sin, a sentence more dire in Cain's case, since the earth will resist his efforts (*Genesis* 4:12). The repetition or mimicry of Adam's tilling of the soil by Cain in the lower purple zone of the illumination enforces the moral lesson.

At the upper border of the portion of the painting with rich purple background, we encounter again the conflict forecast in the painting of the converging rams. Nothing in the biblical texts gives rise to this figure, but it has been suggested that midrashic tradition is in play. Several scholars have drawn attention to a piece of rabbinic commentary about turf wars between the world's first brothers—a consequence of Cain's resentment at having his sacrifice refused by the Lord. We shall meet narrative expansion of this theme below, when considering *Genesis Rabbah* 22.7, in which hostile dealings between the brothers result in separation of territory, and the setting of boundaries not to be transgressed. It has been suggested that the battling rams in our painting could reflect the battle between siblings described in *Midrash Tanhuma* 9:

Cain said to Abel: Let us divide the world! He answered him: Yes. Then Abel took his flocks, and Cain went to till the soil. They agreed not to meddle in each other's affairs. When Abel took his herd, he began to pasture it, but Cain pursued him from the mountain to the plain, and from the plain to the mountain, until they came to blows. Abel defeated Cain and he fell under him. When Cain saw that he was beaten, he began to cry out: Abel, my brother, do no evil unto me! Abel showed mercy to him and left him alone. But Cain rose up and slew him, for it says, "Cain rose up" (*Genesis* 4:8), because he had fallen before.[5]

In the clear demarcation of the brother's territories and occupations at the top of the purple band in the painting Kurt Schubert detected not merely a biblical motif, but pictorial representation of "a conflict over these two spheres of life" articulated by the rabbis as they sought to explain the causes of Cain's fratricide.[6] The collision of rams about to occur may, however, be a more general visual symbol under which the brothers' clash is figured—that is, with no implied reference to anything other than *Genesis'* own narration of the brothers' enmity and its violent conclusion. An image of two bulls about to butt heads (their contest is over a beautiful cow) had become a literary and pictorial commonplace by the time it appeared in a painting decorating a fifth-century CE manuscript containing Vergil's *Georgics.*[7] We may not be able to recover the origin of the image of the rams soon to collide, but the artist's rendition of the story of Cain and Abel leaves little doubt about its fundamental teaching: the violence Cain visited upon his brother was damnable—an offense to God. Humankind is forewarned.

The images of the sons of Adam and Eve at their respective labors can be understood to derive from the single verse in *Genesis* 4:2, and the depiction of the act of murder (which does not hint at protracted chase and wrestling) similarly draws only from what is related in v. 8: "and when they were in the field, Cain set upon his brother and killed him." "Here is Cain when he strikes down Abel, his brother," reads the Latin inscription. The artist of the Ashburnham Pentateuch, however, reveals more about the murder in visual terms than does the biblical text, in any of its translations. Despite the silence of *Genesis*, he is compelled to show how the murder was done—what it looked like. The medium both demanded and allowed elaboration of the narrative.

With a single exception, to which we'll return, the dress of the brothers—white garb worn by Abel and the brown by Cain—consistently identifies them, as surely as do the inscriptions. (The same is not true of Adam and Eve; their dress varies in color within the top two panels.) It is likely that the painter wishes not only to make the page's main characters easily recognizable, but also to make visible the opposition which is the story's primary subject—to clothe the God-approved innocent victim in white, and to show the disobedient and finally vicious killer in shades of brown. The contrast between the sons—their behavior, the consequences of their actions, and especially the steady attention to Cain, humanity's first killer—is what stands at the center of the *Genesis* story, and is portrayed by the Ashburnham Pentateuch's illuminator.

One could argue that our painter was content to represent the Cain and Abel story simply—in some combination of its literal and moral levels of meaning. Special attention is paid to Cain: his offered loaf is rejected, his lie about Abel's whereabouts is confronted, and his labor in the soil signals the penalty for his crime. In his act of murder Cain pulls his brother upward from the ground by his hair in order to deliver the death stroke with his axe (the head of which, we note, is one not of stone, but of good sturdy seventh-century metal). The viewer could not fail to observe in the representations of Cain what happens to the person who is counted unworthy of divine favor, who out of his resentment does evil, and afterward attempts to conceal his crime. The deserved fate of Cain, then, occupies the painter's attention more than any effort to depict Abel's good offering, his righteousness, or his association with God—concerns we shall find explicitly marched out in numerous Jewish (as well as Christian and Muslim) exegeses.[8] Here a clear emphasis falls upon the conflict and the crime per se, and upon God's confrontations with Cain, both at the time of the offering and in the aftermath of his killing of Abel.

There remains, however, evidence that folio 6r *does* want to bring to visual expression a dimension of meaning in the story that is symbolic, running beyond its clearly represented moral lessons. If we return to the portraits of Abel the shepherd and Cain the farmer that stand in the upper section of the purple zone of the page, we may ask whether the painter intends us to consider them *again*—this time as representing the conditions of life of the brothers *following* their fateful altercation. If so, there are strong messages being communicated about the punishments and rewards brought by God to those who choose evil or good—lessons appropriate to a community of Christians in the early medieval West. Not having become "a ceaseless wanderer on earth" (*Genesis* 4:12b), Cain remains in the picture as one bearing the consequences for his sin. He might be understood to symbolize the Cain-like, and their painful prospects both in and beyond their mortal lives. Abel, for his part, robed in a dark cloak which covers his white garment, is at rest—in repose, as if in paradise. This assessment of Abel's fate would have found ready acceptance among many Jewish commentators and their audiences who regarded Abel as a martyr. But for the Christian painter and for those who viewed this scene in a seventh century ecclesiastical context, the presentation of Abel as one bearing the appearance of a nearly enthroned good shepherd who tends his multicolored flock, the reference would have been quite transparent. The understanding of Christ as "the good shepherd who lays down his life for his sheep" derives from the *Gospel of John* 10:11–21, and paintings symbolizing Jesus the savior as a shepherd tending a flock abound in the earliest Christian catacomb paintings. The painter uses typological interpretation (making Abel the fore-type of Christ) easily and deftly.[9]

This brief encounter with an ancient painting of Cain and Abel—the work of a Christian artist intent upon portraying biblical scenes and the inheritor, it can be argued, of influences from extrabiblical Jewish traditions—alerts us, in a preliminary way, to some of the dynamics of interpretation to be found within Jewish, Christian, and Islamic works of art—visual products that are full partners with written works in these communities' searches for sense and significant meaning in the lore that matters to them.

JEWISH COMMENTARIES ON THE CAIN AND ABEL STORY

What characterized postbiblical Jewish interpretations of *Genesis* 4? Interesting and often unforeseen answers are provided in three Jewish writings we shall consider in this section: an Aramaic translation of the Hebrew text, a commentary which preserves the voices of several rabbis discussing the narrative, and an exposition of questions arising from the Cain and Abel story by Philo, the prolific first-century Alexandrian Jewish author.

Targum Pseudo-Jonathan

Sometime around the fifth century BCE the Hebrew Bible (or portions of it) began to be translated into Aramaic, the Semitic language akin to Hebrew that had come into popular use in Persia and the Near East.[10] In the context of Torah study in synagogues from the second century CE, and perhaps earlier, these translations, called *targums*, were being given orally, their Aramaic phrases interspersed between verses of the Torah being read in Hebrew; the translator's "purpose was to interpret the text, and make it meaningful to the congregation."[11] The Aramaic translation of the Pentateuch known as the *Targum Pseudo-Jonathan* (so called because of its false attribution to the teacher Jonathan b. Uzziel, who lived in the first centuries BCE and CE) is, like similar *targums*, a text containing traces of its use and revisions over many years. In the form that we have it, *Pseudo-Jonathan (Ps-Jon)* is aware of the city that was renamed Constantinople in the fourth century CE, and knows also the names of Muhammad's wives. Yet much material within the *targum* originated in the eras of the Tannaim and Amoraim—rabbis in the periods before and after 200 CE, respectively.[12] In its version of the Cain and Abel story, *Ps-Jon* takes us well beyond the truism that any translation into another language necessarily involves interpretation; we see which aspects of the *Genesis* text the translator thought it necessary to clarify and to expand as he repeated in more popularly accessible language the Torah reading from *Genesis* 4.

With the opening verses of *Genesis* 4, *Ps-Jon* startles the reader who knows the biblical account only. John Bowker's English translation of the text italicizes those words that exactly or closely translate the Hebrew, and puts in Roman characters the *targum*'s additions and elaborations:

> *Adam* was aware that *Eve his wife* had *conceived* from Sammael the angel, and she became pregnant *and bare Cain*, and he was like those on high, not like those below; and she *said, "I have* acquired *a man,* the angel of *the Lord.*"[13]

Elements not present in this verse 1 of the Hebrew text quickly catch our attention, and the additions are significant. They serve to address the question: what accounts for Cain's becoming the person he became? *Ps-Jon* is out in front of his narration with this concern, but we must imagine that it is not the first hearing of the text in Hebrew, nor the first time the translator has felt obliged to add a note of explanation about Cain's character, his waywardness. The *targum* deals with the problem by locating the trouble in Cain's begetting, and in his begetters. The elaboration of the verse was, without doubt, either prompted or assisted by Eve's tantalizing claim that she got her son with God's help (the Hebrew word for "knew," with its well-known double connotation, allowing for Adam's cognizance of, but not role in, Cain's conception). So the evil angel, Sammael, takes Adam's place as Cain's progenitor, with the result that Cain was no ordinary human, being "not like those below," but like the spirits above. Of course some of those spirits were unruly—with Sammael, the prince of demons, chief among them. Bowker notes that the translator/interpreter, working to account for Cain's character and behavior, exploited something that was *not* said about Cain. *Genesis* 5:3 told of Adam's third son, Seth, "who [unlike Cain, the targumist infers] was in [Adam's] likeness, after his image." Satan's paternity of Cain ruled out that "likeness," explaining who

Cain was from birth and forecasting who he will be in the story about to be told. *Ps-Jon* constructed his insertion of Sammael out of a difference he noted in scripture's way of describing Adam's relations to Cain and to Seth (born in his "likeness"), and a bold assertion about the character of the divine "help" by which Eve "gained a male child" (*Genesis* 4:1). Cain came from satanic seed.

In *Ps-Jon* 4:2a we meet another addition to the narrative, not so dramatic as the first, but one responding to a question that inevitably occurred to listeners of the creation story: where in the story are the women who will make possible the continuation of the family, the future generations?

> *And* she went on to bear from Adam, her husband, his [Cain's] twin sister and *Abel.*

In this text we notice that Cain's sister and Abel are progeny of Adam, not Sammael. Variations on the theme of the sisters' origins will appear in other Jewish—and Muslim—interpretations.

The *Book of Jubilees*, a work composed in the second century BCE, ventures to give the names of two sisters born with Cain and Abel as Awan and Azura (*Jubilees* 4:1,8), while Josephus, writing in the first century CE, simply notes that along with two male children, Adam and Eve "also had daughters" (*Antiquities* 1:52). We shall see other commentators take up this matter in more detail, bringing two sisters on the scene and involving them in the conflict between the brothers.

Pseudo-Jonathan's rendition of *Genesis* 4:4 reports that the offering brought by the brothers took place on "the fourteenth of Nisan," and on the supposition that the Jewish triennial cycle of Torah-reading in Palestinian Jewish assemblies began in Nisan, *Genesis* 4 would have been the appointed text for the sabbath nearest Passover.[14] Geza Vermes pointed to a "tendency manifest in ancient Judaism (second century BC–second century AD), to date the great events of the past in the month of Nisan, not only the first Passover in Egypt, but also the creation of the world and the sacrifice of Isaac," and continues, "to these, [*Ps-Jon*] adds the first sacrifice mentioned in the Bible and the death of the first innocent man."[15]

Targum Pseudo-Jonathan's most striking and extensive elaborations to the narrative occur at the point just after the report that Lord was pleased by Abel's offering, but not by Cain's. First, the frustrated Cain is told that his *future* actions, not the unacceptable offering (the fault in Cain's offering is assumed, but not explained), will determine when and whether his guilt will be taken away. *Ps-Jon Genesis* 4:7 uses only a few words of the Hebrew of *Genesis* 4:6–7 in its expansion of the narrative. The Lord instructs Cain:

Is it not the case that if you have done your work *well* your guilt will be forgiven you? But if you have not done your work *well* in this world your sin will be kept for the day of the great judgment, and at the doors of your heart, sin lies waiting. And into your hands I have given the power of the inclination to evil, and towards you will be its *desire*, and you will have authority over it for righteousness or for sin.

Earlier in his translation of *Genesis*, at 2:7, *Ps-Jon* had inserted the well-established Jewish doctrine of "two inclinations"—one good (*yetzer hatob*), and one evil (*yetzer hara*). This teaching belonged to the account of the fashioning of the human from dust. Here the targumist expands upon the imagery in *Genesis* 4:7b: "sin couch[ing]" with its "urge" toward Cain. Just before Cain speaks to his brother and invites him "into the field," the voice of God notifies him of the *yetzer hara* and its desire "towards [him]," but at the same time assures Cain that he will have control over this instinct for evil. The choice of righteousness or sin will be his.

A second addition in v. 8 fills in the awkward missing words in the Hebrew text by supplying what Cain said to Abel. *Ps-Jon* inserts a discussion of the ways of the creator and creation, and the brothers are presented as disputants over matters theological (even if they are also personal). Cain, reflecting on the rejection of his sacrifice by God, asserts that

the world was created in love, but it is not ordered by the issue of good works, because there is partiality in judgment; thus it is that your offering was accepted with favor, but my offering was not accepted with favor.

Abel counters:

By the issue of good works [the world] is ordered, and there is no partiality in judgment. But because the issue of my works was better than yours, so my offering has been accepted before yours with favor.

Abel has declared God to be just, and has identified himself as the good and worthy sacrifice-maker in God's sight—in the process denouncing his older brother. The argument intensifies, as arguments between siblings and arguments over theology may be expected to do. Cain pronounces his disbelief in a final judgment, God the judge, and a world to come, while Abel endorses all three, adding pointedly, "there is a good reward to be given to the righteous, and the wicked will be called to account." The next sentences in *Ps-Jon* make plain the narrative requirement that inspired this correction, or fill-in, of the interrupted verse:

> And because of these words they fell into a dispute in the open field, and *Cain rose up against Abel his brother*, and drove a stone into his forehead, and slew him.

The latter phrase, which addresses curiosity about the method by which Cain killed Abel, is a secondary concern in this passage. The answer is generated by the familiar rabbinic technique of using scripture to interpret scripture. Vermes wrote: "This *haggadah* appears to have resulted from an association of Gen. 4:8 with Ex. 21:19 ("If two men dispute and one smites the other with a stone") and 2 Sam. 14:6 ("Your handmaid had two sons. They disputed in the field … and one smote his brother and killed him").[16]

The major purpose of the *targum*'s expansion on this verse is to give the reasons for Cain turning his wrath upon his brother—to account for the jealousy that caused him to commit the world's first murder. Of course there stand behind this straightening-out of the story line other basic interests of *Ps-Jon* as an interpreter of the Torah. He wants to safeguard the Lord's justice from the charge that divine rule operates by favoritism, rather than by strict fairness. The corollary with respect to humans resides in the ethical message that Cain's decisions hold for others: the evil inclination is able to be controlled by human beings. As empowered moral agents, if this sinful urge is not restrained, the responsibility is theirs. Guilt and penalties suffered, then, are results of human fault, not of divine arbitrariness.

From what period in the long life of the text, *Ps-Jon*, do these ideas come? If *Ps-Jon*, in the form that we possess it, dates to at least the seventh century CE, how might we determine what parts of it might be more ancient? This section of *Ps-Jon* holds clues for dating, according to Vermes, who pointed to the fact that these two interrelated themes—the possible tension between justice and love (partiality) in divine action, and the argument that God, having empowered humans to exercise the good, rather than the evil inclination, makes them accountable for their actions—appear, in varying forms, at least by the first century CE, in debates among Jewish sages, in Josephus, and in New Testament writings.[17] The debate of Adam's sons in *Ps-Jon* both fills the lacuna, the unfilled space, in the Hebrew text of the story and also places in the ancient tale questions and claims quite current in the early centuries CE about divine and human actions—a discussion very germane to the targumist and to those synagogue-goers for whom he translates scripture.

Our consideration of this writing's interpretive efforts could proceed along these lines and in this kind of detail to the conclusion of *Ps-Jon*'s account of the Cain and Abel story, but it is preferable at this point to note briefly, and for future reference, only a few of its remaining features. First, unlike other *targums, Ps-Jon* preserves the plural "bloods" of the Hebrew in God's accusation of Cain in vv. 10–11, and does so without comment. (The explanation that the plural of "blood" points both to Abel and to his *potential* progeny is offered as an explanation in *Mishnah Tractate Sanhedrin* 4:5 and in *Genesis Rabbah* 22:9). Second, ambiguity surrounds Cain's words to the Lord in the Bible at 4:13 and also in its slight expansion in *Ps-Jon* at v. 13, which reads: "Severe indeed is my rebellion, more than to be borne, and yet it is possible with you to forgive it."[18] At stake here is the question of whether Cain shows repentance for his deed by speaking of guilt's burden. Does *Ps-Jon* 4:3 convey this? Third, the encounter and negotiations between Cain and the Lord after the crime are given more precision in *Ps-Jon*'s translation. Cain's lament in 4:14 that as a fugitive and wanderer he will be vulnerable to anyone he meets is sharpened: "any *just* person who *findeth me shall slay me.*" Here Cain is presented as acknowledging (and dreading) the workings of God's justice in the world. He seeks protection. Fourth, *Ps-Jon*, like the other *targums*, understands the "seven-fold vengeance" to be taken on Cain's assailant (*Genesis* 4:15) to mean that Cain will survive for seven generations *because* he has acknowledged his crime. We learn this later in the translation, in connection with Cain's own death at the hands of Lamech: "Now *Cain* who had sinned and turned in repentance had seven generations extended to him" (*Ps-Jon* 4.24).[19] Fifth, only *Ps-Jon* among the surviving *targums* relates the character and location of the mark put on Cain by the Lord: "*And the Lord* marked on the face of Cain a letter from the great and glorious name, that *any finding him* should not kill him when they saw it on him."[20] The mark is evil-averting, a safeguard against assault. According to *Ps-Jon*, Cain leaves the presence of the Lord still enjoying God's protection, and wears an emblem denoting God's forbearance and defense. Other commentators will read the verse in different and contrasting ways.

The *targum* known as *Pseudo-Jonathan* labors, as we have seen, not merely to make the Hebrew text accessible to those whose usual language is Aramaic, but also to fill in gaps or to make desired additions to the narrative. These ideas and story elaborations (e.g., the setting of the sacrifices of Cain and Abel within the Jewish calendar at the time of Passover, the doctrinal quarrel between Cain and Abel, the identification of the murder weapon by means of two other passages in the Pentateuch, and the description of Cain's mark) are created by the targumist himself, or drawn from the store of scripture-interpreting traditions he has learned from others.

Pseudo-Jonathan tells us more about what happened between Cain and Abel than *Genesis* 4:1–16 does. In the process the *targum* affects and alters our sense of the story, its actors, and its possible meanings. Does this translation—which is also exposition—amount to a distortion of the biblical text, or is it the translator's and the reteller's necessity, given the character of the biblical text itself? Daniel Boyarin writes:

> The Bible is notorious for the paucity of detail of certain sorts within its narrative. Erich Auerbach described this as being "fraught with background." The gaps are those silences in the text which call for interpretation if the reader is to "make sense" of what happened, to fill out the plot and the characters in a meaningful way. This is precisely what midrash does by means of its explicit narrative expansions. I am extending the application of the term "gap" here to mean *any* element in the textual system of the Bible which demands interpretation for a coherent construction of the story, that is both gaps in the narrow sense, as well as contradictions and repetitions, which indicate to the reader that she must fill in something that is not given in the text in order to read it. . . . There is even a native rabbinic saying for this quality of the text: "this verse cries out, 'interpret me!' "[21]

Our next document presents us not only with noisy texts, but also with rabbis audible in their proposals that "It means this!"

Genesis Rabbah

In the fifth century CE, a collection of rabbinic teachings concerning the first book of the Torah, *Genesis Rabbah* (or *Bereshit Rabba*), was edited and produced within a larger work, *Midrash Rabbah*.[22] One of *Genesis Rabbah*'s modern editors and interpreters, Jacob Neusner, contextualized this writing by pointing to the rise of Christianity in the fourth century, and that dominant religion's strong efforts to suppress Roman polytheism ("paganism") and to weaken the status of Jews and Judaism in the Empire. Neusner described *Genesis Rabbah*'s setting and purpose in this way:

> The issue confronting Israel in the Land of Israel . . . proved immediate: the meaning of the new and ominous turn of history, the implications of Christ's worldly triumph for the other-worldly and supernatural people, Israel, whom God chooses and loves. The message of the exegete-compositors [of *Genesis Rabbah*] addressed the circumstance of historical crisis and generated remarkable renewal, a rebirth of intellect in the encounter with scripture, now in quest of the rules not of sanctification—these had already been found—but of

salvation. So the book of Genesis, which describes how all things had begun, would testify to the message and method of the end: the coming salvation of patient, hopeful, enduring Israel.[23]

Genesis Rabbah (GR) provided a running commentary on the verses of Genesis—*midrash*, or interpretation, deriving from teachers' Torah-lessons and sermons, and featuring explanations and narrative expansions of the sort already encountered in *Ps-Jon*. In *GR*, however, alongside authoritative interpretations attributed to a single sage, or to "the Rabbis," we sometimes find ourselves exposed to exchanges over what a text means, as if the rabbis are in face-to-face discussions. Their modes and styles of argument are clearly evident to us.

Genesis Rabbah recounts the first family's beginnings from its own perspective. Unlike *Ps-Jon* and other commentaries, for example, *Genesis Rabbah* does not spy Sammael in Cain's conception, but assumes Adam to have been Eve's sexual partner. Indeed, Adam is identified as the introducer, with her, of sex: he "made known sexual function to all" other creatures.[24] Three rabbis suggest that in the course of Adam's "knowing" of Eve he "knew"—or realized—that he had "been robbed of his tranquility," and that he had been sexually aroused by his "serpent," who in this case was his temptress, Eve. Rabbi Aha, drawing on the episode in *Genesis* 3:12 ("The man said, 'The woman whom you gave to be with me, she gave me from the fruit of the tree, and I ate'"), makes the lesson explicit in his comment (directed to Eve): "The serpent was thy serpent, and thou wast Adam's serpent" (22.2).

The commentary takes a different turn: Rabbi Eleazar b. 'Azariah states that in a single day (mythic days are lengthy!) three wonders occurred: the fashioning of Adam and Eve, their sexual union, and their production of offspring. A well-known statement of R. Joseph b. Harhah elaborates upon the third wonder: "Only two entered the bed, and seven left it: Cain and his twin sister, Abel and his two twin sisters" (22.2). From the phrase in 4:2, "And again she bore his brother Abel," it is deduced that with Cain were born Abel and the sisters—they were quintuplets, not children of separate pregnancies (22.3).

Another sage makes sense of, or exploits, Eve's comment, "I have gotten a man" (*Genesis* 4:1), with a deduction about conniving women: "When a woman sees that she has children she exclaims, 'Behold, my husband is now in my possession'" (22.2). The gendering of morality and immorality here receives midrashic elaboration: Eve, while not the mother of Cain by Satan/Sammael, is herself likened to the serpent and the serpent's evil, is portrayed as a source of peace-disturbing arousal (as implied in Adam's knowledge of what she "had done to him"), and is suspected to be dedicated, as archetypal woman, to entrapment and control of her man.

A negative valuation of tillers of soil serves as commentary on 4:2. Cain is one of three "who had a passion for agriculture and no good was found in them" (*GR* 22.3). Cain's companion farmers are Noah (*Genesis* 9:20), whose drunkenness is referred to, and King Uzziah (*2 Chronicles* 26:10), whose audacious attempt to do the work of priests—make an offering of incense to the Lord—brought leprosy upon his forehead (*2 Chronicles* 26:16–21). How weighty is this homiletical observation about farmers and their faults meant to be? It is not accompanied by contrasting praise of Abel's vocation as shepherd (with intimation of other shepherds who are prominent among Israel's heroes), but seems (in echoing remarks about Adam's fate as tiller of the ground in *Genesis* 3:17–19, 23) only to offer more, or another, etiological explanation of Cain's evil: you should know what to expect from a worker of the soil.

Turning to *Genesis* 4:3–4, the narration of the two brothers' offerings to God, *Genesis Rabbah* continues a comparative moral assessment of their characters and deeds. The case against Cain intensifies in the rabbis' discussion of his act of sacrifice, and hinges on careful scrutiny of the scriptural text: "that Cain brought [an offering] of the fruit of the ground." From the observation that the passage does *not* specify that Cain brought the *first* fruits of his harvest, he is accused of having brought fruit "of the inferior crops," and of being (as a *mashal*, or parable, illustrates) "like a bad tenant who eats the first ripe figs but honours the king with the late figs" (22.5). Cain is represented as one who treats himself to the best of the crop and then brings to the Lord an offering of second-bests, or "leftovers."

Ps-Jon accounted for the differences in the brothers' offerings only through Abel's claim that he was more virtuous ("the issue of [his] works was better than [Cain's]"), but *Genesis Rabbah* asserts what was defective in Cain's sacrifice: both the substance and the manner of his offering a sacrifice failed to honor the Lord, from whom comes all that is, including the fruits of the field.

In what way, according to the commentary in *GR*, was Abel's offering superior to his brother's, thereby earning God's approval? *Genesis* 4:4 relates: "And Abel, he also brought of the firstlings of his flock and the fat thereof." Rabbis Eleazar and Jose b. R. Hanina are presented as disputing the meaning of the passage, the former proposing that Abel brought not only a burnt offering, but also (in reference to "the fat thereof") a peace offering. (In *Leviticus* 3:3, the content of the peace offering, the *shelamim*, is described as an "offering of fire to the Lord [of] the fat that covers the entrails and all the fat that is around the entrails; the two kidneys and the fat that is on them, that is at the loins, and the protuberance on the liver," and this sacrifice is distinguished [at 3:5] from "the burnt offering which is upon the wood that is on the fire, as an offering by fire, of pleasing odor to the Lord.") Contra R. Eleazar, R. Jose insists that the latter phrase in *Genesis* 4:4, "the fat thereof" signifies "the fat ones," the best from Abel's flock, not an additional offering.

When the subject under discussion changes from a comparison of Cain's evil and Abel's righteousness to the question of when—before or after Sinai—the practice of peace offerings began, we become aware that a rabbinic Torah-lesson or sermon *on another topic* has attached itself to *Genesis* 4:3–4, which clearly concerns itself with what the two offerings revealed about Cain and Abel. As their debate progresses, we learn that its crux has to do with "the Revelation"—the giving of the Law at Sinai. R. Jose's resistance to R. Eleazar's notion that Abel and others among the *avot*, the forefathers, offered peace offerings is born of his effort to sharply distinguish the status of "the Revelation" at Sinai and those who lived under *this* decisive compact with their Lord—Moses and his successors—in the history of God's actions. God's giving of the Law marked a new age in which true worship and life according to the divine will were fully disclosed—even mapped out in specific privileges and commandments. Now, in these times after Sinai, those honoring God would offer not only burnt offerings, but also peace offerings—offerings of thanksgiving. Those, on the other hand, who lived in the age prior to Sinai had made burnt offerings only, not being entitled to, or not being worthy of, the benefits involved in peace offerings.[25] The sermonic transition from the subject of Cain's and Abel's sacrifices to the topic of the Torah, the Law revealed on the mountain to Moses, and its importance for the children of Israel is quite noticeable, but not surprising. It belongs to the nature of rabbinical interpretation to extend and to expand elements which in the exegetes' imaginations reside in or near the biblical text being studied, and of course the honoring of the event of Moses's receiving of the Torah upon Mount Sinai is all-important for the guardians of Israel's identity and purposes subsequent to the destruction of the Temple.

We return to *Genesis Rabbah*'s treatment of *Genesis* 4, which next offers commentary on Cain's demeanor after the rejection of his sacrifice. The exposition of the verse was destined to contribute to a long and strange racialized exegetical history. We are told that Cain's face became like a firebrand—that is, black—since he was described in *Genesis* 4:5 as being "very wroth" (*wayyihar*, from the verb *harah*, to burn).[26] Discussion passes quickly to the Lord's challenging words to Cain in 4:6. What is being proposed or promised to Cain, the rabbis ask, if he does the right thing, or if he does not? The term *se'eth*, with its several connotations, inspires the variety of answers to this question. Cain's future holds either forgiveness (*se'eth* in the sense of God's "bear[ing] with" them) *or* sin overflowing the brim (*se'eth* linked with *se'ah*, a measure which something exceeds, or spills over). R. Berekiah cites *Psalm* 32:1, "Happy is he who is uplifted over transgression, whose sin is pardoned," as the basis for God's instruction to distressed Cain: "this means, happy is he who is [master] over his transgressions, but his transgressions are not [master] over him" (*GR* 22:6).

But what works against the person's mastery—his or her self-control? What can it mean in the text that "Sin couches at the door"? What are the powers and stratagems of sin, which has "its urge toward" Cain (*Genesis* 4:7), or anyone else? The Hebrew word for "couches" (*robez*) is in the masculine, a detail the rabbis do not pass by without noting that initially sin was weak, "like a woman," but in time gained masculine power. Various rabbis speak of sin's strength in similes prompted by biblical texts they count as *apropos*: Sin "couched" or poised opportunistically at a person's door "is like a spider web that eventually becomes like a ship's rope" (R. Akiba, drawing on *Isaiah* 5:18, with its references to iniquity's cords and rope); it is like a traveler who then lingers as a guest, and in time becomes head of the house (R. Isaac, invoking *2 Samuel* 12:4). Rabbi Tanhum b. Marion's similitude is drawn not from biblical inspiration, but from what can be seen on the street: sin couching is like a stealthy Roman dog. The dog lies near the baker's shop and pretends to sleep, waiting for the baker to doze off. He then upsets the stack of loaves, and in the confusion that follows, takes one in his teeth and runs away.

Once more: how is it that sin works against a person's self-control? The sages' thinking turns to images of the Tempter. He is like a robber at a crossroads who held up everyone who came his way until one passerby noticed that he was not strong, but feeble, and proceeded to thrash him. So it happened that the Tempter destroyed several generations, but Abraham saw his weakness, and "began to crush him, as it is written, 'And I will beat to pieces his adversaries before him'" (*Psalms* 89:24). R. Ammi claims that Satan moves among crowds of people, looking for those who strut and preen themselves; he knows that these belong to him (cf. *Proverbs* 24:12).

Whenever the Tempter approaches, the Torah may be called upon for defense. Rabbi Hanina quotes *Isaiah* 26:3 in order to derive two meanings from the word *tizzor*: You may *combat* the evil imagination when it besets you, or you may *create* peace. If you doubt your ability to resist temptation, summon this assurance from the revealed Law—indeed, from the Lord's exhortation to Cain in 4:7: "Unto thee is [sin's] desire, but thou mayest rule over it" (*GR* 22.6). R. Simon provides the section's final admonition about coping with sin: subvert temptation by beating it at its own game. "When the Tempter comes to incite you to levity, gladden it with the words of the Torah," for it is written, "'the evil imagination is gladdened'" (or so R. Siman construes a verb in *Isaiah* 26:3).

Threads of tension and argument are not apparent in these reflections on sin, its *powers*, and the possibility of overcoming it. Rather, a number of sermon-like comments and moral urgings are seen to have been collected in service of (or in attraction to) exposition of *Genesis* 4:7—God's warning that sin desires Cain, and God's assurance that he can withstand sin's powerful wiles.

The multiple voices of rabbis also distinguish *GR*'s attention to the "gap" in v. 8. which leaves the reader of *Genesis* asking *what* Cain said to his brother. It is taken for granted that Cain and Abel quarreled. But about what, or about how many things? To the interpreters, the Lord's different responses to the brothers' offerings is not in itself sufficient cause for the conflict that follows. There must have been additional causes for their clash. One interpretation (seen earlier, in *Midrash Tanhuma* 9) has the brothers agreeing to "divide the world"—one took the land, the other the "movables" (*GR* 22.7). Immediately they clashed over rights and entitlements.

> The former said, "The land you stand on is mine," while the latter retorted, "What you are wearing is mine." One said: "Strip"; the other retorted: "Fly [off the ground]" (*GR* 22.7).[27]

Joshua of Siknin joins the debate, and redirects it:

> Both took land and both took movables, but about what did they quarrel? One said, "the Temple must be built in my area," while the other claimed, "It must be built in mine."

On this view, strife between the brothers was sparked not by their different possessions, but by the zeal of each to own the holiest land, the (future) site of the Temple in Jerusalem. R. Joshua was influenced by his notion that the "field" the brothers went "out to" was that also referred to in *Micah* 3:2: "Zion [i.e., the Temple] shall be plowed as a field" (*GR* 22.7).

Or was it, to return to a popular speculation, that Cain and Abel quarreled about women? Judah b. Rabbi claimed that they fought over "the first Eve"—either Eve, or (more likely) Lilith, the legendary first wife of Adam who deserted him.[28] Rabbi Aibu retorts that "the first Eve" had died by this time, so she could not have been the cause of friction between Cain and Abel. The opinion of R. Huna follows: "An additional twin was born with

Abel, and each claimed her. The one claimed: 'I will have her, because I am the firstborn'; while the other maintained: 'I must have her, because she was born with me'" (GR 22.7).[20]

The reader of GR is left to decide whether one of these more than any other, or all of these combined, led to the fatal clash. Unwillingness to live a life in common, insistence upon prized territory, jealous desire, and competition in love or lust—these seeds of hostility and murder are not ranked, but in each of them the rabbis recognize the weaknesses and woes of humankind, and put them forth both as explanations of what happens next, and as warnings to all who would attend to God's laws.

Genesis Rabbah explains how it was that Cain "rose up" against Abel in a narrative elaboration woven together from themes of virtue, strength (and its vulnerabilities), and the workings of trust and deceit. The brothers continue their dialogue as they wrestle on the ground, the stronger Abel having taken down and pinned his older brother. Cain, at a disadvantage, says to him, "we two only are in the world; what will you go and tell our father [if you kill me]?" Abel's moment of pity for his brother is at once a virtue and a fatal lapse. "Cain rose up against his brother Abel, and killed him." A popular saying generated by this moment in the narrative, according to GR, is a piece of sage advice: "Do not do good to an evil man, then evil will not befall you" (GR 22.8).

The means Cain used in murdering Abel—his method or weapon of choice—is also taken up in this text. Receiving no hint in *Genesis* 4:8, interpreters looked elsewhere in the scriptures, and where better than the next murder mentioned in the narrative—indeed, in the same chapter of *Genesis*? *Genesis* 4:23–24 preserves a piece of ancient lyric poetry in which Lamech boasts of slaying "a man for wounding me, and a lad for bruising me." Tradition and *midrash* expanded on this obscure text also, identifying Lamech's victims as his great grandfather Cain and his own son, both killed in a hunting accident.[30] From this poem two separate inferences were drawn. Because a wound is mentioned, "the Rabbis said: He killed him with a stone." But R. Simeon noted the word "bruising," and concluded that Abel was killed with a staff. R. Joshua, in R. Levi's name, finds in *Psalm* 37:14–15 images that illuminate the murder. The phrase "the wicked have drawn out their sword" describes Cain, and "to cast down the poor and needy" points to Abel. Verse 15 says of the wicked that "their sword shall enter into their own hearts," which Joshua relates to Cain's sentence to be a fugitive and wanderer in *Genesis* 4:12 (GR 22.9). Another opinion, that of R. 'Azariah and R. Jonathan in R. Isaac's name, does not specify the implement, but the point of attack. Reasoning that Cain had watched closely when Adam killed a bullock for sacrificing (*Psalms* 69:32 is quoted in support), these teachers assert that Cain went for Abel's throat.[31]

Genesis Rabbah pauses over the "bloods" (*deme*—plural) of Abel that cry to God from the ground. It is both the blood of Abel and that of his potential offspring that God identifies.[32] R. Simeon b. Yohai issues a challenge to God he finds "difficult" to utter. At issue is the late arrival on the murder scene of the Lord, who appears only after the victim's blood had been spilled:

> Think of two athletes wrestling before the king; had the king wished, he could have separated them. But he did not so desire, and one overcame the other and killed him, he [the victim] crying out [before he died], "Let my cause be pleaded before the king!" (*GR* 22.9).[33]

The rabbi boldly raises two questions, the first explicit: why, God, did you not stop the violence before it brought death? And implicit, through the characterizations of Cain and Abel, there is a differently framed question of theodicy, of divine justice: why was the righteous and innocent brother not protected? An answer is awaited from God.

Abel's bloods are the subject of additional comments at the end of *GR* 22.9. The gore "lay spattered on the trees and stones"—that is, in more than one place, as bloods (plural). And it remains on "the ground" for two reasons. The bloods of Abel could not go underground because no human had yet been buried (blood, as vital and active substance, has options and mobility, it is presumed, but cannot act without some custom to guide its choices). Neither could the blood ascend to the heavens, "because the soul had not yet ascended thither" (*GR* 22.9). This piece of rabbinic reasoning envisions the ascension or resurrection of Abel—if not in soul *and body*, then certainly in soul *and blood* (in the *midrash*, blood as substance is being distinguished from soul).

The remainder of chapter 22 of *Genesis Rabbah* is concerned with the curse visited on Cain in 4:11–12, and on Cain's final discussion (and negotiation) with the Lord. The gravity of being cursed by God is underlined by placing other condemned figures alongside Cain—namely, Korah and his companions who rose up in resistance to Moses and Aaron (*Numbers* 16:1ff.), who were sent down to Sheol as a punishment, and Jepthah (*Judges* ll.35), who, in fulfillment of a fateful vow made in wartime, sacrificed his only daughter as a burnt-offering when he safely returned home. God's pledge to Cain—that though he will work the ground, "it will no longer yield its strength" to him—evokes strong opinions. One viewpoint is that the blood-spilling polluted the earth and caused the creator to withdraw from mankind the earth's fertility and sustenance.[34]

The ambiguity in Cain's response to God in 4:14 is preserved in two opposing comments in *GR*. One interpretation turns on the verb "bear," in the sense of bear with, or abide, even though the question does not now pertain to what Cain can bear (endure), but rather what he thinks God might be expected to treat with understanding. There is (unrepentant) protest in Cain's retort: You can "bear" things heavenly and the earthly, but you cannot bear or abide my transgression? (The remark may be read either as a question or a declaration.) The Lord is being mocked for not demonstrating patience with Cain, who (it might be pleaded) was ignorant that death would result from his attack on his brother. The contrasting opinion keeps the focus on Cain and his act, finding connotations of weight and weightiness in the word "bear." In this picture of Cain, he is more thoughtful as he compares his evil deed with that of Adam: "My sin is greater than my father's. . . . [He] violated a light precept and was expelled from the Garden of Eden; [my] crime is a grave crime—murder; how much greater then is my sin!" (*GR* 22.11).[35]

Genesis Rabbah displays what Ruth Mellinkoff called "a zesty interest in specificity about the mark of Cain."[36] The rabbis' projections about the "sign" reflect their diverse views of Cain's attitude and status following his encounter and dialogue with the Lord. Has he recognized the horror of the murder of his brother and repented of his crime? Or is he insincere and self-seeking, even as he receives his punishment, and attempts to negotiate its terms? What sign does God set upon him? Rab ("Teacher"—the honorific title of Abba Arika, a second-century CE scholar), apparently of the opinion that Cain warrants merciful treatment, claimed that the Lord's sign was the gift of a dog—a protector. R. Nehemiah, on the other hand, sharply questioned that God helped "that wretch!" No, he asserts, God gave Cain a case of leprosy. (The rabbi's application of *Exodus* 4:8 in support of his argument is both ingenious and strained: leprosy is what awaits those who will not respond to God's signs communicated through Moses). Abba Jose suggested that "He made a horn grow out of him" (and horned Cain makes his way into medieval illustrations[37]). The horn was taken to have both positive and negative connotations. Rab saw it was a warning example to murderers, while R. Hanin asserted that it was a sign giving hope to penitents, Cain being recognizable as the murderer who was spared being put to death immediately.[38]

The questions surrounding Cain's character carry over into the final section of *GR* 22. What does it mean that he "went out from the presence of the Lord and settled in the land of Nod, east of Eden"? The verse indicates that Cain shook off God's words and strode away "like one who would deceive the Almighty," says R. Aibu. R. Berekiah colorfully intensifies the point, saying that Cain goes forth like a beast with a cloven hoof who tries to pass as "clean"—that is, as a hypocrite "who deceives his Creator" (*GR* 22.13). R. Hanina b. Issa counterposed to these condemnations a positive construction of Cain's exit, seeing him "rejoicing" because he is about to have another encounter (*Exodus* 4:14 describes such a meeting), this time with his father.

> Adam met him and asked him, "How did your case go?" "I repented and am reconciled," replied he. Thereupon Adam began beating his face, crying, "So great is the power of repentance, and I did not know!" Forthwith he arose and exclaimed, "A Psalm, a song for the Sabbath day: It is a good thing to make confession unto the Lord" (*Psalms* 92.1).

So concludes *Genesis Rabbah*'s exegesis of the story of Cain and Abel and Cain's dealings with the Lord—with an episode in which the breach between God and Adam is being mended through the penitence of Cain, the chastened killer of his parents' other son. Though it strikes the reader as a happy ending, this final happening is not offered as a summary, nor as the proper conclusion finally reached. *All* of the interpretations of Cain and of his terrible crime that are found in *GR* 22 stand; these varied and often contradictory opinions presume and invite ongoing study and debate of the portrayal of Cain in *Genesis* 4. The reappearance of Adam does, however, underline the continuity of the story of God's dealings with humankind. It belongs to the next chapter of *Genesis Rabbah* to enumerate and describe Cain's offspring, and the line of Adam issuing from Seth, whose name carries the meaning "God has provided me with another offspring in place of Abel" (*Genesis* 4:25).

Philo's Writing: *Questions and Answers on Genesis*

No discussion of early Jewish interpretations of the Cain and Abel saga, however selective, can exclude the name and writings of Philo Judaeus, the Alexandrian intellectual—a biblical commentator and philosopher—who lived ca. 20 BCE to 50 CE.[39] Indeed, it is doubtful that anyone in antiquity wrote more about Adam's sons than this expositor of the Bible in its Greek translation, the Septuagint. In his *Questions and Answers on Genesis* (*QG*), and in several other works in which Philo interprets the story of Cain and Abel, we encounter both the "literal" account of what transpired between Adam's sons and also the accompanying figural or metaphorical exegesis— the latter producing a broad range of philosophical-theological observations touching upon the nature of the Good/God, the makeup of human beings, and—especially—definitions and descriptions of virtue and of vice.[40] In David Dawson's words, "The principal nonliteral meaning that Philo discovers in scripture concerns either the moral education of the human soul or the order of the cosmos in which the soul's progress from vice to virtue takes place."[41] Emblematic of Philo's approach is the title which announces that "The Worse is wont to attack the Better." The case in point is Cain's assault on his brother, a narrative capable of being read simply, but one that by its very content invites analysis along philosophical and ethical lines. The allegorical interpretation of literature was by no means novel in the first century, but the ways in which Philo Judaeus undertook this way of reading in his own context was quite distinctive, as we shall observe.[42]

"Why did Cain after some days offer firstfruits of offerings, while Abel (brought an offering) from the firstborn and fat ones, not after some days?" So opens *Questions and Answers on Genesis* (90), with Philo moving to probe both the timing and motivations of the two brothers' offerings. (The phrase "after some days" stands in the LXX version of the verse.) Cain's delay indicates "great wickedness," and marks its contrast to the offering of Abel, a "lover of God" who made sacrifice "without any delay at all or rejection by his Father"—that is, God, the receiver of his offering (*QG* 60). But what inspired Cain and Abel to offer their sacrifices? The ensuing "answer" represents one of Philo's major moral-theological ideas—one he finds in scripture: the "distinction between the lover of self and the lover of God." How is Cain's fault of self-love demonstrated?

In *The Sacrifices of Abel and Cain* Philo places the teaching that "good deeds should be done in a spirit of eagerness" in alignment with two sources of authoritative wisdom. The philosophical tenet "the best of deeds is to do without delay the pleasure of the Primal Good" (*to proton kalon*) he couples with the biblical command in *Deuteronomy* 22:21 ("if thou vowest a vow, delay not to pay it"). One who has received from the giver of all things should give honor to God (and not to himself) "without delay."[43]

People fail to do this in three ways, Philo observes. Least grievous is the case of those who forget their blessings and thereby cheat themselves of the benefit of "the spirit of thankfulness." Others, captive to their own pride, believe they are themselves the sources of the goodness that has come to them, and do not recognize "[Him] who is the true cause." A third group falls between the two in degree of culpability:

> They accept the Ruling Mind as the cause of the good, yet say that these good things are their natural inheritance. They claim that they are prudent, courageous, temperate and just, and are therefore in the sight of God counted worthy of His favours.[44]

In their delay in returning thanks, this last group nods to the benevolent deity, but expects a return nod in recognition of their adherence to the four chief virtues. The good things that have befallen them are as much returns on their investments in achievement as they are divine gifts.

The answer to the question "Why did Cain delay in bringing his offering?" is this: Cain and Abel were motivated by different loves, the one misdirected, the other well directed. In addition to being explanations of what happened, these contrasting loves of self and of God are the models for, and represent the options open to, any reasoning person in the world who enjoys life's benefits.

Put in terms of belief and loyalty, Philo argues, the case of Cain is a study in animated idolatry: the creature's self-love, as a form of strict individualism, is also atheism. Abel, by contrast, represents pure devotion and philosophy: the creature's love of Wisdom/God/the Good, as a form of humility, an acknowledgment of human dependency and gifted-ness. These several aspects of Philo's thinking are distilled, in part of the answer given for the question raised in *QG* 64, into a firm assertion: "It is not proper to offer the best things to that which is created, namely oneself, and the second best to the All-wise." The irony and tragedy of the self-regard of the Cain-like, Philo remarks, is that the chief truth about Cain himself is that he was unable to "possess" (one etymology provided for his name is "Possession") or "rule" even himself. His soul was not well-ordered—it was not controlled.[45]

Question 60 further asks, "Why does He who knows all ask the fratricide, 'Where is Abel, thy brother?'" Philo's response requires us to follow a somewhat abstract line of reasoning. He is not concerned here to correct the question's erroneous depiction of God as a being of limited understanding. The usual philosophical enumeration the divine attributes, including omniscience, would have addressed that *apparent* problem. Rather, Philo's interests as philosopher-theologian close in upon the purposes and effects of the Lord's interrogation of Cain: "[God] wishes that man himself of his own will shall confess [his deed], in order that he may not pretend that all things seem to come about through necessity." Cain's understanding of what has taken place, and why, is being probed against the background of determinist philosophies, on the one hand, and those philosophies, on the other, which underscore the agency and accountability of beings possessed of free will and freedom of action. Philo invokes a well-known Stoic distinction between human acts within, and human acts beyond a person's control when he argues that a person who committed murder "through necessity would confess that he acted unwillingly, for that which is not in our power is not to be blamed" (*QG* 68). That is, had the death of his brother been an accident, Cain would have spoken up—regretful, perhaps, but blameless. But the one who does evil *intentionally* denies his deed, and Philo asserts, denies it for a definite reason: "sinners are obliged to repent." Cain dreads not only being found out, but being required to make amends.

A final comment in the QG 68's answer turns from analysis of Cain's, or the guilty party's, denial of responsibility to the nature of God. However, it is God's justice and fairness, not God's omniscience, that is defended—with support from the Torah: "(Moses) inserts in all parts of his legislation that the Deity is not the cause of evil." (In chapter three we shall encounter Muslim interpreters debating just this proposition.)

Question 69 reads: "Why does he (Cain) reply as if to a man, saying, 'I do not know. Am I my brother's keeper?'" Philo argues that Cain is exposed once more as a holder of atheist opinion, believing that there is no "divine eye [that] penetrates all things and sees all things at one time." Here the character of God as all-knowing *is* declared—over against Cain's lack of regard, captured in his insolent response. But more strongly denounced is Cain's apologia—his self-defending retort-question, "Am I my brother's keeper?" You had only three other humans to keep track of, Philo remonstrates, and to whom else besides your brother might you have been the protector? Continuing to speak with the authority of God's voice, Philo accuses Cain of taking good care of "violence, injustice, treachery, and homicide," but "show[ing] contempt for [his] brother's safety, as though it were something superfluous."

The question (QG 70), "What is the meaning of the words, 'The voice of thy brother calls to me from the earth?'" Philo takes up with enthusiasm. He finds God's words "exemplary":

> The Deity hears the deserving even though they are dead, knowing that they live an incorporeal life. But from the prayers of evil men He turns away His face even though they enjoy the prime of life, considering that they are dead to true life and bear their body with them like a tomb that they may bury their unhappy soul in it.

The crisis of the murder of the good brother by the wicked, and the text's depiction of God finding that the victim's blood remained vocal allows Philo to maintain the continuing "true life" of the righteous dead, to distinguish true life from life in the body, and to register the spiritual-religious point that evil doers, while seemingly alive, estrange themselves from God. Cain and the wicked walk about barren of authentic existence, with misery buried deep within them.[46] In the treatise *The Worse Attacks the Better* Philo describes the fates of Abel and Cain in this way:

> So far as superficial appearance goes . . . Abel has been done away with, but when examined more carefully . . . Cain has been done away with by himself. . . . Abel, therefore, strange as it seems, has both been put to death and lives: he is destroyed or abolished out of the mind of the fool, but he is alive with the happy life in God. . . . What we arrive at is this: the wise man, while seeming to die to the corruptible life, is alive in the incorruptible; but the worthless man, while alive to the life of wickedness, is dead to the life [that is] happy.[47]

QG 76 does not ask simply what the mark of Cain was, but considers its cause: "why is a sign placed upon the fratricide in order that anyone who finds him may not kill him, when it was fitting to do the opposite and give him into the hands (of another) for destruction?" Philo's answer unfolds in related segments. It is important to distinguish, first, between death as commonly understood (i.e., mortality), and the many forms of death—sorrows, fears, hopelessness, and so on—that befall creatures while they still live in the world of sense. Second, the Cain and Abel story establishes, early in the scripture, the "law of the incorruptibility of the soul" to "refute the false belief" (*pseudodoxian*) that only physical existence is "blessed." Philo elaborates:

> For behold one of the two (brothers) is guilty of the greatest evils, namely impiety and fratricide, and yet is alive and begets children and founds cities. But he who gave evidence of piety is destroyed by cunning. Not only does the divine word clearly proclaim that it is not the life of sense which is good and that death is not an evil, but also that the life of the body is not even related to life. But there is another (life) unaging and immortal, which incorporeal souls receive as their lot.[48]

Now Cain was offered an "amnesty" by God, who acted benevolently (as all judges must) in regard to first offenders. It was not that God did not wish to destroy evil, but his purpose in hesitating to deliver punishment, and in offering Cain a protective sign, was to educate him toward mercy rather than cruelty. So the Lord exercised gentleness "concerning the first sinner, not killing the homicide but destroying him in another manner" (QG 76). Cain is not allowed to be counted as a member of Adam's family—that is, not as a human, but "a genus peculiar and separate from the rational species, like one driven out, and a fugitive, and one transformed into the nature of beasts."[49] By Philo's interpretation, Cain's continued existence is sub-human and bestial.

In contrast, murdered but still-existent Abel is in God's company. Question 78, in reference to Eve's exclamation over Seth's birth, "God has raised up for me another seed" (*Genesis* 4:25), understands Abel's name in this way, and draws conclusions in keeping with yet another etymology:

> "Abel" is interpreted as "brought and offered up on high" to God. And it is not fitting to offer up everything, but only what is good, for (God) is not the cause of evil. . . . Wherefore nature separated him from his twin, and made the good man worthy of immortality (*athanasias*), resolving him into a voice interceding with God; but the wicked man it gave over to destruction.

We see that alongside his close scrutiny of Cain's motives and deeds, Philo steadily valorized Abel—exalting him as the one who rightly offered his gift to God. Abel, lover of God, is also Abel sacrificed and Abel triumphant. He exists immortally, having been "brought and offered up on high." The righteous victim who lives on, *invictus*, bears all the marks of a martyr, his endurance rewarded from on high. In the language that described the ultimate fates of the Maccabean martyrs, to whom "God . . . will in his mercy give life and breath" (*2 Maccabees* 7:23) and enjoy the prize of "immortality in endless life" (*4 Maccabees* 17:11–12), Philo proposes that the Creator "will . . . of His own mercy give you breath and life again" (*On the Cherubim* 32, 114).[50] One of the ideas that informs Jewish martyrologies is given full expression in Philo's comment about Cain's "victory over Abel" in *On the Posterity of Cain and His Exile* 11, 38–39:

> In my judgment and in that of my friends, preferable to life with impious men would be death with pious men; for awaiting those who die in this way there will be undying life, but awaiting those who live in that way there will be eternal death.[51]

With his turn to the histories of the offspring of Cain and of Seth (Abel's substitute and continuation), Philo broadens the scope of his application of the chief theme he found at *Genesis* 4: the opposition of virtue and vice, of those oriented to God versus those oriented to self now must also be discussed in terms of two races. Cain's progeny credit themselves with every good they possess, but lovers of virtue, Philo writes, "remain enrolled under Seth as the head of their race." Seth took up and championed his slain brother's way of wisdom. His race is of a "sort very hard to find," being made up of "those who have been well-pleasing to God, and whom God has translated and removed from perishable to immortal races, [being] no more found among the multitude."[52]

Focused as they are upon questions of the two ways taken by the first two brothers, of souls of individuals pursuing virtue being endangered by the evil that "couches," Philo's several treatments of the first murder inevitably expand to consider the social and political inferences to be drawn from the fratricide.[53] I find one example particularly instructive. Toward the end of *The Worse Attacks the Better*, Philo takes issue with Cain's complaint that, barred from God's presence, he will be vulnerable: "groaning and trembling upon the earth, then it will be that anyone that finds me shall slay me" (LXX *Genesis* 4:14). He will be found either by those like him, who are likely to protect him as a kindred being, or by those unlike him, who out of opposition will seek to destroy him. No, Philo argues, Cain is not threatened by *everyone* he meets, and the greater danger is not posed by those unlike him. Rather, "unscrupulous people, given to vices closely akin to his, will prove his guards and keepers. . . . For it is an almost invariable rule that both persons and causes are cherished by those who are friendly and attached to them."[54] So God was right to respond, "Not so" (*Genesis* 4:15) to Cain's fear that anyone might kill him, "since countless numbers have been enrolled on your side." Only "a friend of virtue" will be Cain's "irreconcilable enemy."[55] There follows a set of reflections on the human behaviors and vices that God sought to purge and purify with the Flood. Philo elaborates the particular faults of the worthless man who can neither control his tongue nor his sexual sins (prompted by "ungoverned lust"), and observes:

> Our cities are full of these evils; all the earth is full of them from one end to another; and out of them springs up for mankind, both as individuals and in communities, the war that is waged in time of peace, the war that has no break or pause, and is the greatest of all wars (*The Worse Attacks the Better* 47, 174).

Philo emphasizes the need to resist temptations. It is better to be blind and deaf than to see or hear things injurious to the soul . . . better to have one's tongue cut off than to speak what should not be divulged, "better to be made a eunuch than to be mad after illicit unions."[56] We notice, however, that Philo's counsel extends beyond the dangers to individual souls in order to warn against the social and institutional effects of unrighteousness—namely, continuous hostilities and warfare. Warnings are necessary because the vicious relentlessly desires to defeat the virtuous—in families, in states, and in entire races of people. "Folly is a deathless evil" affecting individuals and societies, Philo concludes, because love of worthless things flares up again and again, imparting to those captured by it, like Cain, "the disease that never dies."[57]

Philo Judaeus's interpretation of the first murder reveals the scope and the connectedness of its lessons for persons seeking to live virtuously, for the citizens and their education, and for all affected by the evils of war. At the end of *The Posterity of Cain and His Exile* he wrote:

The consecrated intelligence, being [God's] minister and attendant, must do all those things in which her Master delights: [God] delights in the maintenance of a well-ordered state under good laws, in the abolishing of wars and factions, not only those which occur between cities, but also those that arise in the soul; and these are greater and more serious than those, for they outrage reason, a more divine faculty than others within us. Weapons of war can go so far as to inflict bodily and monetary loss, but a healthy soul they can never harm. From this it appears that states would have done rightly if before bringing against one another arms and engines of war with the enslavement and complete overthrow of the enemy in view, they had prevailed on their citizens one by one to put an end to the disorder which abounds within himself, and which is so great and unceasing. For, to be honest, this is the original (*archetypon*) of all wars. If this be abolished . . . the human race will attain to the experience and enjoyment of profound peace, taught by the law of nature, namely virtue, to honour God and to be occupied with His service, for this is the source of long life and happiness.[58]

CONCLUSION

In our initial attention to the storyline in the Hebrew Bible's narration of the Cain and Abel saga we trained our sight on those issues within it that would invite or demand follow-up explanations—even extensions of the narrative beyond what the scripture stated. Next, a painting containing signs of Jewish influences was used in order that we might do several things at once: revisit individual scenes in the drama of the murder, think more about the actions of its characters (including God), note the artist's choices of what to emphasize, and (as it turned out) come to some preliminary awareness of how differently a Jew and a Christian might have comprehended this set of images.

The chapter examined three writings about the tragedy of Cain's murder of his brother: *Targum Pseudo-Jonathan*, *Genesis Rabbah*, and Philo Judaeus's *Questions and Answers on Genesis*. At a formal level it was easy to point to the differences in genre and method in these works of commentary on *Genesis* 4, since one is a work of translation (with emendations), one a collection of rabbinic expositions (*midrashim*), and the third an exegete-philosopher's probings of issues arising from the biblical text. We recall *Targum Pseudo-Jonathan*'s need to expand upon the Hebrew text while translating it to Aramaic—and not just in the case where a sentence had been interrupted. The world of *Genesis Rabbah* presented us with rabbis interactively interpreting the characters of Adam's sons. In this collection the value of keeping discussion of topics within the Torah open—for the sake of the community's continuing life with its scripture and its God—was strongly evident. Philo's perspective combined biblical and Greek philosophical ideas in order to mount an argument about two contrasting loves, and their place in the history of the first family, and for that matter, for all individuals and societies thereafter.

Taking up the drama of the first murder, Jewish commentators knew what the Torah had proclaimed about this sin. Its prohibition in one of the Ten Commandments (*Exodus* 20:13, *Deuteronomy* 5:17), and the justification for a murderer's penalty of death (in *Genesis* 9:6) made clear that the victim was precious to God, who created him or her in His own image. *Targum Pseudo-Jonathan, Genesis Rabbah*, and Philo's writings focused upon Cain, whom they condemned in definite language—and made an example of murderous evil.

Intriguing assessments of Abel were also proposed, most of these less inclined to question his role in the strife with his brother than to represent him as an innocent victim, then a model for virtue, and, finally, as a martyr whose reward was life among the immortals.

Finally, the majority of our interpretive data concern Cain, since not only his sin but the reasons for his crime and the character of his punishment by God were of dominant interest. These texts evinced a definite double-mindedness about Cain's culpability and also about his sentence as a murderer. According to the interpreters, Cain's evil consisted in his envy, his disdain of the notion that God acts with fairness, his jealous protection of his privileges as the firstborn son of Adam, his self-serving concern for his and his family's reputation, and so on. But into these commentators' condemnatory assessments of Cain were also woven some theories that modified this consistent record of wickedness. The assertion that Satan was operative in the life of Cain—in his birth and in his particular intentions and deeds—suggested that Cain, a man under the devil's sway, was the secondary actor in his own actions, and only secondarily culpable. While God said to Cain (*Genesis* 4:7) that the sin that was "couched" against his door could be mastered, there was a tendency among some exegetes to see Cain's "evil inclination" as an explanation of his actions.

Moreover, we recall that considerable effort was expended by certain rabbis to "hear" Cain's response to God's sentence (in 4:13)—"my punishment is too great to bear"—as a confession, even an act of repentance. It is as if the commentators wished to treat Cain sternly (his crime was great) but also with some sympathy (he and his situation were more complex than they seemed at first glance). A fundamental contributor to this ambivalent strain in the Jewish interpreters' characterizations of Cain can be located in the Hebrew Bible itself: on the one hand, his murder of Abel is denounced by God, and he is cursed; but on the other hand, Cain receives a delay of punishment. Not immediately suffering the murderer's penalty of death, Cain receives from God a protective mark, and he produces a family. This curious history of Cain contributed to the interpreters' explorations of his person and character—and of God's several ways of treating sinners. Will similar two-sided assessments of the first murderer—including instincts to exonerate him—arise in Christian and Muslim representations of him?

Though we are barely underway in this exploration of the three different religions' ways of owning the biblical-qur'anic narrative, we should conclude this chapter with a multilayered question: what makes the interpretations of Cain and Abel we have just encountered Jewish? There are some obvious answers. Jewish writers, translators, and compilers produced the works we read, and their intended readerships and audiences were Jewish, even though Philo also had non-Jews among his readers. Further, whether in Hebrew, Aramaic, or Greek, it was the Bible of the Jews that occupied *Pseudo-Jonathan*, the rabbis of *Genesis Rabbah*, and Philo; their primary orientation and loyalty was to the mysteries present in their Holy Book, understood by Jews to be a gift from the God of *their* covenant.

These matter-of-fact observations do not, however, address the deeper question about the distinctive Jewishness of the religious vision, nor the cultural and theological perspective encountered in the works of commentary we considered. Perhaps the beginning of an answer about Judaism's characteristic viewpoint can be suggested in an example—namely, by registering the strong pursuit in connection with the strife between Adam's sons of the issue of theodicy. The theme is, of course, rooted in the Hebrew Bible's presentation of Israel's Lord as a just God. The dispute between Cain and Abel over whether the world works in accordance with God's judgment of what is right, or in accordance with God's (unjust) favoritism is best understood in the light of earliest Hebraic understanding of, and belief in, a righteous God—a deity whose dealings with his covenant people are fair and equitable.

There is a reason for leaving open and unfinished a response to the question I have posed about Judaism's distinctive point of view or fundamental vision—one that might be visible in its trajectories of understanding of the Cain and Abel story. A premise of this book is that we best discover in what way a religion's interpretation is Jewish, or Christian, or Muslim through careful comparison. Religious communities' patterns of life and thought take on deeper definition when examined and appreciated side by side—and as we see them influencing each other.

We turn now to early Christians' explorations of the biblical story of Cain and Abel, hoping to discern how and why Christians sometimes held to views and interpretations quite like those of the Jews while at others they discovered and fashioned divergent understandings of this narrative's sense and significance. To what extent did these differences stem from conscious competition and rivalry?

CHAPTER 2

Cain and Abel Christianized

How many ways did early Christian artists and writers understand the story of Cain and Abel, and make new sense of it for their own times, places, and circumstances? Already in writings that would be included later in a canonical New Testament, we find four such invocations of the drama of the first murder. The author of *1 John* attacks separatists in his own community, urging loyalist members *not* to

> be like Cain who was from the evil one, and murdered his brother. And why did he murder him? Because his own deeds were evil and his brother's righteous (*1 John* 3:12).

A similarly combative deployment of the story is found in the *Epistle of Jude*, though there the warning is against intruders who endanger "the faith that was once for all entrusted to the saints" (vv.3–4).

> Woe to them! For they go the way of Cain, and abandon themselves to Balaam's error for the sake of gain, and perish in Korah's rebellion (v. 11).[1]

In the *Epistle to the Hebrews* (a sermon, as scholars generally agree) we find a rollcall of the patriarchs, heroes and heroines in Israel's history who "by faith" won their rewards from God. At the head of the list, at 11:4, we find our story's victim:

> By faith Abel offered to God a more acceptable sacrifice than Cain's. Through this he received approval as righteous, God himself giving approval for his gifts; he died, but through his faith he still speaks.

Matthew 23:29–36 has Jesus deliver the last of his seven woes against Israel's religious leaders—a polemic accusing them of being "descendants of those who murdered the prophets."

> 29 Woe to you, scribes and Pharisees, hypocrites! For you build the tombs of the prophets and decorate the graves of the righteous 30 and you say, "If we had lived in the days of our ancestors, we would not have taken part with them in shedding the blood of the prophets." 31 Thus you testify against yourselves that you are descendants of those who murdered the prophets. 32 Fill up, then, the measure of your ancestors. 33 You snakes, you brood of vipers! How can you escape being sentenced to hell? 34 Therefore I send you prophets, sages, and scribes, some of whom you will kill and crucify, and some you will flog in your synagogues and pursue from town to town, 35 so that upon you may come all the righteous blood shed on earth, from the blood of righteous Abel to the blood of Zechariah son of Barachiah, whom you murdered between the sanctuary and the altar. 36 Truly I tell you, all this will come upon this generation.

An attack on hypocritical piety—that is, the glaring contrast between what is professed and what is done—Jesus's speech at the same time urges upon his community an uncompromised fidelity, since that church's faith, which must be congruent in words and deeds, is, or may soon be, under the pressure of persecution.[2]

In these earliest references to Cain and Abel by Christian writers, we discern their efforts to establish the Jesus movement's place in the divine plan—in God's revelation to them of a "new covenant" in history. Putting forward a fundamental and aggressive question, they asked: whose side are you on—the holy family of God, or the family of the evil one? Abel's or Cain's? The question issues from a confident and, to the Christian groups, an essential presupposition: "We belong to God, and we are like Abel, whose righteousness God approved, for we have been newly created as his people by the revelation in Jesus Christ, his son." We shall meet forms of these arguments in subsequent centuries, when different contexts—and additional adversaries—inspired diverse modes of summoning up the story of Cain's murder of Abel in order to advance the Christian cause.

VISUAL COMMENTARY: CAIN
AND ABEL IN A ROMAN CATACOMB

Discovered in Rome only in 1955, the Via Latina catacomb was constructed in several stages over the fourth century, ultimately expanding to ten burial cubiculas (small chambers or rooms), plus three subsidiary rooms.

Figure 2.1 The offerings of Abel and Cain (with Adam and Eve). Fourth century CE. Painting: 76 x 103 cm. © Pontifical Commission for Sacred Archaeology, Rome. Via Latina Catacomb, Cubiculum B.

Some four hundred burials were accommodated there (see Figure 2.1).[3] The great majority of the fresco paintings decorating its chamber walls and ceilings portray figures or scenes familiar from the Bible of the Christian churches—the combination of the writings from the "old covenant" and from the "new." Alongside these are numerous pastoral scenes replete with animals and birds, and also human figures, male and female, who raise and extend their arms and hands in an ancient gesture of prayer. The cemetery's iconography also includes deities and heroes who frequently appear in Roman funerary art: Minerva, Ceres, Persephone, and Hercules (who is pictured bringing Alcestis back from the nether world to Admetus, her husband). Both Christian and traditional polytheist families appear to have been the owners of this private burial complex.

Cain and Abel do, of course, appear elsewhere in Christian art; we met their scene-by-scene story in the illuminated folio from the Ashburnham Pentateuch (which postdates the paintings within this catacomb by several centuries), and we shall be considering later in this chapter several other scenes of the brothers bringing their sacrifices to God. Nonetheless, this representation of Adam, Eve, Cain, and Abel, painted in Via Latina cubiculum B sometime around 315 to 325, qualifies as a unique piece of Christian artistic interpretation.

This chamber is decorated with a surprising variety of biblical scenes, many of which could be understood to relate to a crisis of life or death, to hopes for deliverance from the world or for the heavenward ascent of souls. More difficult to associate with burial-place consolations are images found at the room's entrance. There is Phineas, who by impaling with his spear the couple joined in intercourse (Zimri the Israelite and the Midianite woman Cozbi) won "a pact of friendship" with God; his "impassioned action for his God" was understood as "making expiation for the Israelites," whose whoring after Moabite women involved idolatry (*Numbers* 25:1–14). Also depicted at the room's opening is God's provision to wayfaring and pious Tobias of a fish whose organs possessed healing powers (in the popular Jewish apocryphal text, *Tobit* (here, 6: 1b–9).

Other images from biblical narratives or from the lives of Old Testament personalities also appear in this richly decorated section of the cata-comb: Rahab's assistance to Joshua's spies in Jericho (*Joshua* 2:15), Absalom hanging from the terebinth tree where he met his death (*2 Samuel* 18:15), Lot's deliverance from Sodom with his daughters (his wife shown being turned into a pillar of salt), and the child Moses being rescued from the Nile by his sister and by the Pharaoh's daughter. In a space on the right side of the cubiculum there are more individual scenes, five of which have to do with a vision, a divine epiphany or a wonder recorded in the Pentateuch: Jacob in Bethel dreams of the ladder which angels traverse (*Genesis* 28:10–13), Abraham receives the three angelic visitors at Mamre (*Genesis* 18:1–8), Joseph has two dreams foretelling his greatness—first of the sheaves of wheat bowing to him, and then of the sun, moon, and stars doing the same (*Genesis* 37:5–9), Elijah ascends to heaven (*2 Kings* 2:9–14), and Balaam (here viewed positively), who with his ass's help, recognizes the angel of the Lord (*Numbers* 22). All of these patriarchs and prophets expe-rienced encounters with God, in the process learning of their special status with him. The two remaining paintings in this zone within cubiculum B share the theme. They depict out-of-order blessings, the extraordinary and propitious bestowals of favor and inheritance: Isaac's choice of Jacob in the place of his older brother, Esau (*Genesis* 27:1–28:9) and Jacob's choice of Ephraim rather than Manasseh (*Genesis* 48:1–20).

Directly above the image of Cain and Abel we are considering is a depic-tion (Figure 2.2) of their parents' eviction from the garden.

A bearded male figure dressed in tunic and pallium who escorts Adam and Eve through a passageway at the boundary of Paradise would seem to be "the Lord ... [who] drove the man out, and [who] stationed east of the garden of Eden the cherubim and the fiery ever-turning sword, to guard the way to the tree of life" (*Genesis* 3:23–24). Here we have God represented in human form, and not merely as a hand extending from heaven.[4]

Figure 2.2 The expulsion of Adam and Eve from Eden. Fourth century CE. Painting: 102 x 99 cm. © Pontifical Commission for Sacred Archaeology, Rome. Via Latina Catacomb, Cubiculum B.

Noting that it stands just beneath the depiction of the banishment of Adam and Eve we return to consideration of the representation of Cain and Abel bringing their offerings. How is the composition to be understood? Do we see in the painting two separate scenes or one? In the left half of the painting Eve and Adam are seen sitting on a rock in the "garments of skins" (*Genesis* 3:21) provided to them in Eden by God. Eve is turned toward Adam, while he stares forward. Both have raised a hand to their faces, and their postures suggest some form of pensiveness or sadness. Quite probably the motif, like its counterpart in the Cain and Abel painting in the Ashburnham Pentateuch, is related to the legend found in the first-century *Life of Adam and Eve*, which tells of their seven days of mourning and weeping after having been driven from the garden.[5]

Within this single image, we wonder how the depiction of Adam and Eve relates to the depiction of Abel and Cain. William Tronzo pointed out that the paintings in chamber B attempt to suggest three dimensionality "in the juxtaposition of opaque darks and lights."[6] The smaller size of Adam and Eve and the comparative darkness of their image may be taken as an indication that they are in the background, while their two sons take their places in the progression of the biblical narrative. This is further suggested by the fact that Abel and Cain move with their offerings to an unseen point—toward altars intimated to be further out front and to the left. Not so prominent, but certainly not to be missed among the painting's subjects, is the serpent, who slithers on the ground (*Genesis* 3:14). In the latter half of *Genesis* 3, God's expulsion of bad actors from the garden of Eden begins with the snake, who is to be more cursed than all cattle and wild beasts. He will crawl on his belly, and will, with all his progeny, forever be under attack by Eve and her offspring.

We might regard the expelled trio of the disobedient—the tempted pair and the tempter—in the left side of the painting as a sequel to the episode depicted in the painting above it—the eviction of Adam and Eve. They are shown in their dejection, and what happened next then appears up front in our painting—the fateful sacrifices offered to God by the world's first offspring, the brothers. Abel, clothed in tunic and pallium and walking with the lamb extended forward in his arms, enjoys a place nearly at the center of the framed scene. At his side, wearing a short tunic, is Cain, bearing in his arms bundles of produce from the field. While Abel's tilt of head and demeanor might strike us as having the effect of showing him more confident than Cain, as if the artist seeks to interpret the young men's moods or prospects as bringers of sacrifices, an expert evaluator of catacomb painting styles notices no such thing, but only that in the case of the brothers, as also elsewhere in this part of the burial complex, the artist could not avoid giving his subjects "a disconcerting cross-eyed look."[7]

Are we to see the serpent as a *continuing* tempter-agitator by virtue of his being as close to Abel and Cain as he is to Eve and Adam? James Stevenson, who viewed the painting not in parts but as a single scene in the post-Fall story of humanity, thought so: "[Adam and Eve] sit clad in skins with their sons standing by them, each holding his offering, and the serpent, symbol of the coming murder, is present in the middle of the picture."[8] The passages from early Christian writings noted at the chapter's beginning were very likely to have been known in third-century Rome—they carry clues about how the painting of Adam, Eve, the serpent, and the offerings being made by Cain and Abel might have been understood, and why several other paintings in cubiculum are shown in proximity to it.

We circle back momentarily to *Hebrews*, recalling that it was addressed to Christians in need of encouragement *and* in need of warning. Conditions of persecution and possible martyrdom compelled a sense of urgency; it was of crucial importance to be found, at the time of *krisis* (the Greek term

for judgment), among those who maintained their loyalty to God. "The
promise of entering [heavenly] rest is still open," (*Hebrews* 4:1)—open
to the faithful among the living and the dead to whom Christ will appear
when he returns "to save those who are eagerly waiting for him" (*Hebrews*
9:27–28)—including those "asleep" in their graves.

Faith, salvation, and "rest" cannot be separated from alarms about their
opposites infidelity, damnation, and lasting torment, but *Hebrews* is more
interested in naming the heroes than the villains. We noted earlier that
Hebrews 11:4 characterized Abel as the brother who gave the "more acceptable sacrifice," and stated that though "he died ... through his faith he
still speaks." Abel lives on as one of the blessed of God, to whose company
will be added others—Enoch, Noah, Abraham, Moses, and all those who
will comprise what the author calls "a cloud of witnesses" to God. *Hebrews*
12:24 goes on to present Abel as the prototype of Jesus toward whom the
faithful make their journey, having come to Zion and to God, "and to Jesus,
the mediator of the new covenant, and to the sprinkled blood that speaks a
better word than the blood of Abel."

Abel is both lesson and type: he exemplifies the good brother, the one
who acts by faith, winning God's approval at history's beginning, and he
stands for the Son of God who comes in history's last days to save the faithful. In a religion celebrating as savior one who made an offering of his own
life, Abel is a superb symbol. There are good reasons for assuming that both
of these meanings of Abel—he who lived by faith and he who prefigured
Christ's death—would have occurred, rather easily, to Christian visitors to
the catacomb.

How does the painting of Cain and Abel fit, in terms of its message, with
these images surrounding it, and do the several paintings, taken together,
help to interpret each other? The two brothers bring offerings, and will
receive different responses from the Lord. To any viewer with knowledge of
the story, the portent of two outcomes is present in that half of the painting. The two siblings who walk in unison with their sacrifices are in reality adversaries. The warning against conflict gains some reinforcement in
the tensions surrounding blessings of younger brothers in nearby images.
The greatness Jacob bestows upon Joseph's son Ephraim is only relatively
greater than that which will come to Manasseh (*Genesis* 48:17–20), but the
earlier story of Jacob's gaining the blessing meant for his elder brother has
sinister tones certainly akin to those of the Cain and Abel saga. "Esau harbored a grudge against Jacob ... and said to himself, 'Let but the mourning period of my father come, and I will kill my brother Jacob'" (*Genesis*
27:42–43). Likewise, key episodes in the Joseph story turn on the question of a God-inspired and -protected son who sparks jealousy in his older

brothers. The image of Cain and Abel going to make their offerings could only remind its viewer of the fatal conflict that yielded an innocent victim and a murderer, one sibling adjudged righteous, and the other adjudged guilty. Indeed, Abel is the recipient of God's approval and, like Jacob, Ephraim, and Joseph, the winner of powerful blessing. On the other side, in a spectrum running from damned to finally repentant, are the losers, those deprived of the needed benediction: Cain, Esau, Manasseh, and Joseph's brothers.

It is perhaps too much to say that cubiculum B's paintings, taken together, present us with a coherent and consistent iconographic program, yet we see in the paintings' subjects several theological concepts and themes that stand in close relation to one other. Chief among these is the idea of divine favor, the inheritance of the promise to be God's blessed ones, God's "chosen portion." The viewers knew that Abel's offering was to be approved, and that God would reward Abraham's hospitality to the angels. They knew also that God blessed Lot's responsiveness to the divine warning concerning Sodom's evil, and would oversee and protect Joseph the dreamer-prophet, in whom the posterity of Abraham, Isaac, and Jacob continued. To be spoken to by God, to behold angels and heavenly realities, or to dream propitious dreams—occurrences in the lives of Abraham, Moses, Jacob, Joseph, and Balaam—were recognized as signs of extraordinary privilege. To be taken up to heaven, as Elijah was, involved both seeing what the future held and waiting no longer for the life promised in the world to come. Another divine gift (to take note of a strong motif present in this cluster of paintings) was to receive a blessing "out of turn," whether from God or from one of the holy fathers—a good fortune shared by Abel, Jacob, and Ephraim.

The fundamental early Christian belief in the imminent judgment that God would bring upon the unworthy is not at all downplayed in the images of cubiculum B. Those who engage in rivalry and envy will receive the punishment they deserve. Cain and Absalom will be held accountable for their murders. Cain's curse is known to the catacomb visitor who sees him striding forward with Abel to make his offering. The portrait of Absalom is a graphic foretelling.[9] Killer of his brother Amnon (*2 Samuel* 13:23–39) and rival of David his father, Absalom will meet his fate while hanging by his hair from a tree, his mule having run out from beneath him. The case of Lot's wife, whose failure of conviction stands in contrast to the resolve of her husband and daughters, is bluntly and forcefully drawn. She is damned, turned into a cautionary monument of salt. Come-uppance of a less drastic sort, one requiring confession and repentance before reconciliation occurs, is featured in the scenes involving Joseph and his brothers.

What of Adam and Eve, here depicted post-Eden, sunk in grief? In their two appearances in chamber B they do not represent hope or redemption—but rather are portrait-statements of the human problem, and of the sorrow they have brought upon themselves and their progeny. (Other early Christian depictions of Adam and Eve, as we shall see below, convey more positive signals about them.)

The paintings in Via Latina's cubiculum B, then, give expression to the double edge of divine judgment, which metes out God's protection and promise of prosperity to the worthy, and condemnation and woes to the unfaithful. To moderns this emphasis on the assize—the divine measure of the ways lives were led—may appear harsh as part of a repertoire in funerary art, which might have been expected to be filled with comforting motifs. It is difficult to imagine, however, that members of the early Christian movement would be spared confrontation with this all-important challenge at any occasion or place of communal gathering—burial grounds included—so crucial was it as an assertion at the heart of the message proclaimed by Jesus, and just as much, in later years, as an incentive for those who undertook initiation into the churches by baptism.

Such a sharp division between the saved and the damned persists in the earliest churches' interpretations of the Cain and Abel saga, pointing to emergent discrimination between the old promise and the new, between the synagogues and the churches, between the way the early Christians see themselves—the new people of God, heirs by faith, as the author of *Hebrews* regularly insists, of the promise—and the way they regard their Jewish adversaries—as forsakers of God's covenant.

There is of course no patent signal of Christian animosity toward Jews and Judaism (represented by Cain) in the portrait, only the setting in opposition of creation's first brothers, one blessed, the other judged. Cain represents a dire warning against resisting God's purposes, of being faithless and thus having no place among the righteous and redeemed. Abel is a sign of hope fully appropriate in a burial context, for though he dies, the voice of his blood, heeded by God, evinces his continuing existence under divine care. The two brothers stand for the lost and the redeemed, the two outcomes possible in lives lived within a covenant with God.

A CLASH OF GNOSTIC AND ANTI-GNOSTIC CHRISTIAN INTERPRETATIONS OF THE CAIN AND ABEL STORY

Sometime around 180 CE, Irenaeus, a churchman-theologian with roots in Asia Minor who became a bishop in Lyons, wrote *Proof the Apostolic*

Preaching. The treatise is difficult to categorize.[10] At first appearance it bears the marks of catechetical instruction designed for Christian initiates, describing the three-personed God—Father, Son, and Holy Spirit—in whose name they are to be baptized. More than half of the treatise contains an elaborate and extensive marshalling of scriptural texts which Irenaeus presents as proofs that the "theophanies," or the approaches by God to humankind recorded in scripture, had been appearances of God's Son (sometimes, of God's Spirit).

"Logos theology" is what scholarship long ago named the kind of emphatic concentration on God's Word that won favor with many early Christian thinkers, Irenaeus included. Irenaeus assumed that prior to its/his incarnation, God's Word was not only active in the creation of all things, but also *was* himself the voice and the appearance of God in the narratives found in scripture. Thus it was the preincarnate Word, or Reason of God, who became audible in Sinai's burning bush, the Word who visited Abraham and Sarah in angelic guise, and the divine Word whose voice spoke to and through Israel's prophets. Irenaeus regarded the case of Abel, as we shall see, as an integral part of this providential design, in which Christ the savior would sum up or complete God's salvific plan for humankind in his sacrificial dying and in his rising again.

Next in his *Proof the Apostolic Preaching*, continuing the Gospels' interpretive practice, Irenaeus argues from this battery of biblical texts ("testimonia," as these collections of "proof texts" came to be called) that all events of the new dispensation of God had been foretold and had come to pass as promised: the incarnation of God's Word by birth from a virgin, Jesus's ministry in the world, his crucifixion and resurrection, and the emergence of a newly favored covenant people—one that included Gentiles—people from the world's many nations. Predictably, this employment of Jewish scriptures to frame and support Christian truth claims was an affront to Jews, who with good reason considered this strategy an attempt to usurp Judaism's covenant with God through arbitrary and suspect interpretations of their own holy writings.

In a section of his treatise that treats the first family's story, Irenaeus narrates Adam's and Eve's tumble from childlike innocence (including their kisses and embraces free of shame) in Eden, and their expulsion into a world of "many miseries of mind and body" (*Proof* 14–17). *Genesis* 4.1–2, after being quoted, is summarized:

> But the rebel angel, the same who had brought the man into disobedience, and made him a sinner, and been the cause of his being cast out of the Garden, not content with this first evil, brought about in the brothers a second one; for,

filling Cain with his own spirit, he made him a slayer of his brother. And thus Abel died, slain by his brother, a sign for the future, that some would be persecuted and straitened and slain, but the unjust would slay and persecute the just. Whereupon God became exceedingly angry and cursed Cain; and it came to pass, that every generation in the line of succession from him became like its forefather. And God raised up another son to Adam in place of Abel who was slain (Irenaeus, *Proof* 17).

In this retelling of the story of the Fall, Irenaeus characterized Satan as an angel stirred to disobedience, and to encouragement of disobedience, by his envy of the favor shown by God to Adam/man. As purposeful and wily apostate, Satan worked in the serpent, and along with the first couple was expelled from Eden, "since the Garden does not admit a sinner" (*Proof* 16). Cain was not genetically evil, according to Irenaeus. Rather, his act of murder was "inspired" by the "rebel angel" and therefore satanically influenced; his deed was not a result of Cain's *being* demonic. Irenaeus sees the dramas within *Genesis* in terms of various individual beings' chosen actions—in terms of freely intended, rather than determined, behaviors. Nevertheless, Cain's fratricide did itself create a pattern in future history: persecution of the just by the unjust. And Cain's deed, through God's curse upon him, caused all in his future family to be like him: murderous.

The momentous intra-Christian battle that erupted between gnostic and anti-gnostic forms of belief in the second century has become widely known and studied over the past half-century. Arguably the most decisive turning point in this religion's history and communal self-definition occurred through the ultimate victory of the anti-gnostic, or self-proclaimed orthodox, Christian thinkers and church communities. Irenaeus was a central personality and force in this drama, his *Against Heresies* (*Adversus Haereses*) being an exposé and refutation of various teachers he regarded as exponents of gnostic—and false—Christianity. Marcion of Pontus (d. ca. 160), in Irenaeus's judgment, was one of the most dangerous of these heretics. Although Irenaeus's treatise devoted specifically to Marcion's teachings did not survive, there are important sections within *Against Heresies* that describe the ideas of "this man [who] has dared . . . more than any others to malign God shamelessly" (*Against Heresies* 1.27.4).[11] The common protest directed against Marcion by Irenaeus and many others targeted his belief that Christ was the son of a God superior to and more merciful than the creator (the biblical God).

Marcion commanded a large following, and a significant number of churches were loyal to him and his teaching. Modern scholars have had some difficulty identifying the core of his Christian doctrines, wondering whether he was, or was not, the gnostic that Irenaeus presumed him to be. Missing from the ideas Marcion is reported to have taught are many of the elements common to the majority of gnostic Christian systems now known to us. His doctrines proposed no vision nor myth, for example, that pictured humans, fallen from a transcendent realm, retaining within themselves sparks of the divine that would make it possible for them to be reawakened, and then ascend to the realm of their origin. Michael Williams, in his splendid *Rethinking "Gnosticism,"* summarized the strongest features in Marcion's religious thought: "his complete distaste for the God of Jewish Scripture," the belief that "the Father announced by Christ had nothing to do with this creation," and the conviction that "Jesus was the Son sent from [the] good and loving Father, not a Messiah who fulfilled the prophecies of Jewish scripture."[12]

Irenaeus contested a number of gnostic Christian teachers' and schools' understandings of the Cain and Abel story, but an interpretational duel he had with Marcion holds particular interest for us. One point of dispute concerned an event believed to have occurred in the history of Christ's mission on earth, *not* in the most ancient of days during which Cain and Abel lived.

A bit of background is necessary. By the second century various Christian writers and theologians were developing a picture (hinted at in passages like *1 Peter* 3:19–20, 4:6, and *Ephesians* 4:8–10) that Jesus, in the three days between his death and resurrection, descended into Hades and there presented himself and his gospel to the righteous and unrighteous "spirits in prison."

Enunciating this belief (which later became an article of faith—"he descended into hell"—in the Apostles' Creed and the Athanasian Creed), Irenaeus wrote:[13]

> The Lord descended into the regions beneath the earth, preaching his advent there also, and [declaring] the remission of sins received by those who believed in him (*Against Heresies* 4.27.2).

This doctrine pictured an opportunity of forgiveness and redemption for all humans, who, having died before Christ's appearance or advent *on earth,* could now hear and respond to him in the underworld.

Marcion also taught Christ's descent into Hell—but, Irenaeus reports, in a blasphemous form:

> [Marcion], speaking diabolically indeed and in direct opposition to the truth, [says] that Cain and those like him—the men of Sodom and the Egyptians,

and other such, and in general all the nations that walked in all kinds of wickedness—were saved by the Lord when he descended into the lower regions, and came running to him and received him into their realm; but Abel and Enoch and Noah and the other righteous, and the patriarchs such as Abraham with all the prophets and those who were pleasing to God, did not share in the salvation which the serpent who was in Marcion preached. For, he says, since they knew that their God was always testing them, they thought he was testing them then, and so did not come to Jesus or believe his proclamation, and therefore their souls remained in Hades (*Against Heresies* 1.27.3).[14]

Irenaeus's fulminations within the passage fail to obscure Marcion's teaching about Christ's appearance in Hades, with its strong clues relating to his wider system of thought. Unmistakable is the stark and startling reversal of the salvific outcomes—the rewards and punishments—that befall the ancient individuals, groups, and nations whose stories fill the "Law and Prophets." Marcion taught that when Christ descended into the realm of the dead, Cain was saved—being among those who recognized and ran toward their redeemer. Remaining in Hell unrescued, however, was Abel, like the others who are celebrated as God's "righteous" in the scriptures. Looking upon Christ with suspicion, Abel and the others held back warily; they remembered that *their* God was one who put before them tests and temptations. Implicit in this contrast, of course, is that Cain and his company recognized Christ to be the son of the Good God who was merciful, while Abel and his companions, to their disadvantage, feared that the Christ they saw came from God the creator, who was a demanding, and even deceptive, judge.

Some of Marcion's chief teachings are preserved in his "antitheses" (written ca. 140), which juxtapose ideas (sometimes, quotations) from the Old Testament with passages from what will become writings of the New Testament. From several ancient sources the great historian of Christian doctrines, Adolf von Harnack (d. 1930), reconstructed some of Marcion's contrasting propositions, including these:

The Creator was known to Adam and to the following generations, but the Father of Christ is unknown, as Christ himself said to him in these words: "No one has known the Father except the Son" (*Luke* 10:22).

The Good is good to all men; the Creator, however, promises salvation only to those who are obedient to him.

The Good redeems those who believe in him, but he does not judge those who are disobedient to him; the Creator, however, redeems his faithful and judges and punishes the sinners.

Both the place of punishment and that of refuge of the Creator are placed in the underworld for those who obey the Law and the Prophets. But Christ and the God who belongs to him have a heavenly place of rest and a haven, of which the Creator never spoke.

Others of the "antitheses" contrast the Creator with Jesus, or differentiate between the expected Christ/Messiah of Jewish scripture and the Christ of the Good God, whom Marcion refers to as "our Christ":

The God of Creation did not restore the sight of the blinded Isaac [*Genesis* 27:1], but our Lord, because he is good, opened the eyes of many blind men [*Luke* 7:21].

The Creator says, "Hear and hear, but do not understand" [*Isaiah* 6:9]; Christ on the contrary says, "He who has ears to hear, let him hear" [*Luke* 8.8, etc.].

The Creator established the Sabbath; Christ abolishes it [cf *Luke* 6:1 ff.].

The Christ [of the Old Testament] promises to the Jews the restoration of their former condition by return of their land and, after death, a refuge in Abraham's bosom in the underworld. Our Christ will establish the Kingdom of God, an eternal and heavenly possession.[15]

In an influential 1924 study, Harnack argued that Marcion was influenced more by St. Paul's counterposing of law and grace (which he pressurized into a doctrine of two Gods) than by gnostic Christian cosmic myths in circulation at the time. Following Harnack's lead, many modern historians have treated Marcion's teaching of a *fremdem* (alien) God as a heresy different from those promoting a saving knowledge, or *gnosis*.[16] It remains true, however, that Marcion's teaching *did* entail the multiplication of Gods—in his case, to two, the lesser being the demiurge, or creator of the physical cosmos described in *Genesis*. This conviction correlates with a number of gnostic Christian theologians who distinguished between a transcendent "Father," on the one hand, and, on the other, the creator or "fashioner" of the physical universe who proclaims himself to be the only God, bears the biblical-sounding name of Ialdabaoth, and is presented as "jealous" (cf. *Exodus* 34:14).

We can perceive from Marcion's "antitheses" how he might have come to his radical picture of a descent into hell of the Good God's Son to forgive and redeem those who were *not* approved by the Creator.

The "antitheses" feature several assessments that draw close to this turning of biblical stories (and their characters) on their heads. Joshua is described as one who conquered "with violence and terror," while Christ prohibited violence and advocated "mercy and peace."[17] Moses was rightly rebuffed, Marcion thought, for acting like a judge when he intervened in two brothers' quarrel, while Christ, when importuned to settle a question of inheritance between brothers, asked, "Who made me a judge over you?" Marcion refers to the Christ of the Good God, who "does not judge those who are disobedient to him."[18] Isaiah, prophet of the Creator, who said: "My bow is strung and my arrows are sharp against them" (*Isaiah* 5:28) is negatively compared to St. Paul, who speaks of defense: "Put on the armor of God, that you may quench the fiery arrows of the Evil One" (*Ephesians* 6:11, 16).[19]

A clear rationale stood behind Marcion's belief in the pardon and redemption of Cain, of the oppressive Egyptians, and of the men of Sodom and Gomorrah, while the ones deemed righteous by the Creator were deemed "souls remain[ing] in Hades." The preeminence of the Good God and his Christ led Marcion to envision deliverance from hell of ancient victims of the vengeful Creator's "justice," and the continuing captivity in that "prison" of those who had once won the Creator's approval.

Among anti-gnostic Christians like Irenaeus, Christ's redemptive action in the realm of the dead (later referred to as his "harrowing of hell") was making its way into developing creeds, with their professions of the *one* God who made all that is, and *his* Son, who in time became a human, "born of the virgin Mary," to bring salvation to fallen Adamic nature.

Marcion's doctrine of two Gods, the Good loftier and nobler than the Creator, drew Irenaeus's strongest fire:

> Marcion of Pontus ... shamelessly blasphem[es] the God whom the Law and the Prophets proclaimed, describing him as the author of evils, desirous of wars, changing his opinions, and [at different times] contrary to himself. But [Marcion maintains that] Jesus [was] from the Father who is above the God that formed the world, and came to Judea in the time of Pontius Pilate, who was procurator of Tiberius Caesar; manifest in human form to those who were in Judea, he abolished the Prophets and the Law, and all the works of that God who made the world, whom he calls the World Ruler (*Against Heresies* 1.27.2).

To defend and maintain his vision of the Good Father of Christ, Marcion edited (Irenaeus says "mutilated") the scriptures, removing from his preferred *Gospel of Luke* and from the Pauline letters any references to the creator God of *Genesis* as the one God, and as the father of Jesus Christ. Also excised were the numerous quotations of Israel's prophets by Jesus, the evangelist, and by Paul—prophecies that, if included, would have compelled a recognition that the biblical God was the Lord of whom Jesus spoke, and the Lord at work in his life and mission (*Against Heresies* 1.27.2).

Just as offensive to "the apostolic preaching," Irenaeus asserts, is the docetism (the presentation of a *seemingly* human Jesus) in Marcion's teaching, with its related tenet (held in common with others like the Valentinian gnostics) that salvation belongs to souls, "while the body, as having been taken from the earth, is incapable of sharing in salvation" (*Against Heresies* 1.27.3).[20] Firm rebuffs to these ghostlike pictures of Christ's presence on earth and to notions of spiritual but not somatic, physical redemption quickly appeared in the "rules of faith" laid out by Tertullian and Irenaeus, who argued that Christians throughout the world held convictions about Jesus's truly embodied existence—belief "in one Christ Jesus, the Son of God, who became incarnate for our salvation. . . . [his] birth from a virgin, and the passion, and the resurrection from the dead . . . and the ascension into heaven in the flesh of the beloved Jesus Christ, our Lord" (*Against Heresies* 1.10.1).

Portions of Books 1 and 4 in *Against Heresies* show us the content and method of Irenaeus's rejoinders to Marcion. The most trenchant accuse Marcion and his followers of abuse and mis readings of the holy writings of the Jews and Christians. More aggressive and detailed interrogations follow. Why do Marcion and those in his churches fail to acknowledge the acts of mercy and forgiveness scripture attributes to the God of Israel, and why do they overlook the actions and words demanding righteousness and promising judgment attributed to the God of Jesus in the Gospels—for example, Jesus's warning in *Matthew* 25:41 to the Gentiles that those who did not greet the Lord in a stranger, visit him in prison, provide food and clothing to him would be told by "the King" at the judgment, "You that are accursed, depart from me into the eternal fire prepared for the devil and his angels!"? Neither the just judgments of God in the Jewish scriptures nor the mercy and gentle forgiveness of Christ in the "apostolic writings" should be exaggerated, Irenaeus insists, for one and the same deity acts with righteousness and with love in both testaments. (Moderns, religious or secular, who are heard to express the view that they "prefer the [compassionate] God of the New Testament to the [judgmental] God of the Old Testment" not only fail Irenaeus's test of an open-eyed reading of both, but also unknowingly participate in and perpetuate Marcion's fundamentally anti-Jewish heresy.)

Also found among the Irenaean salvos are pieces of logic with keen polemical edges. How "good" is your God if he steals what is not his—that is, if he takes away to his supernal kingdom creatures who are children and "possessions" of the "God that formed the world"? And in saving some, but not all, beings in the earth, is not the partiality of your purportedly all-forgiving God a defective "goodness"? If Jesus belonged to a Father above the Creator God, why did he liken his body to bread (which comes from creation) and his blood to the cup of wine? Why would Jesus assert that he was "son of man" (in addition to being "son of God") unless he had "gone through human birth," as creatures do?

These and other lines of argument reveal Irenaeus's sense of what is most threatening in Marcion's heresy, while also making plain what he believes *must* be preserved as orthodoxy—right opinion and belief—for Christianity. Irenaeus makes three firm declarations. First, the "new covenant" offered to those who profess Jesus to be the Christ, God's anointed one, is tied in an unbreakable way to the earlier covenant struck with faithful Abraham. Both compacts, that established in Abraham and that established in Christ, were self-disclosures and gifts from the *same* God, whose presence and mighty acts in the world were recorded in the Law and the Prophets, the scriptures.

Second, upon this continuity hinges the Christians' discovery and presentation of evidence—of "proofs" and testimonies—concerning the veracity of their gospel, and their standing as the new people of God. It is the Bible (or the "old covenant") that contains all the prophecies about the appearance of Christ, the manner of his birth, the character of his message and mission, the resistance he met, and, ultimately, the death he would suffer, with its victorious outcome. Such passages as *Psalms* 118:22–23—"The stone that the builders rejected has been made the chief corner stone. This is the Lord's doing; it is marvelous in our sight"—have been fulfilled in his resurrection.

> Now I shall simply say, in opposition to all the heretics, and principally against the followers of Marcion . . . read with earnest care that Gospel which has been conveyed to us by the apostles, and read with earnest care the prophets, and you will find that the whole conduct, and all the doctrine, and all the sufferings of our Lord, were predicted through them (*Against Heresies* 4.34.1).

A third point essential to Irenaeus's rejection of Marcion's other, Good God relates to what he insists must be the correct and faithful reading of the Cain and Abel story—one that preserves the biblical God's estimate and valuation of the two brothers and their offerings. It can only be a perversion, Irenaeus thinks, to regard Cain as someone to be forgiven and rewarded, while Abel's righteous victimhood is counted for nothing. Marcion's blasphemy against the Creator, the true God known from the testimony of scriptures, generates a true outrage: all measures of good and evil are reversed.

In opposition to Marcion, Irenaeus insists that the righteous and God-approved Abel signifies future saving events. Not by any stretch of het-erodox imagination could Abel become the less worthy of Adam's sons, nor the one who missed his chance for redemption in Hades through fear that Christ who came there was sent by a malevolent trickster, the Creator. Abel the innocent victim whose blood speaks still (*Hebrews* 11:4) was, rather, the providential prefiguration of the scriptural God's Son, who, born in the flesh, was Jesus Christ, crucified, risen, and ascended to the right hand of his Father in heaven. In a stunning summary of his anti-gnostic under-standing of how that salvation of humanity through Christ's incarnation was accomplished, Irenaeus points to

> the only true and steadfast Teacher, the Word of God, our Lord Jesus Christ, who did, through his transcendent love, become what we are, that He might bring us to be even what He is Himself (*Against Heresies* 5, Preface).

IRENAEUS'S ANTI-JEWISH USES OF THE CAIN AND ABEL STORY

Christians promoting what he considered to be false doctrines were not Irenaeus's only declared enemies. Here we scrutinize his deployment of the Cain and Abel story in opposition to Jewish interpretations. In the midst of his discussion of sacrifices and oblations to God (which, he instructs his readers, are not needed by the deity, but do bring glory and benefit to one whose gift is accepted), Irenaeus makes an example of the first offerings (*Against Heresies* 4.17.1–6). His initial observations are familiar to us from interpretations like those of Philo; Abel's gift won divine favor "because he offered with single-mindedness and righteousness," while Cain's offering was rebuffed, "because his heart was divided with envy and malice which he cherished against his brother" (*Against Heresies* 4.18.3). Further exposition of the difference in the brothers' offerings calls into play the view that an acceptable sacrifice cannot be made unless one "assigns to his neighbor that fellowship with him which is right and proper . . . [and unless the offerer] is under the fear of God." At the front of Irenaeus's mind are the guidelines of the church's offering, the eucharistic meal, which called for the resolu-tion of offenses committed against others in the community before they could exchange gestures of "peace" and join in partaking of Christ's "body and blood."[21] A comparison of Jewish and Christian sacrifices comes just before our passage, venturing the dramatic—and prejudicial—point that the tithes of their goods which the Jews consecrated to God, while worthy, were done out of "servile" obligation, while "those who have received liberty set aside all their possessions for the Lord's purposes (Irenaeus cites Jesus's observation in *Luke* 21:1–4 about the widow who gives all she has, two small copper coins, as a Temple offering), since they have hope of better things [hereafter]" (4.18.2). The contrast is a Pauline one between offerings made under the Law—that is, slavishly—and those made freely.

Irenaeus proceeds to argue, however, that what most tellingly distinguished Cain's and Abel's sacrifices was not a matter of being under the law or free from it. Rather, the decisive factors were the dispositions, the inner attitudes, with which each approached his altar. God, Irenaeus writes, knows of a sacrificer's "secret sin," and is not deceived when one offering is proper only in terms of its outward form. Unless the person about to make an offering abandons the evil within him, the sacrifice does not benefit him. Indeed, "by means of the hypocritical action, [his attempted offering] renders him the destroyer of himself" (*Against Heresies* 4.18.3). The argument has been building toward the identification and full vilification of the hypocrites whom Cain prefigured. After quoting another in the group of Jesus's seven woes, that which likens the scribes and Pharisees to whitewashed tombs ("So you also on the outside look righteous to others, but inside you are full of hypocrisy and lawlessness" [*Matthew* 23:28]), Irenaeus asserts:

> While they were thought to offer correctly as far as outward appearance went, they had in themselves jealousy like that of Cain; therefore they slew the Just One, slighting the counsel of the Word, as did also Cain. For [the Word] said to [Cain], "Be at rest" (*Genesis* 4:7) but he did not assent. Now what else is it to "be at rest" than to forego intentions of violence?. . . . [and] when Cain was by no means at rest, He said to him: "To you shall be his [i.e., sin's] desire, and you shall rule over him." Thus did He in the same way speak to Pilate: "You would have no powers at all against me, unless it were given to you from above" (*John* 19:11); God always giving up the righteous one [in this life to suffering], that he, having been tested by what he suffered and endured, may at last be accepted; but that the evil-doer, being judged by the actions he has performed, may be rejected (*Against Heresies* 4.18.3).[22]

Irenaeus's charges are harsh but not unexpected. We know of abrasive relations between second- and third-century churches and synagogues, and of apologetic-polemic strategies well-tooled by Christians, who insisted that their gospel message and their community's status as God's new people superseded the old covenant and the Cain-like religion of the Jews. This last accusation Irenaeus stridently advanced by trumpeting Christianity's "single-minded" sacrifice as the one "pure oblation to the Creator, offering to Him, with thanksgiving, [the things taken] from His creation."

> But the Jews do not offer in this way: for their hands are full of blood; for they have not received the Word, through whom [the pure oblation] is offered to God (*Against Heresies* 4.18.4).

There is an additional sentence proclaiming that neither is a pure offering to God made by "any of the conventicles of the heretics." Both Jews and heretics reject Jesus—the first denying that he is God's prophesied messiah, and the second denying that he is the incarnate Son of the God of creation, the only God. However, in this particular exposition of the Cain and Abel story, the final Irenaean passage we shall treat, there is no question which perceived opponent of Christian truth is this argument's primary target: Judaism can no longer make a pure offering to God, having reenacted Cain's fratricide in the crucifixion of God's own Son. In leveling this charge Irenaeus makes common cause with other early Christian thinkers and preachers in developing a discourse of anti-Judaism which was destined to have a long and damaging history. (At nearly the same time, around 170, in the season of Passover, Bishop Melito of Sardis in Asia Minor presented a sermon, *On Pascha*, that set a standard for virulence in its chastisement of the Jews for betrayal of their God in becoming Christ-killers.) Irenaeus's treatment of *Genesis* 4 came down to this: as Abel belongs to Christians as the antetype of their savior, Cain the envious and hostile brother represents and forecasts the murderous Jewish opponents of Christ, both in his human lifetime and in their continuing resistance to Christians and the revelation they claim for themselves.

The bellicose tone and content of Irenaeus's polemics are neither to be glossed as rhetorical, nor too quickly accepted and accommodated as an unattractive given in the jockeying of competitive groups for their own identities and their own places in the ancient Mediterranean world. Christians' differentiation of their beliefs and practices from those of Jews, and vice-versa, involved and generated social antagonisms affecting history in very significant and often tragic ways. Jewish counterassaults against Christians and their teachings will in turn appear in the following pages, and will require both historical contextualization and the weighing of their effects.

Ireneaus's theologizing, which to readers in any era registers as aggressively anti-Jewish, is, from his viewpoint, positive—a declaration of God's great and decisive act of salvation. As Christian thinker and leader in a vulnerable time in his religion's formation and growth, he aspires to clear presentation of the divine revelation he and his fellow believers have embraced. He regards gnostic teachers who propound biblically unsupported perversions of Christianity and its God as a primary threat, judging from the chief content of his surviving large treatise "Against all Heresies." Armed with a rule of faith, a proto-creed that had developed already in late second-century churches (his contemporary in North Africa, Tertullian, attests to the authority of the "rule" or standard of Christian beliefs as well), Irenaeus forcefully and inventively articulated against his perceived foes the implications of the Christianity he believed to be true to the teachings and person of Jesus Christ, as preserved by his intimate followers and maintained by the apostles' successors, the churches' bishops.[23] His interpretations of scripture constituted a central element in this offensive.

Irenaeus's paramount concern, as we've seen, was to demonstrate that the creator God is the one true God, beneath no other; that this God, the Father, is both just and merciful, and also consistently true to his commitment to his original handiwork. Humankind, once brought into being as good, is his eternal project, its redemption achieved through successive covenants. God sent his Word incarnate in order that Adamic nature—the entire human creature, spirit, soul, and body—might be returned to God's sovereign care, reflecting once again its original divine image. We can repeat what Irenaeus believed his foes should embrace if they were to recognize God's true revelation: that God's Word "bec[a]me what we are, that He might bring us to be even what He is Himself."

CAIN AND ABEL (AND THEIR PARENTS) ON CHRISTIAN SARCOPHAGI: THEOLOGY IN SCULPTED IMAGES

Erich Dinkler, a historian of Christian art, wrote that "the migration of iconographic schemes from one medium to another"—for example, from fresco paintings to carved figures decorating stone sarcophagi—"can be observed everywhere in the fourth century."[24] Several representations of Cain and Abel on carved stone caskets of this period suggest that the brothers' story was not just migrating, but also propagating novel theological teaching.

The sarcophagus pictured below (Figure 2.3) is representative of several "Passion sarcophagi" which typically mark their theme by a central figure of the cross, surmounted by the Chi-Rho monogram of Christ, itself encircled by a triumphal wreath. In our sample, doves stand on the arms of the cross, and beneath them guards are pictured, one alert, the other slumbering.

Figure 2.3 Passion sarcophagus. Fourth century. © Genevra Kornbluth. Vatican Lateran Museum, Rome.

André Grabar wrote: "What we have here is a Christian derivative of the monumental Roman trophy, symbol of victory."[25]

Scenes derived from New Testament and early Christian traditions dominate the artistic program: Pilate interrogates Jesus, who holds a scroll in his hand (at the far right), and Peter and Paul (left and right of the central image, respectively—artists were aware of an early tradition that spoke of Paul's baldness) are being arrested as followers of their crucified and risen leader.

What are we to make of the appearance of Cain and Abel in one of the five tree-framed scenes on the front of the casket? Two pictorial elements in the image (Figure 2.4, detail) of Cain and Abel stand out. First, God is shown in human form, seated (or enthroned) and engaged in the transaction that is occurring, rather than pointing his finger from heaven's clouds. This is a daring, and in early Christian art, quite rare, depiction of the religion's "invisible God."[26] Second, with his right hand God signals his approval of the lamb held by Abel and of Abel himself. In itself that moment in the story of the two brothers does not align itself with the theme of this sarcophagus's decoration, but the artist used Abel's offering as a code

Figure 2.4 Passion sarcophagus. Detail. © Genevra Kornbluth.

for its consequence—his murder by Cain. Hence the image's connection with the others that have been carved: Abel, Peter, and Paul are martyrs for God who can be seen and understood in relation to Jesus's encounter with Pontius Pilate, another forecasting image that signifies his crucifixion.

The artist certainly intends to convey something more, since the cross and Chi-Rho symbol denote the resurrection victory of Christ. Like his fellow righteous victims Peter and Paul, Abel merits and enjoys God's continuing care and protection as one of his saints. But Abel's link to Christ and his passion had a special and particular feature; we recall the language of *Hebrews* 12:24 in which the blood of Cain's victim, dear to God, pointed forward to "the sprinkled blood that speaks a better word than the blood of Abel." The artist-sculptor has fully Christianized the Abel of the Old Testament by incorporating him in the Passion sarcophagus's message, which celebrates the victory of Christ and the victory of his saints, themselves righteous victims.

A different doctrinal purpose inspires the next image (Figure 2.5). In this figure the artist's way of picturing God compels our attention. As in the previous example, the deity is represented with human shape and features. Here, however, it becomes apparent that early Christian thinking and picturing of God as a triad, or trinity, has come to expression in the scene's

Figure 2.5 The Trinitarian God interacting with Abel and Cain. Detail from a fourth-century sarcophagus. © Vanni Archive/Art Resource, NY. Vatican Museo Pio Christiano, Rome.

iconography. How did this iconography of God with Cain and Abel promote new understanding?

In *The Invisible God,* Paul Corby Finney, pointing to the manner in which pre-Constantinian Christian art produced images, not of God himself, but of *tekmeria theou* (tokens or signs of God's activities—such as Jonah being spewed forth, or Isaac spared at the altar, or Daniel safe among lions), discriminated between styles of that time, and those in a future period in which God in anthropomorphic form would be presented to viewers. Here, a fourth-century carver of scenes includes the meeting of Abel and Cain with God—that is, God the Trinity. Prominent in the portrait is God the Father, seated, while the Holy Spirit and the Son (not here distinguishable) are signified in the two male heads set in the background. In bringing their offerings to the Lord, the two brothers are depicted as having face-to-face dealings with the triune deity of Christian theology (as that doctrine of God was being worked toward consistent linguistic formulae—that is, creeds—in this and the next century). As Robin Jensen points out in her analysis of several sarcophagi depicting the three-personed God, fourth-century artists, like the theologians of their era, are being attentive to the "economy of the Trinity"—that is, the entirety of the divine action on behalf of humankind—creation, salvation, and sanctification—and the unity of action of the Father, Son, and Spirit.

The presence of an Adam and Eve scene just to the right recalls the painting from cubiculum B in the Via Latina burial complex, and can perhaps be regarded as a more carefully theologized version of the same scene: Adam and Eve, sinners (though not, here, shown as saddened evictees from the Garden), have their heads turned in the direction of the figure on their left, who is likewise turned toward them. This person holds in his right hand a bundle of grain, which may symbolize the labors awaiting the man and the woman outside of Eden. He is presumed to be God's Son, or Word, who would, "in the fullness of time" (*Galatians* 4:4) become incarnate in Jesus.[27] In another of the Trinity sarcophagi the three-personed God creates Adam and Eve—with the Son, God's creative agent, touching the head of Eve, who has been brought forth from the still supine Adam, while God the Father raises his hand either in command or direction of the act.[28]

This sculptor's trinitarian theological addition to the scene of Cain's and Abel's offerings advances an understanding that the Three who are One God *together* enact the divine plan. The judgment of the offerings of Abel and Cain was, on this understanding, the judgment of God—Father, Son, and Holy Spirit.

Does the adjoining scene of Adam and Eve with the Son, or Word, suggest a further interpretive intention? In the image of God as three in one,
and in the separate figure of the Son, the Word, it is reasonable to see
in this sculptor's program of decoration an effort to represent in particular the triune deity's care for Adam and Eve, Abel, and all of redeemed
humanity, including (in particular) the individual whose body lies in the
sarcophagus.

Scenes of Cain and Abel in sarcophagi of the later fourth century—
especially as they form part of the program of the Passion sarcophagus, and
as they appear standing before the Christian God in trinity—are no longer
snapshots from narratives whose moral lessons and warnings are quickly
discerned by their viewers. In the decades after Constantine, as Christianity
became more institutionally secure and more definite in its theological formulations, symbology reflected the changes. Adam and other figures of the
Old Testament, including Abel, were represented in increasingly sophisticated ways as types of Christ—that is, as God-provided indicators of the
salvation to come in the birth, life, death, and resurrection of his Word and
Son. Furthermore, viewers of typological interpretation, we become aware,
are more practiced; they engage in the two-part movement of perception
intrinsic to this kind of symbolism—seeing first the antetype, and then
seeing through it. Abel becomes transparent to Christ and to Christ's sacrificial death that accomplished salvation.

FAMILY RELATIONS IN ADAM'S HOUSE—JOHN CHRYSOSTOM, EPHREM OF SYRIA, AND SYMMACHUS

We proceed to a very particular set of Christian interests in Cain's intrigues
and Abel's glories. Three authors, John Chrysostom, Ephrem of Syria, and
Symmachus, wanted to tease out the psychologies of those in the first
family, and to that end they exercised their interpreters' liberties, adding narratives concerning Cain's dealings with Adam and Eve after he had
killed Abel.

John Chrysostom

In a sermon on *Genesis* 4:8–15, John Chrysostom (ca. 347–407) reveals his
deep curiosity about Cain's inner self. The "golden-throated" preacher asks
relentless questions about the workings of Cain's mind as he set about and
then accomplished the murder of his brother.

How is it that his hand was not paralyzed? how could it manage to grasp the sword and deal the blow? how is it that his soul did not fly from his body? how did it have the strength to put into effect such an unholy outrage? how is that he did not have second thoughts and reverse his intention? how is it that he did not take stock of his nature? how is it that before the beginning of the exploit he did not think ahead to its result? how could he bear to see his brother's body gasping on the ground after the attack? how could he bring himself to gaze on the corpse flung to the ground without being immediately devastated by the sight? (John Chrysostom, *Homily* 19.5).[29]

Even we, Chrysostom tells his audience, who are familiar with death and have experience of people dying, break down when it occurs. And since we are able to put aside our hatred of an enemy and feel some sympathy when he dies, it is unthinkable that we would not be overwhelmed to see a brother, "whom we had been conversing with just before, child of the same mother and same father, born of the same family . . . lying on the ground, all at once lifeless and inert." What was happening within Cain? The sermon form, and the homilist's desire to make a connection to the lives and motivations of its hearers, have motivated John Chrysostom to probe beneath and beyond what the narrative itself tells us about Cain's psyche.

Similarly, but with greater brevity (in *Homily* 20.13), Chrysostom ponders the inner life of Eve—her grief at the loss of Abel. In his exposition of *Genesis* 4:25, which tells of the subsequent birth of Seth to Adam and Eve, the preacher draws attention to the fact that Eve speaks, as if it were an extension of her new child's name, the words "God has raised up for me another child in place of Abel, whom Cain killed." This was, John Chrysostom remarks, "the comment of a grieving spirit, upset at the memory of what had happened" (*Homily* 20.13). He reports an event not found in the biblical text, but one that he believes was particularly devastating to Eve. Cain had brought Abel's body to his parents, "stretching him on the ground before their eyes, a lifeless corpse—[this son] whom they had bred and cherished."[30] The bishop's hearers are reminded that though Adam had been told that he himself would one day return to dust (*Genesis* 3:19), he had no idea until that moment "what death looked like." Next, Cain seized the moment to rail against his brother, to

let loose against Abel the rancor that had been gnawing at his vitals, and thus provided his parents with a dreadful spectacle to contemplate. For this reason, assuredly, the mother, who had scarcely lifted her head and was able only at this late stage to find some consolation for that unbearable grief in the birth of a son [i.e., Seth], offered thanks to the Lord and immortalized the crime of fratricide (John Chrysostom, *Homily* 20.13).

Exploring the sadness of Eve, the preacher is confident that his words will stir sympathy in members of his congregation.

Ephrem

In his *Commentary on Genesis*, Ephrem the Syrian (ca. 306–373) offers his readers additional insights into the motives of Cain. It is true that "Cain was very angry" because God accepted Abel's offering, rather than his, but "his face became gloomy" for another reason:

> There was laughter in the eyes of his parents and his sisters when his offering was rejected. They had seen that Cain's offering had been placed in the middle of the fire and yet the fire did not touch it (Ephrem, *Commentary on Genesis* 3.3.3).

The premeditation in Cain's fratricide was evident from the fact that when Cain spoke to Abel, he summoned his brother from the hills where he grazed his sheep, inviting him down to his field: "For in the standing grains Cain killed Abel and in the earth easily hid him" (Ephrem, *Commentary on Genesis* 3.5.1).

Ephrem, like other exegetes, projected what transpired when Cain next encountered Adam and Eve.

> After Cain had killed his brother, he persuaded his parents with lies that Abel had entered Paradise because he was pleasing to God, and that his offering was accepted bore witness to his entry; that it was by keeping the commandment that he entered Paradise just as by transgressing the commandment you were cast out from there. Then, just when Cain thought that he had deceived his parents and that there would be no one to seek vengeance for Abel, God appeared to Cain and "said to him, 'Where is Abel your brother?'" (Ephrem, *Commentary on Genesis* 3.5.2).[31]

Ephrem's production of this extra narrative does not simply fill gaps; he has more to communicate about the pronounced evil-mindedness and duplicity in Cain's character. He wishes to underline Cain's animosity toward his parents—for his lies about Abel are meant to torment Adam and Eve as much as to cover his own crime—or at least so it seems.

Symmachus

A remarkable revisioning of the Cain and Abel narrative titled *Life of Abel* was a fifth- to sixth-century Christian writing in Syriac. Its presumed author, Symmachus, we cannot identify apart from the connection of his name to the text. This writing seeks to uncover the drama *not* reported in the biblical account—the interactions between the brothers and the relationships between the sons and their parents which took place off-stage.[32] "Symmachus's interest is in the psychological aspect of the brothers' quarrel, rather than in the mere externals of the narrative," Sebastian Brock wrote, and in exploring this dimension of the first murder, the author takes up "the reactions of the figures in the drama to the course of events, and ... readily employs the device of putting speeches into the mouths of the actors."[33]

Symmachus's narrative additions intensify the events preceding and following Abel's murder.[34] Following the Lord's rejection of his flawed offering, Cain's anger doubles, turning to seething hate; he has failed to mend his ways: "He denied love and rejected brotherhood ... [and] decided in his mind to kill his mother's son. . . . Cain meditated in his heart how he would kill him, and where he could hide his body" (Symmachus, *Life of Abel* 2–3).

A piece of Christian typological interpretation precedes the description of Abel's action in "the valley" to which Cain has called him. Abel responded to his brother's invitation happily and in innocence, even if he had concerns for the flock he left behind in the hills. The account of Abel's slaying held symbols of Christ's passion: he went with Cain joyfully, as Christ greeted his Jewish pursuers without apprehension, saying (in *John* 18:5, 8), "I am he whom you seek," and in a further resemblance to "his Lord's son," Abel died in the month of Nisan: "maybe the day was Friday, too" (Symmachus, *Life of Abel* 5).[35]

Symmachus returns to storyline actions of the sort that most occupy his thoughts. Surprised when his brother suddenly seized him, at first wondering if he was being playful but then seeing that Cain's eyes looked like blood, "his face clothed in green," Abel made an appeal to Cain through his tears. Why this eruption of envy? Why would you kill me, your brother? Why would you subject yourself to the stain of my murder, and bring my parents to grief? What follows in Abel's plea are concerns for Adam and Eve. He asks that his death not take place "in the wilderness," but at home, "indoors," where his parents could see his death and lament it, and where he would be able to be buried in a grave, rather than become food for birds and wild animals. Abel has soulful but reasoned proposals to offer. Haven't their parents had enough pain already, having lost Paradise? And did not the justice of God spare Adam after he had done wrong, while you, Cain, seek to "kill me who have not sinned against you"?

The younger brother's pleas continue—on behalf of his sheep, who will not hear his voice again, and on behalf of Cain himself, whose hands will be defiled by blood. Vows born of desperation come next. The first is in the name of the God who caused water to flow from Eden to the earth—alas, the earth which now will be forced to drink his, Abel's, gore. The second invokes the Lord of creation who, Abel reminds Cain, stripped Adam of the glory that clothed him. Cain should not subject an innocent to a different kind of stripping:

> Do not take off from my limbs my clothes and reveal to the sun in the sky the nakedness of my youth; by Him who was merciful to Adam, be merciful to me, my brother! (Symmachus, *Life of Abel* 6).[36]

(The reference to nakedness, evoking the connection between Adam's and Eve's sin and an awareness of their nudity, is striking, but Symmachus does not report that Abel's body was uncovered before, during, or after his killing. Early Muslim understandings of the story of Adam's sons, however, did seem to brood over the nakedness of Abel the victim, as we shall learn in the next chapter.) Unmoved by his brother's passionate speech—even Abel's request that his brother give him the "greeting of a kiss before I die"—Cain became more angry, and "arose and slew him," being careful not to be spattered by the blood, lest his culpability be obvious.

Symmachus injects two other figures of the future (Christian) revelation at this point, relating first that Abel's hands and arms were stretched out in cruciform as he died, and then that the earth where he lay was somehow "rent," a declivity formed in it: "[Abel] depicted the symbol of him whose body was 'laid in a new grave (see *Matthew* 27:60) wherein no one had been laid (*Luke* 23:53)' " (Symmachus, *Life of Abel* 8).

Typologies like these held as much power for Symmachus as they did for other Christian exegetes, but his *Life of Abel* persists in its special agenda—the exploration of the personalities and motivations of the brothers and of Adam and Eve. We read Symmachus's own version of Cain's effort to hide his crime from his parents, who are anxious about their missing son. Adam goes in search of Abel, but finds only his flock. Later in the day or evening, Adam and Eve ask Cain about his brother's whereabouts, and notice that he is hesitant to speak. Eve, becoming suspicious, challenges her son Cain: "By the life of Abel your brother, tell me where he is!" Unwilling to confess, not out of fear of his parents but in the hope "that there should be no commotion in their home," Cain fabricates Abel's disappearance as a reward by God. He claims he witnessed his brother "on the mountain, suddenly snatched up" and escorted into Paradise (Symmachus, *Life of Abel* 6).[37] Cain's explanation quiets his parents for the time being, but does not silence God, who two days later confronts him. Again Cain temporizes, and for his efforts earns a curse from the Lord:

> For you have taught the earth an evil art ... [and] you have brought suffering upon Adam and Eve, the parents of the entire earth. You are cursed by the entire earth because you have opened the gate of Sheol before the whole earth. You are cursed by the whole earth because you wished to be alone on the face of the whole earth. . . . You shall be shaking and trembling (*Genesis* 4:12) on it because you relied on your own strength and murdered your brother. . . . [and] because you wanted to be [the entire earth's] sole inheritor (Symmachus, *Life of Abel* 14).[38]

Physically affected by this encounter with God, and knowing his "humiliating form" will be noticed by his parents, Cain weighs his options, deciding to go home and tell them what he has done. (Symmachus reveals his self-protective, rather than chastened, reason for doing this: it will be better to get the expected explosion of grief and lamentation over with in a single day.) Mistaken for a stumbling drunk as he enters his parents' presence, Eve then spies his tremors and the sign on his forehead.

> She laid her hands on her head, and from her mouth there poured forth incessant wails. She opened her mouth and uttered in a grief-stricken voice a lament over her two sons: "Abel, my dearest one, went forth yesterday and he is no more, and as for Cain, in whom I hoped to find comfort,—his death would have been far preferable to me than his life. My beloved, the beloved of his father, is no more, and as for Cain, whom I acquired,—it would have been better had I never acquired him. What will become of me? My youngest son is no longer, while the one who is left is staggering while still a youth, and before his youth is up his limbs are seized by shaking and trembling!" (Symmachus, *Life of Abel* 16–17).[39]

After Adam's tears, and the added tears he and Eve "made each other weep," they challenge Cain with questions about Abel. At that point, the "heart of stone [Cain] had acquired was crushed, and his pity was stirred for his brother." Too late, he loved Abel once more.[40] Cain claims that he wishes Abel could live again, and spare him—Cain—his misery.

The household lamentations increase. Eve's wailing is so severe that their dwelling's walls tremble, yet when she is able once more to address Cain, it is not the manner of Abel's death she inquires after, but the location of his corpse:

> Where was it you slew Abel, in what place did you slaughter your brother, where have you butchered my beloved? Come and show us before a wild animal devours him; let us go and find him before the birds of prey tear him up. Give us his body so that we may bury it, return to us the chaste corpse; give me his body so that I may wash away the blood and bury it, for you buried him naked, all bloody (Symmachus, *Life of Abel* 21).

Adam, too, wishes to see Abel's corpse, but his desire is fed by the curiosity that belongs to the world's first man. Seeing his son's body, he will learn the end to which he and Eve will come, and he will come to understand by inspecting the wounds "where death entered him ... and whence his soul departed"—that is, how human creatures expire. We note that at this point Symmachus—or his Eve—knows that Abel was naked and blood-stained when buried.

Once at the place of the murder, where the dirt covering Abel's body is removed, Eve collapses into a grief frenzy, tearing her hair, biting her arms and striking her own face until "blood ran down from her cheeks." In another disconsolate outburst she laments her double-plight. Looking at either son fills her with bitterness.

> Two sorrows have come upon wretched (me) in a single day, two blows have befallen me in a single hour. (If) I turn my eyes to the ground, the corpse of the slain man gives me pain, and if I raise my eyes then I see this man shaking and trembling. It is a bitter blow to me: I do not know which of them I should lament, which of them I should weep for; should I weep for the slain?—but the life of the (son who is) alive is worse for me than the dead one. Should I leave the dead and weep for the living? Abel's corpse will not allow me (Symmachus, *Life of Abel*, 24).

Symmachus makes this scene the climax of his *Life of Abel*, and gives a new dimension to the tale. Woman, the first mother, abjectly wrestles with the dilemmas of loving her sons, and realizes that she has in different ways lost both of them.

The final narrative element in the *Life of Abel* simultaneously completes the story and provides a platform for Symmachus's last piece of theologizing:

Abel's parents brought him and buried him in their vicinity, firstly so that their own bones might (eventually) rest on his [i.e., in a common burial place], and secondly because it would be close by for Eve to go out to weep over him at the grave, and for Cain inside the house (Symmachus, *Life of Abel* 26).

So ends the story of the devastated family, the father bereft, the mother in continued mourning, and Cain still at an existential distance from the sibling he killed, since apparently he is unable or unwilling to visit Abel's grave.

Though anticlimactic, these final sentences reveal Symmachus's creative contribution to the Christianizing of the Cain and Abel story, a process well-advanced by the fifth and sixth centuries. He has himself provided more narrative grist for this mill, but he attributes to others ("they do well to say") the report that Adam, Eve, and Cain "took [Abel] from the valley and buried him in the mountain." More messages about Jesus are also found in the account of Abel's burial. It suggests "the type of Him of whom Mary [Magdalene at the tomb of Jesus (*John* 20:13)] said 'They have taken my Lord, and I know not where to find him.'" Further, the transport of Abel's body to "the mountain" residence of his parents represents, after the initial discovery of him in the lowland wilderness, a second raising—an ascension that anticipates another: "they lifted up Abel from the valley to the mountain, and Christ was lifted up in the body from Bethany to heaven" (Symmachus, *Life of Abel* 27).

The *Life of Abel*'s closing ascription of glory and honor to God reiterates a theme that we saw in earliest Christian interpretive references to the brothers and also in Irenaeus's contentions against Marcionites and Jews. God's justice is praised for its double application—both the punishment of the murderer *and* the rejection of "the rebellious people who had acquired Cain's stiffness of neck" are praised.[41] The other side of this benedictory conclusion to the *Life of Abel* emphasizes the story's meaning for Christians. The deaths of the innocent and righteous, of which Abel's is the first, are symbols of the "slain Son" who is God, and who, as God, "received the offering of Abel." Now, that Son of God, Jesus Christ, is prayerfully asked to "bring quiet in His church and peace in His people, and [to] grant to each one of us forgiveness of sins on the day of His coming." Symmachus, too, writes for a community of believers.

Early Christian expositors of scripture explained and creatively enhanced the stories they retold, or taught, or preached, or debated with others. Their basic goal was to educate and build up the faith of believers. Therefore it fell to them to articulate what the scriptures meant in light of the revelation that called their community into being, that won their loyalty and inspired their hope. It needed spelling out what constituted the new covenant between followers and worshippers of Jesus and the God of Israel. How were individuals and congregations to understand and distinguish themselves over against their rivals—the Jews themselves, and groups and schools of so-called Christians whose teachings they deemed false—indeed, satanic?

In this chapter's pages we have observed the attention Christian exegetes gave to their own historical circumstances—the controversies of their time and place, and the pastoral needs of their communities. More sharply than in the rabbinic interpretations of Cain and Abel, where the debate is largely internal to the community of sages, and more sharply even than in Philo, who *does* have in his sights philosophers whose polytheism is idolatrous, the Christian writers we've encountered were combative. They defended the revelation of God's Son, which they claimed for themselves and embraced as salvation. At the same time Christian apologists like Irenaeus went on the offensive, in order to correct and to denounce those who resisted or falsified the truth that sustained what he regarded as the "right-believing" churches.

While recognizing the strong doctrinal and community-protective motivations in Christian interpretations of the story of Cain and Abel, it is important also to register the imaginative richness of its literary and artistic forms and the diversity of its employments—from the preacher who composed *Hebrews*, to Marcion, to Irenaeus, to the painters in the Via Latina catacomb and the sculptors of the sarcophagi, to John Chrysostom and Ephrem—and to Symmachus, the chronicler of Abel's life and death. The biblical story of Cain's fratricide, with its difficult questions about the onset and causes of violence between human beings, about the character and actions of God, and also with its at once sobering and hopeful lessons, was incomplete ... without interpretive commentary.

Muhammad and his followers, themselves recipients of a new revelation containing the story of Adam's two sons, found the same to be true.

CHAPTER 3

✿

"Tell Them the Story of the Two Sons of Adam as It Really Was"

arly Muslims, like Jews and Christians before and contemporaneous with them, recognized the Qabil and Habil narrative's etiological
sense: it told of the origin and cause of human killing. Also apparent to
them was how much more was involved in the tale than a folkloric just-so
story, for the two sons, their father, and God were players in a tragic drama
whose motivations and deeds needed explication. The commentators were
quick to detect the larger questions residing in the story. What is the
nature of the human being, that this horrible incident could occur? How
does the sovereign God deal with—and attempt to guide—human creatures, who appear to be as free to commit evil as to do good?

Legal and moral issues accompanied these anthropological and theological questions. How is the justice that God demands made plain in the
Qur'an's account of the murder? Qabil's murderous act was heinous, but
by what reasoning was it deemed unlawful? Would all future killers of
human beings be adjudged criminal, and sentenced to a single dire penalty,
or would distinctions need to be made between *kinds* of murders—some
illicit and some not?

Because the focus of this book is on the role of interpreters in the earliest
interactions between the three religions, our main purpose in this chapter
is to discover what distinctively Muslim ideas and themes become apparent
as we consider the painters' and commentators' work. Part of that discovery involves measuring the extent to which Muslim interpreters knew and
utilized *isra'iliyyat* (the Arabic term for traditions of the Jews, but also of
the Christians)—in this case, Cain and Abel traditions.

But first, we take up the qur'anic text, which scholars believe was one of the last revelations given to Muhammad—perhaps in 632 CE/10 AH. The Qur'an's version of the narrative of Adam's two sons, we shall notice, differs in significant ways from the biblical account in *Genesis* 4.

CAIN/QABIL AND ABEL/HABIL IN *SURAH AL-MA'IDAH* *("THE TABLE")*

5:27 Tell them the story
of the two sons of Adam
as it really was: both
presented an offering to God;
it was accepted from one
but not the other, who said, "I will kill you!"
The former said, "God only accepts offerings
from the conscientious.
28 Even if you reach out to kill me,
I will not be reaching out to kill you;
For I fear God, Lord of all worlds.
29 I am willing to let you bring on yourself
my sin as well as your sin,
so you will be among
the inmates of hellfire;
and that is the reward
for the unjust."
30 But he [whose offering God refused] had no qualms
about killing his brother,
so he murdered him,
and thus became one of the lost.
31 Then God sent a raven
that scratched the earth to show him
how to cover up the exposed remains
of his brother.
He said, "Woe is me!
Am I incapable
of being like this raven,
who has covered
the exposure of my brother?"
And he became remorseful.

32 Because of that We ordained
for the children of Israel
that if anyone killed a person,
other than for murder
or corruption on earth,
it would be as if he killed
all the people.
And if anyone saved a life
it would be as if he saved the lives
of all the people.

Typically the Qur'an narrates those stories which also appear in Jewish and Christian scriptures more succinctly—with a kind of brevity presuming that these will be familiar to hearers or readers. Here even the sons' names are not given, though early Muslims knew them. On the other hand, as we just observed in the report of the crow, or raven, sent to educate Qabil, the Qur'an often contains narrative elements nowhere to be found in the biblical accounts.

A summary of the qur'anic storyline may benefit us. God's acceptance of only one of the two brothers' offerings leads immediately to a hostile dialogue. Qabil states his intention to kill Habil, who responds in a manner meant to show his foresight, or to provoke rather than placate his brother—or both. Because, Habil says, he himself is counted among the "conscientious," God's acceptance of his sacrifice is justified. Habil also declares that he will not, in self-defense, attempt to murder Qabil. He fears God (presumably, God's judgment against one who takes another's life). Rather, Habil will be passive, and he states his wish that Qabil will suffer in hellfire, paying not only for his own sins, but also for those of Habil. By the victim-to-be's reckoning, such a punishment would be proper for his brother, one of the "unjust." And so it happens. Qabil, his soul not resisting his inclination to murder Habil, commits the deed, becoming one of the "lost."

We do not learn about the reason for the sacrifices, what the two sons sacrificed, nor how they came to know that one had been approved, and the other not. The dispositions of Adam's two sons at the time they made their offerings are not indicated, except that it is made plain that Habil, under assault, knows why God accepted his offering—and, by implication, rejected Qabil's. Neither the manner of a physical altercation nor the means by which Habil was murdered are told. If we think back on the *Genesis* account, we register that Qabil is not directly confronted by God; we are only told that for his fratricide he is damned.

Surah 5:31 concludes the narrative. On one reading (and construal) of it, the sense is straightforward: a God-commissioned raven demonstrates to Qabil how the ground can be prepared for a burial. (Does the terse text suggest that the raven covered Habil's remains, Qabil looking on? This problem of sense, we shall see, Muslim writers and artists clarified, making the raven's action a demonstration *to* Qabil, who followed the bird's example.) At the etiological level, the episode answers questions about the disposal of corpses, about how the first humans learned to care for their dead. In relation to the drama's plot, however, the appearance and action of the raven is a sign: it awakens Qabil to his duty to cover "the exposure of his brother," Habil.

What is the "exposure," which some Qur'an translators yield as "disgrace"? The meaning of the word used here—*saw'a*—is shame, and it could support the understanding that the "exposure" of Habil's body leads Qabil to recognize the shame of his murder of Habil. More extended meanings—concerning Qabil's failure to bury Habil—have been found by other translators. Tarif Khalidi renders the text:

> But God sent a raven clawing out the earth to show him how he might bury the corpse of his brother. He said: "What a wretch I am! Am I incapable of being like this raven and so conceal my brother's corpse?"[1]

Because *saw'a* has a second meaning (as if to intensify a particular form of shame) that connotes "nakedness," or exposure of the genitals, we find other English translations that take this sense of the word into account. Muhammad M. Pickthall's rendering was:

> Then Allah sent a raven scratching up the ground, to show him how to hide his brother's naked corpse. He said: Woe unto me! Am I not able to be as this raven and so hide my brother's naked corpse?[2]

A. J. Arbury's translation uses a phrase that attempts to combine the two connotations of *saw'a*:

> Then God sent forth a raven, scratching
> into the earth, to show him how he might
> conceal the vile body of his brother.
> He said, "Woe is me! Am I unable
> to be as this raven, and so conceal
> my brother's vile body?"[3]

We can see how the chosen sense of *saw'a* or "disgrace" might influence interpreters of the story—one group emphasizing the killing and burial per se, and others finding grounds for another dimension of Qabil's crime, namely his failure to protect the modesty of Habil's corpse. (The association of the disgrace of Adam and Eve in the garden with their search for leaves to cover their genitals, as related in Surahs 7:26, 7:27, and 20:121, understands *saw'a* in this sense.) While it is not easy to picture how it might have happened that Habil was not only dead but naked, we must recall the fifth- to sixth-century Christian Syriac tradition (in Symmachus's *Life of Abel*) in which Abel's buried body was described as "naked" and "all bloody" by the grieving Eve. Could this piece of Christian lore have provided a background for the supposition of some Muslims, if not the Qur'an itself, that Cain's *saw'a* had to do with, or included, his failure to cover his brother's nakedness? We do know that this suggestion in the text's language did inspire some Muslim Qur'an interpreters to extend the idea. Two medieval scholars, al-Zamakhshari and al-Biqa'i, taught in their commentaries that when Qabil became aware of the uncovered genitals of his brother, he was *further* moved to recognize the grievous character of his own deed of murder. Qabil's coming to remorse, according to these interpreters, had two stages.[4]

For now, we leave these ambiguities about the raven's lesson, the possible meanings of "covering the exposure" of Habil's corpse, and Qabil's response, in order to see this episode from another perspective—one that is comparative. Surah 5:31 represents a confrontation of Qabil the murderer by what he recognizes as a divine message that has to do with his brother's body. In other words, it functions in a way similar to the scene in *Genesis* 4:9–16 where Cain is interrogated by the Lord about his brother's whereabouts, but expresses no regret or guilt about his crime.[5]

The narrative of Qabil's killing of Habil brought to a close, Surah 5:32 provides a summation: God has Muhammad deliver the declaration given to the Children of Israel (*Banu Isra'il*) about the universal import of a single killing (and, alternatively, of a single saving or sparing of a human life). A trenchant final word on the story of Adam's sons, the verse contains the weightiest possible injunction against intentional murder. How many ramifications of this statement will Qur'an commentators and legal thinkers be compelled to address?

QABIL, HABIL, AND GOD'S LAWS—ISSUES UNDER SCRUTINY

The role that the story of Adam's sons played in early Muslim moral-legal discussions about murder was not extensive, but we do find texts revealing diverse interpretations of the behaviors of Qabil and Habil, of the discrimination between kinds of killings, and, not least, of Surah 5:53's proposition of the universal "reach" of a single killing.

The Victim

Before delving into Qabil's crime we must pause to consider the Qur'an's account of Habil's response to his threatening brother, which is problematic. Habil's speech presents us with intertextual tension—that is, discrepancy or strain between different qur'anic teachings. In Surah 5:29 Habil expresses the hope that both his and Qabil's sins will be counted against his brother when, in "hellfire," Qabil suffers the punishment due to him. Elsewhere in the Qur'an we find pronouncements that each human, when the day of judgment arrives, will be held answerable for his or her own deeds, and for no one else's—for example, in 6:164: "No soul gets but what it is due, and no one bearing responsibility can bear the burden of another."[6] Basic to Islamic beliefs about the end-time is the expectation that when the record of a person's good and evil are weighed as if on a scale, each *individual* will be held to account by God.

It is not surprising that several interpreters attempted to change the sense of Habil's comment. Some suggested that when he said "for my sin," Habil meant the murder itself—Qabil's imminent crime against Habil— while "for your sin" referred to Qabil's other faults. Another effort to rescue Habil from his utterance came in the form of a *hadith* that *did* sanction a murderer's being charged with the sins of his victim.[7] We are free to speculate for ourselves why Habil is represented as hoping for what elsewhere in the Qur'an is denied. Is it conceivable that the text itself intimates that even the son of Adam, who was granted God's favor, was not without (a minor, rather than a major) fault—that his expressed hope for a double burden of sins for Qabil revealed Habil, human that he was, not to be a wholly righteous beneficiary of God's approval? Given the range of opinions entertained by Muslim interpreters, we should consider a final possibility—namely, that the doctrine found in 6:164 and in parallel qur'anic passages (each person to be held accountable only for his or her own actions) was not yet so inviolable as to disallow Habil's wish as at least a permissible yearning in the story of an ancient hero—Adam's archetypal good son.

There was also, from Islam's beginnings, scholarly (and probably general) puzzlement over Habil's choice of nonresistance in the face of Qabil's death threat (5:28). Why, under this menace, did Habil embrace a strategy of inaction? For many Muslim exegetes, and for Muhammad, as his opinions were preserved in *hadiths*, the questions about when and when not to resist violence were continuing ones, subject to particular conditions and circumstances. Heribert Busse comments:

> Traditional Muslim exegesis asserts that killing in self-defense was prohibited at the time of Cain and Abel but that this prohibition was later abolished. In support of this interpretation a hadith is cited in which it is declared forbidden for a Muslim to kill another Muslim in self-defense. If he prefers to fight and dies, both he and his opponent will be condemned to the fire. Other hadiths recommend the abandonment of self-defense . . . and according to other commentators, the issue of self-defense is of no relevance in this context because Abel was murdered treacherously.[8]

We shall meet several of these points of view in commentaries soon to be considered. But first, what are we to make of the modern scholarly suggestion that the qur'anic representation of Habil's decision to be a victim rather than a fighter was influenced by Christianity—in particular, by that strain of Christian teaching we met in the previous chapter, which portrayed Abel as a martyr and even as a prototype of the crucified Christ?[9] The teachings and the art of Syriac and Arab Christians concerning the crucifixion and resurrection were well known in seventh-century Mecca, and we do possess clear evidence of Christian-Muslim communications about many aspects of Jesus's/`Isa's life, both in and beyond the time of the revelations to the Prophet. And yet there are reasons to question whether or how the Qur'an might have used these verbal and artistic images of Jesus in relation to Habil, the first victim. Did the Jesus of the Christians imprint the Muslim Habil's passive victimhood?

In the ranks of those martyrs (*shuhada*) who died for their faith, Jesus may not have been singled out by early Muslim interpreters as the obvious model. It is interesting, for example, that a powerful saying attributed to Muhammad about martyrdom's glory (though it does not touch upon defenselessness) carries no hint of Christian influence: "By Him in whose hands my life is! I would love to be martyred in God's cause, and then get resurrected and then get martyred and then get resurrected again, and then get martyred again, and then get resurrected again, and then get martyred."[10] More to the point, however, is the fact (we shall examine this more fully in the book's concluding Part, on Mary, chs. 13–15) that Muslim celebration of Jesus centered not in his death, but in three other things—namely, his miraculous birth to his virgin mother (Maryam), his powerful prophethood and messiahship that preceded the appearance of God's ultimate messenger (Muhammad), and his essential role in dramas of the last judgment, as Islam pictured that event. (One tradition imagined Jesus's presence at the end-time in this way: for twenty years he would preside, from Jerusalem's pulpits, as a just judge.[11])

The speculation that Habil's vow not to defend himself against Qabil owes something to Christian representations of Jesus's crucifixion and death also butts up against another obstacle, one we could call a qur'anic counterinfluence—namely, a denial of the actuality of Christ's death within the Qur'an. In Surah 4:157–158 the Jews are excoriated

> 157 On account of their saying,
> "We killed the Messiah Jesus,
> Son of Mary, messenger of God,"
> whereas they did not kill him,
> they did not crucify him,
> although it was made to seem thus to them.
> As for those who differ on this,
> they are certainly in doubt about it.
> They have no knowledge about it,
> only the following conjecture;
> they surely did not kill him:
> 158 rather God raised him
> up to the divine presence;
> and God is almighty, most wise.

The variety of explanations of Habil's unwillingness to resist Qabil is so great that we might be in danger of forgetting the rather straightforward moral and legal rationale Habil gives (in 5:29) for his decision not to respond in kind to his brother's threat: were he to murder Qabil, Habil would fall under the judgment of the God he fears, and become himself one of the "unjust," the sinners. This piece of thoroughly qur'anic reasoning seems, in comparison with a thesis about a Christian influence, a preferable approach in explaining Habil's nonresistant dying.

The Murderer

Qabil, of course, drew much greater attention than Habil among those who turned to the story with concerns for its moral and legal ramifications. It is his act of murder that evokes God's dramatic reminder (5:32) of what he had decreed to the Israelites: "if anyone killed a person . . . it would be as if he had killed all the people." The phrase pushes the gravity of intentional killing to the utter limit.

But a qualification stands in the middle of this declaration: if anyone killed another person, "other than for murder, or corruption on earth." Though murder is a terrible crime, a drastic evil, the killing of killers *is* permissible. Execution of murderers is *not* unlawful. Rather, this penalty sustains order in human communities, enabling and enforcing the exercise of retributive justice ("an eye for an eye").

Cases of corruption on earth entail apostasy, atheism, and holding erroneous beliefs (e.g., arguing that God's hands are tied in relation to events in the world, or espousing doctrines held by the Jewish and Christian "people of the book"), and the crimes are counted in 5:32's exception as punishable in the world by death, alongside the execution of murderers. God commands such, and the ordering of any just community or society requires the same. So it is that Qabil's act of murder is presented, and then further clarified by the insertion of a qur'anic moral norm: it is forbidden to kill, but there *do* exist killings of humans who have committed grievous crimes. These takings-of-lives are lawful under the rules set for fixing punishments appropriate to the crimes committed. The penalties for thieves are described in 5:38 as divinely ordained deterrents, and other particular cases are fully present in the Qur'an. They would in the next centuries come under the consideration of jurists, and be applied by those responsible for maintaining and enforcing laws in their particular communities, large and small.

Military conflicts made the question of killing—licit and illicit—weightier, more complex, and subject to adjustments. What more do we learn about the issues under debate over *qatala* (the Arabic verb, to murder, to kill)? Some early readers of Surah 5:32's warning about the gravity of a single murder argued that it was directed to the Children of Israel, but not to Muslims. This opinion, undergirded by the thesis that the two sons were not really Adam's, but were Israelites, was resisted, as we shall soon see in al-Tabari's grappling with it. The prevailing understanding was that this qur'anic decree was addressed to Muslims and in fact to all humans, but this more universal application of 5:32, it should be said, was under development from the eighth to the twelfth century CE (and remains so in modernity).[12] It is important not to pass over in silence the similarity of the formula (murder of one human is tantamount to the murder of all) to what is found in *Mishnah Sanhedrin* 4.5; the Jewish teaching of the universal significance of a single killing seems to have been prompted by the *plural* "bloods" of Abel that cried out to God from the ground—for example, the inference that in his death were many.[13]

Surah 5's warnings that Muslims should avoid Jews' and Christians' communal practices and ignore whatever preachments they professed from their scriptures reveal the defensive aspect of its message. We have already seen its other side—the strong claims laid out for the revelations God has charged Muhammad to recite. In relation to the question or the ethics of killing, there remained matters calling for articulation in Muslim terms. One of these basic issues presented itself in a well-known *hadith*:

> Narrated By `Abdullah: The Prophet said, "No human being is killed unjustly [without] a part of responsibility for the crime [being] laid on the first son of Adam, who invented the tradition of killing on the earth" (It is said that he was Qabil).[14]

This quotation prompts questions. Does Muhammad's saying suggest that Qabil will pay, at least in part, for all subsequent murderers' deeds, perhaps lessening their individual punishments? This seems an unlikely sense of the Prophet's statement, in light of our earlier discussion of each person's full accountability for her or his sins. Nevertheless, more must be at stake in his words than an intent to recall memories of humankind's beginnings. Whatever connection is being made between the first and subsequent humans who are guilty of murder is not likely to be rooted in the idea that Qabil's evil infected all human beings with the instinct to kill, similar to Western Christianity's doctrine of the transmission to all of the original sin of Adam and Eve. Muslim belief in the capacity of people to do both good and evil works weighs against such a theory of contamination.

Muhammad's reported designation of Cain as the blameworthy originator of murder hovers, at least in this saying, over Muslim discussions and judgments about illegal and legal killings, about proper punishments and justifiable reprieves. Intentional murders were punishable by death, but there was sometimes more to say. To the major sin of wrongful homicide, certain adjustments were made; a killing was deemed even more grievous, for example, if the victim was a relative, if the killing was of a child (in an attempt to fend off a family's poverty), or if it had occurred in a sacred precinct.[15]

We cannot here gather and analyze a number of cases involving different kinds of life-taking, but it would be a mistake to bypass Surah 4:92–94, which sounds warnings about crucial complexities that surround acts of killing, and requisite compensations:

> 92 It is never right
> for a believer to kill a believer,
> except by mistake;

and one who kills a believer by mistake
is to free a believing slave,
and compensation is to be handed over
to the family of the deceased,
unless they forgo it to charity.
If the deceased was from a people
warring against yours,
yet was a believer,
then free a believing slave.
But if the deceased was from a people
with whom you have a treaty,
then compensation is to be paid
to the family of the deceased
and a believing slave is to be freed.
And if anyone has not the means,
then one is to fast
for two consecutive months,
as an act of contrition granted
as a concession from God.
And God is all-knowing, most judicious.
93 But whoever kills a believer on purpose
has hell for his reward, wherein he will remain;
and God will be wroth with him, and curse him.
94 Believers, when you strike out for the sake of God,
get at the facts,
and do not say to anyone
who greets you with peace,
"You are not a believer,"
seeking the goods of this world,
for there are plenty of spoils with God.
You were thus before,
when God bestowed favor on you;
so get at the facts.
For God is well aware
of what you do.

A *hadith* relates one of these circumstances and its impact upon a combatant:

Narrated By Usama bin Zaid bin Haritha: Allah's Apostle sent us (to fight) against al-Huraqa (one of the sub-tribes) of Juhaina. We reached those people in the morning and defeated them. A man from the Ansar and I chased one of their men and when we attacked him, he said, "None has the right to be worshipped but Allah." The Ansari refrained from killing him but I stabbed him with my spear till I killed him. When we reached (Medina), this news reached the Prophet. He said to me, "O Usama! You killed him after he had said, 'None has the right to be worshipped but Allah?'" I said, "O Allah's Apostle! He said so in order to save himself." The Prophet said, "You killed him after he had said, 'None has the right to be worshipped but Allah.'" The Prophet kept on repeating that statement till I wished I had not been a Muslim before that day.[16]

Of course these questions about lawful and unlawful killing, or discrimination between major and minor sins and their respective punishments, served to aid Islam's organization as a society, and as a religion-defined people expanding eastward and westward from its early capitals in Medina, Damascus, and Baghdad. There was for believers another dimension of meaning in these moral standards and adjudications of justice—one that transcended what transpired "in this world." As Jews and Christians summarized those things God regarded as the principal virtues and the most grievous sins, so did early Muslims declare their visions of what God required:

> Narrated 'Ubada bin As-Sammat: I was among the Naqibs [selected leaders who gave the pledge of allegiance to Allah's Apostle]. We gave the oath of allegiance, that we would not join partners in worship besides Allah, would not steal, would not commit illegal sexual intercourse, would not kill a life which God has forbidden, would not commit robbery, would not disobey (Allah and his Apostle), and if we fulfilled the pledge we would have Paradise, but if we committed any one of these (sins), then our case would be decided by Allah (*Sahih Bukhari*, 9.83.12).

Moral-legal questions present in the Qur'an and in the *hadith* appeared also in the following two authors' treatments of Cain and Abel, but their main curiosities took a different direction. Like Jewish and Christian exegetes who found the *Genesis* account of Adam's two sons in need of further clarification and elaboration, al-Tabari and al-Tha'labi spied a range of things in their scripture's narration of Qabil's murder of Habil that cried out: interpret me!

AL-TABARI ON QABIL AND HABIL

Abu Ja'far Muhammad b. Jarir al-Tabari (839–923 CE), named for the place of his birth in the region of Tabaristan in northern Iran, was particularly celebrated for his *History of Prophets and Kings (Ta'rikh al-rusul wa'l-muluk)*, considered "by common consent the most important universal history produced in the world of Islam."[17]

In a section of the *History* which treats the period "from the creation to the flood," al-Tabari retold the story of Qabil and Habil, joining his to the many opinions of Qur'an commentators he collected.[18] Fundamental to al-Tabari's procedure as a chronicler was the practice of identifying his sources and assessing their antiquity and authenticity. Typically, an interpretive comment was introduced by its *isnad*—its chain of transmitters from the originators of the view expressed. The oldest traditions, especially those coming from the Prophet or his family and intimates, were regarded as the most authoritative.

We are not surprised that questions of cause and motive occupied a prominent place in Muslim commentary on Surah 5:26–31. For what reason or reasons did Adam's sons fall into dispute? One explanation, also present in some Jewish and Christian interpreters' theories, enjoys prominence in Muslim commentary—the prospect of future wives for Qabil and Habil as a chief factor in their clash. "Some say" (al-Tabari lists seven transmitters of the opinion attributed to Muhammad's cousin and companion, Ibn `Abbas) that "every boy born to Adam was born together with a girl. Adam used to marry the boy of one pregnancy to the girl of another, and vice versa."[19] Predictably, many among the Qur'an commentators warmed to the topic, with its complex and multiple possibilities.[20]

Because each son had been born with a twin sister, Adam was compelled to be the first family planner, making decisions about appropriate mates. Between Qabil and Habil a controversy arose, since the former's twin was more beautiful—apparently much more beautiful—than his brother's. Though ordered by Adam to marry his sister to Abel, Cain refused. "I deserve to marry her more (than you do)" he stated, without justifying his claim.[21]

How was this issue to be settled? Al-Tabari carefully sets the stage for the tragedy about to occur:

> Cain and Abel offered a sacrifice to God (to find out) who was the more deserving of the girl. On that day, Adam was absent, as he had gone to have a look at Mecca. God had said to Adam: Adam, do you know that I have a House on earth? Adam replied: Indeed, I do not. God said: I have a House in Mecca. So go there! Adam said to heaven: Guard my two children safely! But heaven refused. He addressed the earth (with the same request) and the earth refused. He addressed the mountains, and they also refused. He then spoke to Cain, who said: Yes! You shall go, and when you return, you will be happy with the state in which you find your family.[22]

Adam returned from his visit to the *Ka`bah*—the "ancient house" (*al-bayt al-`atiq*) in Mecca—to discover that one of his sons was dead, the other a murderer. Deftly, Al-Tabari inserts the qur'anic passage, Surah 33:72:

> We presented the Trust
> to the heavens and the earth and the mountains,
> but they refused to bear it, and shunned it;
> but man took it up, for he is unjust
> and ignorant.[23]

Readers and hearers of al-Tabari's story-elaboration recognized his ingenuity in inserting lines from a qur'anic passage unrelated to Cain and Abel in order to make more ominous his portrayal of Cain. Al-Tabari nonetheless felt obliged to identify the figure mentioned in the last two lines. The reference, he wrote, was to "Cain when he took on the (task of) safekeeping for Adam and did not guard his family."[24]

Cautious decline of Adam's request was the response of nature's personalized elements (who knew their limitations, or the dangerous passion that was astir, or both), while Cain, in some ways the representative human—prideful in his scheming, and acting in his own interest—accepted, and abused "the Trust." The message is a double one, at once particular and universal in import: an unjust and ignorant man was Cain, and Cain is man, or the human creature.

A further incriminating characterization of Cain the volunteer "guardian" follows:

> Cain had always boasted of being better than Abel, saying: I am more deserving
> of her, because she is my sister, I am older than you, and I am the legatee (*wasi*)
> of my father.[25]

Al-Tabari fills in the picture of what transpired when the two brothers stood at their altars.

> For their sacrifices, Abel offered a fat young sheep, and Cain a sheaf of ears of
> corn. Finding a large ear, Cain husked and ate it. A fire came down from heaven.
> It consumed Abel's offering and left that of Cain. Whereupon Cain got angry and
> said: I shall kill you to prevent you from marrying my sister.[26]

Qabil's arrogance is revealed in his taking for himself the best part of his grain offering, and in his anger at the consequence—God's preference for Habil's sacrifice.

What follows in al-Tabari's text is the citation of the Qur'an passage, 5:28–30, concluding with the notice that Cain's soul not only permitted but urged him to commit the murder. Abel flees to the mountains, but Cain tracks him, and the killing itself is told in more detail. Discovering his brother near his herd of small cattle, Cain "lifted a big rock and crushed Abel's head with it. So he died."[27] Ignorant of death and burial, Cain lets Abel's body lie naked. Then two fraternal ravens are sent by God; one kills the other and buries its body. Cain then emits his cry of remorse for his lack of respect for Abel's naked corpse, and more than that, for his horrible act of killing.

Al-Tabari relates (from Muhammad b. Ishaq, through an *isnad*) traditions stemming from scholars belonging to "the people of the first Book." He refers to Jewish sources contending that Cain's concern for this twin sister and his notion of deserving her were based on a qualitative difference between this pair and the rest of the subsequent twinned progeny of Adam and Eve. Cain and she had been conceived prior to their parents' sin at the forbidden tree, and they therefore belonged to a class of their own—a reality evinced in their painless and bloodless delivery by Eve, in contrast with Eve's travails in giving birth to thirty-nine sets of twins after she had fallen to earth. With those pregnancies there had been "cravings and illness . . . pain in giving birth to them, and she saw blood in connection with them."[28]

So it was that Cain rejected Abel's sister as a mate, saying: "We [my twin and I] were born in Paradise, and they were born on earth."[29] Al-Tabari interjects that others among the scholars maintain the view that the issue under dispute actually did concern the pulchritude of Cain's sister, rather than her birth in Paradise, but about this, he says, "God knows best what it was!"[30]

Jewish writers' disparate ideas of what the two sons offered for sacrifices are duly recorded by al-Tabari: Cain, a farmer, brought flour, while Abel brought some firstborn sheep or a cow. It was a "white fire" that consumed the latter's offering, signaling that he deserved as his mate "the sister of Cain [who] was one of the most beautiful human beings."[31] And what of Cain's anger? The cause of Cain's passionate ire was variously explained in the Jewish lore, one view holding that "haughtiness got the better of him, and Satan gained mastery over him."[32]

Referring still to interpretive comments by those "knowledgeable in the first Book," al-Tabari notes that Ibn Humayd spoke of Qabil's perplexity when dealing with his brother's corpse, "for this supposedly was the first killing among the children of Adam."[33] The word "supposedly," as we shall see, denotes a question under discussion among those generating *tafsir* (exegesis) on the Qur'an.

What follows in al-Tabari's text is testimony to his care in collecting textual materials. We encounter "one of the rare instances of a quite literal translation from the Bible (*Genesis* 4:9–16) ... based not on the Hebrew Bible but on one of the early translations, most likely one into Aramaic/Syriac."[34] "He" (Ibn Humayd, again) relates what "the people of the Torah suppose" took place when one son killed the other. Now a portion of al-Tabari's account of numerous readings of the story of Qabil and Habil consists in the Hebrew Bible's description of God's confrontation with Cain, the blood of Abel crying out from the earth, and the combined protection and punishment accorded the murderer.[35]

Yet another theory is advanced about the reason for Cain's murder of Abel. Al-Tabari recounts that he heard this from Muhammad b. Sa`d, whose family members through several generations transmitted the witness of Ibn `Abbas. This commentary is prefaced by an observation about a significant difference between the sacrifices of the two sons and those offered in later times: then, in the days of Cain and Abel, "there were no indigents to be given charity from (from the sacrifice)."[36] Because "sacrifices were simply offered"[37]—that is, they were not part of the ritual-social life of a community—it happened one day as they sat relaxing that the idea of making an offering occurred to the sons of Adam. When Abel's offering of his prize animals received divine acceptance in the form of the descending fire, while Cain's agricultural produce did not, Cain said to his brother:[38]

> Should you (be allowed to) walk among men who have come to know that you offered a sacrifice that was accepted, while my sacrifice was rejected? Indeed not! The people must not look at me and at you (and think of) you as being better than I . . . "I shall kill you."[39]

Cain sees his future reputation to be in jeopardy. The one who makes him appear to be deficient or inferior cannot live.

An abrupt shift takes place at this juncture in al-Tabari's treatment of the Cain and Abel story. He turns his attention to the previously mentioned tradition of interpretation that disputes who the two sacrificers were. Some argue:

> The story of those two men did not take place in Adam's time, and the sacrifice was not offered in his age. . . . The two belonged to the children of Israel. . . . The first person to die on earth was Adam. No one died before him. . . . [The two sons] were not sons from the loin of Adam. The sacrifice took place among the children of Israel. Adam was the first man to die.[40]

An attempt to distance the brothers' clash from Adam is the clear objective of this line of thinking. Under contestation is the question of whether Abel or Adam was the world's first mortality, but more importance seems to attach, as we learn shortly, to the question of who introduced murder among the creatures of the earth. It would be better, of course, if Adam, a prophet of God, did not have a murderer in his immediate offspring. Further elaborations of the saga, however, interrupt and tend to redefine the gist of the dispute. In a challenge to the tradition that Qabil and his sister were conceived in Paradise, some are reported to have said that Adam and Eve had a prolonged, healthy, and productive sexual life a century *after* their fall to earth, producing Qabil and his twin sister first, and then, in another pregnancy, Habil and his sister. Qalima is given as the name of Qabil's twin, and a bit later in the text we learn that Habil's sister was Labudha.[41] Locations are added to the narrative, one of which orients the legend to familiar Muslim sacred landscape: Habil met his death on the mountain slope of Hira'—the site near Mecca where Muhammad meditated in a grotto, and the place where, as it is said, the Qur'an descended to him on the "Night of Destiny."[42] Another tradition, this one attributed to Ibn `Abbas, has Qabil, after murdering his brother, descend hand in hand with Qalima to the foot of Mount Nudh, at which point Adam sends his son away—to his (later) death by a bowman (a reminiscence of the tradition of Lamech in *Genesis* 4:17–24).[43]

Al-Tabari returns to the debate over the identity of the son who murdered his brother, and registers his own opinion. Yes, "one of the two sons of Adam mentioned by God in His Book as having killed his brother *is* a son of Adam's loin."[44] Proof consists in evidence from authoritative *isnads*, one of which is traced to the Prophet. Equal accuracy is believed to attach to the tradition (seen in the *hadith* quoted earlier—and known to al-Tabari) about the son of Adam, Qabil, who shares the blame in every murder, having committed the first.[45]

Al-Tabari persists in his challenge to those who claim that the two sons were "children of Israel." Their argument fails, al-Tabari states, because "killing took place among the children of Israel before Israel and his children existed."[46] By "Israel" he means Jacob, who in the Hebrew Bible (*Genesis* 32:28) after the wrestling with the man at Peniel was told: "Your name shall no longer be Jacob, but Israel, for you have striven with beings divine and human."

Could doubt continue that the two sons were Adam's own, and not children in or after the time of Jacob? "There is no disagreement about this among the early scholars of our nation, since the statement that they were children of Israel is corrupt," al-Tabari firmly asserts. We noted earlier that the verse following the narrative portion in the Qur'an concerning Qabil and Habil, Surah 5:32, contains the teaching that the killing of a single person would be "as if [the killer] had slain mankind entirely." Al-Tabari firmly maintains that the fact that the Qur'an states that this decree was ordained "for the children of Israel" does not displace the story of the two sons from Adam's days to the later emergence of the Israelites.

Invoking an *isnad* originating with `Ali b. Abi Talib, cousin of the prophet and eventually the fourth caliph, al-Tabari presents the tradition of Adam's versified mourning of Abel:

> The land and those upon it have changed.
> The face of the earth is now ugly and dusty.
> Everything tasty and colorful has changed.
> The cheerfulness of a handsome face has become rare.

A reply to the father's wailing presumably comes from Iblis (Satan):

> Father of Abel! Both have been killed.
> The one alive has become like the one slaughtered and dead.
> He brought evil of which he was
> afraid. He brought it shouting.[47]

The verses, themselves commentary, are not expanded upon. "Adam's poem presumably had its origin in the highly imaginative early Islamic literature dealing with Arabian prehistory," Franz Rosenthal wrote in his study of complaint and hope in Medieval Islam.[48] The first four lines register the father's lament at the loss of his son; all beauty and good sensation have passed from his experience of the world. The lines of response add an interpretation of the murder's result. Unsuppressed, the evil that frightened Cain is now "shouting." The allusion is to Abel's vocal blood. In the aftermath of this fratricide, evil and rancor bellow, having been set loose in the world.

At the end of his account of Cain and Abel, al-Tabari briefly expresses his opinion about the number of children Eve bore. The correct number of pregnancies, each producing male and female twins, was, according to Ibn Ishaq's reliable testimony, twenty, not (as some contended) one hundred and twenty. Only some of the names of the first couple's offspring are known, among which the author identifies Cain and Qalima, Abel and Labudha, a daughter, Ashuth, and her twin, and Seth and his.[49]

The movement toward the story's ending is interrupted by a return to the subject of the brothers' strife over the more beautiful sister, but this too gives way to a report with which we'll end our review of al-Tabari's pre-sentation of Qabil and Habil in his *History*. Al-Tabari recounts testimony traceable to Ibn `Abbas and told by one early authority to another while they were performing the Hajj's ritual stoning of Iblis at Mina; it had to do with the destiny of the ram offered to God by Habil:

> That ram remained in custody with God until He let it go as Isaac's ransom
> [when Abraham was offering him as a sacrifice]. [Abraham] slaughtered it upon
> this rock on [Mount] Thabir at the mansion of Samura al-Sawwaf, which is on
> your right hand when you throw the pebbles.[50]

Continuities in divine action and the location of that action in places familiar to Muslim pilgrims (the site of Abraham's sacrifice is known as the *majar al-kabsh*, the "place of the bleating of the ram") are purposefully put forth as features of the story worthy of comment. (The identity of the son Ibrahim attempted to sacrifice to God was a matter of debate in al-Tabari's time—a subject that will resurface in a later chapter.)

QABIL AND HABIL IN AL-THA`LABI'S
LIVES OF THE PROPHETS

Al-Tha`labi (Abu Ishaq Ahmad b. Muhammad b. Ibrahim al-Tha`labi) died just over three hundred years after the prophet Muhammad, in 1036 CE. His composition of the legend of Qabil and Habil reveals his familiarity with the commentaries of his predecessors, especially those present in al-Tabari's *History*. Of particular interest to us in al-Tha`labi's version of the story are the changes and additions, large and small, that color his retelling—particularly those elements that give indications of continu-ing debate among interpreters about the story's sense and its paramount moral lessons.

The source of the conflict between the young men (Habil is said to be twenty in the year he dies—only two years younger than Qabil) remains the same as it was in the exegesis of earlier interpreters—the quarrel is over women, or more specifically, about Qabil's twin (here Iqlima, a variant on the usual Qalima). Desired for a mate by both sons of Adam, Iqlima is no longer portrayed as compelling on the basis of her pulchritude alone. Al-Tha'labi calls her "one of the most beautiful and the finest of character among women."[51] The differing legends about the location of the first twins' begetting appear in al-Tha`labi's *Lives*, and include the proposal, known to us from al-Tabari, that Qabil and Iqlima were conceived in Paradise, prior to their parents' sin—and were therefore, at least by Qabil's reasoning, peerless mates for each other. Such a distinction addressed the concerns found in Ibn `Abbas's dire note about the behavior of the earliest human generations:

> Adam did not die before seeing forty thousand of his children and his children's children. Adam also saw among them fornication, the drinking of wine, and corruption.[52]

Incest, per se, is not in the list, though this possible understanding of the beginnings of the human family was, as it had been for Jewish and Christian exegetes of *Genesis*, difficult for Islamic commentators. It was God who commanded Adam to assign Iqlima to Habil, but al-Tha`labi was obliged to clarify the circumstances:

> At that time, a man might marry any of his sisters that he wished except for his own twin sister. . . . this was necessary because in those days there were no women who were not the men's sisters and who did not have Eve as their common mother.[53]

The argument from necessity—that is, scarcity of possible mates—did not sit well with some scholars, as we learn from a transmitter who asked the scholar Ja`far al-Sadiq whether Adam married his children to each other.

> He answered: "God forbid! If Adam had done so, the Messenger of God would have detested him and Adam's religion would not have been the same as our Prophet Muhammad."[54]

Ja`far al-Sadiq was the celebrated eighth-century figure counted as the sixth imam among the twelve (beginning with `Ali) who are held in honor in Shi`ism as descendents of the Prophet, themselves partakers in his spiritual-royal station. Al-Sadiq's conviction about nonmarriage of siblings obviously seeks consistency between Muhammad's teachings and what was permissible in humanity's earliest days. Indeed, the prohibition against marriage of brothers and sisters is qur'anic, for Surah 4.23 declares: "Unlawful are your mothers and daughters and sisters to you," and the passage, a divine decree, is seen by al-Sadiq to trump the lore long circulated among Jews, Christians, and now by some Muslims, that at creation's beginnings siblings mated—in order to ensure the next generations of humankind.

Al-Sadiq and his allies advanced an alternative view of humanity's continuation. A strategic argument, it featured an add-on creation story—one meant to defend the doctrine of original and continuing purity and holiness in prophetic religion—that is, in the lineage of Muhammad, which extends from Adam to the prophets to the imams. Al-Sadiq's teaching becomes remarkable in its proposal about what *kind* of female mates were available to the sons of Adam. According to his understanding of sacred history, when Cain came of age, a *jinni* was created for him "in the form of a human female," womb included. Her name was `Amalah. God inspired Adam to marry `Amalah to Cain, and he did so. For Abel, when he matured, God created a *houri* as a female and fashioned in her also a womb, naming her Tarakah. When Abel saw her, God stirred Adam to marry this son to her. Cain's mate, then, was a *jinni,* one of the creatures "from the white hot flame of fire" (Surah 55:15) who could be either benevolent or malevolent to humans. Abel's mate, on the other hand, was one of the virginal "companions with large black eyes" (Surah 44:54) who recline on couches with the redeemed in Paradise. Tarakah was a heavenly being now made woman for him. Abel fared better than Cain.

By this line of interpretation, the progeny of Adam and Eve were not the offspring of their children—that is, of brothers and sisters. Incestuous origins of humankind would not have been in keeping with the religion of Adam the prophet, which was one with—indeed, *must* be one with—the religion of Muhammad. Al-Sadiq's opinion, incorporated in al-Tha`labi's *Lives of the Prophets*, stands as an insistent statement about the absolute ethical principles and practices contained in the revelation to Muhammad, and also as a doctrine advocating and protecting the view that the imams, standing in the lineage of the pure, from Adam to Muhammad, were men without blemish.[55] The legend of the *jinni* and *houri* spouses serves both of these purposes. The superhuman mates fashioned by God for Habil and Qabil were, from the viewpoint of al-Sadiq and his Shi'ite community, not only fitting, but essential. Of course there is irony in this narrative, for although Habil receives a purer mate than the one assigned to his brother, he will be a victim of Qabil before his mate-taking can occur.

This Shi'ite twist in the story altered but did not eliminate the grounds upon which Qabil, after the rejection of his offering, could cry foul. Complaining that as the older brother he has more right than Habil to the *houri* mate, Qabil and his father argue about favor and favoritism, and about its source:

[Adam] replied: "My son, favor is in God's hand; He bestows it upon whom He wishes." [Qabil] said: "On the contrary, *you* preferred him to me in your affection."[56]

The accusation's bitterness, and the voicing of criticism of Adam's (as distinct from God's) partiality comes at the conclusion of the testimony of Ja`far al-Sadiq, but sympathy for Cain is made impossible by ensuing statements about his hostile disposition and motives. Al-Tha`labi's commentary reverts to the *isnad*, the chain of transmission running to Ibn Ishaq, that reports Cain's sacrifice of the worst of his crops, which he offered with disdain, "harboring this thought in his heart: 'I do not care whether He [God] will accept (my offering) or not; [Abel] will never marry my sister!'"[57]

The contrast in character and actions between the sons of Adam is further sharpened by an observation that the choice fat lamb, along with milk and butter that Abel offered (as Isma`il b. Rafi` recounted), was the animal he loved most, and often carried on his back. It was "purity of heart" and the lack thereof that dictated God's judgment on the sacrifices. Cain's anger was directed at God for the refusal of his sacrifice, we are told, and this was compounded by the envy and covetousness that he already harbored toward his brother. Cain's threat (Surah 5:28) to do violence to Abel has yet other incentives tagged on at the end—namely, concern for how he was regarded, and for the ridicule that his own progeny will suffer:

> Because God accepted your offering and did not accept mine, so you will marry my beautiful sister and I shall marry your ugly one, and people will be saying that you are better than I and more virtuous, and your son will boast of being superior to mine.[58]

Al-Tha`labi preserves the tradition that Qabil struck Habil with a rock when he found him asleep. But the added testimony of an eighth-century CE commentator named Ibn Jurayj informs us that Cain, not knowing at first how to kill, required instruction from Iblis, who "took a bird, placed its head on a stone, and then crushed it with another stone."[59] In this elaborated retelling of Surah 5:27–31, the portrayal of Qabil as murderous, self-interested, and callous is unrelieved. After the sending by God of the two ravens, with its lesson of how Qabil should dispose of his brother's body, the lamentation voiced by him in 5:31, "Alas, the woe—that I could not be even like the raven and hide the nakedness of my brother" has its apparent meaning subverted. We are told that when the Qur'an reports in 5:31 Qabil's remorse, it means that Qabil suffered deep regret "for having carried him [in a sack for a year], *not* for having killed him."[60]

Adam's absence at the time of the murder is al-Tha`labi's next subject. According to a report attributed to Ibn `Abbas, while Adam was in Mecca, the natural order suffered major disruptions:

> The trees became thorny, foods changed their tastes, fruits went sour, the water
> became bitter, and the Earth became covered with dust. Adam said: "Something
> evil has happened on earth."[61]

It was upon returning from Mecca to learn of Habil's death that Adam offered his lamentations—in verse. The drama of the scene dissolves when al-Tha`labi turns to a discussion among commentators about poetry and its origins. He records differing views—one that calls Adam's despondent cry "the first poem ever composed," while a competing opinion holds that Adam could not have produced poetry because to do so would have been a sin. Once more the consistency of belief and practice binding Adam and Muhammad (and all true prophets in between) is being underlined, as Surah 36:69 is quoted: "We have not taught (Muhammad) to versify, nor is it worthy of him." The status of poetry is a contested and ambiguous question in the traditions appearing in *Qisas* writings, as the concluding comment shows: Adam composed a lament for Habil, but being a Syrian, not an Arab, he could not compose poetry—which is possible only for one who speaks Arabic.[62]

Al-Tha`labi concludes his recounting of the drama of Qabil and Habil by spelling out its consequences: Habil is described as "the first martyr on the face of the earth," and Adam asks Qabil to remember his words of lamentation, "that people may pass them on as a heritage."[63] A penultimate piece of narrative elaboration pictures Qabil's banishment, with Iqlima at his side, to Yemen, where the tempter pays him a visit:

> Then Iblis came to him and said: "The fire consumed your brother's offering only
> because he served the fire and worshipped it. So you too [must] set up a fire that
> will be for yourself and your progeny." [So Qabil] built a fire temple, and he was
> the first to build a fire and worship it.[64]

The story of Qabil's death, complete with an image of his distorted bodily form awaiting judgment on the day of Resurrection, then gives way to a description of his successors, who in addition to engaging in fire- and idol-worship, introduced musical instruments and "were engrossed in pleasure and drinking wine, [and] in fornication . . . and abominations, until God drowned them in the Flood at the time of Noah."[65]

So ends al-Tha`labi's account of the murderous son, the resister of God, who "became one of the lost" (Surah 5:30), as did his children. This Adamic line—Qabil and his offspring—is presented here, as in Jewish and Christian lore, as damned. Apparently Qabil's remorse after the God-sent crow brought him to consciousness of his crime has been unable to cancel or soften the condemnation that al-Tha`labi and other Muslim commentators share with the people of the Book.

And what of the posterity of the murdered Habil—is it utterly gone, cut off? Muslim endeavors to keep alive the testament of the favored son were strong, as will be shown shortly.

Two themes dominated al-Tabari's and al-Tha`labi's retellings of the story of the first murder. One had to do with competition between the brothers for a mate. Each offered his sacrifice in order to attain God's endorsement of his hope, and the rage of Qabil against Habil was understood as a reaction to his being denied Qalima/Iqlima. We noticed that other explanations of the murderer's motives were advanced (his desire to protect his inheritance as Adam's firstborn, his grievance over being regarded as inferior to his brother, etc.), but these did not draw attention away from brothers' quest for the more desirable sister—who, we need to remind ourselves, is a character absent from the qur'anic account. An imagined competition for mates became, thanks to interpreters, a major factor in the story of Adam's sons.

The other strong interest that runs through the commentary presented in al-Tabari's *History* and al-Tha`labi's *Lives of the Prophets* centers in the moral makeup of each of the two sons. Qabil and Habil stand in contrast, countermodels of regard for God and for righteousness. Understandably, Qabil's personality and motivations came under closest scrutiny and criticism; given the terrible blameworthy act he had committed, efforts were made to discover grounds for his anger and reasons for his soul's concession to killing. So steadily do these two writers depict the defiant and hostile Qabil that the distinct emphasis within the Qur'an's presentation of him—upon his "remorse" and possible penitence—seems secondary. Habil is the martyr, and Qabil, finally, remains among the lost.

CONTINUING THE PRESENCE OF THE MURDERED HABIL: TWO EFFORTS

Seth/Shith in Muslim Interpretation

In all three religions, the story of Abel's death by his brother's hand resisted its own ending, wanting to sustain—in some imaginable form—the

righteous victim's vitality. When, in *Genesis* 4, the blood of Abel is audible
to God, there is suggestion of the victim's endurance beyond his mortality.
One method of keeping the murder victim "alive" was to transfer the promise he held to another person—to another son of Adam. And so:

> Adam knew his wife again, and she bore a son and named him Seth, meaning
> "God has provided me with another offspring in place of Abel," for Cain had
> killed him (*Genesis* 4:25).

Seth is Abel's replacement—with the help of God. To Eve and Adam, his
birth is divine consolation, not least because Seth exists as his father's
proper heir and successor. The early Christians understood Abel as a mar-
tyr-prototype of Jesus's death, but particular significance also attaches
to the fact that the single time that Seth's name appears in the New
Testament, it is to identify him as one of Jesus's ancestors, "Seth, son of
Adam" (*Luke* 3:38). Here, Abel's replacement stands at the beginning of
what that evangelist recorded as the revered lineage of the Christians'
Lord and Savior.

How did Muslim traditions connect the first and third sons of Adam,
Habil, and Shith? Although Shith does not appear in the Qur'an, Muslim
exegetes and storytellers included him in their histories of the first family,
both drawing from Jewish and Christian lore and also creating their own
explanations and representations of *these* two brothers.

Al-Tha`labi quotes the report of a certain Salim b. al-Ju`d about Abel's
death and Seth's birth:

> After Cain killed Abel, Adam did not laugh for one hundred years. Then
> someone came to him and said: "God granted you a long life, and made you
> to laugh and not cry." When one hundred and thirty years of Adam's life had
> passed—that was five years after Cain had slain Abel, Seth was born to him,
> whose name means "gift of God"—indicating that God had substituted him for
> Abel. And God taught [Seth] the hours of the night and day and how to worship
> [i.e., revere] creation during each of their hours. God revealed fifty pages to him,
> and he was Adam's heir and successor.[66]

The passage relates several things at once: the grief of Adam (and presumably, Eve too), the gift of Seth as a stand-in for Abel, and the special
attention God gave to this third son—instructing him about the created
order, and bestowing upon him fifty pages from the Book. This Book was
understood to be a heavenly form of God's wisdom contained within one
hundred forty smaller books, and Muslim commentators imagined portions

of these being given as leaves or pages, to the very highly favored prophets. It was said that God gave ten leaves to Adam, fifty to Seth, thirty to Enoch, and, in the most special case, fifty to Abraham, plus writings among which were the *Tawrat* (Torah) given to Moses, and the *Injil* ("Evangel" or Gospel), given as revelation to Jesus.[67]

Muslim interpreters found still other ways to fashion Seth as a continuation of the presence of Abel, the martyr holy to God and revered by the faithful. From the great storyteller al-Kisa'i, who composed his work on the *Tales of the Prophets* sometime around 1200 CE, we have a noticeably different account of the events following Abel's murder. What happened, al-Kisa'i recounted, is that late in the day in which the killing occurred, Adam was concerned that his sons had not returned, and set out to find them.

> [Adam] found Abel slain and was stricken with grief. The earth was drenched with Abel's blood, and the trees and flowers of the surrounding area had withered ... Then Adam carried his son Abel over his shoulders, his eyes weeping and his heart full of sorrow. He and Eve wept over him for forty days, until God spoke to him, saying, "Cease your weeping, for I shall give you another child as pure as Abel, who shall produce prophets and apostles." So their sorrow passed away, and they came together in the Tabernacle of Glad Tidings, where Eve conceived Seth. When her time was accomplished, she gave birth and saw that he was just like Abel and did not differ from him in any way. She called him Hibatullah ["Gift of God"], and from his face shone the Light of our Lord, Muhammad. The angels brought the good news of Seth's birth to Adam ... Seth had a dark mole on his right shoulder, and God granted him children during his father Adam's lifetime.[68]

While unexpected elements appear in this narrative—a description of Adam's role in discovering and dealing with Abel's corpse, and a fuller treatment of his parents' grief—the characterization of Shith is the key interest of this piece of tradition. Identical to his brother in every way, Shith possessed and maintained in himself the presence of Habil. But al-Kisa'i's retelling advances a further claim—one intended to highlight the connection and correspondence of *three* prophets. Habil "lived" in Shith, but the future Prophet Muhammad was in him as well, his "light" shining from the face of Eve's newborn son. Even the storyteller's mention of the mole on Shith's shoulder was by no means incidental—he was aware of the tradition that Muhammad bore this mark, which portended the gift of prophecy.[69]

In al-Tha`labi's narrative of Adam's last days, it is told that Adam wrote and then handed to Seth his testament, warning him to prevent Cain from knowing about it. So Seth and his successors hid this "last will" from Abel's murderer and his children. We also are informed that when Adam died, Seth asked Gabriel to pray for Adam, but the archangel responded:

> "You go first and pray for your father." So [Seth] prayed for him and uttered thirty times: "God is Great"—five of them being (regular prayer) and twenty five of them being out of esteem for Adam.[70]

Our pursuit of Islamic characterizations of Seth has concentrated on strategies for maintaining Abel, the virtuous martyr and true worshipper of God, in these descriptions of the brother who took his place. In a painting to be considered below, we shall encounter yet another means by which Muslims honored their prophet Abel in a ritual of remembrance. But before moving to several painters' interpretations of the Cain and Abel saga, we allow al-Tha`labi to conclude his narrative with a contrast between what befell the progeny of his errant son, and those offspring of the Abel-like Seth:

> They say that the children of Cain invented instruments of entertainment, such as varieties of drums and pipes and stringed instruments, and were engrossed in pleasure and drinking wine, in fornication and fire-worship and idol-worship and abominations, until God drowned them in the Flood at the time of Noah; while the descendents of Seth survived [the Flood]—and God is all knowing" (Brinner, *Lives,* 80).

The story of Adam's sons, as told in the Qur'an and elaborated by subsequent Muslim interpreters, had clear purposes. The narrative warned against the injustice that Cain committed in his passion, and the punishment such anger and violence would receive thereafter; it also held out the promise of mercy to those who avoided, or repented of, such crimes (Surah 5:34). Implicitly, the prophetic lineage, including Seth and his posterity, will, in their fidelity to God, enjoy reward rather than damnation. Death will visit the righteous, of course, but Islamic theology and cherished notions of the character of the bearers of God's warnings and good tidings undergird the drama, encouraging the understanding that "they who believe in God and His messengers and do not discriminate between any of them—to those He is going to give their rewards. And God is forgiving and merciful" (Surah 4:152).

THE REAPPEARANCE OF ABEL: A PERSIAN RITUAL
DESCRIBED AND DISPLAYED

Another notice about Abel is recorded by the great Muslim scholar Abu Rayhan al-Biruni, whose fascinating *Chronology of Ancient Nations* was written in 1000 CE. In the course of collecting and attempting to correlate calendars of various peoples, al-Biruni took care to report what he had learned about the histories, customs, and the cycles of religious observances of numerous groups. Among these were Jews, Indians, pre-Islamic Arabs, Chinese Buddhists, Christians, Zoroastrians, and other groups who posed challenges to Muhammad and early Muslims (like the Sabians).[71]

In the midst of his description of Persia's calendar of festivals the Farwardajan is described—an autumnal seasonal rite that occurred over ten days of the month of Aban. Al-Biruni understood Farwardajan to be associated with an Iranian celebration of the creation of humans, and we quickly recognize which aspect of human life this particular ritual addressed.

> During this time people put food in the halls of the dead and drink on the roofs of houses, believing that the spirits of their dead during these days come out from the places of their reward or punishment, that they go to the dishes laid out for them, imbibe their strength and suck their taste. [The people] fumigate their houses with Juniper, that the dead may enjoy its smell. The spirits of the pious men dwell among their families, children and relations, and occupy themselves with their affairs, although invisible to them . . . The reason of the Farwardajan is said to be this—that when Cain had killed Abel, and the parents were lost in grief, they implored God to restore his soul to him. God did so on the day Ashtadh of Aban-Mah, and the soul remained in him for ten days. Abel was sitting erect and looking at his parents, but it was not allowed to him to speak. Then his parents collected. . . . (a break in the manuscript occurs at this point).[72]

Farwardajan, an annual invitation to the spirits of the dead to return to their families—to eat, drink, enjoy aromas, and to observe the household's affairs—was a rite of reunion in which the distance or the boundary between the living and dead was bridged. Those who practiced it aspired to bring the beloved back, if only for a few days, in order to enjoy their company. Not surprisingly, shared food was an instrument and symbol. This ancient custom took many forms among various Persian communities, and it is known that Farwardajan was observed by Zoroastrians (as it is still). Al-Biruni has chosen the explanation that the festival of "symbolic nourishment for the dead" originated with Adam and Eve, who longed to be reunited with their son Abel.[73] Returning to his parents, Abel, unlike others, seems to have been visible, but we are told that in their presence he was mute. The interrupted text does not allow us to know if he partook of the food and drink laid out for him, or was restricted to savoring the odors.

An artist's illumination (Figure 3.1) of the scene in a copy of al-Biruni's *Chronology* produced three centuries later poses interesting interpretive issues.[74]

What do the postures and gestures of the reunited trio—all with halos—seem to signify? The hands of Eve and Adam are raised in greeting, and Abel's responsive extended right hand is a similar gesture. Are they in conversation? According to the Persian inscription surmounting the image, "He (Abel) was not allowed to speak." We view a poignant moment in the ritual's drama, "all the participants . . . gesturing to one another as if trying to overcome this barrier," which prevents their verbal communication.[75]

Like the careful implanting of Abel's life in Seth, this multiday celebration intent upon experiencing his presence, we need to recall, stems from grief, from the parents' agony over the loss of their son—their *good* son. Adam wailed, we recall, over the first murder's shock waves—in distortions of lands and peoples, in the earth's descent into ugliness, in the dulling of colors and tastes, and in the human countenance, rarely capable of smiling. Cain's crime—his killing of Abel his brother—changed the magnificent

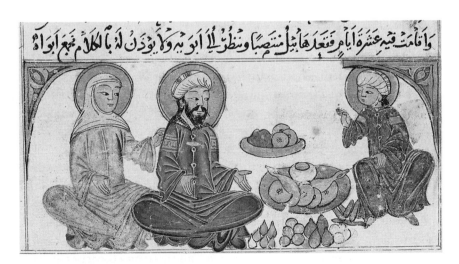

Figure 3.1 Deceased Habil visits his parents. From a copy of Al-Biruni's the *Chronology of Ancient Nations* written by Al-Biruni in 1000 CE. Painting: 6 x 13.4 cm. © Edinburgh University Library, Special Collections Department, Or. MS 161, folio 101v.

creation into a realm of dolor, the deep sadness of loss of, and separation from, the beloved.

Muslim commentators, artists, and festival keepers, expanding upon the qur'anic testimony about Qabil and Habil, labored to protect and preserve the lamented Habil and to build into the community's remembrance his offering acceptable to God, and his innocent martyrdom.

ADAM'S SONS IN *QISAS AL-ANBIYA* ILLUMINATIONS

The history of the representation of human figures in the arts of Muslim societies is complex. Prohibitions of paintings and sculptures as actually or potentially idolatrous are part of the story, as are those periods and places in which paintings depicting the activities of humans enjoyed sponsorship and financial support by Muslim royal houses. We know of paintings in the early fourteenth century depicting Muhammad, and scenes portraying many other prophets recur especially in manuscripts of writings like al-Tha'labi's *Qisas al-Anbiya'* that were produced in the succeeding centuries.[76] The existence of these illuminations in the genre of the lives of the prophets permits us, despite the relative lateness of these books, to compare these artists' story interpretations with Jewish and Christian lore.

One author's Persian version of the "Stories of the Prophets," written in the late eleventh century, is of particular importance to us, since many of the paintings we shall encounter were miniatures placed in later copies of his text. He was called Abu Ishaq Ibrahim ibn Mansur al-Nisaburi.[77] For convenience's sake we shall designate him al-Nisaburi in the pages ahead, even though numerous Muslim notables (like al-Tha'labi) also had their splendid city in northeastern Iran, Nisabur (or Nishapur), in their titles.

The prophets whose stories generated the most paintings in manuscripts, often with scenes from several episodes in their lives, were Adam, Ibrahim, Yusuf, Musa, and Sulayman—and of course, in those *Qisas* which include his life, Muhammad. But the tale of Qabil and Habil also compelled the interest of the artists, one of whose favorite themes was the raven's demonstration of burial to Qabil, who carries his brother's corpse on his back. Curiously, images of the young men bringing their offerings are rare, and depictions of a squabble over potential mates (as we've seen, a particularly popular motif in Muslim written interpretations), or of a physical tussle, do not make their way into the iconographical repertoire.[78]

Habil's Corpse

About this scene as it appears in illuminated *Stories of the Prophets* Rachel Milstein commented:

> The basic formula represents Qabil carrying his brother's dead body on his back in a rural landscape. He encounters two crows; some manuscripts show the birds fighting, while in others one crow dangles his dead victim from his beak, or looks at him buried in a hole. In a few instances, Iblis appears, watching the scene from a remote corner behind the horizon.[79]

This painting, one which graces another manuscript of Nisaburi's *Stories of the Prophets*, shows Qabil intently observing the two birds at what appears to be the moment before the standing raven attacks the raven settled on the stream's edge (Figure 3.2). A large patch of crimson gore appears on Habil's head, above his closed eyes. For those familiar with Surah 5:31 and with subsequent *tafsir* (Nisaburi's commentary on the incident, of course, surrounds the image), the painting recalls the murderer's dilemma, the sending of the raven by God, and Qabil's cry of woe upon witnessing what the bird performs on behalf of *its* victim.

The apparent popularity among painters of this qur'anic episode causes us to wonder how they and the viewers of their images understood and fashioned its depictions. Without doubt their representations of what is described in Surah 5:31–32—the sending of a raven to instruct Qabil about how to bury his brother, and his chagrin and self-castigation upon observing the action—are obvious and "literal." At the same time, there is room, or invitation, in these scenes for a recognition that the raven's action is a divine gift—perhaps not only of basic know-how to Qabil, but also of guidance of a deeper kind. Qabil's gaze upon the birds reminds the viewer of his coming to awareness of what he has not done on behalf of Habil's corpse. This important portion of the story of the sons of Adam "as it really was" drew special attention among the artists doing Qur'an commentary.

Noting that Habil is not shown to be naked in the painting below, we return briefly to an earlier issue. Even if the artists had wished to suggest something of this sense of the disgrace of Habil's body, standards of appropriateness would have hindered them; it is more likely that the artists too took for granted the primary sense of *saw'a* in Surah 5:31 that associated the shame of Habil's corpse centrally with Qabil's act of murder.

The painter has added to the story's depiction an inventive feature. On the hill above the two brothers a brown ram lying on its back, its throat

Figure 3.2 The raven teaches Qabil how to bury Habil's body. From a copy of a ms. of Nisaburi. Painting: 21.3 x 13 cm. © Topkapi Palace Museum, Istanbul. Topkapi Museum H. 1228, folio 11b.

cut, has been visited by flames, while the white animal to its left, similarly sacrificed, has not. The inclusion of this motif telescopes the story, displaying how it came to pass that one of Adam's sons has the bloodied corpse of the other bound to his back with a sash. The white and tan complexions of the brothers correlate to the distinctive colors of their offered animals. Perhaps this subtle association accounts for the innovation of two animals offered to God, rather than the grain and the lamb. And of course the fire consuming Habil's offering addresses the very old discussions over how Qabil and Habil knew the results of their acts of sacrifice. Our painters had commentary to add.[80]

Muslim commentators on the clash between Qabil and Habil were aware of, and quite resourceful in their use of, Christian and Jewish traditions concerning the story of the first murder. There is, nevertheless, noticeable independence in Islam's understandings of the saga. It is incontestable that many of the particularly Muslim approaches to the story owe their chief debt to the Qur'an's representation of the two brothers—portrayals that differ markedly from those in the Jews' Tanakh and in the Christians' Old Testament.

Compared with the *Genesis* narrative, the presentation of the first murder in the Qur'an's Surah 5 presents strong contrasts. In its first half, 5:27–30, the two sons of Adam, as soon as the result from their competition of offerings is known, emerge as personalities with different viewpoints and commitments. When their voices are heard, it is in an impassioned, dangerous dialogue, with both of Adam's sons showing themselves vengeance-minded. Qabil kills his brother, rendering himself a cursed man—one of the damned. This murder is a violation of God's will for humanity, as will be all other unlawful killings that follow; the lesson to be pressed home a few lines later.

The second half of the qur'anic story treats Qabil in the aftermath of his act of murder, but sees him in a manner radically different from the Bible, which relates the tortured continuing existence of Cain. In Surah 5:31 we learn that until God sends a raven to educate Qabil about burial, he is helpless—perplexed about what to do with Habil's corpse. It is only then that Qabil recognizes what his violation of his brother's life means, and bewails his profound shame.

There is no mistaking what the Qur'an presents as the chief—and universal—lesson to be taken from the tale of Adam's two sons. The killing of another human being is disastrous and unlawful. This is a fundamental law of God, even if the challenges of maintaining order in society require punishments of execution, or if warfare necessitates the spilling of blood.

Attention to this principle, we have observed, by no means inhibited interpreters from investigating the actions of those who constituted the first family. The representations of the two brothers' personalities involved creative additions designed to enhance and deepen the story that God insisted Muhammad should recite "as it really was." The commentators' and painters' probings of human dynamics within the qur'anic story, even when they departed from what Surah 5 explicitly revealed, were testimonies to the richness of the content of the Holy Qur'an, and at the same time, lively adaptations intended for the instruction and entertainment of believers. The justice of God, the example of the righteous Habil's restraint, and Qabil's despairing recognition of what he had not done for his brother's corpse are strong features within the qur'anic testimony about Adam's two sons. The retelling and elaboration of sacred narratives in the Qur'an were seen as perpetuating God's wisdom—presenting it afresh to new generations of believers, and continuing to demarcate Muslim teachings from those of their religious opponents.

Comparative Summary

Cain and Abel/Qabil and Habil

Told in different languages and different forms in the scriptures of the Jews, Christians, and Muslims, we saw that the story of Cain's fratricide held many fascinations for its hearers and readers. The three communities' scripture interpreters were eager to probe the drama's plot line and the words and deeds of its main characters, in order that no subtle dimension of meaning be missed. In their writings and in their artistic works we encountered not only differing representations of Cain and Abel, but also of the God to whom they offered their sacrifices.

THE STORY IN TWO FORMS

Genesis 4:1–16, which Jews and Christians had in common, related (1) the notice of the birth of Cain and Abel, their identifications as farmer and shepherd; (2) their offerings to God and Cain's anger at having his offering rejected; (3) God's dialogue with Cain, with its encouragement that he will be able to master the sin that "couches" near him; (4) Cain's killing of Abel; (5) the Lord's interrogation of Cain about Abel's whereabouts, and the assertion that he, God, hears Abel's blood crying out from the ground; (6) the cursing of Cain, who will be "a ceaseless wanderer on earth"; (7) God's answer to Cain's fear of being killed by imposing a mark to protect him, and Cain's departure from the divine presence to the land of Nod, east of Eden. Subsequent verses (17–26) tell of Cain's progeny, one of whom

(Lamech) accidentally slays him. The closing sentences report the birth to Adam and Eve of a third son, Seth, whose name, Eve says, means "God has provided me with another offspring in place of Abel."

Compared with the Bible's *Genesis* narrative, the presentation of the first murder in the Qur'an's Surah 5 presented strong contrasts. In its first half, 5:27–30, the two sons of Adam, as soon as the result from their competition of offerings is known, emerge as personalities with definite viewpoints and commitments. Qabil immediately threatens to kill Habil, and Habil retorts that Qabil and his offering were not deserving of God's approval. Habil declares that he will not resist his brother's assault, adding his own hope that for his evil act Qabil will be held accountable to God for his own and also for Habil's sins. Qabil, his soul impelling him, fulfills his pledge, killing his brother and rendering himself a cursed man—one of the damned. This murder is a violation of God's will for humanity, as will be all other subsequent unlawful killings.

The second half of the qur'anic story, we observed, treats Qabil, in the aftermath of his crime, but does not depict him (as the Bible does) anticipating a tortured existence. Only when God sends a raven to educate Qabil about burial (he is perplexed about what to do with Habil's corpse) is Cain able to see his crime against his brother for what it is, and bewail his most profound shame, his act of murder.

The differences in content between the biblical and the qur'anic versions of the story of Adam's sons proved to be strong factors—though there were others—in the three communities' divergent understandings of Cain and Abel.

The Interpreters

The narrative in *Genesis* 4 conveyed the tensions between Cain and Abel, and between Cain and God, but left its hearers and readers wanting to know more—about the reason for God's preference of Abel's offering, about the speech of Cain (and Abel's probable response) that slipped from the text, about Abel's still-vocal "bloods," about what kind of protective mark God put upon Cain , and, finally, about the birth of Seth. Chapter 1 exposed several Jewish exegetes and commentators in earnest pursuit of these issues. One translator of the Hebrew text into Aramaic, whom scholars dubbed Pseudo-Jonathan, was obliged to clarify some of the narrative's rough spots, and in the case of the missing exchange between the two brothers, to produce one. In his narrative expansion, he had Cain and Abel debate, after only one of the offerings was approved, whether God plays favorites, or whether divine justice is actually at work in the world. Earlier, hoping to explain how Cain became the evil brother, he suggested that Cain had a different father from Abel.

Discussions between Jewish sages captured in *Genesis Rabbah* gave evidence of their ingenuity in using other scriptures to clarify meanings of words and phrases in the Cain and Abel story—a practice that resulted not in unanimous but in richly varied viewpoints and opinions. So it was that attempts to discover root causes for Cain's traits of envy, deviousness, and deep anger differed, generating more deliberation. Some rabbis imagined events that preceded the crisis as causes of the friction between the brothers, or ways in which Satan exercised his influence over Cain. We saw the reasoning behind several guesses about the mark of Cain—whether it appears as a companion dog, leprosy, or a horn, and we also met the daring query about God's inaction while the murder took place. Why did the Holy One not intervene, stopping this murder? The persistent questioning that characterized these rabbinic discourses we recognized to be serving an essential religious purpose: the consistent engagement with, and faithful exploration of, the multiple dimensions of divine wisdom residing in the words of the Jews' holy writings.

Philo's predominant interest in the character and effects of vice and virtue led him to treat Cain and Abel as representations of these two forces. Everywhere and at all times, he insisted, Cain's idolatrous self-love is pitted against Abel's devotion to the Good, or God. To those like Abel immortality belonged. He was also, as innocent victim, an inspiration to martyrdom, should circumstances demand that. Philo, we recall, stated that Abel preferred death in the company of pious friends to life with the impious—for the former would, like Abel, have life forever, while the latter suffer eternal death.

Jewish understandings of the first murder tended to make Cain's crime and his criminal nature the chief point of the story. This was much influenced by the rabbinic distinction between the human being's two inclinations—to the good, or to the evil—which Philo attached easily to Greek philosophy's doctrine (traceable to Xenophon) of the choice between the path of virtue and the path of vice. Abel is not ignored, of course. He is one whose offering God approved, the innocent victim whose voice, still audible, testifies to his immortality. But the earliest question—what caused Cain to kill his brother?—dominates Jewish endeavors to make sense of the story.

Two Christian paintings—one in the Ashburnham Pentateuch and the other in the Via Latina catacomb—also placed emphasis on the enormity of Cain's sin—the one showing him being confronted by the divine voice that asks him where his brother is, and the other depicting the serpent in the company of the brothers as they approach (separate) altars with their offerings. Both paintings contain images of abject Adam and Eve, and invoke the theme so important to some Christian thinking—namely, that the effects of the sin committed in Eden and the resultant flaw in humanity made human malice and murder, horrible as they were, comprehensible. It was St. Augustine who developed the view that humans, ruined by the first sin in the Garden, were unable *not* to sin. Cain's act of violence presented itself as a case study par excellence.

New Testament writings built the argument that followers of Jesus were on the side of God-approved Abel, the righteous brother, and were called upon to battle Cain-like people who threatened them both within and outside their own church communities. Irenaeus's interpretations of the story of the first murder—all of which stressed God's cursing of Cain and his generations while extolling Abel as the victim who "died, but through his faith he still speaks" (*Hebrews* 11:4)—were aggressively directed against Gnostic Christians, Marcion, and Jews. Against the former two, who denigrated the creator God of the scripture and events in his lower realm, Irenaeus championed that biblical Lord's blessing of virtuous Abel and his condemnation of Satan-inspired Cain. Irenaeus combatted those Christian docetists who denied that the savior was ever physically embodied by stressing Jesus's life, death, and resurrection in the flesh. Abel's passion was, he argued, a sign—a prefiguring—of that salvation God would accomplish in Christ.

Contra the Jews, clearly considered to be opponents and rivals of second-century Christians by Irenaeus, another polemical use could be made of the story of Cain and Abel; as the evil brother persecuted the just brother, so did the Jews persecute their prophets—including Jesus—bringing God's disapproval upon themselves. This vehement attack against Judaism drew upon a saying of Jesus (in *Matthew* 23:29–36) as it sought to establish the claim that Christians had displaced, or superseded, the Jews as God's faithful and favored people. There was another aspect—pro-Christian more than anti-Jewish—of the churches' penchant for picturing Abel and Jesus as innocent victims, as we saw in the carved images on sarcophagi. Abel was included among those saints, like Peter and Paul, who died for God, being imitators of Christ.

The sheer drama of what befell the family of Adam continually held fascination for Christian scripture interpreters and preachers, but we paused over writings by John Chrysostom, Ephrem of Syria, and Symmachus, to study their narrative additions devoted to the tumultuous relationships among Adam, Eve, and their two sons both before and after Abel's murder. The terrible grief of Eve and the complexity of Cain's guilt and estrangement required more story, while the Christian point and tenor of these writings were spurred by advocacy of martyrdom and requests that Christ bring peace and forgiveness to all in the churches.

The Qur'an spells out the chief—and universal—lesson to be taken from the story of Adam's two sons. The killing of another human being is disastrous and unlawful. This is a fundamental law of God, even if the challenges of maintaining order in society require punishments of execution, or if warfare necessitates the spilling of blood. The imaginations of Muslim interpreters of the saga of Qabil's act of murder were not riveted to this universal principle in a way that kept them from exploring the dynamics within the first family. The fashioning of the two brothers' personalities involved creative additions designed to enhance and deepen the story that God insisted Muhammad should recite "as it really was." Expansions of the qur'anic story by writers and painters were venturesome, but not regarded as impious by those who encountered them. All such efforts, even those which seemed to wander from what Surah 5 reveals so concisely, were testimonies to the richness of the content of the Holy Qur'an, and at the same time, lively adaptations intended for the enlightenment (and entertainment) of believers. Qur'anic testimony about Adam's two sons undergirded emphases upon God's justice, Habil's passive resistance to his murderous brother, and both the cruelty *and* the remorse of Qabil.

The tale of the first murder survived and thrived through its retellings by Jews, Christians, and Muslims, who were aware of each others' different ways of understanding and valuing the story. Chapter 2 gave strong evidence of growing Christian antipathy for Jewish teachings—e.g., in Irenaeus's strategy of linking innocent victim Abel with Christ crucified, and linking Cain not only with Satan, but with Jews faulted for murdering their prophets, and Jesus. The separation of the two religious communities is well underway, and the rivalry has become harsh and severe. In Muslim commentaries of the story of Qabil and Habil, we took note of several internal differences in doctrine—most memorably, the dispute about whether the interactions between the brothers were predetermined by God, and the insistence of Jaf`ar al-Sadiq and his followers that special female creatures were provided as mates for Adam's sons, since incest with their human sisters would have been impermissible.

PART II

Sarah and Hagar

Mothers to Three Families

Preview, Chapters 4–6

Abraham's Rival Wives

The story of Abraham/Ibrahim is a drama in which the plan of God is regularly in danger of failure—indeed, the divine promises seem possible of fulfillment only against very long odds. Their actualization depends upon the obedience of blessed but all-too-human heroes and heroines, and upon miraculous interventions of angels. God has ordained that Abraham is to become the father of nations, but he is childless, very advanced in age, and married to the barren Sarah. Through a grandly surprising and also troubled series of events, Sarah and her maidservant Hagar are the principal women who give the patriarch his principal sons (there were more), guaranteeing that his offspring will, according to Jewish belief, inherit the blessings and the land destined for them, or will, according to Christian belief, by faith like Abraham's, become citizens of the "heavenly Jerusalem," or will, according to Islamic belief, receive the gift of true worship at God's House in Mecca, and come to honor the prophet Ibrahim's successor, Muhammad, and abide in the true path.

Through the centuries most people telling or hearing a rendition of the saga of Abraham/Ibrahim and his wives and sons counted themselves as part of the story *already come to pass*. Belonging to the patriarch-prophet's family, and having either Sarah or Hagar for a matriarch, the ancient story had become part of theirs, as surely as they enjoyed the promises bestowed on God's "friend"—that is, as surely as they identified themselves as Jews, or Christians, or Muslims.

Sarah/Sara and Hagar/Hajar are the subjects of this chapter—their dealings with Abraham, with each other, with their sons, and with God and his
angels. We shall see these scriptural personalities as they were interpreted
differently and distinctively by Jews, Christians, and Muslims when they
encountered each other, and debated biblical-qur'anic stories.

The rabbis of the first through the fifth centuries are keenly interested in
the character and behavior of each of the two women and in the reasons for
their strife with one another. How are the tensions that led to Hagar's expulsion from Abraham's household to be understood, and what lessons about
God's intentions are to be found in the exchanges between both human and
divine actors in the narrative? As the rabbis inspect the Torah's account of the
events surrounding Abraham's two notable sons, their commentaries open
fresh possibilities of meaning—and, more often than not, add more story.

For their part, the earliest Christian students of scripture read the story
of Abraham, Sarah, and Hagar and their sons attentive to the need to fill in
gaps in the narrative. They were more centrally occupied, however, in working out an understanding, a theologic, of how the promise once given to
Abraham and to the Hebrews was now the promise possessed and enjoyed
by believers in Jesus Christ. St. Paul's early effort to explain this inheritance
(by giving the patriarch's faith priority over Sinai's law) strongly influenced
many Christian retellings of the story of Abraham, his wives, and his sons.

The Qur'an, without naming Sarah, knows her as Isaac's mother and tells
of her reactions upon being told she would give birth to him. Hagar, the
mother of Ishmael, is understood to be present with some of Abraham's
kinsfolk whom he has settled "in a valley without crops near Your sacred
House" (Surah 14:37) in Mecca. Muslim scholars and story tellers elaborated upon these qur'anic passages, while also pursuing whatever information was discoverable about what befell Hagar and Ishmael in the
wilderness, and how Abraham continued to be in relationship with his
cherished firstborn. Together, Abraham and Ishmael were commissioned
to build in Mecca the *bayt Allah*, the "House of God."

Those parts of the Abraham story chosen for representation by Jewish,
Muslim, and Christian artists tell us what messages in the narrative held
the most power for each of the three communities. Sarah and Hagar are not
pictured together (with the exception of a painted scene in the Ashburnham
Pentateuch), so we have from early art very little to compare with the
attention we shall see was given to the drama involving both women by
Rembrandt and many of his contemporaries. With assistance from the
writings of the early exegetes, we shall need at certain points to imagine
those ways in which Sarah and Hagar are sometimes in the picture—that

is, in the minds of viewers of the images—even when they are not actually portrayed.

Because retelling of sacred stories (inevitably with new interpretive twists) was an ongoing activity in Judaism, Christianity, and Islam, we regularly find exegetes and painters from two, sometimes all three, of the religions doing their imaginative work contemporaneously, and aware of their rivals' viewpoints. We shall find that it pays us dividends to spy out how the Sarah and Hagar saga comes to us in carefully wrought Jewish, Christian, and Muslim forms. From the angle of vision or from the faith perspective of the people in one of the communities, the sacred stories rehearsed, studied, and ritually observed were ultimately *only their stories*, holding only *their meanings*.

In the following three chapters representative Jewish, Christian, and Muslim understandings of the saga involving Sarah and Hagar are taken up in that sequence, with attention directed to commonalities and dissimilarities in the three religions' ways of telling and appreciating the story. Passages in *Genesis Rabbah* and a scene from a synagogue's floor mosaic are our foci in chapter 4. For Christian accounts of Abraham's household, we employ treatments by several New Testament writers, by the biblical scholar and theologian Origen, and a fifth-century mosaic image in Rome's Santa Maria Maggiore of Abraham and Sarah entertaining their mysterious visitors. Beginning with the Qur'an's portrayals of Ibrahim's women, which are quite different from the Bible's, our consideration of developing Muslim traditions concerning Sara and Hajar draw upon two chief sources—the writings of al-Tabari, and an intriguing sixteenth-century miniature painting of Ibrahim's family that appears within a copy of Abu Ishaq Ibrahim Nisaburi's Persian *Qisas al-Anbiya'*, composed in the late eleventh century.

Hagar and the
the poor and the
neighborhood.

CHAPTER 4

❧

Sarah and Hagar

Jewish Portrayals

Figure 4.1 Abraham casting out Hagar and Ishmael. Rembrandt van Rijn, 1637. Etching: 15.7 cm X 13.3 cm. © The Metropolitan Museum of Art, New York. Art Resource, NY.

In a drawing made after the mid-1630s Rembrandt focused on the figure of Hagar when she was sent by Abraham into the desert. The theme of the two rival women was a widely depicted subject. . . . Yet only Rembrandt's etching The Expulsion of Hagar really shows the contrast between the triumphant Sarah, gleefully peeping through the doorway with a satisfied smile on her face, and the desolate figure of the weeping Hagar.

Anat Gilboa, *Images of the Feminine in Rembrandt's Work*[1]

Commanded by God to leave his native land and travel to the land of Canaan, Abram (to be renamed Abraham), obeyed, and once at his destination the Lord appeared to him and declared "I will assign this land to your offspring" (*Genesis* 12:7). Some time later, when Abram was told by God that "[his] reward would be very great," he responded, "O Lord God, what can you give to me, seeing that I am childless, and the one in charge of my household is Dammesek Eliezer?" God reassured Abram that Eliezer, his steward, would not be his heir. None would be but "your very own issue" (15:1–4).

> 15:5 He took him outside and said, "Look toward heaven and count the stars, if you are able to count them." And he added, "So shall your offspring be."
>   6 And because he put his trust in the Lord, He reckoned it to his merit.

The declaration in *Psalm* 11:5 that "the Lord tests the righteous" often evokes the memory of God's command that Abraham offer his son as a burnt sacrifice, but the verse could stand over the entire biblical history of the patriarch. It certainly applies to the narrative telling of the birth of two sons to Abraham, first by Sarah's maidservant, Hagar, and then by Sarah herself. The drama involving his two women and their sons is one of conflict, upon which hinges the character of God's different relationships with Abraham's offspring.

In this chapter, after reviewing the Hebrew Bible's presentation of the events, we turn to Jewish interpretations of the story by rabbis and by artists. The community's scripture interpreters will be observed working to ensure that this sacred story presents the origins of Israel's covenant relationship with God in the most powerful words and images possible. We shall also become aware of their awareness of a counterinterpretation by Christians.

SARAH AND HAGAR IN *GENESIS*

16:1 Sarai, Abram's wife, had borne him no children. She had an Egyptian maid-servant whose name was Hagar. 2 And Sarai said to Abram, "Look, the Lord has kept me from bearing. Consort with my maid, perhaps I shall have a son through her." And Abram heeded Sarai's request. 3 So Sarai, Abram's wife, took her maid, Hagar the Egyptian—after Abram had dwelt in the land of Canaan ten years—and gave her to her husband Abram as concubine. 4 He cohabited with Hagar and she conceived; and when she saw that she had conceived, her mistress was lowered in her esteem. 5 And Sarai said to Abram, "The wrong done me is your fault! I myself put my maid in your bosom; now that she sees that she is pregnant, I am lowered in her esteem. The Lord decide between you and me!"

6 Abram said to Sarai, "Your maid is in your hands. Deal with her as you think right." Then Sarai treated her harshly, and she ran away from her.

7 An angel of the Lord found her by a spring of water in the wilderness, the spring on the road to Shur, 8 and said, "Hagar, slave of Sarai, where have you come from and where are you going?" And she said, "I am running away from my mistress Sarai."

9 And the angel of the Lord said to her, "Go back to your mistress, and submit to her harsh treatment." 10 And the angel of the Lord said to her,

> "I will greatly increase your offspring,
> And they shall be too many to count."

11 The angel of the Lord said to her further,

> "Behold, you are with child
> And shall bear a son;
> You shall call him Ishmael,
> For the Lord has paid heed to your suffering.
> 12 He shall be a wild ass of a man;
> His hand against everyone,
> And everyone's hand against him;
> He shall dwell alongside of all his kinsmen."

13 And she called the Lord who spoke to her, "You are El-Roi," by which she meant, "Have I not gone on seeing after He saw me!"

14 Therefore the well was called Beer-lahai-roi; it is between Kadesh and Bered.—15 Hagar bore a son to Abram, and Abram gave the son that Hagar bore him the name Ishmael. 16 Abram was eighty-six years old when Hagar bore Ishmael to Abram.

17.1 When Abram was ninety nine years old, the Lord appeared to Abram and said to him, "I am El Shaddai. Walk in My ways and be blameless. 2 I will establish my covenant between Me and you, and I will make you exceedingly numerous." 3 Abraham threw himself on his face; and God spoke to him further, 4 "As for Me, this is My covenant with you: You shall be the father of a multitude of nations. 5 And you shall no longer be called Abram, but your name shall be Abraham, for I make you the father of a multitude of nations.

6 I will make you exceedingly fertile, and make nations of you, and kings will come forth from you. 7 I will maintain my covenant between Me and you, and your offspring to come, as an everlasting covenant throughout the ages, to be God to you and your offspring to come. 8 I assign the land you sojourn in to you and your offspring to come, all the land of Canaan, as an everlasting holding. I will be their God." . . . 15 And God said to Abraham, "As for your wife Sarai, you shall not call her Sarai, but her name shall be Sarah. 16 I will bless her; indeed I will give you a son by her. I will bless her so that she shall give rise to nations; rulers of peoples shall issue from her." 17 Abraham threw himself on his face and laughed, as he said to himself, "Can a child be born to a man a hundred years old, or can Sarah bear a child at ninety?" 18 And Abraham said to God, "O that Ishmael may live by Your favor!" 19 God said, "Nevertheless, Sarah your wife will bear you a son, and you shall name him Isaac; and I will maintain my covenant with him as an everlasting covenant for his offspring to come. 20 As for Ishmael, I have heeded you. I hereby bless him. I will make him fertile and exceedingly numerous. He shall be the father of twelve chieftans, and I will make of him a great nation.

21 But my covenant I will maintain with Isaac, whom Sarah shall bear to you at this season next year." 22 And when He was done speaking with him, God was gone from Abraham.

18:9 They [the three men who visited Abraham in Mamre] said to him, "Where is your wife Sarah?" And he replied, "There, in the tent." 10 Then one said, "I will return to you next year, and your wife Sarah shall have a son!" Sarah was listening at the entrance of the tent, which was behind him. 11 Now Abraham and Sarah were old, advanced in years; Sarah had stopped having the periods of women. 12 And Sarah laughed to herself, saying, "Now that I am withered, am I to have enjoyment—with my husband so old?"

13 Then the Lord said to Abraham, "Why did Sarah laugh, saying, 'Shall I in truth bear a child, old as I am?' 14 Is anything too wondrous for the Lord? I shall return to you at the time next year, and Sarah shall have a son." 15 Sarah lied, saying, "I did not laugh," for she was frightened. But He replied, "You did laugh."

21.1 The Lord took note of Sarah as He had promised, and the Lord did for Sarah as He had spoken. 2 Sarah conceived and bore a son to Abraham in his old age, at the set time of which God had spoken. 3 Abraham gave his newborn son, whom Sarah had borne him, the name of Isaac. 4 And when his son Isaac was eight days old, Abraham circumcised him, as God had commanded him.

5 Now Abraham was a hundred years old when his son Isaac was born to him.

6 Sarah said, "God has brought me laughter; everyone who hears will laugh with me." 7 And she added,

"Who would have said to Abraham
That Sarah would suckle children!
Yet I have borne a son in his old age."

8 The child grew up and was weaned, and Abraham held a great feast on the day that Isaac was weaned.

9 Sarah saw the son whom Hagar the Egyptian had borne to Abraham playing. 10 She said to Abraham, "Cast out that slave-woman and her son, for the son of that slave shall not share in the inheritance with my son Isaac." 11 The matter distressed Abraham greatly, for it concerned a son of his. 12 But God said to Abraham, "Do not be distressed over the boy or your slave; whatever Sarah tells you, do as she says, for it is through Isaac that offspring shall be continued for you. 13 As for the son of the slave-woman, I will make a nation of him, too, for he is your seed."

14 Early next morning Abraham took some bread and a skin of water, and gave them to Hagar. He placed them over her shoulder, together with the child, and sent her away. And she wandered about in the wilderness of Beer-sheba. 15 When the water was gone from the skin, she left the child under one of the bushes, 16 and went and sat down at a distance, a bowshot away; for she thought, "Let me not look on as the child dies." And sitting thus afar, she burst into tears.

17 God heard the cry of the boy, and an angel of God called to Hagar from heaven and said to her, "What troubles you, Hagar? Fear not, for God has heeded the cry of the boy where he is.

18 Come, lift up the boy and hold him by the hand, for I will make a great nation of him." 19 Then God opened her eyes and she saw a well of water. She went and filled the skin with water, and let the boy drink. 20 God was with the boy and he grew up; he dwelt in the wilderness and became a bowman. 21 He lived in the wilderness of Paran; and his mother got a wife for him from the land of Egypt.

Questions that arise for us as we read these passages—especially those concentrated on the chief characters' motivations and actions—were under discussion among Jews from the time of the Torah's creation and circulation. Readers of the Hebrew understood easily the etymological sense of the names given: the connection of Isaac with laughter; of Ishmael with heeding or hearing of the change from Abram to Abraham, with its connotation of his paternity of many; the suggestion of seeing and being seen in Hagar's naming of the Lord as El Roi (with its implication: I see you, and I am still alive) and El Shaddai, taken to mean "God Almighty." More complex questions concerning the story, however, demanded deeper exploration.

Omitted from the passages above are two parts of the story of Abraham, Sarah, and Hagar that are worth pausing over. Twice while traveling in the lands of powerful rulers, Abraham fears death because of Sarah's beauty—that he will be killed by those who are attracted to Sarah, and wish to obtain her for themselves. Abraham urges her to lie about her identity, calling herself his sister. In *Genesis* 12:10–20, the regent desirous of Sarah was Egypt's Pharaoh, whose taking of her into the palace benefited Abraham (he gained many animals), but brought plagues upon the Pharaoh and his household "on account of Sarai, the wife of Abram" (12:17). Once scolded, Abraham was sent away, with Sarah and "all that he possessed." Though it is not mentioned, are readers to suppose that it was at this time that Sarah came into possession of Hagar, her Egyptian maidservant?

What occurs when Abraham and Sarah sojourn in Gerar (*Genesis* 20) is a near replay of what Abraham's lie earlier caused to happen. King Abimelech learns of Sarah's presence in his realm, and acquires her. In a dream visitation, God corrects Abimelech's misunderstanding of who Sarah is, warning the king that she is not his to possess and enjoy. Sarah's husband, God informs the king, is a prophet of such power that he can make successful intercession for him. Further, Abimelech will die, with all his household, unless he restores Sarah to Abraham. When Abimelech berates Abraham for his deception concerning Sarah, Abraham has a two-part rejoinder, or rationalization:

> I thought, surely there is no fear of God in this place, and they will kill me because of my wife. And besides, she is in truth my sister, my father's daughter, though not my mother's; and she became my wife (20:11–12).

The king's prompt peace-making entails the gift of cattle and slaves to Abraham, followed by the restoration of Sarah to her husband. An additional gift or payment is made: a thousand pieces of silver paid to Abraham—a gesture Abimelech construes and describes to Sarah as an exoneration and public vindication of her.

In the final two verses (17–18) we learn how dangerous the situation had become for the royal house of Gerar:

> Abraham then prayed to God, and God healed Abimelech and his wife and his slave girls, so that they bore children; for the Lord had closed fast every womb of the household of Abimelech because of Sarah, the wife of Abraham.[2]

Since this latter episode falls in Abraham's story just prior to the notice of Sarah's pregnancy, later interpreters, the rabbis in particular, were prompted to discuss what might have transpired between Abimelech and Abraham's "sister" while she was in the king's company. The event impinged, as we shall see, upon important questions not only of morality, but also of genetics—that is, matters of paternity and motherhood.

Driving the Abraham narrative is the insistent claim that God's covenant with Abraham and "his offspring" is with and through Isaac. The Lord's blessing of Ishmael and those whom he will father is of a different order. Nonetheless, chapter 17's concluding verses report Abraham's covenant-prescribed circumcision of thirteen-year-old Ishmael, as well as his own circumcision and that of the other males (home-born and purchased slaves) of his household. Ishmael, on account of his circumcision, and despite the distinction God makes in vv. 19–20, would seem to be included in the covenant, a participant in its obligations and benefits, but this does not prove to be so.

Genesis 21:1–21 is, for the Bible, the climax of the story of Sarah and Hagar and their rivalry. Strong emotions—heights and depths of the characters' lives—are on display. Verses 1–8 celebrate the Lord's fulfillment of the promise concerning Sarah. A great feast marks Isaac's weaning, the end of his infancy.

The drama that follows in vv. 9–21 grows out of Sarah's fearful or hostile attitude toward Hagar and her son. The two-mother, two-son household has come to a crisis. Sarah is reported to have seen Hagar's son playing (the text discloses neither the manner of Ishmael's play, nor whether his half-brother Isaac might have been involved, as many later interpreters will presume), and apparently what she sees stirs her to a strong action. Abraham, on her orders, sends Hagar and her son away the next day, supplying them with bread and water.

Wandering in the wilderness near Beer-sheba, their provisions run out and Hagar foresees their doom. An angel approaches Hagar and directs her actions; God then opens Hagar's eyes to the sight of water, and she and her son are saved.

From this point on, Ishmael and Hagar are virtually absent as *actors* in the Abraham saga. Interestingly, Ishmael surfaces once more in the story, joining his half-brother in burying their father (near Sarah) in the cave of Macpelah (25:9). The list of Ishmael's twelve sons and their region of settlement is preceded by a reference to his mother, "Hagar the Egyptian," at 25:12. That chapter begins with mention of another of Abraham's wives, Keturah, whose six sons are named, as are the descendants of the first two of these, Jokshan and Midian (vv. 1–4). The lesser importance for Abrahamic history of these sons and of others whom he "begat" by concubines is clearly indicated: "Abraham willed all that he owned to Isaac" (v. 5). His other male offspring were given gifts by Abraham and sent "away from his son Isaac eastward, to the land of the East" (v. 6). Ishmael's status is at once similar and different. He too was distanced from Isaac, yet he received from God the blessing of numerous offspring, and of nationhood (16:20, 21:13, 18).

It is necessary at this point to visit the narrative following the expulsion of Hagar and Ishmael and their trial in the wilderness. *Genesis* 21:14–21 resumes the main story of Abraham's dealings with God and his "favored" offspring in telling of the *akedah*—the binding of Isaac. This test of Abraham—taking Isaac, whom he loves, to Moriah to offer him as a sacrifice to God—ends in the boy's (and the father's) deliverance from this obligation, and a restatement and elaboration of God's covenant promise:

> 22:15 The angel of the Lord called to Abraham a second time from heaven, 16 and said, "By myself I swear, the Lord declares: Because you have done this and have not withheld your son, your favored one, 17 I will bestow My blessing upon you and make your descendants as numerous as the stars of heaven and the sands on the seashore; and your descendants shall seize the gates of their foes. 18 All the nations of the earth shall bless themselves by your descendants, because you have obeyed my command."

Jon Levenson, in his *The Death and Resurrection of the Beloved Son*, eloquently spelled out the significance of this divine pledge, in its now revised form:

> It converts the standing promise of Abraham of innumerable progeny into a consequence of the near-sacrifice of Isaac. . . . This is a transformation of enormous import. It renders the very existence of Abrahamic peoples dependent

upon their ancestor's obedience to the fearsome directive to make of his beloved son a burnt offering to his God. The aqedah, in short, has become a foundational act, and its consequences extend to every generation of those whose father is Abraham. Our people exists and perdures, the Israelite narrator seems to be saying, only because of the incomparable act of obedience and faith that the patriarch-to-be carried out on an unnamed mountain in the land of Moriah. In light of the interpretive move that the second angelic address evidences, it is hardly a source of wonderment that, at least since biblical times, Jewish think-ers have continually pondered the troubling story of the binding of Isaac. Nor is it surprising that the pondering is usually most intense when the existence of Jews is threatened, and their survival, to all appearances, miraculous.[3]

Sarah's name does not appear in the story of the near-sacrifice of Isaac, though later interpreters will find a place for her in the event's retelling. Her death at age 127 in Kiriath-arba (Hebron) is recounted in chapter 23, along with Abraham's purchase of a burial site, the cave of Machpelah. The fortunes of Isaac and his successors are the subject of the continuing chap-ters of *Genesis*, and so we read in chapter 24 the colorful story of the mis-sion of Abraham's servant to find a fitting wife for Isaac—someone from the patriarch's homeland, not "from the daughters of the Canaanites" (v. 3). The happy (and destined) result of the servant's search is the beauti-ful virgin, Rebekah, who hails from the family of Abraham's brother, Nahor. The next stage of the history of Abraham's seed has a happy beginning:

> Isaac then brought her into the tent of his mother Sarah, and he took Rebekah
> as his wife. Isaac loved her, and thus found comfort after his mother's death
> (24:67).

Sarah, through whose son the people of the covenant will come into being and ultimately possess the land promised to them, becomes, from the Tanakh's (and later, Judaism's) viewpoint, *the* mate and partner of Abraham. The reality of her prominence in the tradition surfaces in ref-erences to the grave of the "fathers" and their women at Machpelah (in *Genesis* 49:29–33, Jacob, dying in Egypt, requests that his corpse be taken to the land of Canaan for burial in the company of Abraham and Sarah, and of Isaac and Rebekah, his parents.)

We should take note, here, of the appearance of Isaac's name in the recurring formula which identifies the triad of Abraham, Isaac, and Jacob.[4] The unfolding history of Israel cannot be recorded without allusions back to the Abrahamic convenant, and, simultaneously to Isaac, the guarantor of its promise and power.

GENESIS RABBAH ON SARAH AND HAGAR

Genesis Rabbah (GR), an anthology of teachings compiled in the late fourth to early fifth centuries CE, contains a treasure trove of rabbis' ruminations on the scriptural account of Abraham's two women. Sarah and Hagar enjoy their prominence by virtue of being means to a divine end: they are child producers in the service of God's promises that from Abraham's loins nations will come, with future offspring as numerous as particles of dust, grains of sand, stars in the heavens.[5] *Genesis Rabbah* reveals clearly the rabbis' familiar methods for untangling problems and for filling in gaps perceived in the biblical text: a passage under consideration suggests another, in whose light the first may be considered anew. Individual words likewise gain fresh connotations from their appearances elsewhere in scripture. We have already met rabbis' regular employment of examples and parables from outside the scripture to add strength to their arguments.

Genesis 16

In *Genesis Rabbah* XLV we find a set of speculations about Sarah's barrenness, and also the possibility of Abraham's infertility. Reading "Now Sarai Abram's wife bore him no children" in the light of *Proverbs* 31:10 ("A woman of valor who can find, for her price (*mikrah*) is far above rubies"),[6] and recalling in *Ezekiel* 16:3 the term "origin" (*mekuroth*) connotating pregnancy, a line of argument reconstructs the reproductive histories of Abraham's brothers. Calculating that Haran (Abraham's brother) fathered his first child when he was six years old, the rabbis pondered how, with this prodigious procreativity at work among his male kin, it was possible that Abraham could not beget a child. The infertility must have been Sarah's. But this inference is challenged by Rabbi Judah, who reminds his fellow sages that the text states that Sarah bore no children *to him* (Abraham), not ruling out the possibility that she might have produced children with a different mate. R. Nehemiah insists that the text cannot be construed in that way: Sarah was herself infertile. The verse draws comment here because *Genesis Rabbah*'s format is a verse-by-verse *midrash* on scripture, and *Genesis* 16:1 in its vocabulary allows various interpretive options. But there are also other concerns, less grammatically inspired, attaching to this topic. They might be put under the rubric of divine purpose, or providence. How, ask the rabbis, does God's commitment to the covenant made with Abraham come to hinge on the pregnancy of a long-barren woman? Is it the case that God's most important actions—like the promise of land and nationhood—are manifest through wonders and miracles? Sarah's conceiving of Isaac requires careful attention, standing as it does in close relationship to the pregnancy of Hagar, and the biblical record of Abraham's other women and their children.

Scriptural cross-referencing done in connection with the verse, "And she had a handmaid, an Egyptian" also led to diverse opinions—namely, (1) that Hagar was Sarah's property, and thus was a person whom Abraham was obliged to support, but was not free to sell; that (2) Hagar was the Pharaoh's daughter, given to Sarah in the aftermath of that ruler's attempt to wed or bed the one he believed to be Abraham's sister—an explanation attributed to R. Simeon b. Yohai; and that (3) the name Hagar derives from the Hebrew word *agar*, meaning "reward" (*Genesis* 12:7).[7]

Similar exegetical strategies produce a variety of meanings attaching to Sarah's declaration, "Look, the Lord has kept me from bearing," and also to her remark that she too might be "built up" in Abraham's having a son "through" Hagar. Sarah speaks as she does because she understands the cause of things, and does not (like many, apparently, in the social world of the rabbis) seek a pregnancy-inducing amulet or charm. Sarah's being built up, a rabbi asserted, referred to survival or to restoration to life. His idea was confirmed (or generated) by Rachel's plea to her husband Jacob in *Genesis* 30:1, "Give me children, or I shall die." Sarah, childless, is as good as dead, and her building up depends on her becoming a mother—of her surrogate's child.

The rabbis ruminate about Hagar's quick conception of a son to Abraham—arguably as a result of their "first intimacy."[8] To Rabbi Eleazar's claim that this never happens, a rejoinder marshals as evidence the pregnancies of Lot's daughters (*Genesis* 19:36), who presumably had sex with their father only once. Rabbi Tanhuma explains that unusual case with unusual imagery: "By an effort of will power they brought forth their virginity, and thus conceived at the first act of intercourse."[9] A comparison of Hagar's and Sarah's procreative capabilities (and of the qualities of their respective sons) is the yield of a botanical metaphor volunteered by R. Hanina b. Pazzi: "Thorns are neither weeded nor sown, yet of their own accord they grow and spring up, whereas how much pain and toil is required before wheat can be made to grow!" That is, Ishmael is easy, spontaneous, and worthless; Isaac is the product of "labor," is "worthy fruit," and thus of great value.[10]

The rabbis can give explanations for the fact that notable women were sometimes barren: God loved to hear their prayerful requests (*Song of Songs* 2:14 is cited in support), or their infertility caused them to depend on their husbands' support, when their great beauty might have made them self-reliant, or that being barren they might pass their lives without the burdens of having and raising children. These lines of male thinking are capped with one offered by a trio of rabbis: The matriarchs were for a long time barren "so that their husbands might derive pleasure from them, for when a woman is with child she is disfigured and lacks grace. Thus the whole ninety years that Sarah did not bear [a child] she was like a bride in her canopy."[11]

A very different opinion and valuation of Sarah's barrenness is put on the lips of Hagar in a piece of narrative meant to illustrate how, after Hagar became pregnant, "her mistress was lowered in her esteem" (16:4b). A passage in *Genesis Rabbah* reports:

> Ladies used to come to inquire how [Sarah] was, and [Sarah] would say to them, "Go and ask about the welfare of the poor woman [Hagar]." Hagar would tell them: "My mistress Sarai is not inwardly what she is outwardly: she appears to be a righteous woman, but she is not. For had she been a righteous woman, see how many years have passed without her conceiving, whereas I conceived in one night!" Said Sarah: "Shall I pay heed to this woman and argue with her! No; I will argue the matter with her master!"[12]

Sarah's complaint to Abraham about Hagar's disrespect is in the form of curse-like challenge. She wants the wrong done to her to fall on him (16:5). The text, revealing as it does rancor between husband and wife, produces contrasting comments by the sages. On the one hand, Sarah is understood to have made a valid complaint. Her claim that Abraham should himself bear the wrong suffered by her gains credence when it is recalled that Abraham said to God in 15:2 ("seeing that *I* shall die childless"). If he had said "*We* go childless," Sarah would not be suffering humiliation, for a child would have been born to them both.

On the other hand, "the wrong done to me" (*hamasi*) that Sarah speaks of suggests the idea that she scratched (*himmes*, to scratch) Abraham, and this observation triggers a brief cataloguing of bad characteristics of women in general. Sarah is the exemplar of half of these:

> The rabbis said: Women are said to possess four traits: they are greedy, eavesdroppers, slothful, and envious. Greedy, as it says, "And she took the fruit thereof and did eat it" (*Genesis* 3:6); eavesdroppers: "And Sarah heard in the tent door" (*Genesis* 18:10) [when the visiting angel predicted the birth of Isaac in the next year]; slothful: "Make ready [quickly] three measures of fine meal" (*Genesis* 18:6) [understood to imply that Sarah did not eagerly bestir herself to prepare

the meal for the Lord/the angelic visitors]; envious: "Rachel envied her sister" (*Genesis* 30:1).[13]

The sharp exchange between Sarah and Abraham that grows out of Sarah's resentment of Hagar requires, the rabbis think, critical assessment. Sarah's too speedy move to litigation ("Let the Lord decide between you and me") was itself blameworthy, and won her the punishment of a shortened life. She would otherwise have lived as long as her spouse.

Abraham's refusal to take action against Hagar ("Your maid is in your hands") and the subsequent harsh treatment of her by Sarah also required explanation. Supported by a prohibition in *Exodus* 21:8 against selling a servant with whom one has become displeased, the patriarch's line of reasoning is this: "after we made her a mistress [i.e., gave her the status of a wife], shall we make her a bondmaid again?"[14] Finally, there are speculations about the kind of harshness Sarah visited upon Hagar: she kept Hagar from Abraham's bed; "she slapped her face with a slipper," she made her do slave tasks in connection with the baths.[15]

Hagar's flight is clearly the result of Sarah's maltreatment, but whether she leaves Abraham's household in fear, in defiance, or in sorrow is not indicated in *Genesis* 16:6, nor taken up by the teachers of *GR*. What *does* draw the interpreters' attention is the fact that Hagar is three times identified in the text *not* as Sarah's equal (i.e., as wife or mistress in her own right), but as maidservant—by Abraham when he speaks to Sarah ("your maid"), by the angel of the Lord who finds Hagar at the spring in the wilderness ("Hagar, slave of Sarai, where have you come from?"), and in her own response ("I am running away from my mistress Sarai"). The point being registered about Hagar's place in the scheme of things is bluntly and comically put: "So runs the proverb: 'If one man tells you that you have an ass's ears, do not believe him; if two tell it to you, order a halter.'"[16]

When God's angel discovers Hagar in flight, he urges her to return to Sarah "and submit to her harsh treatment" (16:9), and we learn later in the passage that Hagar has obeyed the angelic counsel. She is back in the household of Abraham when she gives birth to Ishmael.

Ishmael is next in line for scrutiny. The rabbis' discourse is evoked by scripture's report that the angel of the Lord said to Hagar that he "will greatly increase [her] offspring," and that she will bear a son to be named Ishmael (*Genesis* 10–11). Rabbi Isaac notes that only three figures in the tradition were called by their names before birth—Isaac, Solomon, and Josiah (in *Genesis* 17:16, *1 Chronicles* 22:9, and *1 Kings* 13:2, resp.). An unattributed opinion follows: "Some add Ishmael among the nations." The distinction being made presumes that although Ishmael shares with Isaac, Solomon, and Josiah the apparent honor of being given his name prior to his birth by the Lord or the Lord's angel, he does not belong in their category. Ishmael, son of Abraham, is counted a non-Jew—one among the nations.

Negative estimates of Ishmael fill the succeeding passages in *Genesis Rabbah*, which address phrases by which the angel described him to Hagar in *Genesis* 16:11–12. The rabbis ponder what it means that Ishmael will be a "wild ass of a man." R. Johanan takes the view that it signifies only that he will be raised in the wild, rather than in civilization, while Resh Lakish asserts, "It means a savage among men in its literal sense, for whereas all others plunder wealth, he plunders lives."[17] And what sense is to be drawn from the prediction that Ishmael's hand would be "against everyone, and everyone's hand against him" (16:12)? The *kol bo* ("against him") of the text suggests his doglike (*kalbo* equals dog) taste for carrion.[18]

It is worth asking what associations the name Ishmael carries for the rabbis as they consider this text in *Genesis*. Their *midrashim* from the early centuries of the common era inevitably link the angel's pronouncement that Ishmael would be a perpetual warrior in conflict with "everyone" to Israel's past history. The progeny of Ishmael had long since held a place in the biblical roll of enemies. In *Psalm 83*, a prayer for God to speak and act in a time when "foes assert themselves against [His] people" and threaten to eradicate Israel's name from mention and memory, the clan of the Ishmaelites, and also of the Hagarites, are identified along with such traditional adversaries as the Edomites, Ammonites, Amalekites, Philistines, and the Assyrians.[19]

We may see this representation of bellicose Ishmael and his offspring also in *Pirke de Rabbi Eliezer* (PRE), a compilation of rabbinic teaching and lore edited in the early centuries after the rise of Islam.[20] Here we read of "six (people) [who] were called by their names before they were created: Isaac, Ishmael, Moses, Solomon, Josiah, and King Messiah."[21] Ishmael's presence in the group is explained simply by referring to *Genesis* 16:11, and giving the meaning of his name a new turn:

> Why was his name called Ishmael? Because in the future, the Holy One, blessed be He, will *hearken* to the cry of the people arising from (the oppression) which the children of Ishmael will bring about in the land in the last (days).[22]

The hostile inversion is clever: Ishmael, the boy called into existence because God "hearkened" to his and his mother's misery, is now an oppressor whose victims God will hear and heed. Elsewhere in the text

Rabbi Ishmael speaks of fifteen travesties that the children of Ishmael will accomplish in Israel—in the future and "in the latter days." Among these terrible actions are measurings of the land, desecration of a cemetery, falsehood's triumph over truth, the removal of statutes "far from Israel," the destruction of writings, the despoiling of the tombs of the kings of Judah, and this:

> They will ... fence in the broken walls of the Temple; and they will build a building in the Holy Place; and two brothers will arise over them, princes at the end.[23]

These prophecies attributed to Rabbi Ishmael are of course retrospective, pointing as they do to the claiming of the Temple mount as *haram* (a sacred place) and the building in the late seventh century of what came to be known *al-Masjida al-Aqsa* (the al-Aqsa mosque, or more literally, "the furthest mosque" from Mecca and Medina), and to the sons of the Abbasid Caliph Harun al-Rashid, al-Amin and al-Mamun, who sequentially held power from 809 to 833 CE.

Future-looking, however, is *PRE*'s expressed messianic hope positioned at the end of the list of woes brought upon the Jews by sons of Ishmael:

> And in their days the Branch, the Son of David, will arise, as it is said, "And in the days of those kings shall the God of heaven set up a kingdom, which shall never be destroyed" (*Daniel* 2:44).

This characterization of the sons of Ishmael as the Muslim foes of Israel is part of a traceable development. Having its origins in the Sarah-Hagar story, the opposition between Isaac and Ishmael already in later portions of *Genesis* became a story of divided and hostile families and nations. Esau (like Ishmael, a firstborn son denied his inheritance) took one of Ishmael's daughters, Mahalath, as a wife (*Genesis* 28:6–9). The Ishmaelites who purchased Jacob's son, Joseph, and took him to Egypt (*Genesis* 37:25ff.) are portrayed as a people quite other than the Hebrews. Needless to say, a thoroughly different perception and valuation of Ishmael took shape in Muslim tradition and commentary, as chapter 6 will demonstrate.

Returning to the exegetes of *Genesis Rabbah*, and to their concerns in their era, we find them pondering what occurs near the conclusion of *Genesis* 16, when Hagar called out to "the Lord who spoke to her." The rabbis considered this unusual encounter and exchange rich in possibilities. Again, the standing of Hagar with God is at issue—a matter seen specifically in relation to, or in comparison with, the divine favor shone to Abraham's other wife:

R. Judah b. R. Simon and R. Johanan in the name of R. Eleazar b. R. Simeon said: The Holy One, blessed be He, never condescended to hold converse with a woman save with that righteous woman [viz. Sarah], and that too was through a particular cause (*GR* XLV.10).

The cause seems to have been God's need to confront Sarah about her laughter, whereas the Lord simply addressed Hagar by way of an announcement to her about her future as a mother. But questions press themselves upon the commentators: was it God, or an angel, who spoke to Hagar? The prevailing opinion is that God communicated with her "through an angel," though the great privilege which came to Hagar via the divine visitor at the spring raises another issue. What did she mean in saying (16:13) "You are a God of seeing"? According to Rabbi Aibu, she meant "Thou seest the sufferings of the persecuted."

There is, however, more to be considered in the latter part of verse 13, which can be translated, "Have I even here (*halom*) seen him that seeth me?"[24] A very positive estimate of Hagar derives from noting the occurrence of this same word, *halom*, in *2 Samuel* 7:18. Upon hearing from the prophet Nathan that God will establish his house and kingship, David responds: "What am I, O Lord God, and what is my family, that You have brought me thus far [or: even here—*halom*]?"—that is, to royal status.[25] *Genesis* Rabbah advanced the view that Hagar's situation was like that of David. From her will issue rulers, as the angel promised—the angel appearing to her, not in the company of her mistress, but "even now" when she, a runaway, was alone at the spring.

The rabbis' interpretations both confirm and destabilize what might seem to be *Genesis* 16's obvious presentations of Abraham and his two women. Nuances attach to Sarah and her ambitious desire for a son for Abraham, her anger at being deprecated, her aggressive challenges to Abraham about which son will be his heir, and her desire for revenge against Hagar. At the same time, the interpreters tease out reasons why Hagar gloats in her pregnancy, demeans Sarah, and attempts to flee her difficulties. Bold in her interrogation of the Lord's angel, who brings her good tidings, Hagar nevertheless accedes to his injunction to return to her household and submit to Sarah's cruel treatment of her. We notice that even while disparaging Hagar, the commentators credit her interactions with God, and honor the privileges with which she is blessed. Abraham, in the midst of the rivalry between the two women, seems to deflect Sarah's charge against him, while at the same time tolerating her maltreatment of Hagar, who has conceived and delivered his firstborn.

Genesis 21:1–21

We turn now to *Genesis Rabbah*'s treatment of the earlier verses of chapter 21, those which precede the final rift between Abraham's two women, and Hagar's being cast out. At considerable length, and with an array of supporting biblical texts, the rabbis celebrate God's faithfulness in keeping his promise concerning Sarah. For God to remember or take note of the pledge of the birth of Isaac to her and to Abraham, as the rabbis reflect on the passage, signifies a number of things. God accomplishes what he decrees when this is for the world's good (though he sometimes postpones or relents from action when he has promised to bring evil— i.e., judgment). Sarah's confidence in the promise is praised. No longer one who laughs, she is imagined exclaiming: "What! am I to lose faith in my Creator! Heaven [forbid]! I will not lose faith in my Creator, 'For I will rejoice in the Lord, I will exalt in the God of my salvation'" (*Habbakuk* 3:18).[26]

Considerable (and amusing) interest centers on the means by which the capacity to produce a child came to Abraham and Sarah. The rabbis speak of youth restored, sexual potency returned to Abraham, the Lord's creation of an ovary for Sarah, the onset of her menses, and the provision of milk for her nursing of Isaac. Concern for Sarah's virtue is great, in order that it not be suspected that she was impregnated by Abimelech, from whose sexual aspirations she had only recently escaped, with God's help (*Genesis* 20). A moral claim is advanced. Sarah, having emerged from the houses of the Pharaoh and Abimelech undefiled, *deserved* to be remembered by God and made a mother to Abraham's son. The fact that the text (21:2) states "bore to Abraham" rules out suspicion; "This teaches that she did not steal seed from elsewhere." Furthermore, Isaac too, like his father, bore "a son in his old age." The rabbis argue in several ways that Sarah's pregnancy was sufficiently lengthy "that it might not be said that he [Isaac] was a scion of Abimelech's house."[27]

A striking legend is inspired by Sarah's versified exclamation in v. 7:

Who would have said to Abraham
That Sarah would suckle children!
Yet I have borne a son in his old age.

The commentators pause and puzzle over "children," in the plural, and then set about their work. Abraham importunes Sarah to put modesty aside, and to bare her breasts so that her miraculous flow of milk can be publicly observed. The milk is then offered to the offspring of many noble ladies who come (while doubting their worthiness) in order "that [their] children might be suckled with the milk of that righteous woman."[28] Sarah's declaration in *Genesis* 21:6 that her God-given happiness will be enjoyed by all who hear of it, becomes a prophecy fulfilled when more miracles occur. The matriarch's being remembered by God—that is, her giving birth to Isaac—released these additional wonders: "many other barren women were remembered with her; many deaf gained their hearing; many blind had their eyes opened, many insane became sane."[29] Verbal connections with other scriptures allow the rabbis to elaborate on the ways that God's fulfillment of the promise of Isaac's birth to Sarah was "a gift granted to the world."[30]

The celebratory tone of *GR*'s treatment of the birth of Isaac and Sarah's happiness echoes *Genesis* 21:1–8. But immediately after the "great feast" marking the boy's weaning, according to vv. 10ff., threatening clouds come over the household of the patriarch.[31] This change begins with the protective mother sensing danger (*Genesis* 21:10–11):

> Sarah saw the son whom Hagar the Egyptian had borne to Abraham playing. She said to Abraham, "Cast out that slave-woman and her son, for the son of that slave shall not share in the inheritance with my son Isaac."

What was the "playing" of Ishmael that so aggravated Sarah? Rabbi Akiba's interpretation leads off a series of opinions. The verb that underlies "playing," or "making sport"—*tsahak*—is the same that appears in the story of Joseph and Potiphar's wife. Failing in her attempt to seduce Joseph, she tells Potiphar that his "Hebrew servant ... came into me to make sport of me" (*Genesis* 39:17). Akiba deduces that "this teaches that Sarah saw Ishmael ravish maidens, seduce married women, and dishonor them."[32] Rabbi Ishmael recalls the use of the term "sport" or "play" in *Exodus* 32:6, which tells of the Hebrews' actions around the golden calf on the plain below Sinai. Sarah, then, spied Ishmael committing idolatry. He is imagined building altars and there sacrificing locusts, the entertainment of a wicked, cruel youth. No, others argue; she saw a violent act. Rabbi Eleazar (drawing on the appearance of "sport" in *2 Samuel.* 2:14, where a battle by sword and dagger is described), asserts that Ishmael committed bloodshed. Aware of the notice that Ishmael became an archer (*Genesis* 21:20), R. Levi recalls images from *Proverbs.* 22:18ff. in which the "play" of a person who deceives his neighbor is compared to the behavior of "a madman who casts firebrands, arrows, and death."

Perhaps because he finds these varied opinions too speculative, or because he has reservations about imputing such shameful behaviors to a son of the great patriarch Abraham, Rabbi Simeon b. Yohai takes a different tack, reading vv. 9–10 together. "Playing" suggests to him mockery—specifically, Ishmael's attitude toward the festive commotion surrounding the birth and childhood of his half-brother, "for when our father Isaac was born all rejoiced, whereupon Ishmael said to them, 'You are fools, for I am the first-born and I receive a double portion.'"[33] Here it is not Ishmael's warlike character that arrested Sarah's attention, but rather his assertion of his rights of primogeniture, expressed in a spirit of disdain and greed. On this reading, Sarah's protectiveness of her son has to do with Isaac's patrimony—she is forcefully reminding her husband of the promise made and now fulfilled by God, and of Abraham's commitments to the covenant.

We recall that Sarah's demand that the "slave woman and her son" be dismissed caused Abraham great pain, "for it concerned a son of his" (21:11). A single scriptural text is brought forth in *GR* by way of comment: "Thus it is written, 'And shut his eyes from looking upon evil'" (*Isaiah* 33:15). The gist of this *midrash* entails a criticism of the patriarch, who "shut his eyes from Ishmael's evil ways, and was reluctant to send him away."[34] One wonders, however, if another meaning may be intended by the citation of the text—a comment more sympathetic to Abraham. The phrase in question in *Isaiah* 33 falls in a number of descriptions of a righteous person "who spurns profit from fraudulent dealings, waves away a bribe instead of grasping it, stops his ears against listening to infamy, shuts his eyes against looking at evil" (v. 15). Is it possible that the rabbis acknowledge Abraham's distress, imagining that he might have considered the banning of his son an unrighteous act, and that for this reason he averted his eyes, and recoiled from it?

The continuing narrative in *Genesis* has God address words to Abraham that seem, while upholding Sarah's admonition to send away the threatening mother and son, consolatory rather than accusatory. Certainly God reinforces Sarah's wish, telling Abraham, "whatever Sarah tells you, do as she says, for it is through Isaac that offspring will be continued for you" (v. 12). Nonetheless, God *does* reassure the patriarch about his first son, saying "I will make a nation of him, too, for he is your seed" (v. 13).

The biblical narrative of the expulsion of Hagar and Ishmael presented puzzles to the commentators in *Genesis Rabbah* that may or may not have held for them the kind of pathos seen in *Rembrandt's* rendering. They wondered how Abraham's action of placing the water skin on Hagar's shoulder was to be construed—positively, in that he showed generosity in providing her with an abundance of water, or negatively, showing Hagar to be a water-bearing servant? Was the father discouraging any impression that the boy with her was his freeborn son with a claim on his inheritance? Why did the biblical text state that Abraham put provisions for the journey, *plus* the child, on Hagar's shoulder as he sent her away? The rabbis were conscious of the problem of seeing Ishmael as a young child (the *GR* comments that he was twenty-seven years old at the time),[35] but their explanations are differently framed. Ishmael had to be carried because he had been made ill by Sarah, who "cast an evil eye on him, whereupon he was seized with feverish pains."[36] Wandering in the wilderness near Beer-Sheba, Ishmael consumed the water in the way a feverish person drinks, and so, with none left, was on the verge of death.

Another question arises from the story. Having put Ishmael under a bush, Hagar separated herself to the distance of a bowshot, "for she thought, 'Let me not look on as the child dies.' And sitting thus afar, she burst into tears" (21:16). Is her thought prayerful? Is it something else—an accusation? The Hebrew word for bowshot calls to mind a similar term that connotes hurling words, or "one who criticizes" (*ke-mateheth*). So, it is proposed, hurling her complaints on high, Hagar spoke

> as a woman who impugned God's justice, saying, "Yesterday Thou didst promise me, 'I will greatly multiply thy seed, etc.' (*Genesis* 16:10), and now he is dying of thirst!"[37]

Hagar is not alone in raising questions of justice. According to R. Simon, ministering angels accosted God and put to him a challenge starkly different from Hagar's. "Lord of all ages, to a man who is destined to kill your children with thirst will you provide a well?" The ministering angels, the rabbis suppose, are presuming that a passage in *Isaiah* (21:13ff) tells of a time when Arabs, Ishmael's descendants, murderously ignored the Israelites in their desperate plea for water.

What follows is a statement regarding the basis upon which God judges, or acts on behalf of, human beings. About the person (Ishmael) whom the angels foreknow will someday be injurious to his children (of the line of Isaac), God asks: "What is he now?" They answer, "Righteous." God declares that he judges the human as he or she is in the present, "at the moment," not on the basis of that person's future character and deeds. The hook on which this argument hangs is an element in verse 17, "where he is," which is taken to mean "as he is at present." So God hears the cry of the boy and one of his angels calls to Hagar from above:

> What troubles you, Hagar? Fear not, for God has heeded the cry of the boy *where he is.* Come, lift up the boy and hold him by the hand, for I will make a great nation of him (*Genesis* 21.17b–18).

The theological argument about God's ways of judging seems at first to stand at some remove from the agonizing of Ishmael and his mother, but of course as a scene depicting the plight of those who are suffering, it naturally raises questions about God—his silence and his inaction, or his purpose and power in relation to the event. The next verse reveals the mode of divine rescue. "God opened her eyes and she saw a well of water. She went and filled the skin with water, and let the boy drink" (v. 19). Two rabbis comment that all people are blind until God opens their eyes. The implication that the problem lay with Hagar is followed by the observation that she lacked faith even after having been enlightened—she filled the water skin because of doubt about the well, being anxious that it might vanish as quickly as it appeared.[38] (We shall see that Muslim interpreters similarly criticized the action of the rescued Hagar, who was said to have attempted to dam, and preserve, the waters of the spring.)

Even though the previous commentary on this incident regarded God's decision to intervene and save Ishmael "where he [was]" (i.e., for what he was *then*) as evidence that the youth was a person of righteousness and merit, concluding remarks about his future life take a negative turn. The two Hebrew words for "became an archer" (*robeh kashoth*) point to two others (*rabbah, kashiuth*) suggesting that Ishmael grew in cruelty. This narrative section's final verse telling of Hagar's finding an Egyptian wife for her son (v. 21) prompts R. Isaac, not without prejudice, to remark, recalling *Genesis* 16:1 ("She [Sarah] had an Egyptian maidservant"), that a stick tossed in the air will fall back to its point of origin.[39]

In the biblical drama of Abraham's family, the cast-out mother and son leave the stage, Hagar not to appear again, and Ishmael returning only to join Isaac in burying their father. *Genesis* pursues the story of Abraham and Sarah through to the events of their deaths and burials in chs. 23 through 25, and then turns to the stories concerning the patriarch's "seed"—Isaac, Jacob, Joseph.

Revealed once again in these pages of *Genesis Rabbah* was the typical mode of rabbinical scriptural analysis—the production of *midrash* that explored, rather than attempted to achieve consensus on, the actions of Abraham, Sarah, Hagar, and Isaac and Ishmael—and their Lord. Rather, holding scripture and all of its parts to be God-given treasure, the rabbis were in search of its rich prizes—its multiple lessons and truths.

ABRAHAM'S FAMILY IN EARLY JEWISH ART: MOSAICS IN THE SEPPHORIS SYNAGOGUE

The 1923 discovery of multiple biblical scenes in a third-century "house synagogue" in Dura Europas (on the Euphrates) fully dispelled the notion that adherence to the commandment against idolatry prevented Jews from producing figural art.[40] Further excavations in Palestine brought to light a number of splendidly decorated synagogues, one of which has a role to play in our search for Jewish artistic interpretations of Abraham's women and their sons.

We should begin by acknowledging that nowhere in early Jewish art does a depiction of Hagar survive. Do we see Ishmael? Very probably, but a case needs to be made for this. Isaac *does* appear, and not infrequently, because of the popularity of depictions of the *aqedat Yitzhak,* the "binding of Isaac" at the time his father prepared to sacrifice him to God.

Sarah is the one to be searched out, and she is believed to be shown in a portion of the mosaic floor uncovered in 1993 by archaeologists Ze'ev Weiss and Ehud Netzer.[41] A small but elegantly decorated synagogue dating from the fifth century was built in the lower Galilean city of Sepphoris. In that era the city, which had long been regarded as an important center for Jewish life, preserved many features of its having been a typical Greco-Roman municipality. It also showed signs of the growing strength of Christianity; several churches (constructed upon the foundations of what had been pagan temples) stood near the cardo, Sepphoris's main street—close to the city's administrative center.[42] It is hard to know the extent to which pagan sights and sounds might have continued in the city in the fifth to sixth centuries, but the proximity of Jewish (a Talmudic report tells of eighteen synagogues) and Christian buildings in Sepphoris allows us to presume some measure of social interaction between Jews and Christians. A bit later, we shall explore how much they knew about each others' beliefs, and interpretations of biblical narratives.

In a summary description of their discovery, Weiss and Netzer wrote:

> The most significant remnant of the synagogue is its mosaic floor which was designed as a single long carpet measuring 16.0 x 6.6 m[eters]. . . . The carpet in the nave is divided into 7 horizontal bands of unequal height, with a zodiac in the center. Some of the bands have internal subdivisions. The floor is made up of 14 panels containing a variety of decorations, some of which make their first appearance in Jewish art here. Dedicatory inscriptions, mostly in Greek, adorn the panels but bear no relationship to the scenes in them. All of the depictions that comprise the main mosaic carpet face in one direction, perpendicular to the nave's longitudinal axis, thus emphasizing the *bema,* the focus of religious activity in the synagogue. Although each panel features a different scene, they are all thematically connected.[43]

The proposal by the excavators that the art program of the mosaic carpet centered in the themes of "promise and redemption" generated lively scholarly discussion, with diverse opinions about what overall sense can be drawn from the multiple panels, which depict images of the ark and two menorahs, scenes of temple sacrifices (the name Aaron appearing next to an effaced figure standing at an altar), a large Zodiac image similar to those found in other synagogues of the period), and two scenes having to do with Abraham.[44]

Bypassing here the discussion of the mosaic floor in its entirety, we close in upon issues of interpretation pertaining to the latter mosaics, which bear directly on this chapter's topic. The first of these (Figure 4.2), largely damaged, showed the head-covering and forehead of a woman standing in a doorway—Sarah, its excavators determined.

Figure 4.3 is a drawing in which Weiss reconstructed what this mosaic showed and suggested.

Figure 4.2 Sarah depicted in a mosaic panel of the Sepphoris synagogue. Fifth to sixth century CE. Courtesy of Prof. Zeev Weiss, The Sepphoris Excavations, The Hebrew University of Jerusalem.

Figure 4.3 Drawing, courtesy of Prof. Zeev Weiss, The Sepphoris Excavations, The Hebrew University of Jerusalem.

Weiss described the scene in this way:

Only small fragments of the original panel are preserved. One figure, stand-ing in a rectangular structure, can be seen on the left of the panel. Traces of two other figures can be identified beside it. One is standing to the right of the rectangular structure, and the other is depicted in a reclining position farther to the right and below the previous one. Traces of a cloth with a fringed hem, which probably covered a table that stood in the picture's foreground, are visible below the reclining figure. Although this scene is poorly preserved, analysis of its remains in light of a close parallel in the presbytery in St. Vitale, Ravenna (mid-sixth century CE), makes it possible to reconstruct what was once depicted here. The three angels reclined in the foreground of the panel next to a low table. Abraham, their host, is located to their left, and behind him, Sarah stands in the tent listening to his conversation with his guests. The presentation of the story of the Binding of Isaac as a direct continuation of the scene of the angels' visit to Abraham is also found in Ravenna (if the identification suggested here is accepted). In Jewish art, this theme makes its first appearance in the Sepphoris synagogue.[45]

The mosaic (Figure 4.4) on the north wall of the church of San Vitale to which Weiss refers postdates the Sepphoris synagogue by approximately a century (San Vitale was constructed in the period 528–547), but it does provide the similar configuration of the Sarah image that gave Weiss and Netzer external support for identification of this mosaic's subject. The two biblical stories in the mosaic pavement initially visible to those entering the synagogue—first, the angels' visitation to Abraham and Sarah at Mamre and second, the depiction of the near-sacrifice of Isaac—appear in the San Vitale wall mosaic aligned on a horizontal plane, and appear, not surprisingly in this Christian context, beneath a cross held aloft by angels.

In the church decoration both parts of the single mosaic scene stand not only as pictorial Abrahamic history but also as symbols understood to prefigure the annunciation of the birth of Jesus and his sacrificial death. As if to hold the two images together and make manifest their connected meaning for Christians, the angels at the center have in front of them as they sit at the table what, in this setting, can only be eucharistic bread.[46]

In the Sepphoris synagogue, the two scenes will of course only convey Jewish meanings, but in the social-religious context of Palestine's—and Sepphoris'—fifth and sixth centuries, it would be surprising if their presentations were not cognizant of, and resistant to, Christianized appropriations of these two important scriptural stories. We want to weigh how the *akedah* scene in the Sepphoris mosaic (Figure 4.5) reveals—or gives strong intimations of—the ideas and perspective of its artists.

Again, a drawing by Weiss (Figure 4.6) clarifies what can be seen in the damaged mosaic.

Weiss describes the two panels on this band of the mosaic floor:

> The two youths whom Abraham has left, together with an ass, at the foot of the mountain, are depicted in the left panel. The ass, which has a colored pack-saddle on its back, stands in the foreground of the scene; behind him is one of the youths who is extending one hand forward and holding a spear in the other. The second youth is seated on the left beneath a tree and grips the reins of the ass in one hand. The continuation of the story in the panel on the right has been largely destroyed. On its left side one can discern a sparsely branched tree to which a ram is tethered by means of a reddish cord; only the head of the ram remains intact. Below it, two pairs of shoes removed by Abraham and Isaac as they approached the site of the sacrifice are visible, a detail absent in other depictions of this episode. In another surviving part of the mosaic in the center of the panel, one can possibly identify the blade of a knife, and to its right the

Figure 4.4 Abraham welcomes strangers, prepares to sacrifice Isaac. Mid-sixth century CE. Mosaic in San Vitale, Ravenna. © Art History Images.

Figure 4.5 Abraham's attendants and the aqedah. A floor panel in the Sepphoris synagogue. Courtesy of Prof. Zeev Weiss, The Sepphoris Excavations, The Hebrew University of Jerusalem.

Figure 4.6 Drawing, courtesy of Zeev Weiss, The Sepphoris Excavations, The Hebrew University of Jerusalem.

remains of a cloak. In the light of the numerous parallels in Byzantine art, it appears that Abraham was depicted in the foreground of the original panel, his body being far larger than the other figures beside him. In his raised right hand he held the knife, while his other hand grabbed Isaac, perhaps only by his forelock. Isaac, probably portrayed on a smaller scale, appeared next to Abraham,

on the right, beside an altar that was located on the panel's right side. The ram
on the left side of the panel completes the portrayal of the biblical narrative.[47]

The content and arrangement conform to another mosaic depiction
of the *aqedat Yitzhak* found in the sixth-century Beth Alpha synagogue
(Figure 4.7).

Distinctive here are the *tituli* in Hebrew, which read (from the right):
"Isaac," "Abraham," "Do not raise [your hand]" (the angel of the Lord's words
from heaven to Abraham in *Genesis* 22:12), and the declarative statement,
"Here is the ram" (22:13).

In the Sepphoris mosaic's *aqedah* scene (and also in Beth Alpha's)
the ram is tied to the tree or bush, rather than caught in it by its horns
(as *Genesis* 22:13 relates). The motif of the ram tethered with a rope is
regarded as a piece of "artistic midrash" meant to clarify and expand what
the ram's appearance in *Genesis* 22:13 signifies: tied up and awaiting this
event, the ram's presence was providential, not accidental.[48] The tethered
animal to be sacrificed in Isaac's stead was in thematic keeping with this
and other artists' interpretive additions focused on divine oversight of the
event—namely, the hand of God shown atop the painting of the *aqedah* in
Dura Europas's synagogue, representing the voice from heaven (*bat qol*), or
the hand pictured in conjunction with the divine command given in letters,
observable above the ram in the Beth Alpha image.[49]

Figure 4.7 Aqedah scene from the Beth Alpha synagogue. Sixth century CE. Photo courtesy
of the Center for Jewish Art at the Hebrew University of Jerusalem.

Significance attaches to another detail concerning the rope that tethers the ram. The artists knew the rabbinic teaching which, expanding upon the description of the scapegoat sacrificed on Yom Kippur (*Leviticus* 16:10), held that the rope was crimson—its symbolism found in *Isaiah* 1:18—"Be your sins like crimson, they can turn snow white." By this motif, there could be put in place a thoroughly Jewish commentary on what the ram was and signified. The animal available to Abraham was the bearer and remover of Israel's sins. Passages in both the *Mishnah* and the *Babylonian Talmud* refer to the crimson thread tied between the ram's horns—the former text noting that the other end of the woolen rope was attached to a rock as the scapegoat was pushed over the precipice.[50]

Rabbinic discourses pertaining to the *aqedah* spend considerable time on Isaac's attitude (willing or questioning) about what is to befall him; by contrast the artists do not portray Isaac as an adult, with the result that greater interest and centrality belongs to the figure of the ram.[51] For example, *Genesis Rabbah*'s extensive commentary on the "binding of Isaac" often takes into consideration thoughts and emotions of Isaac and Abraham as they speak to each other, or of Abraham when he "picked up the knife to slay his son" (*Genesis* 22:10). The angels, in close attendance, are imagined as weeping at the sight.[52]

Further, a passage in *GR* discloses sharp consciousness of Israel's historical situation, and the place of the *aqedah* in Judaism's ritual life. The ram spied by Abraham *ahar* ("behind him") is given a temporal twist, so that R. Judan can say, "After all that happened [i.e., our redemption from slavery in Egypt, the gift of the Torah, etc.], Israel still fall[s] into the clutches of sin and [in consequence] become[s] the victim of persecution; yet [Israel] will be ultimately redeemed by the ram's horn, as it says, 'And the Lord God will blow the horn, etc.'" (*Zechariah* 9:14).[53] R. Hanina b. R. Isaac adds, "Throughout the year Israel [is] in sin's clutches and led away by [her] troubles, but on New Year they shall take the *shofar* and blow on it, and eventually they will be redeemed by the ram's horn."[54] Rabbi Hanina's remark lets us know that the story of the binding of Isaac was read at Rosh Hashana, even though it had earlier been associated with Passover.[55] Christian preaching at Easter, which transformed the bound Isaac into Christ crucified, would have been one of the motivations for moving the reading of the *aqedah* to another feast in the Jewish calendar. As noted earlier, Melito, a second-century bishop in the city of Sardis, had, with strong polemical force, taught his congregation at Easter what the "sacrifice of Isaac" signified for him and his fellow-believers.

The synagogue mosaic emphasized the animal's role in the drama not only by putting the scapegoat's red leash on him, but also by depicting in the upper registers the *menoroth*-surrounding ark, Aaron's priesthood, and the central importance of sacrificial animals, including birds, in the cultic life of the Temple. The ritual consciousness of Jews was being evoked in this imagery, and the relation of these realities to the ram that took Isaac's place as the offering at Moriah was obvious.

In the *Tanhuma Yelammedenu*, a collection of exegeses many of which stem from the fifth through seventh centuries, we find a variation on the interpretations already met:

> *A ram caught in the thicket by his horns.* The Holy One, blessed be He, said to Abraham: "let them blow upon the ram's horn to Me, and I will save them and redeem them from their sins." This is what David meant when he sang: *My shield and my horn of salvation, my high tower (Psalm 18:3).*[56]

And of course our mosaic panel is art in a place of worship, not in a book. The liturgical hearing and seeing of the *aqedah* recalled and confirmed the congregation's sense of identity as God's beloved—tested, protected, and redeemed.

Only in the Sepphoris synagogue's *aqedah* iconography is found the feature of two pairs of upturned shoes, shed by the smaller Isaac and by his father. Weiss notes that in *Genesis Rabbah* 56.2 one meets the tradition that clouds and "the *Shekhinah* (Divine Presence) ... dwelt in the place chosen for Isaac's sacrifice."[57] One recalls God's command in *Exodus* 3:5 that Moses remove his sandals at Mt. Horeb, since it is "holy ground." A place of God's powerful presence and speech requires those who ascend it to proceed with feet unshod.[58] In this detail of the pairs of shoes resides the claim that this mountain in Moriah, like Horeb, is a "mountain of God" and that the *aqedah* ranks in importance with the giving of the Law at Sinai. But the image of the shoes left off at the place of the binding of Isaac may be understood to signify more than proper respect for hallowed space. Over against Christian interpretations of the binding of Isaac in Christological terms, the shoes say: this event of God's pardon took place in *our* holy place, and was revealed to *our* ancestors.

Studying the Sepphoris *aqedah* scene in the light of Christian uses of the image, art historian Herbert Kessler suggested that another detail—a barely noticed omission from the Jewish imagery—can also be thought to serve the cause of a distinctive Jewish claim *adversus Christianorum. Genesis* 21:6's report that "Abraham took the wood for the burnt offering and put it on his son Isaac" fails to appear in the Sepphoris *aqedah* image, and in other Jewish representations of the scene. Christian exegetes and theologians as early as the second century asserted that this biblical detail held the clue that Isaac's sacrifice anticipated and pointed to Jesus's bearing his own cross to the place of his death, and Christian artists *did* show Isaac with the wood in his arms.[59] Kessler's study of miniature paintings of the scene in the *Christian topography* manuscripts (dating from the eleventh through the twelfth centuries, but "surely copied from a 6th- or 7th c. Syrian model and hence . . . rather close to the Sepphoris mosaic in place and time of origin") prompted him to speculate:

> The ubiquitousness of the depiction of Isaac bearing the wood in Early Christian art, and hence of the typological interpretation, may have induced the mosaicist [at the Sepphoris synagogue] to omit it.[60]

In his *Bound by the Bible* Edward Kessler, a historian of Jewish-Christian relations, pursued concerns akin to those of Herbert Kessler by searching for evidence of "exegetical encounters" between Jews and Christians who interpreted the sacrifice of Isaac.[61] Early in his study he remarked about rabbis' responses "to Christian claims about ownership of Scripture," and quoted a passage from the *Tanhuma*:

> When the Holy One, Blessed be He, said to Moses "write" (Ex. 34:27), Moses wanted to write the Mishnah as well. However the Holy One, Blessed be He, foresaw that ultimately the nations of the world would translate the Torah into Greek and would claim, "We are Israel."[62]

Kessler observed that the church fathers, while not abandoning the narrative's strong interest in Abraham's faithfulness to God's command, gave concentrated attention to Isaac as the prototype of Jesus. Kessler argues that the rabbis knew and used concepts from this Christian trajectory of ideas, turning them to their own purposes. Examining a piece of commentary in *Genesis Rabbah* 56.3 which likens Abraham's placing of the wood on Isaac to "a man who carries his cross on his shoulder"—a phrase which was "undoubtedly deliberate"—Kessler noted that this "is as near to an explicit reference to Christianity as we shall find in rabbinic interpretations" of this time period.[63] He continued:

> Rather than associating Isaac with death and martyrdom, the [rabbis'] purpose was to emphasize Isaac's *willingness* to give up his life and suffer torture. This is why the rabbis deliberately failed to associate Isaac with such martyrs as Akiva.... It is Isaac's willingness to give up his life that provides the basis for those interpretations [i.e., those that spoke of his fear of the knife] and appears to be a response to the Christian teaching that Christ was willing to give up his life for Israel. The rabbis argued that there existed numerous biblical figures,

such as Isaac at the Akedah, who were willing to give up their lives on behalf of Israel. These examples showed that no special significance should be given to the willingness of Christ to give up his life. In the words of the rabbis, 'you find everywhere that the patriarchs and the prophets offered their lives on behalf of Israel.' In other words, the sacrifice of Jesus was not a unique event. Isaac was used to counter Christological claims of uniqueness.[64]

We cannot leave unexamined the Sepphoris mosaic's representation of the other half of the band showing the *aqedah*. Abraham's servants may be regarded as biblically required, but the mosaic portrayal of them is provocative. The two men are turned toward each other, with the larger, spear-bearing man on the right speaking and gesturing in the other's direction. Is the viewer of this panel that adjoins the sacrificial scene meant to recognize these two attendants, and to have some idea of what is transpiring between them? Familiar, presumably, were *aqedah* traditions like the one found in *Pirke de Rabbi Eliezer* 31, which gives the names of those who accompanied Abraham and Isaac to the place of sacrifice: Eliezer, the servant, and Ishmael, the patriarch's other son. How did these two, told to stay behind with the ass, occupy themselves during the time Abraham and Isaac went to the mountain top to "worship" (as Abraham says)?

> Contention arose between Eliezer and Ishmael. Ishmael said to Eliezer: Now that Abraham will offer Isaac his son for a burnt offering, kindled upon the altar, I am his first-born son, I will inherit (the possessions) of Abraham. Eliezer replied to him, saying: He has already driven you out like a woman divorced from her husband, and he has sent you away to the wilderness, but I am his servant, serving him by day and by night, and I shall be the heir of Abraham. The Holy Spirit answered them, saying to them: Neither this one nor that one shall inherit.[65]

The exchange resonates with one of the fundamental themes and plot lines of *Genesis*: inheritance rights and competition between sons for these. Ishmael sees his opportunity to lay claim to the rights of a first-born son, while Eliezer, after likening Ishmael's status to that of a rejected wife, bases his own claim upon a life of devoted service. The two men personify values worthy of comparison and judgment in this rabbinic tale, but in its telling the Spirit of God summarily ends the debate. The denial of both men and their claims by the Spirit "points" the listener to the wonder that is transpiring on the mountain. A similar redirection of the eye must have happened to viewers of the mosaic. But we pause over the best preserved part of band 6 because here the artists, no doubt aware of some form of the *midrash* we have in *PRE*, have Ishmael re-entering the

Abrahamic story (back from the wilderness of Paran where he was left in *Genesis* 21:20–21), armed with a spear, rather than the bow which God predicts he will master.

Ishmael's presence in the scene underlines, with a nonbiblical image, this scripture narrative's chief theme: it is to Abraham's son *born to Sarah* (not to Hagar's son) that God's covenant applies. The patriarch has demonstrated his faithfulness, at which point the angel of the Lord reiterates (and as Jon Levenson emphasized, transforms) the blessing: "Because you have done this and not withhold your son, your favored one, I will . . . make your descendants as the stars of heaven and the sands on the seashore; and your descendants shall seize the gates of their foes. All the nations of the earth shall bless themselves by your descendants, because you have obeyed My command" (*Genesis* 22:16–18).

We conclude our consideration of Abraham's family in the figural art of Sepphoris by turning once more to Sarah. Though the artists did not place Sarah anywhere in the band of the synagogue mosaic depicting of the binding of Isaac, she would have been imagined behind that scene by those whose eyes fell on the two panels they met as they entered the building. A main reason for this was that in *Genesis* the account of Abraham's near-sacrifice of Isaac in chapter 22 is followed only a few verses later by the report of the matriarch's death. We know that in some synagogues the two stories, the *aqedah* and the death of Sarah, constituted a single Torah portion to be read to the congregation.[66]

The juxtaposition of the "binding of Isaac" and Sarah's demise prompted speculation that there was a cause-effect relation between the two happenings. A passage in *Pirke de Rabbi Eliezer* tells of a visit to Sarah by Sammael/Satan, who knows of, and is frustrated by, Abraham's fidelity to God at the altar he has prepared for Isaac on the mountain. During the time when Abraham and his son are at the mountain in Moriah, Sammael falsely informs Sarah that Isaac has been slain and given to God as a burnt offering by her husband. Sarah weeps, then wails aloud with three long and three short cries like those of the shofar, and dies.[67] It is the stuff of tragedy—a dangerous deceiver, working off to the side of drama's main action, turns to the woman who had once laughed in incredulity, and brings her to tears of agony and to her death, even while the God of Abraham is rescuing her son, their son, at center-stage. Sympathy for Sarah, even among those who take the moral point about her vulnerabilities, must have brought an image of her to mind.

The latter part of this chapter has been an exploration of how Jewish mosaic artists at Sepphoris chose to represent Abraham, Sarah, and Isaac and Ishmael both similarly and differently from those descriptions we possess in literary texts. Sharply evident in the work of the artists of the

Sepphoris synagogue are indications that the Jews knew themselves to be debating a scriptural story held in common with their rivals. Herbert Kessler's comments about the importance of the synagogue and its art illumine the interactions between religious communities that are this study's principal interest.

> What this new discovery tells us about the relationship of Jewish to Christian art during late antiquity, then, is appropriately complex. It supports the hypothesis that Christians may well have based some of their imagery on Jewish models; but it reminds us, as well, that they did so only within the polemics of who are the Chosen People. Moreover, it suggests that the Jews, in turn, deployed the shared pictorial repertory to stake out their own claims, particularly their faith that their covenant with God had not been abrogated but would, indeed, be renewed. And while Jews may well have taken the lead in deploying Roman artistic forms to their own religious purposes, by the 5th c. they seem to be following the Christians, or at least, to be in dialogue with them. The faceless Helios [in the Zodiac], the omission of Isaac carrying faggots, and even the spectacular representation of Aaron consecrating the Tabernacle might well be responses, not initiatives, in a debate over who was the true heir to God's grace, a debate conducted, in part at least, through pictures. Seen from this perspective, viewed through the lens of Christian art, the Sepphoris mosaic appears even more clearly and uniquely Jewish."[68]

In how many ways and with what intended goals did early Christian interpreters explore the scriptural story of Abraham's two women and their sons? We have already had glimpses of their viewpoint and tactics, but the next chapter treats more fully the manner in which churches' teachers and artists pressed the assertion that the story's meaning became clear only with and subsequent to the appearance of Jesus as God's annointed one—and Son. Two important factors were operative in the churches' appropriation of Abraham's narrative. First, it was Abraham, Sarah, and Isaac, and the covenant of God made available through them and their posterity that Christians laid claim to—not Abraham's other family. Second, originating as a sect within Judaism, believers that Jesus was God's promised messiah asserted that they had become God's favored people, and obviously found themselves immediately (and also permanently) in debate, conflict, and controversy with their parent religion. In the next chapter we shall become acquainted with the churches' determined efforts to Christianize Abraham, Sarah, and Isaac.

CHAPTER 5

⟡

Sarah and Hagar in Christian Retellings

When earliest believers that Jesus was God's messiah claimed that they were now God's covenant people, they were obliged to explain their relation to Abraham, and to his two women. A provocative observation by Elizabeth Clark is a good one to place over this chapter—and to test as we proceed:

> Exegeses of the stories of Hagar, Sarah, and Abraham by the church fathers were born of needs, as they perceived them, of their own days. . . . [Their] main concern is to defend the honor and reputation of Abraham, the forefather of the Messiah, often at the expense of the women with whom he shares the story. That Sarah and Hagar are "used" by the Fathers to illustrate other points of Christian theology shows, above all else, that however little concern they had for these female characters in their own right, they, like women elsewhere, were "good" for men "to think with."
>
> Elizabeth A. Clark, "Interpretive Fate and the Church Fathers"[1]

For Jews and Christians only the couple, Abraham and Sarah, and their son Isaac held central importance. With that "side" of the patriarch's family, the Bible made clear, God's covenant and its promises were operative. Sarah, then, had the status of revered matriarch—it was her son and his own offspring who were especially blessed. Christianity's assertion that it became that Abrahamic "family," the preferred and chosen people of God, was at the heart of Jewish-Christian debate and difference, and will occupy us in the following pages. Islam exults in the divine will that brought into being father Ibrahim the prophet, and celebrates especially Ishmael and his progeny, from whom continued that line of God's emmisaries through the centuries—down to the appearance of Muhammad. Hagar, at one point called "mother of the Arabs," is the wife of Ibrahim to whom Muslims give special honor.

We have seen the rabbis' judgments of Sarah and Hagar in conflict. What kinds of valuations of the two women did early Christians reach, and what became of their personae as scriptural characters when preachers, theologians, and artists expanded upon their identities and their significances? In particular, what interpretive fate will befall Hagar?

ST. PAUL ON SARAH AND HAGAR AND THEIR SONS
Galatians 4:21–31

No early Christian writer's use of Sarah and Hagar "to think with" was more influential than Paul's, even though two other passages in the New Testament effectively fashioned Sarah into the example of wifely obedience (1 Peter 3:6) and of life lived "by faith" (Hebrews 11:11).[2] The recipients of the Epistle to the Galatians, which Paul sent sometime in the early 50s CE, could only have been surprised by his analysis of the Sarah-Hagar story in his letter. Taking liberties with traditional Jewish understandings of the Genesis narrative, Paul radically reimagined Abraham's family in terms consistent with the revelation he himself had experienced. His conversion caused him to leave behind his "earlier life in Judaism" (an account of which he gives in Galatians 1:11–2:14) and become the "apostle [of God] to the Gentiles" (Galatians 2:8; Romans 11:13). Abraham and his family are thus interpreted in a way consistent with the "gospel for the uncircumcised" (2:7) that he preached, apparently persuasively, to the congregations in this area in Asia Minor.

The unexpected meanings Paul derives from the tale of Sarah and Hagar and their two sons have challenged commentators through the centuries, including modern scholars of the New Testament and those who investigate the history of relations between Jews and Christians. Large issues are at stake. Paul asserts in Galatians (1) that obedience to commands of God was not the basis upon which Abraham was "reckoned" or counted righteous; (2) that the revealed Mosaic law was a divine intervention necessary to God's dealings with his people, but that its purpose and effects had been surpassed in the removal of the "curse" upon humankind by Jesus's death on the cross; (3) that the law, which is impossible for men and women to obey in its entirety, is a negative weight, a burden, a form of slavery (a view peculiar to Paul among first-century Jewish teachers);[3] and (4) that "works" or deeds undertaken to satisfy the requirements of Judaic law have no bearing upon the salvation now made available to converts from "the nations," the Gentiles, who through Christ have become children of Abraham and sons and daughters of Abraham's God.

In this letter Paul responds in deep anger to what he has learned of recent events in the "churches of Galatia." When preaching there as one divinely sent he had converted a number of Gentiles to faith in Jesus as the Jewish God's agent of salvation, but subsequently and in his absence other missionaries had come to trouble the faithful there. These rival preachers proclaimed a "different gospel" and sought, he says, "to pervert the gospel of Jesus Christ" (*Galatians* 1:6–7). The revelation that Paul championed among them (when he first was in their midst as a missionary and now ever more firmly in this crisis-moment) was the "good news" that Gentile (polytheist) converts are claimed as God's own by their faith in Jesus Christ, and not through adherence to Jewish legal observance. Having been visited by God's spirit which worked miracles among them (*Galatians* 3:3–5), and having been ritually cleansed from false beliefs and destructive behaviors ("you were baptized into Christ" (*Galatians* 3:27)), these believers are now, together, a "new creation," no longer "Jew or Greek . . . slave or free . . . male or female . . . but one in Christ Jesus" (*Galatians* 3:27–28). Indeed, Paul asserts, the newly initiated faithful have become the authentic "Israel of God" (*Galatians* 6:14–18). Paul's announcement of what has been given to them—freedom from waywardness and the blessing of belonging to God—is threatened by the interlopers. Accordingly, he frames his letter as an *apologia*: that Greco-Roman genre of legal speech and writing designed to refute charges that have been brought.

What, specifically, is Paul protesting in his follow-up communiqué to the Galatian churches? The competing missionaries, with their deviant doctrine, were persuading (male) Gentile converts that to complete and confirm their new conviction that Jesus is their savior, it was necessary for them to become circumcised—to accept as an effective mark of their salvation the traditional sign of inclusion in God's covenant people.[4] Paul denounces his rival missionaries for their failure to understand and accept the new revelation and promise of God—both its accessibility to humankind, and its liberating force. "Accursed" promoters of this alien gospel in the Galatian churches will, he hopes, in their zeal for circumcising, somehow "castrate themselves" (*Galatians* 5:12).

The apostle's condemnation and curse falls also, though a bit less ferociously, upon those "foolish Galatians" who have been duped into taking up Jewish law and its obligations. To do so, he insists, is to forfeit the gift God gave to them in the life, suffering, death, and victory of Christ—that which, under the inspiration of Paul's preaching and teaching, inspired them and led them to their new and saving convictions. Reflective of his postconversion retrospection on his personal religious struggles, as E. P. Sanders convincingly demonstrated, Paul presents a picture of Judaic law that holds it to be a "yoke," a servitude that he is convinced *now* was removed when he came to acknowledge and to believe in Jesus, whose death on the cross entailed taking on himself the sin/"curse" that had separated humankind (and certainly the apostle himself) from God (*Galatians* 5:1, 3:10–14).[5]

Important to Paul's argument against the unwelcome teaching that Gentile believers in Jesus must undergo the Jewish practice of circumcision is his own doctrine that Abraham's right relationship with God came about through the patriarch's faith: "Abraham believed God, and it was reckoned to him as righteousness" (*Genesis* 15:6).[6] It was *not* through the patriarch's observance of divine requirements and demands that he was "justified." Paul's assertion carries the reminder that this encounter and transaction between Abraham and God *preceded* Abraham's circumcision, while it also states the fact (and Paul is adamant in underlining this) that Mosaic law "came four hundred thirty years later" (i.e., than "the promises made ... to Abraham and his offspring," as the preceding v. 16 notes). Sinai, he says, "does not annul a covenant previously ratified by God, so as to nullify the promise" (*Galatians* 3:17). The true gospel he brought to the churches in Galatia is at one with and fulfills its ancient biblical precedent:

> 3:7 So you see, those who believe are the descendants of Abraham. 8 And the scripture, foreseeing that God would justify the Gentiles by faith, declared the gospel beforehand to Abraham, saying, "All the Gentiles shall be blessed in you" [see *Genesis* 12:3; 18:18; 22:18]. 9 For this reason, those who believe are blessed with Abraham who believed.

Passionate and stark ideas and language make up Paul's rebuke to those who reject the truth of his declaration that those "baptized into Christ" no longer stand in need of the law's tutelage or discipline, but are "free" (3:23–29, 5:1–6), are sons and daughters of Abraham, "heirs according to the promise," and thereby "children of God through faith."

When he deploys as part of his *apologia* a retelling of who Sarah and Isaac, Hagar and Ishmael are—the clear lessons he sees in their story—Paul is an interpreter of scripture excited to meet his immediate challenge. The crisis in the congregations in Galatia dictates at every point what he chooses to highlight in his representation of Abraham's women and sons. Paul is impelled to adopt a mode of reading that reconstructs the Sarah-Hagar story in other than literal or historical terms.

The modern reader is struck, no less than the ancient was, by the emotional and intellectual ferocity in Paul's allegory and the verses surrounding it. Radiating from these lines is the forceful, daring, and often overstretched reasoning that is a polemicist's sharpest tool:

4:22 Tell me, you who desire to be subject to the law, will you not listen to the law? For it is written that Abraham had two sons, one by a slave woman and the other by a free woman. 23 One, the child of the slave, was born according to the flesh (*kata sarka*); the other, the child of the free woman, was born through the promise (*di' epaggelias*). 24 Now this is an allegory: these women are two covenants. One woman, in fact, is Hagar from Mount Sinai, bearing children for slavery. 25 Now Hagar is Mount Sinai in Arabia and corresponds to the present Jerusalem, for she is in slavery with her children. 26 But the other woman corresponds to the Jerusalem above; she is free and she is our mother. 27 For it is written,

> "Rejoice, you childless one, you
> who bear no children,
> burst into song and shout, you
> who endure no birth pangs;
> for the children of the desolate
> woman are more numerous
> than the children of the one
> who is married" [*Isaiah* 54:1 LXX].

28 Now you, my friends, are children of the promise, like Isaac.

29 But just as at that time the child who was born according to the flesh (*kata sarka*) persecuted the one born according to the spirit (*kata pneuma*), so it is now also. 30 But what does the scripture say?

"Drive out the slave and her child; for the child of the slave will not share the inheritance with the child of the free woman" [quoting *Psalms* 21:10 LXX, to which Paul has added the final phrase, "of the free woman"]. 31 So then, friends, we are children not of the slave but of the free woman.

A closely detailed exploration of this passage and scholarly debates surrounding it is not possible here. For our purposes it will suffice simply to underline Paul's major assertions—and to see in them a distinctive piece of biblical interpretation.

The passage's opening mode of rhetoric may be classified as diatribe—a pseudodialogue in which the speaker challenges the opponent and then provides, controls, or mutes his responses. Hence the challenging ridicule in Paul's invitation: So you want to cleave to the law. Then let us examine (which is to say: let me lay out for you in unmistakable terms) what the law says.[7] It is not the body of laws nor any particular law in the Torah that Paul then takes up, but rather what scripture teaches in a narrative—that of Abraham's women and sons. He is intent upon making elements in the story "stand for" and speak to the controversy at hand—one in which he argues for the Galatian believers' salvation "in the grace of Christ," rebutting his opponents' teachings, which "pervert the Gospel of Christ" (*Galatians* 1:7).

The dispute over the two definitions of being Christian being advocated in the churches of Galatia is the engine that drives Paul's searching out of contrasts between the two women, each with her son, and what they signify. Opposed are (1) a son marked by slavery and "flesh" versus a freeborn son whose birth fulfilled a divine promise; (2) two women (who "are" two covenants), one linked with Sinai and the Jerusalem of Paul's time, whose children are enslaved, versus the other who "corresponds to the Jerusalem above," she who is free and "our mother." Protecting the divine truth he "received … through a revelation of Jesus Christ" (*Galatians* 1:11–12), Paul's allegory discovers (or invents) contraries, and then sharpens them. Compared to what we have seen in rabbinical interpretations, and even viewed on its own terms as an argument advanced by a biblically informed Jew of the first century, the most startling element in Paul's treatment of Abraham's sons and women in vv. 24–26 is what becomes of Hagar. She signifies Mount Sinai—that is, the Law given to the Hebrews there in the age of Moses. (Paul's support of this curious attribution consists in his report that Sinai is in Arabia, the land with which he associates her, and in his further strict identification of the two: Hagar equals Mount Sinai. This latter construction is so perplexing and untenable as a claim issuing from either history or legend that we suspect that Paul is simply restating, by compression, his trope. Hagar, *or* Mount Sinai, "bear[s] children for slavery" [24.b]. The phrase is not so ambiguous as it is suggestive, and in two directions: it plays on Hagar's status as Sarah's servant—seeing her progeny also as "slaves, "and it points to conditions of life "under the law," in bondage to *that* covenant—that is, life that does not partake in the liberation won for Galatian converts. In choosing to be circumcised, the "foolish" in those churches are choosing to be "cut … off from Christ," who "has set [them] free" (*Galatians* 5:4; 5:1).

The hapless Hagar "corresponds to the present Jerusalem, for she is in slavery with her children" (25b). Enslaved Jerusalem is a metonym for Judaism—the panoply of its beliefs and its practices (and not, it seems, an allusion to Israel's past and present conditions of being invaded and governed by foreign rulers). The Torah covenant is, as Paul argues at various points in his letter, "slavery under the law" (see *Galatians* 3:22–25,

28; 4:1–10; 5:1). The description of Jerusalem and her people as "in slavery" constitutes one of Paul's strongest assaults on the Judaic law and its observers. He disparages in a single phrase precisely that revelation, vision, and community to which he had, until recently, been fully committed.

Paul's interpretation is stunningly contrary. Hagar, who in the scripture is no friend to, and certainly no willing participant in, the divine plan making Isaac and his progeny inheritors of the land promised by God, is here *identified* by Paul with that people of the old covenant. Her slave status qualifies her to represent, or rather, to *be* Jerusalem, Judaism, and its law, and it renders her the foremother of those held in thrall—Jews, and by extension, Gentile converts who resort to circumcision. This radical alteration in the identity and value of Hagar, strange and unprecedented as it is, works to Paul's advantage as a controversialist, and has its justification in that.

Sarah, by contrast, Paul divorces from association with the law or with any servitude "under it." She is free, and the Jerusalem she "corresponds to" is the heavenly, not earthly, one—the holy and transcendent city "above"—the imagined final home of the blessed.[8]

Sarah did not produce her son "naturally" (which is one connotation, for Paul, of "according to the flesh"), but "through the promise," and through its miraculous and divine fulfillment. Paul wants no one to be uncertain about the application of his allegory to the matters at hand in Galatia: "you, my friends, are children of the promise, like Isaac." Those adhering to the gospel Paul presented are heirs born of supernatural "promise" into the "freedom" of salvation, who travel, like their forefather, toward the superior Jerusalem: "And if you belong to Christ, then you are Abraham's offspring, heirs according to the promise" (5:29).

On the other side, Hagar, the present Jerusalem whose children are in bondage, the life according to the flesh which she begets, and "doing works of the law" (3:5) all stand for and identify people outside the saving covenant, unredeemed by God.

In verses 29 through 30 Paul offers an analogy that seeks to make parallel the circumstances of Isaac, of Paul, and of those followers of Jesus who side with him. Aware of the tradition we met in *Genesis Rabbah* that Ishmael "persecuted" Isaac, Paul suggests that his gospel and its adherents are likewise subjected to threat and hostility in "playing" with him. Paul probably refers both to what he regards as the torment he suffers from those Judaizing troublers of Gentile converts of Galatia and also other reported run-ins he and his devotees had experienced at the hands of Jewish foes of his teaching (cf. *1 Thessalonians* 2:15–16).⁹ In the face of such conflicts, he sees no other recourse except that action that was originally taken (*Genesis* 21:10): throw out the slave and her son, and deny to them the inheritance that belongs to "the child of the free woman." Paul is encouraging thoughts of expelling the advocates of circumcision who trouble the churches there, on the grounds that they have no right to the promises God has made available in Christ, but he settles for another division or polarity which he hopes will solidify and encourage his allies: "So then, friends, *we* [unlike our opponents in Galatia and the 'fools' who heed their teaching] are children, not of the slave, but of the free woman." In other words, those who stand with him and his teaching are the ones saved by God, while his opponents have taken upon themselves once more the slavery from which they were released by Christ's sacrificial death and his resurrection.

Again, the point and direction of Paul's allegorical contrast, this time focused on the "free woman," can be given blunt summarization: "Sarah = heavenly Jerusalem = Christianity," as Hans Dieter Betz put it in a formula.¹⁰ The lineage of the "family" enjoying God's particular favor now runs, at least as Paul presents the case here, from Abraham, Sarah, and Isaac to their children in the churches he has called into being. Paul's zeal for his gospel to the Gentiles, fervently articulated in his battle against the "circumcision party," drives a wedge between the new revelation to which he testifies, on the one hand, and Judaism, or any confidence people might put in the Mosaic covenant and the rewards of their faithful adherence to it. Israel's matriarch and her son, "born according to the spirit" and "according to the promise" are, in Paul's view of the history of salvation, coguarantors, with Abraham, of the divine pledge now given to those who will soon be known as "Christians" (*Acts* 11:26).

Romans 4:11–12, 18–21; 9:2–13

By no means a diatribe, Paul wrote *Romans* (ca. 58 CE) with objectives different from those in his letter to the Galatians, and in another mode—one appropriate to the addressees and to present circumstances.

Abraham *is* the model for "a person [who] is justified by faith apart from the works of the law" (*Romans* 3:28), but Paul's interpretation of him is altered. A different audience requires a different and particular approach. Here, when Paul turns to Abraham's story, his emphasis is shaped by his knowledge that both Jews and polytheists/Gentiles make up the chosen community that will greet him in Rome. We see this in a topic he takes up with care: the biblical testimony that Abraham was circumcised—but circumcised *after* his having been found righteous on the basis of his belief in God:

> 4:11 He received the sign of circumcision as a seal of the righteousness that he had by faith while he was still uncircumcised. The purpose was to make him the ancestor of all who believe without being circumcised and who thus have righteousness reckoned to them, 12 and likewise the ancestor of the circumcised who are not only circumcised but who also follow the example of the faith that our ancestor had before he was circumcised.

In this line of argument Paul does not at all have in mind the circumcision-tempted Gentile converts in Galatian churches. Rather, in his "longing to see" members of the Roman churches, he aspires to "share ... some spiritual gift to strengthen [them]" (1:11). One of his chief goals in writing his letter is to create room and complementarity, on biblical and theological grounds, for Gentile *and* Jewish believers in Jesus's messiahship. In pursuit of this goal he amplifies his teaching about what Abraham's circumcision signifies. Paul spells out the meaning of the patriarch's circumcision in terms directly pertinent to those he addresses: Jews who now call Jesus "lord," and count themselves members of "the body of Christ"—that is, congregation members—must count as *secondary* their circumcisions and their adherence to Jewish law, even though those covenant loyalties predate their adoption of new belief and function as holy "tradition" for them. What is *primary* and *essential*—namely, "the righteousness of God through faith in Jesus Christ for all who believe" (3:22)—stands as the key and saving datum. Their loyalty to, and observance of, the law, follows upon this and, in effect, serves only to confirm it: "[Abraham] received the sign of circumcision as a seal of the righteousness that he had by faith while he was still uncircumcised" (4:11).

Only two references to Sarah occur in *Romans*. Hagar goes unmentioned—an intriguing omission to be examined a bit later. In 4:19 Sarah's name appears as part of Paul's testimony to the steadfast trust Abraham had in God's pledge to him that he and his offspring would "inherit the world" (4:13). Paul recapitulates a part of the *Genesis* saga that he thinks very helpful to his letter's purposes:

> 4:18 Hoping against hope, he believed that he would become "the father of many nations," according to what was said, "So numerous shall your descendants be" [see *Genesis* 17:5 and 15:5]. 19 He did not weaken in faith when he considered his own body, which was already as good as dead (for he was about a hundred years old), or when he considered the barrenness of Sarah's womb. 20 No distrust made him waver concerning the promise of God, but he grew strong in his faith

as he gave glory to God, 21 being fully convinced that God was able to do what he had promised. Therefore his faith "was reckoned to him as righteousness."

Paul presents Sarah's barrenness as a descriptive "fact" which, taken alongside Abraham's old age and impotency, only makes her husband's hope more admirable. The Greek regularly rendered "barrenness" is, more literally, a phrase about the *nekrosis* (the deadness or the necrotic state) of her womb, and it is meant to echo Paul's use of the same word-root in calling Abraham's body "as good as dead." In this "note" about Sarah we surmise that Paul was aware of the discussions in rabbinic circles about whether Sarah was infertile (e.g., *Genesis Rabbah* XLV, above, pp. 129-131) and had taken a position on the question. *Genesis* itself reports only that at the time of God's promise of a son to be named Isaac, Abraham wondered (having fallen to the ground, laughing) whether this could happen when he was a hundred years old, and Sarah was ninety (17:17). Though Paul is working imaginatively and with theological intent, his mention of Sarah in 4:19 does not interpret her in the symbolic or allegorical mode. Drawing upon a tradition stemming from exegesis of the Torah, and using it as a "historical" datum, he presents Sarah simply as a woman incapable of pregnancy and childbirth, important insofar as her condition underlines the strength of Abraham's faith, and the wondrous nature of God's power in making the one he called forth from Ur "the father of many nations."

Though Sarah appears in *Romans* 9:9 only in a quotation of *Genesis*, she is there more richly interpreted (than in 4:19) simply by virtue of the passage's place in the midst of Pauline ruminations about God's promise. The surrounding ideas are quite familiar from what we met in the allegory (or at least in half of it) in *Galatians* 4. The "promise" is associated with the (new) covenant, with Sarah's son, and with the "Zion" to be entered when the "day" of judgment arrives, ushering in that salvation that Paul claims is "nearer to us now than when we became believers" (13:11).

The hard and painful question at issue for Paul: Will Israel, the elect of God, be among the redeemed?

9:2 I have great sorrow and unceasing anguish in my heart.

3 For I wish that I myself were accursed and cut off from Christ for the sake of my own people, my kindred according to the flesh.

4 They are Israelites, and to them belong the adoption, the glory, the covenants, the giving of the law, the worship, and the promises;

5 to them belong the patriarchs, and from them, according to the flesh, comes the Messiah, who is over all, God blessed forever. Amen. 6 It is not as though the word of God has failed. For not all Israelites truly belong to Israel, 7 and not

all of Abraham's children are his true descendants; but "It is through Isaac that descendants shall be named for you" (*Genesis* 21:12). 8 This means that it is not the children of the flesh who are children of God, but the children of the promise are counted as descendants. 9 For this is what the promise said, "About this time I will return and Sarah shall have a son" (*Genesis* 18:10, 14). 10 Nor is that all; something similar happened to Rebecca when she had conceived children by one husband, our ancestor Isaac. 11 Even before they had been born or had done anything good or bad (so that God's purpose of election might continue, 12 not by works but by his call) she was told, "The elder shall serve the younger" (*Genesis* 25:23). 13 As it is written, "I have loved Jacob, but I have hated Esau" (*Malachi* 1:2b–3a).

These lines, deploying passages of scripture as "proof texts" and argument-builders, are moving toward Paul's uncompromising declaration in 9:31–32 that "Israel, who did strive for [righteousness] that is based on the law, did not succeed in fulfilling that law," and thereby tripped on the stone God placed in Zion to "make people stumble," and they fell—that is, erred. But here, in 9:2–13, Paul puts his wish for the Jews' conversion to belief in dramatic personal terms, and acknowledges the hallowed glories constitutive of Israel's sacred history. There is a reserve clause even in this recital, however, for by repeating the phrase "according to the flesh," he maintains (though less abrasively than his formulation in the *Galatians* allegory did) the status, over against the ethnic and genetic reality of being Israelites, of those who are now, since Christ's coming, God's true sons and daughters "according to the spirit" or "the promise."

Sarah does her duty in the citation of *Genesis* 18:10, 14–15; she is the mother of the child who fulfills God's promise, an instrument in the plan of salvation for all of Abraham's sons and daughters in the generations stemming from Isaac. The other children of Abraham are not included; Ishmael and his posterity must be most prominently in Paul's mind. But that is not the distinction Paul is most anxious to make at this point in his message to Roman believers. Rather, he is keen to communicate his insight, the fruit of the revelation he received, that those are of Isaac's seed who are children of the promise. "Children of the flesh," on the other hand, are not "counted as descendants" and are not "children of God" (v. 8). God's favor and parenthood hinge not on genetics, but on God's promise as it is given and received. Paul's chosen term, "promise" (*eppangelia*), is a stand-in for "covenant" (*diatheke*), which he does not want to employ; he is intent upon maintaining the difference, central to his understanding of God and salvation, between God's compact with Abraham and his later covenant with Moses, articulated in the law.[11] Only those belong to the seed of Abraham and "count as descendants" who have come to know God's promise, and

have responded—that is, responded by faith and in believing, *not* by undertaking deeds meant to comply with and satisfy the law's demands. By Paul
now redefined and reconfigured as people "born" according to the promise, or spiritually, the descendants and heirs of Isaac have in common not
simply their act of believing (as opposed to efforts at law-obedience), but a
necessarily content-specific conviction: that the Jew according to the flesh,
Jesus, who was crucified and raised up, is none other than God's "messiah,
who is over all."

Counterposing the election of Israel "according to the flesh," with which
he began the passage, to the election of those who, in accepting Jesus as
God's messiah, are children of "the promise," Paul interprets Sarah as he had
in the allegory of his earlier letter: she and her son Isaac, with Abraham, are
the true—that is, the spiritual—forebears of Jews and Gentiles who hear
and believe in the gospel that he, the apostle, preaches.

Paul inserts an additional interpretive twist in 9:10–13 by seeking
enforcement for his claims in the procreative history of Isaac. God's "promise" or election was at work in the case of the sons Rebecca bore him, for
God's word declared that the first of the twins to be born would serve the
second-born. From the prophetic book *Malachi* Paul provides another supportive divine declaration, this one about God's love (or favor, or choice) of
Jacob, and his hatred (or disfavor, or passing over) of Esau. Paul is championing God's freedom to act, and to prefer and elect particular persons
and peoples for his care and protection, "even before they had been born
or had done anything good or bad" (9:11). Covenants are given, or enacted,
Paul again insists, by divine initiative, and do not originate in, nor continue
by, the "logic" or mechanics of human deeds—that is, by "works" that are
assumed to earn God's attention and effect reconciliation with him.

A piece of unfinished business lingers at the end of our treatment of
Paul on Abraham's women. Why is Hagar, so serviceable in his letter to
the Galatian churches, absent from his *Epistle to the Romans*? Why did
he choose to exclude from the presentation of the gospel message he
was forecasting to the Roman Christians his characterization of Hagar
in *Galatians* 4 as "from Mount Sinai, bearing children for slavery....
correspond[ing] to the present Jerusalem"? We have seen that the heat of
his earlier assault on "Judaizers" of Gentile converts inspired his strained,
even bizarre, connection of the woman and son expelled by Abraham with
Judaism and the Law. This allegorical association made no real sense in
terms of the historical legends surrounding her, and therefore signaled
the exegete's reach for a forceful interpretation, however novel. Paul
worked in *Galatians* to distinguish through oppositional images the freedom won for people of the "nations" from what he depicts as the "slavery"
of Judaism.

In the Roman community of believers, he has a much different appeal to make. The association of followers of Jesus who understand themselves as having been called into existence before the eschaton's arrival is made up of Jews *and* Gentiles. Dissension or confusion is not the presented reason for Paul's writing, as it had been in his correspondence with the churches in Galatia, Thessalonica, and Corinth. Together, and by virtue of their common faith in God-sent Jesus the Christ, the believers in Rome, as Paul seems (or hopes) to see them, make up the new people of God, enjoying unity. They are one people "since God is one; and he will justify the circumcised on the ground of faith and the uncircumcised through that same faith" (3:31). In language he would not have used in addressing turmoil afflicting the Galatian churches, he adds: "Do we then overthrow the law by this faith? By no means, on the contrary, we uphold the law." Paul means that he upholds the law for Jews as a confirmation, a sealing, of that righteousness granted to them, on the basis of their faith, by God.

This difference in Paul's audience and thus in his viewpoint, with its emphasis on an inclusive gospel, dictated that Paul *not* employ the Hagar half of his Sarah-Hagar allegory, for though his making her into a metaphor for Judaic law which enslaves and for Jerusalem in bondage spoke to the controversy in Galatia, that argument could only undermine his effort to assure Roman Christians of "the continuing validity of Israel in God's purpose."[12]

Paul's insistence that believers in Jesus enjoyed a convenant with God that superseded the former was destined to stir deep contention and animosity in all subsequent historical seasons of interactions between Jews and Christians. To be historically conscious and conscientious, we are obliged to see this line of reasoning—that is, that members of churches were the covenant people, having taken the place of the Jews who rejected God's messiah—in the context which prompted him to write his letter to the Jesus-followers in Rome. His confident vision of God's most recent actions is that of a first-century Jew who was compelled (miraculously, by his own account) to believe in Jesus as God's agent of salvation—the redeemer of Paul himself, of all the nations, and of those Jews who would honor Jesus as their "lord."

Paul the apostle of Christ *did* in fact use Sarah and Hagar "to think with," presenting both women as representative of something other than "female characters in their own right," as *Genesis* might be said to portray them. Paul's allusions—and adjustments—to Abraham's women, especially in his aggravated letter to the churches in Galatia, symbolize them as figures for spiritual promise, in the case of Sarah, and of enslavement and exclusion from God's saving covenant, in the case of Hagar.

Will we find significant differences in the way one of early Christianity's most stellar scripture scholars (and a deep admirer of Paul) retells the story of Abraham's household, and the conflict between his two wives?

ORIGEN'S *GENESIS HOMILY VII: ON THE BIRTH OF ISAAC AND THE FACT THAT HE IS WEANED*

By the time, around 240, that Origen (ca. 185–254) was regularly preaching to a congregation in the port city Herod had built, Caesarea Maritima, he was a man of significant and widespread reputation.[13] Reports of his life circulated and grew after his death, as we know from a biographical sketch in Eusebius's *Ecclesiastical History*, written before the mid-fourth century, and from notices penned by other Christian writers. He was remembered as a boy in Alexandria whose father's martyrdom inspired in him a desire for the same fate. His zeal for the Christian life (increasingly imagined by some in his circles in ascetic terms) led to his choice as a young man to become, through castration, a "eunuch for the kingdom of heaven"—that is, a person endeavoring to guard against the lures and distractions of sexual appetites. The admiration and authority he gained as a Christian rhetor-philosopher and catechist in Alexandria was a factor in a wrangle with his bishop, Demetrius, and eventually led to his relocation from Egypt to Caesarea Maritima in Palestine. There he was ordained a presbyter and spent the last two decades of his career, having among his duties regular preaching to a Christian congregation in the "liturgy of the word" which preceded the communion meal. Fortunately for us, after a time he allowed stenographers to record his sermons.

What follows is an experiment—a case study in Origen's approach to reading scripture as observed in a single brief sermon, one devoted to our story. In the tracking, point-by-point, of his homily's line of reasoning and the strategies it employs, we have interests that have already been identified. How do his exegetical interests in Sarah and Hagar compare with those of Paul? In what ways does Origen distinguish between and manipulate the kinds of meaning that center on the *Genesis* text's storyline in its literal sense, on the one hand, and those that are symbolic or metaphorical, on the other? In what comes to expression as preached scriptural commentary made accessible for a group of listeners, does his concern for the symbolic meanings overwhelm or abandon the text's historical level of meaning? And we have the larger question of this chapter in view: is it the case that Origen's penchant for underlining spiritual meanings in a sacred story results in a distinguishable early Christian retelling of the story—when compared with the interpretive strategies of rabbinic and Muslim commentators?

Origen's three-year cycle of sermons devoted to texts of the Old Testament included his homily devoted to *Genesis* 21:1–21, the scripture portion recounting the events from Isaac's birth to the trial in the wilderness suffered by Hagar and her son. Its most accurate and succinct title would be, as a biblical scholar labeled this portion of *Genesis*, "Isaac's birth, Ishmael's Expulsion."[14]

About Origen's presuppositions in approaching biblical interpretation we need still more introduction. God's wisdom fills scripture and supports believers in accordance with their current capacities to understand. There is guidance—and salvation—for those who read or hear the text "plainly," in its explicit language. More profound comprehension of God's wisdom awaits those who grow in their abilities to consider the Bible's revelations with increasing care and discernment. Those messages which invite students of scripture closest to the mystery of God's goodness and help are not obvious. Even the silences in scripture are pregnant. When waxing theoretical about this in his *On First Principles*, he wrote:

> One must portray the meaning of the sacred writings in a threefold way upon one's own soul, so that the simple man may be edified by what we may call the flesh of the scripture, this name being given to the obvious interpretation; while the man who has made some progress may be edified by its soul, as it were; and the man who is perfect and like those mentioned by the apostle: "We speak wisdom among the perfect. . . ."—this man may be edified by the spiritual law, which has "a shadow of the good things to come." For just as man consists of body, soul, and spirit, so in the same way does the scripture, which has been prepared by God to be given for man's salvation.[15]

Such are some of the key assumptions informing Origen's writings and those of his oral teachings that survive. His advice is plain: if you intend to be a Christian, be prepared to follow Jesus's precept, "Search the scriptures" (*John* 5:39). Be prepared also to be changed from a child to an adult, from a person whose mode of perception is carnal to one who thinks and sees in a way that is spiritual—who prayerfully reads with eyes opened and upturned.

In this sermon, Origen regularly and firmly declares the rules of the game in encountering scripture. He warns. He teases. He goads the congregation: Are you content with the scripture's most obvious and literal sense? Are you up to the challenge of digging for significant meanings when you encounter in the biblical narrative elements that strike you as unedifying or illogical?

You will not hear what God is telling you in this story of Abraham's family, Origen regularly asserts, unless you press for its deepest meanings, which contain truths relating to you in your own existence. A biblical narrative does not reveal God in its ancient storyness alone, says the preacher: in and through scripture you are being addressed—summoned into your full, mature faith and beckoned toward your Lord.

Origen's homily commences not with a reference to an opening verse in the day's text, *Genesis* 21, but with a prayer that alludes to Paul's teaching about how believers are (and are not) to read and hear scripture:

> Moses is read to us in church. Let us pray [to] the Lord lest, in accordance with the Apostle's word, even with us, "when Moses is read the veil be upon" our "heart."[16]

Origen no doubt hoped that some in the congregation, hearing his invocation, would recall the content of *2 Corinthians* 3:12–18, in which Paul makes the veil that Moses wears in *Exodus* 34 into a metaphor for Israel's current blindness to "the Lord." Imploring both the Lord and the members of his church that this Jewish veil or misunderstanding not obscure "even to us" the text and the sermon, the preacher is asking for a particularly Christian encounter with Moses—that is, with this day's scriptural message from God. Origen's prefatory prayer baldly identifies a wrong way to hear and comprehend scripture, and warns against that misguided way of interpreting, and the people who practice it. It reminds his congregants immediately of who they are as an assembled group (in contradistinction to "Israel").

Significant also in his opening prayer and admonition is that it reveals what he believes about levels or tiers that are involved in pursuit of meaning—levels present both in the sacred story itself and in those in his flock who might learn and be affected by it.

Turning to *Genesis* 21, Origen summarizes its opening verses: Abraham, at a hundred years old, conceived Isaac; Sarah wonders aloud who will inform Abraham that she nurses a child. In a presumed "dialogue" with his audience, the preacher pauses first to consider what is striking in 21:4: "And then Abraham circumcised the child on the eighth day." Origen comments on the fact that it is not Isaac's birthday that is celebrated with "a great feast" (21:8), but the day of his weaning.

> Why? Do we think that it is the Holy Spirit's intention to write stories and to narrate how a child was weaned and a feast was made, how he played and did other childish things? Or should we understand by these things that he wishes to teach us something divine and worthy that the human race might learn from the words of God?[17]

Origen continues his exhortative theme: let us look and listen for the nobler meanings which the Holy Spirit has placed in our scripture; to do otherwise is to remain child-like, to be aware chiefly of our bodily senses, to languish in our carnal states, and worst of all, to miss the feast awaiting the weaned, the spiritual.

Proceeding to the *Genesis* passage's next comment-worthy item, Origen recapitulates the few verses recounting the "play" of Ishmael with Isaac, Sarah's anger (this play is a "disaster" (*pernicium*) to her) inspires her demand that "the bondwoman" be cast out, so that Ishmael not be coinheritor with Isaac. The preacher postpones consideration of these verses (21:8–10) until he can consult Paul, for he wants to probe his mentor's allegory of the two mothers and their sons. How, he wonders aloud, should we take the apostle's words in *Galatians* 4:21–24, where Paul gives contrasting characterizations of the two sons—Ishmael "born of the flesh" and Isaac born "by the promise"?

Is it literally true, Origen asks, that Isaac was *not* born naturally—"according to the flesh"? Wasn't he born from Sarah, circumcised in the flesh, and did he not play with Ishmael "humanly"? What is Paul driving at? Origen observed that "He called things 'allegorical' which were quite obviously done in the flesh."

> His purpose is that we might learn how to treat other passages, and especially these in which the historical narrative appears to reveal nothing worthy of the divine law.[18]

Simultaneously endorsing and interrogating Paul's symbolic interpretation of the passage, Origen seizes the moment to state one of his interpretive principles: some biblical narratives contain no important or "worthy" sense, when read in the literal-historical register of meaning, and these, therefore, beg further examination. As Origen had written some fifteen to twenty years earlier about "the inspiration of divine scripture":

> Our contention with regard to the whole of divine scripture is that it all has a spiritual meaning, but not all has a bodily meaning. . . . Consequently the person who reads the divine books reverently, believing them to be divine writings, must exercise great care.[19]

Sense next has to be made of Paul's remark that as Ishmael "persecuted him who was according to the spirit, so also it is now" (*Galatians* 4:17). Origen argues that the apostle's point was "that in all things the flesh is opposed to the spirit." He wants to move his hearers to consider the several forms this opposition might take, and how close to their own life-situations persecution comes "now." It is possible, he declares, to imagine persecutions in cases involving two quite different peoples or nations, one carnal and the other spiritual. (To this type of conflict he will return.) But within our own community, he says, one finds opposition between members—some who are flesh-bound against some who are spiritual. Persecution and hostility between the brothers, Abraham's sons, is, upon more thoughtful scrutiny, not simply in the past but in our present and, indeed, among and within us:

> For even you, if you live "according to the flesh," are a son of Hagar and for this reason are opposed to these who live "according to the spirit." Or even if we inquire in ourselves, we find that "the flesh lusts against the spirit and the spirit against the flesh and these are contrary to one another" (cf. *Galatians* 5:17). . . . Do you see how great the battles of the flesh against the spirit are?[20]

In suggesting that his hearers can *be* Ishmael, Origen is not speaking, like Paul, to first-century Galatian Jesus-followers conflicted over the place of Jewish observance in their personal and communal life. Rather, his audience consists of third-century Christians conscious of who they are—one group within a religiously diverse populace in a seaport city. He has been transposing Paul's "Jewish" Ishmael—carnal and thus enslaved—into a category applicable to his Christian hearers and the tests and temptations met in their moral and spiritual lives.

However, when he next refers to a still more difficult battle than the ones he has just identified—namely against those "who understand the law 'according to the flesh'"—his audience knows that he is targeting the Jewish community and its leaders—people for whom, as Origen sees things, "spiritual discernment" is out of reach. His anti-Jewish criticism, Pauline, but now Origen's own, surfaces again at this point, but not for the last time in his sermon.

The preacher trains his eye once again on his own listeners, and prepares them to take on another name and a better identity. In a series of conditional phrases ("if you have in yourself," "If only you can say," "if you can be such") he reiterates the challenge that the day's reading poses: as in your carnality you can be Ishmael, being "joint heirs with him who was 'born according to the flesh,' so too you can be Isaac"—"heirs indeed of God, and joint heirs with Christ" (*Romans* 8:17). To which of Abraham's sons do you wish to be related? If it is to the son of "the promise," will you act resolutely upon this choice of yours? Isaac and Ishmael, spoken of as differently "born," have been made subjects for tropological, or moral, exegesis. The hearers are to choose between the two lives that Abraham's sons represent.

Another unexpected and unexplained item in the day's reading catches the preacher's attention. A silence in the text raises questions. What could possibly have been involved in the "playing" of the two boys that so angered Sarah, causing her to demand expulsion of the "son of the bondwoman"? "Certainly no persecution of Ishmael against Isaac is related to have been undertaken, except this play of the infant alone."[21] Origen attributes to Paul an explanation that recasts and idealizes Sarah, and accordingly frames the imagined interactions of the boys at play. If the flesh, or carnality, which Ishmael stands for, "attracts the spirit, which is Isaac, and deals with him with enticing deceitfulness, [and] if it allures him with delights. . . . this kind of play of the flesh with the spirit offends Sarah especially, who is virtue."[22]

Having made the cause of Sarah's anger at the boys' playing into a lesson meant to give ethical guidance, Origen can now ask his hearers to consider Ishmael-like persecutions they themselves have suffered—or committed. He is provocatively conversational.

> You, therefore, O hearer of these words, do not suppose that that alone is persecution whenever you are compelled by the madness of the pagans to sacrifice to idols. But if perhaps the pleasure of the flesh allures you, if the allurement of lust sports with you, flee these things as the greatest persecution if you are a son of virtue. Indeed, for this reason the Apostle also says: "Flee fornication [*1 Corinthians* 6:18]." But also if injustice should attract you, so that, accepting "the countenance of the mighty [Cf. *Leviticus* 19:15]," and because of his artful twisting you render an unjust judgment, you ought to understand that under the guise of play you suffer a seductive persecution in injustice. But you shall also consider it a persecution of the spirit by individual guises of evil, even if they are pleasant and delightful and similar to play, because in all these virtue is offended.[23]

Genesis 21:11–21 describes the fortunes of Ishmael and Hagar, and Origen's interpretation makes room for a new set of insights—ones triggered by details and images in the story of the banished pair. While continuing to use Paul's allegorizing to develop more of his own, Origen introduces a thematic counterpoint, one that, as John Thompson observed in his *Writing the Wrongs*, renders "Hagar truly enigmatic"—and not the object of scorn that the Apostle made her out to be.[24]

A hint of this is present in Origen's treatment of *Genesis* 11–13, where Abraham requests God's consideration for his older son, and receives divine reassurance. Origen at this point thinks about Abraham's sons in a way that qualifies the strict opposition posed in *Galatians* 4:22–29. He is paying heed to what the *Genesis* text literally reports. Ishmael does not become his father's heir, yet "he receives gifts and is not sent away empty."

While Isaac may obtain "the promise," Ishmael is granted a "blessing." Isaac "becomes the people of adoption," but Ishmael becomes "a great nation." There is spiritual sense to be made of the different boons granted to the sons, and the preacher proceeds to identify two groups *within* the Christian church who have become sons of "Abraham": there are "some [who] cling to God on the basis of love, others on the basis of dread and fear of future judgment."[25] The former were born of Abraham and "the free woman," while the latter (the types of the son of the bondwoman) are like one "who keeps the commandments not in perfect love, but … in fear of punishment." Dramatic, consistent warnings about the fiery torment awaiting unbelievers had prompted the pagan philosopher Celsus to tease the Christians for thinking of their God as a periodic "cook" (Origen, *Against Celsus* 5: 14)— and years later Origen gives evidence that the conviction of a dreadful judgment day *is* one in which many Christians are deeply invested. Here he compares two forms of faithfulness—one enjoyed in the freedom of love, and the other, an inferior type, characterized by "slavish fear." The contrast is sharp. Nevertheless, though Ishmael and the Ishmael-like are presented as imperfect, that is, cheerless and judgment-wary sons of Abraham, they are (in his exegesis here) incorporated in the family of God (those "who come to the recognition of God by faith"). Origen's application of his reading recalibrates Ishmael the "blessed" and those Christians like him, even if they have not been fully liberated into the covenant promise. The combination of close attention to what *Genesis* tells about Ishmael's gift from God and his desire to expose two expressions of faith found among people in his congregation moves Origen at least momentarily to an estimate of Ishmael that is not nearly so uncompromisingly negative as Paul's.

Origen then invites his congregation to ponder the expulsion scene:

> Let us see what Abraham does meanwhile after Sarah is displeased. He casts out the bondwoman and her son, but nevertheless gives him a bottle of water. For his mother does not have a well of living water, nor could the boy draw water from a well. Isaac has wells for which he also suffers strife against the Philistines; but Ishmael drinks water from a bottle, but this bottle, as it is a bottle, fails, and therefore, he is thirsty and does not find a well.[26]

Like the rabbis with whom he sometimes discussed scripture, Origen considers his *Genesis* passage with an eye and ear to other biblical texts. He has mentally scanned them, evaluating their homiletic utility. At this juncture in his sermon, scriptural references to bottle, water, and wells suggest creative possibilities. The saying of Jesus to the Samaritan woman at the well about "living water" has become part of the interpretation he will offer, as has the *Genesis* narrative's story in chapter 26 of the wells that Isaac reclaimed (they had once belonged to Abraham) and protected. Because it will serve the argument he wants to advance, Origen alters a detail in the biblical text, having Abraham give the water bottle to Ishmael rather than to his mother (whereas *Genesis* 21:14 relates that the Patriarch "took bread and a skin of water, and gave it to Hagar"). Literal and figural meanings are operating in parallel as Origen describes Hagar as one not possessing "a well of living water" and as he notes that her son was unable to draw water from a well. These motifs are recognizable from the account of Hagar's and Ishmael's dire circumstance in the wilderness (*Genesis* 21:15–16). At the story's literal level, there is that plight to be registered, but another crisis exists at the spiritual level, for it is "living" water that Origen says Hagar does not have access to, while Ishmael is equipped only with the bottle, now empty. The contrast Origen makes with Isaac's wells is at once "factual" and spiritual—even ideological. Abraham's son by Sarah is of "the promise," the primary beneficiary of God's providential care, the begetter of "the people of adoption." He has rights to his father's wells. On the other hand, blessed and destined to be father of "a great nation" though he may be, Ishmael is here again pictured as being, in comparison with his younger brother, inferior in status and significance. Indeed, the water bottle he receives, soon to be empty, puts his life (and that of Hagar) at risk, endangering God's claim about his future. The *Genesis* narrative and elements from Paul's allegory are interwoven but distinct.

Origen turns the lessons he spies in this portion of the text in the direction of his sermon's main themes. You are not like desperate Ishmael, unable to find a well, he tells people in his congregation. You are a son (or daughter) "of promise, as Isaac." Origen rings in *Proverbs* 5:15–16, with its urging that those who aspire to wisdom should drink from their own abundant wells, and benefit from the waters that flow in their streets.[27] He is gearing this image of abundant wells to his present emphasis, which reiterates Paul's use of the two sons of Abraham to draw boundaries between opposing religious beliefs and behaviors. Now, in Origen's era and setting, the sons represent Judaism and Christianity.

> He "who is born according to the flesh" drinks water from a bottle and the water itself fails him and he lacks in many things. The bottle of the Law is the letter from which that carnal people drinks, and thence receives understanding. This letter frequently fails them. It cannot extricate itself; for the historical understanding (*historialis intelligentia*) is defective in many things. But the Church drinks from the evangelic and apostolic fountains which never fail, but "run in the streets," because they always abound and flow in the breadth of spiritual

interpretation (*spiritalis interpretationis*). The Church drinks also "from wells" when it draws and examines certain deeper things of the Law.[28]

Having registered his claim about Judaism's lack of "evangelic and apostolic fountains,"—that is, that it has not believed in the one who promises "living water"—the preacher turns toward his concluding assertions, which expound upon water, wells, and women.

The mystery of the "deeper things" that Christians find in spiritual interpretation sheds light on an episode Origen is anxious to insert in his treatment of what befall Hagar in the wilderness. As a Logos-theologian in the tradition of Justin Martyr, Clement of Alexandria (his predecessor as a catechist there), and others, Origen presumes that when God appears and is heard in Jewish scripture, this is not the high God himself, who in his transcendence is by nature invisible and incomprehensible, but rather God's "Word"/Logos who speaks, appears in angelic form, and who, as God the Son, will "in the fullness of time" be enfleshed as Jesus. There is for Origen no real theological distance between the appearance of the angel-agent who speaks with despairing Hagar, reassuring her that God has "heard" or "heeded" the voice of "the boy where he is," and Jesus's appearance to the Samaritan woman. God visible and audible is, for him and others in his faith community, the Word, who became incarnate in Jesus Christ. The preacher's dominant interest here is in juxtaposing the one dialogue with the angel in *Genesis* 21:17–19 that leads to Hagar's eyes being opened to see a saving well of water (preserving the hope of Ishmael becoming "a great nation") with the episode in *John* 4:7–15 in which a Samaritan woman drawing water from Jacob's well is engaged by Jesus in a discussion about the "living water" he provides—the quickening water she asks him to give to her.

How far will the preacher take this connection between the Samaritan woman, who recognizes Jesus as a prophet, receiving his testimony that he is the promised messiah of God, with desperate Hagar? The two stories have epiphanies of water and a well in common. Hagar leaves Ishmael to himself in order not to see his dying, and while she weeps at a distance an angel appears, telling her: "God has heeded the cry of the boy where he is. Come, lift up the boy and hold him by the hand, for I will make a great nation of him" (*Genesis* 21:17–18). In the next verse we read that "God opened her eyes and she saw a well of water." Origen's license as preacher and exegete enables him to insinuate and apply the Johannine phrase (concerning the water that rescues and preserves life) to Ishmael and Hagar. This, Jesus declares, will become, in those who drink it, "a spring of water gushing up to eternal life" (*John* 4:14).[29]

Origen asserts that Jesus declared to the Samaritan woman "as if he were speaking with Hagar herself," that the one "who shall drink of the water which I give . . . shall not thirst forever." To read the Hagar story in the light of Jesus's promise of "living water," the preacher insists, is to be in the community that "draws and examines deeper things from the Law."[30]

What may have seemed to his hearers (and to moderns) an unexpected, even arbitrary connection of two women and two wells and two rescues flows easily from Origen's repertoire as theologian-exegete-preacher. He capitalizes on obvious but useful and suggestive correspondences. We notice that Origen, renowned for his spiritualizing strategies in exegesis, pays close attention to Hagar's "historical" actions and attitudes, as biblically narrated, and that these observations play a strong role in his representation of her. Her wailing and tears are seen, as the text makes clear, as worthy of divine attention. What John Thompson refers to as "literal Hagar" is in the preacher's mind, and he departs sharply from the negative caricature of her in Paul's allegory, obliged to do so by the content of the *Genesis* text read "historically," for it tells of the good outcome for Hagar and Ishmael in their wilderness ordeal. Origen *is* using Hagar "to think with," but his interpretation of Hagar is not strictly nor exclusively metaphorical and spiritual. His close attention to her actions in the *Genesis* text allows him to keep in sight the woman's "history"—her description in scripture as a character "in [her] own right."[31]

"Allegorical" Hagar does not fare nearly so well, however, as Origen employs her in what he must hope will be a rousing conclusion to his homily. He wonders aloud what significance lies in the biblical claim that the Lord "opened Hagar's eyes":

> How can these words be related to history? For when do we find [in the text] that Hagar has closed eyes and they are later opened? Is not the spiritual and mystical meaning of these words clearer than light, that that people which is "according to the flesh" is abandoned and lies in hunger and thirst, suffering "not a famine of bread nor a thirst for water, but a thirst for the word of God" [see *Amos* 8:11] until the eyes of the synagogue are opened?[32]

Once more a detail in the *Genesis* text—here, something unexplained—sparks an interpretive move. There is no mention of Hagar's blindness or closed eyes preceding their opening, and thus only a metaphorical meaning will suffice. Origen reverts to Paul's association of Hagar with the law that enslaves, but the word that mobilizes his argument derives from *Romans* 11:25, where the Apostle seeks to explain why a "blindness" (or, "hardening of heart") has come upon part of Israel. This lack of vision, Paul asserts, abides until all the Gentiles are incorporated in God's plan, and then "all Israel will be saved." Until the blindness, which is the "veil of the letter," is taken away by God's angel, she—Israel (Hagar's nonliteral, allegorical signifier)—cannot, or will not, see the "living water" offered to her. The final denunciation is stark: "For now the Jews lie around the well itself, but their eyes are closed and they cannot drink from the well of the Law and the prophets."[33]

In the end, as in the beginning of his homily, Origen's criticism, judgment, and warning against Judaism is also brought closer to home—replayed—in an admonition directed to Christians. We Christians too, he says, lie around the well. We hold and read the divine scriptures, "but we do not touch upon the spiritual sense." The "literal" Hagar is enlisted as a model and inspiration. Origen suggests: Maybe there is a need among us, the faithful, for "tears and incessant prayer that the Lord may open our eyes."[34]

Yet another coupling of a passage in the day's reading from Moses with an incident in a Gospel serves the preacher's purpose: even the blind men in Jericho (*Matthew* 20:30) would not have received their sight had they not cried out to the Lord, like Hagar in her desperate need. While quick to reassure his listeners that he is not claiming that their eyes have not been opened, Origen nonetheless states his fear that awakened members of his church may close their eyes again, falling into a slumber so deep that they cannot be "watchful in the spiritual meaning." Or, though aware of dangerous temptations, these may not stir them to labor, to avoid sleep and to "contemplate things which are spiritual." Or they might fall into the errors that beset "the carnal people set around the water itself." A word from the prophet David (*Psalms* 131:4–5) can only be heard as an exhortation: Until a believer "finds a place for the Lord, a tabernacle for the God of Jacob," he will not, or should not, sleep nor slumber. Origen proclaims that this tabernacle is to be fashioned and found within the individual Christian, enlightened and encouraged by things "divine and worthy that the human race might learn from the words of God." Throughout his homily, and emphatically here at its conclusion, Origen promotes his belief that spiritual maturation and the advance toward all that God promises to his people is effected primarily through deepened insight into divine writings. To learn how to hear and to heed God's words in the sacred texts is to become spiritual and free—to be saved.

Origen has reiterated the assertion vital to early Christians that they are heirs of God's covenant promises made to Abraham, continued through Isaac and Jacob. And yet, more than some Christian exegetes and theologians were inclined to do, Origen's sermon revealed his concern to honor the blessing given to Ishmael, ensuring that from him would come a strong nation. This motif, which underlines divine favor shared (though differentiated as greater and lesser), is born of Origen's loyalty to what *Genesis* relates, and it resists (at least in that moment in the sermon) the stark contrast that in Paul's allegory in *Galatians* pits the sons against each other—the one free and saved, the other enslaved and condemned. Of course Origen accepts and enunciates the already entrenched and necessary claim of the church that believers in Christ have been "adopted" as children of Abraham and are heirs of the divine boons given to them. In the imagery of his sermon, the Jews have failed to drink from the well of scripture, and have put themselves at a distance from God—the God now understood as the one who in Jesus Christ provides the "living water" guaranteeing eternal life. Because in Origen's day the Christians enjoy stronger self-definition as a recognized and distinct religion, he spends as much time applying these kinds of arguments to tensions within the churches as he does to tensions between Jews and Christians. Yes, the members of churches are now *exclusively* the children of Abraham and Sarah, through Isaac and Jacob, yet Origen insists that it is *within* Christian communities, in the ethical practices of individual Christians, and even in the ways believers cling to God (in "slavish fear" or in "the freedom of love") that people work out which son—Ishmael or Isaac—they most resemble. Origen's scriptural interpretation by no means ignores the zone of religious competition in which he lives and works. However, he writes and speaks to Christians, and turns the biblical wisdom that he finds inward—directing it to the multifaceted churches and the multifaceted individuals making up their number.

The women of Abraham, in Origen's retelling, are often, it is true, recognizable in their similarity to other idealized and allegorized representations by other authors. And yet, because Origen is obliged to read completely and to work through the day's lection from *Genesis*, he breaks from Paul's one-dimensional caricature of Hagar, including her among those whose eyes opened to see (and to drink from) the well that gives salvation. Likewise, the "blessing" that in scripture God gives to Ishmael is not bypassed, and the elder son is at least briefly, or qualifiedly, presented (contra Paul) as one among those who enjoy God's favor.

The frame for our exploration of Origen's sermon and its interpretive strategy is a comparative analysis of how sacred stories were retold in antiquity in three different religious communities. We have seen Origen and his thinking, especially about Judaism, in the historical context of the "parting of the ways" between Jews and Christians as that separation had advanced in the third century.[35] Origen's treatment of Abraham's women displays not only his dexterous imagination, but also the vibrant multireligious world in which he made sense for himself and for his fellow believers by pursuing Jesus's admonition to "search the scriptures."

CHRISTIAN ARTISTS' INTERPRETATIONS OF ABRAHAM'S WOMEN
The Ashburnham Pentateuch

Unique in early Christian iconography is the following depiction (Figure 5.1) of the conflict between Sarah and Hagar:

A compression of the actions familiar to us from *Genesis* 21:8–13 (and from Origen's sermon), the painted image has both Hagar and Sarah present, standing before the seated Abraham. Ishmael and Isaac also faintly appear in the damaged painting, depicted as young boys, one smaller than the other, "playing"—that is, tussling—in front of their mothers. "Here is Hagar," the Latin superscript above her head tells us. Sarah, the scene's central figure, gestures in Abraham's direction. The Latin (paraphrasing *Genesis* 21:1) that surrounds her relates her speech: "Sarah says to Abraham, 'Behold, (the) son of my servant will not be (an) heir!'" Abraham is given no words, but his extended hand is interpretable as a request for the women's testimonies, or more likely, his response to Sarah's declaration. In its content, the image freezes that part of the narrative in *Genesis* 21:1–14 the artist wishes to present. It may be simply a report, graphically displayed. Yet the viewer is supposed to understand what this tension-filled moment resolved, and what it "states." Sarah is the actor. In this contest, she is also the victor. Her demand, approved by God (*Genesis* 21:12), secures Isaac's inheritance. Ishmael and his mother Hagar are to be sent away.

The scene is only one of seven that fill folio 18a in the Ashburnham Pentateuch. The illuminations depict episodes from chapters 19 through 21 in *Genesis*, a narrative section that begins with the story of Lot and the destruction of Sodom and Gommorah and ends with the ejection of Hagar and Ishmael from Abraham's household. At the bottom of folio 18a another critical incident in Sarah's life is shown (Figure 5.2) in two scenes abutting the one just described.

In a picture to the left side of the page we are shown Abimelech sleeping on his bed, with his queen and Sarah identified as the two women seated nearby. (Abimelech's queen does not appear in the *Genesis* narrative; perhaps the artist believed that her appearance in the king's bedroom would heighten the drama and implications of his having "taken" Sarah.) Some of the words spoken to Abimelech in his dream-state dialogue with God are related in the Latin. "Here the Lord tells King Abimelech that Sarah is the

Figure 5.1 Sarah makes her case to Abraham. Ashburnham Pentateuch. © Bibliothèque nationale de France, Paris. Ms. lat. nouv. acq. 2334, folio 18r.

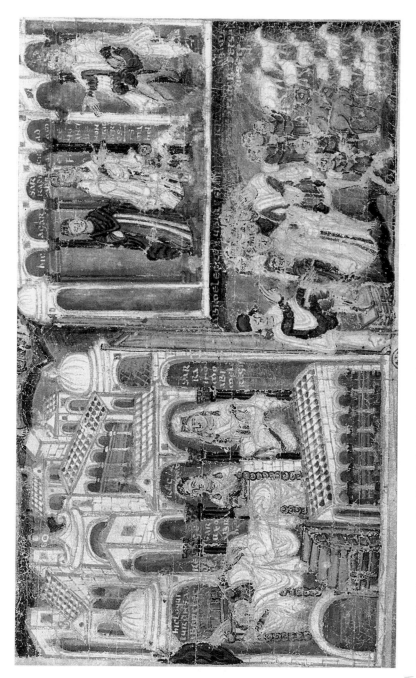

Figure 5.2 Sarah's encounter with Abimelech. Detail. Ashburnham Pentateuch. © Bibliothèque nationale de France, Paris. Ms. lat. nouv. acq. 2334, folio 18r.

wife of Abraham"—his wife, not his sister. Abimelech, so informed, heeds God's warning and is spared the death that would have come to him had he had intercourse with Sarah and had he not returned her to her husband.

The adjoining lower scene depicts this dangerous episode's conclusion. Abimelech on his throne dispatches Abraham and Sarah to safe settlement somewhere within his territory. "King Abimelech, where he restores Sarah to Abraham and gives to him sheep and oxen and male and female slaves" (see *Genesis* 20:14). Oscar von Gebhardt described the body-language of the scenes' characters: Abimelech "holds his right hand aloft, as if for an oath; with the left hand he surrenders Sarah to Abraham, who seizes her left hand with both hands and inclines his head towards her."[36]

It is worth asking whether the three panels featuring Sarah—in Abimelech's chamber, departing from Gerar after her close encounter with the king, and before Abraham, making her case against Ishmael and his mother—are simply graphic repetitions of the text. Has the painter simply rendered the literal/historical account in images and with identifying Latin tags? Or is it more likely that the artist intended in these scenes more than sheer chronicling? The incidents selected for portrayal have in common an occupation with decisions, choices, ethical quandaries, and the actions of God in such human dramas. In their alien residence in Gerar, there was Abraham's fear of his own death, should his wife Sarah be desired, Abimelech's threatened "integrity of heart" as he sought to "approach" the woman he believed to be unmarried, and God's intervention which protected and rescued Sarah. Abimelech's return of Sarah to Abraham followed upon a truth-telling encounter between the two men (*Genesis* 20:9–13), and was accompanied by the gifts depicted in the painting. Endangered virtues are preserved. Other moments in Sarah's life, and in the interactions between the patriarch's wives, could have claimed space, but these images represent what the artist wished to set forth as the centrally important outcome of the scriptural narrative: the covenant promise of God to Abraham rests with the child promised to, and born of, Sarah—Isaac. Without having a hand of God pointing toward Sarah as she speaks to her husband, the person viewing the painted scene recalls that this was God's decree. Sarah is defending the God-preferred heir, and the people of his lineage. In what seem to be straightforward renditions of biblical happenings concerning Sarah and Hagar, there reside discernible lessons and teachings.

We are left, however, with an intriguing question. If these paintings were created with moral instruction in mind, how is Sarah depicted, and what is her message in ethical terms? In the first of the scenes depicting Sarah's life, she sits composedly in Abimelech's chamber, but no particular indication is given either of her state of mind or her actions. Indeed, the image may have its focus not so much in Sarah (and Abimelech's queen) as in the sleeping king. For the biblically informed viewer the scene calls to mind what transpired in the king's dream: God's disclosure about the married status of the woman he has claimed for himself. Not holding her responsible for complying with Abraham's falsehood, we are free to see Sarah as an innocent participant—even a pawn—in a portentous struggle or negotiation involving two males (three, with the Lord counted in)—all of whom have a vital investment in what decisions are made and what actions are taken. Similarly, Sarah's presence in Abimelech's send-off of the pair carries no obvious and perceptible moral importance—except to those who know that in the *Genesis* text she has been exonerated of any suspicion by the king, who tells her, "you are completely vindicated" (20:16b). Another, arguably greater, significance belongs to Sarah, at least in the minds of those who know the narrative well, for in the succeeding lines we learn that Sarah, having escaped becoming Abimelech's concubine, conceives and gives birth to Abraham's child, in accordance with what God had promised (21:1–2).

The content of the final scene, which takes us to the separation of Abraham's two sons and wives, has only Sarah as a speaker. Very probably the artist sees her as a paragon of virtue in two important senses—she is not one of the morally compromised characters in this artistic composition (the art does not present us with the Sarah who scoffs, nor with the Sarah who is irate), *and* her worthiness expresses itself as responsiveness and loyalty to what God has revealed that he will do with her. The claim that she makes is based in God's own proclamation that the heir of the covenant with Abraham would be Isaac. Further, depiction of the conflict between the two boys would serve to justify Sarah's fear that her son is vulnerable to Ishmael's aggression, which itself challenges the providential plan of God. Hagar and Ishmael are present in the painting as antagonists, but Sarah is adamant. She is the foremother of the covenant people of God, who, for those gathering for worship in a church in the sixth century, are themselves and their fellow-believers in Christ.

The Ashburnham Pentateuch's painting of Abraham's two women and two sons in his presence must finally be deciphered not simply as literal or historical, but rather as a component part in an artistic presentation that, mediated through its selection of actions to be portrayed, strives toward pictorial ethical education. Its strategy is not allegorical—rather, the painted scenes' persons, deeds, and their fates, for good or for ill, serve as moral examples.

In the Roman church dedicated to the Virgin Mary and created under the auspices of Sixtus III, pope from 432–440, we find this beautifully executed two-tiered depiction of Abraham's hospitality to special visitors (Figure 5.3).

Figure 5.3 The hospitality of Abraham. A mid-fifth-century CE mosaic. Santa Maria Maggiore, Rome © Art History Images.

With bended knee and outstretched hand, the patriarch, his advanced age well captured in his white hair and beard, extends his welcome to the angels, one of whom is distinguished by the translucent mandorla surrounding him. (We recall that in *Genesis* 18 Abraham extends his hospitality to "three men," but one delivers the promise of the birth of Isaac within a year, and the repeated announcement is attributed, at *Genesis* 18:13–14, to "the Lord.") The mosaicist is Christianizing the scriptural scene in an unmistakable way: in accordance with Christian Logos-theology, it is the Word of God, the Son, who is present to Abraham and Sarah as the Lord—he who would become incarnate as Jesus, God's anointed one, the Christ.[37] (The oval mandorla, in this period and after-ward, most frequently surrounds images of the resurrected Jesus, or of Mary.)

The lower scene is two in one, with Abraham in the foreground turned toward Sarah (her head covered and her dress a handsome combination of white, black, and bright orange). Presumably he asks that Sarah prepare a meal of cakes (Genesis 18:6), but his countenance could be thought to register something between anxiety and consternation. At a deeper dimen-sion in the image, Abraham turns to the table, about to set before his angel-messenger guests "the calf, tender and good" (Genesis 18:7). Two of the angels look toward their host, the center one reaching toward the plat-ter as if to receive it.

We have seen this basic iconography before, both in the floor panel in the Sepphoris synagogue and in the mosaic within the Ravenna's sixth-century church of San Vitale. The visitation of the angels to Abraham, with the event's main purpose implied—the promise concerning the birth of a son to Sarah—was for both Jews and Christians a sacred story, but one that Christian artists, as well as theologians, were especially keen to reimagine and reimage.

We take note of a small detail in this mosaic artist's transformation of the biblical narrative into a Christian one. Above the door lintel of the small building (the "tent") behind Sarah appears a cross. This marking of the camp of Abraham as Christian is in keeping with a typological understand-ing of the Lord's/angels' announcement that Sarah will give to the patri-arch a son. High above this scene in the church's great arch there appears the depiction of the other annunciation which it anticipates, Gabriel's visit to Mary (Figure 5.4).

For fifth-century Christians who gathered in the great church of Saint Mary, the portrait of Abraham and Sarah was a visually readable fore-cast and celebration not only of the parents-to-be of Isaac, but also, and more profoundly, of the young virgin who would become "the mother of God."[38]

Biblical interpretations of Abraham's two women as we encounter them in the two quite different visual commentaries—the folio in the Ashburnham Pentateuch and Sta. Maria Maggiore's mosaic—reveal, espe-cially when considered alongside New Testament passages and Origen's sermon, the variety with which these Christians thinkers re-told and re-presented their sacred stories. Taken together, our texts and art in this chapter demonstrate the strong tendency toward seeking moral, typo-logical, and spiritual meanings that emerged immediately and grew in

Figure 5.4 The Annunciation, a mosaic decoration in the triumphal arch of Sta. Maria Maggiore, Rome. Mid-fifth century CE. © Art History Images.

creativity (and complexity) in Christian literature and art of the early centuries of the common era.

These modes of interpretation also appeared in Jewish writings—admittedly less so in the *midrash* of the rabbinic period than in Philo's readings of scripture—and also in Muslim *tafsir* and art. While Christians did not come to ignore the literal and historical elements in the texts, and Jews and Muslims did not shy away from moral, philosophical, and theological or spiritual implications they found in the texts they studied, it is still quite noticeable in the case of interpretations of Abraham's women how strongly Paul and Origen, in particular, pursued, and led others to pursue, meanings beyond the "letter."

Qur'an interpreters, while honoring Sarah and counting her son Isaac a prophet of God, were most occupied by the fortunes of the other half of Abraham's family, Hagar and Ishmael, who dwelled in the vicinity of "God's house" in Mecca. To Muslim visions and understandings of Abraham's women, compared with those of the Jews and Christians, we now turn.

CHAPTER 6

ᴄᴧᴐ

Hagar and Ishmael, Abraham's
Family in Mecca

In Islam's strong vision of a history in which God's messengers offer right guidance to all of humankind, Abraham, Ishmael, and Hagar take center stage as God's family of special choice. Much of their dramatic story unfolds in the vicinity of Mecca, where God's "first temple [was] set up for humankind" (Surah 3:96).

Even if the 245 references to Abraham in the Qur'an were collected and read all at once, they would strike someone familiar with the extended narrative cycle in *Genesis* 11–25 as being spare and episodic. There is no mistaking, however, what it is about the life and role of Abraham and his progeny that *this* scripture declares. The Qur'an knows Abraham as God's "friend" (*khalil*) and as "upright" (*hanif*). This chapter traces Muslim interests in Abraham's women and sons, first in the Qur'an and then in the writings by storytellers and commentators intent upon explaining and elaborating upon the Qur'an's testimonies.

SARAH, HAGAR, AND THEIR SONS IN THE QUR'AN

Sarah is identified in the Qur'an as "his [Abraham's] wife," but there is no direct reference to Hagar. We find in Islam's scripture no treatment of the relationship between the two women. Absent is any notice concerning how Hagar came to be Sarah's servant, or any mention of the troubled dealings between these two mothers of Abraham's sons that resulted in Hagar and Ishmael being sent away—to a wilderness. The Qur'an regularly presumes that its hearers and readers possess broader background knowledge about the events recited by the Prophet. The more complete history of Abraham's dealings with his wives and their sons, then, is not unfamiliar.

The Visit of God's Messengers

Two passages describing the visit of the "messengers" to Abraham (Surah 11:69–76 and Surah 51:24–30) provide brief glimpses of "his wife." Abraham becomes suspicious and apprehensive about the visitors when they do not eat the food he has offered them, but the tension is broken when they declare their news. In one of the recountings of this episode, however, there is ambiguity in what prompts the response of Sarah:

> 11:69 And Our messengers came to Abraham
> with good news: they said, "Peace."
> He said, "Peace," and without delay
> set out a roasted calf.
> 70 But when he saw they did not touch it,
> he felt offended by them,
> and had foreboding fear of them.
> They said, "Do not fear; for we were sent
> to the people of Lot."
> 71 Then his wife, who was standing there, laughed;
> but We announced to her
> good news of Isaac, and of Jacob after Isaac.
> 72 She said, "Woe is me!
> Shall I give birth now
> that I'm an old woman
> and my husband an old man?
> This is a indeed a strange thing."
> They said, "Do you marvel
> at the order of God?
> The mercy and blessings of God
> are on you, the people of the house.
> Truly God is most praiseworthy,
> most glorious!"

Sarah's responses to the messengers' announcements are somewhat puzzling. What, exactly, causes her to laugh? And what kind of reaction is her "Woe!" to the tidings that she and Abraham, in old age, will be parents to Isaac (and perhaps Jacob? the language allows this possibility)? The announcers chastise Sarah for regarding her predicted motherhood as a "strange thing" rather than a gift from God. Later interpreters will sort out the confusions.

In Surah 51:24–37 the sequence of the visitors' two messages is reversed, and that to which Sarah reacts, though she reacts differently in this case, is clear.

> 51:28b They said [to Abraham], "Don't be afraid," and announced
> good news to him of a very wise son.
> 29 Then his wife approached
> in an uproar; striking her forehead,
> she said, "A barren old woman?"
> They said, "Thus has spoken your Lord,
> Who is the epitome of wisdom, and of knowledge."

In this instance, the patriarch's wife cries out and strikes herself— gestures that catch up in themselves some combination of perplexity and disbelief. For their part, the messengers make a retort that expresses a basic element in qur'anic representation of Allah as creator: God says "Be!" and a being comes to life. God's will to generate life is a force not to be denied—whether in extraordinary or ordinary circumstances.[1] Following this exchange, Abraham inquires about his visitors' mission.

> 51:32 They said, "We have been sent
> to a people guilty of sin
> 33 to bring upon them stones of clay
> 34 marked for trangressors
> in the presence of your Lord."

Believers were to be rescued in these doomed cities, but these could be found in "only one household of people who submitted to God" (51:36). Lot's wife is not among the redeemed; she, with Noah's wife, is an example of "those who scoff" (i.e., disbelieve), both having betrayed their husbands, God's "righteous servants" (66:10). The voice of God speaks the lesson: "We left a sign there for those who fear the agony" (51:36–37).

We recognize within these episodes elements of the biblical legend—and also lessons couched unmistakably in the vocabulary of qur'anic think- ing. Abraham's wife is not like Lot's. Though she greets the news about her motherhood with surprise and consternation, she is understood to have acquiesced to God's plan articulated by the messengers (or God) as a believer, a Muslim.

Hagar

Where do we see Hagar? The question directs us to a number of places in the Qur'an. She is present, but only implicitly, in a passage that tells of the birth of a first son to Abraham, and of the second, Isaac, born to (similarly implied) Sarah. Within these verses there also occurs the narrative of Abraham's near-sacrifice of his son. Already at an early point in the period in which Islam's history unfolded alongside that of Judaism and Christianity, the meaning of the text was questioned and debated. At issue: which of Abraham's sons was taken by him to be offered to God as a sacrifice? Surah 37 ("Those who stand together") follows notices of God's extolled envoys (Noah, Moses, Aaron, Elias, Lot) with a narrative about Abraham's challenge to his father and his father's community: they worshipped "deities other than God" (37:85–92). When Abraham proceeded to knock down the images, and was threatened with being burned alive, he declared his intention to go to his Lord. In this journey to God, his emigration, Abraham trusted that his God would guide him (37:99). The *ayat* that follow are these:

> 37:101 "My Lord, grant me sound progeny."
> So We announced joyful news to him,
> of a good-natured son.
> 102 Then when he had come of age
> to work together, he said, "My son,
> I see in a dream that I sacrifice you.
> Now let's see what you think."
> He said, "Father, do what you are commanded;
> You will find me, God willing,
> bearing it calmly."
> 103 Then when both had acquiesced
> and he lay him down, on his forehead,
> 104 We called to him, "Abraham!
> 105 You have already authenticated the vision."
> For that is how We recompense
> those who do right;
> 106 for this was certainly an evident trial,
> 107 as We redeemed him
> through a tremendous sacrifice,
> 108 and We left for him in future generations
> 109 "Peace upon Abraham!"
> 110 That is how We recompense
> those who do right;

111 for he was one of Our faithful servants.

112 We also gave him good news

of Isaac, a prophet, a man of integrity.

113 And We blessed him and Isaac too;

but while some of their descendants are good,

some are clearly oppressing their own souls.

Abraham's prayer request for "sound progeny" yields the unnamed "good-natured" son who proved himself, in time, to be prepared to submit to God's will that he be a sacrifice. He is spared on account of his father's meeting the test of obedience to God. There follows the birth to faithful Abraham of a second son, the prophet Isaac, who gains, with his father, God's blessing. The mothers are not identified. Those who hear the Qur'an read or come to recite it know who they were. More important to recall and emphasize, it seems, than the women who bore Abraham's offspring, are other things: Abraham, who trusts in God for guidance, has his prayer answered; a first son is born to him, and together father and son submit to God's testing and gain their reward; Isaac the second son comes to the patriarch as another gift, and the sons are together counted worthy of God's blessing.

How are we to weigh the concluding line, which combines observation and an alert? From the seed of both of these God-sent sons, Ishmael and Isaac, came children of Abraham who (in the qur'anic revelation's present) do or do not abide by the guidance of God. The entire passage poses questions and also evokes curiosities in us, as we shall see that it did in the earliest Muslim interpreters of the story of Abraham and his two families. But we must return to the Qur'an itself—to other portions in it that point to the two women, and here, Hagar especially.

Does the Qur'an know or tell of the fortunes of Hagar after her banishment from Abraham's household, or her plight in the wilderness, when she and her son were at the point of death, due to thirst? Two qur'anic segments preserve strong suggestions of Hagar and her actions.

At the beginning of Abraham's speech addressed to God in Surah 14:35–41 he petitions his Lord to make the land in which he dwells secure, and to divert him and his sons from the idols who have led so many into error. Verses 37–38 contain Abraham's report to God of one of his own actions:

14:37 "Our Lord, I have settled

some of my children

in a valley without crops

near Your sacred House,

our Lord,
that they may keep up prayer;
so make the hearts of some people
fond of them,
and provide them with fruits,
that they may be grateful.
38 Our Lord, you do indeed know
what we conceal and what we reveal;
and nothing whatever is hidden from God,
on earth or in the sky."

The "land," Syria, from which Abraham speaks is clearly different from and some distance from the uncultivated "valley" near the "House" where some of Abraham's family are meant to maintain prayer, attract others, and enjoy friendly associations. Subsequent commentators on the Qur'an presumed that Abraham's comment referred to his compliance with Sarah's demand that he take Hagar and her son not simply to some far place, but to Mecca, which the commentator al-Tha'labi writes was "at that time a place of thorny shrubs, acacia, and thistles."[2] If the Qur'an interpreters were correct in believing that 14:37–38 *did* resonate with Jewish and Christian scripture's narration of the casting out of Hagar and Ishmael to a wild place, then this passage indeed incorporates Hagar, as matriarch, among "my children" (presumed to be Ishmael and his descendants) whom Abraham settled near the "sacred House." Major emphases in the text, however, bear no correspondence to the biblical narrative: it is for prayer that this band of Abraham's kin have been sent to this valley where God's holy *bayt* is found, and furthermore, Abraham gives voice to a hope that his people in the barren place will find acceptance and support there. There is a coding in the text, and Muslim exegetes will relish deciphering it.

A second passage which points to Hagar occurs in Surah 2:158:

Note that the mountains
Safa and Marwa are among the emblems of God:
so whoever makes the seasonal pilgrimage
to the House,
or an off-season pilgrimage,
it is not held against anyone
if he circles them both.
And if anyone willingly
does what is good,
God is appreciative and cognizant.

The ritual running, the *sa'y*, between these two hills at Mecca by those on pilgrimage (the greater, *al-Hajj*, or the lesser, *al-'Umrah*, the "visitation"; the text marks a distinction) re-enacted Hagar's search for help when Ishmael was at the brink of death. Her running may indeed be seen as her test, a trial analogous to that met by Abraham when asked to sacrifice his son. The *sa'y* becomes for those who travel to do their devotions at Mecca a prescribed circumambulation undertaken after prayer at the place Abraham stood, and after drinking from the water of the Well of Zamzam—the water source believed to have possessed, and to possess still, the powers of salvation and healing. We cannot be certain how fully developed this particular ceremonial "running" was at the time of the Qur'an, but our verses approve of the action on the part of pilgrims to Mecca—the prayerful runners "[do] what is good." There is more at stake in this endorsement than is evident, since it is a monotheist and specifically Muslim displacement and reform of earlier religious practices at the site: the kind of *sa'y* endorsed in the Qur'an and given more narrative authority by later commentators is, Reuben Firestone noted, actively "substituting Hagar's actions for the pre-Islamic practice of running between the idols that graced the peaks of the two hills."[3]

Hagar, then, can be said to be present in the Qur'an no less than Sarah, the wife. The two texts, 14:35–41 and 2:158, without giving her name, invoke memories of Hagar's significant place in the Muslims' foundational story—the discovery of the place of the Ka`ba, its building by the patriarch and his first son, and the institution of proper prayer in that holy place.

Though their mothers go unnamed in the Qur'an, Ishmael and Isaac are referred to often—in interesting patterns. Firestone observed two idiomatic phrases that occur, the first not unexpected by those familiar with the Bible, namely, "Abraham, Isaac, and Jacob," and another which appears several times, "Abraham, Ishmael, Isaac" (2:133), and an extended form, "Abraham, Ishmael, Isaac, Jacob, and the tribes" (2:136, 140; 3:84; 4:163).[4]

Because Ishmael had become a name associated with Israel's foes, the Ishmaelites, in the time of the rabbis, and because Christianity understood its own covenant with Abraham's God to have come via kinship with Isaac, moderns familiar with those religions can only be struck by Ishmael's status and prominence in the qur'anic groupings of God's favored ones, his envoys and prophets. Certainly Isaac is regularly counted among those righteous servants sent by God to warn and guide humankind, both together with Ishmael and independent of him.[5] Surah 29:27 stands in parallel and in contrast to *Genesis* 17:21–22. ("As for Ishmael ... I will bless him and make him fruitful and exceedingly numerous; he shall be the father of twelve princes, and I will make him a great nation. But my covenant I will

establish with Isaac, whom Sarah will bear to you this season next year.")
The qur'anic form of the divine promise to Abraham that will be sustained
through Isaac reads:

> 27 And We bestowed Isaac and Jacob on him,
> and We placed prophecy and scripture
> on his descendants,
> and We gave him his reward in the world;
> and at the end he will certainly be
> one of the worthies.

To Isaac and Jacob were granted prophecy and scripture—that is, the
revelation manifested through Muhammad's recitations of God's words.

Another mode of listing Abraham's sons names them both, but
separates them.

> 38:45 Remember also Our servants
> Abraham, Isaac and Jacob
> Endowed with ability and vision:
> 46 We purified them by a pure quality,
> remembrance of paradise;
> 47 and they were to Us
> among the chosen, the best.
> 48 And remember Ishmael and Elisha,
> and the holder of responsibility;
> every one of them was one of the best.

In the first three verses Abraham, Isaac, and Jacob are saluted for their
power and wisdom, and for the blessing that made them capable of remem-
bering—that is, yearning for—Paradise. Here and elsewhere Ishmael is
found *not* in immediate association with Abraham and Isaac, but in other
clusters of renowned prophets. At the end of this passage (38:48) he is
grouped with Elisha and with "the holder of responsibility" (as our translator, Thomas Cleary, renders Dhul Kifl, commonly understood to be Ezekiel).
A similar phrase puts Ishmael in the prophetic company of Idris (Enoch)
and Ezekiel, and notes their shared qualities of patience and steadfastness
(21:85). It is not evident what elements in the lore surrounding these three
heroes served as a qur'anic rationale for their association—or for the attraction of Ezekiel and Enoch to the name of Ishmael. Was it Elisha's wondrous
healings and his capacity to confront an unrighteous ruler? Enoch's being
"taken up" to heaven by God? Ezekiel's visionary powers, enabling him to

see a chariot in the heavens and a valley in which human skeletons were resurrected? The same mystery surrounds Surah 6:86, in which Ishmael and Elisha are joined by Jonah and Lot, the latter two not identified by a particular trait (what attributes or virtues might early hearers of the Qur'an have thought linked Jonah and Lot—and Ishmael?), but who with all the prophets earlier listed gained God's (unranked) favor among his creatures.[6]

In one instance Ishmael, by himself, is described. Surah 19:54–55 reads:

54 And mention Ishmael in the Book,

for he was true to his promise

and was a messenger, a prophet.

55 He used to enjoin prayer

and charity on his people,

and he was acceptable to his Lord.

What is distinctive about Ishmael, according to these verses? A parallel passage in Surah 21:73 steals much of his individual thunder in that it attributes also to Abraham, Lot, Isaac, and Jacob the virtues of establishing true worship ("perform[ing] the prayer"), urging *zakat*, and living in submission to God.[7] What remains particular to Ishmael, alone, is the claim that "he was true to his promise." Later commentators, as we shall see, knew or fashioned stories to substantiate the claim. Reuven Firestone argued that despite the dozen references to Ishmael in the Qur'an we learn little about him, his slender characterization a result of his being a comparatively minor character in a drama strongly focused on his father.[8]

Perhaps the same argument applies to the others in Abraham's family. Insofar as Hagar and Sarah and Isaac gain notice in the Qur'an, it is as if they are small planets circling Abraham, *khalil Allah*. And yet the sacred book's placement of Hagar and her son in the arid land near God's House, the running between the two mountains there, and Ishmael's placement near the Ka`bah, are rich soil for the further cultivation of Islam's celebration of the guidance it received from God, the Merciful, the Compassionate.

THE STORIES OF IBRAHIM'S WOMEN, INTERPRETED

In taking up that portion of his *History of the Prophets and Patriarchs* that tells of Sarah, Hagar, and their sons, we gain access to the kinds of inquiries and discussions that fascinated both the predecessors and contemporaries of al-Tabari. And yet he does not merely report; at various points we learn also of his own intellectual and interpretive leanings and conclusions.

Moving from the Qur'an to literature that seeks to understand and to expand upon its messages, we notice quickly that Hagar and Sarah become more visible—and audible. Islamic *tafsir* shows awareness of biblical materials developed by Jews and Christians, and of pre-Islamic Arabic remembrances of Abraham and members of his household. Ardent *Muslim* interest in the religion's great ancestor, Abraham, brings with it a new and important shift of emphasis, one that Barbara Stowasser highlighted:

> Among all of sacred history's female images ... Hagar's may have been the most productive of ongoing change and interpretation in the Islamic imagination. Inasmuch as the palpable tensions embodied in the scripturalist tales on Sarah and Hagar have to do with the Islamic processes of acceptance of the Biblical heritage while also establishing its own, the figures of Sarah and Hagar symbolize Islam's selfdefinition as continuation, but also corrective completion, of the monotheistic tradition. During the early medieval period, the stories of Isaac's (Syrian) and Ishmael's (Meccan) role as Abraham's chosen sacrifice both appear to have existed side by side for a while; thus, these sons' mothers were then also more ambiguously ranked. With the ninth and tenth centuries, however, the Mecca-Ishmael-Hagar tradition rose in prominence, and with it, Hagar's rank as one of Islam's most important female figures, a symbol of Islamic identity.[9]

The section on "Abraham, the Friend of the Merciful" in al-Tabari's multivolume history gives a colorful presentation of Hagar, but necessarily commences with questions and opinions about Sarah's genealogy (questions taken up by the rabbis as well) that motivated al-Tabari to provide two accounts of the origins of Sarah's belief—of her becoming a Muslim. The first tells that, being the daughter of Haran the Elder, Abraham's paternal uncle, she was among the early followers who, impressed by the prophet's deliverance from King Nimrod's fiery furnace, believed in the God who saved him. An alternative explanation of Sarah's faith in God drew upon a tradition that she, the daughter of the king of the land of Harran, had herself resisted the polytheism of her people, "so [Abraham] married her, since he would thus have a believing wife without having to convert her."[10] When his father, Azar, and his people refused Abraham's call to honor the single God, he and his small company, Sarah included, took up the "fugitive" life of wayfarers (Surah 19:41–50).

The trauma caused by Sarah's "goodness and beauty" in their sojourns is at once familiar and yet, in Muslim interpreters' tellings, particular in its presentation. The troublesome "lie" of Abraham to the ruler who asks to meet the virtuous and stunning Sarah is given a justification by way of an argument for *religious* kinship. Fearing for his life should the king desire her, and believe him to be her husband, Abraham says to Sarah:

> This tyrant asked me about you, and I told him that you are my sister. So do not give me the lie when you see him. You are my sister in God, for in all this land there are no Muslims except ourselves.[11]

Her marriage-minded (and aroused) host, once Sarah is within reach, suffers repeated frustration. Paralysis overwhelms his arm as he attempts to touch her. Each time the paralysis is eased by Sarah's prayer, which she offers on the pledge that he will not try again to grab or fondle her. Declaring finally that he has been brought a devil, not a human, the tyrant ejects Sarah from his presence, sending with her Hagar—as a gift, or as an act meant to guarantee that the powerful Sarah will not visit harm on him and his house. Sarah reports to Abraham that God protected her "from the unbelieving libertine and has given me Hagar as a servant." We note that Hagar comes to Sarah from God, and only secondarily from the tyrant. Following these words al-Tabari reports:

> According to Muhammad b. Sirin: When Abu Hurayrah related this account, he would say, "This is your mother, O Arabs!"[12]

A tradition attributed by Abu Ja`far to Ibn Ishaq recounts Sarah's later decision to make Hagar, a person of "good appearance" and a "clean woman," available to Abraham, that he might gain a son from her: "So he had intercourse with Hagar, and she bore him Ishmael."[13] Again, we meet an interjection that preserves conversation among the sages. The first part, whose chain of transmitters stems from Muhammad and ends with Ibn Humayd, reads: "When you conquer Egypt, treat its people well, for they are kin (to you) and deserve protection." Al-Zuhri (also listed in the *isnad*) was asked, "What is their kinship that the Messenger of God mentioned?" and he answered, "Hagar the mother of Ishmael was one of them."[14] These scholars are eager to know how many ways Hagar should be identified and understood. She, the matriarch of the Arabs, hailed from Egypt (from the Pharaoh's household) and this ties her and her native people to the future (or, at the time of al-Tabari's writing, the past) mission and expansion of Islam. The Egyptians are a kindred people; they are to be accorded favor and defense. In the *Qisas al-anbiya'* of al-Kisa'i, composed four centuries later, the elaboration of the importance of the mother is shown to have extended to the son. Though from Isaac's loins many prophets would issue, from Ishmael would come a "prophet whose name would be Muhammad, the Seal of the Prophets."

Indeed, it is told that when Hagar "was delivered of Ishmael … [his] face radiated the Light of our Prophet Muhammad like the moon."[15]

The Qur'an's telling of the visit of the Messengers to Sarah and Abraham undergoes elaboration in the sources preserved by al-Tabari. Knowing that Lot's people were doomed because of their "vile deeds" and their heedlessness despite prophets and good advice sent to them, God had his traveling angels stop at Abraham's camp, "commanding him to leave their [i.e., the people of Lot's] community"—that is, to sever any relations with his nephew's folk. The other reason for the visit had to do with the tidings to Sarah and Abraham of the coming of Isaac "and also of Jacob who was to come after him." Eager to give hospitality and awed by his guests, grander than any to whom he'd previously extended his generosity, Abraham determines that only he will cook for and serve them. When the messengers do not reach for the fare, their host is chagrined and fearful. What next transpires, al-Tabari the commentator tells us, is what the Qur'an indicates about this encounter and Sarah's reactions.

> They said, "Do not be afraid! We are sent to the people of Lot" (Surah 11:70). Sarah was standing nearby, and when she heard of God's command, she laughed, knowing what she knew of the people of Lot. Then they told her of the coming of Isaac and, after Isaac, of Jacob—that is, they told her she would have a son and grandson. She struck her face (in surprise) and said, "Woe is me! How can I have a child when I am a barren old woman?" (Surah 11:72)[16]

The reasons for Sarah's reactions are clarified, as is the relationship of Jacob to Isaac. Firestone notes that it was to Jews and Christians that early Muslims turned for information concerning this event, which, while being a prominent moment in the biblical tale, was not part of any "pre-Islamic Arabian consciousness" or legend concerning Abraham. Hence the etymological connection in Hebrew between Sarah's "laughing" and the name "Isaac," having no consonance in Arabic, dropped from Muslim commentary as a detail.[17]

The event next recorded in al-Tabari's chronicle—God's command that Abraham build "the House" in which worship and the speaking of God's name will occur—receives the author's focused attention. Where does the building of the Ka'bah fit in Abraham's history? Several of the preserved Muslim traditions make no reference to what, besides God's injunction, may have preceded and affected the journey.[18] But our chronicler writes that some

> have said that … the reason he took Hagar and Ishmael to Mecca with him was that Sarah was jealous of Hagar's having borne Ishmael by him.[19]

Holders of that opinion told an arresting narrative, features of which are known in rabbinic *midrash*, that expands upon the measures Sarah took in her jealousy and anger:

> Sarah said to Abraham, "you may take pleasure in Hagar, for I have permitted it." So he had intercourse with Hagar and she gave birth to Ishmael. Then he had intercourse with Sarah, and she gave birth to Isaac. When Isaac grew up, he and Ishmael fought. Sarah became angry and jealous towards Ishmael's mother and sent her away. Then she called her back and took her in. But later she became angry and sent her away again, and brought her back yet again. She swore to cut something off of her, and said to herself, "I shall cut off her nose, I shall cut off her ear—but no, that would deform her. I will circumcise her instead." So she did that, and Hagar took a piece of cloth to wipe the blood away. For that reason women have been circumcised and have taken pieces of cloth down to today. Sarah said, "She will not live in the same town with me." God told Abraham to go to Mecca, where there was no House at the time. He took Hagar and her son to Mecca and put them there."[20]

We are most struck, encountering this brief tradition, by the reference to Sarah's ultimate choice of circumcising Hagar, on the grounds that that would *not* deform her—at least in terms of public visibility. It has the character of an etiological tale that, as William Brinner suggested, "probably reflects the antiquity of the practice of circumcision (both male and female) among the Arabs, which antedates Islam."[21]

We saw that rabbis whose views were preserved in *Genesis Rabbah* speculated freely about the play or sport which Ishmael entered into with his younger half-brother. Al-Tha'labi reports simply that "one day Isaac and Ishmael fought as boys do," stirring Sarah's anger toward Hagar, whom she wanted to deface, before Abraham convinced her to relent. He advised: "Lower her status and pierce her ears," which Sarah did.[22] Within this same piece of lore we find an episode combining the competition between the boys and the source of Sarah's jealousy. After presiding over an archery contest between his sons, Abraham takes Ishmael, the winner, onto his lap, while placing Isaac next to himself. In her ire Sarah says to him: "You have turned to the son of the servant-girl and have seated him in your bosom, whereas you have turned to my son and seated him at your side, while you had vowed that you would not injure me or do any evil to me." So it happened that "the jealousy that overcomes women overcame her."[23] In both al-Tabari's and al-Tha'labi's stories of the clash between Abraham's women we see the traces of available biblical and ante-Islamic lore, but these sources contribute to a decidedly Islamic representation of the Abraham narrative—one that leaves the figures of Sarah and Isaac behind, moving forward to the religion's full exposition of Abraham's service to God—at Mecca.

Although ready and willing to obey God's call to build the House (cf. Surah 2:124–128), Abraham, according to Muslim interpreters, needed help in discovering its destined location. The guidance, some scholars said, was provided by Gabriel. Many others favored the view that the "Shakinah" led the prophet to the propitious site. Drawn from imagery of the cloud-like divine presence, the *shekinah*, which stood over and accompanied the Israelites' tabernacle in their long journey in the wilderness (*Exodus* 40:34ff.), this motif was adapted and altered by Muslim interpreters as they considered what kind of divine helper could reveal the location of the *bayt Allah*—the Ka'ba.

The Shakinah that leads Abraham toward Mecca takes many forms in the traditions al-Tabari cites—a two-headed strong wind that, having arrived at the place intended for the Ka`bah, coils, snake-like, to mark it, or a wind with a single head and wings, or, most colorfully of all, a wind-being equipped with a voice who proclaims three times, while circling the sacred site's location, "Build on me!" We are reminded more than once which branch of Abraham's family has traveled southward with him. Hagar and Ishmael are present, and the notice in the Qur'an (14:37) of Abraham's settling some of his family "in a valley without crops near Your sacred House" hovers over the now expanding narrative. Indeed, in a tradition traced to the eminent eighth-century CE scholar Ibn Ishaq, Hagar receives privileged and prior information concerning the location of the "Temple," or House:

> Sa`id b. Salim, who got it from `Uthman b. Saj, who got it from Muhammad b. Ishaq, told us: It reached me that an angel came to Hagar, the mother of Ishmael, after Abraham settled her in Mecca, before Abraham and Ishmael raised up the edifice of the Temple, and showed her the Temple, which was a round, red hill, and said to her, This is the first temple for mankind on earth, and it is the Temple of God. Know that Abraham and Ishmael will erect it for mankind.[24]

Commentators, aware of speculations about the earliest histories of God's holy places, wondered about the antiquity of "the House." Did it have an earlier existence, Adam having built, Shith/Seth having rebuilt, and Noah having protected it? Yes, according to the source just quoted. Abraham and Ishmael in their digging found the foundation put in place by Adam, discovering a stone so large that "three men could not surround it. . . . then [Abraham] built on the first foundation of Adam."[25] No, there was no earlier sanctuary, one tradition dependent on a saying of `Ali b. Abi Talib argues, "but it [i.e., this construction] was the first House built with the blessing of the standing-place of Abraham, and whoever enters it will be safe."[26]

Numerous legends speak of the process of the Ka`bah's construction, and about the roles played by Abraham and his assistants. The patriarch is credited with building the structure up to the last and necessary capstone. He then turned to Ishmael for assistance. In one account, the boy is absent, having wandered away to do his own project. In others, Abraham does not like the stone offered him and sends Ishmael on another search. Or, Ishmael sets out to find a proper capstone and returns with one in hand.

> But he found that Abraham had already set the Black Stone in place. He said, "O my father, who brought you this stone?" Abraham answered, "Someone who did not rely on your building brought it to me. It was Gabriel who brought it to me from heaven." Then the two of them finished it.[27]

Mixed in with the themes of wonder that explain the completion of the "sacred house" are the slightly comic and disparaging glimpses of Ishmael—a curious feature that may serve to contrast the son's youth (seen alternately as "a baby" or "a boy") with the preeminence of his father, the especially favored servant, God's obedient one.

Quite different conclusions to the story of the discovery and building of the Ka`ba appear in two reports in the *History*. In one a hierarchy of authority among the actors is made plain through the dialogue between angel and prophet.

> At last they reached Mecca, which at that time was nothing but acacia trees, mimosa, and thorn trees, and there was a people called the Amalekites out-side Mecca and its surroundings. The House at that time was but a hill of red clay. Abraham said to Gabriel, "Was it here that I was ordered to leave them?" Gabriel said, "Yes." Abraham directed Hagar and Ishmael to go to al-Hijr, and settled them down there. He commanded Hagar, the mother of Ishmael, to find shelter there. Then he said, "My Lord! I have settled some of my posterity in an uncultivable valley near your Holy House"... [with the quotation of Surah 14:37 continuing until] "that they may be thankful." Then he journeyed back to his family in Syria, leaving the two of them at the House.[28]

In renditions like this one attributed to Ibn Abbas, Hagar's voice is heard:

> As he was leaving, Hagar called out to him, "O Abraham, I ask you three times, who commanded you to set me down in a land without grain, without cows' udders, without people, without water, and without provisions?" He said,

"My Lord commanded me." She said, "Verily, He will never lead us astray." As Abraham was retracing his path (back to Syria) he said, "O Lord! You know both the sadness we hide and the sadness we reveal. Nothing on earth or in heaven is hidden from God."[29]

By a deft addition to the drama, Abraham's poignant acknowledgment of his pangs is given scriptural weight in his concluding quotation of the verse in Surah 14:37. Yet Hagar's earlier response to the answer she has drawn from Abraham is the central element in the passage. Testifying to *her* trust in God she identifies herself as a Muslim woman, expanding upon earlier recognition of her as matriarch of the Arabs, and also upon what may have been presumed about Hagar's faithfulness on account of her accompanying Abraham in his journey toward the place of the *bayt Allah*. Sarah's status as a believer having been established in the earlier part of Abraham's history, Hagar now commands the spotlight, and states her confidence in God's protective oversight of her and her son in the barren place where Abraham has deposited her. Her faith, we know, is put to an immediate test.

The revelation of the spring of Zamzam that rescues from death Hagar and Abraham's beloved first son, the guarantor of the line that will produce Muhammad, is remembered in numerous ways. Details vary. Ishmael is an infant, still nursing, or he is a young boy. Hagar is identified as one who, in flight from Sarah, used the hem of her garment to cover her tracks (and, in another etiological tale, as "the first Arab woman who voided ordure and dragged the edges of her garment over it").[30]

In her search for water Hagar hears no sounds, or she hears the noise of beasts, causing her to rush back to where her son languishes. Ibn Abbas is credited with the report that at one point in her running, Hagar

> heard a faint voice. Being unsure that she had really heard it, she said "Hush!" to herself, until she was sure of it. Then she said, "You have made me hear Your voice, so give me water, for I am dying and so is the one with me."[31]

The saving stream gushes forth, and it is the work of Gabriel, or of Ishmael—one or the other digs with his heel. We are told that when Zamzam began flowing, Hagar hastily worked to gather the water into her depleted waterskin—an action that is criticized by Muhammad, the commentators recall, on the grounds that without her frantic intervention, "Zamzam would still be a free-flowing spring." The source and rationale of this accusation is obscure. It does not seriously diminish the maternal heroism that is understood to have summoned God to act in mercy, redeeming the promising son of Abraham.

Ishmael's mother is celebrated as "the first person to run between al-Safa and al-Marwah,"[32] and on account of this she stands alongside Abraham as one whose ancient deeds of faith constitute the foundations of Islam's pilgrimage rituals. Further narrative development of the tradition preserved by al-Tabari is seen in the writing of his successor Al-Tha`labi:

> She heard a sound coming from al-Marwah and ran, taking pains not to run like an exhausted person. She was the first to run between al-Safa and al-Marwah (as is the custom of the Hajj). Then she climbed al-Marwah and heard a voice, as if disbelieving her hearing, then she knew for certain, and began to call out: "Ishmael!" by which she meant: "God, You have made me hear your voice, so help me, for I and he who is with me will perish." Suddenly Gabriel stood before her, asking "Who are you?" "Abraham's concubine," she answered, "He left me here with my son." He said: "To whom did he entrust you?" "She said: "He entrusted us to God." He said: "Then he has entrusted you to One [who is] Generous and Sufficient." Their food and drink had run out and he brought them to the place of Zamzam, where he thrust his foot into the ground and a spring burst forth. Therefore Zamzam is called "The Foot Thrust of Gabriel."[33]

Recognizably biblical motifs resonate in the recognition that Ishmael's name, in Hebrew, means "God hears" (*Genesis* 16:11), and in the notice that Hagar, confronted by an angel, identifies herself here, as Abraham's concubine (while in *Genesis* 16:8, as Sarah's slave girl). But Muslim pilgrimage practices hold sway over the episode—in the mention of the Hajj, in the prescribed way of running, in the enunciation of God's attributes, and in the reminder that Muslims refer to the spring as the angel's "Foot Thrust." Worshippers at Mecca run in the steps of Hagar the believer, the mother who stands at the beginning of their heritage. As Michael Wolfe wrote of modern pilgrims in his *One Thousand Roads to Mecca*, the *tawaf*, or seven circuits of the Ka`ba, is succeeded by a period of refreshment at the Zamzam well, prior to the *sa`y*:

> To perform it, pilgrims cross the mosque to the east side of the building, where a course about a third of a mile long, the Masa`a, stretches between the Safa and Marwa hills. Here Ishmael's mother, Hagar, is said to have run back and forth seven times in a frantic search for water in the desert. During her final lap, the child cried out. Returning, she found an unearthed desert spring. Today this rite gives pilgrims a participatory taste of a timeless drama in which parental

love and religious faith are weighed in the balance. At an ethnic level, the story explains the survival of all Arabs, Ishmael being their progenitor.[34]

Though it is to be expected, we should pause to notice that in these traditional Muslim representations of Abraham's Mecca-settled family all traces have vanished of rabbinic deprecation of Ishmael, whose "sport" was thought by some to be idolatry—the playing at sacrifices—and of similar charges against his mother, who in desperation in the wilderness (according to Rabbi Eliezer and others) is said to have sought help from the gods of her former people.[35]

The Muslim Hagar's story is its own. Barbara Stowasser captures and highlights in a few lines what has emerged from our engagement with Hagar in al-Tabari's *History*, and in other Muslim commentary:

> Islamic interpretation has not seen Hagar's expulsion from Abraham's household at Sara's hands as an occurrence of female oppression but as part of the divine plan to establish God's true sanctuary and its pure rituals in the wilds of a barren valley far away. Hagar had to endure the distress and danger that have typically marked the careers of God's historical agents. Like God's prophets, Hagar persevered, and thus her name and memory came to be part of Islam's sacred history and ritual.[36]

Our inspection of Muslim perceptions of Abraham's women can very nearly be concluded at this point, even if later episodes in Abraham's life bring them back on the scene (for example, each is portrayed as the mother of the son which Abraham prepares to sacrifice). Al-Tabari's *History* moves from the events at Zamzam to other stories relating to Mecca and the establishment of true worship there. A people named the Jurhamites, spying birds above the spring, come and succeed in gaining from Hagar the privilege of living near her and Ishmael in the valley. When Hagar dies, according to one account, Ishmael marries a woman from the Jurhum people. Multiple reports are given of Abraham's later journeys to Mecca. He hopes to see Hagar and Ishmael, and then, when it is known to him that Hagar is dead, he visits Ishmael's home and tests the hospitality of his successive wives. These narratives regularly begin by noting the conditions Sarah imposed on Abraham's trip: he is not to settle there; he is not to get down from his camel! The stories in which Abraham sees to it that his son dispatches one wife and finds a proper one are best understood as serving to promote and celebrate the Ka`ba and the Hajj in particular, providing an origin-story for the *maqam Ibrahim*, the prophet's "standing place" that comes to adorn the sacred precinct of God's House. One account has it that while extending the courtesy of washing the head of her unknown visitor (Abraham, her father-in-law), Ishmael's second wife made use of a stone standing place—a place for his feet to rest. Several traditions assume that the building of the Ka'ba occurred at this time, after Hagar's death, and in connection with Abraham's return to the site where he had settled her and her son. So, after the building's completion, narrative context is provided for a number of important qur'anic statements, especially the exhortation found in Surah 22 (*The Pilgrimage*) at *ayat* 27–29:

> 22:27 And announce the pilgrimage
> to the people: they will come to you on foot,
> and on every lean mount,
> coming from every recondite mountain pass,
> 28 that they may bear witness
> to the blessing they have
> and remembrance of the name of God
> on special days
> over domestic animals
> God has provided them.
> So eat from them
> And feed the poor in distress.
> 29 Then let them clean themselves up,
> fulfill their vows, and circle the ancient House.

Standing on the stone Abraham performs God's command to announce the pilgrimage. All beings and things in heaven and earth hear him. Al-Tabari wrote:

> And his voice reached even those yet unborn in the loins of men and the wombs of women. All who believed among those of past generations in God's knowledge that they would perform the pilgrimage between then and the Day of Resurrection answered Abraham, "Here I am, my God, here I am."[37]

Another element in the collected stories has Abraham initially hanging back, pleading lack of capacity ("O Lord! What will my voice reach?"), only to be reassured by God ("Proclaim! The reaching is my responsibility").

Early Islam is eager to blot out any recollections of pre-Islamic cultic activity at Mecca and at the Ka'ba, and the commentators work assiduously and enthusiastically to locate (and secure) the *first* worship done at Mecca in the story of Islam's patriarch. Nowhere is this effort made in such detail as in al-Tabari's record of the testimony of ʿUbayd b. ʿUmayr al-Laythi:

> [Abraham] took Ishmael out and went with him on the day of Tarwiyah and stayed at Mina with him and with the Muslims who were with him, and he prayed with them the prayers of midday, afternoon, sunset, and late evening. Then he spent the night with them until they arose, and he prayed the dawn prayer with them. In the morning he went out with them to ʿArafah, and spoke to them there until sunset drew near. Then he joined the two prayers, midday and afternoon, and then he went and stood with them at the thorn bush which is the standing-place of ʿArafah, where the prayer-leader stood teaching him and demonstrating to him. When the sun had set, he urged on the prayer leader and those who were with him until they came to al-Muzdalifah. There he joined the two prayers of sunset and late evening. Then he spent the night with him and those with him until, when the dawn broke, he prayed the morning prayer with them. Then he stood with them at Quzah of al-Muzdalifah. This is the standing-place where the prayer leader stands. When day came, he demonstrated and explained to them what to do, including the throwing of the great stone. He showed them the sacrifice-ground of Mina, then performed the sacrifice and shaved his head. From Mina he went into the crowd to show them how to perform the march around the Kaʿbah. Then he took them back to Mina to show them how to throw the stones, until he had completed the pilgrimage and proclaimed it to mankind.

Al-Tabari appends the teaching of the Messenger of God and some of his companions, preserved by Abu Jaʿfar: "Gabriel was the one who showed Abraham the ritual acts when he made the pilgrimage."[38]

This description of the initial pilgrims' ordered acts of worship is based on a testimony deriving from a contemporary of Muhammad. One of its effects is to represent in the narrative of Abraham's Hajj exactly those patterns and practices well-known in Islam's first century. The text outlines the activities of al Tarwiya (the day of "deliberation"), the *tawaf,* prayer at the *maqam Ibrahim,* the drinking of Zamzam's water and the sʿay, and the night spent at Mina; the day's "standing" or "waiting" at Mina with its led prayers and recitations of the *talbiyah*, the statement of preparedness and confession (*Labbayka allahumma labbayka*, "Here I am, my God, here I am"), the feast of sacrifice, ʿId al Adha, and the collection of stones for casting at the pillars at Mina, the offerings at the sacrifice ground, followed by the cutting of hair. Throughout this text, Abraham, along with stationed prayer leaders, is shown to model and preside over the devotional acts of the Meccan pilgrimage. He has purified God's house, and now leads in true worship "those that shall go about it and those that stand ... those that bow and prostrate themselves" (Surah 22:26).

There are still other narratives concerning Abraham's women that the writers of *tafsir* and *qisas al-anbiya* take up and deploy. Two parts of their stories remain—one confusedly intertwined, and the other having to do with the deaths and burials of each. A significant amount of text in al-Tabari's *History* pertaining to Abraham's life is spent on the two opposing opinions Muslim commentators held in the discussion of whether it was Isaac or Ishmael that he offered for sacrifice. Both in al-Tabari's chronicle and in the larger body of traditional commentary-literature, the groups of "those who say" that it was Isaac, and "those who say" it was Ishmael are nearly equally divided.[39] While giving full treatment to the two schools of thought, al-Tabari sides with the view that the near-victim was Isaac. His argument and choice (one which will not prevail among Muslims in subsequent centuries) depends upon his interpretation of the relevant (and, as we saw earlier, debatable) qur'anic passages.[40] In relation to our subject, this debate among Muslim sages about which son of Abraham was chosen for the *dhabih* results in a dramatic scene in which *either* Sarah *or* Hagar is present. Satan's effort to tempt Isaac's mother during the time Abraham journeys toward the place of sacrifice we encounted earlier in Jewish legend.[41] Its counterparts in Islamic story-telling feature both Sarah and Hagar. In one account, Ka`b tells Abu Harayrah:

> Satan visited Abraham's wife, Sarah, in the shape of a man whom Abraham's people knew, and asked her, "Where is Abraham going so early with Isaac?" She said, "He went off early on some errand." Satan said, "No, by God! That is not the reason. . . . He took him out early to sacrifice him." Sarah said, "There is no truth to that, he would not sacrifice his own son." Satan said, "By God, it is true." Sarah said, "And why would he sacrifice him?" He replied, "He claims that his Lord ordered him to do it." Sarah said, "If his Lord ordered him to do that, it is best that he obey." Then Satan left Sarah.[42]

In a different report, attributed to "Ibn Humayd—Slamah—Ibn Ishaq—certain scholars," we read of Iblis being rebuffed in his attempts to dissuade Abraham, and then Ishmael, from obeying the divine command. (It is this attempt of Satan to tempt Ishmael that underlies the Muslim Hajj ritual practice of the lapidation—the hurling of stones at the three large columns (*jamarat*) at Mina.) In his last attempt to frustrate the purposes of God,

> Iblis went to Ishmael's mother Hagar in her dwelling and said to her, "O Mother of Ishmael! Do you know where Abraham has taken Ishmael?" She said, "He took him to gather wood for us on the trail." Iblis said, "He took him only to sacrifice him." Hagar said, "Never! He is too merciful to him and loves him too much for that." Iblis told her, "He claims that God commanded him to do it." She said, "If his Lord commanded him to do it, then one should surrender to the command of God."[43]

The event takes place in the vicinity of Mecca, with Abraham taking his son to Mt. Thabir, and a definitive qur'anic tone sounds at the end of Iblis's failure to tempt: the enemy of God rages, and the narrator notes that "the family of Abraham . . . had all refused to deal with him, by God's help, and they had agreed with God's command, saying, 'To hear is to obey.'"[44]

Some Muslim Qur'an commentators familiar to al-Tabari believed that the near-sacrifice of Isaac took place when he was on pilgrimage to the House with his father and his mother (Abraham sending Sarah back to the Ka`ba after the lapidation, at which point he proceeded with his son to al-Jamra al Wusta in Mina). This view gave way, over time, to that tradition within Meccan pilgrimage associated with the killing of an animal, the `Id al-Adha on the 10th Dhu-l-Hijjah—namely, that Hagar's son Ishmael was the one redeemed by the *dhabih*, the "mighty sacrifice" (Surah 37:107) which God provided in Ishmael's stead. This identification of Ishmael as the son intended for sacrifice, and the location of the divine intervention in one of Mecca's hills (al-Tabari, in arguing for Isaac, was forced to contend with the tradition that the horns of the victim were known to be on display in the Ka`ba), brought into play the story of Hagar's *sa'y* between Safa and Marwa, and also remembrance of her as one who, faced by Iblis, reaffirmed her trust in God—Abraham's God and hers.[45]

Information about the deaths of Sarah and Hagar do not present us with any particular narrative drama; these notices are summary statements about the progeny of Abraham (who, with two later wives, fathers eleven more sons). The interest in these passages centers in the extension of the children of Abraham into future generations. Al-Tha`labi's obituary information for the two mothers reads:

> The men with knowledge of the accounts of past generations have said, "Sarah died in Syria when she was one hundred and twenty-seven years old, in a town of the Jababirah of the land of Canaan, that is, in Hebron, in a field that Abraham

had bought, and she was buried there. Hagar had died in Mecca before Sarah, and was buried in the Hijr."[46]

He writes that at age one hundred thirty-seven, Ishmael died, "and was buried in the Hijr near the tomb of his mother Hagar." To this al-Tha`labi appends a colorful saying by `Umar b. `Abd al-`Aziz to the effect that

> Ishmael complained to his Lord of the heat of Mecca, whereupon God revealed to him, "I shall open for you one of the gates of the Garden from which its breeze will blow upon you until the Day of Resurrection," and at that place Ishmael was buried.

Reference to the Hijr brings us to the end of the story of Hagar and her son, and also to the continuation of their memory in Muslim celebrations of God's signs in Mecca. The Hijr being referred to in these texts is the semicircular area adjacent to the Ka'ba's northwestern wall that is within the circuit of pilgrims' *tawaf* (circumambulation). Much discussed by modern scholarship in relation to this space's use and understandings by pre-Islamic visitors to and inhabitants of the site (the era Islam tagged as al-Jahiliyya—the time of pagan "ignorance"), the area possesses significance for our commentators of the early centuries of Islam precisely because what al-Kisa'i calls the "rock" at the Hijr contains the bodies of the religion's heroine and her son by Abraham. As holy spaces within the Ka`ba's sacred precinct, the tombs of Hagar and Ishmael make a triad with the *maqam*, or standing place, that commemorates Abraham's blessed presence and accomplishment there. We observe how carefully the Islamic narrative concerning Hagar and Ishmael, the patriarch's family in the valley near the House, both inspires and is reinforced by the "true worship" established and continued there as generations of pilgrims come to make their prayers at this holiest of places.

THE FAMILY AT MECCA

Here we discuss interpretations of the family at Mecca in a painting (Figure 6.1), and in the text of a manuscript of al-Nisaburi's *Stories of the Prophets*. The viewer's eye takes in both the central figures around the door, and also the elaborate building which seems too prominent in the painting to be simply backdrop. In their publication of the image in *Stories of the Prophets: Illuminated Manuscripts of Qisas al-Anbiya*, Milstein, Rührdanz, and Schmitz supplied the caption, "Ibrahim and Isma'il praying after the building

Figure 6.1 The angel Jabril visits Ibrahim's family. From a 1577 copy of Nisaburi's *Qisas al-Anbiya*. © The New York Public Library, Astor, Lenox, and Tilden Foundations. Spencer Collection, Persian Ms. 1, folio 33b.

of the Ka`ba."[47] Did they correctly identify the illustration's subject? It does not seem to be the case that Abraham and Ishmael are praying, nor is it at all evident that the mosque's completion is the focus of the action portrayed.

Some literary and artistic archaeology is called for. The manuscript containing our painting is a sixteenth-century copy of al-Nisaburi's Persian *Qisas al-anbiya'* which was composed in the eleventh century.[48] Al-Nisaburi's version of the collected histories and legends of the prophets was itself reliant largely upon Bal`ami's edition-revision of al-Tabari's *History* forty years after the latter's death in 923 CE—a little less than three centuries after the death of the prophet Muhammad. Our manuscript, then, while not itself early, bears the clear marks of its primary source, the work of the Islamic chronicler and Qu'ran commentator now familiar to us, al-Tabari.[49] At the same time, it is important to note that we find in Nisaburi's narrative significant additions to al-Tabari's story of Abraham's women and sons, and to these narrative elaborations we shall want to return, for they interject a quite surprising turn of events into Abraham's saga.

We return to the painting in order to investigate more closely its content and possible intended meanings. Present in the scene are five recognizable figures, three with halos. To each side of the black door we see Abraham (on the left) facing winged Gabriel. Standing behind his father is the prophet Ishmael, a beardless youth. On the right, in back or to the side of the angelic messenger, are two women—Sarah the closest, I infer, and then, Hagar. There are onlookers nearby and at a distance in the background. Gabriel's proclamation to Abraham (and his family) of the coming birth of Isaac/Ishaq is the painting's subject—definitely this, and *not* the establishment of the Ka'ba and the prayers of its builders. Gestures of response to Gabriel's tidings take the form of extended hands by the principals in the drama, while onlookers strike poses indicating a range of attitudes from curiosity and wonder to earnest gazing, or devotion. In taking up this subject, the painting is, to my knowledge, unique—that is, without a parallel among the extant Muslim *qisas* illuminations of the story of Abraham.

Are we able to know why the artist chose to produce a painting of this event, and why he opted to have the Ka`ba as its setting?

One piece of explanation lies in the format of al-Nisaburi's book, which our painter seems to have taken seriously. His *Stories of the Prophets,* including that portion dedicated to Abraham's saga, is presented in brief and clearly delineated segments (each termed a "story" and each devoted to a particular incident). So, for example, we find the story of the early encounter of Abraham with Nimrod his persecutor, and a later one telling the birth of Ishmael, and at the end, a story telling of the patriarch's death.

Al-Nisaburi's narrative plan has a feature that becomes noteworthy after studying the painting: a brief story that treats the birth of Isaac follows *immediately* the story of the building of the Ka'ba. The textual transition between the incidents gives no indication of a change of scene. The artist has, then, pictorially heeded the conjunction of the two episodes—one (the twenty-sixth story) centered on the Ka'ba's construction, the other (the twenty-seventh) on Gabriel's declaration of God's gift to Abraham and Sarah—their son, Isaac.

The writing that stands above and below the painting is the continuous text of al-Nisaburi's *Qisas* in its sixteenth-century form—not an inscription nor an identifying description of the picture per se. The passage from the page preceding the text at the top of the illumination and running to the end of the writing above the image reads:

> After completing their praying, Gabriel came and said: "Behold, Abraham! 'Invite people to pilgrimage to the House (Surah 22:27).'" Abraham said: "My God, who can hear my call?" God responded: "You proclaim. I shall spread the calling." Then Abraham said: "People! Truly the Almighty Lord ordered me to build the Ka'ba. I did build it and brought its construction to completion according to his command and his call. So now, answer His calling to [text continues in the space above the painting] make the pilgrimage. The Most-High God will forgive you." The Most-Holy Lord brought the voice [of Abraham] to all people, even those in the loins of the fathers. And all who would make the pilgrimage someday between then and the Day of Judgment answered: "Yes!"[50]

In red letters beneath the painting, we find the next episode's heading, "Twenty-seventh story: Birth of Isaac (peace be upon him)," followed by this story's opening words:

> When Gabriel (peace be upon him) gave Abraham (peace be upon him) the news of the birth of Isaac, then after seven days Sarah got pregnant, and after nine months she gave birth. When Isaac (peace be upon him) was born,

The text continues on the next page,

> One thousand stars gathered in front of Abraham's house, and he asked, "My God, what sign is this?" And God responded through his angel, "I decided that one thousand prophets would issue from Isaac's seed." Abraham was pleased, and praised God. Then he asked, "My God, you gave this mercy to Isaac—what about Ishmael who is also my son?" And God said, "Abraham, do not worry. Leave him and his progeny to Me. I shall bring from among his offspring a

prophet who is more exalted than a thousand prophets, even more than one hundred twenty-four (thousand)."[51]

The artist's inclusion of the Ka'ba and the divine promise of Isaac's birth in a single scene is, therefore, fully explicable on the basis of the sequencing of stories or incidents in al-Nisaburi's Abraham narrative.

The twenty-seventh story's account of the birth of Isaac is, interestingly, the author's second reference to the event. Earlier, in the twenty-fourth story, al-Nisaburi narrated Gabriel's tidings to Abraham that Sarah will have a son and that Lot, his nephew, will be spared from the destruction of Sodom. There it was reported that Sarah was pregnant within the week, and further, that her delivery of Isaac, her first born, was difficult. Hagar's derisive laughter at Sarah's distress in labor is given as the cause of Sarah's anger, explaining her demand that Hagar and Ishmael be expelled. Upon his birth, Isaac is declared a "good and great child" from whom a thousand prophets of the people of Israel will issue.[52] We may surmise that those closing sentences about the great succession of prophets to issue from Isaac prompted al-Nisaburi's return, three stories later, to the subject of Isaac's birth, which occurred subsequent to the construction of the Ka'ba.

The twenty-seventh story stands, therefore, as an embellishment and corrective variant on what was told in the twenty-fourth. When a thousand stars gather in front of his house and he hears the divine declaration of the thousand prophets to come from his second son, Abraham is filled with delight. But this revelation also causes him to make a plea for the good fortune of Ishmael, his firstborn—the passage quoted above, in which God speaks about Ishmael's posterity, and promises the appearance of that "prophet who is more exalted" than all the others—Muhammad.[53] In this episode's recalibration of the status of Ishmael in relation to Isaac, Abraham's first son gains more prominence—in his progeny there will be more than a thousand prophets.

Other parts of this *Qisas*'s account of Abraham and his family prove consequential. In the twenty-fifth story, we learn that during one of his periodic visits to the valley (this one allowing him to interact with Ishmael's second wife, an Arab), Hagar (still alive) and Ishmael came on the scene. Abraham "saw them" and rejoiced.[54]

Upon receiving the command to construct the Ka'ba, Abraham summons (from Syria) Sarah and Isaac, along with others loyal to him. Abraham then informs Sarah that the time has come for her to be at peace with "my son and his mother."[55] Sarah does not resist her husband's request, even though there follow grudging comments. Sarah claims that God has shown partiality to Hagar and Ishmael, showering them with greater mercy and property, blessing them in their residence in Mecca, and giving them good and bounteous offspring. For story-teller al-Nisaburi, Sarah's muttering recalls the element of her resentment in the two women's earlier dealings, but it has a more important purpose as a distinctly Muslim counterplay to biblical teachings about the privileges and favored status of Isaac. Jewish and Christian estimations of Sarah's preeminence are being rebuffed.

When Abraham's wives and sons are present in Mecca together, mutual forgiveness takes place. Sarah and Isaac pardon Hagar and Ishmael, and they reciprocate, Ishmael extending, as the text says, "great kindness to Sarah."[56]

According to al-Nisaburi, the completion of the Ka`ba's building took three years, and a few years afterward Abraham, having circumambulated the House, took his family members to a mountain, where they raised their hands and prayed. For those who would make the Hajj, Abraham made his petition on behalf of learned Muslim leaders, asking God that these be rewarded and blessed in the Day of Reckoning. In the same formula, Ishmael prayed for the males sixty years old or older, Isaac for the young, Sarah for every Muslim, and Hagar for every religiously trained Muslim woman who aids women making the pilgrimage.

Abraham's family functions as a quintet of worshipful patrons seeking divine beneficence for all who will come to the Ka'ba. Though this is presented as a unified and comprehensive act of prayer, it is not to go unnoticed that in relation to the hierarchy of Muslim believers represented, from the educated elders and leaders down to the young males and the observant women, the prayers of Mecca's primary human trio—Abraham, Ishmael, and Hagar—are aligned with, and are designated to, ask God's blessings upon the most worthy and eminent among the believers. The next words in the twenty-sixth story are those that commence above our painting: "After completing their praying, Gabriel came and said: 'Behold, Abraham! Invite people to pilgrimage to the House, etc.'" (cf. Surah 22:27).

This tour of al-Nisaburi's literary portrayals of Abraham and his women and sons indicates that however dependent his *Qisas* may be upon traditions from al-Tabari, it adds remarkable twists to the tale. Together these fresh elements constitute and advance a strong Muslim vision and perspective. In its unexpected resolution of a fractured family's bitter tale, al-Nisaburi's narrative locates the healing of grievances and the subsequent prayers for a united community of believers in Islam's sacred precinct, and thereby shows these dynamics to be entirely a part of the pilgrimage, the ritual entering upon "the straight path, the path of those You have favored" (Surah 1:6–7).

It is difficult to believe that those who surveyed this image would have missed its iconographic assertion: the prediction of Isaac's birth—an event that Jews and Christians (and perhaps many Muslims) understood to have happened near the oaks of Mamre at Hebron—is here firmly placed in Mecca. How many issues and possibilities of meaning might be at stake in this happening's relocation? Most obviously and most significantly, those stories which we saw the commentators elaborating as they shifted the Abrahamic saga's center of gravity to Islam's cultic center—namely, the rescue of Ishmael and his mother at Zamzam, the building of God's House, the "great sacrifice" of the ram at Mina, which preserved Ishmael's life—now exercise their influence in this painter's revisionist theme. It is difficult to imagine a more forceful way to illustrate this claim than to have the fortunes of both of Abraham's sons, his first and his second, shown as unfolding near his standing place in the Ka`ba.

Present in both al-Nisaburi's narrative additions and the painting's scene are innovative messages that secure deeper meanings in the sacred history of Muslims. The pilgrimage from Syria by Sarah and Isaac, as well as the presence in Mecca of Sarah at the time of Gabriel's promise of a son, communicate the loyalty of the other half of Abraham's family to the God whose name is worshipfully pronounced at the Meccan House, and what transpires there between family members—especially the accomplishment of *salaam* between the patriarch's two wives, the mothers of the Israelites and the Muslims—signals reunification of the Abrahamic household. This regathering of his family is, of course, effected by the help and power at work in the pilgrimage commanded and blessed by God.

So runs the narrative of Abraham and his family as it approaches its conclusion in al-Nisaburi's telling, and so is revealed the imaginative artistry of the painter, whose image freshly interprets what the scene of the promise of Isaac's birth signifies—in terms Muslims recognize and honor. The legacy of Abraham, Hagar, Ishmael—and, yes, also the reconciliation of Sarah and Hagar and their sons—is a matter of Meccan celebration.

Muslim understandings of the story of Abraham's women and sons, and the processes by which Islam took ownership of the story, give clear evidence of "exegetical encounters" with Jewish and Christian rivals. We noticed in the Qur'an's account of the messengers' visit to Abraham and "his wife" its correspondence to the biblical narrative in *Genesis* 18, but also that there was no reference to Hagar's experiences in the patriarch's household, or as someone expelled from it. Rather, a passage in which Abraham tells God of his settling of some of his family in desolate terrain near God's house provided for interpreters a basis for recounting Gabriel's rescue of Hagar and Ishmael at the spring called Zamzam. Muslim Qur'an interpreters and tellers of the stories of the prophets, while very much aware of Jewish Abrahamic traditions, chose to generate a continuance of the story of *this* half of the prophet's family by situating them in Mecca and involving them in the prayers for which the Ka'ba was dutifully, and wondrously, built.

Because of the mother and son in Islam's foundation story, and because of the lineage from them that includes Muhammad, Islam's Ibrahim is neither Judaism's nor Christianity's Abraham. This orientation of Muslim religious history and loyalty is consistent, as we have seen in the Qur'an, in the tradition-building revealed in the writings of al-Tabari, al-Tha`labi, and al-Nisaburi, and in the splendid painting that makes unmistakable the holy place, Mecca, to which Abraham has gathered his family, that they might "keep up prayer" (14:37).

Comparative Summary

Sarah and Hagar: Mothers to Three Families

How did Jewish, Christian, and Muslim scriptures and their interpreters treat the relationships between Sarah and Hagar—and between their sons? This guiding query in chapters 4 through 6 produced, more than anything else, our discovery of profound differences in viewpoint and fundamental beliefs between the three religions. Narratives of Abraham and his two women, when fashioned to serve each community, resulted in Sarah and Hagar becoming mothers to three families—three diverging religions.

The clash between Sarah and Hagar described so vividly in *Genesis* chapters 16–18 and 21 attracted further exploration and comment in *Genesis Rabbah*, where we found rabbis intensifying the women's animosity. Hagar's arrogance and ill-will were increased in further (imagined) incidents, explaining and justifying some of Sarah's harsh actions toward her. (The biblical traditions that identified the Hagarites and the Ishmaelites as enemies of the Jews were obviously influential in the exegetes' expanded characterizations of Abraham's two women.) The wonder of Sarah's birthgiving received celebrative treatments, to which were added reports of miraculous healings accomplished by her milk. Because the scriptural account did not explain what Sarah witnessed in Ishmael's "playing," the rabbis provided numerous opinions—for example, that she saw him threatening Isaac with his archery, or "ravishing maidens," or committing idolatry. These actions explained Sarah's defense of Isaac, and her demand that Hagar and Ishmael be sent away. Abraham's pangs of concern for Ishmael, his firstborn son, were treated sympathetically by the rabbis, we noted, and the theologizing about how God found Ishmael worthy of being saved when he (and his mother) were at the point of death, was ingenious. What presides over, and is woven into, these many elements of commentary in *Genesis Rabbah*, we recognized, was the claim so firmly established in the *Genesis* account—that the covenant made by God with Abraham belonged to those children of his whose foremother was Sarah, and who stemmed from the line of Isaac—and Jacob, and Joseph.

In a panel in the mosaic floor of the Sepphoris synagogue we saw the bare remnants of the scene in which this promise that Sarah would bear Isaac was delivered by visitors. The commonalities and the differences in Jewish and Christian understandings of this episode—and of the near-sacrifice of Isaac by Abraham—brought to our attention the close familiarity of each religion's scripture interpreters with the others' lines of reasoning and distinctive religious convictions. Matters under debate strongly and directly influenced the production of their diverging interpretations of the same story.

Attempts by Christian interpreters to make the Bible's account of the strife between Abraham's two women and sons serve the churches' best interests were definite and aggressive. The apostle Paul's bold (and idiosyncratic) allegory of Abraham's family and its divisions (Hagar representing Mt. Sinai and slavery under the law, and Sarah representing heavenly Jerusalem and freedom) commenced, only a few decades after Jesus's public ministry, the construction of a radical Christian claim: the covenant blessing God first bestowed upon Abraham and his successors through Isaac had passed from the Jews to the new community (composed of both Jews and Gentiles) who believed Jesus was God's promised messiah. The sermon on the birth of Isaac by the theologian and biblical scholar Origen showed us his careful attention to the story, his way of using (differently from Paul) Sarah and Hagar "to think with," and his consistent push to bring the biblical episode's challenges directly to the lives and life decisions of his hearers. Were not the characters of the two brothers, and tensions between them, now present in the churches, where some believers clung to God out of fear, while others turned to God with the "freedom of love"?

A remarkable painting in the Ashburnham Pentateuch of Sarah and Hagar together, their boys skirmishing in front of them, showed Sarah asking the enthroned Abraham to deny any inheritance to Ishmael. We found this characterization of Sarah to be not only literal—that is, true to what the biblical text describes—but also thematic, since Sarah's demand upholds and defends the covenant promise that belongs to their son Isaac and to those who stand in his line. Sarah's uprightness and confidence in God was similarly reflected in two contiguous scenes which portrayed (1) her endangerment in the palace of Abimelech, whose dreams warned him not to seek sex with her, since she was Abraham's wife, not his sister, and showed (2) her release, vindicated, from the king's house.

In the splendid mosaic within Sta. Maria Maggiore which depicted the three men who visited Abraham, and were fed by him and Sarah, we met another Christian interpretive presentation of Sarah: the angelic promise of her wondrous pregnancy and the birth of her son symbolically prefigured the event principally pictured in the great Roman basilica—Christ's birth to Mary.

We learned that not in the Qur'an, but in Muslim commentaries treating Abraham and his sons, and particularly in the genre of stories of the prophets, we gain access to many other traditions about Sarah/Sara and Hagar/Hajar. Those sources, replete with isra'iliyyat—traditions from the Jews and Christians—treat and elaborate upon the competition and conflict between the women and their sons. There is qur'anic reference to Ibrahim's wife (with Sarah the person being indicated), but Hagar goes unmentioned (since the relationship between the two women is not reported), even though it is implied that she was among those whom Abraham sent to a barren place near God's "sacred House." Hagar's importance appears, we noted, in the Qur'an's endorsement in 14:37 of Meccan pilgrims' sa'y, the running between the hills of Safa and Marwa, as she desperately had done, looking for help for Ishmael, when he lay dying of thirst.

The rise and development in the ninth and tenth centuries CE of Muslim traditions concerning Mecca, the fortunes of Hagar and Ishmael at the well of Zamzam, and the commission of Abraham and Ishmael to build God's house did not prevent writers like al-Tabari and al-Tha'labi from revisiting the lore of Sarah's harsh relationship with Hagar, speculating about whether circumcision was the punishment inflicted by the mistress on her slave, or what kind of playing by Ishmael led to the expulsion of him and his mother from Abraham's household in Syria. However, it was not the portrait of Hagar, oppressed, that prevailed in Muslim cultural consciousness. Rather, her endurance of trial and testing when the water supply ran out for her and her son, the miracle of the gushing forth of the spring, and more fundamentally, as Barbara Stowasser wrote, her being "part of the divine plan to establish God's true sanctuary and its rituals" marked her as one of God agents, an exemplar of faithful submission and duty. This honor of Hagar was, and is, preserved, in her burial—and her son, Ishmael's—near the prophet Abraham's maqam, or standing place, at the Ka'ba.

Finally, the imagination of Muslim interpreters of Abraham and his women took us to a new chapter—a grand conclusion—in the saga. A

painting illuminating a manuscript of al-Nisaburi's *Qisas al-anbiya* we discovered to be not a celebration of the completion of the Ka'ba by Abraham
and Ishmael, but the depiction of a reunion of the two halves of Abraham's
family (Sarah having been required to forgive and reconcile). Gathered
together before God's house (as al-Nisaburi had imagined in his story-
expansion), the angel Gabriel announces that Sarah will give birth to Isaac.
The painting and the text's narrative present a reunion of Abraham, his
women, and his sons, and accomplishes this in a decidedly Muslim denouement of the story—centered in Mecca, the place of true worship and of
true blessings from God the merciful.

The significantly different values and goals that became transparent
as we plumbed several Jewish, Christian, and Muslim understandings of
Abraham, Sarah, Isaac, Hagar, and Ishmael provided compelling evidence
not only of the three communities' knowledge of each others' belief systems and traditions, but also the sharpening social divergence due in significant measure to debate over their scriptures' messages and meanings.

PART III

Joseph's Temptation by His Egyptian Master's Wife

Preview, Chapters 7–9

Joseph/Yusuf and the Temptress

Joseph, son of Jacob, grandson of Isaac, and great-grandson of Abraham, was a prodigy as a boy and throughout his life, which, as it is recounted in the Hebrew Bible, involved two challenges—his life in separation from his family, due to his brothers' abandonment of him at a young age, and his rise from the status of a Jewish slave in Egypt to being the Pharaoh's protégé. In the individual scenes of the biblical narrative (*Genesis* 37–50), from Joseph's dreams and dream-reading to his wise and often crafty leadership, we meet a new kind of biblical actor and a new brand of Hebrew patriarch. Steadily thumping beneath the narrated events that make up his life story are promises having to do with the future of his people—that branch of the Abrahamic lineage stemming from the house of Jacob.

In the historical period we are considering, Jews knew the grand tale of Joseph primarily in the languages of Hebrew, Aramaic, and Greek, and Christians in Greek, Syriac, and Latin, while Muslims first heard Yusuf's story in Arabic. All three religions revered Jonah/Yunus; he was an ancient hero and kinsman—a renowned victor through many trials and tests, God being constantly "with him." Jews will call him "the righteous," Christians will include him among the saints of what they term the "old covenant," and Muslims will celebrate him as one of the prophets of God—each faith community understanding Joseph's/Yusuf's history in the idioms of its own patterns of thought and custom.

The attempted seduction of Joseph by his Egyptian master's wife and Joseph's resistance to her stands out among the many drama-filled moments in his saga. Its tensions are palpable, the motivations of its actors complex, and its possible messages, moral and otherwise, provocative. Rabbinic, early Christian, and early Muslim students of their respective holy books found much to discuss in this transparently salacious—and dangerous—incident. Their comments, speculations, and "narrative expansions" invite a comparative consideration of the three communities' ways of reading and using the arresting story of Joseph's narrow escape from the scheming woman.[1]

All three traditions explore what kind of encounter took place between Joseph and Potiphar's wife—or between Yusuf and Zulaykha, to use their names in the Muslim tradition. A key interest in the three chapters to follow is one of the more provocative issues taken up by early commentators—namely, Joseph's response to his mistress's insistence that he submit to having intercourse with her. Wedging apart two closely related terms, the focal question is: was Joseph not only *tested* but also *tempted*?

Rabbinic producers of *midrash* and Muslim composers of *tafsir* debated the degree of Joseph's involvement and complicity in his encounter with his master's wife. Though their questions and responses bore directly on their understandings of the virtue (and the status) of a patriarch or of a prophet, this did not preclude speculation about the susceptibility of the handsome young Joseph/Yusuf to the lustful woman's advances.

It may be the case that Joseph's status as one of the church's saints qualified the kinds of questions early Christian biblical commentators might ask about his vulnerability to the lure of Potiphar's wife.[2] We want to know whether the fathers of the church, in making use of the narrative of *Genesis* 39, were able to entertain the idea of Joseph's temptability—his potential for misstep, sin, and guilt. For Muslim commentators, the subject was necessarily open for consideration and discussion, since the qur'anic account of this incident acknowledged Yusuf's readiness to match the desire of his would-be seductress with his own.

This portion of the Joseph story, with its early histories of interpretation among Jews, Christians, and Muslims, opens, I think, upon a broader set of questions that I hope at least to sharpen, if not resolve, as these three chapters proceed. How and why does the representation of Joseph/ Yusuf undergo changes in the traditions of Jews, Christians, and Muslims alike? Do efforts to fashion him into an exemplar of a specific virtue rob him of human qualities, and rob the scriptural accounts of some of their most searching and entertaining pictures of human motivations? Were other factors and dynamics—namely shifts of viewpoint occurring within the communities of interpretation over the course of time—the sources of these *re*presentations? The early Christian characterizations of Joseph, which tend to understand him as above temptation, may be sheer efforts at idealization of a biblical hero, but we shall see that other interests and goals influence the Christians' ways of picturing and understanding him.

We encounter a particular surprise in some Muslim representations of the wife of the Aziz. An older, wiser Zulaykha emerges in poetry and commentary beginning in the fourth Islamic century, giving her a place nearly as lofty as Yusuf's: she comes to personify a worthy form of desire.

CHAPTER 7

∾

Joseph and Potiphar's Wife

Jewish Interpretations

Figure 7.1 Marc Chagall, *Potiphar's Wife*. 1958. The Haggerty Museum, Marquette University, Milwaukee, Wisconsin. © 2014 Artists Rights Society, New York/ADAGP, Paris.

L ike many painters before him, Chagall found the subject of Joseph's escape from the sexual aggression of Potiphar's wife an irresistible subject (Figure 7.1). Not only was the scene attractive to artists because of its vivid pictureability, it was also understood to be a defining moment in the biblical history of the life of the young slave who would become an official in Egypt capable of sustaining and protecting his own people, the Hebrews. How was a young man to resist the advances of a mature woman—one who held power over him?

Into the brief account in *Genesis* 39 of Joseph's encounters with Potiphar's wife are woven several dominant themes of the Torah's first book—preeminently, God's selection and calling of certain individuals to be prophets and seers. A review of the better known elements in *Genesis* 37–50 is called for: Joseph's revelations of the youthful dreams foretelling his grand future, combined with his being favored and adorned with a splendid coat of many colors by his father, leads his brothers to hate him, abandon him in a pit, and deceive Jacob with evidence of his death (37); rescued by wayfarers and sold as a slave to the Egyptian official Potiphar, the adroit Joseph quickly becomes the overseer of his master's affairs; the attempted seduction of Joseph by Potiphar's wife, who claimed that *he* had been the sexual aggressor, lands him in prison; Joseph's liberation is due to his usefulness to the Pharaoh, first, as a dream-analyst, and thereafter as a shrewd and skilled director of Egypt's lands and commerce (37, 39–41); Joseph marries Aseneth, the daughter of an Egyptian priest, with whom he has two sons, Manasseh and Ephraim (41); difficult and emotion-laden dealings with his brothers occur when, coming from Canaan to purchase grain, they do not recognize him; Joseph proceeds to put his brothers to a series of tests (42–45); Joseph is reconciled with his father, who comes with his people to reside in a place within the Pharaoh's lands called Goshen (46); at the end, after Jacob the father's death, Joseph forgives his fearful brothers.

Joseph's conclusive merciful act comes with a two-part explanation: he, Joseph, is not God (to judge them), and all the events of his history had transpired providentially, "to preserve a numerous people" (50:20) against that day when the Lord himself "will bring you up out of this land to the land that he swore to Abraham, Isaac, and Jacob" (50:24). By this statement in Joseph's farewell speech to his brothers, the narrator fully communicates his own understanding of the place and significance of Joseph in his people's history—past and future.[1] Joseph, frequently endangered in the course of his life but steadily blessed by having the Lord "with him," is the pivotal figure: he ensured the survival of the Hebrews who one day would, passing through Egypt's waters, gain freedom to journey toward what would be their homeland.

For Jews and for Judaism, the entire drama of Joseph is enfolded between the scripture's account that precedes, running from the Creation to the calling of Abraham and his progeny, and by what follows—the exploits of Moses and his successors. The adventure, or misadventure, of Joseph that now occupies us—his dealings with his master's impassioned wife—is more than a small but vivid bit of Joseph's longer life story. Within this engagement, as narrated, its actors' motivations, words, and deeds, are multivalent; questions suggest themselves about the temptress, yes, and her husband, but even more about Joseph, this Hebrew favored son of Jacob, who now finds himself in peril while in the service of an approving Egyptian master.

Hearers of this part of Joseph's story were titillated both by its content and by the questions it posed, finding much to discuss and debate. What stood behind the actions of the woman, of her husband, and of Joseph himself? We, in the course of reading these twenty-one verses, are able to anticipate what in the narrator's account would most spark curiosity.

Genesis 39

1 When Joseph was taken down to Egypt, a certain Egyptian, Potiphar, a courtier of Pharaoh and his chief steward, bought him from the Ishmaelites who had brought him there. 2 The LORD was with Joseph, and he was a successful man; and he stayed in the house of his Egyptian master. 3 And when his master saw that the LORD was with him and that the LORD lent success to everything he undertook, 4 he took a liking to Joseph. He made him his personal attendant and put him in charge of his household, placing in his hands all that he owned. 5 And from the time that the Egyptian put him in charge of his household and of all that he owned, the LORD blessed his house for Joseph's sake, so that the blessing of the LORD was upon everything that he owned, in the house and outside. 6 He left all that he had in Joseph's hands and, with him there, he paid attention to nothing save the food that he ate. Now Joseph was well built and handsome.

7 After a time, his master's wife cast her eyes upon Joseph and said, "Lie with me." 8 But he refused. He said to his master's wife, "Look, with me here, my master gives no thought to anything in this house, and all that he owns he has placed in my hands. 9 He wields no more authority in this house than I, and he has withheld nothing from me except yourself, since you are his wife. How then could I do this most wicked thing, and sin before God?" 10 And much as

she coaxed Joseph day after day, he did not yield to her request to lie beside her, to be with her.

11 One such day, he came into the house to do his work. None of the household being there inside, 12 she caught hold of him by his garment and said, "Lie with me!" But he left his garment in her hand and got away and fled outside. 13 When she saw that he had left it in her hand and had fled outside, 14 she called out to her servants and said to them, "Look, he had to bring us a Hebrew to dally with us! This one came to lie with me; but I screamed loud. 15 And when he heard me screaming at the top of my voice, he left his garment with me and got away and fled outside." 16 She kept his garment beside her, until his master came home.

17 Then she told him the same story, saying, "The Hebrew slave whom you brought into our house came to me to dally with me; 18 but when I screamed at the top of my voice, he left his garment with me and fled outside."

19 When his master heard the story that his wife told him, namely, "Thus and so your slave did to me," he was furious. 20 So Joseph's master had him put in prison, where the king's prisoners were confined. But even while he was there in prison, 21 the LORD was with Joseph: He extended kindness to him and disposed the chief jailer favorably toward him. 22 The chief jailer put in Joseph's charge all the prisoners who were in that prison, and he was the one to carry out everything that was done there. 23 The chief jailer did not supervise anything that was in Joseph's charge, because the LORD was with him, and whatever he did the LORD made successful.

MODERN SCHOLARS' LINES OF INQUIRY

Recent decades' scholarly attention to this section of the Joseph story will set the stage for turning, in a few pages, to our chief interest: the diverse interpretations put forth by Jewish scholars of the early centuries of the Common Era. Quite a few of the questions tackled by modern exegetes occupied their forebears as well. These interests will not, for the most part, surprise us, since it is all but impossible to read *Genesis* 39 without wondering at certain points what is really being said, or implied, in the text.

For over a century a beguiling question has occupied students of the Bible who necessarily have in their purview other literatures of the ancient Near East: does the story of the attempted seduction of Joseph by Potiphar's wife depend upon a much earlier and apparently widely known Egyptian tale of "Two Brothers," which "tells how a conscientious young man was falsely accused of a proposal of adultery by the wife of his elder brother, after he had actually rejected her advances"?[2] In one portion of this story, the unnamed wife of the older brother (Anubis) attempts to seduce the younger brother, Bata—a person who performed significant labor in his brother's service, and was exemplary in his goodness. On a certain day, working in the fields with his brother, Bata was sent home to collect more seed for sowing, and there his sister-in-law interrupted him in his task, inviting him to stay a while and have intercourse with her. His reward, she promised, would be fine new clothing of her own making. Angered "like a leopard in a rage," Bata declared that to succumb to her wantonness would be an act of disloyalty: "See here—you were like a mother to me, and your husband is like a father to me! Because—being older than I—he was the one who brought me up."[3] Spurned, and worried about the consequences of her overture, Anubis's wife proceeded to bruise her body so that, upon her husband's return, she might provide evidence supporting her accusation that Bata tried to force himself upon her. The tense happenings conclude when, at the end of his pursuit to kill Bata, Anubis is convinced by his younger brother's words and deed (Bata, distraught, dismembers himself) that guilt is not his brother's, but belongs to his wife. He then dispatches her, throws her corpse to the dogs, and mourns Bata's self-exile.

While some scholars have resisted the view that the author of *Genesis* 39 was cognizant of, or significantly influenced by, the tale of the Egyptian brothers, others have thought otherwise, calling attention to close similarities. The former see the Egyptian text in its entirety as too mythological and fanciful to have served as a basis for the realistic mode of the *Genesis* account of Joseph's history.[4] Claus Westermann strongly maintained the competing view—that the fashioner of the biblical story of Joseph and Potiphar's wife knew a version of the "Two Brothers" saga, and used it well in his own narrative. Westermann's argument holds that in

> the parallel course of the narrative there are almost word for word points of agreement. It is said of the younger brother, who is in service of the elder, that his work was particularly fruitful, "the strength of a God was in him," and that because of him his brother's property increased. The motive for the refusal is almost the same. Like Joseph, the brother describes the proposed adultery as a "great sin" or crime.[5]

While varied presuppositions about the character of Hebrew scripture as holy and inspired may to some degree affect assessments about "outside influence" and the content of ch. 39 itself, our interest here centers in the manner in which the writer of the narrative worked to make *this* attempted seduction story one that concerned a tradition-particular hero who is in the midst of difficulty and danger. Though imagining the origins of the story differently, both groups of scholars see in *Genesis* 39 a specific portrait of Joseph—one intent upon detailing his traits and characteristics, his reactions to both promising and perilous events that befall him.

Modern scholars highlight the strategies by which the narrator unfolds his story of the attempted seduction of Joseph. In the space of only twenty three verses, key themes are regularly sounded, and the plot gains both momentum and sense through frequent repetition of phrases, or in some cases by their transfer from one character to another. The early and repeated identification of Joseph's master as Egyptian (vv. 1, 2, 5), for example, is meant to remind the biblically aware listener or reader of what the Lord had said to Abraham in a vision (15:13–14): that his people would be for four hundred years strangers and slaves in a land not their own, but then liberated.[6] In these verses, it is a subtle rather than thunderous motif, but it is one crucial to the storyteller's contextualizing of Joseph, for it is he who will be responsible for the presence of his people in this alien land.[7] All modern exegetes call attention to the fact that only in this chapter in the Joseph story is the divinely disclosed name *YHVH* (rather than the more generalized `*Elohim*) employed—with the intent of conveying, as Nahum Sarna notes, that "events in the odyssey of Joseph are key elements in God's plan for the people of Israel ... [giving] an appropriate nuance to this wider national inflection in the narrative."[8] It is by design rather than accident that in v. 8 ("How then could I do this most wicked thing, and sin before God?") the author supplies the word `*Elohim*, for in this instance Joseph speaks to a non-Hebrew, his would-be seductress.[9] Helping to explain how a "spoiled lad of seventeen, utterly alone in a foreign land and in dire adversity" (again, Sarna) is able quickly to mature and display admirable character, the advisory phrase that the Lord (*YHVH*) "was with Joseph" occurs four times in chapter 39; "[he] can rise again and again in situations that would surely have crushed others."[10]

The shifting language about what responsibilities his master has left in his charge evokes scholarly comment and speculation: what innuendos reside in the phrases, taken together, in verses 6 and 9—"the food that he ate" and "his wife."[11] One scholar submits that the single excepted activity of Joseph—that of food preparation—reflects the author's knowledge of "a general Egyptian concern that non-Egyptians were unaware of how properly to prepare food ... or, more likely, because of ritual separation at mealtimes."[12] But others suspect a less prosaic sense—namely, taking the meaning to be that Potiphar's wife is the one thing that has not been left "in Joseph's hands," and speculate that she is being referred to as "the food that he ate." Commenting on vv. 6–9, Eric Lowenthal wrote:

> Joseph has now become Potiphar's overseer, no longer expected to give his master an account. To ascertain the meaning of the seemingly simple words, "anything except for the bread he ate," we have to compare them with the way Joseph paraphrases them in vv. 8ff., "Lo, with me [around], my master knows nothing . . . nor has he withheld anything from me *except yourself*" (emphasis added). "The bread he ate," then, is a euphemism for sexual intercourse.[13]

This last line of interpretation assumes the author to be clever—and innuendo-prone. Still another approach can be entertained, one that follows the textual sequence more literally, but also spies sexual implications: does the comment that Potiphar paid no heed to anything but the food he ate suggest that his (overlooked) wife had some reason to be interested in the physique and attractiveness of the household's new and privileged slave?[14]

The early verbal exchanges between the temptress and Joseph also manifest evidence of careful production. As one commentator notes:

> Potiphar's wife does more looking than talking. Her propositioning of Joseph is terse. She says only two words to him: *sikeba `immi*, Lie with me (v. 7b), which she later repeats (v. 12). By contrast, Joseph's rejection of her advances is much lengthier (vv. 8–9).[15]

Obviously the narrative is meant to demonstrate the Lord-strengthened character of the righteous youth under threat, and to allow Joseph to give voice to his cherished values—loyalty and respect for his master and what is his, and abhorrence of adultery, which he counts as a "sin before God." (Scholars ponder the grounds upon which the narrator, describing an event prior to the revelation of God's Law at Sinai, declares adultery a sin, some seeking other scriptural supports for the teaching.)[16] Variously evaluated by scholars is the persistence of the woman in her invitation (or is it, rather, her command?) to Joseph, culminating in the day of opportunity (with no one else in the house) when she seizes his garment (vv. 8–9). Some emphasize the build-up from a compromise proposition—that even if he will not have sex with her, he should lie beside her (v.v. 10)—to the aggressive insistence of Potiphar's wife when she grabs him by his clothes, presumably to pull him toward her bed. Others are inclined to wonder how much Joseph might have had to endure—and with what degree of compliance—in order to avoid invoking the wrath of his mistress.

Joseph's escape, leaving his garment in his pursuer's hands, sets the stage for the two protestations made by Potiphar's wife—first to her servants, and then to her husband. In the first instance she prefaces her account of what has happened by an accusation directed toward her husband: "Look, he had to bring us a Hebrew to dally with us!" Eric Lowenthal described her behavior, tactics, and viewpoint in this way:

> She toadies to the domestics by disparaging their master and places herself on their level by saying "us." She also makes them feel superior to Joseph, telling them that the upstart is but one of the impure Hebrew pastoral people (cf. [Genesis] 43:32; 44:34), whose very admission to their race-pure Egyptian home by their master had been an insult, not to mention the master's intention to have him toy with them and with her.[17]

We encountered the Hebrew word tsahak (equals "sport," "toy," "dally") earlier, in Sarah's accusation of what she saw Ishmael doing with or to Isaac, and noted there that the term had sexual connotations, with the sense of mocking as an alternative. Is there any suggestion or intimation in the remark of Potiphar's wife that Joseph had, or might have, acted promiscuously toward several in the household? (The issue arises explicitly, as we shall see, in the qur'anic telling of Yusuf's story.) Scholar-exegetes are quick to point out that though Potiphar's wife tells her husband "the same story" (v. 17–18)—that is, that Joseph came to "dally" with her, but at her loud screaming he fled, leaving his garment "in her hand"—her presentation to him employs different language.[18] To her husband, Joseph is "the Hebrew slave" (not the Hebrew he had foisted upon her and her household), and there is no suggestion that others were or could have been subjects of his purported sexual harassment. In keeping with the novella's mode of developing not only the characters and their actions, but also dropping strong clues about motivations and changes of temperament, vv. 7–18 relate how the woman's desire for and pursuit of Joseph grew in intensity until, frustrated by his resistance and, finally, his flight from her, her anger at him erupted. Her loathing of him, combined with her instincts for self-preservation, led her to attribute to Joseph her actual behavior, and claim for herself the innocence belonging to him. An interesting detail in her scheming appears in v. 16, in which the narrator comments that, in preparation for her husband's arrival, she "kept [Joseph's] garment beside her," wanting to produce evidence that Joseph had begun to undress when he came to her.[19] In seeking Joseph's punishment, she labors to free herself from any suspicion.

Modern commentators note the ambiguity attaching to the fury of Potiphar upon hearing his wife's report of Joseph's attempted assault.

Against whom is the master's wrath directed? Is he enraged to hear of Joseph's violation of his trust? Does he harbor questions about his wife, but realize what the cost would be to his reputation, privileged position, and his estate's stability should he challenge and expose her? What next happens, according to the scholars, holds suggestive clues. On the one hand, Joseph is given no opportunity for rebuttal, and might be understood in his silence to be either aware of his powerlessness in this circumstance, or (as at least the narrator would gauge the situation) exercising his patience, knowing that his fortunes will be determined by his God.

The woman states her case, the accused is silent, and Potiphar passes his judgment. An episode built upon observations of human passions, intrigue, and tension comes to an abrupt climax. Some biblical scholars do not find this surprising—Potiphar, under pressure, has done the only thing he can do with his wife's complaint, even if he regrets and resents the loss of his trusted servant. Joseph, for his part, is in no position to protest. But another way of assessing this abruptness—namely, asking what might be hidden between the lines of those verses—is properly inquisitive. Nahum Sarna, using evidence from another part of Joseph's story, projects an alternative way of understanding what finally transpired on his last day in Potiphar's household:

> It must not be assumed that Joseph silently accepted his unjust fate. The narrative is mute on this point; but it also recorded no reaction from Joseph when he was thrown into the pit (ch. 37), while a subsequent incident reveals that he had indeed pleaded with his brothers for his life (42:21). Here, too, it is reasonable to assume that he defends his innocence in a manner that at least raises some doubts about his guilt in his master's mind.[20]

According to this view, the author trusted hearers and readers to fill in gaps in his story of Joseph and his resistance to the wife of the Egyptian. Indeed, the brusque conclusion of this episode virtually begged for more explanation. Perhaps, the early Jewish exegetes will suggest, there was some discussion about the garment that Potiphar's wife held in her hand, or an unexpected challenge put to her accusation of Joseph at the time. Elaborations of the narrative designed to clear Joseph of the charge that he had attempted to rape his master's wife quickly arose—in Philo's writings, in early Christian exegesis, and in the Qur'an.

When considering the final verses of chapter 39—Potiphar's placement of Joseph in prison, and the events which make him an unusual prisoner—biblical analysts of our era identify again some of the purposes and strategies of the author. Pattern and repetition are carefully employed by him: Joseph, whose life had earlier been endangered by his siblings' throwing him into a pit, is now for a second time placed in an enclosure, his prospects bleak. The grabbing of Joseph's garment by Potiphar's wife recalls the action of his brothers in taking from him the brightly colored coat bestowed upon him by Jacob. Endangerment, and subsequent escape, or, as Westermann wrote, sequences of "advancement, fall, advancement," here, as elsewhere in *Genesis* 37–50, signify important turnings in the span of Joseph's life.[21]

Potiphar's decision to jail his trustworthy servant undergoes close scrutiny by modern commentators. That action itself is seen to reflect a solicitude for Joseph, for he is not incarcerated among the common criminals, but put "where the king's prisoners were confined" (v. 20). The next verses relegate the entanglement with Potiphar's wife, and the period of Joseph's relationship and dealings with Potiphar to the past, marking a transition in the longer narrative. In a new setting Joseph's talents and powers earn for him the trust of the "chief jailer," who makes the managerially gifted Joseph a prisoner of special status. He is again an overseer—of all the inmates. The narrator has returned his focus to Joseph, whose life, even in hardship, cannot lose the promise it carries, "because the Lord was with him, and whatever he did the Lord (JHVH) made successful" (v. 23).

I have wanted in these opening pages to present the text of *Genesis* 39 and to give general attention to its place and role in the larger Joseph narrative cycle. Familiarity with some of those questions that have absorbed modern biblical scholars of the text allows us now to examine (and enjoy) the interpretive work of their ancient predecessors. The scripture's portrait of Joseph's success and his endangerment in his master's household received new and sometimes unexpected adjustments by those specially trained interpreters who lived between the second century BCE and the fifth century CE.

Joseph with Potiphar's Wife

One aspect of the biblical account of Joseph—lured, pursued, and at one point in the clutches of his master's wife—became a matter of special and often entertaining debate. Was he tested and *also* tempted in the course of this encounter? Looking back at Joseph's words to her in *Genesis* 39:8–9, it seems evident that he resisted her lust-driven invitation out of loyalty to his employer and because he believed that having intercourse with this woman would be "wicked" and a "sin before God." He did not yield to her demands. But is there any suggestion in the text that Joseph found her alluring? That he felt desire for her? That he might in some way have played along with her attempted entrapment, either because he weakened in his resolve, or because he was quite willing to participate in the "dallying"?

Both pro and con opinions about Joseph's temptability appear in existing Jewish writings, and this chapter will take them up, first, by returning to three rabbinic discussions of this and other questions arising from *Genesis* 39. Joseph's *yetzer hara* toward immoral thoughts and deeds, according to these writings, gives reasons for imagining his behavior in the company of Potiphar's wife. A second inspection takes up another set of writings—products of Jewish authors living in Hellenized communities. These latter texts, written in Greek and for the most part "thought" in Greek intellectual categories, present Joseph as a particular moral type, and use his behavior with Potiphar's wife as a laudable example. Joseph personifies a virtue, and thus cannot be depicted as vulnerable to the vice to which he is superior. In contrast, promiscuity, or any form of slavery to passions, is represented in the woman's erotic beckonings, and in her deceptive tactics.

The way was paved for the exposition of these Jewish writings by two important studies: James Kugel's *In Potiphar's House*, a masterful case-study in the workings of "the interpretive life of biblical texts," and Erich Gruen's *Heritage and Hellenism*, which lays bare the aims of certain Jews writing in Greek who were anxious to give fresh salience to stories of heroes like Joseph, sometimes boldly departing from strictly biblical representations and valuations of them.[22]

Hebrew Texts

Before turning once again to the early fifth-century collection of midrash, *Genesis Rabbah*—this time to survey its treatment of Joseph in Potiphar's house—there are interesting things to learn about interpretations of Joseph from two brief passages in the *Talmud* and in the work titled *Jubilees*.

The talmudic tractate *Yoma* is thought to preserve results of deliberations among several first-century CE Jewish sages (Hillel included) and a section of it concerns the problem of those with predilections for various ways of busying themselves, with the result that they avoid studying the Torah. *Yoma* 35b prescribes how a challenge is to be put to a man whose diversion of choice is chasing women for sex:

> When a wrongdoer is asked, Why did you not study the Torah, if he should reply that he was of handsome appearance and distracted by his sexual passions (*yetzer*), he is asked: Were you more distracted by your sexual passions than the

righteous Joseph? It was reported that each day the wife of Potiphar tried to seduce the righteous Joseph with words. The clothes she wore for him in the morning she did not wear in the evening, and what she wore in the evening she did not wear in the morning. She said to him: Yield to me, but his answer was: No. She said to him: I will have you put in jail. He replied: "The Lord releases the imprisoned" (*Ps.* 146:7). She said to him: I will put down your haughtiness. He replied: "The Lord raises up those who are bowed down" (*Ps.* 146:8). She said: I will blind your eyes. He replied: "The Lord opens the eyes of the blind" (*Ps.* 146:8). She offered him a thousand talents of silver to yield to her, to lie with her, to be with her, but he refused to yield to her, to lie with her in this world, [lest he then] be with her in the world to come.[23]

The righteous words and deeds of Joseph chastise the sexually preoccupied person, for Joseph, though pressured by the woman's insistence, was sufficiently versed in the study of scripture to be able to use its contents in neutralizing her threats. The text does not suggest that he was unaffected by her enticements. Rather, he was "distracted by sexual passions" during his striving against her. (We should note, however, that the prospect of being joined to her in the afterlife was forbidding, if not horrific, to him!)

The Book of Jubilees contains an extension of the narrative that not only elaborates on Potiphar's wife's importunings of Joseph, but also fills in a gap in the *Genesis* text by introducing information about how, prior to Sinai, Joseph was aware of a divine prohibition of adultery:

> She loved him and besought him to lie with her. But he did not surrender his soul, and he remembered the Lord and the words which Jacob, his father, used to read from among the words of Abraham, that no man should commit fornication with a woman who has a husband; that for him [i.e., the fornicator] the punishment of death has been ordained in the heavens before the Most High God, and the sin will be recorded against him in the eternal books continually before the Lord. And Joseph remembered these words and refused to lie with her. And she besought him for a year, [yet] he refused and would not listen. But she embraced him and held him fast in the house in order to force him to lie with her, and closed the doors of the house and held him fast; but he left his garment in her hands and broke through the door and fled from her presence.[24]

Clearly drawn here, in a work composed in Hebrew in the second century BCE, are Joseph's virtue under unremitting pressure *and* the sources of his motivation and action.[25] *Jubilees* 39.6–9 imagines what Joseph recalled and put to use in order to withstand the woman's aggression—even her final attempt to enclose him in the house and in her arms. The question of whether he found himself titillated or tempted by her, however, seems to be left open. That he did not "surrender his soul" to her could suggest that either his attraction to her, or his apprehension of being susceptible to her entreaties, *required* the recollection of the Lord and of the teachings that Joseph marshals as the grounds for his fleeing. Did his struggle, his test, consist only in fending off Potiphar's wife as dangerous nuisance, or did it require a soul-enforcing disciplinary effort within Joseph, a young man vulnerable to her steady invitations and her ultimately physical embrace?

Genesis Rabbah

A lengthier consideration of the daily enticements Joseph received from his master's wife appears in *Genesis Rabbah*. In its treatment of ch. 39, *GR* sets forth pieces of information (or conjecture) about this drama's main actors, and spends considerable energy trying to discern or tease out their motivations, their limitations, and their strengths—those elements of an individual's character that help to explain his or her choices.

The latter half of *Genesis* 39:1 refers to Potiphar's purchase of Joseph, and *GR* preserves a piece of commentary that gauges his new status by familiar cultural expectations of slaves:

> All slaves cause loss to their master's house [i.e., by "being careless with his property"], but as for this one, "The Lord blessed the Egyptian's house for Joseph's sake" (39:5); all slaves are suspected of theft, but here, "And Joseph gathered up all the money . . . and Joseph brought the money into Pharaoh's house" (47:14); all slaves are suspected of immorality, but this one "Hearkened not unto her, to lie with her, or to be with her" (39:10).[26]

The purchase of Joseph raised questions about Potiphar, and what he found appealing in his young servant. The *GR* contains a midrash on the Hebrew term *seris* that denotes both castration, and, given the Egyptian context, a high minister to a superior.

> A Eunuch of Pharaoh. This intimates that he was castrated, thus teaching that he [Potiphar] purchased him for the purpose of sodomy, whereupon the Holy One, blessed be He, emasculated him. This may be compared to a she-bear that wrought havoc among her master's children, whereupon he ordered, "Break her

fangs." In the same way we are taught that he bought him for the purpose of sodomy, but the Lord emasculated him. Hence it is written, "For the Lord loves justice and does not forsake his saints" (*Ps.* 37:28), which is actually written "His saint," and refers to Joseph.[27]

This divine intervention—God's prevention of the sexual violation of Joseph by emasculating his heathen owner—adds unanticipated dimensions to the story of Joseph in his master's house. "The Lord was with him" in a very active manner, thwarting Potiphar's sexual intentions toward him. After applying the notion of direct divine action to Potiphar (with his nefarious plans), this bit of interpretation invokes the tradition of God's love of justice and his safeguarding of his saints—Joseph in particular. Of course there is a further implication. For what new reason, knowing what we now know, might the master's wife be so keen to bed the "well-built and handsome" young household servant?

In drawing near to the verses telling of Joseph's challenge from the single-minded mistress of the house, *GR* frames its interpretation of these goings-on in its usual manner. Juxtaposing *Genesis* 39:7–23 and *Proverbs* 7:6–20 just prior to its investigation of the behavior of both characters, the content of the latter passage associates Joseph with "a young man void of understanding" (*Proverbs* 7:7b) while Potiphar's wife is likened to "a woman . . . dressed like a harlot, and wily of heart." Ensuing verses in the *Proverbs* passage indicate why the rabbis found its application so appropriate to Potiphar's wife, and also to a way of imagining what transpired between her and Joseph.

> She lays hold of him and kisses him;
> Brazenly she says to him,
> "I had to make a sacrifice of well-being;
> Today I fulfilled my vows.
> Therefore I have come out to you,
> Seeking you, and have found you.
> I have decked my couch with covers
> Of dyed Egyptian linen;
> I have sprinkled my bed
> with myrrh, aloes, and cinnamon.
> Let us drink our fill of love till morning;
> Let us delight in amorous embrace.
> For the man of the house is away;
> He is off on a distant journey (*Proverbs* 7:10–19).

In *Genesis Rabbah* we discover that new and often conflicting story details have emerged in the rabbis' discussions. R. Abin tells how and why Joseph did not succumb:

> She drove him from room to room and from chamber to chamber, until she brought him to her bed. Above it was engraved an idol, which she covered with a sheet. [Joseph said to her,] "You have covered its face [for shame]; how much more [should] you be ashamed before him of whom it is written (*Zechariah* 4:10), 'The eyes of the Lord, that run too and fro through the whole earth'"! [that is, God will see no matter what you do.][28]

Joseph, invoking but also feeling the divine gaze, wants out of the bed.

GR next conveys elements in the debates among its sages about the question standing at the heart of this and the next two chapters: was Joseph aroused by Potiphar's wife? One passage seems to capture a popular curiosity about this. A noble lady asked R. Yose if it were possible that Joseph, "at seventeen years of age, with all the hot blood of youth," could have resisted Potiphar's wife, refusing to listen to her. The rabbi shared and enforced her skepticism, arguing that Reuben and Judah, his brothers, who lived at home and in the presence of Jacob, had indulged their lust, while the more vulnerable Joseph "was younger and his own master"—that is, by himself, far from the influence of his family.[29] The lady and the sage together presume Joseph's temptability; it is only by implication that they entertain an outcome between Joseph and Potiphar's wife different from the scriptural report—that is, that Joseph fled from her.

The remark in *Genesis* 39:10 that Joseph one day entered the house "to do his work" stirs up strong opinions about what transpired and about Joseph's intentions. The viewpoints, and the direction in which some of these tend, are worth quoting in full:

> R. Judah said: On that day there was a fête in honor of the Nile; everyone went to see it, but he went into the house to cast up his master's accounts. R. Nehemiah said: It was a day of theatrical performance, which all flocked to see, but he went into the house to cast up his master's account.[30] R. Samuel b. Nahman said: TO DO HIS WORK is meant literally, but that AND THERE WAS NOT A MAN [INSIDE]—on examination he did not find himself a man [i.e., He actually went in to sin, but found himself impotent], for R. Samuel said: The bow was drawn but it relaxed, as it is written, "And his bow returned in strength" [*Genesis* 49:24, which alludes to God's keeping Joseph's bow taut and his arms strong when he is assailed by archers]. R. Isaac said: His seed was scattered and issued through his finger-nails. R. Huna said in R. Mattena's name: He saw his father's face, at which his blood cooled.[31]

Knowledge of various male sexual performance difficulties makes its way into the exegetical reasoning of several of the rabbis.

Speculations about Joseph's wish to satisfy the desires of Potiphar's wife as well as his own obviously occupy (and entertain) the rabbis. The questions surrounding Joseph's willingness remain unsettled, though unsurprisingly every opinion advanced in the midrashic tradition takes it for granted that Joseph did not ultimately have intercourse with his master's wife. While taking pleasure in being flies on the walls of rooms where the rabbis discussed and sometimes disputed each others' understandings of the Torah, we are obliged not to miss the profundity of what their various interpretations show—namely, the ingenuity at work in their retelling and reshaping of the stories it was their vocation to comprehend and to teach. These glimpses of the way rabbis went about their obligation to tease out and amplify the sense of their scripture are best captured and explained in James Kugel's trenchant observation about rabbis' close examination of Joseph with Potiphar's wife:

> If this picture of Joseph shows us less than the paragon of virtue . . . it should not be adjudged inferior for all that. For Joseph the Guilty not only helps out with the rabbinic problem . . . of justifying the ordeal of his lengthy imprisonment (that is, although Joseph was not, in terms of strict justice, guilty of adultery, his initial willingness and intention to sin may have been sufficient to warrant, within the divine plan, his suffering the punishment of imprisonment, all the more so if it enables him to emerge, at the end of his sufferings, as the thoroughly virtuous Joseph we know in the rest of the story). But apart from this, presenting Joseph as sorely tempted by Mrs. Potiphar, indeed, bringing him to the brink of submission, offered an advantage to exegetes intent on using the Joseph story (as so many biblical narratives were used) as a model of ethical conduct. For to hold that Joseph was not tempted for a minute by Mrs. Potiphar is, as it were, to put him outside the range of normal human emotion. But to say, on the contrary, that Joseph was indeed tempted, and that events indeed brought him to the very point of complying—this is to present a Joseph of flesh and blood with whom others can identify, and whose example of sudden repentance others might seek to emulate.[32]

Jewish Writings in Greek

The title of Erich Gruen's book, *Heritage and Hellenism: The Reinvention of Jewish Tradition*, strongly signals the thesis he develops in splendid detail within. The convergence of the cultural heritage of Israel with that of the Greeks and Romans was, as moderns now say, a significant "game-changer."

For Jews there were challenges of adaptation to a social, political, and intellectual world now strongly marked by that engine of Hellenism spreading across and influencing eastern Mediterranean areas and beyond. Joseph, "reinvented" for Jews (and others) in this changed world, is one of Gruen's favorite examples, as we shall see.

Special attention falls here, also, upon the conceptions and representations of Joseph when he is tested in Potiphar's house. Do Jews writing in Greek, and influenced by many of its categories of thought, see this episode in ways noticeably different from those who have thought and written about it in Hebrew? Are there shifts in the way the two characters are imagined and portrayed? What are the chief features of the redesigned Joseph's response to his master's wife? What, according to the three writers selected here, was the woman like? How difficult was it for Joseph to discourage her impassioned requests and actions?

Testaments of the Twelve Patriarchs

This writing, which includes Joseph's testament, is believed to date from the same century as Jubilees (second century BCE, though some Christian interpolations from the second century CE are evident within its manuscript). The section in the work dedicated to Joseph purports to be his end-of-life summary of his deeds, replete with moral admonitions to his successors. Among the twelve patriarchs born of Jacob and Rachel, Joseph is singled out for his chastity, shown in his encounters with Potiphar's wife. Joseph's own voice reports (in more detail than *Jubilees* gave) what it was like to be exposed to her fervent coaxing and her increasingly desperate propositions.

> The Egyptian woman annoyed me relentlessly. In the night she would come to me, pretending a mere visit. Because she had no male child, she pretended to consider me as a son. For a time she would embrace me as a son, but then I realized later she was trying to lure me into a sexual relationship. I spoke to her the words of the Most High, hoping He might divert her from evil desire. Publicly she honored me for my self-control, while privately she said to me, "Have no fear of my husband, for he is convinced of your chastity." Then she began to approach me for instruction, so that she might learn the Word of God. And she kept saying to me, "If you want me to abandon the idols, have intercourse with me, and I shall convince my husband to put away the idols, and we shall live in the presence of your Lord." But I kept telling her that the Lord did not want worshipers who came by means of uncleanness. On another occasion she said to me, "If

you do not want to commit adultery, I shall kill my husband by a drug and take you as my husband." Later she sent me food mixed with enchantments. I told her: "Now then understand that the God of my father revealed to me through an angel your wickedness. In order for you to learn that the evil of the irreligious will not triumph over those who exercise self-control in their worship of God, I will take this [charmed food] and eat it in your presence." So I prayed aloud, "May the God of my fathers and the angel of Abraham be with me." And I ate. . . . So you see, my children, how great are the things that patience and prayer with fasting accomplish. You also, if you pursue self-control and purity with patience and prayer in humility of heart, the Lord will dwell among you, because He loves self-control.

Joseph the chaste declares his abhorrence of and resistance to sex outside of the marriage bond. According to this Jewish writing in Greek, Joseph's steadfastness in sexual abstention is born out of his commitment to his God, and to the teachings of his religion. Here Joseph's innocence and purity are cast in the sharpest possible relief by the elaborated descriptions of the growing exasperation and forceful antics of Potiphar's wife. She offers to convert to his religion, and to murder her husband. She threatens suicide if Joseph, the servant of the house, does not submit to her—all this while she has been putting unspecified "enchantments" (aphrodisiac drugs, we are encouraged to think) in Joseph's food.

Joseph's powers of resistance are not due entirely to the Lord in whom he believes and the force of the teachings gained from his forebears. It is also the case that he possesses, internally and as a feature of his character, another strength—one much valued and championed in Greek and Roman philosophy and ethics. Unmistakable traces of a new and *Hellenized* Joseph, are manifest, for the author puts on prominent display (alongside those strengths drawn from his heritage) the parallel and complementary resource that made his resolve firm: it was that he practiced that "self-control" (*sophrosune*) loved by God, and thus was able to master his emotions and passions. Joseph's capacity to remain chaste—to rebuff Potiphar's wife—had become an attribute, a quality of his mind or soul, a product of his moral discipline.

4th Maccabees

4th Maccabees, a first-century CE Greek work, proposes to retell, from a philosophical perspective, the story of noble Jews who had been made martyrs by the harsh Seleucid ruler Antiochus IV Epiphanes three centuries earlier. To the drama of the torture and execution of Eleazar the scribe, and of seven brothers and their mother, already narrated in a historical mode in *2nd Maccabees*, this author brings an argument meant to explain their courageous behavior in the face of death—their ability to maintain their loyalty to Jewish Law. He holds that "reason is [the] absolute master of the passions"—able to accomplish and guarantee all thoughts and deeds of genuine nobility. Other heroes of the Jewish tradition—Joseph, Jacob, Moses, Daniel—are also singled out as exemplars of virtue, each combatting a species of dangerous passion by his exercise of "devout reason." Deploying a teaching quite similar to that in the *Testament of the Twelve Patriarchs, 4th Maccabees* celebrates Joseph's success in withstanding the wiles of Potiphar's wife:

> The temperate Joseph is praised, because through his own rational faculty he gained mastery over his sensuality. Though a young man at the prime of his sexual desire, he quenched the burning ardor of his passions. And not only over the fiery passion of sexual desire does reason evidently exercise control, but over all desire.[33]

The word "temperate" characterizes Joseph. Through the exercise of reason, *logismos*, he is able to practice self-control, which in this circumstance is chastity. Described as a process, temperance is that continuing action by which he "gained" control and "quenched" heated passions.

What does this portrait, expressed exclusively in Greek philosophical and moral terminology, suggest about Joseph's temptability? Was his "devout reason," like a component in place, sufficient to meet the test of the brazen wife of Potiphar, or was it an attribute developed and steeled precisely because, throughout his dealings with her, he was tempted, and yet did not succumb? The language of the passage seems to favor the latter view, and is apparently due to the author's understanding that the exercise of reason could modulate and correct those passions that are part of the makeup of a human being—indeed of the soul itself. For the Platonists, negotiations between the rational and less rational (the passions, or emotions) were intrinsic to and never absent from human life. The author of this text, then, stands at some distance from the early and classic Stoic view that passions were intrusions on the soul that disturbed its tranquility—and that they must be kept out, or if they gain entrance, be extirpated. By strict Stoic standards the wise person is to enjoy *apatheia*—complete freedom from the invasion of agitating external *pathe* that generate fear, jealousy, sadness, and so on ... including the "burning ardor" to which a person early in his manhood might be susceptible. The writer of *4th*

Maccabees employs the ethical language of the Stoics, but he has adopted the Platonists' view of how reason can tame the self's own passionate (and less fully rational) inclinations.

Philo's *De Iosepho* and Its Audience

No one in Jewish antiquity was more at home in reading scripture and Jewish history in such philosophical ways than the learned Philo of Alexandria, whose style of exegesis we encountered earlier in his treatment of the Cain and Abel story. Among the writings in which he presented the allegorical and ethical lessons to be learned from the lives of the great personages of Hebrew tradition—for example, Abraham and Moses—he devoted deep attention to Joseph. His treatise's subtitle discloses what Philo thinks most praiseworthy *and* most commendable to his audiences: *On Joseph—that is, the Life of a Statesman.*[34] The treatise's chief subject and theme concern the ingenuity and energy which, despite his trials and setbacks, led to Joseph's political successes in the world of the Pharaoh—that is, the place (now under Roman imperial rule) that the author and his community in Alexandria inhabit in the first century CE. Philo's rendering of the episode in *Genesis* 39 extends the perspective of Hellenized Judaism we have been considering—namely, the interpretation of events through philosophical lenses, and the attention that will be given to new circumstances in which many Jews live their lives.

The position Joseph achieved as the manager of Potiphar's affairs and household—a role analogous, in terms of the political dexterity required, to that of a statesman—was less the decision of the one who purchased him than "nature's doing," for the Hebrew teenager was endowed with "nobility of character."[35]

In a narrative that utilizes allegorical and moral interpretations to valorize Joseph's admirable life, what does Philo hope to discover in the tale of his near-seduction?[36] Was the young Joseph's virtue a "natural" gift, unimpeachably constant, even under the pressures imposed by his Egyptian master's wife?

Having been "placed" by providence in indentured servanthood to the eunuch Potiphar (the Septuagint employs the Greek word *eunochos* in translating *Genesis* 39:1), Joseph's skills became apparent.

> But while he was winning a wide reputation in household affairs, his master's wife made him the object of her designs, which were prompted by licentious love; for wrought up to madness by the beauty of the youth, and putting no

restraint on the frenzy of her passion, she made proposals of intercourse to him which he stoutly resisted and utterly refused to accept, so strong was the sense of decency and temperance which nature and the exercise of control (*sophrosune*) had implanted in him.[37]

The ideas and language are familiar from our two previous samples of Hellenized characterizations of the woman and Joseph. The Hebrew phraseology about the Lord's presence with Joseph has been captured and restated in the Greek word *phusis* (nature), and the desires of Potiphar's wife, while presented in an animated narrative form, transparently reveal the moral allegory: this is how the passions function when they go unchecked—that is, when they are no longer controlled by rationality. Joseph's behavior epitomizes the virtue of reasoned restraint. It is possible to see both in the narrative and in the allegory the championing of a devout reason that is not, in this threatening encounter, shaken or affected by the passion that it confronts. Philo's retelling continues:

> Since, as she fed the fire of lawless lust till it burst into a blaze, her constant efforts to gain him . . . constantly failed, at last in an accession of passion she was [willing] to employ violence. She caught hold of his outer garment and powerfully drew him to her bed by superior force, since passion which often braces even the weakest gave her new vigor. But he showed power which was more than a match for the untoward situation and burst into speech with a frankness worthy of his race. "What," he said, "are you forcing me to? We children of the Hebrews follow laws and customs which are specially our own. . . . with us a courtesan is not even permitted to live, and death is the penalty appointed for women who ply this trade. Before the lawful union we know no mating with other women, but come as virgin men to virgin maidens. The end we seek in wedlock is not pleasure but the begetting of lawful children. To this day I have remained pure, and I will not take the first step in transgression by committing adultery, the greatest of crimes. For even if I had always hitherto lived an irregular life, drawn by the appetites of youth and following after the luxury of this land, I ought not to make the wedded wife of another my prey."[38]

Not to be missed in these lines is Philo's assumption (needing to be broadcast in his social setting in which Jews and non-Jews coexist) that the ideals of Jewish law and custom are fully authoritative *and* fully consonant with the highest ethical standards articulated by Greek and Roman philosophy. Indeed, he has Joseph remind his pursuer that what is commonly practiced in Egypt and other cultures falls far short of the expectations upheld among Jews. In Philo's addition to the story, Joseph continues at length (indeed, tediously) to verbalize his grounds for rejecting the advances of Potiphar's wife, defending himself with what is, in fact, a speech of moral instruction. Apparently it is for the benefit of the readers only:

> Thus he spoke long and wisely, but she remained deaf to it all. For lust is powerful to becloud even the keenest of the senses. And seeing this he fled, leaving in her hands the garments which she had grasped.[39]

The narrative representation of pious and praiseworthy Joseph is interrupted, briefly, by Philo's intriguing criticism of Potiphar at the time his wife made her accusation of Joseph. His first "great error" was his verdict against Joseph without giving him an opportunity to answer the charges leveled against him. Potiphar's second mistake, according to Philo, involved his dullness in not regarding carefully the garment which his wife offered as evidence damning Joseph, since it gave indication that

> violence was not employed by him, but suffered [by him] at her hands. . . . if force were used by him he would retain his mistress's robe, but [if force were used] against him he would lose his own.[40]

Philo, taking one of the available descriptions of Potiphar's line of work, pardons the man for his lack of judicious intelligence when he has arrived home from his labor as the Pharaoh's chief steward and chef; the smoke and gore of the kitchen in which he saw to the preparation of his master's food was sufficient to compromise his capacity for reason and reflection.[41] Philo's consistency of perspective is impressive, for even this constructed picture of Potiphar's failings is presented in categorical terms of reason and unreason—the latter in this case being those things that cloud and distract concentrated good judgment.

We have in these few sentences the first suggestion that the question of who was the aggressor in the "dallying" might have been illuminated by closer consideration of the garment of Joseph which was left in the hand of Potiphar's wife. Philo's elaboration of what *might* have happened when Potiphar was presented with his wife's complaint will be further elaborated by subsequent exegetes—Jewish, Christian, and Muslim. Philo himself quickly returns to his main subject—Joseph's frame of mind, or state of soul, when Potiphar's wife made her most fervent and physical approach to him.

That Philo's Joseph feels himself vulnerable to the passion of the woman—that in her presence or grasp he wrestles with his own desires— is nowhere indicated in this text. Joseph's comment in which he wonders "what would be my inward feelings" if he capitulated to her request argues against his having reached a point at which his rational powers gave way to being aroused by her. Rather, he is—and represents—sexual purity, or sexual righteousness, a Torah value restated in the language of Hellenistic ethics. It would be both wrong and ungracious to have sex with her, he asserts, since her kind husband had played a part in turning him from "a captive and an alien" into "a free man and a citizen as far as he can do it."[42] This last phrase works, of course, to support the larger portrait of Joseph "the statesman" who deserves the attention of Jews living in circumstances akin to Philo's, where opportunities for social advancement present themselves.

What follows in Philo's exposition is another run-through of *Genesis* 39—this time concentrated on the relation of certain of its features concerning Joseph's trial and triumph to the important task of finding, owning, and exploiting one's status and potency in a land not one's own—that is, within a population in which Jews are not the dominant community. A summary statement about Joseph's gifts of "shepherd-craft," "household management," and "self control" (here the Greek term employed is *enkrateia*) points to lessons for governance: when dissolute behavior infects a nation, a display of continence is needed in order to stabilize the people, turning them toward "the acquisition and enjoyment of perfect blessings."[43] A eunuch who purchases a statesman is an allegory: the masses (eunuch) are unable to be productive, even when they seem to be faring well; the masses require a wise governor.

Further, it makes symbolic sense that a eunuch takes a wife, Philo asserts, likening the eunuch's wife to what the masses desire most of all:

> Like a licentious woman the desire of the multitudes makes love to the statesman. "Forward, lad," she says, "forward to be my mate, the multitude. Forget your own ways, the habits, the words, the actions in which you were bred. Obey me, wait on me, and do all that gives me pleasure."[44]

This capitulation to her, "the desire of the multitudes," the reasoning goes, will gain for the statesman freedom, exacting only the cost of his independence of judgment and action (*autopragia*). But, Philo responds, it belongs to a statesman to resist this compact, since he "regards himself as a free man, and shapes his activities to please his own soul."[45]

The Joseph of Philo's treatise is, then, not only the exemplar of chaste resolve—a model for those individuals vulnerable to sexual arousal and susceptible to "licentious" acts. Even in his behavior when tempted and taunted by Potiphar's wife—the self-control he maintained when pulled toward her bed—points to what statesmanship in the wider society requires and entails. Both contexts and both levels at which Joseph's character is drawn—as biblical hero, and as Temperance in action—show him as tested, but not in a state of frenzied excitement or agitated temptation.

For each and all of the interpretive representations of Joseph in the Greek writings we've just surveyed, Erich Gruen's insight holds significance:

> The ambiguous personage who appears in Genesis, gifted and competent, faithful and sensitive, but also devious, arrogant, and domineering, is flattened out . . . transformed into a one-dimensional paragon of virtue.[46]

To see in Hellenized Jews' literary portraits a Joseph who represents "unblemished ethical purity" is to be reminded of this patriarch's malleability for interpreters, since we recall Kugel's conclusion that the rabbis pictured Joseph as a man "of flesh and blood with whom others can identify, and whose example of sudden repentance others might seek to emulate."[47]

Varying depictions of Joseph, with their divergent estimates of his vulnerability to the wiles of Potiphar's wife, no doubt stemmed from a number of causes: the free unfolding of interpretive processes in different locations, the common hermeneutic procedure of reading a text with the help of another (producing novel but biblically informed meanings), and the influence of new directions and trends both in legal discourse and in philosophy.

We are encouraged by Gruen's analysis to see in Philo's *De Iosepho* something of the relational dynamics between Jews and their non-Jewish neighbors characteristic of, and required by, his own era and social setting. The last line of *Genesis* 39 relates that "whatever [Joseph] did the Lord made successful." Of the several Jewish Hellenistic treatments of Joseph, Gruen writes:

> Jewish intellectuals had a free hand in reshaping, excerpting, expanding, or even ignoring the Genesis narrative. The ostensibly cavalier attitude toward Scripture, however, did not constitute irreverence or creeping secularism. The adaptation of Jewish legend and the appropriation of Hellenic forms marched in tandem to reassert the admirable values and superior attainments of the Jews. The images of Joseph, in all their disparate manifestations, had that mission in common.[48]

It will be worth asking in the next chapter whether and in what ways early Christian writers' and artists' understandings of Joseph similarly molded themselves to changes in the empire's political-religious landscape, as these affected Christians in their diverse locales and environments.

SIGNS OF JEWISH MIDRASH IN EARLY CHRISTIAN PAINTINGS OF JOSEPH AND POTIPHAR'S WIFE: A CASE OF SHARED EXEGETICAL TRADITIONS

The image which follows (Figure 7.2) pictures Joseph's escape from Potiphar's wife. Called by Herbert Kessler "the most sumptuous manuscript to survive from the early Christian period," the Vienna Geneis is believed to have been created in Syria or Palestine in the sixth century. It contained in its original form the Septuagint text of *Genesis* (slightly abridged) and an estimated 400 separate scenes painted on 96 two-sided leaves, or folios."[49]

Page 31 in the Vienna Genesis displays beneath the Greek text a painting with an upper and lower register. Several scenes fill it. The painting confronts us with problems of interpretation of the sort that have long vexed historians of text and art: while the drama pictured in the opening scene at the top left is familiar, it is no easy matter to ascertain the sense and import of the adjoining images. If one presumes that the scenes difficult for us to decipher were understood by the painters (and their clients) as parts of the narrative involving Potiphar, his wife, and Joseph, the study of their contents becomes all the more intriguing. *Visual* expansion of narrative is obviously in play, but what is being shown in the additions made by these artists, and what inspires their extrabiblical pictorial commentary?

The painting's initial image is straightforward enough, showing Joseph's attempt to flee from Potiphar's wife, who holds part of "his garment in her hand." In light of the chief question we have been pursuing, note should be taken that the content of the image gives no encouragement to an opinion that Joseph was tempted, nor that he (with some eagerness) had been in her bed. While searching for traces of Jewish traditions in the paintings of the Vienna Genesis, it is important to acknowledge that it is a Christian book. It is quite possible that a Christian painter or a painter for a Christian client, for reasons to become clear in the next chapter, would not have been inclined to depict Joseph in any compromising position.

The Greek text that stands above the illumination on the folio runs from the middle of v. 9 to the middle of v. 11 in *Genesis* 39—from Joseph's refusal to do the "wicked thing" his master's wife has proposed, to his "fleeing outside." What immediately follows in the text is the episode in which, on the day he came to "do his work," the woman once again exhorted Joseph, "lie with me" (in the Greek: *koimetheti met' emou*), and then clutched and held

Figure 7.2 Joseph runs from Potiphar's wife, and other scenes. The Vienna Genesis. Sixth century CE. Painting; 16 × 26 cm. © Österreichische Nationalbibliothek Bildarchiv und Grafiksammlung, Vienna. Nationalbibliothek, cod. theol. gr. 31. Page 31.

fast to his garment as he fled. This initial scene and the content of the text are synchronized.

None of the subsequent scenes within this two-tier painting, however, portray people or happenings to be found within the *Genesis* text. To modern interpreters of the book's ancient artist interpreters, these scenes' identifications have become fair game.

Art historian Kurt Weitzmann's 1977 description of scenes in the two panels is confident where it can be, and properly tentative where it must be:

> Dressed in a transparent garment, the temptress sits on the edge of a gilded bed before a double-rowed colonnade, suggesting a stately palace chamber; she grasps the edge of Joseph's purple mantle, which he tries to slip out of. Next Joseph is repeated looking back at the open door through which he has just escaped. To this point the illustration is biblical, but the rest of the upper zone and all of the lower are additions which once were regarded as "novelistic," but which . . . must be interpreted as features of Jewish legends, although in this particular case a satisfactory explanation has yet to be offered. Here a wide area of future research has just opened. The figure at the top right in a star-studded mantle and holding a spindle has been explained as an astrologer, and the woman bending over the cradle once more as Potiphar's wife, holding a rattle over a baby which, on the basis of Jewish sources, has been thought to be Osnath (Asenath in Greek), an adopted daughter whom Joseph is later to marry. Even less surely identified are the figures in the lower register, a woman holding a naked baby and two seated women spinning, the one at the right clad like Potiphar's wife in the first scene in a transparent garment. Only the two trees can be dismissed as "space fillers."[50]

More than a century of scholarly combing of Jewish literature for clues about what some of the scenes represent has produced abundant but varied and often conflicting answers. The problem, which may be one of too many possibilities, can be appreciated when one reads the book-length collection of Jewish legends about Joseph compiled (from sources early and late) and woven together by Louis Ginzberg to make a coherent summary of Joseph's career.[51] Aware of this body of Jewish lore, anyone would be inclined to match some of these colorful exegetical add-ons with the more indefinite scenes in the Vienna Genesis' Joseph paintings.

Drawing upon medieval Jewish texts presumed to contain earlier pieces of midrash and legend, James Kugel ventures (with due caution) to produce a more comprehensive identification of the several unbiblical scenes that appear in our painting: Joseph, minus his mantle but safely outside of the room, looks back towards it; the woman closest to Joseph is Potiphar's wife, who leans over to wash the child, who is "in reality . . . probably none other than Aseneth, Joseph's future wife."[52]

Joseph Gutmann made different sense of the iconography. Seeing the woman bending over the child as a maid-servant (her clothing seems quite unlike that of Potiphar's wife, despite the suggestion by Weitzmann and others that it is similarly "transparent"), he proposed another "reading":

> Could this scene possibly allude to the child mentioned in a very late Jewish source, which relates that "there was a child there eleven months old, and the Lord opened the mouth of the child," who testified before Potiphar that: "my mother speaks falsely and utters lies; this is how the affair occurred."[53]

Already in the early third century the Christian exegete Origen wrote of a tradition he had learned from "Hebrews" that does not specifically link Asenath with the child shown in the Vienna Genesis image, but does report her action in defense of Joseph which apparently occurred, not immediately after his escape from the woman's bed-chamber, but later:

> Asenath brought charges against her mother in the presence of her father, stating that she had laid a trap for Joseph, and not Joseph for her. For this reason, therefore, Potiphar gave her in marriage to Joseph, in order to prove to the Egyptians that Joseph had committed no wrong of this kind against his house.[54]

Scholars acknowledge that their efforts to identify the scenes filling the painting's lower register must be speculative, and Kugel states simply that it "shows three women, one of whom now holds the baby," while Michael Levin entertains, but counts as "not very probable" the notion that the image of the woman with the young boy at her side may attempt to invoke the exegetical tradition that had "Potiphar's wife trying to seduce Joseph by pretending to adopt him."[55]

A second Vienna Genesis painting (Figure 7.3) is of special interest. It portrays Potiphar, his wife, and *perhaps* Joseph, in its two scenes. Even though the painting's main characters and their actions initially seem recognizable, there are intriguing riddles to sort out.

The painting's upper register shows Potiphar (on the left) approaching his house, while within it his wife, shown to be elegant and of high station, speaks to three males, with a female servant in attendance behind her. Kurt Schubert offered this interpretation:

> The upper half on page 32 is clarified by the following midrash tradition: "When they all returned from their idol worship, including the women, they came to

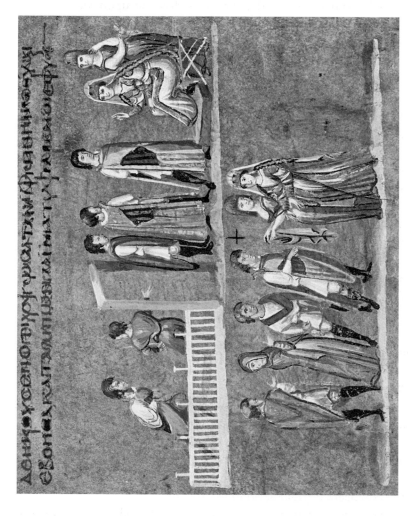

Figure 7.3 Potiphar's wife displays Joseph's garment. The Vienna Genesis. Sixth century CE. Painting: 16 x 26 cm. © Österreichische Nationalbibliothek Bildarchiv und Grafiksammlung, Vienna. Nationalbibliothek, cod. theol. gr. 31. Page 32.

visit her." In our depiction, three court officials, having already arrived, wait on Potiphar's wife, who speaks to them, while Potiphar himself is hurrying to them from outside. The identification of the hurrying figure with Potiphar is suggested by the midrash, according to which the entire household was at the Nile feast.[56]

Schubert's exposition has the virtue of drawing upon what *Genesis* 39:14 recounts—namely, that prior to her husband's arrival, Potiphar's wife told the servants of the act committed by the "Hebrew" whom her husband sent to "dally with us." But it seems strange that the servants called out to by their mistress are represented by three men, with the lone woman pictured behind Potiphar's wife not among the trio being directly addressed.

Other interpretations suggest themselves. Could Joseph himself be one of those in the room, the center of attention, and subject of the raised hands of his accuser? The artist could have exercised painter-exegete's liberty here, imagining Joseph standing present and hearing the false charges Potiphar's wife reported to the household just before Potiphar's return home from the festival. The woman's anxious effort to cast blame on her victim, with him being there, could have the effect of intensifying the drama—one of its moments of (un)truth.

James Kugel suggests, alternatively, that this scene could be, in "garbled" form, the pictorial germ of what in time becomes a favorite episode in the retellings of the Joseph story. In some of its more developed iterations (e.g., in the Qur'an, in *tafsir*, and in numerous Muslim paintings), the incident involves a party or assembly of women invited for a light meal, and their distraction when Potiphar's wife brings before them the beguilingly handsome Joseph, as if to display the reason for her lust for him. Kugel, then, sees in this illustration a very early suggestion of Joseph being shown off to people, with some explanatory or self-justifying comments by Potiphar's wife's about her passion for him. Again, we are haunted by not finding it easy to choose confidently from among these three interpretations, while supposing that for viewers of the scene in and after the sixth century, its sense was probably not obscure.

The lower scene on page 32 does not contain such great ambiguity. Potiphar's wife (she and her servant clearly recognizable by comparison with the previous scene) has Joseph's mantle held up before her husband as evidence of her accusation against his trusted servant. Schubert sees additional possibilities in this part of the image, drawing still upon the later Jewish source, *Midrash Gadol Genesis* (which, as we shall see later, shares this and other exegetical commentary with the Qur'an and Muslim commentaries):

Having returned from their idol worship, the wives of the dignitaries ask Potiphar's wife,

> Why are you so distressed? Indeed, you have perhaps made eyes at this servant? . . . Then they say to her: You have no other recourse but to tell your lord to have him locked up in prison. Then she said to them: If I complain of him to my husband, he will not believe me. But if you will tell all your husbands that Joseph tried to force you, then I will also tell my husband and he will have him imprisoned.

The lower picture column on page 32 actually appears to be a pictorial translation of this tradition. At the far right, Potiphar's wife is bringing her charge against Joseph, whereby the handmaid is presenting Joseph's abandoned garment as proof. Behind Potiphar stands a man, who is distinguished by his dress from all other men in this picture. This is either Joseph—albeit otherwise attired than on the preceding pages—or someone who is also hearing the charge against Joseph. Behind this figure stands an Egyptian couple, supporting the charge against Joseph by indicating with their hands the damning garment.[57]

The late midrash adds texture to the viewer's appreciation of things that might have been going on behind the event as depicted—in this case, the efforts of Potiphar's wife to secure support for her case from the husbands of her female confidants. It is easy to see the painter's depiction of others gesturing toward the garment which Potiphar's wife hopes will have the force of damning Joseph. Could this not be a reasonably natural enhancement of what is related in *Genesis* 39:15—that is, the incorporation of other people (showing their responses) when she declares to Potiphar what Joseph has done?

We are reminded of the origins of the Vienna Genesis, and made to pause in the search for signs of Jewish midrash, by noting that mixed within this painting's motifs, one in particular does not yield to that approach. A clearly painted cross stands at the top of the scene, just above the garment being held up as evidence against Joseph. What is this symbol supposed to convey? Is it the blessing of the garment of a righteous and Lord-blessed man? Will Christian commentators on Joseph's trial in his dealings with Potiphar's wife clarify what may be the cross's significance, placed as it is in this scene? And if they do not do so specifically, what inference might we draw from this Christian graphic declaration itself? The question arises again, as we shall see shortly, in the depiction of Joseph in prison, where a cross appears outside the building, but above him. I'll not offer here a hypothesis, but suggest that we await Christian interpreters' ways of associating Joseph with Jesus.

With one eye directed to the particularities we shall meet in Christian and Muslim interpretations of Joseph with Potiphar's wife, I want to conclude consideration of these Vienna Genesis paintings that bear directly upon Joseph's near-seduction by highlighting a few motifs in the artists' pictorial elaborations of the story. The first has to do with the cradled child positioned next to the second depiction of Joseph, who stands just outside the chamber. Sitting upright and seeming to gesture, the baby faces Joseph, who has escaped from the attempted sexual coercion of Potiphar's wife, and faces also the earlier image of his effort to get free from the garment seized by her. There is reason to believe, as Kugel observes, that the child's presence is a narrative enhancement serving a purpose additional to that of introducing Asenath, Joseph's destined future wife. What may have been an early tradition—that an infant spoke, testifying to Joseph's innocence of the charge that *he* was the aggressor in the grappling with Potiphar's wife—could be one of the artist's chief reasons for this scene, an explanation or justification absent from the text of *Genesis*, in which no defense of Joseph is given.[58] Some rabbinic interpreters declare that the infant was not Aseneth, but the *son* of Potiphar and his wife (born as a result of Joseph's prayer!), whose mouth God opened that he might defend Joseph against his mother's deceit. These sources also report, as we have seen, that Asenath, well beyond infancy, informed her foster-father Potiphar of his wife's duplicity and Joseph's innocence.[59] How will the infant whom God enables to speak be understood and represented in the literary and artistic exegeses of Christians and Muslims?

Each of the three religions shows interest in gaining and disseminating (by means of interpretation) more information than the Jewish scripture itself gives about Potiphar's *actual* opinion concerning the testimony of his wife. Could there have been an exchange between him and Joseph, his theretofore reliable servant? And if Joseph himself was not given opportunity for self-defense, could God, who was "with Joseph," have acted in a way favorable to him in this crisis—something like an intervention through the preternatural speech of an infant?

Yet another account of intervention on Joseph's behalf circulates among rabbinic interpreters: Potiphar's wife, during intimacies with her husband (and knowing that he would be most amenable to her wishes then), urges him to punish Joseph for his audacity, while hoping (successfully) that Joseph will be jailed rather than executed.[60]

Figure 7.4 Joseph in prison. The Vienna Genesis. Sixth century CE. Painting: 16 x 26 cm. © Österreichische Nationalbibliothek Bildarchiv und Grafiksammlung, Vienna. Nationalbibliothek, cod. theol. gr. 31. Page 34.

Finally, because traditions emerge that tell of the wife of Potiphar's continuing longing for and pursuit of Joseph, we should be aware of yet another painting in the Vienna Genesis (Figure 7.4) that runs well beyond what *Genesis* 39 narrates: this scene features the moment (in *Genesis* 40:9ff.) in which Joseph the dream-interpreter reveals to the baker and the butler their respective fates (the artist shows their responses). Outside the jail, the painting shows a woman speaking with a male figure who is sitting.

A modern critic finds the identification of the woman as Potiphar's wife to be arbitrary, a product of much too energetic efforts to use rabbinic teachings to decipher elements in paintings from the Vienna Genesis, but others are confident in their interpretation, given Jewish texts' references to her visits to the jailed Joseph, where she persisted in trying to convince him to capitulate to her and her sexual yearning for him.[61] Joseph comments in *Testaments of the Twelve Patriarchs* that he received many messages while imprisoned saying, "Acquiesce in fulfilling my desire and I will release you from the fetters and liberate you from the darkness."[62] *Genesis Rabbah* 85:10 preserves a rabbi's comment concerning her extreme efforts to capture the imprisoned Joseph's attention, and his resistance:

How far did she go [in this]? Said R. Huna in R. Aha's name: She went so far as to place an iron fork under his neck so that he would have to lift up his eyes and look at her. Yet in spite of that he would not look at her. Thus it is written [in *Psalm* 105:18], *His feet they hurt with fetters, his person was laid in iron.*

The application of this psalm verse has particular force, since it comes from a section within *Psalm* 105 that relates in its own manner the ways in which the Lord sustained Joseph in Egypt:

> 16 He called down a famine on the land,
> destroyed every staff of bread.
> 17 He sent ahead of them a man,
> Joseph, sold into slavery.
> 18 His feet were subjected to fetters;
> an iron collar was put on his neck.
> 19 Until his prediction came true
> the decree of the Lord purged him.
> 20 The king sent to have him freed;
> the ruler of nations released him.
> 21 He made him the lord of his household,
> empowered him over all his possessions,
> 22 to discipline his princes at will,
> to teach his elders wisdom.
> 23 Then Israel came to Egypt;
> Jacob sojourned in the land of Ham.

By invoking this particular passage from the *Psalms*, the rabbinic teaching starts from the wider perspective of God's providential care for the people of Israel and Joseph's singular role in that history which had Jacob join his son in Egypt. Nonetheless, the verses quoted are taken to be fully relevant to the case of persistent harassment of Joseph by Potiphar's wife.

On the supposition that the woman depicted in page 34 *is* Potiphar's wife requesting to see or speak with him, the artist leaves us wondering how long Joseph's test endured, and how it was ultimately resolved. Muslim exegetes, philosophers and painters in particular, explored with care the longer history of Yusuf and Zulaykha (as Potiphar's wife was, in time, named by them).

Once again we have encountered a Christian book whose paintings reveal knowledge of Jewish (alongside Christian) commentary on a biblical story. Like the Ashburnham Pentateuch's portrayal of the sacrifices of Cain and Abel and the ensuing fratricide, several illuminations in the Vienna Genesis present us with graphic artists' exegeses and elaborations of the story of Joseph with Potiphar's wife. The scholarly theory in circulation for many decades—that the Christian artists had access to Jewish books with paintings that supplied them with iconographic prototypes—has, for lack of physical evidence of such books, come upon hard times.[63] What is beyond question, however, is the fact that those who provided paintings for Christian books were familiar with the contents of Jewish scriptural exegeses and commentaries. As we shall see in the following two chapters, cross-fertilization of Jewish, Christian, and Muslim literary and artistic interpretations of Joseph's encounter with Potiphar's wife was a vital contributor to all three religions' different developments of the story.

Present in *Genesis* 37 through 50 are theological ideas met elsewhere in this first book of the Jewish bible—particularly the narrative presentations of God's covenantal relationship to his people, with its promises and demands, and the election of persons to be leaders, prophets, and special agents in the unfolding of providential history. Joseph the dreamer, the endangered, the one whose prospering is God-supported, belongs to the wider biblical vision, and yet his story is styled differently than others in the book. His circumstance of being a Hebrew slave in Egypt, his trials, and his contribution to future prospects of the Hebrew people are distinctive, supporting a novella that is unique within the Pentateuch. *Genesis* 39 has its own emphases as it reimagines the ways God accompanies one of his beloved servants—one whose existence is filled with desperate crises and splendid deliverances. Joseph's multifaceted life introduces new contours to Jewish understandings of how human beings participate in and advance the purposes of God and God's chosen people. A talent-blessed but tactless and abrasive boy becomes "a successful man" (39:1), exercising his wits and political dexterity to preserve the future of his people: "The Lord was with him, and whatever he did the Lord made successful."

Was Joseph seriously tempted by his would-be seductress, or did he stand the test, proving invulnerable to her intensifying come-ons? Conflicting answers emerge from our study of ancient Jewish interpretation—the midrash of rabbis and the moral-allegorical exegesis of Jews influenced by Greek philosophy. Joseph the man of "flesh and blood" *was* tempted by Potiphar's wife. He visited her with every intention of meeting her sexual desires with his own. Joseph the personification of self-control, by contrast, was free of perturbation and fully able to fend off his wicked pursuer. Exercising his devout reasoning, he established his iconic stature among Judaism's worthies as the champion of chastity.

To which of these two perceptions of Joseph did Christianity incline, and why? We turn next to the views of the early churches' biblical commentators, preachers, and artists.

CHAPTER 8

cᴎᴐ

Joseph Put to the Test

Christian Sermons and Art

*G*enesis' final chapters chronicle the tormented and yet charmed life of Joseph—his precarious but God-supported existence that became a grand success, establishing him as a man of worldly might. The career of *this* champion from the line of Abraham was rich in what it suggested about human possibilities and the effects of divine sponsorship in an ancient saint's perseverance and glory. Preachers and teachers in the churches also approached Joseph's story as a mine of moral instruction and symbolic, spiritual meaning. To be discovered through allegorical interpretation and through analogy was the likeness of events in Joseph's life in the "old covenant" to things revealed in the "new"—especially in the life of Jesus.

Genesis 39's drama was a salient part of Joseph's history, and Christian scripture interpreters did—as much as Jewish, and later, Muslim exegetes—speculate about what "actually" transpired between Joseph and his temptress. What, they asked, was the significance of this test of Joseph? What did it convey about this ancient hero, and what did the tale reveal about human behavior, with its extremes of passion, strained loyalties, and miscarriages of justice?

JOSEPH'S CHASTITY: THE CHURCH
FATHERS' TEACHINGS

The early churches' treatments of Joseph's encounter with Potiphar's wife fall into three categories. The first is that of capsule idealization.

Continuing in the vein of philosophical-ethical exposition already seen in Hellenistic Jewish writings, numerous writers and homilists invoke the name of Joseph in short notices, in formulaic characterizations. He represents sexual purity, or continence. So Joseph the modest youth, pursued by his master's wife, set the example for chastity "because he did not defile his conscience with the crime" (Novatian); he was morally superior to his father on account of his *monogamia* (Tertullian); far from being a tree that withered in the trial of being grabbed by a woman, Joseph bore the fruits of self-control (*enkrateia*) and chastity (*sophrosune*) (Origen); "For chastity's sake," he rebuffed "the intrigues of an unchaste woman" (Basil); his patriarchal attribute, as strictness was Samuel's and zeal was Elijah's, was chastity (Gregory of Nyssa); his aversion to Potiphar's wife's touch illustrates the force of Paul's advice—"It is well for a man not to touch a woman"—in *1 Corinthians* 7:1 (Jerome); the "chaste Joseph" was held up as an example by the parents of Symeon the future pillar-standing saint (Theodoret); for "carry[ing] off the greatest prize of chastity when a woman burning with desire sought to draw him by force to an unlawful bed," Joseph is both a subject (and even a refrain-singer) of the Christian virgin Thecla's hymn in Methodius's *Symposium*.

A second group of texts, interesting to read alongside Jewish and Muslim interpretations, supply somewhat more narration. I do not wish to generate suspense, and then disappoint: unsurprisingly, one finds in these early Christian sources very little discussion of Joseph's inclination to take up his pursuer's invitation, nor suggestions that Joseph became so intensely involved with Potiphar's wife that he was sexually aroused. His soul, or his reason, or his heart was the location of the contest, if indeed he suffered one. A cluster of familiar ideas used by early Christian scripture interpreters and theologians—the makeup of the human being and the workings of the soul and the passions within, divine and human will and deed, in their relation and interaction—these are themes not far beneath the surfaces of the following three interpreters' reconstructions of Joseph's challenging moments in the locked chambers of Potiphar's house.

Writing in the late second and early third centuries, Clement of Alexandria asserts in his *The Instructor* that Joseph conquered the Egyptian "harlot" because his chastity, maintained through self-discipline, was stronger than her sexual wantonness. Contrasting a comedy's portrayal of harlotry and its sad outcome to Jesus's admonition to pluck out the offending eye, Clement suggests that even "languishing looks . . . [are] nothing else than to commit adultery with the eyes, lust skirmishing through them. For of the whole body, the eyes are the first destroyed."[1] In his *Miscellanies* the figure of Joseph is a guide for the life of a Christian of true knowledge, who "never prefers the pleasant to the useful; not even if a beautiful woman were to entice him . . . wantonly urging him; since Joseph's master's wife was not able to seduce him from his steadfastness . . . he divested himself of [his coat]—becoming bare of sin, but clothed with [propriety] of character." Clement notes that though Joseph was invisible to Potiphar within the house, God could see him, the God who discerns the inner thoughts of humans, those things "from which the speaking and the looking proceed."[2] Next, Clement lays out two ethical strategies for the good Christian. The first envisions a believer's soul as trained "like the body of an athlete":

> He is prudent in human affairs . . . having obtained the principles from God above, and having acquired (due to the soul's resemblance to the divine) moderation in bodily pains and pleasures. And he struggles against fears boldly, trusting in God.[3]

Such a soul, having made itself a temple for God's Holy Spirit, consequently is able to face challenges in a second, more elevated way:

> This is the really good man, who is without passions; having through the habit or disposition of the soul endowed with virtue, transcended the whole life of passion. He has everything dependent on himself for the attainment of the end. . . . He, then, who faultlessly acts the drama of life which God has given him to play, knows both what is to be done and what is to be endured.[4]

In the descriptions of Joseph's behavior by Philo Judaeus and by the author of *Jubilees* we met this language which cut a distinction between a life of moderation and a life of passionlessness. Clement, the learned and sophisticated teacher of Christians in Alexandria, presents them as stepwise ethical ideals. The "true Gnostic," by which he means the serious and thoughtful Christian, with the Holy Spirit (of New Testament teaching) present in his or her soul, will stand above the storm of passion and do the good. Having aspired to and attained that brand of *apatheia* that steeled Joseph when he was in the grasp of his master's wife, the knowledge-filled believer will make no compromises with evil, proving capable of meeting life challenges imperturbably.

A remark in Origen's *Genesis Homily 15* is on the same trajectory of thought as Clement, his predecessor, but it is concentrated on a moral definition of "living." Origen tells his listeners that when we read (or hear) in *Genesis* 45:26 that Jacob is told, "Joseph your son is living," the words should not be taken in the usual—that is, literal—sense:

> If we should assume that [Joseph] could have been overcome with lust and sinned with his master's wife, I do not think that this would have been announced ... to his father Jacob: "Your son Joseph is living." For if he had done this, without doubt he would not be living. For "the soul that sins, the same shall die" (*Ezekiel* 18:4).[5]

Eusebius of Caesarea shows in his *Preparation for the Gospel* an expansive flair as he recounts the story of Joseph and Potiphar's wife. He warms especially to the description of the woman's attempt to "drag [the] young and beautiful [Joseph] into licentious and amorous intercourse ... to cajole him with words ... [and] with entreaties ... at last [trying] to lay violent hands upon him, ... [having] recourse now to immodest and shameless embraces."[6] But Joseph acts the hero, inspired by "memory of the piety of his forefathers."[7] It is only *after* he has escaped her clutches, according to Eusebius, that Joseph reflects "with sober reasoning" on what has happened,[8] at which point he makes the moral observations which in the *Genesis* text Joseph addressed directly to Potiphar's wife (in 39:8–9). Consequently, God crowned Joseph with the rewards of virtue, giving him governance over his master and over Egypt itself. Echoes of Philo's presentation of Joseph as successful "statesman" sound here in Eusebius's account, but with the Christian twist and claim which is at the same time *adversus Judaeos*. Eusebius adds that all this happened to Joseph "as a Hebrew of the Hebrews, and not a Jew (because the Jewish nation did not exist)," with the result that Joseph "has been received among the thrice-blessed and most highly favored friends of God."[9] To this last theme—the manner in which Joseph belongs (exclusively? particularly?) to the Christians—we shall want to return.

Commentary on Joseph with Potiphar's wife by two fourth-century bishops and champions of Christian teaching—John Chrysostom in the Greek-speaking East, and the Latin church's Ambrose, bishop of Milan—represent a third kind of interpretation—one that probes more fully the workings of Joseph's psyche under the pressure of temptation. They too ask the arresting questions: in what did Joseph's temptation consist? Was he at any point atremble? Was his virtue unwavering, or was his chastity at risk? If the latter, how did he prevail against the woman and her stratagems?

John Chrysostom on Joseph's Test

John Chrysostom gives over the latter half of his *Homily LXII* (on *Genesis*) to Joseph's career, and puts themes in place prior to taking up this particular happening, which he sees as instigated by the devil's rage at seeing Joseph "becoming more commendable as each day passed."[10] "The Lord was with Joseph," (*Genesis* 39:2)—that is, grace from above consistently supported him, allowing him to meet difficulties without alarm or doubt. God's usual practice with virtuous people was not to free them from trials, but to give them more challenges, and thus, more opportunities for victories and celebrations. Virtue, "wherever it appears, . . . prevails over all things . . . just as darkness is driven out with the rising sun . . . [and] so too in [Joseph's] case every evil is absent with the approach of virtue."[11]

Chrysostom is not preparing his congregation for a moment of crisis or trauma in the story he relates. When his master's wife approached Joseph,

> aflame with satanic desire, he did not submit, nor did he accept the invitation. . . . He realized . . . the great ruin it would bring him; and instead of thinking of himself, he was greatly concerned . . . to deliver *her* from this folly and improper desire . . . So he offered her advice calculated to awaken her to a sense of shame.[12]

Chrysostom (like Philo before him, we recall) provides Joseph with an ample speech of moral education. It has little effect, and after days of relentless propositioning Potiphar's wife grabs Joseph "like a wild animal grinding its teeth."[13]

What next occurs is carefully phrased: Joseph is involved both in a contest and in something "light and easy":

> After making whatever effort he could and giving evidence of his struggle for continence with great intensity, [he] enjoyed abundant help (*summachias*) from above, and all at once prevailed.[14]

It was thanks to cooperative action by God that Joseph "slipped from the clutches of that lustful woman . . . emerging divested of his clothes but garbed in the vesture of chastity, as though escaping unharmed from some fiery furnace."[15] At work in Chrysostom's narration is the Greek church fathers' familiar and favored notion of divine and human *synergeia*, or, collaboration, but there is no ambiguity about the sequence of initiatives, either in the description of Joseph's victory or in the preacher's exhortation at his sermon's end:

> Then it is that grace from on high reaches us in generous measure, when we too give evidence of great virtue . . . since he had resisted valiantly, accordingly he enjoyed great reward.[16]

(How differently the actions of Joseph can be framed is seen in Jerome's use of the story against the Pelagian Christians, where he argues that there is no mention of the power of free will in the patriarch's heroics—all follows from the Lord being with him [*Genesis* 39:2].)[17] In Chrysostom's retelling of Joseph with Potiphar's wife, Joseph is a martyr put to the test by the satanic female. The danger is real. He prevails through a combination of his own effort (exertion apparently free of inner turmoil or distress) and divine help.

The scriptural incident's lesson? It is possible to "shun completely the devil's wiles and enjoy great help from on high."[18] The Joseph of John Chrysostom's sermonic presentation is tested but not tempted. That is, when the young Hebrew is confronted by the temptress's pleadings, demands, and threats, he resists, God cooperating with his effort, and he withstands her invitations to sin.

Ambrose on Joseph's Test

Ambrose's *De Ioseph* is thought to have been a sermon delivered around 388. However, its length (fifty pages of Latin text!) points to a later amplification of his homily into a full treatise.[19] Ambrose's presentation of Joseph as "a mirror of purity" owes a great deal to Philo's treatise, but also contains distinctive motifs. One theme in particular began with the argument that although he was much loved and desired by his mistress, "scripture did well to absolve [Joseph]," for "he refused" her (*Genesis* 39:8).[20] In response to the initial beckonings by Potiphar's wife "[Joseph] overcame her attack through a struggle in his heart (Latin: *mentis congressione*)," during which the servant showed moral mastery, "not feel[ing] the bonds of the seducer," and aspiring to freedom from sin.[21]

On what grounds did Joseph refuse her? He recognized his commitments both to Potiphar and to his own blamelessness (*innocentiae*). Held by the garment, he was not seduced in his soul (*non potuit animo capi*); though stripped, he was not naked, but covered by chastity.

However, by Ambrose's account, at one moment in the contest Joseph *was* vulnerable. He refused to listen for long to the woman's words, fearing "contagion," and apprehensive that "incentives to lust (*libidinus incentiva*) might pass over to him through the hands of the adulteress."[22] Her touch might have proved irresistible. Here Ambrose comes as close as any early Christian commentator does to the rabbinic speculations about the hero's susceptibility to the temptations of Potiphar's wife. Ambrose relates, however, that the decisive threat to Joseph's virtue was averted. Wrongly accused, rightly rewarded, Joseph was imprisoned, a martyr for the cause of *castitate*.[23] Though tempted, Ambrose's Joseph prevails in the trial posed by his would-be seductress.

So far, our survey of representative early Christian commentary on Joseph with Potiphar's wife yields a hero whose moral characterization and whose range of possible actions are set within fairly restricted parameters. We have Joseph the type, the ideal of sexual purity—his name the label or shorthand for chastity and modesty. And we have, in Chrysostom's fuller exploration of his trial, one of the witnesses dear to God who in the frenzied grasp of his master's wife was tested but, by means of divine assistance, did not waver—and was not compromised. Ambrose's portrayal of Joseph is of a different texture, approaching at least momentarily the figure Kugel saw in some rabbinic commentary: "a Joseph of flesh and blood with whom others can identify"—one "that events indeed brought . . . to the very point of complying."[24] It remains accurate to say, however (with Ambrose's account included), that for early Christian exegetes and teachers, Joseph is—in the midst of his struggles against the requests of Potiphar's wife—a champion of virtue, a holy example of sexual purity.

In this, patristic writers had a great deal in common with the Jewish authors of *Testaments of the Twelve Patriarchs, 4 Maccabees*, and Philo, whose portraits of an idealized and sanitized Joseph (he is, in the book of *Genesis*—as Gruen noted—a canny, wily, and multifaceted character) were much influenced by the working categories of Hellenistic ethics and the working modes of allegorical exposition. By contrast, the rabbis brought to bear on their elaborations of the Joseph saga a fair measure of that haggadic realism interested in pursuing questions of human motivation and also in considering foibles, even those of the tradition's heroes.

SOME CONTRIBUTING FACTORS IN CHRISTIAN DEPICTIONS OF JOSEPH

Perhaps excepting Ambrose, the church fathers portray Joseph the ancestor and saint as tested, but not susceptible to the perils of being tempted.

If, in ways unlike the rabbinic (and, as we shall see, the Muslim) interpretative traditions, Joseph and his actions seem to have become predictable and one-dimensional, and his character less complex, are we to attribute this to a fundamental and weighty moralizing tendency in early Christian thought, reading, writing, and teaching? Was narrowing the range of acceptable, or meritorious, human intent and action—or to put it differently, was some form of modesty or prudery—a dominant and shaping force in the early church communities, and in their interpretations of scripture?

I think the inferences from these questions could lead to an understanding of Joseph in early Christian texts that is itself too flat and abstracted. In this comparative exploration, some other reasons for this particular profile of Joseph the pure need considering. Here we engage the wider story of Joseph, as adapted by Christian interpreters. The combination of Christology, typological exegesis, and interactions between Christians and Jews is the best starting point.

At the earliest opportunity in his hagiographical sermon *De Ioseph*, Ambrose reveals his interpretive frame of reference. The young boy Joseph's dream vision of the sheaf that stood while others bowed down (*Genesis* 37:5–8) was a forecasting of the resurrection of Jesus, as the second dream of stars and planets bowing before him (*Genesis* 37:9–11) pointed to that day when *the other Joseph*, with his Mary and with the disciples, would worship the true God in the body of Jesus Christ.[25] An etymology of Joseph's name that means "expression of God the highest" leads to the view that the one who was sold is the subject of the hymn in St. Paul's *Philippians* 2—the one who, though exalted, took the form of a servant. And Ambrose adds the distinctly Christian supersessionist comment: "we would not have bought Him, unless his own people had sold him."[26] Typology entails a claim of ownership: insofar as Joseph "is" Jesus, only the Christian community can count Joseph *their* saint, *their* God-sent holy example.

To re-engage our segment of the Joseph saga, *Genesis* 39, this time in conjunction with the wider early Christian hermeneutic: if our hero consistently prefigures Jesus, and if this is *a*, or *the* key Christian exegetical and interpretive hinge, there are ramifications in two directions. First, it is inevitable that representations of Joseph the servant of Potiphar, exposed to his wife's temptations, will be shaped by the figure of Jesus. Under these terms, what can be imaginatively entertained as having transpired between a beautiful young man and his desire-frantic pursuer? The controls and restraints are strong, since Joseph is not merely or even really Joseph, but a figure whose story and whose actions are read in the light of, or backward from the story and actions of, Christ. A change of heart that interrupts and cools the passion he feels for the woman and her enticements is not a likely scenario for the Joseph viewed as the type of Christ.

Second, and in the other direction, Joseph's saga is being presented with more than passing interest and investment in matters of Christology. All that befalls Joseph, but especially his responses to and actions in the midst of trying events, point beyond the *Genesis* narrative, registering or suggesting points about the Christian savior. In the specific matter of his being tested by Potiphar's wife, Joseph as Christ-type cannot have been tempted, since sexual attraction and desire are not understood by early Christian thinkers to be among those challenges confronted by Jesus either at the outset of his ministry in the wilderness or thereafter. Nor did Christian writers believe that erotic temptations or occasions of illicit sexual intimacy were among those tests Jesus had in common with other humans that he met without sinning (see *Hebrews* 4:15).

We can see how readily Ambrose moves the incident of Joseph with Potiphar's wife toward this second purpose, a Christological one: he speaks of "that true Hebrew" whom "no corrupt or worldly pleasure could subvert."[27] Other parts of the argument follow closely: "At the last, when he was grabbed by his bodily garment by the adulterous hand of the synagogue, as it were, He stripped off the flesh and ascended free of death."[28] (The earlier figure—of Joseph naked without his garment, but clothed in chastity—here undergoes sharp adaptation.) From this interpretive orientation, which is in Christology's direction, Ambrose is able to find in Benjamin, Joseph's younger brother, the apostle Paul, whose delayed conversion and joining of the band of Christ is the setting aside of "the veil which is set over the heart of the Jews," an image in one of the apostle's letters (*2 Corinthians* 3:13–18).[29] Jacob's unwillingness to travel to Egypt to his son Joseph has, for Ambrose, clear predictive import: the Jews were invited to leave "the narrow limits of Judea . . . to pass to the people of God that was gathered from all tribes and peoples, and was made into a great people. What could be clearer?"[30]

Use of the Joseph story to underscore the revelation celebrated by Christians and to criticize the Jews' supposed intransigence began early and was continuous: *The Epistle of Barnabas*, a late first or early second-century writing, saw in Jacob's blessing of Ephraim, Joseph's younger son, a sign that "the greater shall serve the less"—that is, "that this [new] people is the first and the heir of the covenant," and Cyprian in the third century repeated the claim in his *Testimonies Against the Jews* under the rubric that gentiles rather than Jews would believe in Christ.[31] Epiphanius compared the bloody robe given by Joseph's brothers into Jacob's hands with the flesh the Jews held and possessed in persecuting and crucifying Jesus.[32] It is impossible to pass over the same author's entertaining declaration of his more personal sense of association with the tempted Joseph. Recounting his difficult encounters with various Christian gnostic groups, Epiphanius comments specifically about those known as the Barbelites:

> I happened on this sect myself, beloved, and was actually taught these things
> in person, out of the mouths of practicing Gnostics. Not only did women under
> this delusion offer me this line of talk, and divulge this sort of thing to me. With
> impudent boldness moreover, they tried to seduce me themselves—like that
> murderous, villainous Egyptian wife of the chief cook—because they wanted
> me in my youth. But he who stood by the holy Joseph then, stood by me as
> well. . . . Though I was reproached by the baneful women themselves, I for my
> part laughed to hear women like that whispering to each other, scornfully if you
> please, "We cannot save the youngster; we leave him in the hands of the archon
> to perish." (For whichever is prettiest displays herself as bait, so that they claim
> they "save"—instead of destroy—the suckers through her).[33]

Yet another piece of exegesus strains to make its supersessionist point: Augustine takes the meaning of Joseph's name, "addition," to refer to the divine plan: Joseph sold into Egypt represents Christ passing over to the gentiles from the Jews; from then on, to Joseph (or Christ) the gentiles belong, and thus the addition. Later, when Joseph's bones went out from the land of Egypt with Moses (*Exodus* 13:19) in the exodus, the passing of the faithful through baptism was presaged.[34]

The penchant of early Christian interpreters for finding prefigurements of Christ and the church in the Bible they shared with the Jews had, inevitably, anti-Jewish content; these ramifications remind us of the social and religious rivalry affecting the writings and pieces of art we have been considering. Christian exegetes' portrayals of Joseph, whose face, person, and characterization yield to that of Jesus, linked with defamations of the Jews that cannot be discounted as mere rhetorical commonplaces, belong to the churches' presentation of their revealed truth and thereby to their efforts to achieve social consolidation and also political credibility in the opening centuries of the common era.

Joseph, Temptation, and Christian Monks

We may wonder to what extent the picture of sex-abstaining Joseph was a symbol not only of a particular virtue, but of the energy and momentum of asceticism as it gained prominence in institutionalized Christianity. We read in the *Sayings of the Fathers* of monks gathered while a brother reads the history of Joseph from *Genesis*; they debate its meanings in a style much like that of the rabbis.[35] Found in works having to do with the ascetic or monastic life are several notices of Joseph coping with the overtures of Potiphar's spouse. A monk tells Abba Poemen that his "heart becomes luke-warm when a little suffering comes [his] way." Poemen's counsel is succinct: "Do we not admire Joseph, a young man of seventeen, for enduring his temptation to the end? And God glorified him."[36] Abba Orsisius sounds a familiar monastic theme and concern in proclaiming that "the man with a carnal disposition of soul who has not been in the fire through fear of God like Joseph, utterly disintegrates when he accepts a position of authority."[37] We should note what these two invocations of Joseph emphasize: they ring Joseph in as a challenging and appropriate example for those who *do* suffer temptation—of weakened resolve, or of fleshly attractions. A tested and a tempted Joseph apparently could be related to by monks who opted to live the life of disciplined self-deprivation.

Elsewhere, ascetic writings celebrate Joseph's humility, since he suffered injustices—being sold, and being imprisoned—in silence; humility led to his becoming the great man of Egypt.[38] Yes, in addition to the underlining of his purity, the theme of Joseph's success also finds a place in monastic lore and teaching: it was his entrepreneurship that was copied by the industrious Palestinian monk Theodosius when he founded a hospice on ground above his cave, and organized maintenance of his crowd of visiting clients.[39]

Attention to the Joseph figure, and to his conquest of Potiphar's wife in her scheming, abounds in this literature—in a letter sent by Jerome to recruit a Roman soldier to the ascetic life ("Imitate Joseph and leave your garment in the hand of your Egyptian mistress!"), in a hymn of Ephrem which promises a glimpse in paradise of the one "who stripped off and cast away the lust that flared up among the senseless," and in the report of James the Syrian hermit's vision of saint Joseph at the "summit of virtue."[40] A passage in Theodoret's epilogue to his *History of the Monks of Syria* capsulizes that portrait which held sway among promoters and practitioners of asceticism.

[Joseph's] friendship with God neither envy could destroy, nor slavery quench, nor the wheedling of a mistress remove, nor threats and terror extinguish. . . . But he remained the same, looking at the Beloved and fulfilling his laws.[41]

In one of his hymns, Paulinus of the monastic community in Nola, embraced the life of Joseph in more personal terms:

May my love be pure, and may sinful love disgust me; then, like the unpolluted Joseph, I may shun the enticements of the flesh and, having cast off the chains of the body, I may be free of sin and leave to the world the spoils of the flesh. It is time to put embraces at a distance.[42]

The growth of Christian monasticism and its capacity for presenting a strong profile of this burgeoning religion in the late Roman world both drew upon and affected the ways of telling the Joseph story in the patristic era. For the early churches' teachers and preachers, Joseph conducted himself, when he was accosted by Potiphar's wife, with honorable restraint and obedience to divine law. Though certain ascetics embraced the notion that he suffered the throes of temptation, the patriarch Joseph's ethical manner was part of a program of heightened morality that churches sought to commend both to their own and to onlookers as Christianity gained greater purchase on a position of acceptance and authority in the empire.

SCENES FROM THE LIFE OF JOSEPH: A CHRISTIAN SARCOPHAGUS AND AN ARCHBISHOP'S THRONE

In the preceding chapter, we exploited surviving pages of the Christian Vienna Genesis in order to discern signs of Jewish exegetical motifs in its depictions of Joseph. At this juncture, two other works of early Christian art command our attention, for each reaches beyond the incident of Joseph with Potiphar's wife to explore what other meanings the persona and career of Joseph held for members of Christian communities. The first two, Figure 8.1 and Figure 8.2, are details of the same fourth century Roman sarcophagus fragment.

Discovered in 1943 beneath St. Peter's in Rome, in a grotto adjacent to the subterranean chapel honoring Pope Clemens VIII (d. 1605), this marble sarcophagus lid's iconography presents an unusual combination of subjects. A central plaque (uninscribed) that is held on each side by a winged Victory divides the separate biblical stories.

Figure 8.1 Joseph scenes on a Roman sarcophagus. Detail. Vatican collection. Fourth century CE. St. Peter's Basilica, Rome. © Biblioteca Hertziana.

Figure 8.2 Adoration of the Magi, sarcophagus. Detail. Vatican collection. Fourth century CE. St. Peter's Basilica, Rome. © Biblioteca Hertziana.

On the right half, the three wise men, their camels nicely sequenced behind them, bring their gifts to the Christ child. Jesus, sitting upright on Mary's lap, holds up before them, or extends toward them, a laurel wreath—itself a symbol of victory or laudation. At the far right, in the shadow behind Mary, a cross is visible—a *signum* that begs for explanation. Is it incorporated in, and does it relate to, the artist's representation of his subject, the infant Jesus receiving the adoration of the magi?

The left side of the lid contains two scenes from Joseph's history. One of these portrays Joseph, the vizier of the land of Egypt, selling grain to his brothers. This image captures the beginning of Joseph's devious but purposeful dealings with them; he will finally disclose his identity, be reunited with his father Jacob, forgive his treacherous brothers, and bring his family to Goshen in Egypt (*Genesis* 41:39–47:27). The other narrative scene, closest to the center, shows Joseph being extricated by Midianite traders from the pit into which his brothers had cast him (*Genesis* 37: 28). The rescuer's camel visually answers those of the magi.

Can we determine what is being suggested by the juxtaposition of two moments from the life of Joseph and one of early Christianity's earliest and most popular images—the visitation by the sages from the East, who recognize the child as the new king promised by God? Minimally, the coupling of the two sacred stories and their chief figures in itself asserts the Christians' association of the two—undoubtedly, judging from the texts studied above, as ante-type to type, as anticipation to realization. The life of Joseph, in some of its selected aspects, pointed to the life of Christ. I do not find it difficult to suppose that the artist recollected that the wise men (in *Matthew* 2:6) told Herod that the child they looked for would be the shepherd—or the ruler—of the people of Israel, and then called up the image of his prototype—Joseph, Egypt's virtual ruler, whose actions redounded to the benefit of the line of Jacob, and ultimately, to the Hebrews' deliverance from slavery in the land of the Pharaohs.

More specific iconographic intentions fall more in the realm of speculation. May we presume that the selection of these two particular Joseph episodes out of several the artist-sculptor might have chosen was fully and carefully intentional? Are we being shown Joseph, the Lord being "with him," saved—delivered from death—and also playing a salvific role? As the governor of Egypt's lands, he provides sustenance, through his brothers, for the famine-threatened people of Jacob in Canaan—and then protects them in Goshen until that day when their progeny will, by God's might, make their exodus from slavery. The appearance of the cross behind the child Jesus, if we entertain the possibility that it is not mere space-filling decoration, but is meant to interpret the scene, speaks equally of danger, persecution, and death on the one hand, and deliverance and victory on the other. On this kind of reading of the carved scenes on the left, Joseph is being rescued from the certain death he would meet in the well, and then, presides in power as a governor of affairs, involved in a transaction (on many levels) with brothers ignorant of his identity. These two Joseph scenes can be understood to "match," and anticipate what is pictured on the right side of the marble lid: the adored newborn Jesus, the Christ, who will, God being "with him," suffer travail, gain triumph, and rule. The cross in the background adds that dimension of meaning to an already well-established Christian image of the visit of the magi to honor the infant Jesus.

We are reminded of that painted scene in the Vienna Genesis in which Joseph's garment is being displayed by Potiphar's wife as evidence of his crime. The clearly painted symbol of the cross above the piece of clothing was suggestive, if not transparently clear, in what it might have signified to its viewers. The cross as Christian *signum* may be a blessing—an affirmation of Joseph's steadfastness against the woman's wiles. But the cross may rather (or at the same time) invoke persecution and trial, Joseph's crisis in Potiphar's house belonging firmly in that category. Joseph, one of God's favored ones, is both on trial, and enduring a trial of his faithfulness.[43] In the previous chapter I asked whether a Christian interpretation of the cross in this image from the Vienna Genesis might connect Joseph's garment with that of Jesus at the time of his execution (Mark 15:24). Epiphanius, the fourth-century bishop of Salamis (in Cyprus) *did* make such an allusion, though he referred to Joseph's many-colored coat, splattered with blood by his treacherous brothers before they presented it to Jacob: "In the same [way] did the Jews have the flesh of him who was crucified, [similar] to the garment of Joseph, and through precaution they laid him on a bier, and for yet greater caution sealed up the sepulcher."[44]

Though Christian commentators (like Philo before them) play on the idea of Joseph's lack of nakedness, since he is "clothed" in his blameless chastity, there is at least one other reference possibly being made by the cross that stands over Joseph's garment—a likening of it to the tunic stripped from Jesus at the time of his crucifixion. Seen in that light, an early Christian painter-commentator might well have recalled the description (in *John* 19:23–25) of Jesus's clothing in the hands of those seeing to his execution. If this association is implied in decorating with the sign of the cross that dramatic moment when Potiphar hears his wife's false accusations against Joseph, an emphasis on the parallel meanings of the stories of Joseph and Jesus, both innocent victims and God-protected victors, however shorthand the icon of the cross may be, is similar to its use on the marble coffin lid we have just inspected.

The magnificently decorated throne (Figure 8.3) has been identified and dated on the basis of the monogram at the center of the panel just below

Figure 8.3 Episcopal chair of Maximianus, Bishop and Archbishop of Ravenna (546–556). Museo Arcivescovile, Ravenna. © Art History Images.

its seat, which is interpreted to read MAXIMIANUS EPISCOPUS. Its construction probably marked his election in 546 as bishop, a position second
only to that of the pope, given the fact that the city had become the de
facto capital of Italy.[45] The *cathedra* of Maximianus is thought to have been
carried in the city's Christian processions, displaying on its seat liturgical
objects—ornate crosses and Gospel books—as it was borne along streets
and roads.[46] Another opinion pictures the archbishop enthroned on important liturgical occasions—in particular during baptisms, in the course of
which he would have conducted the questioning of the candidates and
heard their confessions of faith.[47]

The original wooden frame supported the throne's elegant ivory images,
the majority of which depict events in the life of Christ. Our interest in
the Ravenna *cathedra* centers on the presence of ten ivory panels (five on
each side, from the level of the arm-rest to the lower base) illustrated with
episodes from *Genesis 37–50*. On these Joseph's story is adjoined with
that of Jesus. The Vienna Genesis illuminations and the Roman sarcophagus lid revealed that this interest in Joseph was not without precedent in
early Christian iconography, but in this case we have the largest (surviving) collection of images having the patriarch, Jacob's son, as their subject. Furthermore, their use in the decoration of a *cathedra* built for a high
church official raises new questions about the variety of reasons exegetes
and artists had for Christianizing the Joseph of the old covenant.

Art historian Meyer Schapiro opened a 1952 investigatory essay in
this way:

> Why was the story of Joseph represented on the great ivory throne of Archbishop
> Maximianus (546–554) beside scenes from the life of Christ? Until now the
> choice has been explained by the notion common among Christian theolo-
> gians, from Tertullian to Pascal, that the patriarch Joseph was an antetype of
> Christ: betrayed by his brothers, lowered into the well and sold to the Ismaelites,
> he was in the end the savior of the Gentiles and the Jews. *This striking parallel of
> Joseph to Christ does not account sufficiently, however, for the unique place of Joseph
> as a theme on a bishop's throne* [emphasis added].[48]

Schapiro's question *and* his explanatory thesis inform many of my conclusions about the use to which Joseph's saga is being put in this particular
artifact. We begin with a description of the carved ivory panels and their
subjects, turning then to consider the artist's modes of interpretation in a
few scenes from the Joseph story.[49]

By chronological order of the biblical narrative, the carved images portray
these events: (1) Joseph is put in the well by some of his brothers, while others slaughter a kid in order to place blood on his coat; (2) the brothers inform

Jacob of Joseph's death, displaying his tunic; (3) Joseph's brothers sell him to the Midianites; (4) Ishmaelites sell Joseph to Potiphar; (5) Potiphar's wife attempts to seduce Joseph, after which he is led to his imprisonment; (6) the Pharoah dreams of seven "well-formed" cows who are consumed by seven "scrawny . . . and emaciated" cows (*Genesis* 41:17–21); (7) Joseph stands before the Pharaoh, interpreting his dream; (8) Joseph, now in office as Egypt's governor, detains his brother Simeon, while his other brothers are allowed to return to Canaan (*Genesis* 42:18–26), or Joseph listens to a plea from Judah that he and his brothers not be required to bring Benjamin, Jacob's youngest son, to Egypt (*Genesis* 44:18–33); (9) Joseph observes as his brothers fill sacks of grain to take back to famine-struck Canaan; (10) Joseph is reunited with his aged father Jacob (*Genesis* 46:29–30: "[Joseph] presented himself to him and, embracing him around the neck, he wept on his neck a good while. Then Israel [Jacob] said to Joseph, 'Now I can die, having seen for myself that you are still alive.' ")[50]

It is noteworthy that the subjects of the ivory carvings on Maximianus's throne encompass the greater part of Joseph's life—from his boyhood to his reunion with his father, Jacob, but *also* striking that these scenes on the ivories incorporate and interweave those twin plot lines that animate the last chapters of *Genesis*: Joseph's rise to success through hardship and trials until he becomes (as Judah remarks in *Genesis*. 45:18) "the equal of Pharaoh," on the one hand, and on the other, Joseph's ingenious and emotion-wracked resolution of his breach with his brothers, bringing to an end his separation from his long-suffering father. The two scenes featured here highlight Joseph's change of station from humility to great power. The introduction of Joseph to slavery, and to the lust of his master's wife, are the subjects of Figure 8.4.

In the upper scene we see Joseph the Hebrew youth's introduction to life as a slave in Egypt. He approaches the house of his master, Potiphar, while the man's wife looks on interestedly. Below, tussling in front of her stately bed, Joseph is shown to be resisting the seduction efforts of his master's wife. No space is given to what came next—the loss of his garment to his tormenter's grasp. More unique is the adjacent scene, which adds narrative even as it compresses the story. Potiphar, having come to his judgment against Joseph, is present as Joseph, bent over and bound at the hands, is led away. The fig-ures looking on from the prison have been identified as a "prisoner staring sadly out of a window while his jailer sits nodding in the doorway below."[51]

The scenes carved on this ivory are spare in their narrations—that is, they communicate much less than the Vienna Genesis' comparable images concerning the characters involved and the tensions and consequences generated by that "certain day" in which Potiphar's wife sought forcefully to seduce Joseph. It may be that they are iconographically abbreviated,

Figure 8.4 Joseph's sale to Potiphar and his punishment after accusations by Potiphar's wife. Ivory from Maximian's cathedra. Ravenna. Sixth century CE.
© Photo: Alfredo Dagli Orti/Art Resource, NY.

due to space limitations. Possibly, however, the combination of events in this one plaque carries its own message, moving Joseph from Potiphar's household to the jail, from which he will—due to rumors of his expertise as dream interpreter—be conducted to the palace of the Pharaoh.

Upon proposing that Egypt store grain in the cities during the years of bounty in order to ward off famine in the lean, Joseph (he who had been as a boy blessed with dreams of his future powers) is recognized by Pharaoh, who in *Genesis* says to him:

> There is none so discerning and wise as you. You shall be in charge of my court, and by your command shall all my people be directed; only with respect to the throne shall I be superior to you. . . . See, I put you in charge of all of the land in Egypt (*Genesis* 41:39–42).

Now in the scriptural text emerges the mature and competent Joseph, one who wears the Pharaoh's signet ring, fine robes and a gold necklace. When he passes by in the chariot of Egypt's second in command, the people bend their knees in obedience and honor (*Genesis* 41:42–43). Figure 8.5 depicts Joseph overseeing grain sales to his unsuspecting brothers.

This ivory panel depicts Joseph in lordly authority; from his governor's seat, he questions his unwitting brothers, who have come seeking famine relief. In the central image, Joseph oversees their grain purchase. This is

Figure 8.5 Joseph oversees provision of grain to his brothers. Maximian's Cathedra. Ravenna.
Sixth century CE. © Photo: Alfredo Dagli Orti/Art Resource, NY.

part of his continuing plan for confronting the brothers who had betrayed him (42:18–26).

Taken as a whole, what is the burden of the message that is communicated in the episodes from Joseph's life that adorn Archbishop Maximianus's sixth-century throne? I have circled back to Meyer Schapiro's doubt that typology—Joseph's prefiguring of Jesus—fully accounts for the range and meaning of the ivory representations of Joseph on this very particular piece of furniture.

The chair's Joseph scenes, Schapiro proposed, had another purpose—namely, the employment not only of the chaste but also the just and competent Joseph as a model for effective ecclesial leadership. On the assumption that the exquisite throne was a gift from the emperor to the newly elected bishop of a key city, one art historian has wondered whether there was built into its utilization of Joseph's history a message about power relations: "perhaps the parallel to be drawn from these scenes is that Maximian was expected to be to Justinian what Joseph was to Pharaoh," an honorable and obedient subordinate.[52] A quite different understanding of the intent of the Joseph ivories was reached by Schapiro, who based his analysis on writings (both before and after the episcopal reign of Maximianus) that render advice and guidelines concerning the proper character, values, motives, and actions—even the correct pastoral sympathy—of Christian clergy.

The post-Constantine rise of Christianity as a social and political force positioned (and obligated) a bishop like Ambrose of Milan—himself a working colleague (and sometimes challenger) of emperors—to pay heed to the effectiveness of priests under his authority. In his treatise, *On Duties* (*De officiis*, which borrows both title and numerous ideas from Cicero), Ambrose explicitly addresses church leaders, even while assuming a wider readership.[53] The employment of biblical exemplars of ethical behavior is a strong feature in this work, and analyses of Joseph's deeds appear frequently. An early general profile of his virtues contains, Ambrose believes, clues for the priest who will be worthy:

> Joseph—he had seen the sun, moon, and stars all bowing down to worship him in a dream, yet he submitted to his father with a ready devotion. He was so chaste that he would not listen to a single word if it was not pure. He was so humble that he endured slavery; so modest that he ran for his life; so patient that he put up with prison; and so ready to forgive those who had treated him unjustly that he even did them good in return.[54]

The author imagines ordinary circumstances in which this kind of advice would be relevant: Joseph fled Potiphar's wife and left his cloak behind "rather than listen to proposals which affronted his modesty. For if one person shows that he likes to hear such things, he incites another to come out with them."[55] Bringing the value of Joseph's virtue of modesty to bear on a regular, but he thinks dangerous, practice in fourth-century Christian communities, Ambrose speaks of the conditions that ought to apply when women are visited by men:

> There is no reason for younger men to go near the houses of widows and virgins, unless they are on an official visit. Even this should be done in the company of older men—namely the bishop, or, if the situation is serious, with the priests. Why should we give worldly people occasion to criticize us? Why should such visits take on some significance by the frequency? What if one of these women were by chance to fall? Why should you come under reproach because someone else has fallen? Think how many men there are, strong men, too, who have been taken by charms like these! Think how many there are who have given no occasion for any kind of transgression, but have given plenty of occasion for suspicion![56]

Just after commenting that the best ways of commending oneself as a leader is "by showing [people] love and by earning their confidence," he points to another of Joseph's strengths:

> Since one particularly good way of winning people over is by giving them good advice, prudence and justice are desirable in every situation. Indeed, this is just what most people are looking for: they want to place their confidence in someone who possesses these virtues, for they know that he is in a position to give useful and reliable advice to anyone deserving it. . . . think of Joseph, even when he was in prison, he could get no rest from being consulted about things that were uncertain. His advice proved so valuable to the whole of Egypt that the country did not feel those seven barren years, and was even in a position to alleviate the plight of other peoples who were suffering in the grip of the terrible famine.[57]

Governance of the Pharaoh's lands, according to *Genesis*, entailed close attention to crops, grain, and granaries, and to Egypt's commerce and trade in these goods. The duplicitous and taunting negotiations with his visiting brothers presented a special case, of course, tied as it was to the restoration and continuation of the house of Jacob. But the dramatic intrigue in the story and its bearing on the continuance of the Abrahamic line was not the only appeal this part of Joseph's story held for the bishop of Milan.

The justice with which Joseph sold grain to all who could purchase it, pressuring no buyers with "too dear a price," Ambrose contrasts with the "daylight robbery" he knows some of his contemporaries commit. They inflate prices, raise interest rates, and sell to the highest bidders, like auctioneers.[58] "Why," he asks, "do you put an evil curse on everyone, making out that the famine will only get worse . . . that next year's is set to be even worse for crops?"[59] Joseph is the counterexample:

> Holy Joseph opened the granaries to all; he did not shut them up. Instead of chasing the higher prices that could be had from one year's crop, he built up a reserve for the years to come. Rather than getting anything for himself, he had the foresight to make arrangements which enabled the people to deal with the famine that would recur in the years ahead.[60]

Whether the worst of the hoarders and profiteers included bishops and their appointees or not, these matters were, in the days of Ambrose—and of Maximianus two centuries later—official episcopal business, and in his ethical arguments about duties Ambrose once again brought the exemplar Joseph to the fore.[61] So, while Ambrose wrote unambiguously about "the holy Joseph who is [Christ's] prefiguration, receiv[ing] a choice blessing so that he may be held in honor among his brothers," he also saw in the patriarch attributes important for leaders in a religion that had now gained firm and positive status in the Roman empire.[62] Joseph is admirable for things that bishops and priests can learn and develop in themselves.

> He longed for freedom, of course he did, yet he put up with the harsh bonds of slavery. How submissive he was as a slave, how consistent in the virtue he displayed, how generous in his time in prison—he was wise in the interpretations he gave, moderate in his use of power, far-sighted in times of plenty, and just in times of famine! He brought an order to all his affairs; he timed everything right; he showed such moderation in discharging his duties that he was able to dispense justice to entire nations at a time.[63]

Ambrose translates Joseph's world of maintaining the lands and markets of Egypt with the help of his own knowledge of the fourth-century Roman realm, in which the churches have received gifts of land and are obligated to manage the commerce generated from them. In other words, the overseers or bishops charged with these practical duties must uphold—against what Ambrose presents as not uncommon practices of exploitation—Joseph's manner of fair dealings on behalf of the people and their best interests.

On the basis of treatments of Joseph like these from Ambrose as well as other similarly focused descriptions occurring in sermons of Peter Chrysologus, who served as Ravenna's bishop from ca. 430 to ca. 450, Meyer Schapiro advanced a new and more comprehensive picture of the Hebrew slave who became the Pharaoh's viceroy—a picture serviceable to Christian leaders in changed circumstances.

> It is [a] richer conception of the patriarch Joseph as a figure of Christ and a model of the bishop who is both priest and statesman that underlies, I believe, the choice of the Joseph story for the symbolic decoration of the Maximianus throne. The likening of the bishop to Joseph must be understood historically, that is, with respect to the character of the episcopal office in the sixth century. By that time, the bishop had advanced far from his earlier status as a presbyter to a position of great power, with civil as well as religious functions. . . . With the decline of the Roman state, the bishop's role in secular affairs increased immensely. The laws of Justinian assigned to the bishops important duties in the state. . . . the governor [in a province] could hardly resist the all-powerful bishop, who spoke at the same time in the name of the Emperor from whom he drew his prerogatives and of God himself whose representative he was.[64]

Just as the very particular social conditions in which Philo and his readers lived stirred him to reinterpret and reconstruct Joseph as the righteous and adroit "statesman," so were the likes of Ambrose and Peter Chrysologus refiguring him as a "churchman" in an age when bishops were also leaders possessing broad social authority and responsibility. Joseph became the model of a consecrated priest and politician.[65]

By Christian exegetes and preachers, Joseph was elevated above some of the quite human attributes and actions clearly present in the biblical presentation of him. We have seen several causes for that editing out, or laundering, of Joseph. It was not driven, as we might have guessed, by instincts to censor the dramatic sexuality in part of his story, but by a search for the ways in which he might be an exemplar for virtuous behavior, a source of inspiration for ethical, spiritual, and administrative accomplishment. Some Christian writers and artists, in the same vein as the Hellenistic Jewish idealizers of Joseph, fashioned him as the personification of chastity. Represented in his purity, in his endurance of persecution and victory, and ultimately as a victor, Joseph could be understood as scripture's forecasting of Jesus Christ, but this portrait would necessarily result in muted or ignored suggestions that Joseph might actually have been tempted by the invitations of Potiphar's wife. This typology had the effect, once the lineage from Joseph through Jesus was extended to the clergy—the vicars of Christ—of enshrining Joseph as the wisest and most just ruler and administrator. He could even be presented as the kind of person or priest or bishop in whom anyone could in full trust confide, seeking counsel. Exegetes, preachers, carvers of images in marble sarcophagi or ivory plaques were able to preserve *and* elaborate the ways in which the Joseph of *Genesis* 37–50 was the paragon of control of the passions, the holy saint whose word and deeds pointed to the messiah the churches celebrated, and (as Christianity moved from the edges to the center of imperial life), the example par excellence of an ecclesiastical overseer, a bishop-administrator reliable in his morals, his maintenance of justice, and his astute and wise execution of his duties.

Our survey of early Christian understandings of Joseph and his encounter with his master's spouse yields a strong picture of his deployment as the one tested and found to be faithful in his commitment to sexual continence. Yet the question of whether he was not only tested but also tempted remains unresolved, on the basis of the texts we have considered. Although as Christ-figure Joseph cannot have been inclined to the sin offered him, Ambrose did imagine him as tempted, as a man mulling over the risks of touching the woman, before he resists. And the monks, insofar as they sometimes enlisted Joseph as a proto-ascetic, should have him (as Abbas Poemen and Orsisius seem to) experiencing temptation and yet overcoming it; their perception of Joseph's testing is more closely oriented to the *Genesis* account. In this matter, as it shapes the representations of Joseph in early Christian writings, a genuine tension exists both between and among patristic accounts and within the work of a single author, Ambrose, who imagined that Joseph did not succumb to the woman's temptations, but did wrestle with his fear that being touched by her would have brought upon him incentives to lust.[66]

My observations—first, about the roles of Christological-typological exegesis and of the ascetic movement in the church fathers' world of religious competition, and second, concerning the new imaging designed for bishops—have taken a page from the work of Erich Gruen, who noted an altered portrait of Joseph by Philo and other Hellenistic Jewish writers as reflective of certain Jews' new and promising status and situation in the diaspora. For Christians too, Joseph's victory in the midst of temptations was a compelling and serviceable holy story. So also did the church's growing profile, necessitating means of instruction and reinforcement for church leaders being thrust into new imperial relations and daunting obligations, call for lessons from Joseph's spellbinding successes and rise to power. To adapt only slightly a sentence of Gruen's: a strong strain in early Christianity pushed beyond accommodation and sometimes endangered status to stress Christian advantage and superiority. The pliable portrait of Joseph suitably ministered to those objectives.[67]

How different from Christian perspectives and teachings about Joseph and Potiphar's wife are those found in the Qur'an's Surah 12, Yusuf, and in the works of exegetes and storytellers in the succeeding years? What meanings and layers of meaning were early Muslims able to detect in the revelation concerning this prophet's temptation by the wife of the Egyptian who purchased him?

CHAPTER 9

༄

Yusuf with Zulaykha

Pivotal qur'anic ideas about knowledge, revelation, kinds and levels of awareness and understanding are concentrated in Surah 12, permeating and giving shape to Yusuf's story.[1] Its opening verses declare as much:

> 12:2 We revealed it as an Arabic recital
> so that you would understand.
> 3 We tell you the best of stories
> in revealing this Recital to you
> in spite of your former ignorance.[2]

This recitation, given in the Arabic in order "that you might understand," is deemed the "best of stories." Its superiority consists in its clarity, in its accessibility to those who seriously hear it, and exercise their reason. Knowledge of the truth, knowledge of such depth and precision as to be conscious of outcomes in human lives (like those of Yusuf, his father and his brothers, the Aziz and his wife, and the Pharoah) belongs to God alone. All other levels of knowing and foreseeing are, by comparison, limited.

To what extent or degree do Yaqub the father and Yusuf the son possess and manifest the knowledge that comes from their God? Yusuf the boy is gifted with prophetic dreams—about his future prominence, and his family's ultimate bowing to honor him. His father warns him of the (satanic) envy and hatred his visions have caused in his brothers, but also informs him that in the future he will indeed be elevated in this way by God, "who will impart to you some understanding of the inner meanings of the happenings" (12:6). Joseph's dreaming and his capacity to interpret dreams are arrows in his quiver—significant in his particular giftedness—but not, apparently, the exclusive stuff or full set of powers contained in his prophethood.[3] There is more for the young Joseph to learn. God informs Muhammad of an increase in Joseph's powers at the time he arrived in Egypt: "And when Joseph reached maturity, We gave him judgment and knowledge. And thus We reward the doers of good" (12:22). The young prophet is one who gains in discretion, gains in wisdom, and gains in favor with God.

Neither is the mature prophet Yaqub blessed with certainty or invincible foresight. He harbors doubts concerning his sons' report that Yusuf was victim to a wild animal, his dubiety grounded, it seems, in his conviction that the boy's dreams would be fulfilled. However, Jaqub is depicted more than once as turning in his grief to God, on the grounds that God alone knows what has happened, and what will be disclosed in the future.

At nearly every point in Surah 12, then, we are made aware that there are levels of knowledge and awareness that range from the omniscience of God to the dire limitations of the ignorant. God is fully conscious of all that happens in Yusuf's life—from the caravan-travelers' discovery of him in the pit, to what will transpire when, years later, his brothers come to Egypt, to what his last recorded words will be, late in his troubled but splendid life:

> 12:101 My Lord, You gave me some authority, and
> taught me some interpretation of stories.
> Creator of the heavens and earth,
> You are my protector
> in the world and in the hereafter:
> take my soul in a state of acquiescence,
> and unite me with the upright.

It was in the residence of the unnamed Aziz ("the mighty one," or "lord," or "master") that Yusuf was provided with a learning-experience—one with ramifications for his future. This episode comfortably fits the entire surah's emphasis on the divine disclosure of knowledge, and the variety of responders and responses. In Surah 12, Yusuf's authority in speaking and acting is presented as the fruit of his belief, of his servanthood to God. So it is that Yusuf, in 12:37, does not turn to deciphering the dreams of the two young men in prison with him before he recounts how his skills are "part of what my Lord taught me." He continues, "I have left behind the religion of those who do not believe in God and who scoff at the hereafter, and I follow the religion of Abraham, Isaac, and Jacob."

This young dream interpreter, however, is not a possessor of sure knowledge, fully conscious of what must transpire. His story is filled with happenings not anticipated, and with results that do not yield to his precise planning. "God knows," or "God knows best" are qur'anic phrases with theological weight: *only* God knows.

SURAH 12:19–35; 50–56: YUSUF AND ZULAYKHA

The Qur'an, and especially its early exegetes, regard Joseph as one whose behavior with Zulaykha merits close scrutiny. According to a doctrine of `isma, or "prophetic sinlessness," Yusuf's behavior might be expected to be above reproach, but this teaching impedes neither the Qur'an nor its interpreters from pondering Yusuf's motives and psychology—even his weaknesses. This is another point at which Surah 12 contributes to a fresh aspect in Muslim understanding of the prophet. What does God's testing of the young and handsome Yusuf by the wanton Zulaykha signify? Is such an experience needful—even ordained—in the case of this prophet?

Pursuit of Yusuf by the impassioned Zulaykha is told, first, in a few verses, though the incident's repercussions crop up at later points in the surah as well.

12:22 And when he gained maturity,
We gave him judgment and knowledge.
That is how We recompense
Those who do good.
23 But she whose house he was in,
tried to seduce him against his will;
she shut the doors and said, "Come!"
He said, "I take refuge in God;
For my master has made my abode agreeable.
Surely oppressors will not succeed."
24 Yet she did desire him,
and he desired her but for the fact
that he saw evidence of his Lord.
Thus it was, so that we might divert
Evil and indecencies from him;
For he was one of Our purified servants.
25 The two raced to the door,
and she tore his shirt from behind.
And they found her husband at the door.
She said, "What is the due of one
who desires evil of your wife

but imprisonment or torture?"
26 He said, "She tried to seduce me,"
and a witness from her household testified,
"If his shirt is torn from the front,
then she is telling the truth, and he is a liar.
27 But if his shirt is torn from the back, then she is lying,
and he is telling the truth."
28 So when he looked at the shirt,
it was torn from the back; he said,
"This was a trick of you women.
Your trick is serious indeed!
29 Joseph, turn away from this.
And, you, wife, seek forgiveness
for your sin; it was you
who were in the wrong."

In verse 24 the divine narration tells not only the actors' words, but their feelings and intentions—especially with regard to those of Yusuf. Other translations of 12:24, while acknowledging that young Yusuf's disposition was conditioned by the sign he saw ("he would have inclined to her"), more sharply state the correspondence of the woman's and Yusuf's desire for sex:

She wanted to involve herself with him [*hammat bihi*] and he wanted to involve himself with her [*hamma biha*], if he had not seen God's *burhan* ["proof," "evidence," "sign"].[4]

That Joseph was excited and aroused by Zulaykha is fully acknowledged in the Qur'an, a difference from the scriptural accounts known to Jews and Christians. There was mutual enthusiasm for the sexual encounter. In this test, Joseph was tempted. How are the two actors evaluated?

Prevented from succumbing to Zulaykha's plan by a *burhan*, a sign from God, Joseph was turned aside from evil. A fundamental notion of God's workings among humans who might not come to knowledge and obedience of him is here condensed in a single statement. Joseph made his decision to desist from what he illicitly desired *after* and on the basis of the *proof*, a revelation from his God. The avoidance of sinning—the triumph of his virtue—occurred in this way.

In the Qur'an, Joseph's shirt is torn from behind as he rushes for the door. The Aziz is met there, and Zulaykha and Yusuf are called upon to provide a classic "she said, he said" exchange. A witness from Zulaykha's family damns the woman by urging an inspection that will disclose how (and by whom) the shirt was torn. Here, unlike the narrative in *Genesis* 39, Joseph seizes the opportunity to defend himself against the woman's lie. Zulaykha's husband sees the truth, cursing the scheming of women (plural), and asking Joseph to let the matter rest. The Aziz then bluntly and forcefully demands that his wife ask forgiveness from Joseph for her sin (12:28).

The ensuing passage (12:30ff.) tells of the banquet given by Zulaykha for women of the city who had been gossiping about her.[5] Description of this event is intrinsic to the Qur'an's presentation of Yusuf, and more especially, to its characterization of the women and Zulaykha:

12.30 Women in the city said, "The wife of the grandee
is trying to seduce her manservant;
he has infatuated her.
We see she's in obvious error."
31 Now when she heard of their conniving,
she sent for them and prepared them a banquet;
she gave each one of them a knife,
then told Joseph to come out before them.
Now when they saw him,
they praised him,
and they cut their hands;
and they said, "God forbid! This is not a human being;
this is no less than a noble angel!"
32 She said, "Here you have the one
about whom you censured me.
I did indeed try to seduce him,
But he resisted.
And if he does not do
What I order him to,
he will be imprisoned
and will be one of the despised."
33 He said, "My Lord, prison is preferable
to me to what they are inviting me to;
and unless You divert their cunning from me,
I would be attracted to them,
and would behave foolishly too."
34 So his Lord answered him,
diverting their cunning from him.
For God is the all-hearing, the all-knowing.
35 Then it appeared to the men,

after they had seen the signs,
that they should imprison him
for a while.

During the meal the condemnatory women are given knives (presumably to carve fruit served to them) and when Yusuf is brought into the
hall they slice into their own hands, entranced by his dazzling appearance.
Zulaykha's guests now have experience of the young man's disorienting
allure. With a kind of confrontative defiance Zulaykha is putting on display
the one who inspired her lust and led her to her seduction attempt, which
she, with no trace of shame, admits to them.

Zulaykha's last comment to the women (12:32) indicates that she
schemes still, insisting that Yusuf now yield to her demands, lest he
loose his privileged position and be put in prison. Only at this point is
Joseph imprisoned, and then at his own request. His reasons are given in
12:33–34: unless the Lords (it is Lord Aziz in v. 33, the Lord God in v. 34)
remove Joseph from the sphere of the women's guile, he will desire them,
and falter, becoming one of the "fools"—the unenlightened sinners.
Significantly, Yusuf is represented as recognizing his vulnerability to their
further temptation.

The incident's sequel in 12:51–56 returns to this problem. Summoned
to the Pharaoh's service because of his reported talent in dream-reading,
Yusuf resists.

50 Now the king said,
"Bring him to me,"
but when the emmisary
came to him, he said,
"Go back to your master
and ask him about
the intention of the ladies
who cut their hands;
for my Lord is well-acquainted
with their cunning."
51 The king said,
"What business did you ladies have
trying to seduce Joseph?"
They said, "God forbid!
We knew no evil against him."
The wife of the grandee said,
"Now the truth has become manifest;

I tried to seduce Joseph,

so he was telling the truth."

52 [At this, Joseph remarked:] "This is to let him (the Aziz) know

I didn't betray him in secret,

and that God does not guide

the planning of betrayers.[6]

53 Yet I do not exonerate myself;

for the self is certainly compulsive with evil

unless my Lord has mercy;

for my Lord is most forgiving and most merciful."

54 Now the king said,

"Bring him to me;

I would reserve him for myself."

Then when he spoke to him, he said,

"Today you are secure and safe with us."

55 [Joseph] said, "Put me in charge

of the storehouses of the land;

I am very attentive and very expert."

56 Thus did We establish Joseph on earth:

he lived anywhere he wanted.

We pour Our mercy on whomever we wish,

And we do not neglect the reward of those who do good.

Barbara Stowasser observed:

> In the qur'anic rendition of the story of Joseph and the women, the themes of
> female seductiveness and cunning figure with some prominence. Both appear in
> the Hadith as symbolized in the concept of *fitna* ("social anarchy," "social chaos,"
> "temptation") which indicates that to be female is to be sexually aggressive, and
> hence, dangerous to social stability. According to tradition, God has instilled an
> irresistible attraction to women in man's soul, which works through the plea-
> sure he experiences when he looks at her or deals with anything related to her.
> She resembles Satan in his irresistible power over the individual.[7]

Joseph seeks assurances that the women who cut their hands when
they first laid eyes on him will not be given opportunity to ensnare him.
The king demands the truth about their earlier encounter with Joseph, his
question (12:51) presuming (without any correction) that the women at
the banquet sought to seduce him. Silent about their own actions, they
simply clear Joseph of culpability. The Aziz's wife does, however, make a
full confession of her intentions.

The voice in 12:53 definitely belongs to Joseph/Yusuf, who in the midst of being cleared of the charge of attempted seduction of Zulaykha declares that he was not entirely blameless in what occurred; the self, or soul, he explains, compels evil unless or until God's mercy comes. Yes, God intervened, delivering Yusuf from his pursuer in an act of mercy. Nonetheless, Yusuf is acknowledging his own fault, his having yielded to sexual temptation. This happened on account of his humanity, his makeup as a person—for his human "equipment" includes a soul (*nafs*) that by its very nature compels evil—*ammara bi's-su*—seeking opportunities for immoral actions. This piece of Muslim anthropology maintains a doctrine akin to Judaism's teaching of the "evil impulse" (*yetzer hara*), explaining Yusuf's vulnerability to the overtures by the mistress of his house and, by extension, to those of the women of the city who might accost him if he leaves his confinement in prison.

Zulaykha's confession is forced by what has been revealed; again, one of this surah's primary concerns—the workings of revelation and rationality—is in play, in this case confronting an unbeliever. "Now the truth has become manifest," says Zulaykha; "I tried to seduce him, so he was telling the truth" (12.51b).

Yusuf's confession of his own susceptibility to sin presents itself as an attainment of self-knowledge and wisdom. He did not have sex with that woman, but in the midst of her most energetic seduction effort he was affected by the passions within himself. In this testing he was tempted, but then brought from fevered to sober mind by the *burhan*, the evidence that appeared to him. It was only in this way that he was able to remain faithful to his God.

Near the end of *Surah Yusuf* it is proclaimed about the prophets that:

12:110 When it came to the point
where the messengers lost hope,
thinking that they had been misrepresented,
Our salvation came to them;
and those We wished were delivered.
But Our severity is not averted
From people guilty of sin.
111 There is certainly advice in their stories
for those who have reason.

Trials and persecutions have brought prophets to crises, and they have endured, with God's assistance. Yusuf's test at the hands of Zulaykha falls in that category and belongs to that history—it is necessary for the actualization of his own prophethood.

Most distinctive in the Qur'an's presentation of Yusuf's success in resisting Zulaykha is what is captured in Surah 12:24 and 12:53, where his struggle with temptation is not implied but described. However designed or willed or engineered by God this "test" may have been, it belonged to Yusuf to choose and to do the right thing, in spite of his strong impulses. His soul's compulsion, which threatens his goodness and his loyalty to the Aziz and to his Lord, must be battled, and overcome. A much-quoted *hadith* is relevant:

> God, exalted be He, says: "If a servant of Mine [merely] desires to do a good deed, I shall count this [desire] as a good deed; and if he does it, I shall count it tenfold. And if he desires to commit a bad deed, but does not commit it, I shall count this as a good deed, seeing that he refrained from it only for My sake."[8]

The last part of this teaching was given classic formulation by the twelfth-century Persian scholar Zamakhshari, who maintained that "the moral significance of 'virtue' consists in one's inner victory over a wrongful desire, and not in the absence of such a desire."[9]

The Qur'an's Yusuf is portrayed as one who is in the process of accomplishing the virtue of a prophet, of surrendering to the will of God. His Lord was "with him" both as one who endowed him with powers of judgment between good and evil, and watched over the challenges to his commitment to faithful servanthood. His own actions in resisting the temptress and the women, while not those of a literal martyr, mark Yusuf's victory over oppressive evil, personified in the wife of the Aziz, and his own conquest over his (lower) soul's penchant toward sin. In resisting Zulaykha's beckonings, the young Yusuf acts in the manner of one God elects to be one of his envoys.

JOSEPH'S DESIRE: A FASCINATION OF THE EXEGETES

Muslim Qur'an interpreters and storytellers relished the story of Yusuf's close encounter with Zulaykha—and not least because of its libidinous character. Two especially rich collections of the opinions and narrative elaborations of exegetes and storytellers are found in the tenth- and early eleventh-century works of al-Tabari and al-Tha`labi. Both authors record multiple and varying opinions of Yusuf's reactions to the enticements of the mistress of the household.

Surah 12:24, predictably, was the verse that compelled consideration of Yusuf's desire for Zulaykha—and his actions when with her. Like some of their Jewish counterparts, Muslim exegetes and commentators moved fairly directly and graphically to the subject of what might have occurred—and to speculations about the body-positions of the pair, as well as Yusuf's trousers. Al-Tabari reports that Ibn Waki and three of his colleagues say that after "she locked the doors . . . he went to loosen his trousers, when suddenly the figure of Jacob appeared to him" with warnings that intercourse with Zulaykha would leave him like a defenseless animal.[10] "So," the text continues, "Joseph tied his trousers up and left at a run," though she was able to tear off the tail of his shirt.[11] Ibn 'Abbas was asked by his colleagues, "'How far did Joseph go in following his desires?' And he said, 'She lay on her back for him and he sat between her legs removing his clothes'" until God diverted him from his desire by giving him a sign—"the image of his father Jacob, biting his fingers."[12] Other scholars held that the warning proof was a qur'anic passage written on the wall: "Do not come near to adultery. Verily it is an abomination and an evil way" (Surah 17:32).[13]

In the *Qisas al-Anbiya* compiled by al-Tha'labi in the eleventh century, the events believed to have taken place behind the closed doors of the woman's chamber included dialogues of different sorts. One had much in common with a tradition well known to Jewish exegetes. When Yusuf was secured within the room,

> the wife of the ruler walked over to the idol [within it] and covered it with a cloth. Joseph asked her about this and she replied, "I was ashamed that he would see us." Joseph said to her, "Are you ashamed before one who neither hears, nor sees, nor understands? Should not rather I be ashamed before Him Who created all things and knows all things?"[14]

Another exchange between the two involved love- or lust-talk, from Zulaykha, prompting defensive retorts by Yusuf:

> She said, "O your beautiful hair, Joseph!"—"It will be the first thing to decay when I die." "Your beautiful face, Joseph!"—"My lord formed me in the womb."—"Joseph, you have emaciated my body with the shape of your face!"—"The devil will help you with that."—"O Joseph, the little garden has caught fire, come and extinguish it."—"If I extinguish it, I will have to burn for it."—"The little garden is thirsty, Joseph, arise and water it."—"The one who holds the key has more right to water it than I."—"O Joseph, a carpet of silken hair has been spread out for you, arise and gratify my wish." "Then I will lose my share of the Garden."—"Come with me under the cover, Joseph, and I will hide you."—Nothing can conceal me from my Lord if I disobey Him."—"Joseph! Put your hand on my breast and you will cure me."—"My master has more right to that

than I."—"Ah well, your master! I shall give him a cup with mercury in it to drink so his flesh will fall off and his bones will disintegrate. Then I shall throw him onto a gold-embroidered silk cloth and drop him in the qaytun"—which is a small storage room—"and no one will know of it and I shall put you in charge of all his possessions, the small ones and the large." He said, "But payment will come on the Day of Repayment." She said, "Joseph! I have much in pearls, sapphires, and topaz, and I shall give all of that to you so that you may spend it to please your master who is in heaven." But Joseph refused.[15]

The increasingly aggressive offers made to Yusuf by Zulaykha appear also in Jewish commentaries, but here the imagery and language of Islam (the Garden of Paradise, the debt owed at the Judgment) permeates the exchange. More than a touch of comedy is in the byplay as Yusuf's resistance impels Zulaykha to more and more drastic measures. And in keeping with this surah's themes, Zulaykha's cravings mark her as a person who lacks reason, who is unable to discriminate between good and evil. She is a deluded nonbeliever, one of the unknowing.

Yet the commentators agree that Yusuf had not been able, by his speech, to avert a deeper entanglement with her, or for that matter, to quell his own desires (at least before he received the *burhan*). There are many variations on this scene's actions, with differing understandings of Yusuf's undressing:

"If you do not do as I wish," she screamed, "I shall kill myself this very instant, and you will be put to death on my account!" And she put her hand on a knife as if to kill herself (but it was just a ruse on her part to trick Joseph). Hastening toward the knife, he snatched it from her hand and threw it aside. Then she threw herself upon him and untied seven of the knots of his trousers, one after the other. *She resolved within herself to enjoy him and he would have resolved to enjoy her* (12:24), had not just then Gabriel descended in the form of his father Jacob, biting his fingertips. When Joseph saw the Proof, he hastened toward the door, but Zuleikha dashed after him.[16]

Or,

Then, according to Ibn ʿAbbas, the devil rushed into the space between the two, putting one arm around Joseph and the other around the woman and drew them together. Ibn ʿAbbas said, "Now Joseph's desire grew so strong that he undid his waistband, and lay down next to her, in the manner of a man about to commit adultery."[17]

A further account of Joseph's behavior, thanks to the elaboration of a commentator, is put on the lips of the wife of the Aziz as she addressed the women who were her guests:

> I asked of him an evil act, but he proved continent. . . . After he had loosened his trousers, he remained continent. I do not know what appeared to him. But if he does not do what I [now] order—[that is, have intercourse]—truly he will be imprisoned and brought low.[18]

Again we are made aware that the qur'anic account has Joseph remaining on the scene after the shirt-tearing chase and making his counteraccusation; he is jailed later in the story. Surah 12:53, following interrogation of the women and the wife of the Aziz by the king, contains Joseph's admission of his culpability. This too prompts a narrative addition: it was Gabriel who asked Joseph, "'Did you not desire her even for one day?' And Joseph said, 'I do not excuse myself. The soul does indeed drive us to evil (12:53).'"[19]

We have seen that interpreters variously understood the character of the burhan, the proof or sign that riveted Yusuf's attention, calling him back from his passionate state to his senses. Additional pieces of lore deserve mention: the appearance of his father himself—that is, not the angel in Yaqub's guise—shames Yusuf, or the father strikes his son's chest, his fingertips draining sexual desire from him.[20] Jacob is reported also to have spoken, warning Joseph, according to one commentator, that if he succumbed to Zulaykha's wiles he would become like a dying bird plummeting to the earth, or like a fallen ox—both defenseless against being consumed by ants and scavengers.[21]

A particularly sharp-edged version of Yaqub's imagined warning against the adultery his son is about to commit takes this form: "Will you do the deed of fools when you are inscribed in the register of the prophets?"[22] The challenge is inspired by the content of Surah 12:24: "Thus it was, so that We might divert evil and indecencies from him; for he was one of Our purified servants." This later interpretation of the burhan invokes, simply by referring to the illicit sex act as the work of fools, a summons to the awareness and understanding from which virtue stems. Also at work in these pictures of the proof that deterred Yusuf from sinning is the rhythm, or the sequence regularly met in the Qur'an's descriptions of dealings between God and those being called to servanthood: the Lord provides signs of his presence, and of what he requires of those who will follow the right path. Yusuf sees and comprehends, and then forsakes the evil that has attracted him. Even—or especially—the life of one destined to be one of God's messengers consists in testings—in training.

Speculations abound concerning the identity of "a witness from her [the Aziz's wife's] family" who implored the Aziz to see how Yusuf's garment was torn. One opinion was that "the shirt itself and the tear in its back" spoke up in Yusuf's defense, but a human voice seemed more likely.[23] A cousin of Ra`il (another name given to the Aziz's wife), presumably an adult, was a candidate, while others favored the view that the one who spoke was a "child in his cradle." Al-Tabari comments:

> This version has come down from the Messenger of God by way of al-Hasan b. Muhammad—`Affan b. Muslim—Hammad—`Ata' b. al Sa'ib—Sa'id b. Jubayr—Ibn `Abbas: The Prophet said, "there were four people who spoke when they were small," and he mentioned among them this witness of Joseph's.[24]

THREATENING WOMEN

Why were the women at Zulaykha's banquet dangerous to Yusuf at the time, and also later, when he stated his preference to stay in prison rather than have any further dealings with them?[25] The Qur'an has the Aziz chastise them along with Zulaykha not only for their "typical" female scheming, but also on the grounds that they too sought to have intercourse with the angel-like young servant. From an early point Muslim *tafsir* sought to explain more fully the incident of the hand-cutting. It was for cutting citrons, or an array of fruits, that the women's places were set with knives. The questions were: just how distracting was Yusuf to those who had criticized the wife of the Aziz for being smitten with him, and what did their hand-cutting either actually entail or signify? Progressively extreme accounts are given:

> He filled them with awe and they were speechless "and cut their hands" with the knives, thinking they were cutting the citrons and other fruits. . . .
>
> Qatadah said, "They kept cutting their hands until they made them fall off, but they became aware only of the blood, yet experienced no pain because their minds were preoccupied with Joseph." . . .
>
> Wahb had been told that seven of the forty women died during that session out of ecstasy of love for Joseph. They exclaimed, "God preserve us!"—which means the same as "God save us!"[26]

In the minds of the storytellers, Joseph's physical attractiveness, when displayed to the women by their hostess, awed them, and immediately impassioned them. While the interpreters' descriptions of the blood-letting do explain why he sought protection from them, even when, later, he was to be released from his imprisonment by the Pharoah, these expansions on the women's behavior evince their authors' notions of female sensuality and its inclination to frenzied, hysterical behaviors. The drama of Zulaykha's tea party is the subject of Figure 9.1, which captures its motifs.

A vivid artistic rendering of the event participates in those interpretations that made more grave the degree of distress and disorientation caused by Joseph's appearance at the banquet. Our artist commentator suggests that blood-red pomegranates were offered to the assembled ladies, that the knifes provided to them were of dangerous size, and that Zulaykha, seated in her raised and throne-like divan, raised her hand while beckoning the flame-haloed Yusuf (whose black and gold outer coat matches hers) to enter the room. Reactions to his beauty vary. Closest to him two women are in the pose the Qur'an itself suggests—gazing at him while attempting to slice into the fruits, while just below is a woman who is being held by another guest, having fallen into a swoon (or died). A single squatting woman in the lower portion of the painting seems to be reaching toward the hand of one of three distracted ladies near her. Two maids stand to one side of their mistress, carrying a large platter of the fruit, while Yusuf carries the large ewer from which he will pour tea for the ladies. Gayan Karen Merguerian and Afsaneh Najmabadi commented:

> The scene [in the Qur'an] in which Yusuf appears before the women of the town deserves some attention. Unlike much of sura 12, it has no parallel in Genesis. . . . The simultaneous cutting of hands, triggered by the sight of Yusuf's beauty, is a dramatic image. Later commentaries have interpreted it as a scene of collective menstruation and a display of female sexuality. What in the text has lent itself to this overwhelmingly popular interpretation? In fact, it is Yusuf's reaction to the cutting of hands, his pleading to the Lord to shield him (12.33)—using exactly the same word as was used in the earlier seduction scene, when he had been approached by al-`Aziz's wife and the Lord had shielded him (12.23)—that defines the women's bleeding as a sign of sexual threat. His words thus transform the scene from one of collective empathy by the women of the town for Zulaykha into a scene of collective seduction. This interpretation and the consequent association of female heterosexual desire with danger and guile become cemented more firmly and explicitly in later commentaries.[27]

Figure 9.1 Yusuf appearing at Zulaykha's gathering of Egyptian ladies. From a Nisaburi *Qisas* ms. Ca. 1580. © The New York Public Library, Astor, Lenox, and Tilden Foundations. Spencer Collection, Persian Ms. 46, fol. 48b.

It probably needs to be recalled, in light of this assertion, that it was not Yusuf but his master, the Aziz, who first generalized his wife's sexual advances as the cunning characteristic of (all) women. The point stands, nonetheless, that Yusuf's repeated expressions of fear of any future exposure to the women who had been present at the banquet (or any impassioned women of their ilk?) keeps alive in the Qur'an narrative and encourages in Muslim commentary more and more intense portrayals of the women. One might argue that these intensifications have as their main purpose the exaltation of young Yusuf's beauty were it not for the fact that the interpreters' attention seems entirely absorbed in narrating the antics—increasingly abandoned and senseless—of women in their states of sexual excitement. This, more than an attempted justification of Zulaykha's hot pursuit of Yusuf, or even a narrative signal that he had learned his lesson from God's *burhan* and was now properly and energetically cautious of would-be-seducers, spurs the writers' and painters' interest in the women who cut their hands.

ZULAYKHA'S RECOVERY

Standing in conspicuous contrast to the persona of the lecherous, deceitful woman determined at all costs to have sex with her husband's servant, a favorable portrait of Zulaykha came into being—a creature of interpreters' enduring interest in her. This positive view of the wife of the Aziz, which transformed Zulaykha into a character to be esteemed, even emulated, hinges on two kinds of reconsideration of her. One involves a significant addition to her life story, in the course of which she undergoes a radical change, becoming a woman worthy of Yusuf's love. While adopting the longer saga of the woman, the other innovative mode for revisioning Zulaykha involved an allegorical reading of her uncontrollable desire—in spiritual terms. The passion-stirring beauty of the luminous Yusuf "stood for" the divine source of light and truth, which a pious soul earnestly pursues.

Zulaykha: Redeemed and Restored

An early account of the life which Ra'il/Zulaykha lived subsequent to Joseph's imprisonment and his rise to authority as the Pharoah's vizier, appears in the *History* of al-Tabari, who traces the story to the reliable keeper of tradition, Ibn Ishaq:

> When Joseph said to the king, "Set me over the storehouses of the land, for I am a skilled custodian," the king said, "I hereby do it." It is said that he appointed Joseph to Potiphar's post, dismissing Potiphar from it. God said, "Thus We gave Joseph power in the land. He was its owner where he pleased. We reach with Our mercy who We will. We do not fail to reward the good." (12.56) It is said—God knows best—that Potiphar died around that time and that the king, al-Rayyan b. al-Walid, married Joseph to Potiphar's wife Ra'il. When she was brought to him, he said, "Is this not better than what you desired?" It is said that she answered, "O honest one, do not blame me, for as you see I was a beautiful and graceful woman, comfortable in my possessions and worldly goods, and my master did not have intercourse with women. And you were as God made you, with your beauty and appearance, and I could not control myself, as you saw." They said that he found her to be a virgin and had intercourse with her, and that she bore him two sons, Ephraim b. Joseph and Manasseh b. Joseph.[28]

While Joseph points to marriage as better for the expression and realization of mutual desire and love than an illicit encounter of the kind she had earlier sought, Yulaykha is more explanatory than repentant of her temptation of him. So irresistible was Joseph, how could she possibly have restrained herself? Her situation was comfortable—that is, undisturbed—before he was purchased as a slave, becoming a member of the Aziz's household. And there was the other factor spurring her strong attraction to his beauty: her husband's lack of sexual interest in women.

Other tales of what befell Zulaykha during the years Yusuf served in the king's court vary wildly, but most recount her fall from glory, her becoming destitute: the Pharoah displaced her husband as Aziz, or vizier, giving the post to Yusuf (as seen in Ibn Abbas's report), and she suffered in her husband's decline. Or, she was divorced by him. Or, disowned by her family, she fell into poverty when the seven lean years (prefigured in the Pharoah's dream) came. Most commentators report that as a result of her incessant weeping (out of her love of Yusuf) she became blind. In her decrepitude an ugly old woman, Zulaykha is said to have found shelter in a hut near the road the lordly Yusuf often traveled on horseback with his retinue. His passings-by stirred again and again her implacable yearning for him. In time, by a decisive act of frustration, she threw down the image of the God to whom she had long directed her devotion and prayers and called upon Yusuf's God for help.

Some of these motifs occur in al-Nisaburi's eleventh-century *Qisas al-anbiya*, where the narrative is more developed than al-Tabari's.

Zulaykha asked to be taken to his [Yusuf's] way [or road], poor, weak, blind and humbled ... When Yusuf came close by, Zulaykha was told. Like a beggar she stood on a height and said, "Know that whoever has patience and does not commit treason, even if he be a slave he becomes a king. And if he were a king and not patient and went after passion and desire, he would lose kingship and become a slave." When Yusuf heard Zulaykha's voice, he lost consciousness fearing God Almighty. Then he got up, halted his horse and said, "O Zulaykha!" Zulaykha passed out, hearing Yusuf's voice and from joy Yusuf shed tears. When Zulaykha came to, Yusuf said, "Where is your grandeur, your splendor, and your generosity?" Zulaykha answered, "I lost them in grief for you."

He said, "Where is your wealth?"
She said, "I sacrificed it, giving it to whoever brought me news from you."
He said, "What made your back bent?"
She said, "The severity of grief in being separated from you."
Yusuf said: "What do you want now?"
She said: "Give me eyesight so that I can see you. I have no desire in this world but to see you." Yusuf was surprised. He said: "O Wonders! You still have my love inside you, such that even after you have suffered thus, you still want me?" Zulaykha said: "If you want to know of the fire inside my heart give me a cane." Yusuf gave her a cane made of bamboo stalk. Zulaykha held it against her mouth and sighed. Instantly the cane burnt throughout. As Yusuf saw that, he felt sorry and wept, and ordered that she be taken home. Yusuf returned himself and asked his father to pray and Yusuf prayed too, so that Zulaykha's youth would be restored. Instantly, Gabriel appeared and told him that God Almighty has answered his prayers and restored Zulaykha's youth. Zulaykha became as she had been at the beginning. Yusuf took her for his wife and they both fulfilled their desire. The people of Egypt celebrated for seven nights and seven days . . . They lived eighteen years and had seven children, five sons and two daughters.[29]

Al-Nisaburi's expansion of the story presents his readers with a Zulaykha forgiven, restored, and "fulfilled [in her] desire." Her former youth and beauty are returned to her—yet in her reconstituted self there is freedom from bedevilment, from evil intentions, and from what had once been her ("natural") female sexual scheming. Earlier a passion-crazed woman and one of the unknowing (the pagans), she has been redeemed by the combined actions of father and son prophets at prayer, God's merciful response, and Gabriel's confirming message.

Ideas and themes deeply rooted in Surah 12 are much in evidence—Zulaykha's testing was costly to her, but resulted in a hard-won and worthy submission. She came to comprehend the significance of Yusuf's virtue, and she now commends the lessons of his obedience to all who will heed his story. The re-encounter of Yusuf and Zulaykha causes in both of them a black-out, a loss of consciousness—a signal of the Lord's role and activity in this destined reconciliation. The climax is of the "they lived happily ever after" variety, but the storyline throughout has involved unfortunate and tragic struggles on Zulaykha's part. It is not to be overlooked, therefore, that the rehabilitation of the now-Muslim Zulaykha brings with it a most splendid reward: her marriage to a prophet and the gift to her of children from him.[30]

It is Yulaykha *rediviva* who occupies the expanded Yusuf story. Her wanton lust is replaced by appropriate love. Licit sexual union of the pair, finally, is better than the adulterous gratifications would have been. Now their love is mutual and their lives filled with contentment and peace. Further, the sharp opposition found in the Qur'an and in many early interpretations between Zulaykha's vice and deceit and Yusuf's virtue is a prior history, a chapter one that prepares for chapter two, in which Zulaykha, forgiven and redeemed, shares with Yusuf both loyalty to God and the gift of divine favor.

Completed in this way, we might think that the narrative of Yusuf and Zulaykha had run its course, exhausting its commentators. But the longer narrative lent itself to yet another kind of interpretation, one that elevated and altered the woman's agonized longing for the one she craves. Zulaykha, in her strainings to have the handsome young Yusuf, can also be heard voicing the soul's pining after Beauty itself—after the elusive Beloved.

ZULAYKHA AND THE SOUL'S YEARNING

Though it cannot qualify as an early commentary on a qur'anic story, we must give some attention to the Zulaykha presented in Hahim Nuruddin Abdurrahman Jami's 1483 lyrical poem, *Yusuf and Zulaykha*, a classic of Persian literature. While living a luxurious and carefree life, the young girl Zulaykha experienced a dream with the "eyes of her heart," beholding a young man "or rather a pure spirit, a radiant apparition from the realm of light."[31] Jami continues:

> Seeing such superhuman beauty and grace, which was unknown even among the sprites and the houris of paradise, she fell in love with all her heart—what am I saying?—with all her hundred hearts. The image of that incomparable form remained forever engraved in her mind: love had been planted in her heart. All her patience and faith were consumed in the conflagration within her breast. Her soul was captive to every perfumed hair on the head of that apparition; the sight of his eyebrows made her groan, as she slept there drenched with tears; her heavy heart melted like sugar with desire for his mouth; and at the sight of his teeth, pearly tears formed on her eyelashes. God, what a vision! At length the graceful phantom vanished; but it left an ever increasing impact in Zulaikha's mind. She was beside herself with shock; but she stopped short of grasping the true significance of her experience. If only she had been aware of that deeper meaning, she would have numbered among those who have joined the path of Truth; but being captivated by the outward form, she was oblivious at first to the underlying reality.[32]

Only after she has married (mistaking the Aziz for the dream-promised beautiful man), does Zulaykha behold Joseph, whom she adores in his outward form, while she is not yet able to discern who, in his inward form, he represents. She is not alone in her confused passion, says Jami, for all of us, like her, are misled by appearances—and helpless: "If reality did not peep out from behind appearances, how would the sincere of heart ever reach the fashioner of appearances?"[33]

The clue to the veiled meanings in this rendition of the story of Yusuf and Zulaykha is given at the poem's outset.

This childhood dream of Zulaykha introduces a wider vision of what her encounter with Yusuf must signify. The tensions and traumas of the slave boy and the vexations of the mistress of the Aziz's house—that is, the literal sense of the story—now are invested with a loftier plot and sense: Zulaykha's passionate desire for handsome Yusuf, allegorically interpreted, is yearning of another kind: the soul or mind desires the brilliant Beauty by which Joseph was made luminous. Like a lover bereft of her beloved, Zulaykha models the bodily love that transposes into spiritual love—that desire that longs for God, the "fashioner." Jami, drawing upon the ideas and images of poets before him—Ibn Arabi and Rumi among them—portrayed Zulaykha as a *nafs*, or soul, to be "purified by boundless love and its resultant fathomless sorrow."[34]

Zulaykha's pursuit of Joseph, her attempt to bed him—is readable as an inner story of her frustration and travail. She symbolizes the love-sickness of the soul. Separated from the One, the soul longs to draw closer. The reader of Jami's poem is urged in explicit terms to hear and to recognize in its recitation both a woman crazed by unfulfilled appetites and the experience of the highest part of the self bewailing the Beloved's distance, inaccessibility, absence.

Jami composes his extravagant portrait of Zulaykha pursuing the handsome Yusuf: she draws him into an inner chamber of her palace, where he will not look at her, though his downward turned eyes cannot avoid images on the carpet of the two of them locked in a variety of sexual embraces—her cries and gestures are more, not less, impassioned than those recounted in other commentaries. In the mystic poet's perspective, the heat of the soul's desire for God invites embellishment of Zulaykha's passions.

> Oh Yusuf! I beseech you in the name of that God, who is master of the masters of the world—by the world-conquering beauty with which he adorns your face—by the light that radiates from your forehead, and forces the moon to bow down before you—by your beguiling brow and your bewitching eye, your cypress-stature and slender waist—by the sweet smile playing on your rosebud lips—by the tears of longing in my eyes, and the burning sighs your absence causes—by the total dominion which love for you has over my whole existence, and your utter indifference to whether I exist or not: have pity on this wretched, love-crazed woman! Untie this knot that has caused me so much anguish! My heart bears the scars of a lifetime of longing for the perfume of your garden. Oh Yusuf, be for one moment the fragrant, healing balm of my heart! I am starving in the famine of your absence: I beg you, restore life to me at the table of love![35]

Jami's *Yusuf and Zulaykha* sustains a story-long double-entendre—an interpretation that praises and intensifies desire, and regards both its physical and mystical expressions as fully intertwined and complementary. It is a single story in two registers. Zulaykha is reformed, but she represents precisely in her passionate intentions (that had elsewhere compelled her categorization as a woman of cunning and vice) the most important and lofty human pursuit, the journey Godward. Zulaykha, the female striver for closeness to God, is to be extolled, not scorned.

The attraction of Zulaykha to Yusuf translates, then, into a philosophy and mystical piety that quickly and enduringly becomes a serviceable "best" story for Muslims drawn to Sufism and to other forms of mystical devotion. This Zulaykha is loved by Muslims for her passionate love of God.

THE STORY PAINTED: IMPASSIONED PURSUITS

Surviving illuminations reveal the interest of Muslim artists and their patrons in specific events in Yusuf's life. Paintings abound of Yusuf being placed by his brothers in the well, where he is sometimes shown to be accompanied in the dark space by his angel protector. Yusuf's discovery by members of the merchant caravan and his later sale as a slave in Egypt are often chosen as subjects. Various in iconography but frequent in its appearance in manuscripts is the poignant scene of Joseph's reunion with elderly Jacob.

We turn now to two Persian paintings that concern pursuit of the one desired—in one instance, Yulaykha's aggression toward Yusuf, and in the other, the reverse. What each image portrays seems evident, touching close to a main theme in this and the previous two chapters: the degree of Yusuf's temptation when his virtue was tested by Zulaykha's invitations to sex. Due to the extension of the Yusuf and Zulaykha narrative into their later years, however, we should be on the alert for the artists' presentation of other possible interpretations of these chase scenes.

Zulaykha's Pursuit

In its vertical placement above Yulaykha, the idol commands a place of prominence in the painting (Figure 9.2). From her childhood to her old age, according to Jami, she was a fervent worshipper, in her later years offering sorrowful prayers that her blindness be healed. The scene draws upon an exegetical tradition familiar to us also in Jewish commentaries: it was her God's potential gaze upon her hoped-for copulation with Joseph that worried the temptress, while at the same time the sight of the statue provoked young Yusuf's greater concern about his God, from whom nothing could be veiled or hidden.

The sense of this painting may be considered to reflect Jami's account of what transpired in the woman's chamber. A Victorian-era attempt to capture Jami's verse in English, despite its quaint language, is worth quoting:

> She sugared his lip with a touch of her own
> One arm was his collar and one his zone [i.e., belt].[36]
> With a long sweet kiss on his lips she hung,
> And an eager arm round his neck was flung.
> [Then, made aware in the *burhan* of being seen by his God]
> From the fond dream of rapture he woke;

Figure 9.2 Zulaykha reaches for the fleeing Yusuf. A miniature in a sixteenth-century Persian text of Jami's *Yusuf and Zulaykha*. Painting: 133 x 100 cm. © The National Library of Israel, Jerusalem.

From the arms of Zulaikha he struggled and broke.
With hasty feet from her side he sped,
And burst open each door on his way as he fled.
Bolt and bar from the stanchions he drew—
All opened before him as onward he flew. . . .
But Zulaikha caught him, with steps more fast,
O'er ever the farthest chamber he passed.
She clutched his shirt as he fled amain,
And the coat from his shoulder was rent in twain.
Reft of his garment he slipped from her hand,
Like a bud from its sheath when the leaves expand. . . .
[Zulaikha:] "Ah, woe is me for my luckless fate!
He has left my heart empty and desolate.
Ah, that the game from my net should slip!
Ah, that the honey should mock my lip!"[37]

The soul's frustrations in seeing only through obstructions the source of light, we recall, are contained in, and come to expression through, the earth-bound lamentations of the seductress. Zulaykha's failed plan to seduce Yusuf is, in terms of Jami's mystic projections, love denied but still straining after the Beloved.

Yusuf's Pursuit

Though this painting, like the previous one, is by no means an "early" Islamic product, it warrants our attention, picturing as it does an aggressively amorous, rather than appalled and resistant, Yusuf (Figure 9.3). Attempting to read the artist's intent poses an intriguing dilemma for us. From what portion of the saga of Yusuf and Zulaykha does this illustrated event come, and what assumptions about the levels of meaning in their dealings with each other might be operative for the artist depicting it?

The image could have been inspired principally by the Qur'an's testimony about Yusuf—that "he wanted to involve himself with her [*hamma biha*]," and by later exegetes' musings on how far he went in pursuing intercourse with her before he relented.[38] The chase takes place in the palatial courtyard rather than the bed-chamber of the Aziz's wife, and once again, given the moment represented, neither nakedness nor torn clothing is shown. Rather, it is the eager body language and enthused expression on Yusuf's face (not that Zulaykha's countenance bears signs of fear or disapproval) that draw our attention. As commentary on the story of Yusuf

Figure 9.3 Yusuf grabs Zulaykha from behind. A miniature in a Persian ms. of Jami's *Yusuf and Zulaykha*. Eighteenth-century Kashmir, India. Painting: 14.4 x 7.8 cm. © The National Library of Israel, Jerusalem. NLI Yah Ms. Ar. 1025.

with Zulaykha, the painter seems to invite recollection of the sexual zeal aroused in Yusuf, who can be understood to be participating fully in the temptation that is part of the divine testing of his virtue. The moral victory achieved, once the sign recalls Yusuf to his obligations, needs, according to this artist's choice of his subject, to be appreciated in light of what preceded: Yusuf's strong wish and hope "to involve himself with her." Placed in the frame of reference that takes seriously the qur'anic assertion that both Zulaykha *and* Yusuf felt sexual desire for each other, the painting holds a set of meanings on one plane.

Another perspective, however, gained as if by the turn of a kaleidoscope, alters the image's sense in an emphatic way. Expanding upon the story of the redeemed Zulaykha, converted from her idolatry and repentant of her earlier wantonness, Jami tells of a later drama, a turn-about in the life of the unified and serene couple. Yusuf's deep devotion to Zulaykha, expressed in his relentless affection and sexual ardor for her, became a burden: "He was constantly striving to please her and win her favor, placing his cheek against hers, his lip to hers; and so abundantly did he water the green field of delight, that he was often short of water himself."[39]

What was happening? Jami's report either blurs the line dividing the woman's story from the allegory of the soul or fuses the two:

> It was thanks to him [Yusuf] that the curtain before Zulaikha's eyes was finally torn asunder; and a ray from the sun of Truth struck her with such overwhelming brilliance, that Yusuf was lost in it like a mote in a sunbeam. For after a lifetime of obstacles had been melted down in the crucible of earthly love, when that sun of Truth finally arose, not a single obstacle remained. Reality now held such an attraction for her, that she gave up everything which she had formerly deemed indispensable.[40]

To recall the language of her girlhood dream, Reality has peeked through, has penetrated appearances, and the brilliance of the Fashioner of all things becomes manifest—dimming everything else. Her longing for the figure in her youthful dream, long supported and sustained within and under the cover of her earthly passion for the luminous Yusuf, is dramatically altered. The beauty of Yusuf is now like a speck or a particle barely detectable "in a sunbeam." Divine perfection has shown itself to her. This is the stuff of the Islamic mysticism inscribed by the Sufi poet upon the commentators' tale of Yusuf and Zulaykha.

But the story of Zulaykha's spiritual break-through, or rather of her visitation by a burhan directed to her—God giving her evidence—had an important addendum. We learn of her attitude, in her newly heightened consciousness, toward her husband's too persistent amorous affection.

> One night, as she was trying to slip out of Yusuf's grasp, she ran stumbling from him in confusion. He managed to seize the hem of her dress—and tore it down the back. "You see!" cried Zulaikha: "once upon a time I tore your shirt: now it is your turn to tear mine. Now we are partners in crime, and I no longer feel at a disadvantage. When it comes to tearing shirts, we are both on an equal footing!"[41]

Beneath Zulaykha's clever inversion of the speech of one who feels over-pursued, a crucial change in her is being expressed.

So impressed was Yusuf by his wife's newfound wisdom and piety that he constructed in her name a glorious pavilion suffused with "the light of happiness." It was to be an oratory, a place of prayer for her. Though the death of Yusuf, as well as her own, lies ahead in the narrative, the poet pictures the saga's proper conclusion: Zulaykha "sitting on the throne of sovereignty, liv[ing] happily in the knowledge of Yusuf's love and God's grace."[42]

The artist, providing an illumination for a manuscript containing Jami's *Yusuf and Zulaykha*, does his painting in proximity to the Persian text telling of Zulaykha's being struck by the "sun of Truth." The scene does not have as its subject the youthful and lustful Yusuf who shared Zulaykha's desire, but rather the older Zulaykha attempting to get free from the distractions that her husband's conjugal enjoyments pose for her. Now summoned to a holier observance, to a visionary lover's concentration upon the divine Beloved, Zulaykha flees, leaving part of her garment in Yusuf's hands.

This second estimate of the painter's understanding and intent in representing the scene is, of course, different from, and in some ways at odds with, the first estimate of the intended meaning—that is, that of Yusuf's impassioned chasing after Zulaykha. It is probably a mistake, however, to say that the painting's message is ambiguous. Rather, as the work of a painter aware of the Zulaykha who emerged through Muslim interpretations and retellings of the story, it gives expression to the two intertwined dimensions or levels of the saga, incorporating Jami's insistence on the continuum of human love and desire and the soul's love and desire for God.

The mutual physical yearning of Yusuf and Zulaykha opened upon their shared longing for God, and here it is Zulaykha, a symbol of agonized and laudable pursuit of the divine, who is valorized. In Jami's words:

> The lover who sincerely commits himself to the path of love will himself ultimately attain to the title of the beloved. Such a sincere lover was Zulaikha, whose whole life, from start to finish was sacrificed to love.[43]

While Zulaykha the instrument of Satan held and holds her place in Muslim consciousness (the celebration of Yusuf's victory over temptation requires her evil persona), Islam celebrates the converted Zulaykha, who became (and continues to be) "the courageous, strong heroine willing to bear anything for the sake of her Beloved."[44] She is symbol and model for the hope that human love participates in and enables advancement in the soul's desire more fully to know and experience its divine source and inspiration.[45]

At chapter's end, we should review some of the ideas and emphases that make Muslim interpretations of the story of Yusuf with Zulaykha so decidedly Muslim. First, in its entirety Surah 12's "best of stories" distinctively presents itself as revelation especially designed for reasoned hearing. The range of characters heard or seen in Yusuf's history either know, are among the knowing, gain in knowledge, or turn, at their own peril, from what is there plainly to be recognized about the virtuous life, commended and commanded by God. Revelation beckons to rationality, and the actions of Yusuf—as well as those of Zulaykha, the Aziz, the Pharaoh, Joseph's brothers, Yaqub, and all the rest, are interpretable on these terms.

We concentrated here, as in the previous two chapters, on young Yusuf's sensual eagerness for Zulaykha. Though this theme correlates with a strain of rabbinic commentary also interested in his flesh-and-blood personhood, it stands in higher relief in Islam—due both to the Qur'an's comment "and he desired her," and to the additions to bedroom scenes contributed by entertained and entertaining commentators and storytellers. With this second theme an important Muslim teaching about anthropology—the makeup of human beings—is introduced and then explored; the discussion's trigger is Yusuf's admission that his soul, his *nafs*, necessarily incites him to passion, a factor in his relationship with Zulaykha and with those who "cut their hands." This compulsion, intrinsic to every human, is a factor in enduring tests and temptations, and in Yusuf's dedication to become one of the knowing, a servant of God who follows the right path.

Among the scriptures of the Jews, Christians, and Muslims, only the Qur'an records the incident involving the "women of the city" who gossiped about Zulaykha's improper love for one of her slaves. This banquet story, a third and quite colorful feature of Islam's Yusuf and Zulaykha traditions, reveals Zulaykha's taunting self-defense against haughty ladies. In presenting Yusuf as irresistibly handsome, the episode pays tribute to the prophet while justifying her obsession with him. At another level, however, the narrative identifies and criticizes women, who, according to the Aziz and Yusuf, are naturally prone to scheming with a specific purpose—namely, the satisfaction of their sexual appetites. The frenzy, first in Zulaykha, and then in her tea-party guests, is a female trait, and one rife with implications: the *nafs* of women make them threats to men—hence the suggestions that they are Satan-inspired. The account of Zulaykha's gathering of the ladies, as depicted in the Qur'an and as exaggerated by subsequent commentators, contributed to a strongly negative representation of women's wiles and their "pathetic" (emotive) attraction to males.

Finally, in texts and in two paintings we met the invention by commentators and poets of Zulaykha's later life, and of her double-being as woman spurned and a soul in deep sorrow because of her distance from her Beloved. In a way unparalleled in Judaism and Christianity, Islam converts the would-be seducer of Yusuf into the redeemed and spiritualized Zulaykha who cast aside her former God for the true God, and was reunited, in purity, with Yusuf. The allegorization of her life, especially by Jami, rendered her obsessive desire a parable that endorses and celebrates the passionate longing of the human soul for true, unobstructed light. Zulaykha, perceived in this way, became the popularly appealing example of that human love which mirrors the believer's spiritual quest to love entirely the Creator.[46] (So too, by implication, were the women so distracted by Yusuf's beauty that they cut their hands, interpretable as soulful, rather than merely lustful, spiritual aspirants.[47])

Fully human in his appetites (the view early Islam shared with some Jewish commentators), tempted in the course of the test put to him in his youth by the wife of the Aziz, instrumental in the recovery and restoration of Zulaykha, with whom he shares a virtuous and happy marriage (and the yield of progeny), the Muslim Yusuf is portrayed, through his trials and triumphs, as a prophet of God. Exegetes and artists, even in elaborating upon his saga, sustained the Qur'an's own estimate of Yusuf as one divinely tutored in the exercise of power and the interpretation of dreams, a virtuous Muslim determined to die as one of the righteous (2:100–101).

Comparative Summary

Joseph's Temptation by His Egyptian Master's Wife

The preceding three chapters concentrated on only one part of the story of Joseph—the tense episode in which Jacob's son, a slave in Egypt, resists an attempted seduction by his master's wife. To compare and contrast Jewish, Christian, and Muslim understandings of Joseph in his predicament, I posed this question: when Potiphar's wife, or Zulaykha, set about enticing him, was Joseph/Yusuf not only tested, but also tempted?

Jewish commentators produced conflicting views of the beautiful young man who had his Lord "with him" at all times, and yet was required to meet challenges to his virtue. In Rabbinic writings (e.g., *Talmud Tractate Yoma*, and *Genesis Rabbah*) we found the assumption that the human—and physical—nature of Joseph was taken into consideration as the sages discussed his susceptibility to the sexual overtures of his temptress. Rabbi Yose acquiesced to a noblewoman's expressed doubt that a seventeen-year-old, "with all the hot blood of youth," could have been unaffected by the woman's urgings. We read the rebuke of a student who suggested that his failure to study Torah was due to his sexual distractions: did he think that Joseph had not struggled with and overcome this challenge? In *Genesis Rabbah*, three rabbis entertain the idea that Joseph approached Potiphar's wife on the day the household was empty, fully intending "to sin, but found himself impotent"—because, according to Rabbi Huna, he envisioned his father Jacob's disapproving face.

In tension with these views that Joseph suffered temptation were arguments put forth by certain authors well-versed in Greek philosophy and
ethics. In *4 Maccabees* and in a treatise by Philo, Joseph became the personification of moral steadiness. The key to these presentations was the
argument that through his reason, which inspired moderation or psychic
imperturbability within him, Joseph did not waver when tempted by
Potiphar's wife. We recall Philo's statement that Joseph was able at every
point to resist the woman's "frenzy of passion . . . so strong was the sense
of decency and temperance which nature and the exercise of control had
implanted in him."

As much to examine the extent of knowledge of Jewish *midrash* by
religious competitors as to find further examples of it, we turned to several paintings devoted to Joseph and Potiphar's wife in the splendid
sixth-century Vienna Genesis, a Christian book. The reward was significant, since elements in Jewish lore shed light upon intriguing features
and details in this sample of the churches' retellings and picturings of the
story—for example, colorful additions to the scenes in which the woman
offered to her husband and others evidence that Joseph had attempted to
seduce *her.*

Early Christian interpreters, nearly without exception, upheld the view
that Joseph consistently repelled the would-be adulterer, untroubled by
temptation. At least two rationales supported this celebration of Joseph's
virtue by the fathers of the church. Most exegetes and preachers shared
(and were indebted to) the philosophy-based argument of Philo—that by
his reasoning the young man exercised moderation, valiantly resisting the
seductress's scheming. Ambrose, the fourth-century bishop of Milan, came
closest to imagining that Joseph was tempted, picturing the young man's
fear that he would yield to "incentives to lust" if her hands touched him.

The other grounds for denying that Joseph was temptable derived from
the Christian practice of reading scriptures (what would become their Old
Testament) typologically—in this case searching in Joseph's history for
signs that anticipated or prefigured Jesus's life and deeds—for example,
having God with him, undergoing tribulations, and being innocent of the
charges for which he was punished. If Joseph was Jesus's forerunner, he
could not easily be considered a person vulnerable to temptation and sin.
Therefore, the revered patriarch Joseph was understood to have been tested,
but also to have been impervious to any attraction to Potiphar's wife.

It is important also to recall turnings of Christian typological arguments
about Joseph into biting anti-Jewish polemic. Joseph's coat, bloodied by
his brothers, was likened by Epiphanius to Jesus's crucified and bloodied
flesh, which the Jews held, and then buried, attempting to prevent his body

from being stolen. Augustine, making an argument that the covenant with God had gone to the Christians, allegorized Joseph's going to Egypt as a signal of that future in which the Christ/Messiah of God would *pass over* to, and be embraced by, the Gentiles.

Christian monastic literature, too, championed the view that Joseph, befriended by God, was superior to temptation, his loyalty and faith undaunted by the woman's tauntings. An interesting exception is recorded, however: a monk, discouraged by the turbulence stirred by his sexual thoughts and fantasies, is counseled to make Joseph his model and inspiration, since Joseph did, like him, suffer temptation, and struggled *through* that, winning and persevering in his continence.

We took note of the sarcophagus fragment discovered beneath St. Peter's in Rome that coupled an image of the Magi adoring Jesus with scenes from Joseph's career. Its iconography boldly proposed parallels between the two figures' tribulations and their ultimate triumphs. A similar linkage was created in the ivories that decorated the sixth-century throne of Maximianus, archbishop of Ravenna, on which scenes of the life of Christ and the life of Joseph were carved. Here, as Ambrose had suggested two centuries earlier, attention was directed to themes of rulership and governance, for again, Joseph's rise to power in Egypt and his gathering of his people there could be understood as a foretelling of the majestic reign of the risen and ascended Christ.

In the Qur'an and in Muslim commentaries concerning Yusuf the prophet, his endangerment by the temptress was real, and his escape from her clutches was hard-won—a close call. Yusuf's sexual restraint was the result of his timely change of heart (a theme also present in Jewish lore concerning Joseph), which was induced by God's merciful intervention—the *burhan*, or sign of warning presented to him.

We noted earlier that Yusuf's sensual eagerness for Zulaykh appears in higher relief in Islamic tradition—as a consequence of the Qur'an's comment "and he desired her," and also of his later confession that his soul (*nafs*) necessarily incited him to passion, making him susceptible to female desire for him—that of Zulaykha and also of the women who, gazing upon his beauty, "cut their hands." For Muslim interpreters this reality of the compulsive power of the *nafs,* and its acknowledgment in Surah 12, opened the question of whether God has dealings with any humans—including prophets—who are exempt (by dint of some kind of "constitutional" perfection) from suffering tests and temptations? What obstacles, it was worth asking, stood in the way of the person who will become, or will fail to become, one of the knowing, a servant of God who follows the right path? This last ideal—to become one of those who know, and rationally respond to the revelation of the Qur'an's "best of stories"—was, we recognized, a strong and consistent feature in the Surah 12's presentation of Yusuf.

The Aziz and Yusuf both characterized women as prone to scheming with a specific purpose—namely, the satisfaction of their sexual appetites. The frenzy over young Yusuf, first in Zulaykha and then in her tea-party guests, was presented as a singular female trait, and one rife with implications: the souls of women make them threats to men—hence their not-infrequent designations as Satan-inspired. Zulaykha's gathering of the ladies became a vehicle for subsequent exaggerated accounts of what transpired on that afternoon—and contributed to negative imagings of women's wiles—the traps they, by (their female) nature, will set for men.

The invention by commentators and poets of Zulaykha's later life and of her double-being—as desirous woman and lovesick soul—worked against this disparaging view of her persona and her gender. In a way unparalleled in Judaism and Christianity, Islam turned the would-be seducer of Yusuf into the redeemed and spiritualized Zulaykha. The extension of her narrative allowed her to come to her senses, cast aside her former God for the true God, and to be united in unsullied love with Yusuf. The mystical allegorization of her life by the poet Jami rendered her obsessive desire the passionate longing of the soul for the divine Beloved. Seen from that perspective, Zulaykha was not the dangerous female, but rather, the popularly appealing example of that human love which mirrors the believer's spiritual quest to love entirely the "fashioner"—God the creator.

In our treatment of two Persian paintings—one showing Zulaykha, the other showing Yusuf, as the impassioned pursuer—we entertained the view that both images needed to be interpreted in connection with the later life of the two lovers, and along the lines of Jami's mystical themes that conjoined physical human love and the soul's yearning for God—as corresponding and closely related loves.

Our comparisons of the three religions' developing understandings of the temptress's attempt to seduce the beautiful Joseph yielded a number of both complementary and diverging features. Rabbinic and Muslim exegetes had in common an interest in exploring the extent of Joseph's temptability (did he help the woman untie the knots of his trousers?), They discriminated, using Joseph's case to do so, among intention, near-action, and completed act—that is, sexual intercourse with his temptress. Hellenized Jews and the great majority of Christian interpreters, on the other hand, steered clear of such speculations—the first, for distinctive philosophical reasons, and the second, due to both philosophical and Christological commitments.

Ultimately, however, Jewish, Christian, and Muslim writers honored Joseph/Yusuf for the virtue that he practiced in not, finally, succumbing to his temptress, and each religion counted him an ideal of chastity—a Hebrew paragon for resisting adultery, a Christian Old Testament "saint" (and prefigurement of Jesus) firm in his sexual continence, and a Muslim prophet empowered by a *burham* to avoid sin and submit to God's will.

PART IV

Jonah the Angry Prophet

Preview, Chapters 10–12

"The One of the Fish"

The fantastic account of Jonah—first captive in, and then freed from, the whale—has enjoyed centuries of popularity, appearing in the scriptures of the Jews, Christians, and Muslims, and also in their respective histories of interpretation of sacred stories. The next three chapters explore the similarities and the differences in these religions' understandings and uses of Jonah and his adventures.

Precisely because the saga of the prophet sent by God to condemn the city of Nineveh does include the extraordinary episode of Jonah's being swallowed and then "vomited forth" from the belly of what the Hebrew Bible calls a "great fish," any discussion of the story is obliged to cope with the obvious question it poses: is this narrative to be approached as a tall tale, or does the narrative, in the forms we find it in the Hebrew Bible, the Christian Old Testament, and the Qur'an, represent the encounter of Jonah and the whale as a historical—in other words, a more-or-less factual—event?

In the Gershwin brothers' 1935 American folk opera, *Porgy and Bess*, the character "Sportin' Life" sang:

> Oh Jonah he lived in de whale
> Oh Jonah he lived in de whale
> For he made his home in dat fish's abdomen
> Oh Jonah he lived in de whale

The song's title, and assertion, is repeated in the refrain:

> It ain't necessarily so
> It ain't necessarily so
> De things dat yo' liable to read in de Bible
> It ain't necessarily so. . . .

Jonah's sojourn in the fish seems so far beyond the range of what could be considered true by the criteria of empirical, testable evidence, that many readers and hearers—ancients and moderns alike—incline to a symbolic reading—sometimes finding in its exaggerations equal parts of message and grand entertainment. Others, firm in their commitments to literal interpretation of scriptural narratives, have maintained the facticity of Jonah's adventure in the whale.

The two points of view were much in evidence following an event in February of 1891, when one James Bartley was reported to have survived being swallowed by a sperm whale off the Falkland Islands; he was recovered, alive, from the whale when it was caught and sliced open the next day. The title of a 1993 article, "James Bartley—A Modern Jonah or Joke?," presents, rather than judges, the numerous conflicting views of whether the claims made about Mr. Bartley's survival were possible—and credible.[1] The testimonies, however, revealed investments in both scientific and biblical literalist modes of reasoning. A sometime-teacher at Oxford, the Rev. A. J. Wilson had argued in a 1927 issue of the *Princeton Theological Review* that "the gastric juice would be extremely unpleasant but not deadly. [The whale] cannot digest living matter, otherwise it would digest the walls of its own stomach."[2] Wilson's opinion was considered supportive of the view of "thousands who believe that Jonah was indeed swallowed by a whale and cast up later alive."[3] A scholar of whaling, R. C. Murphy, sharply criticized the story of James Bartley, denouncing it as "unadulterized bunk," adding: "I might be asked how I can prove such an uncompromising opinion and statement. My answer is that it is unnecessary to do so, because the burden of proof is entirely on those who make or credit the yarn."[4]

Early Judaism, Christianity, and Islam each maintained teachings that insisted upon giving serious attention to a scriptural passage's plain, historical, or literal sense—but only as *one* of its several other possible kinds of meaning—for example, allegorical, moral, and mystical. It will prove interesting to see in these three chapters how the Jews, Christians, and

Muslims of the late-Roman, Byzantine, and early Islamic eras viewed the Jonah story as defensible history while at the same time approaching it as a writing pregnant with supra-literal meanings.

In his first-century *Jewish Antiquities,* Josephus feared the story of Jonah might draw ridicule from his Roman readers, so he edited out its more fanciful parts, hoping to keep the narrative and its hero plausible and admirable. In the next century the pagan theologian Celsus poked fun at the Christians, suggesting that Jonah had accomplished greater things than Jesus. To meet challenges of this sort, something other than a defense of the story's literal truth was required of the church's exegetes. Muslim commentators on the story of Yunus considered miraculous events in it as "signs," as God-given revelations manifested in time, while also finding in the story precious metaphorical-mystical elements.

The overarching interest in the following chapters is not whether the Jonah saga could have "actually happened," but concerns another brand of credibility: what was it in the story of Jonah that commanded earliest interpreters' respectful attention to it and excited their ambitious searches for its several levels of possible sense? In what ways and for what reasons did the three religions *credit* the narrative, holding it in honor? And how did these faith traditions develop understandings of this prophet and his dramatic story so different from each other that finally it is possible—even necessary—to speak of the Jewish Jonah, the Christian Jonah, and the Muslim Yunus?

Such divergent pictures of God's prophet Jonah/Yunus are not solely the result of the scriptural interpreters' tailorings of this sacred story to their own particular faiths' bedrock convictions and modes of ritual and prayer, though each religion's interest in accommodating and thereby "owning" a sacred story was a vital one. A prior and more basic factor in a parting of the ways in Jonah/Yunus understandings had to do with the differences in the ways Jonah was portrayed in the three religions' scriptures. The Hebrew Bible's fifth-century BCE *Book of Jonah* located him within Israel's lengthy history of God's prophets and drew particular attention due to the fact that Jonah flagrantly disobeyed his Lord's command—to prophesy. The early Christians worked from translations of the Hebrew text of *Jonah*—initially in Greek, but then in Latin and Syriac. The early churches claimed for themselves the Hebrew messengers of God, believing these prophets' predictions both foretold and confirmed the Christian revelation; but Christians also incorporated into their imaginative rethinking of Jonah a New Testament saying about him by Jesus that was destined to change in significant ways the figure and message of the prophet to Nineveh. The Qur'an's several intriguing passages concerning Yunus, along with several *sunnah*, or sayings, of the Prophet Muhammad, set the terms *and* the distinctive tones for Muslim appreciation of Yunus's life—one in which his dealings with the Ninevites, his "wrongdoing," and his prayer from the great fish's belly were stages on the way to his submission (*islam*) to his God.

CHAPTER 10

cx/ɔ

Jonah, Nineveh, the Great Fish, and God

Jews Ponder the Story

Figure 10.1 The opening column of *Jonah*, Xanten Bible, Germany. 1294. © The New York Public Library, Astor, Lenox, and Tilden Foundations. Spencer Collection.

In this rare illuminated manuscript of the Hebrew Bible now in the New York Public Library's Spencer Collection, an artist's choice of an image to accompany the opening word in *Jonah* (Figure 10.1) shows the prophet either being swallowed or spewed out by the "great fish." A marginal note just to the left of the fish's head tells that this book is read at the afternoon service on the Day of Atonement.

The *Book of Jonah* is one among the group of twelve writings of minor prophets included in the Hebrew Bible. Only forty-eight verses fill its four chapters, making Jonah the shortest writing in the Tanakh. Here we need no summarization of the sacred story at hand; it can easily be read. An alert, however, is in order: serious students of *Jonah* regularly describe it as a seemingly simple story, or a deceptively straightforward narrative. Anyone taking it up is well advised to keep asking what, or how many things, the book is about.

THE BOOK OF JONAH

Chapter 1:1 The word of the LORD came to Jonah son of Amittai:

2 Go at once to Nineveh, that great city, and proclaim judgment upon it; for their wickedness has come before Me.

3 Jonah, however, started out to flee to Tarshish from the LORD's service. He went down to Joppa and found a ship going to Tarshish. He paid the fare and went aboard to sail with the others to Tarshish, away from the service of the LORD.

4 But the LORD cast a mighty wind upon the sea, and such a great tempest came upon the sea that the ship was in danger of breaking up. 5 In their fright, the sailors cried out, each to his own god; and they flung the ship's cargo overboard, to make it lighter for them. Jonah, meanwhile, had gone below into the hold of the vessel where he lay down and fell asleep. 6 The captain went over to him, and cried out, "How can you be sleeping so soundly! Up, call upon your god! Perhaps the god will be kind to us and we will not perish."

7 The men said to one another, "Let us cast lots and find out on whose account this misfortune has come upon us." They cast lots, and the lot fell upon Jonah. 8 They said to him: "Tell us, you who have brought this misfortune upon us, what is your business? Where have you come from? What is your country, and of what people are you?" 9 "I am a Hebrew," he replied. "I worship the LORD, the God of heaven, who made both the sea and land." 10 The men were greatly terrified, and they asked him, "What have you done?" And when the men learned that he was fleeing from the service—for so he told them—11 They said to him: "What must

we do to you to make the sea calm around us?" For the sea was growing more and more stormy. 12 He answered, "Heave me overboard, and the sea will calm down for you; for I know that this terrible storm came upon you on my account." 13 Nevertheless the men rowed hard to regain the shore, but they could not; for the sea was growing more and more stormy about them. 14 Then they cried out to the LORD, and said: "O please, Lord, do not let us perish on account of this man's life. Do not hold us guilty of killing an innocent person! For You, Lord, by Your will, have brought this about." 15 And they heaved Jonah overboard, and the sea stopped raging.

16 The men feared the LORD greatly; they offered a sacrifice to the LORD, and made vows.

Chapter 2:1 And the LORD provided a huge fish to swallow Jonah; and Jonah remained in the fish's belly three days and three nights. 2 Jonah prayed to the LORD his God from the belly of the fish. 3 He said:

> In my trouble I called to the Lord,
> And he answered me;
> From the belly of Sheol I cried out,
> And You heard my voice.
> 4 You cast me into the depths,
> Into the heart of the sea,
> The floods engulfed me;
> All your breakers and billows
> Swept over me.
> 5 I thought I was driven away
> Out of your sight:
> Would I ever gaze again
> Upon Your holy Temple?
> 6 The waters closed in over me,
> The deep engulfed me.
> Weeds twined around my head.
> 7 I sank to the base of the mountains;
> The bars of the earth closed upon me forever.
> Yet you brought my life up from the pit,
> O Lord my God!
> 8 When my life was ebbing away,
> I called the Lord to mind;
> And my prayer came before You
> Into Your holy Temple.
> 9 They who cling to empty folly
> Forsake their own welfare,

10 But I, with loud thanksgiving,
Will sacrifice to You;
What I have vowed I will perform.

11 And the LORD commanded the fish, and it spewed Jonah out on dry land.

Chapter 3:1 The word of the LORD came to Jonah the second time: 2 "Go at once to Nineveh, that great city, and proclaim to it what I tell you." 3 Jonah went at once to Nineveh in accordance with the LORD's command. Nineveh was an enormously large city, a three days' walk across. 4 Jonah started out and made his way into the city the distance of one day's walk, and proclaimed: "Forty days more, and Nineveh will be overthrown!"

5 The people of Nineveh believed God. They proclaimed a fast, and great and small alike put on sackcloth. 6 When the news reached the king of Nineveh, he rose from his throne, took off his robe, and put on sackcloth, and sat in ashes. 7 And he had the word cried through Nineveh: "By decree of the king and his nobles: No man or beast—of flock or herd—shall taste any thing! They shall not graze, and they shall not drink water! 8 They shall be covered with sackcloth—man and beast—and shall cry mightily to God. Let every one turn back from his evil ways and from the injustice of which he is guilty. 9 Who knows but that God may turn and relent? He may turn back from his wrath, so that we do not perish."

10 God saw what they did, how they were turning back from their evil ways. And God renounced the punishment He had planned to bring upon them, and did not carry it out.

Chapter 4:1 This displeased Jonah greatly, and he was grieved.

2 He prayed to the LORD, saying: "O LORD, Isn't this just what I said when I was still in my own country? That is why I fled beforehand to Tarshish. For I knew that YOU are a compassionate and gracious God, slow to anger, abounding in kindness, renouncing punishment. 3 Please LORD, take my life, for I would rather die than live." 4 The LORD replied: "Are you that deeply grieved?" 5 Now Jonah had left the city and found a place east of the city. He made a booth there and sat under it in the shade, until he could see what happened to the city. 6 The LORD God provided a ricinus [gourd] plant which grew up over Jonah, to provide shade for his head and save him from discomfort. Jonah was very happy about the plant. 7 But the next day at dawn God provided a worm, which attacked the plant so that it withered. 8 And when the sun rose, God provided a sultry east wind; the sun beat upon Jonah's head, and he became faint. He begged for death, saying, "I would rather die than live." 9 Then God said to Jonah: "Are you so greatly grieved about the plant?" "Yes," he replied, "so deeply that I want to die."

10 Then the LORD said: "You cared about the plant, which you did not work for and which you did not grow, which appeared overnight and perished overnight. 11 And should I not care for Nineveh, that great city, in which there are more than a hundred and twenty thousand persons who do not yet know their right hand and their left hand, and many beasts as well?"

This chapter contains (1) a brief survey of modern biblical study of this text; (2) an excursion through early Judaism's interpretations of Jonah's story; (3) a study of the connection of Jonah with synagogue observances of Yom Kippur; and (4) attention to the interesting puzzle of Jonah's seeming absence from the repertoire of the earliest Jewish graphic artists.

In the preview of the Jonah story I briefly addressed the issue that has long accompanied discussion of Jonah's dwelling within, and then being freed from, the great fish: is this narrative to be regarded as factual or figurative? Such true-or-false categories do not enter most modern biblical scholars' study of Jonah and the fish. Having before them an ancient story with miraculous features, their analyses focus on *Jonah*'s literary type, its genre. Uriel Simon wrote:

> One characteristic of nonrealistic writing is that the author is quite uninterested in whether the events described are possible and makes no attempts to buttress their plausibility. Thus the miracle of the fish focuses on the fact that Jonah is swallowed and spewed forth; the more difficult problem of his protracted stay in the belly of the fish, without air or food, is passed over in silence. . . . In nonrealistic writing, stories derive their force not from resemblance to the known world but from their freedom from its constraints.[1]

Another kind of literary interest informs scholar Jack Sasson's discussion of the whale. The Bible participates in ancient Near-Eastern cultures' creation of stories and legends in which animals have extraordinary roles to play. Against this background Sasson identifies what is singular about Jonah's swallower: "a fish, albeit uncommonly large . . . become[s] inextricably linked with the protagonist of the whole tale," something even more unusual than another biblical "example of an animal with a major role"— the serpent who appears (with a speaking part) in *Genesis* 3.[2]

The use to which the author of *Jonah* put the great fish in spinning his story, not the factual feasibility of its ingesting the prophet, is what most interests those scholars who today examine and interpret the nature and contents of *Jonah*. It might, for example, be pointed out that when the Lord provides "a huge fish to swallow Jonah" (2.1) this is only one in a series of divine and supernatural provisions that propel the narrative: the wind and intensifying storm that endangered the ship, setting the stage for Jonah's being cast overboard; the calm that followed; the gift of a gourd plant to shade Jonah as he sulked over God's pardon of Nineveh; and finally, the plant-killing worm and the hot east wind that caused Jonah to beg, a second time, for death. Such preternatural happenings belong to a style of thought and imagination which an earlier generation of biblical scholars were happy to label, positively, as "mythopoetic" (myth-making).

THE BOOK OF JONAH: ISSUES AND THEMES

This chapter's main interest—the varied understandings of the Jonah story held by Jews in the early centuries of the Common Era—will be illumined by a brief sketch of what some current biblical scholars find intriguing—and complicated—in *Jonah*.

One text-history problem is a good point of entry. The versified psalm (or prayer) attributed to Jonah in chapter 2—the book's only nonnarrative portion—has undergone microscopic examination. Did some version of this psalm predate the composition of *Jonah*, standing on its own before being incorporated in, and perhaps adapted to, the book? How do these verses correspond to other pieces of Hebrew poetry, including biblical psalms of distress which also contain words calling for help, or voicing thanksgiving? What is to be made of language in the prophet's beckoning of God that is unparalleled—like the arresting phrase, "the belly of Sheol"? Do the contents of the psalm fit what the three chapters of narrative convey about Jonah? In the runaway prophet's prayer from the deep what do the references to the Temple and to sacrifice (2:5, 10) signify? Does his prayer (particularly in vv. 7–8, 10) actually give evidence of his sense of regret and repentance over fleeing God, as has long been suggested?[3]

Many distinctive episodes comprise the book, each possessing its own focus and interest. Uriel Simon divides his commentary on *Jonah* into seven segments, ones we can recognize from our own reading: "The Command and Its Violation," "The Storm-Tossed Ship: The Sailors' Fear of the Lord versus Jonah's Rebellion," "In the Belly of the Fish: Submission," "The Repeated Injunction and Its Fulfillment," "In Doomed Nineveh: The Repentance of the Sinners," "Outside the Pardoned City: Jonah's Second Rebellion," "East of Nineveh: Acquiescence."[4] Each of these episodes has its own narrative integrity, but the several parts of the story raise the question of the whole: where is the unity, the overall coherence, the connecting thread of *Jonah*, to be found? The biblical book, we recall, is only seemingly simple.

Earliest commentators will find most captivating in *Jonah* not a single, but three dominant themes: the transaction between God and Ninevites, resulting in the city's being spared; the disagreement between Jonah and his Lord over prophecy and its purposes; and the closely related universalizing notions that, first, there is no place to go where Jonah's God will not be present *and active*—and, second, the insistence that gentiles, the "nations," are also subject to the judgment and the care of Israel's God.

THE RABBIS TAKE JONAH'S MEASURE

Both worthy and wayward, Jonah the personality posed a challenge to teachers of his story. His status as one of God's elected spokespersons stood in tension with what was best known about him—the defiance of his Lord's command to prophesy to the Ninevites. The rabbis did count Jonah a true prophet, but not without discussion. They knew of the fulfillment of his proclamation in the time of Jeraboam II (2 *Kings* 14: 23–27), but had to work through other instances in his career. One voice in the *Babylonian Talmud* posited that his flight to Tarshish to avoid his mission to Nineveh (*Jonah* 1:1–3) made him "one who suppresses his prophecy," for which a penalty of flogging existed.[5] Absurd, responded Rabbi Hisda. This debate moved then to the question of whether a prophet was informed what would be the result of his speaking the word of God in particular situations. It could be argued that Jonah was in the right, and spoke the truth, since:

> In the case of Jonah [the Ninevites] did repent, yet Jonah himself was not informed! Jonah was originally told that Nineveh would be turned, but did not know whether for good or evil (*Talmud Tractate Sanhedrin* 89b).[6]

A less complicated view of Jonah made reference to the name of his father, Amittai, in which the Hebrew word for truth (*emet*) is contained. Etymologically and genealogically, then, Jonah was to be celebrated as the son of "truth." An expansion of his pedigree, calling him "equal to Elijah" and Elisha's anointee, is attributed to the great first- and second-century sage Rabbi Eliezer.[7] A first-century text named *Lives of the Prophets* adds more weight to the approval of the prophet by claiming that when the great Elijah raised from the dead the son of the widow of Zarephath (1 *Kings* 17:7–24), that child was Jonah.[8] Legends elevate him, and praise abounds for him, a bona fide prophet.

Jonah is also grouped among certain of Israel's storied ancestors whom God saved from life-threatening danger.

> A man acquires for himself a patron, and he is arrested for his crime, and the
> judge sentences him to be thrown into the sea: where is he and where is his
> patron? But with God it is not so. Jonah was cast into the sea, and yet God saved
> him. Whence this? For it is said, [*Jonah* 2:11] "And the Lord spoke unto the fish,
> and it vomited out Jonah" (*Deuteronomy Rabbah* 2. 26–30).

Others listed with Jonah as having God for their patron are Moses standing before the Pharaoh, Daniel imperiled by the lions, and Abraham escaping Nimrod's furnace. With Noah, the three young Hebrews sentenced to the flames by Nebuchadnezzar (*Daniel* 3), and with Susanna the falsely accused and persecuted (*Daniel* 13), Jonah is regularly associated. They were all in crises, and their Lord preserved them.

Not all rabbinic treatments of Jonah, however, regard him as completely praiseworthy. Jonah's flight from God's command to go to Nineveh draws various criticisms. One piece of rabbinic *midrash* (*Exodus Rabbah* 4.3) puts Jonah in the company of two other reluctant prophets—Moses, who attempted to decline God's summons to become a spokesperson on the grounds that he was clumsy and slow of speech (*Exodus* 4.13, 18), and Jeremiah, who asked to be exempted from this calling because he was "still a boy" (*Jeremiah* 1.7).

A particularly stringent critique concerns Jonah's stated defense of his rejection of God's mission for him in *Jonah* 4:2: "That is why I fled beforehand to Tarshish. For I know that You are a compassionate and glorious God, slow to anger, abounding in kindness, renouncing punishment." The assertion that Jonah was a deficient prophet appears in a *midrash* in *Mekhilta de Rabbi Ishmael:*

> Jonah said, "I will go outside the Land of Israel, to a place where the Divine
> Presence is not revealed, so as not to render Israel guilty"—because the Gentiles
> are quick to repent. . . . There were thus three prophets: one asserted the dignity
> of the father [i.e., God] and the dignity of the son [i.e., Israel]; one asserted the
> dignity of the father but not the dignity of the son; and one asserted the dignity
> of the son, but not the dignity of the father. Jeremiah asserted the dignity of the
> father and the dignity of the son . . . For this reason his prophecy was repeated . . .
> Elijah asserted the dignity of the father and not the dignity of the son. . . . Jonah
> asserted the dignity of the son and not the dignity of the father, as it says "Jonah
> arose to flee" (1:3), followed by "the word of the Lord came to Jonah a second
> time" (3:1)—He spoke with him a second time, but not a third time![9]

The comparison of the three prophets, with its specific criteria, is triggered by Jonah's attempted flight to a place where Israel's God is not known. His purpose in fleeing, implied in his own speech, is here spelled out: since gentiles readily repent, so the Ninevites will, and their release from God's impending judgment will reflect badly on Israel. (The presumption is that "the son"/Israel is stubborn in the face of God's call for righteousness, and will be threatened with, or will suffer, punishment.) The valuations—best, good, poor—of Jeremiah, Elijah, and Jonah are thought to be revealed in the number of times each received from God his prophecy: his message to announce.

What is the gist of this criticism? Jonah's concern for his own people caused him to attempt escape from his assignment—and from what he believed would be that prophecy's result. This motive led him to his willingness to be cast into the sea, and manifested itself later in his deep anger when he was compelled finally to voice God's warning to the people of Nineveh, and to witness their response. Jonah's protectionist attitude on behalf of Israel—his nationalism—impaired his understanding of, and his loyalty to, his Lord. He fell short of the highest performance expected of God's nevi'im.

The balancing act of being God's particular people and being God's "light" to the nations, who are also God's peoples, involves strain and tension. Jonah is Israel's prophet, and in a book composed during a time when some Jews were emphasizing that God is not simply the protector of one people, but the creator whose concern and providential care is universal, Jonah is vulnerable to the charge of tribalism, or of limited-vision patriotism. He is found guilty in the rabbinic teaching in Mekhilta de Rabbi Ishmael, but to this harsh judgment an alterative and softer one is appended. Rabbi Nathan labors to spare Jonah from condemnation by characterizing him as a noble person of self-sacrifice: "Jonah went only to throw himself into the sea, as it is stated, 'Lift me and cast me into the sea' (1:12). So too you find that the Patriarchs and the prophets gave themselves on behalf of Israel."[10]

A remarkable portrayal of Jonah, quite different in kind from those just considered, is given by Josephus, the notable first-century CE Hellenistic-Jewish historian.[11] In order to be able to commend to his Roman readership the biblical hero Jonah, Josephus resorted to drastic redrawing of his story and character. Removing from his account of Jonah any reference to the penitence of the Ninevites and their forgiveness by God, Josephus emphasizes (more than Jonah itself does) Jonah's status as an honorable prophet. There is no place for mention of Jonah's petulance at being asked to announce doom to Nineveh, nor for a description of his morose chagrin when his prophecy was taken to heart by the people of the "great city," and, later, when his protective gourd plant expired. Writing an audience-conscious encomium of Jonah, Josephus took care to omit his faults.

A part of Josephus's strategic laundering of *Jonah* involved his assertion that Jonah's threat of damnation to Nineveh *did* come to pass. Building this piece of history by referring to the prophetic work, *Nahum*, which tells of the city's later destruction, Josephus was able to leave out any report of what most frustrated the prophet. Having had his prediction of the devastation of Nineveh confirmed in *Nahum*, Jonah is, by Josephus's criterion, a presentable "true"—that is, reliably accurate—prophet. There is no reason, in this retelling, for Jonah to be angry, to have a grievance with his Lord. In addition, Josephus suppresses any suggestions of Jonah's stubborn nationalism—his desire to protect Israel from God's judgment. Josephus's goal was to make the history and traditions of the Jews more attractive, more compelling to his audience of lettered and powerful Roman leaders.

Projection of the nobility of Jonah in his *Jewish Antiquities* impelled Josephus to play down the miracles that might have prompted in his readers skepticism—or worse, ridicule. To this end he writes, in the manner of historians like Herodotus, "the story has it" that Jonah was swallowed and regurgitated by a huge fish. Josephus is aware that his readers are accustomed to discriminating between fanciful and factual kinds of happenings. Did he himself hold to the view that Jonah's experience in the great fish was a symbolic, myth-like tale—and not history? Maybe, yet all we can say with confidence is that the tastes and expectations of his readers shaped Josephus's account of the prophet.[12]

Eager to characterize Jonah as a figure his readers would admire, Josephus knew why and how Jonah's profile had to be altered—which elements to soften or delete, and which to improve or, if necessary, invent. Taking the pliability of this biblical Jonah for granted, the purposeful historian-exegete crafted the Jonah he needed.

Having sampled the rabbis' varied estimates of Jonah the protagonist, we turn to these commentators' treatments of individual events related in *Jonah*. Predictably, more information was wanted than the biblical text gave about what transpired during Jonah's residence in the whale during those three days and three nights.[13] Particular interest centered in the recalcitrant prophet's presumed "change of heart"—clues about what turned Jonah around.

The *Book of Jonah* itself does not indicate that Jonah repented; his prayer makes no clear plea for forgiveness.[14] Many Jewish interpreters nonetheless believed the text suggested otherwise—and set about imagining when and why that act of remorse and apology occurred, and what form it took. They looked for confirmation of their view in chapter two, where the prophet is described as crying out from the belly of the fish, ultimately vowing to do his God's bidding.

What incentive caused the prophet to acknowledge and confess his sin? One rabbinic explanation wins the prize for inventiveness and entertainment. It seems that the prophet was first swallowed by a great fish whose interior was like a commodious synagogue with good windows. Gazing upon the wonders of the deep, Jonah's journey was carefree. In the third day, the pleasure cruise was interrupted when God arranged for his prophet's transfer to a second huge fish.

> Three days Jonah had spent in the belly of the fish, and he still felt so comfortable that he did not think of imploring God to change his condition. But God sent a female fish pregnant with 365,000 little fish to Jonah's host, to demand the surrender of the prophet, or else she would swallow both him and the guest he harbored. So it came about that Jonah was transferred to another abode. His new quarters, which he had to share with all the little fish, were far from comfortable, and from the bottom of his heart a prayer for deliverance rose to God on high. The last words of his long petition were "I shall redeem my vow," whereupon God commanded the fish to spew Jonah out. At a distance of 965 parasangs from the fish he alighted on dry land.[15]

The force of this piece of narrative expansion, with its introduction of the female fish (the feminine form of "fish," *dagah*, crops up once in the *Jonah* text),[16] is plain enough. Only under the pressure of unpleasant circumstances (sharing passage with thousands of embryonic fish) would Jonah come to his senses—that is, recognize his plight and make an earnest plea for God's help. Regret about his situation, rather than an acknowledgment of any fault, comes to expression in the passage. Some, however, inferred from the prayer Jonah's penitence for his own actions. This last supposition will reappear in the pages below.

Another important approach to the Jonah saga—one more philosophical and mystical in its orientation—deserves mention. The medieval (thirteenth-century) book the *Zohar*, relates:

> In the story of Jonah we have a representation of the whole of a person's career in this world. Jonah descending into the ship is symbolic of a person's soul that descends into this world to enter into the body. Why is Jonah aggrieved? Because as soon as the soul becomes partner with the body in this world she finds herself full of vexation. The human being, then, is in this world as in a ship that is traversing the great ocean and is like to be broken, as it says, (*Jonah* 1:4) "so that the ship was like to be broken."[17]

In this text's perspective, the symbols and their meanings easily shift. Here the great fish is not presented as the other player in the drama at sea, but rather the ship, which Jonah boards. Then, the tale is read metaphorically, or existentially, rather than as a narrative "back then" in history. The *Zohar* discerns significant truths in Jonah, advancing in just these few lines a theory of the soul/mind in its relation to the body—and picturing the latter as storm-tossed and destructible by nature. The interpretation also takes for granted the preexistence of souls—their independent being prior to their incarnation—or their ship-boarding. Among its several pictures of afterlife the *Zohar* presents an understanding of resurrection at the end of time, and employs Jonah as a symbol of this.[18] The development of this idea owes a significant debt to the important text we now consider.

THE *PIRKE DE RABBI ELIEZER*: A STRONG REVISION OF JONAH'S LIFE

The centerpiece in our survey of rabbinic commentary on Jonah's story comes from *Pirke de Rabbi Eliezer* (hereafter, *PRE*) a work we encountered earlier when considering Jewish traditions concerning Hagar and Ishmael. An eighth-century writing, it contains teachings that hail from much earlier centuries.[19] To make our way through the portion of *PRE* titled "History of Jonah" is to see that in the course of filling what were considered gaps in *Jonah*'s narrative, rabbi-exegetes freely introduced supplements, often venturing unexpected views about the story's wider (and more current) meanings. We are helped in understanding this text—why it departs so easily from the biblical story, and what its operative mentality is—by recognizing that here, in effect, the rabbis are creating a new storyline, one attuned to an emergent theology of anticipation, messianic hope, within Judaism.

The day of Jonah's calling by God to go to Nineveh fits two calendars. In reporting that it was "on the fifth day [that] Jonah fled before his God," the text purposely recalls the tradition (stemming from *Genesis* 1:21) of the creation of the Leviathan on the same day of the week—the very first Thursday. The great monster of the deep and Jonah have been destined to meet since the beginning of time. Is this the great fish who will swallow the prophet, or some other watery creature?

A second way of dating Jonah's mission is set in terms of Jonah's earlier prophecies. Successful in delivering God's word, Jonah son of Amittai was effective in restoring the contested border of Israel in the days of King Jeroboam II (eighth century BCE; *2 Kings* 14:23–27). Summoned to prophesy in Jerusalem—that God would destroy it—Jonah's second effort was also successful, at least on the Lord's terms, who acted "in accordance [with] His tender mercy and repented of the evil (decree), and He did not destroy it." (Worth noticing is the absence of any reference to Jerusalem's change of heart and behavior—it is as if the text claims that God's intrinsic compassion saved the city.) In the aftermath, however, Jonah suffered ridicule, being called "a lying prophet" (*PRE* 65). Placed in this chain of events, Jonah's excuse for his flight from God gains a rationale:

> On the third occasion, (God) sent him against Nineveh to destroy it. Jonah argued within himself, saying, I know that the nations are [close] to repentance, [and] now they will repent and the Holy One, blessed be He, will direct his anger against Israel. And is it not enough for me that Israel should call me a lying prophet; but shall also the nations of the world [the Gentiles] (do likewise)? Therefore, behold, I will escape to a place where His glory is not declared (*PRE* 65–66).

According to this embellishment of *Jonah* 4:2–3, Jonah reasoned that the repentance of the Gentiles would motivate God to direct a threat of judgment to the people of His covenant. Further, Jonah was sure that his reputation as a prophet—that is, one whose prophecies come true—would now become null and void, turning him into an international laughingstock. Jonah's win-loss record of successful prophecies has the intended effect of explaining Jonah's resistance and reducing his blameworthiness. This attempted defense loses some of its effect, however, when seen against the backdrop of Judaism's normative presumption that a worthy prophet will honor and obey the deity's commands.

The episode describing Jonah in flight, and his arrival at the port from which he hoped to depart, also attracted commentators' attention. We are told that the ship he might have taken was already two days' distance away (a test put to Jonah, the *PRE* states enigmatically)—until God "sent against it a mighty tempest on the sea and brought it back to Joppa" (*PRE* 66). Jonah saw this wonder and rejoiced, saying to himself, "Now I know that my ways will prosper before me" (*PRE* 66). The addition is curious, either indicating that the prophet believes the God he seeks to escape is aiding his cause, or, more ironically, illumining Jonah's ignorance about the divine purpose and the manner in which his Lord intervenes in humans' lives. The exegetes also add specificity to another of God's actions: the tempest that threatened the shipwreck of the craft that bore Jonah enveloped only *that* patch of the sea, while ships nearby made easy progress on tranquil waters.

The opinion that the men on Jonah's ship were "of the seventy languages," making its inhabitants representative of the whole world, is
attributed to Rabbi Chanina, as is the observation that "each one had his
god in his hand" while agreeing that whichever deity proving to have power
to save them "shall be God" (*PRE* 67-68). The captain, when calling Jonah
to add his prayers to those of the other endangered passengers, is shown to
know something about the religion of a Hebrew: "Arise, call upon your God.
Perhaps He will work (salvation) for us according to all His miracles which
He did for you at the Reed Sea" (*PRE* 68).

Expanding on *Jonah* 1:14–15's quotation of the men on board—to the
effect that they feared being held guilty of killing an innocent person by
dispatching Jonah into the raging waters—Rabbi Simeon comments:

> The men would not consent to throw Jonah into the sea; but they [had] cast lots
> among themselves and the lot fell upon Jonah. What did they do? They took
> all their utensils which were in the ship, and cast them into the sea in order to
> lighten it for their (safety), but it [did not help]. They wanted to return to the
> dry land, but they were unable. . . . What did they do? . . . They took him (and
> cast him into the sea up to his knee-joints, and the sea storm abated. They took
> him up again to themselves and the sea became agitated again against them.
> They cast him in (again) up to his neck, and the sea-storm abated. Once more
> they lifted him up in their midst and the sea was again agitated against them,
> until they cast him in entirely, and forthwith the sea-storm abated (*PRE* 68–69).

The moral-religious scruples of Jonah's shipmates are noticeable—and
will be featured again in this rendition of Jonah's adventures.

All that is told in *Jonah* was transpiring according to the plan God made
during the six days of creation. According to Rabbi Tarphon, God not only
"provided the huge fish" (2:1), but constructed its interior in such a way
that Jonah "entered its mouth just as a man enters the great synagogue,"
and can stand there (*PRE* 69). Either by the great fish's window-like eyes
(R. Tarphon) or by an illuminating pearl (R. Meir), light shined within, also
giving Jonah opportunity to see "all that was in the sea and in the depths,
as it is said, 'Light is sown for the righteous'" (*PRE* 70). The estimation of
Jonah in this quotation from *Psalm* 97 is striking; he is not regarded as the
wayward and problematic prophet, but in these terms:

> *Psalm* 97:10 O you who love the Lord, hate evil!
> He guards the lives of His loyal ones,
> saving them from the hand of the wicked.
> 11 Light is sown for the righteous,

radiance for the upright.
12 O you righteous, rejoice in the Lord
and acclaim His holy name.

Rabbi Meir's connection of the light provided for Jonah in the fish with the psalmist's words is interesting in its interpretive possibilities: is Jonah presumed to be one who loves the Lord, being "loyal," and "upright," or do these verses contain imperatives as well—to "hate evil," be "upright," to "rejoice in the Lord and acclaim" Him? This question has relevance for our sense of the Jonah being represented in *PRE*; the grumbler against God may be in the process of being eclipsed by the man of God, elected as a servant of his Lord's will.

The tale of Jonah's sojourn in the huge fish is being reshaped in *PRE* by ideas dear to the Jewish sages of the early centuries of the common era, and its plot now moves in an unforeseen direction. The great fish in which Jonah is carried is not simply a holding-station for him, but rather a character in a larger drama. Now an imminent danger arises. Jonah needs to be briefed:

> The fish said to Jonah, "Do you not know that my day has arrived to be devoured in the midst of the Leviathan's mouth?" Jonah replied, "Take me beside it, and I will deliver you and myself from its mouth." It brought him next to the Leviathan. [Jonah] said to the Leviathan, "On your account I have descended to see your abode in the sea, for ... in the future I will descend and put a rope in your tongue, and I will bring you up and prepare you for the great feast of the righteous." [Jonah] showed [the Leviathan] the seal of our father Abraham (saying) "Look at the Covenant (seal)," and Leviathan saw it and fled before Jonah a distance of two days' journey. [Jonah then] said to the fish, "Look, I have saved you from the mouth of the Leviathan, (now) show me what is in the sea and in the depths" (*PRE* 70).

A popular Jewish apocalyptic vision and hope has found its way into the rabbis' retellings of Jonah and the fish. Enter the Leviathan, the fierce sea monster with his announced diet of one huge fish per day.[20] Jonah's transporter is aware that his time has come. The God-sent fish that saved Jonah from drowning now needs protection, and his passenger-prophet is shown to act forcefully. Drawn within earshot of the Leviathan, Jonah makes plain who he is, first, by telling of his own future capture and killing of the threatening monster, so that *its* flesh may be the food at the banquet celebrating the appearance of God's messiah, and then, second, by displaying his circumcision "seal"—so potent in its marking of Jonah as one reliant upon the God of Abraham that the monster rushes away to (temporary) safety.

We pause over a phrase in Jonah's threat to the Leviathan: he will "put a rope in [his] tongue" and hoist him to the surface. Similar words appear elsewhere in the Hebrew Bible, in *Job* 40:25 (where the phrase is "press down his tongue with a rope") and would have been familiar and convenient to the rabbis as they sought images and language for their elaborations upon what befell Jonah in the deep. The phrase inserted by the exegete comes from *Job* 40:6–8, when God "replies to Job out of the tempest"—a vehement answer to him who complained against his Lord, and impugned his justice (40:6–8). The text reads:

> *Job* 40:25 Can you draw out Leviathan by a fishhook?
> Can you press down his tongue by a rope?
> 26 Can you put a ring through his nose,
> Or pierce his jaw with a barb? . . .
> 31 Can you fill his skin with darts
> Or his head with fish-spears?
> 32 Lay a hand on him,
> And you will never think of battle again.

Job's audacity in arguing with God has been answered with a proclamation of the Almighty's greatness and sovereignty over all that he has made. The Leviathan is God's creature; every "you" in these verses is like a challenging finger poking Job's chest. What powers do *you* have to show?

A closely similar theme from what scholars designate as Jewish scripture's "wisdom literature" actually appears in the *Book of Jonah* itself—in God's final confrontation with the prophet over his grief (and grievance) that the shade-providing gourd-bush has been removed, threatening Jonah's life (4:5–11).[21] The plant you cared for, says Jonah's challenging Lord, *you* did not plant nor grow.

It is not in order to humble Jonah, however, that the rabbis invoke the phrase in *Job* about putting a rope around the Leviathan's tongue. Rather, in this episode in *PRE* a very bold statement is made about Jonah's powers; speaking God's words with the confidence he possesses as prophet and agent in God's service, he, Jonah, will defeat the ancient nemesis.[22] On the day of the Messianic Banquet, Jonah it is who will have drawn him up from the depths—a feast for the redeemed people of God.[23] The runaway and churlish prophet has vanished. In his place is an honorable and mighty servant of God.

How did Jonah change? When, and how? After recounting his confrontation with the Leviathan, the rabbis take up these questions—necessarily producing more narrative.

Still within his "host" great fish, Jonah requests a sightseeing journey in the deep. The itinerary includes the seas surrounding the earth, the waterway of the Red Sea "through which Israel passed," the pillars of the earth, "the lowest Sheol," and Gehenna (PRE 70–71).

Each underwater location is linked by the interpreters to elements in Jonah's prayer—the Red Sea, for example, is likened to the "weeds that entwined" him in *Jonah* 2:6. The whale-guide has been doing God's work, as we learn when Jonah is taken to the waters underneath the Temple of God in Jerusalem. Standing and praying around the *Eben Shethiyah* (the Foundation Stone), Jonah saw the "sons of Korah"—those rebels who defied the authority of Moses and Aaron in the wilderness, and were swallowed up by the earth, descending alive into Sheol (*Numbers* 16–17).

> They said to Jonah, "Behold, you stand beneath the Temple of God, pray and you will be answered." Immediately Jonah said to the fish, "Stand in this place where you are, because I wish to pray." The fish stood (still), and Jonah began to pray before the Holy One, blessed be He, and he said: "Sovereign of all the Universe! Thou art called 'the One who kills' and 'the One who makes alive.' Look, my soul has reached all the way to death. Now restore me to life." [Jonah] was not answered until the word came forth from his mouth, "'What I have vowed I will perform' (*Jonah* 2:9), namely, I vowed to draw up Leviathan and to prepare it before You. I will perform (this) on the day of the Salvation of Israel [i.e., the day of Judgment], as it is said, (*Jonah* 2:10) 'But I will sacrifice to You with the voice of thanksgiving'" (PRE 71–72).[24]

This narrative moment captures the prophet Jonah's plea to God, or his turning to God, in the *PRE*. We need to weigh the text's words and implications carefully. Do they convey Jonah's *repentance* expressly, and is this the passage's chief interest? The sons of Korah who address the prophet can be taken to represent condemned Hebrews begging forgiveness for their sin. It is in their presence and at their urging that Jonah makes his prayer-offering—precisely from the place that guarantees God's hearing. The content of his words, nonetheless, fail to communicate confession or contrition about his flight from God. Rather, Jonah pleas for deliverance from near-death. The Lord, as in *Jonah* 2:10–11, refrains from responding until Jonah makes his vow. More important to the *PRE*'s exegetes than whether Jonah has acknowledged his fault and declared his repentance, it is safe to assume, is the provision of an interpretive follow-up on the prophet's reference to the Temple in *Jonah* 2:8: "When my life was ebbing away,/I called the Lord to mind;/And my prayer came before You,/Into Your holy Temple."

Strikingly, Jonah's vow does *not* pertain to prophesying to the Ninevites—that is, fulfilling the mission that is a chief concern in the biblical Jonah story—but rather, has to do with his prophecy to the Leviathan, that Jonah will capture him, and provide him as grand fare when the "great feast of the righteous" occurs.

But how will Jonah be available when that day arrives? An explanation that flies in the face of traditions about Jonah's tomb declares:

> Jonah's suffering in the watery abyss had been so severe that by way of compensation God exempted him from death: living he was permitted to enter paradise (*Midrash Tehillim* 26, 220).[25]

Revised in accordance with the end-time urgencies expressed by the story's commentators, Jonah's purposes and actions are not those in the book bearing his name. The conclusion of Jonah's adventure in the whale must be a novel one. So it is that Jonah's promise of a sacrifice in his prayer in *Jonah* 2:10 is fulfilled in his (future) capture and slaughter of the Leviathan. As soon as Jonah made his vow, "forthwith the Holy One, blessed be He, hinted (to the fish), and it vomited out Jonah upon the dry land" (*PRE* 72).

Resuming the plot line of *Jonah*, the *PRE* continues it only long enough to relate the consequences of Jonah's underwater encounters with "his" whale, then the Leviathan, and finally, his Lord. The sailors, privileged to see all that took place in the sea, and all that God "did to Jonah," instantly rejected their hand-held idols, the images of their own deities. According to the text, they were responding to the cautionary saying (at 2:9) in Jonah's prayer from the deep—another piece of Hebrew wisdom-philosophy: "They that cling to empty folly forsake their own welfare" (*PRE* 72).

From Joppa, these witnesses of Jonah's experiences traveled quickly to Jerusalem, where they "circumcised the flesh of their foreskins" (an action "explained" in connection with the earlier shipboard crisis described in 1:16: "And the men feared the Lord exceedingly, and offered a sacrifice unto the Lord"). *This* sacrifice, the *PRE* clarifies, refers to the blood of circumcision, "which is like the blood of a sacrifice" (*PRE* 72). Each of the seventy men then pledged to bring all in their households to faith in Jonah's God, and upon doing so "they made vows and performed them." A final phrase, drawn from the *Shemoneh Esreh*, or Eighteen Supplications ("Hear O Israel, the Lord your God"), then calls them "proselytes of righteousness" (*PRE* 72),[26] giving a nice ironic touch at the end of *PRE*'s "History of Jonah." To the men from "the nations" God provided a path to conversion—through their observation of Jonah, whom they first met as he was fleeing his Lord's command to prophesy to the great city of Gentiles.

We noticed that Jonah's destined encounter with the Ninevites dropped out of sight in the section of *PRE* devoted to his history. It was displaced by his prophecy that he would ensnare the Leviathan at the time of the resurrection and judgment. Later in this same rabbinical work, however, the subject of Jonah's mission to Nineveh *does* appear.

"The Power of Repentance" stands out as a thematic chapter set between retellings of stories—the Exodus on one side, and Israel's war with its arch-foe, Amalek, on the other. Its viewpoint and concern are clear:

> Repentance and good deeds are a shield against punishment. Rabbi Ishmael said: "If repentance had not been created, the world would not stand. But since repentance has been created, the right hand of the Holy One, blessed be He, is stretched forth to receive the penitent every day, and He says, 'Repent, you children of men' (*Ps.* 90:3). Know, all of you, the power of repentance" (*PRE* 337).

The last sentence, an exhortation, recurs as various instances of penitence and divine forgiveness are described: King David, with a pestilence sent upon Israel and an avenging angel hovering over Jerusalem, clothing himself in sackcloth and ashes and confessing his sin (*1 Chronicles* 21:7–14), and Rabbi Simeon ben Lakish, turning from thievery to Torah study and care for the poor ("He did not return any more to his evil deeds, and his repentance was accepted," Rabbi Ben Azzai reported). In the mix of materials there is a parable that likens a person who has not acknowledged his sin and repented in this lifetime (there will be no later opportunity) to a voyager at sea or a traveler to the wilderness who did not take care to supply himself with food and drink (*PRE* 338, 240).

Intoning "Know the power of repentance!," a certain Rabbi Nechunia produced an unexpected narrative about the Pharaoh who in Moses's days rebelled against God, saying in *Exodus* 5:2: "Who is the Lord, that I should heed his voice!" At some point the ruler repented, was raised from the dead, and then "went and ruled in Nineveh." The stage is well set for the prophet's entrance:

> The men of Nineveh were writing fraudulent deeds, and everyone robbed his neighbor, and they committed sodomy, and such-like wicked actions. When the Holy One, blessed be He, sent for Jonah to prophesy against (the city) its destruction, Pharaoh hearkened and arose from his throne, rent his garments and clothed himself in sackcloth and ashes, and had a proclamation made to all

his people that all the people should fast for two days, and all who do [not do] these things should be burnt by fire.[27] What did they do? The men were on one side, and the women on the other, and their children were by themselves; all the clean animals were on one side, and their offspring were by themselves. The children saw the breasts of their mothers (and they wished) to have suck, and they wept. The mothers saw their children and they wished to give them suck. [The fast was observed, however, and] by the merit of four thousand one hundred and twenty-eight children more than twelve thousand men (were saved). . . . And the Lord repented of the evil which he said he would do to them (3:10: "God saw what they did, how they were turning back from their evil ways. And God renounced the punishment He had planned to bring upon them, and did not carry it out"). For forty years was the Holy One, blessed be He, slow to anger with them, corresponding to the forty days during which He had sent Jonah. After forty years, they returned to their many evil deeds, more so than their former ones, and they were swallowed up like the dead, in the lowest Sheol, as it is said (*Job* 24:12), "Out of the city of the dead they groan" (*PRE* 342–343).

More striking even than the proposition that Egypt's king arose to rule again—this time in Nineveh—or the detailed drama of his people's resolute penitence, with mothers abstaining from nursing their children, is this passage's focus on who "know(s) the power of repentance." The Ninevites turned away from their evil ways, and the same language— "turning from"—noticeably characterizes God's own decision to honor the city's contrition for its faults, and to relent from punishing its inhabitants.

Jonah is not an example of those who knew and experienced the effects of the power of repentance, but simply the one who sounded the alarm for Nineveh. This is consistent with what we saw in his history, set earlier in the *PRE*—namely, that Jonah, when within "his" whale, was not sorting out his troubled relationship with his Lord, but was instead fully occupied in his confrontation with the evil Leviathan whom he would defeat in the day of resurrection. Atonement for sins is not associated with Jonah the prophet.

Given its particular vision of where history stands, we can imagine why this rabbinic text passes over Jonah's quarrel with God, making him instead a prophetic harbinger of the triumph to occur at the dawning of the new age. The Jonah characterized in *PRE* represents a significant shift and reorientation in rabbinic mentality. In transforming Jonah into a prophet-agent for the coming Messiah, the exegetes are responding to and advancing an apocalyptic urgency alive within Judaism. *PRE*'s revised story of Jonah ably serves that theology's hope for the future.

How do representations of Jonah in this early period of Judaism finally sort out? Did some (or most) Jewish sages question Jonah's status as one of God's honored prophets on the grounds that he resisted his Lord's command, or, was it broadly believed that Jonah *had* confessed his fault and expressed his penitent regret in his prayers from the deep, thus turning back to God? *Jonah* 2:2 ("Jonah prayed to the *Lord his God*") indicated, strictly speaking, only his submission to the divine will, but it could have been taken to say more.[28] *Had* Jonah repented while in the great fish, however, the difficulty remained of his resistance when, finding himself back upon dry land, he became angry with God for the mercy shown to Nineveh, and angry—again, to the point of wishing he could die—about the here-one-day, gone-tomorrow gourd plant that had protected him. This problem was solved by *Midrash Jonah's* revised ending of the story:

> But the sun smote the gourd [so] that it withered, and Jonah was again annoyed by the insects. He began to weep and wish for death to release him from his troubles. But when God led him to the plant, and showed him what lesson he might derive from it,—how though he had not labored for the plant, he had pity on it,—he realized his wrong in desiring God to be relentless toward Nineveh, the great city, with its many inhabitants, rather than have his reputation as a prophet suffer taint. He prostrated himself and said: O God, guide the world according to Your goodness.[29]

Jews seem to have had no choice but to grapple with two Jonahs (or two sides of Jonah) difficult to reconcile: the oppositional or the penitential messenger of God. A choice of one over the other was not necessarily the sole option, of course. Jonah could be lived with in whatever complexity readers and hearers of *Jonah* discerned in him; he was, after all, an instrumental protagonist in one of scripture's best-loved sacred stories.

THE DAY OF ATONEMENT AND THE *BOOK OF JONAH*

As observed in synagogues, the Day of Atonement (or Yom Kippur) recalled and adapted to the Jews' new circumstances after 70 CE those traditions and rituals hailing from the days when the Temple stood: sacrifices and acts of purification by the high priest, and the fasting and prayer required of Israel's people. Yom Kippur had as its central concerns the annual confession of sins and requests for forgiveness—from God and from people—in hopes that through their repentance and the correction of their lives, worshippers' names would be recorded in the Book of Life. In this liturgy's several services, in its words and actions, thanksgiving for the mercy and compassion of their God was steady and insistent.

The reading of the *Book of Jonah* has played a significant role in Yom Kippur observances since the fifth century or earlier, as we know from a notice in *Talmud Megillah* 31a; Jonah was to be ritually recited in its entirety as part of the afternoon service, or *Mincha*.[30] This, with the usual addition of three verses from the *Book of Micah*, served as the *haftarah*, or selection from the prophets (*Nevi'im*), that succeeded an earlier passage from the Torah (i.e., the Pentateuch, or five books of Moses). Particular readings from the prophets were chosen both because they related to chief themes of the Sabbaths and festivals to which they were attached, and because they were "believed to instruct by means of comparison or analogy with the Torah portion."[31]

Illustrative of both points are the Torah and *haftarah* readings traditionally prescribed for the morning service on the Day of Atonement. Segments of *Deuteronomy* 29 and 30 describe God's offer of his covenant to the Hebrews, with the following straightforward and comprehensible instruction:

> See, I set before you this day life and prosperity, death and adversity. For I command you this day, to love the Lord your God, to walk in His ways, and to keep his commandments, His Laws and His rules, that you may thrive and increase, and that the Lord your God may bless you in the land that you are about to enter and possess. But if your heart turns away and you give no heed, and are lured into the worship and service of other gods, I declare to you this day that you shall certainly perish (*Deuteronomy* 30:15–18a).

The Day of Atonement's morning *haftarah* comes from *Isaiah* 58, in which God redefines and intensifies just the kind of repentance that is satisfied with those things the day's observance requires: fasting, humble postures, the wearing of sackcloth and the imposition of ashes.

> Do you call that a fast,
> A day when the Lord is favorable?
> No, this is the fast I desire:
> To unlock fetters of wickedness,
> And untie the cords of the yoke
> To let the oppressed go free;
> To break off every yoke.

It is to share your bread with the hungry,
And to take the wretched poor into your home;
When you see the naked, to clothe him,
And not to ignore your own kin (*Isaiah* 58:6–7).

The Torah lesson concerning the benefits as well as the demands of being in relationship with God, and the *haftarah*'s prophetic warning that acts of penitence unaccompanied by acts of justice fail to gain God's favor, are fully appropriate to the solemn holy day on which they are read, complementing each other.

Did the selection of *Jonah* as a Yom Kippur *haftarah* have so obvious a rationale? We want to know what understandings of Jonah made ancient Jews believe that *this* text was especially well-suited to an annual fast—one given over to acts of atonement for sins, and to prayers for God's reconciling forgiveness.

We examined earlier some of the ambiguities that surround Jonah's behavior toward his Lord, including the absence in the writing itself of the prophet's confession of his fault. Can we discover, or at least infer, the ancient synagogues' reasons for instituting the entire *Book of Jonah* as a prophetic reading appropriate for the Day of Atonement? If we chase this question in the pages of the *Talmud*, will it be clarified or not?

The *Babylonian Talmud's Tractate Yoma* contains rabbis' deliberations on festivals held in the days of the Temple, and on ritual rules that govern the synagogue observances of their own time. A passage in *Yoma* reads: "On the Day of Atonement it is forbidden to eat, to drink, to anoint oneself, to put on sandals, or to have marital intercourse" (*Talmud Yoma* 73b). This holy day's raison d'etre and terms of compliance are plainly stated: penitence at the time of death or at Yom Kippur brings atonement; penitence atones for minor sins, but penitence for major sins does not effect atonement until the next Day of Atonement arrives; those who regularly sin and repent, taking forgiveness for granted, will no longer be given opportunity to confess their sins, and those who plan to sin, presuming future atonement on Yom Kippur, will be disappointed. Equal in importance is a further rule that demonstrates social-communal dimensions of confessing and acting upon one's sins: "A sin towards God, the Day of Atonement atones for; but a sin towards his fellowman is not atoned for by the Day of Atonement so long as the wronged fellowman is not righted."[32]

Tractate Yoma gives several reports of people making amends on the eve of Yom Kippur, but none is so dire (and soberly comic) as this description of Rabbi Zera's dealings with a determined grudge-holder:

When R. Zera had any complaint against any man, he would repeatedly pass by him, showing himself to him, so that he may come forth to [pacify] him. Rab once had a complaint against a butcher, and when on the eve of the Day of Atonement [the butcher] did not come to him [to ask his forgiveness] he said: I shall go to him to pacify him. R. Huna met him and asked: Where are you going, Sir? He said: To pacify So-and-so. [R. Huna] thought: Abba (i.e., Rab) is about to cause one's death. [Rab] went there and remained standing before him [the butcher], who was sitting and chopping an [animal's] head. He raised his eyes and saw him [i.e., Rab], then said: You are Abba, go away, I will have nothing to do with you. While he was chopping the head, a bone flew off, struck his throat, and killed him (*Talmud Yoma* 87b).

Repentance before God and before certain members of one's community is the gateway to forgiveness, to reconciliation. *Yoma* consistently cites biblical texts to enforce its calls to penitence and its promises that sincere contrition will gain a hearing with God. Special consideration is allowed to a pregnant woman who, while fasting, catches the scent of meat, and is overwhelmed by hunger. (The woman in question *could* have been given something dipped in the meat's sauce. She chose, however, to persist in her self-restraint; significantly, the child she bore was the esteemed Rabbi Johanan.)[33]

When *Tractate Yoma* turns to matters of repentance and forgiveness, passages from both the Torah and the Nevi'im are selected to support various claims, as these examples demonstrate.

R. Aqiba said: Happy are you, Israel! Who is it before whom you become clean? And who is it that makes you clean? Your Father which is in Heaven, as it is said: [*Ezek*.36: 25] "And I will sprinkle clean water upon you, and ye shall be clean"; and it further says: [*Jeremiah* 7:13] "Thou hope of Israel, the Lord!" Just as the fountain [*mikveh*] renders clean the unclean, so does the Holy One, blessed be He, render clean Israel (*Talmud Yoma* 85b).

R. Mathiah b. Heresh asked R. Eleazar b. Azariah in Rome: Have you heard about the four kinds of sins, concerning which R. Ishmael has lectured? He answered: They are [only] three, and with each is penitence connected. If one transgressed a positive commandment, and repented, then he is forgiven, before he has moved from his place; as it is said: [*Jeremiah* 3:14] "Return, O backsliding children." If he has transgressed a prohibition and repented, then repentance suspends (the punishment), and the Day of Atonement procures atonement; as it is said: [*Leviticus* 16:30] "For on this day shall atonement be made for you . . . from all your sins." If he has committed [a sin to be punished with] extirpation or death through the Beth din [house of law], and repented, then repentance and the Day of Atonement suspend [the punishment thereon], and suffering finishes the atonement, as it is said: [*Psalm* 89:33] "Then will I visit their transgression with the rod, and their iniquity by strokes." But if he has been guilty of the profanation of the Name, then penitence has no power to suspend punishment, nor the Day of Atonement to procure atonement, nor suffering to finish it, but all of them together suspend the punishment and only death finishes it, as it is said: [*Isaiah* 22:14] "And the Lord of hosts revealed Himself in my ears; surely this iniquity shall not be expiated by you, till you die" (*Talmud Yoma* 86a).

It is startling to discover that among the numerous biblical citations in this talmudic tractate's references to the Day of Atonement—and particularly to matters of repentance, the seeking of forgiveness, and the active compassion of Israel's God—there appears no quotation of any part of the prophetic book *Jonah*, nor any reference to Jonah himself. This absence is all the more surprising when we recall that early producers of *midrash* were quite attracted to the story, eager to explore its possible meanings, and when we observe that the book was chosen at an early date to be one of the *haftarot* chanted during Yom Kippur. The role of *Jonah* in this most solemn of the Jewish "Days of Awe" is perplexing: how was this book understood to relate to the atonement for sins, the holy day's concentrated purpose?

In fact, depending on what might be taken as key themes in the *Book of Jonah*, strong clues do exist that take us closer to the rabbinic rationale for the Yom Kippur recitation of *this* prophetic text. In *Jonah* 3:5–8, we will remember, a fast of penitence is described with considerable attention to detail—the community members covering themselves in sackcloth, crying out to God, and striving to rid their lives of evil and violence. The rituals and actions of the Ninevites bespeak immediate and sincere efforts to atone, and their prayers for forgiveness are answered. What passage from a prophetic book in Hebrew scriptures could be more relevant for those observing the Day of Atonement in their synagogue communities? The story of a city that, warned by God, did its penance and actually changed its ways was perfect in its emphases. The tale *did* pose a challenge to Israel as penitence-resistant in comparison with the Ninevites, but those who gathered for Yom Kippur were more attentive to the day's chief business—facing their demanding God, and coming to terms with those they had wronged.

What might a sermon (*derashah*) at *Mincha* have sounded like? The second- to fourth-century writing now known as Pseudo-Philo has within it a homily "On Jonah"—one suspected of being "the earliest extant Yom Kippur sermon."[34] A point of particular interest lies in what the text adds to *Jonah*'s description of the Ninevites' fast of repentance and its outcome:

(38) They were prepared to confront the love of the Lord of human kindness, (or rather) to accept his pronounced threat on account of their sins. They put on their formal attire: if the prophecy was to retain validity despite the declaration of [their] penance, then they could count these clothes as the clothing of corpses; but if the human kindness of the Lord gave them life in response to their supplication, then they could just as well hold the feast of salvation in this same attire. And so it came to pass. When the deadline of the death sentence had passed, they unexpectedly saw themselves (still alive), and all brought their thanks to God. (39) Again they convened a meeting of the people and ordered from the elders a speech of Thanksgiving. As the people insistently demanded their presence, the elders stepped forward, forgetting sorrow and horror and proclaiming the following:

"As far as we were concerned, dear (friends), we were (already) dead. We had passed judgment on ourselves, which condemned us and the whole city to collapse—and (now) we live by the goodness of the Lord! Under these circumstances it is only right and proper that we give thanks through (this) our life to him from whom we have received life as a part of his mercy."

Thus it was with the Ninevites. They were resolutely and honestly determined, through their fear of God, to demonstrate their acknowledgement of the (received) beneficence. (40) The prophet did not remain in the city, however, after he had delivered the speech that had been ordered. . . . but only fled from the people and awaited their fate from afar. He sought for himself a vantage point from which he could observe the inescapable drama. His place was in the shade afforded by the branches of the pumpkin shrub—a beautiful, inviting shade, a comfortable arrangement. Yet, as he was waiting to see the city reduced to ashes, he saw (its inhabitants) adorned in a festive way. Thus the prophet returned to the Ninevites, as if a gratifying change in their suffering had occurred; the grief of the Ninevites, however, had now transferred to him. For the city's salvation could not please him as much as he was sorry about the lack of fulfillment of (his) prophecy. (41) When he caught sight of the citizens of Nineveh, saw (them) dancing and heard the accord of their instruments, he clapped his hands and cried out: "That's why I fled! Not in order to elude the all-seeing eye, but to preserve my respect and reputation" (*Pseudo-Philo, De Jona*, 38–41).

The actions and experiences of the Ninevites, the homilist proposes, reveal what devout atonement and the celebration of the forgiveness of sins is like.

Worshippers, *Talmud Tractate Yoma* indicates, knew what was required of them in order to effect reconciliation with the One they knew to be a "compassionate and gracious God, slow to anger, [and] abounding in kindness"—a phrase spoken by Jonah that is recited multiple times during the Yom Kippur observance.[35] A fast of repentance, described in *Jonah* 3 in the day's *haftarah*, had every likelihood of being a chief theme for the *derashah*. For those in the midst of the discipline of Yom Kippur, the enacted penitence of Nineveh was an excellent motivating model.

The other important factor in the choice of *Jonah* as a reading for the day, I believe, is the language concentrated in its description of the actions of Nineveh and God. In the cluster of verses running from chapter 3:8 to 4:3 two nearly synonymous Hebrew verbs—*sh-w-v* and *n-ch-m* are their roots—appear with the sense "turn (back from)," "repent," "relent," and "renounce."[36] These verses reward close scrutiny. In 3:8, Nineveh's king says, "Let every one *turn back* (*sh-w-v*) from his evil ways and from the injustice of which he is guilty." He continues in 3:9 with a statement of speculative hope: "Who knows but that God may *turn* (*sh-w-v*) and *relent* (*n-ch-m*). He may *turn back* (*sh-w-v*) from His wrath, so that we do not perish." (The language carries echoes of the ship captain's words to Jonah in 1:6, "Perhaps the god [Jonah's god] will be kind to us and we will not perish.") *Jonah's* narrator reports, "God saw what they did, how they were *turning back* (*sh-w-v*) from their evil ways. And God *renounced* (*n-ch-m*) the punishment He had planned to bring down upon them, and did not carry it out" (3:10).

Phyllis Trible's observations about this section of Jonah bear directly upon our subject—the connection seen by the sages between *Jonah* and the Day of Atonement. She notes that the king's hope of the "turning" of Nineveh (from wickedness and violence) in 3:8 is matched by the "turning" of God (3:10) from his anger (or more literally, "from the burning in his nostrils"). Trible also captures the gist of 3:10: "the Ninevites have done more than perform proper deeds of penance. They have changed inwardly."[37]

Yet another reference to repentance occurs in 4:3—this one in Jonah's prayer (or self-justifying lament) to his Lord: "That is why I fled beforehand to Tarshish. For I know that You are a compassionate and gracious God, slow to anger, abounding in kindness, *renouncing* (*n-ch-m*) punishment." Angrily the prophet complains that justice was not visited upon Nineveh, but mercy. Jonah's bitterness is so great that he asks God to take his life.

Who, then, in the *Book of Jonah*, repents? In the confession and correction of their iniquities, the people of Nineveh do. So too does God, repenting of his plan to overthrow all life in the great city. Repentance—a crucially important transaction in the dealings between people and God, belongs to the non-Jewish city of Nineveh, and to the God who was pre-pared to damn it.

To Jonah belongs resentment. That is the biblical book's unambiguous portrait of him, even though it was subject to revisions both subtle and stark. To hear the story read was to be free to rethink Jonah, altering his profile in the process. Perhaps many early Jewish hearers of *Jonah* on Yom Kippur so registered its force as scripture telling of a pardoning God that they did not suffer undue cognitive dissonance about Jonah's characteriza-tion in the text; they may have found his aggravated behavior overshad-owed by the interaction between Israel's God and Nineveh—penitence rewarded with forgiveness. It is also quite possible that Jews gathered for the fast came to believe that Jonah *had* performed some effective atone-ment for his faults during the "distress" after which "God answered [him] from the belly of Sheol" (2:3).

They were certainly encouraged to see Jonah in this way in another pas-sage in Pseudo-Philo, *On Jonah*, where we encounter the preacher's imag-inative liberty in retelling what transpired when Jonah, from inside the beast, offered up his penitential prayer:

> (18) Because it appeared that the prophet took refuge in the belly of the monster, but was actually protected by the hand of God, he prayed inside the animal, as we heard (from the Bible). He used the mouth of the beast for (his) prayer. Thus a whole new miracle was to be seen, with a sea monster becoming an advocate for the salvation of the prophet. It opened its mouth in order to allow the prayer to ascend, allowing its tongue to be used to articulate words. The prophet oper-ated it [i.e. the tongue] just as a musician plucks an instrument with his finger. (19) His invocation was as follows: "If it was your intention to have me suffer comprehensive retribution, then I (clearly) see that the extent of my sins would have deserved an even graver castigation. Yet because you wanted to repay the sins only so far as I learned from you the impulse for human kindness—for I was not supposed to disappear entirely from view, rejected and far from your eyes, nor was my mouth supposed to be sealed toward you or toward others—I now look toward you with the eyes of my heart and activate my tongue, over which you have granted me freedom to pray for myself. Thus do you answer the prayers of sinners!"[38]

Not only are the hearers of this *derashah* treated to the extraordinary picture of cooperation between the sea monster and the prophet in pluck-ing the prayer that moves heavenward, they are assured that Jonah *did* experience deep regret for his sins, confess them, and, in consequence, express gratitude that God accepted his call for help. With the "eyes of [his] heart" he looks up to the one who hears and forgives sinners. Concern to have Jonah's repentance and forgiveness on record spurred this reworking of the prayer in *Jonah* 2.[39]

Micah 7:18–20: An Important Haftarah

From an early time, three verses from *Micah* (the prophetic book which follows *Jonah*) were appended to the *haftarah* for the *Mincha*. The text reads:

> *Micah* 7:18 Who is a God like you,
> Forgiving iniquity
> And remitting transgression;
> Who has not maintained His wrath forever
> Against the remnant of his own people,
> Because He loves graciousness!
> 19 He will take us back in love;
> He will cover up our iniquities,
> You will hurl [or: cast] all our sins
> Into the depth of the sea.
> 20 You will keep faith with Jacob,
> Loyalty to Abraham,
> As You promised on oath to our fathers
> In days gone by.

Following upon *Jonah*'s unsettled ending, with the prophet in silence, the *Micah* verses reassure. In their chanting is heard Yom Kippur's message, paying tribute to God's capacity to forgive transgressions and withdraw his wrath against "his own people." Returning the focus of the Lord's mercy from Nineveh back to Israel, *Micah* 7:18–20 directly addresses those penitent people bound to their God through the covenant promise.

In all likelihood it was the reference to the casting of sins into the "depths of the sea" (7:19b) that attracted the *Micah* verses to a conjunction with Jonah's story, and with Yom Kippur. There is more to tell, however, about the role of these three lines of prophecy in Jewish liturgy. Perhaps as early as the fourth century CE *Micah* 7:18–20 (without *Jonah*) served as the *haftarah* at Rosh Hoshanah's afternoon service. In later centuries the reading sponsored a ritual that drew its name, *tashlikh*, from *Micah* 7:19 (*Ve Tashlikh*, "And you will cast"). As part of the observance of the New Year, individuals in medieval Europe ceremonialized the atonement of their sins by symbolically "affixing" them to pieces of bread—which then were cast into water currents and carried away—into "the depths."[40]

An adaptation of the sending out the sin-bearing scapegoat practiced in the Jerusalem Temple, *tashlikh* was akin to a very similar expiatory action associated some centuries later with the Day of Atonement—the *kapparot*, in which a white fowl (carefully *not* among the creatures sacrificed at the Temple), after being spun three times around a penitent's head and declared to be the sinner's "substitute," was sacrificed, its meat or its value donated to the poor.[41]

The hearing of the verses from *Micah* (and, in time, the ritualized gesture of *tashlikh*) denote a commencement at the New Year of a period of penitence that will culminate on the Day of Atonement (which also, in time, will include the *kapparot* ceremony).

Sexual Sins

Why were sexual prohibitions the subject of the Torah read during the afternoon liturgy of the Day of Atonement? My investigation of the role of Jonah and of the book bearing his name in the ceremonies of Yom Kippur has bypassed, until now, the Torah selection that preceded the afternoon *haftarah* recitation of *Jonah* and *Micah* 7:18–20. *Leviticus* 18 contains God's instructions to Moses about prohibited sexual relationships and acts—those violations which would defile the land to which God has been leading them. If the sexual abominations and iniquities committed there by the Canaanites are repeated by the Hebrews, God's promised land will be defiled, and the perpetrators "vomited out" from it. Prohibitive commandments in *Leviticus* 18 spell out what kinds of sexual contact are illicit, and center upon sex acts between family members (broadly conceived)— that is, incestuous relations. The euphemisms "approach" and "uncover" (i.e., a person's nakedness) do little to soften the text's condemnation of a wide range of sexual couplings—those with parents, stepmothers, sisters, step-sisters, grandchildren, aunts, sisters- and daughters-in-law, and so on. Though victims might be nearer or more distant kin, all of these are, for the potential or actual sexual aggressor "[his] flesh," or inseparably part of his life and personhood. To couple with any of them "is depravity" (cf. 18:17). Other sexual violations (intercourse with a neighbor's wife, or with both a woman and her daughter, or an unclean woman) are also specified, and a crime different in kind, the sacrifice of children to Molech, as reported in *2 Kings* 23:10, appears in the text and is declared a profanation. The listing of sexual defilements resumes, concluding with references to sex between men (an "abomination") and sex with animals ("a perversity").

God's statutes for the people of Israel concerning sexual relations are sharply contrasted with the immoralities practiced in other lands (i.e., "nations" with *their* deities):

> The Lord spoke to Moses, saying: Speak to the Israelite people and say to them: I am the Lord your God. You shall not copy the practices of the land of Egypt where you dwelt, or the land of Canaan to which I am taking you; nor shall you follow their laws. My rules alone shall you observe, and faithfully follow My laws. I the Lord am your God (*Leviticus* 18:1–4).

Canaan receives special attention, since its sins—especially its sexual crimes—polluted the holiness that had once belonged to that land, holiness that must be restored and maintained. The same theme, contrasting the immoral practices in lands of the Gentiles with the undefiled behavior demanded *now* for *this land* and its people (including non-Israelites within it), closes the chapter:

> You shall keep My charge not to engage in any of the abhorrent practices that were carried out before you, and you shall not defile yourselves through them. I the Lord am your God (*Leviticus* 18:30).

Returning now to early Judaism's synagogue observances of the Day of Atonement—and its combination in the afternoon service of the Torah segment of *Leviticus* 18 with the *haftarah* reading of *Jonah* and *Micah*—we are able to appreciate why the first text, with its concern about sexual crimes that not only defile individuals but also destabilize families and communities, and even an entire land, was selected to be read. The *Leviticus* reading called worshippers to consciousness of those sexual practices disapproved by God which blocked their reconciliation with him. In both the public and communal confession (the *vidui*) and in individuals' personal confessions (often using a formula beginning, "O God, I have sinned"), sexual transgressions had to be included. Yom Kippur's *Leviticus* lection in effect mandated recollection and full, honest confession of *these* sins—along with others. Such soul-searching was the proper work of those who kept the fast.

In *Jonah*, the "wickedness" of the Ninevites that has "come before (God)" (1:1–3) is not elaborated upon, nor does the king's recognition of his people's "evil ways" and the "violence that is in their hands" specifically point to sexual immorality. We noticed, however, that by the time of the composition of the *PRE* in the eighth century, rabbinic opinion held that, along with business fraud and rampant robbery, people in this Gentile city "committed sodomy, and such-like wicked actions."

Early Judaism's Yom Kippur prescribed that illicit sexual relations be addressed in its scriptural readings, in corporate and individual prayers, and in ritual actions. The linkage of sexual immorality with people of other lands, Gentiles, could well have suggested the appropriateness of exposing the positive example of the Ninevites, who set about their repentance so quickly and assiduously. If the subject of the repentance and redemption of Nineveh was the chief reason for the *haftarah* selection of *Jonah*—all forty-eight verses of it—we are able to detect a rationale for the combination of this prophetic book, the three *Micah* verses, and the Torah portion, *Leviticus* 18. While *Jonah* can be understood as trumpeting God's oversight and sovereignty over all nations, not simply one, those who in the early centuries of the Common Era determined its placement in the liturgy of the Day of Atonement may well have been more interested in the text as a demonstration of a nation's successful negotiation of a threat of divine punishment—through a resolute undertaking of ritual penitence over sins committed. A closely observing God turns away from the destruction intended for this wayward great city and grants a pardon.

There is no reason to think that the rabbis wished to idealize the Ninevites to Israel's disadvantage. They are quick to provide a historical follow-up, recounting the total destruction of Nineveh forty years later, upon God's discovery that the city's wickedness had grown worse than before. For the rabbis the story of Nineveh's repentance in *Jonah* functioned, rather, as an instrument of teaching and encouragement. The annual observance of Yom Kippur had its attention steadily fixed upon Israel's standing with God, with the need to expiate those evil actions that distanced its people from their Lord's merciful love. So it is that *Micah*'s verses 7:18–20 exalt the God who pardons evil, covers over sins, stamps wickedness underfoot, and casts these iniquities into the deep. And which of the world's peoples can most confidently call upon God?

> You will keep faith with Jacob,
> Loyalty to Abraham,
> As you promised on oath to our fathers
> In days gone by (7:20).

These verses of *Micah*, addressed to God's covenant people, complement the preceding Torah reading from *Leviticus* 18, also firmly directed to "the people of Israel" who must not commit those acts which defiled other nations: Egypt, Canaan, and, as the rabbinic sages would point out, Nineveh, before it repented.

The chief reason for ritual recitation of *Jonah* at the afternoon Day of Atonement service has to do with its description of a penitential fast properly undertaken, with Nineveh's acts of contrition and moral reform, and with God's repentance of his plan to overthrow its inhabitants. The congruence of a primary interest in all three of the assigned readings, then, becomes evident. Though texts of very different kinds, the *Leviticus*, *Jonah,* and *Micah* passages spoke to and mutually supported the synagogue ceremonies' central concern for its members' confession and forgiveness of sins.

In comparison with that part of the narrative of *Jonah* that describes Nineveh's repentance, and, in response, God's own, Jonah's own story is of secondary importance in the context of Yom Kippur—except insofar as he is acknowledged to be the bearer, ultimately, of God's warning, or is understood to have himself repented. At least this appears to be the case, given this holy day's goals and purposes: "For it is a Day of Atonement, on which expiation is made on your behalf before the Lord your God. Indeed, any person who does not practice self-denial throughout that day shall be cut off from his kin" (*Leviticus* 23:28b–29). Earnest penitence—the necessary prompter of the Lord's compassion—is Yom Kippur's concentrated effort and hope. Enforcement of that goal for worshippers comes in dramatic form from *Jonah* 3—Nineveh's repentance, and God's turning from punishment—more than from the story of Jonah's struggles with his Lord over what the results of a prophecy must be.

JONAH IN EARLY JEWISH ART?: A PUZZLE

In the third- to fifth-century catacombs constructed in and around Rome, scenes from Jonah's life (on the ship he boards, being cast into the sea where the great fish awaits him, his being swallowed, being spit out toward "dry land," reclining beneath the leaves of a gourd plant) far outnumber other popular subjects—like the near-sacrifice of Isaac, Noah in his box-like ark, Adam and Eve, Shadrach, Meshaq and Abednego in the fire (*Daniel* 1–3), Daniel between the lions, or (from the Christian New Testament) the frequent depictions of Lazarus emerging from his tomb, or of Jesus's baptism.

Jonah scenes appear often in paintings or as carvings on sarcophagi that were made for Christian use—as evidenced by surrounding paintings or carvings featuring "the good shepherd," the visitation of the magi, or a miracle-working Jesus. In the company of these painted or incised subjects,

Jonah under the gourd tree, a particularly popular image, carries its own message, one distinctively interpreted, as we shall see, by Christian commentators and artists.

It is curious that by the judgment of art historians writing over the past century, not one among the more than one hundred representations of Jonah discovered in Rome's catacomb paintings and decorated sarcophagi can be identified with certainty as Jewish—that is, as having belonged to a specific Jewish context, and created for members of that religious community.

Two artifacts, beginning with Figure 10.2, give us a glimpse of the identification issues.

Believed to have been broken from a larger glass vessel and placed near a catacomb burial, this image captures Jonah's being cast directly into the great fish's mouth while three men on his ship look on. The inscription is a single Greek word, written in Latin characters: *ZESIS*—"May you live!" Nothing in the imagery or in the inscription's content necessarily prevents this image in gold-glass from being considered a Jewish artifact. Jews in Rome and elsewhere in the diaspora used Greek and Latin, in addition to Hebrew and Aramaic, in their inscriptions, and the inclusion in a picture showing Jonah being swallowed, with its graphically expressed hope of a new life for the deceased, makes as much Jewish as Christian sense. On the basis of what it shows, this image might just as well have been created for use by a Jewish, as by a Christian, individual or family.

The second object (Figure 10.3) is similarly ambiguous.

One is free to wonder whether this carnelian gem, with its several Jonah scenes on one side, might have been made for a Jew, despite its description in a modern catalogue as a Christian artifact.[42] We see in it no feature nor accompanying symbol suggesting that it was made by or for a Christian; its iconography is unusual only in that it includes a scene of an angel who greets the naked Jonah on the dry land. (Chapter 12 treats the popularity of this motif in Islamic paintings of the fourteenth century and after.)

A great number of recovered Jewish sarcophagi and epitaphs, the paintings in the "house synagogue" of Dura Europos, and several synagogue mosaics, demonstrate that Jewish communities from the third century and following were eager, rather than reticent, to produce symbols of Judaism (dominantly, the torah shrine and the menorah, often with lulab and ethrog), and also to create figurative art depicting Judaism's sacred events and their heroes. We find portrayals of Abraham's visit by the angels, of his binding of Isaac for sacrifice, episodes in Moses's life, including a representation of the Israelites' miraculous escape from Egypt through the Red Sea, Elijah bringing the widow's infant back to life, and Ezekiel beholding the

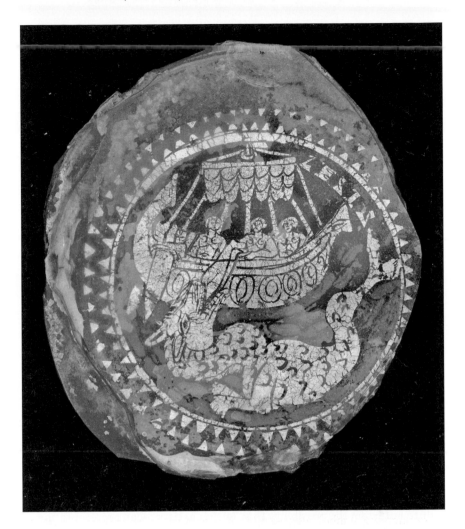

Figure 10.2 Jonah and great fish. Decoration in a gold glass bowl. Fourth century (diameter 11 cm). Provenance unknown. Louvre Museum, Paris. Durand collection, the Louvre. © Art Resource, NY.

re-enfleshment of the "dry bones." David playing his harp appears in a fine mosaic from the synagogue at Gaza, while in a village in the Golan Heights was found a large stone block showing Daniel praying between two massive lions.[43]

Such a wide range of subjects found in early Jewish art makes it all the more puzzling that images of Jonah made for Jewish use cannot be confirmed in this period. This phenomenon could be an accident in the survival of antiquities, but other possibilities exist as well. Some images of Jonah may have been misidentified and incorrectly catalogued, due to

Figure 10.3 Gem incised with cycle of Jonah scenes. Ca. 300 CE. Width 1.9 cm. Photo courtesy of Christian Schmid and Dr. Jeffrey Spier.

single-minded zeal among some archaeologists in past centuries for locating evidence of early Christianity.[44] We have no reason to suspect that Jews purposely omitted visual representation of Jonah among Judaism's hallowed figures, given the fact that the *Palestinian Talmud* groups Jonah in the fish, the three young Hebrews in the flames, and Daniel and the lions as excellent examples of God's rescue of helpless humans.[45] Further, it is difficult to entertain the possibility that Jewish artists ceded representation of Jonah and the fish to the Christians on account of the latter group's great enthusiasm for picturing the story.

In all likelihood Jews, like Christians, *did* commission art for their homes and their burial places that featured Jonah scenes, and carried this practice over to gold-glass pieces, gems, and amulets. The great interest among Jews in Jonah, in the wonder of his residence in the great fish, and in his mission to Nineveh, is manifest, as we have seen, in rabbis' commentaries and the early synagogues' incorporation of the recitation of *Jonah* in Day of Atonement observances. For Jonah *not* to appear on a surviving Jewish sarcophagus or fresco painting in a Jewish catacomb, or in what survives of the painting program in the "house synagogue" of Dura Europos, remains an oddity.

A Christian bowl (Figure 10.4) made in the fourth century illustrates some of the intriguing intersections and interconnections between Jewish and Christian traditions.

Discovered around 1870 in the vicinity of the ancient city of Doclea in Dalmatia (today's Croatia), the bowl's artistic program shows that it was produced for use by a Christian individual or family; its subjects include scenes both from the churches' Old and New Testaments—plus one image that derives from an early church tradition about Peter, Jesus's apostle.

The *akedah*, or Abraham's "binding" of Isaac for sacrifice in Moriah, was, we have seen, prominent in early Jewish art (for example, in a painting just

Figure 10.4 The Podgoritza Cup. Date and provenance unknown. Width: 28 cm, depth: 5 cm. The State Hermitage Museum, St. Petersburg, Paris. © State Hermitage Museum. Photo by Svetlana Suetova and Konstantin Sinyavsky.

above the Torah shrine in the third-century house-synagogue discovered at Dura Europos, in a scene in the floor mosaic of Beth Alpha synagogue, and in the floor mosaic of the synagogue in Sepphoris). Also important to Christians, who took the sacrificial theme as a prefiguring of Christ's crucifixion and victory over death, the *akedah* image appears centrally not only in the Podgoritza Cup but also in other Christian objects (e.g., on the Boulonge dish, where the Chi-Rho symbol stands just beneath it, on a beautifully executed gold glass disk from a Roman catacomb, and also on a dish found in Trier).[46]

The theme, the essential message, of all the Podgoritza cup's scenes combined, becomes clear in its visualization of the drama told in *Genesis* 22: God intervenes on behalf of the endangered. By the voice of God that startled Abraham (the artist makes this clear) and stopped his knife stroke, Isaac was spared from being sacrificed, while an animal substitute was provided. The deity's hand reaches downward through the clouds: divine rescue of a person dear to God is what the etching displays—or graphically proclaims.

The surrounding biblical images make the same visual declaration. Jonah (at the top, right) is delivered from the deep, and (moving counterclockwise) Susanna calls for God's defense in a time of trial, the three Hebrew youths pray for rescue from the (unpictured) "fiery furnace," and Daniel, threatened by two open-mouthed lions, appeals for divine assistance, his arms raised in the usual *orans* posture. The next two scenes continue the portrayal of biblical personages seeking and receiving divine help: Peter (identified as such in the inscription) draws flowing water with his rod—a Christian recasting of Moses's similar miracle in *Numbers* 20:7–11,[47] and Jesus summons Lazarus from his burial place—not, as is usual in early Christian representations of the scene, from a cave or tomb entrance, but from a stone casket, through which the viewer is able to see him. The etching's superscription reads, *DOMNUS . . . LAZARUM*, with the verb *resuscitat* standing below, in lower case script: "The Lord raises up (or rouses) Lazarus again." Next appear Adam and Eve on each side of the serpent-entwined tree—for both Jews and Christians a portrait of *the* human plight, and the need for God's help and mercy.

Having returned to the depiction of Jonah's story, we pause to consider it in a bit more detail: on the left the men on the ship observe his being swallowed by the dragon-like great fish, while to the right the same creature looks toward Jonah, already safe and at rest beneath the gourd plant. The inscription carved over the Jonah scenes deserves special attention, since its language echoes an early Christian prayer for the dead.[48] The Latin DIVNAN DE VENTRE QUETTI LIBERATUS EST is translated "[Jonah] is delivered from the belly of the sea monster." Jeffrey Spier observed that:

> Both Christian and Jewish prayers for salvation invoked similar biblical epi-sodes in which individuals were saved by God: Noah in the flood, Abraham and Isaac, Moses and the Israelites crossing the Red Sea, Jonah swallowed by the "great fish," Daniel in the lion's den, and Susanna falsely accused. Jewish exam-ples of this sort of prayer were already in existence, notably the *zikronot* (remem-brances) recited (then and now) at the New Year. . . . [one of which concludes] He who answered Jonah in the belly of the fish, He shall answer you and hearken this day to the voice of your cry. Blessed art thou, O Lord, who answerest in time of trouble.[49]

Spier's exposition underlines the fact that the early Jews' and Christians' invocations of the figure of Jonah were contemporaneous, often sounding the same thematic key, even if some of their interpretations diverged in order to make religion-particular assertions and arguments.

The questions surrounding the figure of Jonah in, or not in, Jewish art must be left here—engaged, but not settled. What is *not* in question is the interest among Jewish scripture commentators in the Jonah saga, nor the interconnections of some of their interpretations with those of their Christian counterparts.

CONCLUSION

Jewish commentators regarded Jonah as a man of many faces. Remembered and honored by the rabbis as God's servant and prophet in the age of King Jeroboam II, they held him to be the equal of Elijah—indeed, the young child once brought back to life by him. Jonah, then, stood firmly within the ranks of Israel's honored *nevi'im*, those called to be God's prophetic messengers.

Jonah was also a person worthy of divine help: delivered from his pre-dicament in the great fish through God's action, the prophet was a frequent example of those who were tested, redeemed, and God-favored—like Noah, Daniel, Susanna, and the three young Hebrews in the fire.

We have seen, however, that the high approbation bestowed upon Jonah did not go unchallenged. Some exegetes regarded his agitated resentment at Nineveh's redemption a distinct weakness—lowering him in rank com-pared with Jeremiah and Elijah, on the grounds that he, unlike them, hon-ored Israel more than he honored God.

The use of the *Book of Jonah* at Yom Kippur presents another angle of vision: this ritual *haftarah* recitation trumpeted not the honor of Jonah, but rather, the merit of the responsive Ninevites, who heard and acted upon the prophet's delivery of God's warning to repent. Only if it was inferred by hearers of the text, or proposed in a Yom Kippur homily on the text, could Jonah have been showcased as an admirable penitent before God.

But a noble agent of God he became. Making a change in Jonah's biography, the rabbis of *the Pirke de Rabbi Eliezer* presented him as a hero. Bold and authoritative in his confrontation with Leviathan, this Jonah—understood in terms of early Judaism's urgent hopes for history's "last things"—retains no vestiges of his God-resenting misery. Rather, he was fashioned as an activist for his Lord, a visionary cognizant of the imminence of God's triumphal day, when the "great feast of the righteous" would occur.

These rich and varied representations of Jonah, Nineveh, the Great Fish, and God sprang from Judaism's ways of living with, and worshipping with, its sacred stories. Jonah was problematic, even blameworthy, resenting his Lord's actions of forgiveness. He regretted his disobedience—or at least one could choose to picture him this way. And certainly Jonah was redeemable, as added narrative concerning him revealed him to be a necessary and positive participant in the coming Day of the Lord.

Here it makes sense to ask about possible outside influences on these Jonah traditions. We noted Josephus's adaptation of the biblical story so as not to draw criticism of Jonah (and of Jewish lore) from his Roman readers. How do we weigh the probability that one factor in the development of the narrative about Jonah's slaying of the Leviathan for the future messianic feast was awareness of, and eagerness to rebut, Christian beliefs about Jesus's messiahship? Could Jews of the era in which *PRE* was composed—some hundred years after Muhammad's death—have been as familiar with the store of Muslim opinions about the prophet Jonah/ Yunus as we find Muslim commentors in following decades to have been with Jewish lore concerning him? The next two chapters shed light on these questions.

Who was Jonah to become in the imagination of a community committed to the belief that the Messiah, the Son of God, had been revealed? To the formation of an unmistakably Christian Jonah we now turn.

CHAPTER 11

꒰ꕥ꒱

Jonah and Jesus

In One Story, Two

Figure 11.1 Jonah and the whale, from a page of the Melk Missal. Late twelfth century. Photo: 17 x 26.5 cm. © The Walters Art Museum, Baltimore, Maryland. The Walters Museum Ms. W 33, folio 9r.

The image of Jonah emerging from the great fish stands in the letter R of this missal's opening chant for Easter Mass: "I arose, and I am with you still. Alleleuia!" (Another missal's painting accompanying the Easter hymn depicts, not Jonah, but Jesus, risen and standing before tombs, Roman guards pictured nearby. That scene likewise fills the upper loop of the R.)[1]

The variety of Christian understandings of Jonah expanded over the churches' initial centuries, but one of the most influential of these new readings of *Jonah* appeared quite early—in one of the Gospels.

"THE SIGN OF JONAH," AND *MATTHEW*'S ADDITION

In the Gospels of *Luke* and *Matthew*, Jesus promised his hearers a sign, "the sign of Jonah," but their versions of his words, though similar, do not agree. It is intriguing to compare them.

> *Luke* 11:29 When the crowds were increasing, he [Jesus] began to say, "This generation is an evil generation; it seeks a sign, but no sign shall be given to it except the sign of Jonah. 30 For just as Jonah became a sign to the men of Nineveh, so will the Son of man be to this generation. 31 The queen of the South will rise at the judgment with the people of this generation and condemn them, because she came from the ends of the earth to listen to the wisdom of Solomon, and see, something greater than Solomon is here! 32 The people of Nineveh will rise up at the judgment with this generation and condemn it, because they repented at the proclamation of Jonah, and see, something greater than Jonah is here!"

> *Matthew* 12:38 Then some of the scribes and Pharisees said to him, "Teacher, we wish to see a sign from you." 39 But he answered them, "An evil and adulterous generation seeks for a sign; but no sign will be given to it except the sign of the prophet Jonah. 40 For as Jonah was three days and three nights in the belly of the whale, so will the Son of man be three days and three nights in the heart of the earth. 41 The men of Nineveh will arise at the judgment with this generation and condemn it; for they repented at the preaching of Jonah, and see, something greater than Jonah is here! 42 The queen of the South will arise at the judgment with this generation and condemn it; for she came from the ends of the earth to hear the wisdom of Solomon, and see, something greater than Solomon is here!"

Among the similarities found in these two accounts of Jesus's declara
tion, we notice that both *Luke* and *Matthew* link Jesus with the Jewish
apocalyptic figure, the "Son of man," whose identity and role will be manifest on the coming day of judgment. The "sign of Jonah" signifies an unmistakable threat of divine punishment; Jesus is harking back to the prophet's
proclamation to the Ninevites: "Forty days more, and Nineveh will be overthrown" (*Jonah* 3:4). As if the "sign of Jonah" is not dire enough, Jesus
further dramatizes the plight of the generation he speaks to by prophesying that when its time of condemnation arrives, special visitors from
the past will be in attendance and will participate in this people's judgment by their righteous God. They can expect to see the Queen of Sheba,
who sought and followed Solomon's guidance, and also the Ninevites
themselves, who heeded Jonah's sign, his warning. The significance of
the selection of *these* two parties as judgment-day witnesses would not have
been missed by first-century Jews, among whom we would include many
of the initial Jesus-followers. Jesus's words reveal and amplify an important message in *Jonah*: the queen and the Ninevites were Gentiles—people
from the nations who through their repentance were saved, and are thus
qualified to play a role in judging this (forewarned) Israelite generation.
Referring to himself, the Son of Man, Jesus declares, "Something greater
than" Solomon and Jonah "is here!"

Variations in the ways *Luke* and *Matthew* present this strong saying of
Jesus prove to be equally interesting. Two different audiences are described
as hearing Jesus, and the intent of their requests contrast. Jesus's potential
or real followers in *Luke*, the "crowd," crave (in seeking a sign) even more
grounds for belief and loyalty, while the "scribes and Pharisees" in *Matthew*
are opposition figures who demand a wonder, but are unwilling to accept
Jesus's claims or authority even if he accomplishes a miracle. It is a detail
worth noticing that to *Luke*'s "evil" generation, the writer of *Matthew* adds
the adjective "adulterous," calling to mind judgment themes from Hebrew
prophetic books like *Hosea* and *Isaiah* which likened Israel's violation of
God's covenant to the breaking of marriage vows.[2]

The most striking discrepancy between the *Matthew* and *Luke* accounts
of what Jesus proclaimed about the sign of Jonah appears in this sentence:

> For as Jonah was three days and three nights in the belly of the whale, so will
> the Son of man be three days and three nights in the heart of the earth (*Matthew*
> 12:40).

When compared with the sequence of thought in the passage in *Luke*,
this statement looks very much like something added. The author of

Matthew, an interpreter in his own right, has expanded the sense of Jesus's words by providing a *midrash* on "three days and three nights" mentioned in *Jonah* 1:17.

It is impossible to overestimate the significance of this one verse in subsequent Christian understanding—and use—of Jonah. In adding to Jesus's words the amount of time Jonah was in the whale's belly, and in linking it with the "three days and three nights" the Son of man would be "in the heart of the earth," *Matthew* radically altered the meaning of the sign of Jonah. Without *Matthew*'s inventive insertion, Jesus's saying foretells divine wrath, but under the influence of *Matthew*'s expansion, the sign of Jonah points to two divine deliverances—of a man from a whale, and of the Son of Man from death.

The resurrection of Jesus—predicted when spoken by Jesus in this text, but believed to be already accomplished when *Matthew* writes ca. 85 CE—is the new, thoroughly Christianized interpretation of Jonah, hinging on the three days and three nights of captivity experienced by both.[3]

Matthew created a typology: Jonah's crisis and deliverance prefigure the crisis and deliverance of Jesus. His exegesis makes Jesus visible in Jonah, and one vivid result of this way of seeing is that Jonah becomes for Christians a sign or symbol of resurrection, and of peace after death. Not only in his being vomited forth from the whale's belly after the third night, but also in his reclining beneath the leaves of the gourd plant outside of Nineveh, Jonah is an antetype of Jesus resurrected *and* of the hopes of afterlife among those who believe in him. One sacred story has become two.

CHRISTIAN USES OF JONAH IN CARE OF BELIEVERS, THEOLOGY, AND CONFLICTS WITH RIVALS

Christian authors found in the Jonah saga a storehouse of lessons for the faithful, grounds for an intriguing theological proposition, and an armory of arguments, defensive and offensive, with which to contend against foes. In the churches' deployments of Jonah treated in this section, the three elements—pastoral, doctrinal, and apologetic—will often be intertwined. Christianity, like its religious competitors in the late Roman period, was required to support its adherents, build and tend its belief system, and both defend and advance the truths that gave the community its definition and identity. It will not be surprising to see a thread running through these writings and being applied in quite different ways—namely, extensions of *Matthew*'s added interpretation that enabled Jesus Christ as a saved savior to be represented in Jonah.

Christian Prayer and Jonah

Tertullian, Origen, and Aphrahat, theologians of the second, third, and fourth centuries, respectively, had good reasons to refer to Jonah in their writings about prayer.[4] After a brief commentary on the Lord's Prayer, Tertullian turned to a survey of worship customs he knew to exist in the churches of North Africa. Critical of practices that were immodest and ostentatious, and also of rituals he deemed unnecessary, Tertullian commented on hand-washing before prayer (an empty observance; the baptized are already clean), removing cloaks before praying (an imitation of the fashion of pagans approaching their idols), sitting after prayers (might God see this as a complaint that worship has tired us?), and exempting dedicated virgins from wearing the head-covering expected of women at prayer (are not the virgins also women?).

Early Christian art abounds in images of women and men raising their arms in prayer; this was the proper posture for Christians addressing God, even if it was a gesture common in other religions. Tertullian disapproved, however, of hands raised too high and too boldly—as if the person praying was calling for attention. The authority for Tertullian's advocacy of modesty in prayer derives from *Luke* 18:9-14, which contrasts the demeanor and petitions of a Pharisee and a tax collector offering their prayers in the Temple. The parable allowed Tertullian to take up the problem of the *noisiness* of some Christians' praying; it is in this connection that Jonah's prayer (*Jonah* 2) serves Tertullian's purposes.

> We commend our prayers to God when we pray with modesty and humility, with not even our hands too loftily elevated, but raised temperately and becomingly; and not even our countenance over-boldly lifted. For that publican who prayed with humility and dejection not merely in his supplication, but in his countenance too, went his way "more justified" than the shameless Pharisee. The sounds of our voice, likewise, should be subdued; otherwise, if we are to be heard for our noise, how large windpipes should we need! But God is the hearer not of the voice, but of the heart, just as He is its inspector. . . . Do the ears of God await a sound? If they did, how could Jonah's prayer find its way out to heaven from the depths of the whale's belly, through the entrails of so huge a beast; from the very abysses, through so huge a mass of sea? What superior advantage will those who pray too loudly gain, except that they annoy their neighbors? (Tertullian, *On Prayer* 17).[5]

Tertullian made sharp and humorous use of Jonah's prayer—one uttered out of God's earshot. (With God all things are possible, but the

theologian concedes, for this lesson's sake, that nature, distance, and matter are factors in divine operations.) Tertullian hoped that his comments
would discourage worshippers whose actions were capable of disturbing a
church community's life, but his point carried additional weight of a spiri-
tual-devotional sort: God's concern is with what occupies the worshipper's
heart—his or her inner thoughts.

Aphrahat, the fourth-century Christian thinker known as the "Persian
sage" and particularly honored for his championing of ascetic life, makes
a claim quite different from Tertullian's about the travel-mode of Jonah's
prayer:

> Jonah also prayed before his God from the depths of the sea, and he was heard
> and answered, and was delivered without suffering any harm; for his prayer
> pierced the depths, conquered the waves and overpowered tempests; it pierced
> the cloud, flew through the air, opened the heavens, and approached the throne
> of majesty by means of Gabriel who brings prayers before God. As a result the
> depths vomited up the prophetic man, and the fish brought Jonah safely to dry
> land (Aphrahat, *Demonstration* 4.8).[6]

Origen insists in *On Prayer* 13.2–4 that if Christians want to praise
God for good things in their lives, praying of a certain kind will take them
beyond "the sterility of their own governing reason and the barrenness of
their own mind"—indeed, the Holy Spirit will inspire in them words and
"visions of the truth."[7] He wrote: "we know that fugitives from God's orders
who have been swallowed up by death, which at first prevails over them,
have been saved through repentance from so great an evil, since they did
not despair of being able to be saved even though they had been made captive in the belly of death."[8] (Origen takes for granted, we notice, Jonah's
prayerful repentance, which accounted for his ejection from the great fish,
his rescue.)

A mode of prayer that seeks the higher divine mysteries, rather than
being satisfied with supplications for small and earthly needs, will demand
self examination. Jonah's crisis, *not* considered in its obvious and literal
sense, for example, can be made a window on a person's own life:

> The one who has been persuaded what sort of whale the one that swallowed up
> Jonah was a type—if he should ever find himself through some disobedience in
> the belly of the whale, let him repent and pray, and he will come out of there.
> And if he comes out and is faithful in obeying the orders of God, he will be able
> by the kindness of the Spirit to prophesy to those who are now Ninevites on
> the brink of destruction and be for them a cause of salvation, since he did not

despair of the kindness of God or seek that God should remain in His severity toward them when they repented (Origen, *On Prayer* 13.4).[9]

With the assistance of the Holy Spirit, Origen urges his reader, your spiritual prayer will be cognizant of the thoughts and deeds that have led to your confinement, will seek the divine mysteries that set you free, and will embolden you to be a Jonah to people in your time and place. Jonah serves, first, as an example of the fruit of prayer, and, second, as an invitation to make his story a vehicle for personalizing both the prophet's plight (what sin binds *you*?) and his restored mission (who, in his or her despair, can *you* urge toward a redeemed life?). A teacher and preacher in the church, Origen is alert to individual believers' dilemmas and hopes.

Theology: A Jonah-Inspired Christian Theory of Salvation

In Origen's *On First Principles*, a treatise that shows him performing theological and cosmological explorations undergirded by his scriptural interpretations, there appears a passage that advances a succinct and intriguing claim about Jesus:

> He has come who according to Job has "subdued the great fish" and who has given to his true disciples authority to "tread on serpents and scorpions and over every power of the enemy," without being in any way harmed by them (Origen, *On First Principles* 4.1.5).[10]

It is Jesus the Christ, or Messiah, Origen asserts, who has snared the dangerous Leviathan spoken of in *Job* 3:8 and 40: 25–32. In doing so Jesus has performed the act which, as we saw earlier, the rabbis of the *Pirke de Eliezer* reserved for Jonah on the Day of Judgment. From the early Christian viewpoint, Christ's death and resurrection vanquished Satan and his army of malevolent spirits, stripping them of their powers. To register that point Origen quotes *Luke* 10:19, in which Jesus declares that with the arrival of God's kingdom, the sting of the threatening evil belonging to demons and poisonous creatures has lost its potency.

A century and a half after Origen, an admirer of his thought, Rufinus of Aquileia, became one of the first to transform the idea of Christ's capture and defeat of Satan into what has long been termed the "fish-hook" theory of salvation.[11] The Evil One, imagined as a watery beast, was fooled by the son of God in the flesh (i.e., incarnate) and took the bait—Jesus's human and physical form—with the result that he was snared and overwhelmed by the conquering divinity which lay underneath. The Jewish idea of a messianic banquet echoes in Rufinus's description: "Having swallowed it, he was immediately caught. The gates of hell were broken, and he was, as it were, drawn up from the pit, to become food for others."

Jonah in Christian Disputes with Jews: Jerome and Cyril of Jerusalem

By the fourth century, when Jerome composed his *Commentary on Jonah*, there existed in the churches numerous writings critical of Jews—their beliefs, scripture interpretations, religious practices, and their resistance to Christianity. Early in his new book's pages, Jerome condemns those, in the past and in his time, who heard Jesus's declaration that "something greater than Jonah is here!" and failed to respond:

> The generation of the Jews is condemned, while the world has faith and Nineveh repents. Israel the disbeliever dies. The Jews have the books themselves, [but] we have the Lord of the books; they hold the prophets, we have an understanding of the prophets; "the letter kills" them, "the spirit makes us live" (*2 Corinthians* 3:6); with them Barabbas the robber is released, for us Christ the Son of God is freed (Jerome, *Commentary on Jonah*, Prologue).[12]

Jerome has absorbed Paul's teachings in *Galatians* and *Romans*: for him, the Lord of Jonah has adopted a new covenant people. Israel has been displaced by the community of believers in Jesus, whom they worship as God's son.

Bishop Cyril of Jerusalem (sometime around 350 CE) took up the problem of how the newly baptized should counter the Jewish critics of their beliefs. When defending Jesus's resurrection, neophyte Christians were to put the Jonah story to good use, since Jews *did* believe that the prophet survived his three days in the whale's belly. Faced, themselves, with the question of the prophet's ability to breathe during that time, Jews explain (says Cyril) that "the power of God descended with Jonah when he was tossed about in hell."[13] Then on what grounds, the bishop (modeling debate tactics) asks, do Jews deny Jesus's being raised from the tomb? Cyril reminds his hearers, whose candidacy for baptism has involved the study of scripture, what supports exist for their assertions:

> Does the Lord grant life to his own servant [Jonah], by sending His power with him, and can He not grant it to himself [God the Son] as well? If that is credible,

this is credible also; if this is incredible, that also is incredible. For to me both alike are worthy of credence. I believe that Jonah was preserved, for "all things are possible with God" (*Matthew* 19:26); I believe that Christ also was raised from the dead (*Matthew* 14:18, 20). . . . Of this our Savior the Prophet Jonah formed the type, when he prayed out of the belly of the whale, and said, "I cried out in my affliction," and so on; "out of the belly of hell" (*Jonah* 2:3), and yet he was in the whale; but though in the whale, he says that he is in Hades; for he was a type of Christ, who was to descend to Hades. And after a few words, he says, in the person of Christ, prophesying most clearly, "My head went down to the chasms of the mountains" (*Jonah* 2:7); and yet he was in the belly of the whale. What mountains then encompass you? I know, [Jonah] says, that I am a type of Him, who is to be laid in the Sepulchre hewn out of the rock. And though he was in the sea, Jonah says, "I went down to the earth" (*Jonah* 2:7) since he was a type of Christ, who went down into the heart of the earth (*Matthew* 12:40). And foreseeing the deeds of the Jews who persuaded the soldiers to lie, and told them, "Say that they stole Him away," he [Jonah] says, "By regarding lying vanities they forsook their own mercy" (*Jonah* 2:9). For He who had mercy on them came, and was crucified, and rose again, giving His own precious blood both for Jews and Gentiles."

Cyril gives a careful demonstration of how his typological interpretation of *Jonah* proceeds and succeeds, especially that element to which *Matthew's midrash* opens the way. There are implications for modern historians in this passage, especially those who wonder to what extent the theologizing of early Christian writers could be accommodated by ordinary believers. We are justified, I think, in presuming that those being baptized in fourth-century Jerusalem were capable of understanding Cyril's defense against skeptics of Jesus's resurrection *and* of recognizing and following the biblical references out of which it was constructed.

The Role of Jonah in Debates Between Christians and "Pagans"

Promoters and defenders of the traditional Greco-Roman deities did not pass up opportunities to discuss the miracle of Jonah and its relation to Jesus. Critics of nascent Christianity tested the ingenuity of the churches' apologists. We look first at a passage in a treatise by Origen which preserves and then responds to an attack by Celsus, an influential opponent of the movement he regards as a novel superstition.

Celsus: [You Christians] assert that a man who lived a most infamous life and died a most miserable death was a god. A far more suitable person for you than

Jesus would have been Jonah with his gourd, or Daniel, who escaped from wild beasts. . . .

Origen: [Celsus] wants us to regard Jonah as god rather than Jesus; he prefers Jonah who preached repentance to the single city of Nineveh over Jesus, who preached repentance to the whole world and had more success than Jonah. He wants us to regard as god the man who performed the portentous and incredible feat of spending three days and three nights in the belly of the whale. But him who accepted death for mankind, to whom God bore witness by the prophets, Celsus would not regard as worthy of the second place of honor after the God of the Universe, a position given to him on account of the great deeds which he did in heaven and on earth. And it was because he fled to avoid preaching the message that God had commanded him that Jonah was swallowed up by the whale. But it was because Jesus taught what God wished that he suffered death for mankind (Origen, *Contra Celsum* 7.53, 57).[14]

The caustic Celsus, concerned to combat the growth and spread of the churches, asks why Christians did not choose a savior more deserving of admiration and devotion. Rather than dying in a pathetic way like Christ did, Jonah in the fish withstood an ordeal and thus became, like Herakles, a divine hero. Origen, writing decades after Celsus's death, framed a reply. Here, he argued, is what makes Jesus more worthy—and indeed, worthy of worship: the gospel about him spreads everywhere, benefiting many, and he died a death that saved humankind. Celsus's taunting proposal, a polemical challenge, compelled Origen to frame an argument that did not fuse, but rather compared and contrasted, Jonah and Jesus.

Augustine Versus Polytheists in Carthage

In the early fifth century a priest in Carthage named Deogratias wrote to Augustine seeking help with a potential convert who was troubled by doubt concerning several Christian beliefs. Among these was the claim that Jonah spent three days in the whale, and survived. Deogratias described how pagan skeptics frequently treated the story as "a matter of jest and with much laughter."[15] They said:

The thing is utterly improbable and incredible, that a man swallowed with his clothes on should have existed within a fish. If, however, the story is figurative, please explain it. Again, what is meant by the story that a gourd sprang up above the head of Jonah after he was vomited by the fish? What was the cause of this gourd's growth? (Augustine, *Letter* 102.6).[16]

Augustine counsels Deogratias first to confront his would-be convert with the illogic of his doubt. Since the man accepts the truth of Christ's raising of Lazarus and of Christ's resurrection on the third day, how can he reject the Jonah miracle?: "Either all the divine miracles are to be disbelieved, or there is no reason why they should not be believed."[17] But the case of Jonah in the whale *does* present challenging issues, and Augustine attempts to address them. If one doubts that a man could fit within a whale, Augustine writes, he should inspect the skeleton displayed in Carthage and see that it could have contained many men. The argument is a scientific, not a symbolic one. It was not Jonah's clothing that prevented his injury as he passed through a narrow opening of the whale's mouth and throat—no, he was quickly swallowed and "inside the monster before he could be crushed by its teeth."[18]

Augustine credits the critics' observation that the heat and digestive juices in the whale's belly would not have allowed Jonah to survive, but calls upon another of God's saving miracles as counterevidence: when the three young Hebrews were thrown in Nebuchadnezzar's furnace, were not the natural properties of fire and flames curtailed by the power of God? His argument requires that the pagans accept a different (biblical) miracle in order to believe Jonah's. As if aware of the weakness of this kind of reference, which is internal to Christian understandings of divine wonders, Augustine changes his tactic, arguing that if the story of what happened to Jonah and the whale appeared in *The Story of the Golden Ass* as something that befell Apuleius, "no laugh would spread over [your] faces, but [rather] proud elation."[19] Augustine taunts the pagans: it is not as if you polytheists do not have room in your imaginations for divine wonders!

Augustine's advice to Deogratias has been moving toward a response to the man's query about whether the tale of Jonah in the whale is figurative. Here, predictably, *Matthew* 12:40 is the springboard for the symbolic explanation that Augustine hopes his friend's potential, but hesitant, convert should consider:

> As Jonah went from the ship into the belly of the whale, so Christ went from the tree into the tomb, or into the abyss of death; and as Jonah was sacrificed for those endangered by the storm, so Christ was offered for those who are drowning in the storm of this world, and as Jonah was first commanded to preach to the Ninevites, but his prophecy did not come to him until after the whale had vomited him out, so the prophecy made to the Gentiles did not come to them until after the resurrection of Christ.[20]

After taking up the question of the gourd that grew up for Jonah, and the worm that destroyed it (the worm, among other things, is a figure for the lowliness of Christ's humanity), Augustine concludes by declaring that all mysteries and obscurities in Christian scripture take an entire life to study and understand. It is better, he tells Deogratias, if the pagan he hopes to bring to the baptismal pool settle the questions about the general resurrection of the dead, and why Christ appeared so late in time, and then accept the faith, looking forward to deep study of other matters as one in the company of "faithful souls."[21]

EPHREM THE SYRIAN: *HYMNS ON JONAH*

The historical circumstances of Ephrem, a preeminent commentator on the story of Jonah, are worthy of review. Born in the early years of the fourth century to Christian parents, Ephrem's life-trajectory was framed by the church in Nisibis and by his association with its leaders. One of these, Bishop Jacob, attended the Council of Nicea in 325, and returned home buoyed by the emergence of Constantine's Christian-friendly powers, and fully committed to that church synod's understanding of God as a trinity—Father, Son, and Holy Spirit.

Appointed the church of Nisibis's interpreter (of scripture, presumably), Ephrem developed strong and boldly expressed convictions in the course of his career as theologian, exegete, and writer of hymns, metrical sermons, and prose works. Writing in Syriac, the Aramaic dialect of his region, Ephrem's subjects included liturgies, biblical commentaries, doctrinal treatises, and polemics against heresies and also against the emperor Julian, the "apostate," who during his brief reign in 361–363 aspired to reinstate classical polytheism to the Roman Empire.

Denunciations of the teachings of Marcion, of the followers of Bardaisan (an Edessene who embraced the gnostic Christianity of Valentinus), and of Mani are prominent in Ephrem's *Hymns against Heresies* and *Hymns on Faith*. His decision to use a particular form of Syriac poetry in defense of the creed of Nicea was quite deliberate; use of these poetic "teaching songs" (*madreshe* in Syriac) had in the previous century won significant support for the brands of Christianity, now under Ephrem's attack, advanced by Bardaisan and by Mani.[22]

Ephrem's theological convictions were formulated and honed in the context of his church's battles with opposing religious viewpoints both within Christianity and external to it—especially those of the Jews.[23] Kathleen McVey writes of Ephrem's studies of the Old Testament that "the uniqueness of his endeavor lay in the fact that he taught in a city where the rabbinic traditions were well-established and sophisticated and where the Jewish community may have been more prosperous and numerous than its Christian counterpart."[24]

The location of Nisibis between the Tigris and Euphrates, north of modern-day Mosul, made it a hot-spot in the territorial conflicts between the Persian and Roman empires. Shapur II (309–379) found Constantine's communications haughty and the Christian communities within Persia untrustworthy—and thus deserving of punitively heavy taxes. During Emperor Constantius's reign (337–360), Shapur laid siege to Nisibis twice, the second (again unsuccessful) effort in 350. It was a series of Persian military incursions into Roman territory in Mesopotamia that motivated both Constantius and his successor, Julian, to pursue a strong campaign against Shapur. The collapse of Julian's effort, which he had supposed would be a victory supported by the traditional deities to whom he rendered worship, caused the next Roman emperor, Jovian, to give over to Persian control the city of Nisibis, from which all Christians were compelled to remove themselves.

In 363 Ephrem took up residence in nearby (but Roman) Edessa, where a confident community of Christians celebrated its distinctive traditions. The church in Edessa traced its origins to the visit of one Addai, or Thaddeus, whom the apostle Thomas himself was believed to have sent to convey the gospel message concerning Jesus. According to this lore Addai also brought to King Abgar as a special gift a portrait of Jesus. It was a visible proof of the sort appropriate to receive from the apostle who doubted. By the sixth century this painting was believed to bear the impression of Jesus's face on a cloth, the famous *mandylion*, an icon "not made with hands."[25] Until his death in 373, then, Ephrem was in a city whose Christian community was vital and durable—strengthened even more, as he himself claims in one of his hymns, by the transfer of the apostle Thomas's bones to the basilica there. Again, however, the city's cultural and religious diversity was much in the foreground, with a significant Jewish community, and strong traces, still, of the region's traditional protective deities—Baal (or Bel) and Atargatis—whose festivals continued to be celebrated.

It was here that Ephrem, probably in his sixties, was ordained a deacon, and continued his work as a teacher (dominantly of those being prepared for baptism) and as a theologian and biblical commentator writing in prose and verse. His curriculum was broader, however: we are allowed glimpses of his training of women choirs to sing the church's hymns, including his own compositions. Also in Edessa he continued to produce writings (some

400 hymns survive) that even in his lifetime were translated from Syriac into Greek, gaining the praise of, among many others, Jerome, whose influential *In Ionam*, a commentary on *Jonah*, was completed in 396–397, more than two decades after Ephrem's death.

Ephrem's *Hymns on Jonah* appear toward the end of a larger cycle of fifty hymns that, despite the variety of subjects treated therein, gained the title *On Virginity*. Its first three hymns encourage the "chaste"—that is, both celibates and married couples pledged to nonsexual relationships.[26] Particular attention and exhortation are directed to "the consecrated virginity of the 'daughters of the covenant' "—that is, to the sexual abstinence of Christian women who through baptism have not only entered the church, but also the higher, paradise-like new life open to them.[27]

Jonah receives adventurous and searching interpretations from Ephrem, whose Syriac hymns were based on patterns of syllables allowing for their singing; names of melodies, but not the music, survive in sixth-century manuscripts. The striking content and style of Ephrem's poems owe much to his love of contrast and paradox, which are fully in play as he fashions theological parallels and moves his observations and arguments to their forceful conclusions.

Especially acute awareness of Jewish beliefs and Jewish biblical interpretations pervades Ephrem's studies of *Jonah*. We meet in his writings an exegetical version of the sociological axiom that close relationships inspire more intense conflict: a climate of rivalry encompassed Christians and Jews in fourth-century Syrian cities, and Ephrem's sensibilities to these tensions are quite transparent. His assignment to tend to the content and quality of life within the churches, however, most directly accounts for his desire to advance a distinctive Christian spirituality. Several themes fundamental to that effort are featured in his *Hymns on Jonah*.

Ephrem on Jonah's Stature and Standing Among the Saints of God

In comparison with the rabbis' challenge in balancing the flaws of Jonah with his standing as a true prophet of God, the Christians, we would think, were in a more difficult situation: for them the problematic Jonah was not only an authentic prophet, but also, for those with ears to hear and eyes to see, the prefiguration of Jesus the savior.

Nonetheless, maintaining a steady separation between what God accomplished through Jonah, on the one hand, and the prophet's own humanly errant choices and actions, on the other, Ephrem is relentlessly critical of

God's messenger. The poetic device of building strophes on the basis of contrasts gives a keen edge to Ephrem's enumerations of Jonah's faults. Comparisons of Jonah to model figures of the Hebrew past are most often bluntly to his disadvantage:

> 44.1 That Sodom not be overthrown Abraham prayed.
> That Nineveh be overthrown Jonah hoped.
> 2 That man prayed for [a city that] abused Watchers.
> This man was angry at a city that made the Watchers rejoice.[28]

Ephrem obviously takes it for granted that those who hear his hymns will recognize his references to biblical events (in this case, *Genesis* 18:22–33, *Jonah* 4:1–5, and *Genesis* 19:1–11), and will also register not only the contrary wishes of Abraham and Jonah for the fates of the two cities, but also the second contrast in the treatment and response of the angels.

Criticism of the irascible Jonah appears also in *Hymn* 47. Here, tribute is paid to the Ninevites, the people's tears of repentance being represented as fruits "the Heavenly One desired," "tasting remorse" in them (47. 7–8). The metaphors build: sin was displeased by the abatement of evil, the penitents' tears placated God's anger, "the sentence of fasting released the sentence of judgment" (17–18). The last image is carried further: fasts are like a rudder on a ship that negotiates waves (that is, temptations and sins).

> 47.20 For Nineveh had become a ship.
> Anger shook it; pity steadied it.
> 21 Every sailor rescues his ship.
> Jonah expected to sink his ship.
> 22 They threw him over into the sea so he could learn
> not to over throw the city on land.
> 23 A man sank; by mercy he came up.
> The one whom [mercy] rescued, expected to sink.
> 24 By mercy he came up, but he forgot mercy.
> What he learned at sea, he rejected on land.[29]

Ephrem has closed in upon Jonah's resistance to mercy—both that shown to the great city and *also* to him. Jonah was not only an unworthy captain, he was stubbornly forgetful of his own deliverance.

One of Ephrem's other critiques has to do with Jonah "deeply grieving about the plant" (*Jonah* 4:9). Having proposed that the fruit of Nineveh's repentance constituted a vineyard—one that "put to shame the vineyard of My beloved"—that is, Israel (*Isaiah* 5:7)—Ephrem captures the force

of *Jonah*'s final verses: Jonah's fig tree and pardoned Nineveh are inter-
changeable. What did Jonah the prophet of God do?

> 49.25 Jonah lifted his axe to uproot
> the fig tree that suddenly had acquired health.
> 26 Since he wanted to cut down the beloved of the King,
> the worm cut down his beloved young plant.
> 27 Since he did not rejoice in peace as a son of peace,
> he was poured into the sea as a contentious man.[30]

Resentful of the fig tree's vitality (Nineveh's repentance-won new
life), Jonah was punished by the death of the gourd plant he cherished.
In verse 27 Ephrem freely alters the sequence of events in *Jonah* in order
to underscore the prophet's resistance to the purposes of God: it was
after Jonah's display of anger at Nineveh's salvation that he went to the
seaport, and there met his more serious punishment—being cast into
the sea, and being swallowed by the great fish. We shall see in the next
chapter that some Muslim commentators also—and for interesting
interpretive reasons—had Jonah's visit to Nineveh precede his flight
to the sea.

The rabbis ultimately were able to find ways to "own" Jonah in his
doubleness—in his justly criticized weaknesses *and* in his positive (albeit
resistant) role in the workings of God's plan. Ephrem, too, was able to pay
tribute to this second, serviceable Jonah, calling him in one instance a
"good man" through whom God saved the thousands in Nineveh (42.6).
The attempt to combine, or at least adjust, the two sides of Jonah was a
trickier matter, but one of Ephrem's hymns reveals a distinctly Christian
strategy for "resolving" the prophet.

Hymn 49 begins with the contrast between Jonah, a circumcised healer
sent to "circumcise the heart of the uncircumcised people," and Moses at
Sinai, where the rebellion and worship of the golden calf by his circumcised
people revealed "the uncircumcision of [their] heart" (49.1–4). Presenting
the events of Sinai and of Nineveh—both involving forty days—as a contest, Ephrem declares the Ninevites the victors, since "instead of their bodies they circumcised their hearts," while there was hidden among Moses's
people "the leaven of Egypt"—namely, the evil accompanying idolatry
which they knew from their years of enslavement there. That yeast-like
force emerged, turning their hearts to "strangeness"—to the worship of
the "molten calf" (*Exodus* 32:2–5).

What for the rabbis was a properly prophetic reproach against Israel's "hardness of heart," became for Ephrem an opportunity to deliver an already established Christian argument *adversus Iudaeorum*. The hearer of Ephrem's song is brought back to the contest between Jonah and Moses—and the contrast between the people to whom they spoke:

> 49.12 Jonah lifted Nineveh up as if at the judgment seat,
> and for forty days he tortured it with his words.
> 13 Moses taught; the People apostasized.
> The healer was irritated that his remedy did not avail.
> 14 Nineveh repented; it grieved Jonah.
> The healer was irritated that his medicine triumphed.
> 15 The medicine of which one of the healers
> has healed myriads of the sick?
> 16 The medicine of penitents came down from the height.
> He [God] scattered pardon among the sins.
> 17 As much as you are irritated, Jonah, rejoice
> that of all the prophets your medicines were most triumphant.
> 18 As much as you are irritated, be joyful, sailor,
> that your oarsmen have rescued the sunken ship.
> 19. The High One answered the sunken ship,
> for the sunken ship was all of the penitents.
> 20 He answered at sea; He answers on land.
> He rescued on land as at sea.
> 21 Jonah's voice became a medicine of life.
> He sowed death with it, but life sprouted.[31]

Christians of the fourth century—and Jews, had they heard them—would have immediately understood the polemic woven into these verses: Moses's medicine at Sinai failed: "the People apostasized." Jonah's medicine brought healing, even if he resented this outcome. The success of Jonah's medicine was due, Ephrem insists, to what the "High One" accomplished through him; Jonah should have rejoiced rather than sulked. Easily recognizable between the lines of this passage is the poet's assumption that even an irritated Jonah is a figure for Jesus Christ the healer-savior, who is the true deliverer of the "medicine of life" that vivifies Christian communities.[32] The case of Moses and his unrepentant or "hard hearted" people fades at this point, giving way to Ephrem's completion of Jonah's tale as a celebration of the redemption of penitents. Ephrem has characterized Jews as those whom Moses could not turn back to their God, while Ninevites

(Christians) are seen as beneficiaries of God's rescue, proclaimed through Jonah's (Jesus's) voice.

God's Favored Ones: What's in a Name? Free-Will and Grace

Describing Ephrem as unique among early Christian writers in the degree that ancient Mesopotamian, Hebrew, and Greek influences met in him, Sebastian Brock wrote of a particularly Jewish theme that greatly occupied him: "the creative tension between God's Grace (*tabuta*) and Righteousness (*kenuta*)."[33] Brock cites a passage from Ephrem's versified homily *On Faith*.

> The scales of Your balance are Grace and Righteousness;
> how and when they are balanced, You alone know.
> Though they may not seem to be balanced,
> they are balanced all the same
> since they are not divided against the One Lord of all
> (*Faith* 12:4).

Under this heading of justice and balancing scales we turn to Ephrem's understandings of how the actions of peoples and individual persons are "weighed" by God. Three interrelated topics are at hand: (1) comparisons of Nineveh and Israel, (2) the distinction between outward and inward circumcision which renders names (of nations or people) irrelevant, and (3) the theologian's clear teaching of the connection between human freedom and sin.

Ephrem's repeated and polemically-tooled assertions of Israel's inferiority to the Ninevites has the energy of four centuries of Christian supersessionist theology behind it. The Christians are the new covenant people of God, and even the story of the Jewish prophet's resentment of the salvation of a Gentile people can "stand for" the obstinacy and blindness of the Jews—and their fall from God's proprietary care. In *Hymn* 44 Ephrem employs a bold tactic in his effort to dismantle the claim of Israel's specialness to God. Christ (i.e., the Word of God) speaks to Jonah about the success of his preaching to Nineveh (44.3), but associates him with those (Hebrews) who "broke the yoke" (became disobedient to the master, God) while the people of Nineveh rushed to take it on themselves. The Word of God says: while you, Jonah and Israel, counted on your lineage, being the people of circumcision, the Gentiles in Nineveh proved that to God the uncircumcised were acceptable—even preferred. Ensuing passages mount an assault on Israel's privileged relationship with its God, demolishing the "rights" thought to stem from being in the lineage of Abraham, Isaac, and Jacob, and overturning the measures by which God favors (or rejects) people or a person. Ephrem has God's eternal Word continue:

44. 8 I chose the circumcised, but they have rejected themselves.

I rejected the uncircumcised, but they have dedicated themselves.

9 Election, therefore is not [a matter of] names,

for deeds enter and dismiss the names.

10 The furnace of testing of the name is the deed.

In it is tested whether it is the true name.

11 For there is fruit that is very splendid,

but its taste is the opposite of its beauty.

12 Even the despicability of the bee,

the most despised of all, is a spring of sweetness.

13 Splendid names—the house of the Hebrews—

are sweet things that make bitter things flow.

14 The mention of their name is sweet to the ear.

The taste of their fruit ravages your mouth. . . .

17 He whose body is circumcised but whose heart is

uncircumcised is circumcised outwardly but

uncircumcised in secret.

18 But he whose heart is circumcised but whose flesh is

uncircumcised is circumcised for the Spirit but

uncircumcised for the eye.

19 In the name of his circumcision the circumcised fornicates.

With the cup of his purity he drinks mire.

20 By a circumcised heart the uncircumcised becomes holy. In the

bridal chamber of his heart dwells his Creator.

21 It was not his name [that] made Abel fair.

Because he desired innocence, his name was desirable.

22 Eve chose the name of Cain,

but since he hated his brother, his name was hated by all,

23 The Assyrians! Inflammatory names!

They gave fruits of desirable tastes![34]

The prophet Jeremiah's metaphor of circumcising the heart's foreskin (*Jeremiah* 4:4), which denotes an inner and more profound commitment to repent and submit to God's will, is an exhortation to Israel alone, and it warns that the wrathful judgment of God will fall upon the people of Judah and the inhabitants of Jerusalem unless their evil stops.[35] For his part, Ephrem has made the outer and inner circumcisions distinguishing marks between peoples (and individual persons) who will garner God's disapproval or favor. Though the speech he imagines God giving principally refers to Jonah's case (even to the end, with the approbation of the Assyrians'—that is, the Ninevites'—fruits), Ephrem's parallel (and more important) judgments pro-Christianity and anti-Judaism are once more close to the foreground, simultaneously proud and chastening in content and tone.

The active mercy of God is the subject of Ephrem's *Hymn* 48, which, after recounting the narrative of Jonah and Nineveh proceeds to offer strong messages about the story's challenge and promise for his fellow Christians. Favorite images of the poet propel a spare, linear retelling. The lot that identified Jonah on the ship "became for him a judgment seat" and "the fish snuffed him in like a judge" (48.2). Transferred from the sea to the fish was "the miserable one [who] fled from the Great One," Jonah's flight making him food for the fish, and leaving the unvisited Ninevites to become "food for death" (5-6). Crisis intervention was needed—and supplied:

48.6 The Gracious One Who makes straight all perversities

set in order Jonah's contradictions.

7 For him He returned from within the fish.

Nineveh he snatched from the mouth of the greedy one. . . .

10 Mercy rushed to straighten the perversities,

and contradictions were set in order.

11 He ordered the fish to spit out the man

and to return to being food for us.

12 He chided the evil one, and he released Nineveh.

The captured one recaptured her captor.

What, or how many things, does this sacred story teach? Ephrem spells them out. His first observation is that the world's disruptions and evils are the products, the consequences, of human freedom; contrariwise, order and being "made straight" issue from divine grace. This, the theologian and observer of history and human behavior writes, is a constant tension and dilemma—the way things have been since the foreparents' disobedience in Eden.

14 Our freedom does not cease to pervert.

His grace does not cease to make straight.

15 Freedom made hateful the beauty of Adam

that he might be god . . . human.[36]

Ephrem calls upon eastern Christianity's persisting doctrine (and view of human nature) that the image of God in humans was effaced (but not thoroughly ruined) in the sin of Adam and Eve. They were to be godlike creatures, but their exercise of freedom (narrated *and* symbolized in the violation of the command not to eat the fruit of *that* tree) overturned and perverted them, and affected—or frustrated—God's good intent for them. However, "The Gracious One Who makes straight all perversities" worked a remedy. At this point Ephrem's hymn becomes a rhapsody of proclamations:

> 16 Grace adorned its [the human's] flaws,
>
> and God came to be human.
>
> 17 Divinity flew down
>
> to rescue and lift up humanity.
>
> 18 Behold the Son adorned the servant's flaw,
>
> so that he became god as he had desired.
>
> 19 To You be glory, Straightener of every fault!
>
> To you I give thanks, Adorner of all flaws!
>
> 20 Since our freedom ceases not to break through,
>
> Majesty wearies not to repair.
>
> 21 Your grace accompanies our evil—
>
> the spring of peace for a raging fire.
>
> 22 Since wherever the fire kindles its flame,
>
> the light of Your mercy presses hard to extinguish [it].[37]

Within these few lines Ephrem is able to make several declarations of real importance to him: (1) the incarnation of the Word of God rescues humanity from its own sinning and condemnation; (2) grace's "adorning" of human "flaws" restores humankind's likeness to God (the doctrine of *theosis* or divinization, frequently expressed in some form of the proposition 'God or the Word became human, that we might become divine,' was firmly entrenched in fourth-century Christianity); (3) the descent of the Divine to lift up humanity was decisive—the event that defeated Satan and death, calling Christians into being; and (4) though the victory has been won, the contest continues between freedom's temptations (flames and fire) and God's "mercy [that] presses hard to extinguish it." The last point—that freedom still inclines humans (indeed, even redeemed Christians) to disorder and evil—was a theological proposition, but also something more. Ephrem's church was regularly forced to deal with this reality—the return of human "flaws"—in members of its holy community.

God's Judgment Against Jonah, and Against Christians
Who Sin After Being Baptized

For all early Christian communities, including those in Nisibis and Edessa, there were two very basic concerns: (1) how was a person to appropriate, to take to herself or himself, the salvation accomplished in Christ's death and victorious resurrection? and (2) upon having received forgiveness of sins and a new, pure life, how was she or he to keep these secure? The simple answers, put in the form of invitations to converts, were these: first, trust in what God has accomplished for you and many others in Jesus's victory over death, and become baptized into the "body of Christ," the church which God's Holy Spirit sustains and inspires; second, having made this your faith and way of life, enjoy it, always safeguarding the gift of your baptismal purity from temptations to sin, to "fall again." Problems inevitably complicated this second solution, since backsliding into the old life *did* occur, requiring that churches distinguish between less serious (menial) sins, for which relatively light penance could be done, and grievous (mortal) sins, which called for a sinner's chastisement and separation from the church, and from its central shared and binding experience, the eucharistic meal.

By the third and fourth centuries, procedures existed for dealing with church-members who, by their major sins (apostasy, murder, adultery) had violated their baptismal vows and, in effect, excommunicated themselves. What was the status of these lapsed believers? If they appealed for mercy and undertook arduous penitence in the hope of gaining God's pardon, might they be reinstated as members of the body of Christ?

The initial three of Ephrem's *Hymns on Virginity*, and one pertaining to Jonah, breathe the air of these actual spiritual and social crises, and address them. We are reminded of the set of human woes and hopes for help that were captured in Judaism's Day of Atonement fasts—and of Rabbi Jose b. Judah's judgment that if a person commits a transgression a first, second, and third time, he or she is forgiven, but *not* the fourth. But now the language and actions are Christian. Can grievous sins committed after the purification of baptism be atoned? The question is pivotal for sinners who wish to repent (again), but also pivotal for communities' own investments in their holiness and good faith, which they cherish as marks and guarantees of their redeemed lives—their salvation.

Another religious-social factor—present in other churches, but apparently exquisitely pressurized in the Syriac-speaking churches—informs Ephrem's discussions of baptism and sin. I mentioned earlier that his *Hymns on Virginity* gained that title because its opening three hymns are addressed to virgins contemplating or already engaged in the "angelic" discipline of sexual abstinence, and warn against threats to their chastity. The language and ideology of the Syrian churches' ascetical practices was succinctly laid out by Sebastian Brock, who noted that the term *idihaya*, used to denote a "celibate," held connotations of "single," and "single-minded," which allowed its association with a description of Christ as *Ihjidaya* (Only-Begotten, or "single" Son of God). The term gave weight to an understanding of the celibate as one walking in the path of the Christ. Brock explains:

> It would appear that by St Ephrem's time the term *ihidaya* normally included two categories of people, the *bthule*, "virgins," both men and women (in other words, celibates) and the *qaddishe*, or married people who had renounced marital intercourse. The latter term, meaning "holy" or "sanctified," had taken its origin from *Exodus* 19, verses 10 and 15. Together these groups constituted *qyama*, conventionally translated "covenant," and they were known as the members (literally, "children") of the covenant. Evidently they had undertaken ascetic vows at their baptism (which would still usually have been in adulthood), and they lived in small groups or communes serving the local church in a variety of different ways.[38]

A question presents itself: was the crime of those who had succumbed to sexual temptation, having formerly committed themselves to lives of chastity, equivalent in seriousness to the mortal sins of rejection of the faith, murder, and adultery? Clues to an answer exist in Ephrem's *Hymn* 46, which features an intricate paralleling of the story of Jonah and the Ninevites with the poet's picture of the plight of Christians' "letters of bondage"—their sins—which they will carry with them to the resurrection day when all are to be judged by God.

The lot Jonah received on the ship initiates Ephrem's treatment of sin and forgiveness. Marking his sin as a fugitive from God, the lot—this judgment on Jonah—did not immediately confront him, but waited until after he had been submerged and raised up.

46.1 Jonah intended to go down to the sea
to flee on a ship from God.
2 But waves rolled him about like avengers.
A lot seized him and gave him to the waves.
3 The lot caught him for the name of fugitive,
but not immediately and at once did it judge him.
4 It submerged and brought [him] up and then judged him.
That he would sink and emerge, it prophesied to him.

5 It portrayed a symbol even of our sins
that after the resurrection will rebuke us.
6 The lot portrays him who would come to save
Nineveh since it resulted in delivering her [from] death.
7 The lot that resulted as if for death
saved one hundred twenty thousand.
8 One judgment that took place at sea
annulled the judgments of thousands on land.
9. The writ that judged the one
tore up twelve myriad letters of bondage.
10 Therefore the letter of bondage of sins that is hidden
within us is well-silenced now so that it may cry out at the End.
11 With us it is buried; with us it rises.
When the judgment seat is established it will cry out to rebuke.
12 Insofar as tears are found in our eyes,
we will blot out with our tears the letter of bondage of our sins.
13 Insofar as just deeds are in [our] hands,
we will close up with our just deeds all the breaches.
14 Who gives us [the possibility] that by visible things
an invisible wound may be healed?[39]

The poem's reference to "twelve myriad letters of bondage" (i.e., bondage to sin, and to the Evil One) is not fully explained by its association with the number of people in Nineveh; it bears also upon those Christians for whom Ephrem writes. Even after the decisive forgiveness which baptism bestowed, Christians will, when Judgment Day arrives, carry within themselves sins requiring atonement. They can use their good works to fill gaps formed by their faults —God enables them to offer their visible tears as penance for their concealed sins. Ephrem acknowledges that "debts" do accumulate in those once-forgiven and baptized persons; these sins will have to be accounted for when the Kingdom of God is realized—when the living and those raised from the dead face divine judgment—to salvation or damnation. Measures can be taken to ready oneself for further mercy. Fully aware of the penitential disciplines enacted in his church, Ephrem proceeded to draw lines between kinds of sins, and the daunting challenges to obtaining forgiveness for some of these.

We meet an allusion to an event that Ephrem's readers or hearers must have caught, even though modern interpreters have difficulty identifying it.[40] The action Ephrem mentions, however, is clear enough: it describes the benefit to some of "the baptized" from washing the feet of unspecified "holy ones." The poet does not pause to explain, though we wish he had. Rather, he is interested in its implications for sinners.

> 46.17 The baptized washed the feet of the holy ones,
> so that there is no baptism [but] there is sprinkling.
> 18. The spattering of sins after you have been baptized
> can be washed with the washing of the sick.
> 19. Justice encompassed and confined us.
> There is a chance for us again—grace.
> 20 Lest we be ravished, justice confined us.
> Lest we succumb, grace had mercy on us.
> 21 Since there is no baptizing again, there (should be) no
> sinning again,
> 22 but since there is spattering, there is sprinkling.[41]

What recourse was available to Christians who had "spatterings of sin" accumulated after their once-for-all baptismal purification? Whether Ephrem's counsel is strictly metaphorical, or refers also to actual liturgical practices of anointing (e.g., the sick, which sinners are)—he offers hope. Justice—or judgment—which has the effect of condemning and keeping us in bondage, is countered by the grace that brings mercy. There is no start-over, no second baptism available to those who repent of their sins—but "since there is spattering" (of sins) upon them, they may receive a merciful sprinkling that cleanses. Again, we are not able to ascertain the precise mode of this "sprinkling" that Ephrem presents as a still-possible remedy.

Upholding the importance of Christianity's initiation of persons into its sanctified company through its sacrament of baptism that remits all sins, Ephrem must also avoid driving the church's backsliders to a despairing hopelessness. The prospect of some form of repentance and recovery must be given to them. At the same time, however, Ephrem is obliged to warn Christians of the consequences of their sinning. Foremost in his thoughts are those who have adopted the vocation of virginity, the "brothers and sisters of the covenant," whose commitments might be softened by wine, by falling in "hateful love," or by being captivated by infatuations.[42]

Concluding with the force of a hortatory sermon, the hymn celebrates the gift given in baptism, warns about the difficulties in atoning for sins (especially postbaptismal ones), and, finally, reassures even those bearing the deepest blemishes from their faults that they may receive a miraculous healing.

22 He Who gave hope in baptism
   gave repentance lest hope be cut off by Him.
   23 But harsher is the work after you have been baptized
   than that work before you have been baptized.
   24 Sins before baptism
   by simple work are able to be atoned.
   25 And if the imprint of scars sullies [the Christian],
   baptism whitens and wipes clean.
   26 But sins after baptism
   with double works are able to be overturned.
   27 When works and mercy have truly healed,
   the imprint of scars will call for a miracle.[43]

We conclude that Ephrem took with absolute seriousness the Book of Jonah's presentation of the recalcitrance of the prophet. The dramatic intensification of the prophet's sin, however, serves a theology whose idiom is paradox, and whose climax is a reversal of perversity and contradictions. For Ephrem Jonah is, finally, a stark symbol of human "freedom [that] made hateful the beauty of Adam," but also a symbol of rescue accomplished by the one described as "straightener of every fault . . . adorner of all flaws" (48.15, 18). Jonah, through whom God saved "thousands," is important to the poet-theologian in his steady promotion of Christian life exercised in chaste spirituality.

Both Jonah the character and personality and the lively narrative of *Jonah* proved to be powerful engines for Christian writers' ethical and spiritual teachings, for their fashioning of doctrines, and for aggressive defense and advocacy of their religion. For Ephrem, especially, the demands of righteousness and the gift of mercy that he found in *Jonah* informed a careful consideration of the rituals and rules by which the church communities might encourage the vital purity of their faith. These writings present strong claims for the exceptional character of Christians; they are people different from and superior to the polytheists in their societies, and, by the Jews' default, now are especially God's own, covenant-privileged and covenant-bound. When not turned toward to their opponents, but turned inward to matters within the churches, these interpreters evince deep concerns for the welfare of dedicated individuals and communities who counted themselves members of an uncorrupted "body of Christ." These things most occupied early Christian writers. Was it the same for the artists?

JONAH INTERPRETATIONS IN EARLY CHRISTIAN ART

Which among the many and varied perspectives on Jonah found in the writings by early Christians also came to visual expression in the works of the graphic exegetes—the artists? Here we shall consider two (out of a great many) portrayals of Jonah's story which clearly were made for use in a Christian context—carving on a sarcophagus and on an ivory diptych.

In the previous chapter's search for definitely Jewish images of Jonah in art of the early centuries of the Common Era, we noted the dominant popularity of representations of Jonah and the whale which have survived in Christian burial spaces. Robin Jensen wrote: "In the pre-Constantinian era, whether in extant catacomb frescoes or on sarcophagus reliefs, Jonah occurs more than seventy times, of which at least thirty are series of three or four episodes."[44] The usual three aspects of Jonah's story—his swallowing and containment within the whale, his ejection, and his rest in the shade of a protective bush (rarely, with an added image—of Jonah praying, or preaching)—translated easily to Christ's death (and his activities during the three days "under the earth," his being raised up, and, after his ordeal, being "at peace").

For Christians viewing representations of the Jonah episodes, then, a first-level symbolism was all but impossible to miss; it had been early implanted by *Matthew* 12:40. Beyond that symbolic translation was another extended and applicable one that heightened the possibility that Jonah scenes would decorate tombs and individual burial sites: Christ's being raised up as "first born of the dead" (*Colossians* 1:18 and *Revelation* 1:5) signified for Christians not only that their Lord possessed a supreme power, but also that they too would be raised up at the general resurrection of the dead. This was the hope of fervent believers that the kingdom of God would come imminently. No doubt other (less eschatologically minded) believers anticipated an existence beyond their mortality—an afterlife in which tranquility would be enjoyed. Whether present in paintings near the burial, on in gold glass images fixed into cement nearby, or carved into stone caskets, scenes of Jonah gave expression to families' hopes for the peace of their dead—either in the near future, resumed at the day of resurrection, or uninterrupted in their still-vital souls.

About the stone casket we want now to examine (Figure 11.2), a modern art historian wrote: "The individualized portrait of the resting Jonah . . . shows that the Christians wanted to incorporate into the biblical story wishes for the deceased as they were expressed in the prayers [of the church communities for the dead]."[45]

Figure 11.2 Marble sarcophagus with Jonah scenes, ca. 260–300. Length: 192 cm. Provenance uncertain. © The Trustees of the British Museum, London.

Despite some irregular features, the Jonah moments on the face of this burial chest are identifiable. In scene one, on the left, the men on board eye the sea serpent, and vice-versa. (Their ship did not have a hole in it until it was transposed—in England—into a water-fountain of some sort.) Curiously, in comparison with many other images of this episode, Jonah is nowhere in sight—that is, we do not see the typical representations of his jumping or being cast into the sea, or directly into the sea monster's mouth. Perhaps the artist intends for the figure elevated to the height of the ship's rail to be seen as the prophet poised to plunge into the sea—or, alternatively, expects the viewer to understand Jonah as no longer visible, already having been swallowed. (How are we to read the sea monster's attitude and body language?)

Scene two, at the lower right, is less ambiguous, showing Jonah emerging from the sea monster's mouth naked, with his arms extended. The two images, with the implied swallowing and the demonstrated spitting forth of Jonah toward dry land, are carefully and gracefully cut, with attention to the ship's details, the waves, and the monster's features. Taken together, the two scenes, carved to the same scale, suggest a symbolic shorthand: capture/death and release/salvation—a single graphic narrative.

What prevents such a simple interpretation of the two lower scenes, however, is the magnification of the third, which places greatest emphasis upon Jonah at rest beneath the branches and leaves of the gourd bush. There is, of course, no hint of the prophet's disgruntlement at Nineveh's salvation. He abides in peace after the "three days and three nights in the belly of the whale." Sculpted in a size commanding attention, Jonah (who is also Jesus) *in pace* functions as more than a biblical memory—the Christian entombed within the splendid stone casket, visitors to his burial place trust, also rests in peace.

Jonah Reclining: The Endymion Factor

Over many years art historians have noted the close similarity of early Christian representations of Jonah in repose to Greek and Roman depictions of the youthful Endymion, who reclines in slumber, awaiting nocturnal visits from the moon goddess, Selene (Figure 11.3). The story centers in the youth's irresistible beauty and the goddess's desire for him—an attraction so strong that she prevents his mortality, ensuring the duration of their amorous encounters.[46] The romantic-sensual theme of the myth made paintings of it popular in the homes of Romans, while the theme

Figure 11.3 Marble sarcophagus with Jonah scenes. Detail. © The Trustees of the British Museum, London.

of Endymion's eternality and resting led, inevitably, to the image's use in funerary art.

The early third-century Roman sarcophagus panel in the Getty Museum collection shown below (Figure 11.4) portrays Endymion in his usual pose, one elbow supporting him, while his other arm is raised to his head—a gestural commonplace denoting sleep. Hypnos, the god of sleep, with the help of an eros, or cupid, either pulls away or replaces the upper part of Endymion's cloak. Whether his tryst with Selene is about to occur or has been completed is not fully evident, but Endymion's repose is more centrally framed by the goddess's (more prominently emphasized) approach than by her departure, where she gazes back toward her lover after ascending her chariot.

However much those artists' Christian clients who employed Jonah scenes in art of the catacombs may have been aware of the myth of Selene and Endymion, I think it certain that they easily recognized the biblical prophet and the whale, as well as its metaphorical reference to Christ's death and resurrection—and understood this, rather than resonances of Endymion, to be the primary content and sense of these artistic representations.[47] If some Christian viewers of a painting or carving of Jonah reclining beneath the vine generalized its meaning, linking it with Endymion's sleep, we know of at least one early father of the church who was intent upon having believers clearly comprehend the differences between pagan and Christian views of the soul's location after death. David Balch cites the

Figure 11.4 Sarcophagus depicting Selene and Endymion. Detail. Ca. 210 CE. Photo: courtesy of the Getty Museum, Los Angeles, California. Getty Museum 76.AA8.

insistent teaching of Tertullian, who disparaged the view that Christians, upon their deaths, would "have to sleep high up in ether, with the boy-loving worthies of Plato . . . or around the moon with the Endymions of the Stoics." No! life in Paradise with the Lord awaits the faithful.[48] Whether all or most Christians were so concerned, in their mourning and in their commemorations of the dead, to adhere to church-taught notions of the afterlife, we cannot know. One early believer's epitaph, however, reveals just this conviction, articulated as part of his discouragement of grave robbers:

> Neither gold nor silver
> but bones lie here
> awaiting
> the trumpet call. Do not
> disturb the work of God the begetter.[49]

The Cloud-Borne Lamb

We must return to the iconography of our Jonah sarcophagus, where we passed over without comment a noticeable element (Figure 11.5). More significant for our reading of the casket's symbolism than the model figure

Figure 11.5 Lamb reclining on cloud, marble sarcophagus with Jonah scenes. Detail.
© The Trustees of the British Museum, London.

of Endymion is the image suspended above the actions involving Jonah and the sea monster.

What did the sculptor mean to convey by placing the cloud-supported lamb in the area of the Jonah scenes, at the upper left? How are we to understand this figure's relationship to the drama that fills the main part of the panel?

This carved image shows the lamb of God and presents us with an unusual piece of visual exegesis of the saga of Jonah and the whale. The heavenly lamb places Jesus squarely in, or over the Jonah imagery—as a recognizable interpretative enhancement.

Numerous biblical texts could have inspired this connotation. John the Baptist, according to *John* 1:29, saw the approaching Jesus and declared him "the lamb of God who takes away the sin of the world," invoking the Jewish tradition of sacrifices—and perhaps the prophet Isaiah's description (*Isaiah* 53:7) of the suffering servant of God who "was like a lamb that is led to the slaughter, and like a sheep that before its shearers is silent, so he did not open his mouth."[50]

Such themes were part of the Christian imaginary by the time the sarcophagus was produced, and can plausibly be thought to have inspired the carver of this figure of the cloud-borne lamb. With his image of the *agnus dei* placed above the casket's Jonah scenes, another level of meaning is introduced: to the peace of the risen Jesus that Jonah's repose foreshadows is added the dimension of Christ's *sacrificial* death that won freedom from sin for human beings—including the Christian buried in the sarcophagus.

My interpretation of the artist's innovation—the suspended lamb of God meant to convey another sense of the Jonah story—gains support from later Christian art. By the sixth century we find unmistakable and more refined representations of the *agnus dei*, who appears, for example, with a gold halo and surrounded by stars, in a vault mosaic in the church of San Vitale in Ravenna, and also in an ivory decorating the front of the throne of Maximianus, which depicts the lamb held in John the Baptist's hand.[51]

Circling back to the time and occasion in which the artist filled the Roman sarcophagus that concerns us with carved renderings of three episodes from Jonah's story and gave the heavenly lamb a significant place in his image-making, we can entertain the possibility that, over and above the identification of Jonah's and Jesus's ordeal of three days and three nights, Christians spied a further graphic and celebratory "alleleuia"—in the form of the lamb whose death and resurrection was understood to have expiated the world's sins.

Figure 11.6 Jonah scenes on the Murano Diptych, an ivory leaf of a multipiece book cover. Detail. Sixth century CE. Museo Nazionale, Ravenna. © Art Resource, NY.

Jonah and the Christ the Victor: The Murano Diptych

The second Christian artistic representation of the Jonah story we want to examine is a sixth-century ivory diptych that now resides in a Ravenna museum. In the lower register of an iconographic program centered upon the image of Christ enthroned, a panel depicting Jonah's encounter with the *ketos* and his repose beneath the gourd reveals some interesting features (Figure 11.6). We begin here.

The maritime setting of the right-hand scene is well presented, the ship with its rudder, and the varied fish in the background supporting the full action of Jonah's being hurled overboard, head-first. The waiting and apparently

Figure 11.7 Christ enthroned. Murano Diptych. Sixth-century CE ivory book cover. Height 35.5, width 30.5 cm. Museo Nazionale, Ravenna. ©Art Resource, NY.

enthused sea monster is quite large enough to ingest the prophet. The narrative's conclusions are compressed on the left—with the result that disgorged and naked Jonah, as tranquil as he might be beneath the leaves of the plant, seems to recline not on dry land, but the monster's back. Leaning toward Jonah is an angel whose raised arm suggests that he addresses the prophet— a scene absent from the *Book of Jonah* (and from the usual Christian iconography of Jonah scenes).[52] This set of Jonah scenes in Figure 11.7 requires being interpreted in the light of its companion images on the ivory leaf.

The diptych's uppermost panel, which might initially strike the viewer as generalized Christian decoration, has messages to communicate. The two angels (still playing the functional role of classical Victories) hold aloft the emblem of Christ's resurrection triumph—the cross, encircled by a wreath. A motif familiar in sixth-century Ravenna, the same image appears on the south wall of the presbytery in the church of San Vitale, positioned just above a representation of Abel and Melchisedek making their offerings at an altar. We should pause over the obvious: the cross is in the heavens, and bears quite different meanings from its depictions in early Byzantine crucifixion scenes, in many of which the witnesses (and a bit later, the hovering angels) are shown in sorrow.

Despite their small size, the two other angels in the upper corners add important detail to the artist's interpretation. There is little doubt that they represent the archangels Gabriel and Michael, in this case showing as their attributes or accoutrements long-staffed crosses and disks marked either with crosses or with the Greek letter X (the first letter of the title *Christos*).[53] The circular objects are not shields but orbs, or globes, representing the cosmos. In the well-known fourth-century Junius Bassus sarcophagus Jesus reigns from his throne, the orb-like cosmos (personified) under his feet.[54] The Murano ivory's iconography incorporates the globe differently, however, for each of two archangels holds an orb, the sphere signifying the triumphant reign of Christ over all things.[55] More closely inspected, then, images of the angels can be seen to promote an understanding of Christ as ruler of the cosmos. This distinctive Christological theme gains fuller definition in the diptych's other scenes.

The diptych leaf's central image bears all the characteristics of an icon, with its suggestion of timelessness: a frontal portrait of Christ in majesty (with his saintly courtiers) is to be beheld. It is not an overinterpretation to regard the two crosses above Christ the king's royal canopy as reflecting, or participating in, the more dominant heavenly cross pictured just above. Beside and behind Christ's throne are sainted apostles, at least two of whom are identifiable, thanks to Paul's baldness, which distinguishes him from Peter on the right.

Four healing miracles of Jesus positioned around Christ, reigning in majesty, are pictured in a mode that is not strictly literal or historical, and this is obviously the artist's intent. The Jesus of Nazareth that the Gospels describe in the days of his earthly ministry is not represented, but rather Christ resurrected, who is equipped with his cross of triumphant power. The actualized kingship of the Son of God and its potencies are either read back into the narratives of his wonder-working, or—more probably—made visible in a Christology in which the almightiness of his deity was never absent.

It is relatively easy to identify the episodes. On the left Christ heals a blind man—most likely Bartimaeus, who in *Mark* 10:46–53 shouted out when he learned that Jesus the wonder-worker was passing along the Jericho road where he did his begging, and upon "regain[ing] his sight . . . followed Jesus on the way." Below, a devil is exorcised from a man (the Gerasene demoniac in *Mark* 5:1–13 is described as having been restrained by chains). Jesus calls Lazarus out of his tomb, alive (*John* 11:1–44), in a scene on the opposite side of the ivory, and beneath that the paralyzed man in Capernaum (*Mark* 2:1–12) is cured, and prepares to depart with his "mat," or cot, on his shoulders. Here, as in two of the other scenes, Christ's raised and extended hand signifies his potent blessing. To this point, the separate scenes carved in the ivory weave together two aspects of a single theme: Christ reigns as conqueror, since he was raised in triumph from Satan's realm of death, *and* his divine power was fully at work in his miracles, themselves battles against demonic forces. An unambiguous sign of victory and power, the cross is present and important in every scene.

We have met in both Jewish and Christian writings the grouping together of biblical heroes as examples of those who endured trial and were delivered by the hand of God. The smaller scene carved beneath the regal Christ is a familiar one—the three young Hebrews, their hands raised in prayers for help, stand in the midst of high flames. The artist has gone beyond the usual iconography of God's holy ones being tested in order to sustain the consistent vision of this ivory's interpretation: an angel touches the cross to the fire—to quench it, and so accomplish the victims' salvation.

Arriving once more at the lower panel, we have a loose end to repair. After examining the images on the Murano diptych leaf in their particulars, but also with a view to their coherence in relation to each other, it is compelling to understand the unexpected angel facing the reclining Jonah as the bringer of God's endorsement. The angel, like Jesus in the portraits of healings, but without a cross in hand, blesses Jonah, whose life, delivered to the deep and then raised up again, is a deliverance accomplished by God. Not only is Jesus's victory anticipated by what happened during and after Jonah's three days and nights in the huge fish's belly, the angel symbolizes, for this artist, God's mercy and strength, revealed most completely in the person of Christ, the incarnate redeemer, who—the diptych demonstrates—now reigns over earth and heaven.

Generalizations about the interpretations of Jonah in early Christian art are barely possible—especially in light of the fact that I have chosen to focus upon only two objects. It goes without saying, nonetheless, that, like the exegetes, preachers, and poets, the artists accepted as standard the evangelist *Matthew*'s typological argument that made the one story of Jonah also the story of Jesus. What is striking in the cases of our two artistic interpretations is the innovative freshness of their symbolic additions, which stand at some distance from the Christian writers' favored themes. This is especially evident in the introduction of the *agnus dei* image to an otherwise familiar Jonah iconography. The novel insertion created an unexpected perspective on the story. But the same holds true for the incorporation of the Jonah story into the Murano diptych's representation of Christ as ruler over the cosmos (*cosmocrator*), which gives evidence of that artist's ingenuity.[56] Again we discover that the early Christian painters, sculptors, mosaicists, and gem-carvers who treated biblical stories were not content to fashion mere illustrations—the graphic version of literal interpretations. They too were convinced that sacred stories compelled commentary, and they provided these in their own idioms of choice. To study the literary and figural understandings of the Jonah story together, or interfaced, is to be reminded once more of power of this and other biblical-qur'anic narratives to stir imaginations.

The Christianization of Jonah in the churches' early writings and art was carefully considered and culturally conscious. Cognizant of Jewish teachers' judgments which both criticized the prophet for his resistance to God and valorized him as one saved by God, early Christian exegetes found in *Jonah* many lessons parallel to those of the rabbis. The greatest energy at work in Christian appropriation of Jonah, however, stemmed from the identification of his ordeal in the deep with Christ's crucifixion, death, and resurrection. What we saw in the case of Joseph in Egypt is even more strongly present here: the typological strategy which makes the story of a biblical (for the Christians, an Old Testament) figure into a platform for staging the story of the Christian savior. The popularity and effectiveness of this mode of interpretation, with its impressive adaptability to the different needs and purposes of the likes of Tertullian, Origen, Augustine, and Ephrem of Syria, and the sculptor who decorated the Jonah sarcophagus, has, I hope, been fully demonstrated in this chapter. The story of Jonah kept elaborating itself in rabbinic discourse—with ramifications for Israel's self-understanding, even as that regularly was refreshed in ritual. So too did Christians extend the biblical story's meanings in ways at first surprising to us—for example, in transforming a rabbinic account of Jonah's promise that he would capture the Leviathan into a Christian theory of salvation: the great sea monster's defeat when he took the bait, closing his jaws upon the fleshly Son of God. Similar extension or elaboration became apparent in Ephrem's interpretation of Jonah's lot as an anticipation of the divine judgment that all believers would face. And again, this interpretive ambition stirred the carver of the sarcophagus to place the cloud-borne lamb of God above the scenes depicting the prophet's adventures in the whale.

The story of the interpretations of *Jonah* is as rich as the biblical narrative itself. In Jewish and in Christian exegetes' hands, the scriptural text is firmly in place, but it opens to a wealth of meanings important to the communities who retell it.

We now turn to Yunus, "the man of the fish," both as the Qur'an presents him, and as Muslim commentators and artists sought to uncover and comprehend how many things his encounter with God revealed.

CHAPTER 12

⋈

Islam's Yunus

From Anger to Praise

Figure 12.1 Yunus beneath the vine, and the fish. Illumination (1314–1315) in Rashid al-Din's *Jami al-Tawarikh* (*Compendium of Chronicles*). Painting: 11.7cm X 24.3 cm.
© Edinburgh University Library, Edinburgh. Special Collections Arabic ms. 20.

Art historian Thomas Arnold, commenting on this "remarkable" paint-ing wrote in 1928: "The fine drawing of a Chinese carp, as the fish that had swallowed Jonah, is evidence of the influence under which the artist was working in Tabriz; it seems to be gazing with a certain degree of sympathetic interest at the unfortunate prophet, lying exhausted under the gourd tree, after the trying experience of his three days' ordeal."[1] Rashid al-Din's great work treats Jonah under two headings—the history of the prophets, and the history of Israel. This painting, which appears in the former section, depicts a naked and languishing Jonah, and the fish, whose figure dominates the scene.[2] The surrounding text is the author's retelling of the story, relevant qur'anic passages presented in the larger letters. Does this iconography of Jonah reclining—similar in its features to that of Christian artists—bear significantly different meanings?

Yunus stands securely within the Muslim heritage as a prophet-precursor of Muhammad. Answerable to the God who discloses his story in the Qur'an, Yunus is presented and evaluated there according to the expectations of a *rasul* (messenger) and *nabi* (prophet). The tale of the man swallowed by a great fish was in circulation in Muhammad's time and place and was, we know, the subject of discussions with Jews and Christians. Yet several major elements in Jewish and Christian portrayals of the story of Jonah play no significant role in qur'anic and early Muslim tellings of Yunus's life. The difference between Israelites and Gentiles, for example, which was so important in the Hebrew Bible and to the rabbis, barely registers in early Islam's accounts of the prophet's mission to Nineveh. Neither, of course, is the Muslim Jonah seen as a prefigurement of the one Christians worshipped as God's son.

Although Jewish and Christian iterations of the narrative of Jonah and the fish were familiar, the Qur'an and its commentators knew Yunus from what the Prophet was charged by God to recite about him. How does the Muslim Yunus sound and look? What does he signify in *this* religious community's vision of human beings' dealings with their God and with each other? And how might a believer benefit from the example of Yunus, who was simultaneously noted for being a "blameworthy," prayerful, and redeemed prophet?

YUNUS IN THE QUR'AN

The Qur'an's six references to Yunus vary in kind, but I treat them here in a sequence intended to indicate how they most coherently relate to one another. We begin with two passages that identify Jonah in the Muslim understanding of history: he merits God's endorsement, since he, like Muhammad and other men, was a recipient of revelation.

> Surah 4:163 We have inspired you, [O Muhammad]
> as we inspired Noah and the prophets after
> him; We inspired Abraham, and Ishmael, and
> Isaac, and Jacob, and the Tribes, and Jesus, and
> Job, and Jonah, and Aaron, and Solomon;
> and We gave David the Psalms.

> Surah 6:84 And We gave him Abraham, Isaac and Jacob.
> We guided them all.
> And we guided Noah before that;
> and from his descendants David and Solomon
> and Jacob and Joseph and Moses and Aaron.
> Thus do We recompense those who do good.
> 85 And Zacharias and John
> and Jesus and Elias.
> Each of them had integrity.
> 86 And Ishmael and Elisha and Jonah and Lot;
> and each of them We blessed over all people.

Surah 10 has *Yunus* for its title. Only once, however, is he named within it. In a pregnant statement of contrast concerning humanity's responses to God's summons to righteousness, Jonah—or rather, a Jonah-related action—is singled out for praise:

> 10.95 And do not be of those
> who repudiate the signs of God,
> for then you will be losers.
> 96 It is the very ones against whom
> the word of your Lord has proven true
> that do not believe
> 97—even if every sign has come to them—
> until they see the agony.
> 98 Why was there not
> a populace who believed,
> so its faith profited it,
> besides the people of Jonah?
> When they believed, We removed from them
> the torment of disgrace in the world,
> and we let them enjoy life for a while.

Given the disappointing reality that even those blessed by receiving divine words and signs persist in disobeying God, it is extraordinary what happened with "the people of Jonah," Surah 10:98 extols as unparalleled the effective repentance of *all*, not just some percentage of, the Ninevites. Early Muslim Qur'an interpreters will suggest a tighter and more familiar connection between Jonah and the city of Nineveh than appears in Jewish and Christian traditions.

Narrative and Biography

The qur'anic renditions of episodes in the life of Yunus are quite brief, reminding us again of an important difference between the Bible's penchant for extended narrative and the Qur'an's mode, which "simply presents a summary of the story and gets directly to the religio-moral point, each aspect of which is, in fact, central to the Islamic message."[3] In reading two of the passages that Muhammad is charged to recite about Yunus's life (in Surahs 37 and 21), we see a complementary factor in play: fuller knowledge of the prophet's story is presumed.

> Surah 37:139 Jonah was one of the emissaries too.
>> 140 When he fled to the loaded ship,
>> 141 he cast lots and was condemned.
>> 142 Then the whale swallowed him,
>> and he was blameworthy.
>> 143 If not for the fact that he
>> was one who glorified God,
>> 144 he would have remained inside its guts
>> until the day they are resurrected.
>> 145 But We threw him into a wasteland, ailing;
>> 146 and We caused a gourd vine
>> to grow over him,
>> 147 and We sent him as a messenger
>> to a hundred thousand or more.
>> 148 and they believed,
>> so We let them live for a while.

This portion of the qur'anic portrait of Jonah the messenger *is* direct in its religio-moral characterization. The hearer or reader recognizes why the prophet is subject to punishment, and there is no question about the character of his crime. The English translation indicates that he "fled," but the sense of the Arabic term employed is noteworthy, since it derives from a verb, *abaqa*, used to describe a slave's abandonment of his master. Yunus, `abd Allah*, the servant of God, has forsaken his *islam*, his submission, his obedience, to God's will. He has escaped (or so he thinks) from his Lord's realm of authority.

The repair of this breach is described matter-of-factly. Yunus is included in a group who "glorified," or exalted, God. It is important to pause over this passage's key word. "The glorifiers" (*al-musabbihin*) is a participle of the verb *sabbaha*, or "to pray." The prophet Yunus, then, took his place among "performers of prayer"—that is, those who acknowledged and glorified God. Pertinent is a further consideration: the verbal noun stemming from *sabbaha, tasbih*, designates the practice (i.e., doing *tasbih*) of saying "subhana llah"—"God is removed from imperfection!"[4] We shall see momentarily that the Qur'an quotes Yunus himself—as an individual—using this term in reference to God. To discern the significance of his utterance from the deep, later interpreters exegete with great care the prophet's prayer language.

But we return to Surah 37:143 with a question. Though it is clear that Jonah's captivity was ended by his act of praising or glorifying God, is it to be taken for granted that in becoming one of God's worshippers, he confessed and repented his blameworthiness? Some translators have assumed so, making insertions—for example, Abdullah Usuf Ali's rendering: "Had it not been that he (repented and) glorified Allah/He would certainly have remained inside the Fish till the Day of Resurrection."[5] Muslim commentators developed their own ideas of this passage's meaning by considering it in conjunction with other qur'anic references to Yunus.

In Surah 21, *Al-Anbiya'* (The Prophets), the divine injunction to make mention of Yunus occurs between similarly pithy summarizing notices about Solomon, Job, Ishmael, Idris (who is thought to be Enoch) and—after Yunus—Zachariah and Maryam (Mary). The brief notice about the prophet, however, discloses important information, including his own words spoken from within the fish's belly:

> 21:87 And there was Jonah:
> when he went off in anger,
> he thought that We had no power over him.
> But then he called out in the darknesses,
> "There is no God but You;
> glory to You—I was in the wrong!"
> 88 So We answered him,
> and rescued him from affliction:
> thus do We rescue those who believe.

The passage intimates the cause of the prophet's anger, and seems to suggest the character of his crime—namely, his flight. Yet will those who later retell this story find other possible meanings in this abbreviated piece of narrative? Jonah, running away, did not believe that God would hold him to account, but upon finding himself captive in the fish's belly and in the deep ("the darknesses"), he uttered aloud—what? Two confessions, different in kind: first, a declaration of faith proper to a believer: You alone are God, You are most glorious—and then, second, a statement of repentance, an acknowledgment of his own sinfulness.

In Yunus's first utterance we encounter language from Islam's basic statement of faith, the *Shahadah* ("There is no god but God, and Muhammad is his prophet"). In Yunus's direct address we find, naturally, "You" (*anta*) in the place of "God" (*allah*). In saying next, "Glory to You," or, as it might be translated, "You are removed from imperfection (*subhanaka*)." With the last phrase of his prayer, the prophet's confession of sin comes to unambiguous expression. He declares that he was (before now...before this declaration) one of the misguided, the errant.

Finally, we learn more about what transpired between Yunus and his Lord in a piece of moral instruction given to Muhammad:

> 68:48 Be patient for the judgment of your Lord,
> and don't be like the one in the whale,
> as he cried out while he was depressed.
> 49 If not that a favor from his Lord overtook him, he would have been thrown
> onto the naked shore while he was censured.
> 50 But his Lord selected him
> and made him one of the righteous.

This teaching presumes that it was an agitated Jonah who urgently cried out to God from within the great fish—that he was unable to wait for the decision and action God would take in his case. The patience recommended to Muhammad is unlike and superior to the behavior of Dhu-n-Nun, the man of the fish. Because hostility to Muhammad and his message is a theme that runs through this Surah, Al-Qalam (The Pen), some modern interpreters suggest that the advice given in 68:48 relates to the Prophet's own situation, urging that Muhammad not "give in to despair or anger at the opposition shown to him by most of his contemporaries in Mecca, but to persevere in his prophetic mission."[6] The force of the criticism of Yunus remains clear and intelligible: as if he did not trust in God's plan, Yunus's crying out was a distress call pressing, rather than trusting, God, for a result—for his salvation.

Surah 68:49 contains another "if x had not occurred" claim, but here the actor is not Yunus, glorifying God. Rather, a "favor"—an act of divine mercy—is what delivered the prophet onto the dry land, *pardoned* for his offense against God. Had Jonah not been shown this favor, or grace, by his Lord, he would have landed, condemned, on the shore and died as one among the sinners, still "blameworthy." Surah 68:50 sums up the passage: It was God's initiative to elect Jonah and place him among the righteous. In all likelihood we are to infer, on the basis of 21:88, that God's gracious act came in response to the prophet's confession, even though this sequence goes unmentioned here.

The qur'anic references to Yunus might be summarized in this way: a receiver of revelation, he was one of God's elected prophets and messengers (4:163; 6:86); the "people of Jonah" in Nineveh were unique in the quality of their repentance and belief, and thus were spared divine punishment—for a time (10:98); fleeing and boarding a ship, blameworthy Yunus, after lots were cast, was thrown into the sea and swallowed by the fish; after his prayer—the acknowledgment and praise of his God—God rescued Yunus and dispatched him, ailing, on a shore, where God grew a gourd vine to protect him; God then sent him to bring to belief the "hundred thousands, or more" (37:139–148); angry Yunus (in a parallel account), believing he could escape to a place beyond God's reach, found himself in the "darknesses," and from there made his profession of faith, admitting his wrongdoing (21:87–88); Yunus's impatience with God's purposes was a warning to Muhammad; thanks to his Lord's favor and mercy, Yunus was rescued and was made one of the righteous (68:48–50).

Retellers of Yunus's story, his dealings with God and with the people of the city of thousands, will present us with several unexpected questions. Is Yunus a Jewish prophet sent to a foreign city, or does he himself hail from Nineveh? Did Yunus's encounter with the great fish happen before or after his mission to Nineveh? How many prophetic encounters did he have with the city, and what is it that prompted his attempted flight to the seacoast? The Qur'an seems to have suggested to its interpreters a sequence of events different from that found in the biblical *Book of Jonah*.

Like the Jewish and Christian exegetes, Muslim Qur'an commentators also wrestled with Jonah's contradictions. On the positive side of the ledger, he was a prophet who brought God's salvation to the people of the great city "for a while," and was singled out for his glorifying of God. On the other side, Jonah was angry, impatient, and defiant in resisting the guidance of God.

Where, then, does Yunus the Muslim prophet stand in the ranks of God's preferred ones? Some such question had arisen early, as an authoritative *hadith* reveals: "The Prophet said, 'None of you should say that I am better than Yunus'" (*Sahih Bukhari* 4.55.642).

No superiority was to be accorded to one prophet over the others, according to Muhammad. That Yunus *was* talked about as one less worthy, however, created the need for the Prophet's defense of him.

Closely related to this notion of the equality of the prophets was a doctrine developed by Shi'a thinkers in the eighth century that won widespread Muslim approval thereafter. God's messengers were invulnerable to sin and error because they had been granted `ismat al-anbiya, "protection of the prophets."[7] This piece of prophetology maintaining the principle of their freedom from sin retained its force even though the faults and sins of particular prophets like Yunus were plainly chronicled both in the Qur'an and in later works recounting the "lives of the prophets." The Muslim commentators on Yunus's life and behavior to whom we now turn will be seen negotiating, or finessing, the problem in their religion's ways of honoring a once "blameworthy" messenger of the Most High.

YUNUS FROM SCRIPTURE TO LEGENDS: THREE NOTABLE MUSLIM COMMENTATORS

Relatively compressed qur'anic notices of Yunus invited further exploration of his dramatic saga; additions to, and adaptations of, the narrative were inevitable. Muslim exegetes and storytellers were aware of the many Jewish and Christian Jonah traditions in circulation and did, in varying measures, include these in their representations of the prophet. Particular elements in the Qur'an's picture of Yunus, as well as Muslim assumptions about the character and actions of God are, however, the primary components in their interpretations.

The sweep, the common threads, and the changes in Muslim understandings of Yunus and the lessons of his story are best seen by considering important sections in the commentaries of three celebrated interpreters: Ibn Ishaq (704–767), al-Tha`labi (d. 1036), and al Kisa'i, who composed his *Stories of the Prophets* just prior to 1200 CE.

Ibn Ishaq

In the century following Muhammad's death, the well-traveled scholar Ibn Ishaq settled in the new city of Baghdad, under appointment to tutor the son of the Abbasid caliph, al-Mansur. Renowned as a collector of *hadith* reports, Ibn Ishaq shared earliest Islam's interest in Jewish and Christian teachings about God's prophets, and put his knowledge of these sources to excellent use in his major work, the *Sirah* (*The Life of the Prophet*). A three-part history, the *Sirah* recounted events from the world's creation to pre-Islamic Arab times, recounted Muhammad's life in his early years (up to the onset of the divine revelations to him), and then gave major attention to the remainder of the Prophet's career—the migration to Medinah, his religious and military feats, and the circumstances of his death.[8] Ibn Ishaq's *Sirah,* Gordon Newby wrote, "helped form an image of Muhammad that accounted for the rise of Islam, explained the course of the history of the world, established the primacy of the Quranic text as scripture, and installed Muhammad as the central religious authority of Islam."[9]

The *Sirah*'s opening section, filled with "sacred biographies" of prophets who preceded Muhammad, includes an intriguing portrait of Jonah.[10] Ibn Ishaq placed Jonah chonologically after Jesus, exposing his supposition that the prophet's father was not the biblical Ammitai (*Jonah* 1:1) but rather Mattai, or Matthew, one of Jesus's disciples (*Mark* 2:14, *Matthew* 9:9) and, according to early church teachings, one of the Gospel writers. A tradition stemming from one of Ibn Ishaq's favorite sources, Ibn `Abbas, then opens his recounting of the Jonah narrative:

> God, the Most High, sent Jonah to the people of his town, and they opposed what he brought to them and resisted him. When they did that, God revealed to him: I am going to send them a punishment on such-and-such a day, so go from their midst, and tell the townspeople what punishment God has promised them.[11]

In Ibn Ishaq's recounting there is no hint that Jonah comes from Israel, or that he is a Jew about to confront a people to whom he is a stranger. Rather, the influence of Surah 10:98 is at work: wherever the prophet is sent *from*, God is directing him to address his fellow Ninevites.

How are we to understand the sequence of events Ibn Ishaq reports? After approaching the people of his city with "what he brought with him," the prophet was rebuffed. In response to this, God chose to announce the precise time of the drastic punishment that will fall upon the city, revealing the appointed day to his prophet. Jonah is to declare this warning to the Ninevites, and *then* heed the Most High's' command to depart—to remove himself from the location of the imminent catastrophe.

At this juncture in Ibn Ishaq's rendition of the story, we notice that Jonah's departure from the people's midst was counseled by God. The prophet obeyed. Also evident in his narration is its contrast with the Hebrew Bible's account in *Jonah* 3, where nonresistant compliance to God's warning by Nineveh's king and people and animals occurs, and is a pivotal element in the scriptural plot line.

Believing, according to Ibn Ishaq, that the containment of their prophet within Nineveh would forestall the divine judgment, the people in Jonah's town kept him under close watch. Nevertheless, on the eve of the appointed punishment of Nineveh, Jonah withdrew from the city. Within Nineveh, the anxious and fearful inhabitants took their own action, begging God's mercy—and receiving it.

> Meanwhile Jonah was waiting for the report of the town and its people. A passerby came, and Jonah said, "What did the people do?" He said, "When their prophet left their midst, they knew that he had told them the truth about the punishment he had promised them, so they cried out to God and repented to Him, and He accepted it from them." Jonah was angry at that and said, "By God, I will not return to them as a liar, ever! I promised them a punishment on that day, and then it is turned from them." Anger passed over his face, and the Devil caused him to make a mistake.[12]

Ibn Ishaq asserts that Yunus grew angry at *this* point, upon learning that God had cancelled the punishment of Nineveh, overriding what he himself had prophesied. Yunus promptly vowed that he would never return to his city, for God's pardon had rendered him a lying, or false, prophet. Echoes of Jewish and Christian representations of Jonah's deep agitation and its cause are evident here—and also in the added suggestion that the prophet's "mistake" was influenced by Iblis, the evil one.

If falling under Satan's sway was Yunus's fundamental problem, interpreters did not believe it was his only one. Ibn Ishaq quotes a tradition stemming from Wahb b. Munabbih the Yemenite, who reported that he had heard that Yunus

> was a righteous servant but was narrow of frame, so that when the weight of prophethood came to him, he could only bear it a little, breaking under it . . . [and that] he threw it in front of him and went fleeing from it.[13]

Not at issue in this opinion was the physical bulk of prophethood, of course, but Yunus's incapacities and failings. As Yunus fled, God spoke to him about the need for patience (Surah 68:48), the absence of which caused him to cast off his Lord's command. To this criticism of Yunus are added the words in Surah 21:87: "when he went off in anger, he thought that We had no power over him." The prophet's wrath was coupled with what can be regardeded as disregard for, or defiance of, God's sovereignty.[14]

Various other explanations of Jonah's anger—often in its relation to the behavior of the Ninevites—gained popularity. In rapid order Ibn Ishaq reports differing hypotheses:

> It is asserted that Jonah's townsfolk did what they did (i.e., repent) unaware that a prophet of the Lord would be annoyed and would regard their actions as important. Jonah was angry at their chief and had gone away from his people angry, for they had done a serious thing [i.e., in repenting] which they had (ear-lier) disavowed. This is the reason that those who say Jonah went away angry from his Lord differ about the reason for his departure. Some of them say that he only did what he did because of an aversion to being among a people who had put him to the test. Others say that it was because of the discrepancy about what he had promised them (i.e., punishment) and their being spared, and he did not know the reason that the trial was lifted from them. Some of those who said this said that there were those among his people who would kill anyone who tested by means of a lie, so perhaps they would kill him because of his promise of punishment and its not coming down on them as he had promised.[15]

The passage shows us a Muslim interpreter wrestling, like his Jewish counterparts, with opposing understandings of Jonah's prophesying: was he a true prophet, in that he was called by God and because God's pur-poses *were fulfilled through him*, or was he a false prophet, a liar, because what he foretold did not come to pass? The varied opinions about Jonah's anger Ibn Ishaq stacked together in a mix of arguments and in notices about misunderstandings between the prophet, the people of his city, and God. New subtleties come to the surface. How, Yunus wonders, could the firm-minded people he unsuccessfully warned have changed their minds, and repented? The Ninevites, on the other hand, cannot imagine that their prophet would be unhappy at their turning toward God. Was it the contrast between what Yunus promised and what the people actually experienced, that so deeply aggravated him? Ibn Ishaq leaves all of the questions stand-ing, and unresolved.

We have been marking significant differences in the three religions' understandings of the same stories, and here we meet yet another clear and tell-tale example: Ibn Ishaq draws upon qur'anic suggestions that Yunus's rebellion was motivated by what occurred *in* Nineveh—not (as the biblical text of both the Jews and Christians proposes) when he was first commanded to travel there to pronounce God's command that they repent from their sins. Ibn Ishaq's attitudes toward the prophet's character—and especially the grounds for his displeasure with and hostility toward his God—were thus influenced and shaped by the Qur'an's different suggestions about what things happened, and in what sequence.

According to Ibn Ishaq and his sources, what befell Yunus when he was swallowed by the fish and then spit out on the shore? The author's narration draws upon a *hadith* reporting Muhammad's view that God, wanting to make him a captive in the fish's belly, "inspired" the fish to ingest him without doing damage to his flesh or breaking his bones. God will similarly stimulate his wayward prophet.

> When he arrived at the bottom of the sea, Jonah heard a noise, and said to himself, "What is this?" God inspired him while he was in the belly of the fish, and he [Jonah] heard angels praising Him. They said, "O, our Lord, we hear a weak voice in a faraway place." God said, "That is my servant Jonah, who was rebellious to me, and I have imprisoned him in the belly of a fish in the sea." They said, "Is that the righteous servant from whom there used to ascend good deeds to you every night and day?" He said, "Yes." So they intervened for him, and God ordered the fish to cast Jonah up on the shore, as He said. He was emaciated, and his emaciation was as God described: the fish cast him on the shore as a newborn child without flesh and with broken arms.[16]

Ibn Ishaq obviously pushes the storyline beyond what the Qur'an itself discloses. Among "those who exalt God" (37:143) are now found angels whose praises are audible even to the prophet sunk in the sea's depths. These angels then hear his weak voice (is the prophet uttering his statement of faith, and confessing his fault?), but God must identify "rebellious" Jonah to them.

The drama of the angels' intercession with God on behalf of Jonah is rich both in imagery and implications. Recalling to God Jonah's fine deeds that preceded his obstinacy, their testimony, it appears, is sufficient to cause God to retrieve the prophet from his imprisonment. The qur'anic testimony about God's responsiveness to the penitence of "the people of Jonah" leaves little doubt about what sways the divine will. Yet in this piece of commentary, while the angels make the case that prior to his wrongdoing Jonah's record of righteousness and noble actions was superlative, it is as if the angels' intercession—in itself—won the prophet's redemption. Perhaps the prophet's confession from the deep—that he was among the wrongdoers—is understood to have taken place, but God's identification of Jonah as rebellious, rather than penitent, does not enforce that assumption. In Islamic eschatology, various angels play key roles at the Judgment in identifying (and negotiating) a human being's faithfulness and virtue.[17]

Ibn Ishaq's introduction of Jonah's winged intercessors improvised on these teachings.

Finally, God's "inspiration" of the fish to preserve Jonah intact at the time of his swallowing apparently did not fully protect the prophet during his time within its belly, nor during his ejection. Jonah emerges "ailing," a damaged and fragile man. Ibn Ishaq believes himself to be clarifying the Qur'an's description of Jonah's illness (the Arabic term *saqim* [37:145] means "sick," with no special connotations) with his odd picture of "newborn" Jonah. The image is reminiscent of a passage in the Christian Jonah hymns of Ephrem of Syria, in which the prophet's being first "conceived and born as in nature," is contrasted with the event in which he was "once more conceived unnaturally." Who, Ephrem had asked, ever saw "a fetus delivered from a mouth"?[18]

But something more must be involved in Ibn Ishaq's description of the weakened Jonah who is vomited forth. It is a picture more curiously provocative than informative—unless some kind of symbolic meaning is being advanced in this imaging of the rescued prophet. Has Yunus survived, but only barely, a test put to him by his Lord? Does he now require further angelic assistance—healing and the covering of his nakedness? Other Muslim interpreters, especially painters, will keep these questions alive.

Ibn Ishaq's Yunus account provides an early display of Muslim exegetes' and storytellers' awareness—and selective adaptations—of the many Jewish and Christian Jonah traditions in circulation and ready for use. Dominantly, however, particular elements in the Qur'an's representation of Yunus, as well as Muslim assumptions about the ways of God and humans (prophets in particular), undergird the interpreters' expositions.

Al-Tha`labi

Writing more than two and a half centuries after Ibn Ishaq, al-Tha`labi opened the Jonah portion of his *Lives of the Prophets* with an intriguing correction of a prevailing tradition, asserting that Amittai was a woman, not a man. Significance attaches to the full name of the prophet, therefore: "the ancestry of none of the prophets is ascribed to his mother except Jesus, son of Mary, and Jonah, son of Amittai."[19] The claim and its positive connotation will become clearer when we examine the title of Jesus in this book's concluding study of Mary/Maryam; it suffices at this juncture to notice that the author points to a particular—and lofty—status that belongs to the prophet Jonah by the unusual virtue of bearing his mother's rather than his father's name.

Al-Tha'labi's introduction of Yunus as the one about whom Muhammad remarked, "It is not proper for anyone to say, 'I am better than Jonah,'" is followed by what appears to be a defense of Jonah's credentials: Surah 21:87, with its acknowledgment of the prophet's angry flight, followed by his cry from the darkness, "There is no God but You—I was in the wrong."[20]

Citing the reports of other scholars, al-Tha'labi locates the pious, God-serving Yunus upon a mountain in Nineveh, in the region of Mosul. Because his people were idol-worshippers, God urged Yunus to challenge their unbelief, summoning them to monotheism. In the description of the prophet's practices we find strong intimations of Muhammad's practice of retreating from Mecca to the nearby hills, and particularly to the cave named Hira, seeking places he might use for contemplation and prayer. But a problematic feature of Yunus's character has also influenced the commentator's placement of him:

> Jonah was a pious man who could not endure the people, so he stayed on the mountain to worship God there. He recited beautifully and the wild beasts listened to him as they had listened to David in his time. But anger would take hold of him and therefore the Messenger of God forbade anyone to be like him in the haste and unsteadiness that appeared from him. God said, "So bear with patience, as the apostles who were constant bore" (46:35). And God also said, "and do not be like the one of the fish" (68:48) because he had little patience with his people and little sociability.[21]

The hermit-like Ninevite is described by the saying attributed to Muhammad that Ibn Ishaq had invoked: "Jonah, son of Amittai, was hasty and unsteady, and when he took the burden of prophecy upon himself, he fell apart under it, and his people fell apart under the heavy burden, and therefore for that reason he left them in anger." Al-Tha'labi noticeably extends the effects of Jonah's collapse to his people, whose faltering contributes to the prophet's damning attribute.

Al-Tha'labi, like his predecessor, lets his readers know that the cause of Jonah's anger is a topic much debated. Some discovered the origin of the prophet's ire in an earlier episode in his career. Jonah, a native of Palestine, had resisted an order by the Jewish king, Hezekiah, to use his prophetic threats to bring some of Israel's tribes under his sway. Isaiah had recommended Jonah to the king on the grounds that he was "strong and faithful." But receiving a negative answer when he confronted Hezekiah with the question "Has *God* ordered you to send me out?" Jonah dismissed the king and his orders, noting that other prophets were also "strong and faithful"—and available: "They reviled him and he departed in anger [directed] towards the prophet (Isaiah), the king, and his people . . . [and] came to the Mediterranean Sea and certain things happened to him there."[22]

Al-Hasan al-Basri (d. 728), an important Muslim intellectual we shall meet again in this chapter, held the view we encountered earlier—namely, that the anger of Yunus was directed to his Lord, who urged the prophet to go *immediately* to his (own) people to warn them of their answerability to Him. "Being a man in whose character there was anger, he said, 'My Lord has hurried me so that I cannot grab my sandal.'"[23] Another version of the same argument was attributed to Ibn `Abbas:

> Gabriel came to Jonah and said to him, "Hurry to the people of Nineveh, and warn them that punishment has already reached them if they will not repent." Jonah said, "I should like to seek a riding animal," but Gabriel said, "the matter must be faster than that." So Jonah became angry and departed for the sea. He boarded a ship and certain events took place with him.[24]

Al-Tha`labi comments that these accounts of Jonah's anger suggest that Jonah's mission took place *after* his escape from the fish's belly, finding support in Surah 37:14: "We sent him to one hundred thousand men or more." Others, he reports, see the sequence differently—believing that Jonah's anger was subsequent to his encounter with his people (in Nineveh) and God's pardon of them, at which time he departed for the sea, having been made a liar ("I promised them punishment on a certain day and it did not come").[25] A further rationale (again, familiar to us, but now more developed) was given for the prophet's flight:

> In some accounts it is said that his people had the custom of killing those against whom they proved falsehood, so when the punishment that he promised them did not come at the appointed time, he feared that they would kill him, and that is why he became angry. He said, "How can I return to my people when You failed to keep the promise to them?", not knowing the reason why punishment was diverted from them, having already departed from their midst because of the impending punishment.[26]

This interpretation is a twist on the problem of Jonah's (self-concerned) complaint against God as it appears explicitly in the biblical *Book of Jonah* and in the commentaries of the rabbis, for here the issue (and purportedly the cause of the prophet's ire) is the danger posed to Jonah by his townsfolk, who executed false prophets.

Again we should note that in these writings there is scant suggestion that the resentment of Yunus stems from his antipathy for the Ninevites (even though they are "idolaters") as a people, a race, or a nation foreign to him. While some rabbis had criticized Jonah for not recognizing God's sovereign care for all nations, Muslim exegetes and storytellers regard the people in the "city of Jonah," prior to their redemption, as belonging to the errant masses among humankind who do not follow the path of truth, who do not heed the God to whom they will answer in the Day of Judgment.

Al-Tha`labi asserts that Jonah's prophecy to the Ninevites was a protracted process, and that those who believed in him were few (initially, only one scholar and an ascetic). "Ibn `Abbas, Ibn Mas`ud and others" held that part of Jonah's warning—delivered thirty-seven days into the period before God's punishment would arrive—included the prediction that the Ninevites would change in color.[27] When he saw that this transformation occurred on the night of the fortieth day, Yunus departed, certain that the people were doomed. And indeed, on the next morning, "the punishment had covered them." One description of this phenomenon features an ominous smoking cloud that settled on their city, turning the people's skin black, and sending them, in vain, to search out "their prophet Jonah."[28] In desperation they assembled with their children and animals in the hills, and begged for—and received—God's forgiveness: "This happened on the day of `Ashura, it was said it was a Wednesday in the middle of Shawwal."[29] There was good reason for al-Tha`labi to note the date. He knew that Muhammad, made aware of the Medinan Jews' observance of the Day of Atonement, had adopted it and recommended it to his followers—naming `Ashura (the tenth of Muharram)—as a day set apart for fasting.[30] In connection with the drama of Yunus's life, the author has especially marked the event of the dramatic repentance and salvation of the prophet's people, paving the way for a description of the Ninevites' penitential fasting and their reformed mode of living: "they rescinded all the injustices among themselves, so that if a man came to a stone upon which he had placed the foundation of his building, he would remove it and return it."[31] All former transgressions were atoned for, great and small.

Thorny and important theological questions appear next in al-Tha`labi's retelling of Yunus's story. Discussion of the prophet's attitude and action pivot on the qur'anic statement in 21:87, where the words of God declare that the prophet, going away in anger, "thought that We would not decree [anything] upon him," as if (adds al-Tha`labi) "to say that We would not sentence him to punishment."[32]

Fundamental issues in Islam's understandings of theodicy—God's justice—recognizably stand behind these few pages in al-Tha`labi's commentary. Just what in the lives and actions of his creatures does God control—or do? Were the very intentions and actions of Yunus preordained—his disobedience and his punishment anticipated and effected by God?

The majority of the exegetes, al-Tha'labi says, take a view based on "what the Arabs say"—namely, that "God decrees a thing that He decrees by predestination, and determines his decree by power."[33] Reinforcement of this viewpoint, al-Tha'labi writes, came from qur'anic passages like Surah 87:3, which describes God as the one "who has destined and guided." One implication of such a strong view of fore-ordained actions would be that Yunus was helpless not only in his attempt to flee his Lord's realm of influence, but also helpless in the first place to resist doing the evil he committed—since his disobedience was a thing decreed. Advocates of this picture of God's omnipotence pointed to the language of Surah 13:27: "Say, God lets anyone wander at will," understanding it to signify that God's allowing is God's action in a person's wandering.

Al-Tha'labi could not have chosen a more prestigious foe of predestinarian thinking than al-Hasan al-Basri, who within a century after Muhammad's death challenged this doctrine of God, being an early Qadaraite—a believer in free will. His arguments and the qur'anic texts supporting them are preserved in a letter requested by the caliph 'Abd al-Malik, who was concerned about rumors he'd heard of al-Hasan's controversial teachings on the subject.[34] Writing in the final years of the seventh century, al-Hasan commenced his apologia to the "Commander of the Faitful" by pointing to the words in Surah 51:56: "I did not create the jinn and humankind except to worship me."[35] By al-Hasan's reasoning, "God is not one to create them for a purpose and then intervene between them and it (to prevent them from fulfilling it) because God does not wrong (His) servants" (citing Surah 3:182). God, that is to say, would not interfere in his creatures' free efforts to worship and obey him.

When his opponents supported their predestinarian doctrine by holding up Surah 4:78's assertion that "all is from God," al-Hasan responded by referring to the words preceding it: "What comes to you of good is from God, but what comes to you of evil, [O man], is from yourself."[36] To think of God as one who "destines and guides" all that occurs is erroneous, al-Hasan warns, on two grounds: first it attributes evil to God—suggesting that God leads astray his creatures, and second, it gives license to some who "declare themselves innocent and attribute iniquity (*zulm*) to their Lord."[37]

In light of his insistence that the covenant between God and his creatures preserves to the latter their freedom of will and action, we are prepared for what al-Hasan is quoted by al-Tha'labi as having said about Jonah's flight and God's decree. According to him, it happened that: "when Jonah did wrong and went off in anger towards his Lord . . . it was Satan who made him err, so that [Jonah] thought that God would not be able to act against *him*"—that is, since Satan was responsible.[38]

Al-Hasan cleverly pictures Yunus's calculation of *which* actor—both making free choices to resist God—will be held responsible for his anger and flight from God. His interpretation is not fashioned for entertainment's sake. It is significant that al-Hasan gives some agency to Satan for Yunus's evil deed. The idea at work here and elsewhere as far as the Qadarites (and later, the school of thought called the Mu'tazalites) are concerned is to make sure that evil deeds are not attributed to God under any shape or form, for, after all, God is good and God cannot be the author of evil.[39]

For al-Hasan, the phrase "he thought" in 21:78 indicated Yunus's sinful conviction (inspired by Satan) that God's decree (that he would be judged for his disobedience) *could not* impede Yunus's choice to flee from God's realm of authority. In other words, chosen actions either to obey or disobey, rather than the irresistble force of what God decreed beforehand, are operative at the heart of the Yunus narrative—and at the heart of correct understanding of the relationship within which God and his creatures interact. In his letter to the caliph, al-Hasan makes an observation about the deeds—or misdeeds—of two other prophets of God that is fully consistent with his treatment of what Junus "thought" in Surah 21:78. The scholar Michael Schwarz, who translated and analyzed the text, wrote:

> [Al-Hasan] quotes verses from the Koran in which Adam says that he has "wronged his own soul" (Koran VII, 23) and Moses describes his sin of murder as "the work of Satan" (Koran XXVIII, 15-16). Moses did not think his sin had come from God, nor did Adam deem his to be of God's decree and determination (*qada' wa-qadar*). Nobody would like to be considered the "author of wrong" (*sahib al-zulm*). So how dare these people attribute to God what they would not have approved when applied to themselves?

Like the crimes of Adam and Moses, Yunus's anger and his decision to flee from God was Satan-inspired, *but also his fault*. Al-Hasan rejected as blasphemous the belief that the prophet's wrongdoing "had come from God."

What Jonah thought or imagined about God's decree remained a matter of debate, the various proposed solutions leaving different pictures of the prophet's character, and of his cognizance of the God he intended to defy. For the Shi'a Muslims there were deep reservations about acknowledging (and certainly about calling attention to) the faults of Yunus and other prophets, since they were believed to enjoy protection against sin and error. But from a wider and more comparative perspective, we meet again—in Muslim rather than Jewish and Christian frames of thought—

the commentators' dilemma in weighing not only the workings of God's fairness, but also the virtues and vices of him about whom Muhammad said, "None of you should say that I am better than Yunus [son of] Matta."[40] And once more, surrounding that judgment are questions of the freedom, or kinds of freedom, accorded to the creature of a providential deity.

Before leaving this passage in al-Tha`labi's commentary that is concerned with theodicy, we cannot pass over in silence one quite odd result of doing comparisons: two predestinarian theologies protect God's providence with strikingly different tactics and results: on the one hand, St. Augustine concluded that the human being, damaged by original sin, was incapable of *not* sinning (by God's decree of punishment for consuming the fruit in the Garden); on the other hand, the predestinarianism of al-Hasan's foes led them to claim that humans cannot be held answerable for sin, since those deeds owe their origins to God's decree and determination (*qada' wa-qadar*).

Another important theme in al-Tha`labi's *Qisas al-Anbiya'* has to do with Jonah's prayer, or cry, from the deep.

> Sa`id b. al-Musayyab related [this], on the authority of Sa`d b. Malik, who said, "I heard the Messenger of Allah say, 'When the name of God is invoked, He answers; and when something is requested by His name, He gives the prayer of Jonah, son of Ammitai.' So I asked, 'Messenger of Allah, is [the prayer] the exclusive possession of Jonah, son of Ammitai, or does it belong to the community of Muslims?' He responded, 'It is the special possession of Jonah and of the community of Muslims as a group when they invoke His name. Did you not hear the words of God—*Then he called out from the darknesses: [There is no god other than You, all glory to you; surely I was a sinner. We heard his cry and saved him from anguish.] That is how We deliver those who believe*' (21:87–88)—When Jonah invoked it, the angels pleaded that God command the fish, so He cast him up on the shore of Nineveh."[41]

Some commentators, we noted, argued that Jonah offered up his prayer in extreme distress—as an act of desperation—when he heard sea creatures exalting God. Al-Tha`labi offers a very different proposal: the prophet's words from the deep held particular force, meriting God's favor. Again, a saying of Muhammad contributes to the honoring of Jonah's prayer. He underlines the desirability of having it as a supplication of special power in the petitionary worship of all Muslims. Modern Muslim teachers and websites continue to recommend this particular "glorious verse" (*ayatul karima*), 21.87, as a prayer available and useful to persons hoping to fulfill a worthy desire, or to ward off afflictions, or to endure hard times. The virtue—and power—of Jonah's prayer, similar in language to the *Shahadah*, its endorsement by Muhammad, and its ensuing popularity among wor-shippers, contributed mightily to Islam's positive estimate of "the man of the fish."

A change is noticeable when al-Tha`labi turns to conclude Yunus's story; his final portrait of the prophet unfolds in the style of a folk-tale expected to resolve problems and finish properly. Departing Nineveh as God's judg-ment descends upon it, the prophet encounters a young shepherd boy who, when asked, identifies himself as being "from the people of Jonah." The boy is told to inform the people of Nineveh that he has met Jonah, and he makes a perspicacious reply: "If you are Jonah," he says, "then you know [our city's custom] that if I do not have proof [of what I say], I will be killed. So who can bear witness for me?"[42] Jonah addresses the valley in which they stand, then a tree, and a sheep, commanding the three to be the boy's witnesses when testimony is required. Predictably, the city's king, hearing that the lad had encountered Jonah, sentenced him to death—as a liar. Crying out that he had "evidence," the boy was allowed to take witnesses to the location where he would have his claim verified:

> They came to the valley, the tree, and the ewe, and he said, "I beg you, by God, did Jonah make your swear?" "Yes," they answered, and the people [with the boy] returned frightened. They said to the king, "The tree, the earth, and the ewe have borne witness for him." The king then took the boy's hand and seated him on his throne, saying, "you are more worthy of this place than I." He remained with them, and that boy put their affairs in order for forty years. In the meantime, they had gone out and searched for Jonah. They found him, rejoiced in him, and believed in him, and he [too] put their affairs in order.[43]

Grandly acknowledged and "believed in," the prophet is celebrated by his fellow Ninevites. It is striking that our commentator felt compelled to elab-orate further, this time intent upon reflecting yet another facet of Yunus's worthiness:

> It is said that when the tree, the earth, and the ewe bore witness for the boy, it was the ewe . . . that said to them, "If you want Jonah, go down into the wadi." They went, and lo, there was Jonah. They dropped to his feet, kissing them, and asked whether he would enter the city with them. He replied, "There is no need for me to be in your city." But they cried and implored him, so he consented to go with them. He was brought a wagon of silver and was seated on it, but Gabriel appeared to him, biting his fingers, proclaiming, "This is the seat of oppressors," and Jonah jumped off the wagon and began to walk, until he entered the city with them. He remained with his family and his children for forty nights. Then

he departed, journeying, and the king departed with him, and the shepherd boy became king of this city, as we have related. The two travelers continued worshipping God until they died. The prophethood of Jonah was in the time of the petty kings. But God is All-knowing.[44]

These last scenes in al-Thaʿlabi's legend of Jonah incorporate old and new themes, all of them doing the service of paying high—but the proper kind of—honor to the prophet. We learn that the Ninevites' adoration of their messenger from God poses a danger when Gabriel appears, making the same gesture he had made during Yusuf's temptation by Zulaykha. Gabriel's declaration that the accoutrements of kings signal oppression causes Yunus to leap from the royal carriage, and make a humble re-entry of the city, walking amidst his people. In the enthronement of the presumably guileless shepherd boy, the thematic critique of monarchs and the importance of just and compassionate rule gain emphasis, even though the last lines of the passage fail to identify the "petty rulers" or the time in which Jonah encountered them. That was for God to know.

Also detectable in this passage are signs of another development coming to the fore in the commentator's own era—the emergence of holy men who practiced intense disciplines of prayer, often attracting disciples (and onlookers). Enthused devotion led to ritual celebrations of prophets, and to the establishment of acts of reverence at their tombs. Similar honors were paid to esteemed teachers and ascetics. In full bloom as a signal feature of Sufism, these kinds of observances characterized a broad movement within Islam, even though some criticized these practices of popular piety centered on prophets and saints on the grounds that they diluted or misdirected the holy honor and recognition due to God alone. We notice that al-Thaʿlabi is entirely comfortable in creating a final scene for Yunus's life that extends his prophethood in such a way that it incorporates the image of an adept in worship (*zikr*) who is capable of training another. Initially known as the one whose prayer for deliverance from the fish was effective (and imitable), Yunus in his last days, according to al-Thaʿlabi, manifested another dimension of his servanthood to God, becoming a holy man entirely consumed in praying.

Al-Kisa'i

Writing just before 1200, al Kisa'i (Muhammad ibn ʿAbd Allah al-Kisa'i) produced in his "Tales of the Prophets" an extraordinarily vivid account of Yunus's life. The story commences in the Jewish world, where the prophet was wondrously born to elderly parents, Mattai and Sadaqa. Destitute after her husband's death, Sadaqa deposited the seven-year-old Yunus with a small group of scholars and ascetics under whose guidance he offered his prayers with diligence and rigor.

Sent fatherly advice in a dream, at age twenty-five Jonah sought out a wife in Ramla; she—Anak by name—was to be found in the household of a prophet named Zacharias. Likewise alerted to these happenings in a dream, Zacharias received Jonah and gave his approval to the marriage. Prior to the wedding, however, a strained verbal exchange took place between the two men. Finding his future father-in-law Zacharias in the marketplace, a well-dressed and very good-humored merchant in herbs, Jonah could not suppress his disapproval: "These are not the characteristics of a prophet!"[45] Jonah's judgment on Zacharias's mixing with the people and doing business in such a gregarious style provoked a cutting reply:

> "Jonah," said Zacharias, "know that merchants are liars, except the merchant who takes only what is due and gives in return what is due, performs his prayers, and pays his alms. I am of that kind. As for my merriment, it is to attract the hearts of the poor and unfortunate" (Al-Kisa`i, *Tales*, 322).

Whether the young and dour Jonah is able to appreciate Zacharias's counterstyle of prophethood we are not told, but A-Kisa`i is interested in putting the challenge to him.

Two additions to Jonah-lore quickly appear in al-Kisa`i's rendering. First, a history of hostile relations between Jonah's native people and the people of Nineveh is recalled. Second, and more unexpectedly, Jonah's wife and offspring become part of the drama relating the difficult relationship in which the prophet and his Lord are engaged.

When God summons Yunus of Jerusalem to prophesy to Nineveh, the city is described as one ruled by a tyrant, Thaalab ibn Sharid, whose forces had raided, killed, and captured Israelites. Upon suggesting that someone else be sent, the resistant Jonah was sharply (and successfully) confronted: "Go and do what you have been commanded to do and do not disobey my command!"[46] The reader of al-Kisa`i's Jonah narrative then learns of the prophet's family, which joins him as he heads toward Nineveh. The crossing of the Tigris brings tragedy when one of Jonah's sons, having been placed on the far bank, is snatched away by a wolf (who warns the pursuing father that this action is according to God's will). In the next passage across the water, the younger son is also lost, having fallen into the river, along with all of Jonah's possessions. To complete the disaster, when searching for his wife on the river bank, Jonah cannot find her. What do these happenings signify?

> God spoke to him, saying, "You complained of the burden of family, so I have relieved you of that. Now go and do what you've been commanded to do, and then I shall restore to you your family and possessions" (Al-Kisa`i, *Tales*, 322–323).

According to al-Kisa`i, the education of the grave and easily agitated prophet was underway *before* he encountered either the great city or the great fish.

The character of the pronouncement that Jonah makes to the Ninevites when he arrives is noteworthy:

> Confess that there is no god but God and that I, Jonah, am His servant and messenger! (Al-Kisa`i, *Tales*, 323).

The prophecy consists in a more complete *Shahadah*-formula than is found on Jonah's lips when the Qur'an reports his prayer from the whale's belly (21:87). Here he announces himself as the bringer of God's ultimatum.

Repeating for forty days this warning to profess the truth and be saved, al-Kisa`i tells us, Jonah bore abuse from the increasingly haughty and disbelieving inhabitants of the city. Counseling Jonah to withdraw, God informed the prophet that Nineveh would come to belief only after it suffered torment. To enact this tribulation Gabriel enters the scene, ordering the guardian of hell to send upon the city sparks of fire "the size of thunderclouds." Now under severe and palpable threat, the king and his people repent, imploring the "God of Jonah" to forgive them, which God does. Meanwhile Jonah refuses to return to the city and begins his flight to the seaport, complaining, "O God, they have denied me, and you have pardoned them."[47]

Al-Kisa`i's provision of hell-fire as a further incentive for the "people of Jonah" to repent is dramatically effective. It makes the city's plea for forgiveness perfectly reasonable. But the storyteller also noticeably gives new content to the prophet's repeated message: Jonah is declared to be God's "servant and messenger." Al-Kisa'i is making the same effort seen in the *hadith* quoted earlier: despite Jonah's disapproved resentfulness (however that anger is explained), he is not to be demeaned; the authenticity—and divine approval—of his prophethood is unquestionable.

Al-Kisa`i reports that once the runaway Yunus had gained passage on a ship, his stated reason for not joining the crew's prayers during the tempest had to do with the loss of his family. His excuse did not, however. impede the sailors' suspicion that it was Yunus's presence aboard that threatened their lives and cargo. Lead balls, each bearing the name of a person on the ship, were the lots cast into the sea, all sinking except that of Yunus.

> Then a great fish appeared with its mouth open and cried out, "Jonah, I have come from India in search of you." Jonah threw himself in the sea, and the fish swallowed him up (Al-Kisa`i, *Tales*, 324).

The Jonah whom, on God's command, the great fish spit out on the bank of the Tigris, emerged "like a featherless chick, for he was no more than skin and bones and had no strength to stand or sit, and his vision was gone."[48] Once Jonah was in place under the gourd vine that God caused to grow up over him, the archangel paid another visit—this time, as a therapist-healer:

> Gabriel came to him and rubbed his hand over Jonah's body, causing his skin and flesh to grow again. His sight too was restored. Then God sent a gazelle to give him milk as a mother does her child. Under the plant was also a spring in which [Jonah] made his ablutions and the water of which he drank (Al-Kisa`i, *Tales*, 322–23).

Nonetheless, reported al-Kisa'i, the recovered prophet was moved to resentment rather than thanks for these mercies, and to God's concern for the "hundred thousand" Ninevites Jonah remained obtuse.

Jonah, traveling in the region of his city, still stands in need of divine instruction, and a colorful series of human encounters contain this guidance, *if* he is able to discern God's purposes in them. In the first case, Jonah frets when he sees villagers uprooting fruit trees, and he chastises them. This evokes God's challenge to his conscience: "Jonah, you feel sorry for fruit trees, but you do not feel sorry for my people!" Another opportunity for illumination follows immediately:

> Then he went to another village, where a potter took him into his house. God spoke to him saying, "Jonah, order him to break his pottery!" When Jonah told the man to do this, he said, "I received you as a guest tonight because I thought you were a pious man, but you are a fool with no intelligence to order me to break the pottery I have made. Go away from me!" And the man turned him out in the middle of the night. God then spoke to [Jonah], saying, "You told the potter what you told him, and he put you out of his house, yet you wished the destruction of a hundred thousand and more!" (Al-Kisa`i, *Tales*, 324).

God's point is clear enough: the potter was jealous and protective of his creations, while Jonah cared little for the fates of God's creatures in Nineveh. If Jonah seems confounded by this event and its implications, it may well be because he is distracted by his concern to be held in high regard. He was aggrieved by the potter's sharp rebuke. Nonetheless, the pouting slow-learner may, under al-Kisa`i`s narrative management, be on the verge of comprehending the nature of his fault and flaw.

Resuming his journey, Yunus walked by a farmer who implored him to request that God bless his crop. Yunus's prayer took immediate effect, waist-high growth erupting, but God just as quickly informed Yunus that locusts would come to destroy the produce. Once more chagrined, the prophet was told that his feelings for the crop were not matched by his concern for God's "faithful people" in Nineveh. Finally he responds, "My Lord and Master, I shall not do it again!" Insight is a form of repentance. Yunus's wrongdoing—his resistance to his God's purposes and actions—he has now vowed to correct. The prophet's testing and his ultimate redemption as one of God's messengers take place, in al-Kisa`i's history of Jonah, not only in the whale's belly, nor upon his being released from it, but in subsequent challenges to his wisdom and faithfulness.

The plot of al-Kisa`i's extended Jonah-narrative requires that God's early promise be fulfilled—that the prophet's lost family should be restored to him. Our storyteller delights in relating how this came to pass. Still journeying in the territory surrounding his city, Jonah hears a man in a village cry out at the roadside: "Whoever takes this woman to the city of Nineveh to her husband, Jonah son of Matthew, will have a hundred dinars."[49] Recognizing his wife, Jonah asks her advertiser for information about her life since they were separated. He is told:

> She was seated on the banks of the Tigris. The lord of this village noticed her and took her off to his castle, where he attempted to entice her to sin, but his hands withered. He asked her to pray God that he be comforted and he would never again approach her; so she prayed and God pardoned him. Then he asked about her husband, and she said that she was the wife of Jonah son of Matthew. He sent her to me and gave me this gold for her and for the expense of transporting her to her husband (Al-Kisa`i, *Tales*, 325).

Satisfied, apparently, by this report about how his spouse, with God's help, withstood a strong man's sexual advances (an adroit redeployment of the story of Sarah's experiences in the households of rulers—the Pharaoh and Abimelech in the Hebrew Bible, and an "unbelievable libertine" in al-Tabari's *History*), Jonah reclaims his wife (and the gold coins) and resumes his journey.[50]

Promise-fulfilling events follow in rapid order. Jonah purchases a fish and finds within it his lost fortune. He next spies his younger son in the company of a man riding an ox. In the midst of their reconciliation, Jonah inquires about what had transpired after his son was lost in the river. The man reports that he, a fisherman, had once caught the boy, still alive, in his net; the youth (like his father, saved from the waters) told the fisherman whose son he was. Soon thereafter Jonah (accompanied by his wife and younger son) sees a shepherd tending his flocks, and recognizes him. When taken by this shepherd, his eldest son, to the owner of the sheep, Jonah again wishes to know his son's history. The owner of the sheep, sharing his delight, relates that once, while his herd was grazing, a wolf approached with the boy "and spoke to me in an eloquent tongue, saying, 'This boy is given in trust to you by God.' I took him with all devotion: now receive your son safe and sound."[51]

The story of Jonah in al-Kisa`i's inventive retelling has reached its providential climax. In need of preparation for his role as servant and messenger of God, the prophet required discipline. Through his trials, each of which tested his incomprehension of himself and his mission, Jonah ultimately came to hear and understand God's expectations of him. Resolved, at last, are the tensions between the Master and his servant, and blessings abound.

> They all went to Jonah's own city, and when the people there saw him they rejoiced. He remained among them, exhorting them to do justice and chastising them for evil, until he died (Al-Kisa`i, *Tales*, 326).

Although different in style and in the degree of creative freedom to move beyond the Qur'an's brief presentation of Yunus, Ibn Ishaq, al-Tha`labi, and al-Kisa'i made the character of Yunus their primary subject, displaying a strong commitment to play out the narrative's sense. The prophet's bad-temper and its causes, the Qur'an's assertion that Yunus did not think he would be held to account for his rebellion against God's command to him, the circumstances in which Yunus gained release from the belly of the fish and the role of his prayer in his deliverance—these subjects, along with attention paid to his condition when he was spewed out "ailing" on the shore near the gourd vine, most occupied these (and other) Muslim exegetes and storytellers. Inevitably, interpreters created new chapters in the life of Yunus, as we saw in Ibn Ishaq's commentary and especially in al-Kisa`i's incorporation of the prophet's family in the narrative and his addition of tales about what occurred between Yunus and his fellow-Ninevites in the aftermath of the city's penitence and pardon.

Notably, our three Muslim writers gave particular consideration to Jonah's crying out from the deep, an act that made plain both his faith in God's oneness and glory and also the prophet's own contrition. Those things that are deemed virtuous and honorable in the (expanded) story of Yunus outweigh and lessen the force of his (Satan-assisted) wrongdoing, resulting in a more positive and less ambivalent evaluation of him and his prophethood. Indeed, by the time al-Kisa`i has characterized him as the wise, empowered, and finally humble returnee to his people, Yunus's holy heroism has come to the fore.

Needless to say, the circulation of the prophet Muhammad's sayings which defended and upheld Yunus and his prayer were of considerable influence in enhancing his reputation, especially in shifting the focus from the prophet's fault to his virtue—his glorification of his God. To make exactly this point the earlier *hadith* of Muhammad's about Jonah took a new form. The scholar al-Tabarani (873–970 CE) reported:

> Ibn Abbas says that the Prophet Muhammad said: "It is not appropriate for one to say: 'I am a better *worshipper of God* than Jonah bin Mattai.'"[52]

Alongside the characterization of Yunus's prayerful piety, the other picture of him persisted. No less than in the Jewish and Christian treatments of Jonah, the Muslim texts we have considered regularly sustain the theme that the runaway prophet is undergoing a trial put to him by his God, and that his captivity in the whale is both a rescue from death *and* an ordeal, a divinely sent discipline to be met and borne. Jonah's response to the sounds of animals in the sea praising God *might* have been one of continuing irritation; we are encouraged by the commentators, however, to believe that God's challenges to Yunus's anger were succeeding. Testing was, after all, God's manner of preparing his messengers for their service.

MUSLIM PAINTERS AND RUMI THE POET INTERPRET YUNUS AND THE FISH

The sheer drama of his fantastic story no doubt prompted the inclusion of Yunus among the prophets whose stories made up the *Qisas* literature, and for the same reason, when portrayals of traditional and historical human figures rose to prominence in Islamic art in the fourteenth century, scenes depicting Yunus were among the most frequent. A few of these provide an opportunity to learn and to compare the interpretive tendencies shown in several manuscript illuminations, and also, along the way, to learn of some other writers with whom these artist-exegetes shared ideas.

Gabriel to the Rescue

The presence of an angel, presumably Gabriel, with Jonah, is not an exclusively Muslim idea or image, as we know from two objects discussed earlier—the carnelian gem engraved with Jonah scenes, one of which shows the angel bringing a cloak to the just-ejected prophet, and the sixth-century Christian Murano Diptych which depicted the angel moving toward Jonah as he reclined under the gourd plant. It is noteworthy, however, that paintings representing Jibril meeting Yunus as he is vomited forth from the fish are quite common in illuminated Arabic and Persian manuscripts from the fourteenth century on. Not surprisingly, these works reveal some familiarity with Christian Byzantine iconography, but a dominant sense of the scene is rooted in the Qur'an itself—namely, Surah 37:145: "But We threw him onto a wasteland, ailing." The commentators, we've observed, could not resist elaborating on the prophet's sickness: he was emaciated, he was like a tender (and skinless) newborn babe, or a featherless bird; he could not sit or stand, and he suffered from blindness. All of this language connoted a life damaged and diminished. The cause of Jonah's condition is not ambiguous. While the artists may have wished to register some indications of the physical effects of three days within the fish, a theological theme is also present: having challenged God's purposes, Jonah suffered the travail deserved by one who thought his Lord could not and would not hold him accountable.

This disgorged Jonah, then, was not likely to become what the Christians made of him—a symbol of rest and peace. Rather, Yunus would be represented as someone helpless and in need of mercy. A new turn in the story, then—that God spewed Yunus out upon the shore "ailing"—called for new imagery. We recall that Al-Kisa`i, himself responding to this qur'anic image of Yunus, imagined Gabriel coming to his rescue with a reinvigorating massage. For Muslim artists the scene of the angel of revelation's flight to assist the distressed prophet had become a figural *topos,* a commonplace—one that gave opportunity for iconographic variations on the theme. Here, in Figure 12.2, we meet one of these.

This splendid painting in a manuscript of Rashid al-Din's history displays resplendent Jibril ready to lend protection and assistance to the clearly disheveled and wearied prophet. Yunus crouches on the fish's lower

Figure 12.2 The angel Jibril flies toward Yunus. From a Persian ms. of Rashid al-Din's *Compendium of Chronicles*. Ca.1400. Painting: h: 33, w: 49.5 cm. © The Metropolitan Museum of Art, New York. Art Resource NY.

jaw, his nakedness a signal of his helpless condition. Jibril (his Mongolian appearance due to the image's creation in the period of transition from Mongol to Timurid painting styles) flies toward the prophet, bringing clothing.

Does the imagery leave room for a positive interpretation, one that celebrates Yunus's survival of his test in the fish's interior as a victory? The inscription on the prophet's arms reads, "The sun's disk went into darkness, Jonah went into the mouth of the fish," lending a cosmic dimension and corollary to the prophet's descent into the "darknesses" (Surah 28:37)—and, we may infer, to his reappearance in the light. The inscription's language combines astrological and qur'anic ideas, if we accept its kinship in theme with the text associated with the next painting.

A Muslim form of the practice of seeking auguries, or prognostications (*falnama*), about one's life (travels, business ventures, marriage prospects, etc.) sometimes entailed the use of paintings; their subjects were understood to provide a seeker with clues about his or her future with promised, or suggested, possible outcomes. Happily for us, a *falnama* painting of Jonah's escape from the fish (Figure 12.3) survives, along with an explanatory text.

Figure 12.3 Jibril flies to Yunus, who emerges from the fish. From a Persian Falnama. Iran. Ca. 1570–1580. © Topkapi Palace Museum Archives, Istanbul. Topkapi Palace Museum Ms. H. 1702, f. 27b.

The haloed Yunus eyes his rescuer, who, rather than hovering with clothing, actively grabs his arm and shoulder, pulling him to freedom from the fish's jaws. The painter emphasizes Yunus's struggle to escape from his captivity more than his captor's willing response to God's command to cast him out on the dry land. Standing at the top of the page, in Arabic, appears Surah 37:144: "he would have remained inside its guts until the Day they are resurrected." A phrase usually spoken after a qur'anic oral recitation is here given in written form: "God has spoken the truth."[53] The succeeding verses in Persian read:

> Yunus, the Messenger, by the decree of the Living One,
> the Dispenser of justice,
> Spent a forty-day period inside the fish's stomach, weeping.
> (and at the bottom of the page)
> Finally, God's aid became his guide.
> Through that supplication he came out of the fish like the sun.

According to these lines, the rising of Yunus from the fish was not an ordeal, but a meaningful sign: the Persian word for "fish" is the same as the Zodiac sign, Pisces. The author associates Yunus's coming out of the fish with the sun's emergence from Pisces. Astrological forecasts of an omen-seeker's future are laid bare in this part of the inscription, even while it rehearses the drama of Yunus's forlorn state, and then his release. The imaginative logic of the transaction is straightforward: God's aid "guided" Yunus, just as this predictive painting of Yunus (and Jibril) bears upon on the client's concern, giving help and direction.[54]

The written response (on the page facing the painting), which blends wisdom from the Zodiac with theology, practical exhortation, and religious instruction, reveals the assumptions and the dynamic of the *falnama*. It is too intriguing not to present in its entirety.

O augury user! Know and be aware that the prophet Yunus, peace be upon him, has come up as your augury—the one who came out of the belly of the fish with great difficulty by the decree of God. It indicates attainment of desires and goals from a place you did not consider. The star of your ascendant has come out of the depth, and you are liberated from grief because all your circumstances will be according to your desire. Immense mercy and blessing will turn to face you, and you will receive riches and a robe of honor from a grandee, will govern a group of people, and profit from your profession and trade. Legitimate fortune will come to you from some place, and you will become rich, on the condition that you behave bravely in this intention and show no uncertainty. Even if it is difficult in the beginning, it will be pleasant in the end, and its pleasure is greater than the difficulty. Since the pleasure is larger than the difficulty, proceed and entrust yourself to God, and what you desire will certainly be attained. There will be good news from the one who is absent, and your beloved will fulfill your wishes. The prophet Daniel says if you intend to travel east, go, because your wish will be attained after forty days. If your intention is a relationship, marriage, or partnership, do it, because the circumstances will conform to your heart's will. "After forty days" is because the prophet Yunus, peace be upon him, stayed for forty days in the belly of the fish and safely left the belly of the fish after forty days without harm. Now, O augury user, even though the intention you are stepping toward is difficult in the beginning, there is pleasure in the end. However, you must not neglect your prayers so that you may achieve your desire. Say, "If the exalted God wishes."[55]

The omen, spelled out, differs in content from an important part of the painting in that it neither mentions nor invokes the angel Jibril as a bringer of God's assistance. While the painter suggests the struggle involved in the prophet's escape from captivity, and brings Jibril into the drama as a strong helper, the text points solely to Yunus's experience in, and then freed, from the belly of the fish. The augury quickly associates this with difficulty that ends in pleasure—and with people desirous of a new, positive, development in their lives. Clearly designed to serve the differing needs of any number of "augury users," the painting and the text presuppose the applicability of the image and story of Yunus and the fish to particular clients' wishes and objectives.

The next painting (Figure 12.4) exposes us to a fascinating, but quite different, way that an image of Yunus's emergence from the fish connected "interactively" with experiences of a large number of Muslim viewers. The gourd plant awaits Yunus on the shore, but our eyes are drawn to his body and his gestures as he comes out of the fish. Yunus is not, as in other representations, a naked, enfeebled man, but rather, one whose arms, and his hands—one turned upward, the other down—reveal him in the posture of a dervish, one who in and through his gyrations offers his prayers.

In and beyond the twelfth century, Sufism was a widespread form of Muslim popular piety. The painter's graphic translation of this climactic moment in Yunus's story to Sufi spiritual ideas and practices of his own era was to be expected—we may assume that he saw no great distance in meaning between his portrayal of Jonah's escape from the fish (in answer to his prayer) and the men represented below (Figure 12.5), who perform their *zikr*, or remembrance of God, to the sounds of flute and drum.

In an earlier chapter we witnessed the Sufi writer, Jami, transforming Zulaykha from a craven temptress of the prophet Yusuf into a model for the soul's desire for the divine Beloved. Here, it serves our purposes to turn to the well-known Jalal-al-Din Rumi (1207–1273), who devoted several of his poems to the story of Yunus. In articulating the system of Sufi thought and spirituality that had been in the air in the decades preceding him, and by developing a genius for making qur'anic stories personally relevant to their hearers, Rumi's poetry drew wide attention. His versified

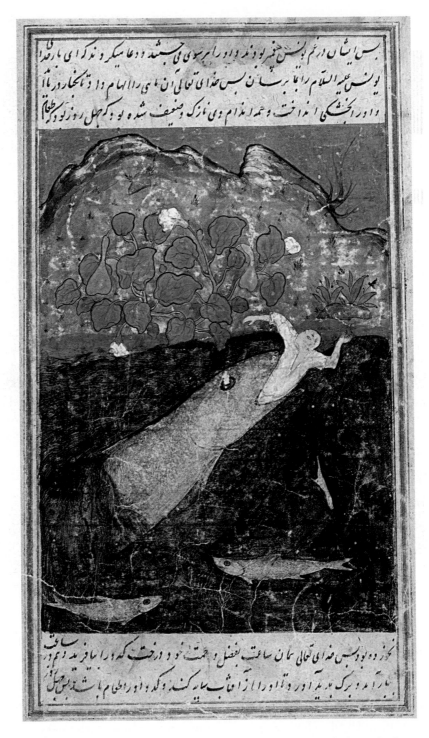

Figure 12.4 Yunus emerging from the fish. From a copy of Juwayri's *Qisas al-anbiya*, ca. 1574–1575. Painting: 23.4 x 13 cm. © Columbia University Library, New York. Smith collection, MS X 892.8 Q1/Q.

Figure 12.5 Dervishes. From Kamal al-Din Husayn Gasurgahi's *Majalis al-`ushshaq* (*"The Assemblies of the Lovers"*). Shiraz, Iran, ca.1590–1600. © British Library, London. British Library I.O. Islamic 1138, f. 43.

Yunus belongs to the social-religious ethos in which our painting was created and, without doubt, understood by its viewers. The "man of the fish" certainly does not come forth from the fish depleted and feeble—he ascends, praying.

Four of Rumi's major themes concerned the soul's longings for the Beloved; the encouragement of the exercise of so holding God in memory and in love that the self is forgotten (or annihilated); love's superiority over intellect; and the human soul's capacity to see beyond the visible and invisible worlds, and to have experience of God. These ideas, fundamental to Rumi's religious-philosophical vision, virtually guaranteed how he would approach Yunus's story.

Closely akin to the interpretive mode we have called "spiritual/mystical" (as distinct from "historical" or ethical) in reference to a number of Jewish and Christian writers, Rumi consistently turned elements in the narrative of a qur'anic figure into applied spiritual counsel for seekers after God. Such is the case when, in his collection of poems, the *Mathnawi* (or *Masnavi*), he takes up the saga of Yunus.[56] Rumi's ideas on the prophet's captivity and liberation moved immediately to the life circumstances of any Yunus-like person (including the poet himself), who is trapped in a darkened existence, and yearns for release. There is available, Rumi wants the hearers of the Yunus story to know, a journey, or a new condition of the spirit, or a liberation from the mundane through which an earnest seeker may experience her or his self yielding to God. In Rumi's recommendation of a mystical *islam,* or submission, there is no mistaking what the Yunus story is about:

> You're Jonah, who inside a whale spent days,
> But managed to escape it through God's praise;
> The belly of the whale would otherwise
> Have been his cell till that day *all must rise* [Surah 37:144]—
> Through praising God, Jonah escaped at last;
> Praise is a sign that points back to *Alast*
> (Mojaddedi, *Masnavi* 2.3146–3148).[57]

We may count the ways that these verses of Rumi connect the ancient adventure of Yunus with prayerful individuals' present existential dilemmas and aspirations. While the prophet's plight as recorded in the Qur'an is Rumi's resource, he steadily generates from it a set of questions and opportunities intended to benefit any person who desires, or might be awakened to desiring, the Beloved. "*You* are Jonah," he asserts.

Dear to Sufi thinkers, Rumi among them, was the primordial Covenant of *Alast*—a compact made between God and the not–yet–embodied spirits of Adam and his children. Challenged by their Creator's question, "Am I not (*alast*) your Lord?" they responded, "Yes!" (Surah 7: 172). The question and its affirmation symbolize the remembrance of God which was a compact established "in the beginning," but the verbal exchange also functions as an affirmative reality to be acknowledged daily—or better, at all times. *Alast* defined the soul's first true loyalty and also its ever-present commitment. *Zikr*, or prayer, in Sufi understanding, consists in remembrance of God's sovereign presence—worship that comes to expression in many forms of ceremony and ritual, including the honoring of God through self-abandonment in ecstatic dance. Here Rumi's attention to prayer as remembrance of God finds a vehicle in the Jonah story—in its vital importance to the prophet's escape from the deep and the fish.

Had Yunus not performed *zikr*, giving himself over to exalting God, to holding the majesty of God in remembrance, he would still be in the great fish's belly—as the Qur'an's Surah 37:143–144 declared. What, then, given Yunus's example, is an individual seeker of God's intervention and rescue to do? When in the deep, Yunus heard fish exalting God, and came to recollection. Now, Rumi insists, think of *your* Yunus-dilemma, and be discerning. Surrounding you are voices to be heard.

> If you have forgotten that glorification (rendered to God)
> By your spirit, hearken to the glorifications uttered by
> Those Fishes (the prophets and saints).
> Whoever has seen God is of God: whosoever has seen
> That Sea is that Fish.
> This world is a sea, and the body a fish, and the spirit is the
> Jonah debarred from the light of the dawn.
> If it be a glorifier (of God), it is delivered from the fish;
> Othewise it becomes digested therein and vanishes.
> The spiritual Fishes abound in this sea (the world), (but)
> You do not see them, (though) they are flying around you.
> Those fishes are brushing against you: open your eye, so that
> You may see then clearly.
> If you are not seeing the Fishes plainly—after all, your ear
> Has heard their glorification of God
> (Nicholson, *Mathnawi* 2. 3149–3155).[58]

Literal (or worldly) sense gives way to metaphor and allegory in Rumi's mystical interpretation; the sea, the fish, the whale, and Yunus now make up the narrative and drama of anyone who desires closeness to God. To advance requires two things: a clear acknowledgment of the character of the seeker's captivity, and the fortification of spirit that results in praise of the Almighty.

If the self, or the Jonah-spirit of a person, has so distanced itself from its Creator as to have lost memory of its first gratitude toward and praise of God, there is recourse. You can study the sounds and ways of "spiritual fishes"—that is, prophets, saints, and spiritual messengers attempting to communicate with you in the world ("ocean"). Alluding to the earlier Muslim commentators' ideas of what "awakened" prayerfulness in Jonah while he was captive in the deep, Rumi finishes his exhortation with the argument that even if you are unable to see clearly those fish of a mystic kind, their praises of the Most High will be audible to you.

But will these spiritual tactics *certainly* achieve the objective of the lover of God? Is there a way of glorifying God, of rendering worship, that can secure and guarantee the success of one's endeavor to glorify the Most High? Rumi, thinking back to the Qur'an's description of the flaw of Yunus that Muhammad was to avoid, inverts the prophet's impatience, making its opposite the decisive virtue for any believer who seeks freedom from his or her own "belly of the whale." The poet offers a prescription:

> To practice patience is the best of ways—
> Be patient, for that's the best form of praise!
> No (form of) praise (excels) to a similar degree—
> Practicing patience is the soul of all praise:
> Be patient! *For relief it is the key* [Qur'an 68:48].
> Patience is heaven's bridge which must cross hell. . . .
> (Mojaddedi, *Masnavi* 2.3156–3158a).

To risk my own prosaic paraphrase of Rumi's counsel: Your concentrated and steadfast trust in God's will and purposes *is* the praise that carries you to Him.

My effort to provide background for this last painting of Yunus emerging from the fish, dervish-like, calls for yet another passage of Rumi's poetry. In it he offered his own elaboration on the *hadith* reporting that Muhammad had once declared that no one should call himself more excellent than Yunus ibn Mattai:

> The Prophet said: "No preference is (to be given) to my
> ascension as being superior to the ascension of Yunus.
> Mine was up to heaven, and his was down below (in the belly of the
> Fish), because nearness to God is beyond calculation."
> To be near (to God) is not to go up or down: to be near to

God is to escape from the prison of existence.
What room does non-existence have for "up" and "down"?
(Nicholson, *Mathnawi*, 3, 4513).

This is a strong statement. Jonah's *mi`raj* from the great fish was equal to Muhammad's ascent—his "night journey" to the Most High. Each of the two prophets' ascensions achieved intimacy with God and both ascensions deserved celebration as prodigious feats, however much they were enabled by divine grace. Was God's practice of testing his prophets involved in these experiences of Yunus and Muhammad? Yes, according to Rumi, who endorsed this teaching of the commentator al-Nisaburi: "five prophets, Nuh (Noah), Ibrahim, Yusuf, Ayyub (Job), and Yunus, glorified God in their moment of suffering, thus giving an example to the angels. Following them, Muhammad set an example to the angels during the trial (*mihna*) of his *mi`raj*."[59] Rumi's interpretation of Yunus made clear that the possibility of *mir`aj* was not, in Muslim mystical thought and practice, limited to prophets and angels. Annemarie Schimmel, in a chapter in her *Mystical Dimensions of Islam* titled "Man and his Perfection," wrote:

> The main object of mystical meditation was ... Muhammad's night journey, the *mi`raj*, his ascent through the spheres—a topic only touched upon in the introductory verse of Sura 17, but lavishly elaborated upon in later legends. The connection of the *mi`raj* with daily prayer—which was experienced by Muhammmad as the repetition of the joy of ascension—made such an ascension into the divine presence possible for every sincere Muslim. The mystics applied the ascension terminology to their own experiences in the rapture of ecstasy.[60]

In all of its components, Rumi perceives Yunus's release from the fish as the accomplishment of freedom from ignorance, which is, paradoxically, the triumph of fervent and impassioned love over the powers of the intellect. Rumi has made Yunus an exemplar for what Shahzad Bashir calls "the two ultimate aims of the Sufi path ... annihilation in God (*fana' fil-lah*) followed by subsistence in the divine reality (*baqa' billah*)."[61] There is no question that this ennobling of Yunus puts into nearly total eclipse the anger and impatience regarded by the Qur'an and the earlier commentators as a moral weakness deep-set in his character. Our painting's imagery, showing Yunus's exit from the fish as the *mi`raj* or ascent of a dervish, is a strong reimaging that depicts, first, what kind of struggle, or labor, occurred while the prophet was contained in the great fish and, second, the kind of *zikr* manifested as he came forth. The painter conveyed a meaning of the prophet's "rising" in the religious symbolic language of his era and location, dominantly influenced by the energies of Sufi piety and practices.

The Perils of Jonah, and of His Family

Mirkhwand's fifteenth-century chronicle of prophets, kings, and caliphs contains a comprehensive account of Jonah's life and career—one that combines the several strands of tradition we traced above in the writings of Ibn Ishaq, al-Tha`labi, and al-Kisa`i.[62] Mirkhwand's text surrounds the painting below (Figure 12.6), and is in midnarrative: having been identified by the casting of lots as the person whose presence endangers the ship, Yunus requests to be thrown overboard. Those on board hesitate to do so, arguing that the use of lots is unreliable. Twice more lots are cast, however, and Yunus's name appears again each time. God then commands the fish to circle the ship with its mouth open. Whichever side of the ship its occupants move to, they are confronted by the fish with its expectant jaws. Finally, being helpless, they give up Yunus to his fate.[63]

The painting belongs to the period of the Safavid dynasty (the sixteenth through eighteenth centuries), a Shi'a culture intent upon rejuvenating consciousness of Persia's ancient glories. Its presentation of a portion of Yunus's story owes a particular debt to themes we saw in al-Kisa'i's elaborated narrative, which are continued in Mirkhwand's account. A scene in its right upper half—on the hillside abutting the upper boat scene—recalls the inclusion of Yunus's wife and sons in his saga. The visual narrative shows the wolf's capture of the prophet's older son, and in the ship to the left we are probably correct in surmising that Anak, the prophet's wife, looks upon the kidnapping from the helm, while her other son stands on the prow. Under orders to prophesy to the people of Nineveh, Yunus's crossing of the Tigris River brought danger to him and his family. According to Mirkhwand's retelling, Yunus "knew that a calamity sent from above was impending over him."[64] We remember that in al-Kisa`i's rendition of the loss of his sons and wife, God told Yunus in a tone of rebuke, "You complained of the burden of family, so I have relieved you of that."

The painting's primary image is striking on several counts. Do the postures and facial expressions of the men on the ship suggest some kind of consternation at what is transpiring—perhaps the artist's effort to show their hesitancy over casting the prophet overboard? They have been confronted by the circling wide-mouthed fish who came for Yunus.

Figure 12.6 Yunus's ordeal. From an illuminated copy of Mirkhwand's *Rauzat-us-Safa'* (*Garden of Purity*). Circa 1600. Painting: 240 x 140 cm. © The Israel Museum, Jerusalem. Y. Dawud bequest, London 903.69.

Half-swallowed, Yunus retains his grandeur. The fine flame nimbus surrounds his head, and his noble countenance, in view of his situation, is remarkably unperturbed. The prophet's confinement in the great fish is just beginning.

In giving attention to and blending two episodes in a more expansive tradition of the story of Yunus—the catastrophe involving his sons and wife, and the fish's swallowing of him—the painter brought more narrative within his "frame," while also highlighting a definite and provocative theme. Again, the trial of the prophet is central to the image's meaning, even if Mirkhwand and the painter, tutored in the Shi'a-favored doctrine of the prophets' `ismah—their protection from sin and error—may have been somewhat reticent to condemn him. Yet the wayward Yunus *is* being challenged by God in a test. And bound together with his own ordeal is also the misfortune suffered by his family—this motif captured in the image of his son's being carried away by the wolf.

What the artist chose to incorporate in the painting records a familiar and basic Muslim truth and value: history, and in this case, the story of Yunus, reveals, to those of who are discerning and capable of humility, God's strong guidance and oversight of his creatures. Yunus, being swallowed, and his son, being kidnapped, will be reconciled—at a time God determines.

To review and compare these paintings is to recognize that they represent not only different episodes in Yunus's story, but also strongly varied perceptions and representations of him. In the first, a solicitous Jibril brings clothing to the prophet, whose crouched position on the fish's lower jaw gives every indication that he is in a post-traumatic state. The prominence of the archangel and his action is a pictorial testament to God's mercy and forgiveness, a feature possessing more piquant force when understood as part of the wider drama of a prophet's ordeal, his standing the divine test. Having sunk, like the sun, into the darkness, Yunus the survivor has now been risen to receive, through Jibril, God's care.

The *falnama* painting of Jibril working to wrest the prophet from the fish's firm jaws is a different type. I suspect that its imagery of Yunus's liberation was correlated to the image's use as a visual omen or prognostication—one that warned of forty days of difficulty, like those of Yunus in the fish's belly, before a happy fulfillment of its prediction.

The angel was absent from the third painting we considered, which portrayed Yunus emerging, dervish-like, from the fish's mouth. The artist presented a quite different notion of the prophet's condition as he emerged. He showed Yunus not as a man languishing, a bare survivor, but rather as a man performing his *zikr*, spinning Godward in his rising—his *mir`aj*—and modeling the journey of the spirit which other true worshippers could and would undertake.

The last of the paintings, from a copy of Mirkhwand's *Garden of Purity*, while depicting the dramatic moment of the prophet's being swallowed, shows as part of this event his son's being captured by a wolf, and intimates all that will happen to Yunus and his family members in the future. It, too, is a piece of artistic interpretation that, fully attuned to elaborations on the Yunus story by storytellers, shows its own touches.

More than the literary commentators, it seems, the artists elevated the importance of Jibril's visitation to the ejected Yunus, at least partly because this element in the story all but demanded pictorialization. But the variety in types of Yunus images, together with the variety in their efforts to explain or highlight distinctive themes, give ample evidence of artists' roles in promulgating, beyond what was given in the relatively spare notices of Yunus in the Qur'an, fresh understandings—adapted to their respective circumstances and times.

CONCLUSION

Our consideration of Yunus as he is revealed in the Qur'an and interpreted by writers and artists between the seventh and sixteenth centuries makes plain that he, Yunus, is not Jonah—that is, not the same figure or scriptural actor who is found in the scriptures of the Jews and Christians and described in those two traditions. Yes, the three religions held in common the view that he was a prophet of God, that he rebelled against his Lord's command to him, that the great fish who swallowed him was sent by God to rescue, test, and then "deliver him," and that the Ninevites, receiving a divine warning through him, came to repentance. The prevailing Muslim portrayal of Yunus, however, possesses features all its own.

The Qur'an's testimony about the prophet is what exercises the greatest influence upon what early Muslims believed and found compelling about Yunus, "the one of the fish." If we recapitulate the chief qur'anic claims concerning him, we see Jonah first as one of those, like Noah, Abraham, Moses, Solomon, John the Baptist, and Jesus, who received revelation from God, becoming a prophet—one of the favorites of the Most High. The Ninevites, unique in their community-wide conversion to faith in God, were "the people of Jonah," though interpreters would narrate difficulties in his relations with them. Most distinctive in the depiction of Yunus by the Qur'an, compared to the biblical narratives, was what followed upon descriptions of his anger and impatience—the definiteness of the prophet's penitential turning back to God.

Two pieces of narrative form the basis for Muslim understanding of Yunus's dealings with God. From one, Surah 37:139–148, comes the portrait of the prophet fleeing to a ship, where the casting of lots identified him as the one to be thrown overboard. Swallowed by the fish while "he was blameworthy," he would have remained there had Yunus not joined those who glorified God. God then *did* cast him out of the fish, and provided a protective plant for him—prior to his mission to the "hundred thousand or more." The Ninevites believed in God, and were spared a devastating punishment. The second passage, Surah 21:87–88, repeats the narrative, but tells more: it was in anger that Yunus fled, supposing that he could travel beyond the range of God's justice. Once captive in the great fish, however, he cried out from the darkness, submitting to God, offering praise, and confessing his evil. In response God counseled the fish to spew him out on the shore. We recall a further notice in the Qur'an, at Surah 68:48-50, that encourages Muhammad to be patient in awaiting God's action, unlike Yunus, and suggests that God, who could well have put the prophet on the shore still under condemnation, instead visited favor on him, electing him and causing him to be one of the righteous.

This brief review underlines the fact that the qur'anic texts concerning Yunus, differing from the *Book of Jonah* in the Bible of the Christians and Jews, strongly determine what issues do and do not occupy the first Muslim interpreters—the exegetes, storytellers, and artists. Yunus, for example, is a person who, in his distress, repented of his sin, declaring, "I was in the wrong." There was no need, then, for Muslim commentators to strain over the question of whether Yunus ever acknowledged his fault. The Qur'an account did not necessitate wrestling with an image like that in the biblical *Jonah*—of an unredeemed figure, still sullen at the story's conclusion. Nonetheless, the cause of Yunus's anger bore investigation, and we saw Muslim exegetes debate whether it was "natural" to him or was the result of Satanic influence. A number of their speculations about the prophet's ire were, predictably, similar to those put forth by Jewish and Christian interpreters.

The presumption that Jonah was a citizen of Nineveh removed from Muslim consideration of his prophethood a dynamic intrinsic to the biblical story of Jonah—that is, the presentation of Jonah as a Jew commissioned to bring the challenge of Israel's God to foreign unbelievers in "the great city." Even when Muslim commentators included *isra'iliyyat* in their accounts of Yunus's origins, this theme of Jewish-Gentile antagonism was all but incidental to their narratives. Rather, in Yunus was seen a prophet receiving a message from the God of Muslims, and then delivering it to his own community—composed, it was sometimes said, of idolaters.

The aspect of ordeal or divine testing in the story of Yunus undergoes extension in works like al-Kisa'i's commentary and the folio painting within Mirkhwand's *Garden of Purity*, with the result that the prophet, strange to say, continues in his own obtuseness about his true role even after the drama's chief "moment"—the calling of Nineveh and of Yunus himself to submission to the single sovereign Lord of the universe. It is the story-tellers' fascination with Yunus's character (especially the pride, egoism, *and* temptability that accompany his anger) that produces the many lively embellishments of the prophet's activities and dealings—for example, his clash with his future father in law, his hermit-like unsociability in Nineveh, his awkward transaction with the potter, and the angelic warning not to mount, though he would like to, the silver carriage of a king.

A bit of ambiguity attends one's enjoyment of these tales of the prophet's continuing education by God. The reader/hearer of these additional tales recognizes in them the writers' indulgences, since the Qur'an plainly asserts that Yunus, through his prayer and by God's mercy, had been made one of the righteous at the time he was ejected from the fish's belly. To take the Qur'an at its word, then, is to consider Yunus to be, once he lands on the shore, a *formerly* unrepentant sinner. Before being released from the fish, Yunus had wholly surrendered to his God, whom he glorified.

What most clearly sets the Jonah of Muslim understanding apart from the biblical and Jewish and Christian interpreters' renderings of him is the prayer, or confession of faith, which he speaks in Surah 21:87: "There is no God but You; Glory to You."

Though all prophets of God were, by definition, obedient and worshipful, Yunus (the once angry and impatient messenger) is renowned and especially honored for his words of prayer. He submitted to the one God in *Shahadah*-like language, and there was in his spoken glorification of God a celebrated uniqueness. Nothing demonstrates this more clearly than an addition to a famous saying of Muhammad—his prohibition of anyone claiming to be superior to Yunus. The *hadith* had taken a significant turn by the time of al-Tabarani, who reported the Prophet's declaration that it was wrong for anyone to assert that he was "a better *worshipper of God* than Yunus."

Ultimately, Muslim consciousness and celebration of Yunus centered in his praying and prayer, his *zikr*. He became Yunus who exalted God, Yunus the one favored by being redeemed, and Yunus who undertook, like Muhammad would do at a later time, his *mi`raj* to his Beloved. A champion and keen example of the remembrance of God, Yunus uttered the prayer in which he turned back to his Lord. Any and all Muslims thereafter would be able to speak the prayer of Yunus, the "glorious verse" (21.87), when they called for help from *ar-Rahman*, the Merciful One.

Comparative Summary

Jonah the Angry Prophet

The Jews' Jonah: the aggrieved prophet who did not repent—or the rehabilitated agent of God, who would slay the Leviathan.

The Christians' Jonah: two in one—a rescued prophet and the resurrected Jesus he prefigured.

The Muslims' Yunus: the angry, then penitent, prophet who excelled in glorifying God.

These distinctions oversimplify but accurately distill what we learned in the previous three chapters about the ways by which Jewish, Christian, and Muslim scripture interpreters imagined and portrayed Jonah/Yunus.

Jewish commentators were compelled to understand Jonah's resistance to God as his chief characteristic, since the *Book of Jonah* portrayed him as aggravated throughout his dealings with his Lord, and churlishly silent at the story's conclusion. This wayward strangeness of Jonah, in comparison with other esteemed prophets, caused Jewish commentators to puzzle over the causes of his disobedience and his persisting disenchantment with God's merciful treatment of the Ninevites. An additional and alternative ending to the story of Jonah was needed, and the rabbis created it, transforming the grim prophet into a strong agent of God.

Though the same problematic Jonah in their scripture, Christian artists' and writers' interests in his motives and faults gave way to a greater enthusiasm for the message in the *Gospel of Matthew* (12:40) which likened Jonah's "three days and three nights in the belly of the whale" to the same amount of time Jesus spent "in the heart of the earth" before he was raised from death. The growth of this celebratory Christian line of argument about the true significance of Jonah was steady; we saw it imaged in the sixth-century Murano ivory plaque that placed Jonah scenes beneath the representation of Christ as ruler of the universe, his angels surrounding him.

The Qur'an's narratives of Yunus, like the Jews' and Christians' *Book of Jonah*, told of his anger and impatience, but contained a unique account of his prayer from the fish—one that included his confession of faith *and* his confession of wrongdoing. Obligated to explain and explore that piece of qur'anic narrative, Muslim interpreters increasingly extolled Yunus's prayer as his singular distinction among God's elect messengers. The depiction of Yunus emerging from the fish as a dervish in prayer, painted nine centuries after Islam's beginnings, captured this understanding of Yunus, who came to exemplify a mystic's path to God.

Much evidence in these chapters indicated that Jewish, Christian, and Muslim interpreters were aware of each others' ideas and traditions; there was borrowing, and there was contestation over meanings. Muslim retellings of Yunus's story recognized him as a prophet from Israel (al-Tha'labi), but also as a prophet in and from Nineveh (Ibn Ishaq). Familiarity with this and other Jewish Jonah traditions was obvious, but it was noteworthy that Muslim investments in Yunus and his story did not include an issue of significant importance in *Jonah*'s narrative: the distinction between Jews and Gentiles (the Ninevites). The framing of Jonah's adventures in relation to Islam's understanding of God's messengers—and the challenges they faced—predominated.

Jesus's sharp denunciation of the "evil and adulterous generation" that sought a heavenly sign from him targets, in the *Gospel of Matthew*, the scribes and Pharisees, and throughout succeeding centuries Christian commentators advanced stronger and more biting anti-Jewish polemics. The Jews, Christians early argued, had a shameful history of resisting and sometimes murdering their God-sent prophets, and this they did to Jesus, God's anointed one. Further, Christian apologists complained that even after Jesus was raised from the dead, Jews not only refused to believe in him, but set out to revile him, calling his resurrection a hoax perpetrated by his disciples (who stole his body from the tomb). Such accusations revealed, of course, more than simple familiarity with Judaism and its teachings. Christian interpreters, knowing themselves to be engaged in an often bitter rivalry, continued their castigation of Jews, proposing to Christian believers that Jewish resistance to Christ and his followers was a confirmation of their new revelation.

To conclude this brief review of the three religions' awareness of, influence upon, and competition with each other, we revisit the Jewish *Pirke de Rabbi Eliezer*, the collection (edited ca. 820–830 CE) of rabbinic teachings. This writing, which gave Jonah a new lease on life and on honor, served Jews in a time in which apocalyptic hopes were active: the occasion of the arrival of Israel's messiah would call for Jonah's capture and killing of the Leviathan. Without underlining its counterclaim in explicit terms, the new account of Jonah renounces and rebuts Christian beliefs about the messiahship of Jesus. More frontal are the attacks waged within *PRE* against Muslims, even if their understandings of Yunus were not addressed nor criticized. Again from the perspective of its urgent calendar consciousness, this rabbinic collection sees Muslims as those who will do battle against Israel in the historical traumas expected to precede the true messiah's coming.

Jewish, Christian, and Muslim artists and writers, we have seen, spent much of their energy as apologists, interpreting scriptures in ways that combatted, where necessary, the meanings their opponents found in the same narratives. Their efforts as commentators concentrated on the moral direction and spiritual care of their own people, but these chief interests could rarely be pursued, as if strong competition did not exist between them and the other peoples of the book.

Jonah's story was a cautionary tale for Jews, probing what constitutes obedience to God, and true repentance. Christians read and heard it as a God-sent forecast of Christ's victory over death, taking that hope to themselves. For Muslims, Yunus's testing by God rendered him a prophet not to be denied his full honor, for in his penitence, this prophet undertook true *zikr*, the steady remembrance and consciousness of God.

PART V

Mary, Miriam, Maryam

Preview, Chapters 13–15

Mary Through the Eyes of Three Religions

Although Mary appears initially in the New Testament, she belongs to the three religions. In Christianity's early centuries she would come to be addressed as "Mary, virgin Mother of God." Jews of the same era knew her as that Miriam who was no virgin (as her son Yeshu was no messiah). From the time of the Qur'an onward, Muslims revered Maryam as the virgin mother of one of Muhammad's greatest predecessors, `Isa (Jesus) the messiah-prophet of God, but (contra the Christians) not his divine Son.

That a young woman bearing a familiar Jewish name, Miriam, gave birth to a child named Yeshu during the rule of King Herod or his successor in Judea was not a matter of debate among Jesus-followers and Jesus-resisters, whether Jewish or pagan, who responded to her story in the first through seventh centuries. But strong arguments *were* advanced over the question of who and what Jesus was, and what significance could be claimed for him. Earliest Christian presentations of the nativity of Jesus were creative—the work of interpreters who, with only scant reports about his early years available to them, fashioned legends congruent with their understandings of his public ministry and his death, resurrection, and ascension to heaven. Not only the Christian writers and exegetes, but also their Jewish and Muslim counterparts, worked to fill gaps in the information concerning the birth of Jesus. Predictably, their interpretive story-extensions assumed both pro-Jesus, pro-Mary and anti-Jesus, anti-Mary forms.

Once more, as with the stories of Cain and Abel, Sarah and Hagar, and others we have met in these pages, it is possible to see the varying evolutions of a sacred story. Given the significance of Jesus to Christians and their claim that he was the promised messiah, Judaism was obliged to challenge devotion to Mary and her child and to annul their places in the divine scheme of things. Similarly, Mary's story required significant tailoring in order for it to be aligned with Islam's comprehension of the oneness and singularity of God. The Christians, for their part, wasted no time in imagining and reimagining the role and significance of the Virgin in the salvation they celebrated and the prayers they offered up.

These concluding chapters will trace the radically different ways that Miriam/Mary/Maryam takes on a life to be remembered. Christians within a few centuries will so enhance Mary's profile and persona that she becomes the object of deep devotion, and will accord her not only the highest rank among its saints, but a heavenly place in proximity to her son. From her initial appearance as an unnamed mother in one of Paul's letters, she becomes elevated to Mother of God, in whose name sinners will seek Christ's forgiveness. Of major importance in the increase of Mary's grand reputation for holiness is a second-century Christian writing titled *The Protevangelium of James*. In its colorful narrative-biography of Jesus's mother are found not only seeds of Mariology (the doctrines concerning Mary) that blossomed beginning in the late fourth century, but also the specific teaching of the immaculate conception of Mary by her mother, Anna.

During the years in which the followers of Jesus made the transition from Jewish sect to Christianity, not Judaism (as Ignatius, Bishop of Antioch distinguished the two in the early second century), rabbis and other Jewish writers resisted the claims they heard about Mary's divinely sponsored and prophesied virgin birth. We possess evidence, especially in *Toledoth Yeshu*, a "life of Jesus" in parody, of the energy spent in collecting damaging stories about Mary's lifestyle, her impregnation, and the identity of her son's actual father. Another rich text, *Sefer Zerubbabel*, a seventh-century Jewish apocalypse, presents us with a response, or counter, to the Mary of the Christians: it presents an alternative powerful mother—of the *now* imminent messiah of the Jews.

Within the Qur'an, and especially in the *surah* bearing her name, Maryam, the reader finds admiring (and intriguing) accounts of her purity as a child, her miraculous conception of the boy to be named ʿIsa, his boyhood wonders, and her faithfulness to God in her prayers and in her actions. As the Mary-tradition is expanded by Muslim exegetes and historians, debate erupts over what kinds of praise and devotion are appropriate for her—some are judged as going too far, while others are deemed entirely fitting in the celebration of Maryam, the one God chose "above the women of the worlds."

The ancient sources on Mary compel an alteration of the format followed in the previous four studies, in which the scriptures of all three religions, chronologically sequenced, served as our points of departure. The books of the Hebrew Bible predate the first century and contain no record of the lives of Mary and Jesus. We proceed nonetheless—for postbiblical rabbinic writings and treatises present us with an abundance of Jewish commentary on Mary and her son. It is not at all surprising that images of Mary and Jesus do not appear in early Jewish art, but this absence reduces the figural interpretations of Mary we may consider to two of the three traditions.

Christians' beliefs in the miraculous nativity of Jesus and his anointment as God's promised one, while serving the churches' message and purposes well, drew early and sustained protests. To polytheist or pagan theologians those claims about Jesus and his mother were both ludicrous and troublesome. Counternarratives concerning Miriam and Yeshu were expected Jewish responses in a cultural setting marked by lively religious competition. While the typical polemics of antique writing (ridicule, disdain, and both high and low humor) were fully in play, there were, nevertheless, grounds for a serious and sharp dispute over scriptural interpretations. *Did a reference to the birth of Jesus exist in the Bible of the Jews, as Christians claimed?* Jewish teachers and scholars challenged, from an early point, the Jesus-followers' argument that the birth of their Lord from a virgin fulfilled a prediction in the recorded words of the Hebrew prophet Isaiah. Whose Greek translation gave the correct reading of the Hebrew? Whose exegesis was forced and errant? Whose was attuned to divine wisdom?

A very different set of questions occupied Muslim and Christian interpreters of their holy books following the revelation to Muhammad, since the Qur'an's portrayal of both Mary and Jesus was in many ways consistent with that of the Christian tradition. Yet the Qur'an represented Maryam and 'Isa in terms of Islam's own theology and piety—often strongly at odds with Christian doctrine and worship. That Jesus Christ was not to be counted as divine, or a "partner" to God—or, worst of all, a son of God—was a foregone conclusion, but in interesting ways the events surrounding Mary's pregnancy and birth made her own status another matter, and another matter under contestation. Was the observed Christian practice of offering worship not only to her son, but also to her, as if she were divine, a distortion of the revelation?

Acknowledged in the three faith traditions as the Jewish girl who gave birth to Jesus, Miriam/Mary/Maryam takes mulitiple forms in representations that emerged in first-through seventh-century Judaism and

Christianity, as well as those found in the Qur'an and among its exegetes, in the seventh century and beyond. She will be thought of as a Jewish girl who becomes a "God-bearer," a promiscuous woman with a penchant for carpenters, and a righteous and pure girl commissioned by God to bring one of his testifiers, his prophets, into being.

The ingenuity of the three faith communities' retellers of Mary's story as they pursue their distinctive goals is fascinating to observe. Often seen to be working in awareness of each others' ideas and convictions, the three religions' interpreters of Mary's story were keen to learn from, as well as to correct and amend, what their counterparts set forth in their developing sacred lore. Once again the writers and artists give us a window that opens upon the splendid curiosity and creativity through which a revelation is, on the one hand, challenged and set to the side, or on the other hand, accepted and enhanced, giving both continuity and new energy to a people's cherished beliefs and rituals.

Because each of the religions pits its Mary against the understanding of her held by its rivals, the literature is ripe with contestation and sharp disagreement. These exchanges—seen frequently in earlier parts of this book—are seemingly intensified around the case of Miriam/Mary/Maryam. Perhaps we gain clarity about this phenomenon of biased polemic in the name of faith from a plain definition of its character. Gavin Langmuir elucidated this dynamic. Anti-Judaism, he wrote, is a

> total or partial opposition to Judaism—and to Jews as adherents of it—by [people] who accept a competing system of beliefs and practices and consider certain genuine Judaic beliefs and practices as inferior.[1]

Of course the same definition is applicable to anti-Christianity and anti-Islam. We shall encounter ample evidence of all three in the pages below. The authors and graphic artists who are the subjects in this book, and in these three chapters, were no strangers to the world of exclusive claims of religious truth and special peoplehood, nor to attitudes and arguments that sought to challenge, criticize, and hold at a distance those who were not included in a saving revelation they believed to be theirs alone.

CHAPTER 13

⚭

Mary in Christian Imagination

From Jewish Maiden to Ever-Virgin
to Heavenly Advocate

Out of the rich and multifaceted history of the rise of devotion to Mary in Byzantine times I have chosen here to concentrate on the evolution of two parts of her story: the nativity of Jesus (in three versions), and the end of her life (unrecorded in the New Testament but produced by Christian preachers, writers, and artists).[1]

One face of the revolutionary increase of Mary's purity and powers (what historians referred to as the rise of her "cult" before that term took on negative modern connotations) can be discerned in a change in the consciousness of Christians between the time when Paul, speaking of God's sending of his son, mentioned simply that he was "born of a woman, born under the law" (*Galatians* 4:4) and the era in which church leaders (like Archbishop Germanus of Constantinople in the eighth century) directed their prayers to heavenly Mary, the pure and majestic, celebrating "the mercy of [her] unchanging patronage" on behalf of sinners.[2]

The other aspect of Mary's greater prominence reflected Christianity's cultural successes. The Virgin's image replaced the goddess Victory on coinage and was, for example, displayed both in Constantinople's churches and its public spaces. She (by means of her icon or a relic) had already displayed her powers to protect the waters surrounding the city and its walls from invaders by 626 CE when a siege by Avars and Persian Sassanids was turned away. In the next two centuries Mary would repel Muslim navies more than once.

In concentrating upon the growth of traditions around the youthful Mary who gave birth to Jesus and, then, around the circumstances of her life's end, this chapter inevitably bypasses important events in her life during Jesus's ministry—for example, her presence at the wedding in Cana, the incident in which Jesus rebuffed his mother and his brothers when they approached him, and Mary's presence at her son's crucifixion.[3] Nor do we visit *Revelation* 12—an eschatological vision of a dragon-attacked celestial woman who gave birth to "a male child who is to rule all the nations with a rod of iron."[4] She has long been understood to be a symbolic representation of Mary.

Confident that a reliable, if partial, understanding of how Mary gained more defined personhood and achieved greater status can be gained from interpretations of her virgin motherhood and from the traditions that gave pictures of her last days, I move first to characterizations of Mary in birth narratives. With these portaits we shall compare fascinating, and baldly competitive, Jewish and Muslim understandings of Mary's motherhood.

MARY AND THE BIRTH OF JESUS: THREE EARLY CHRISTIAN ACCOUNTS

The independence of *Matthew* and *Luke* in their sources of information about Jesus's beginnings is difficult to miss when the two texts are read side by side. The former dates Jesus's birth a decade earlier than the latter (ca. 4 BCE and 6–7 CE, respectively), and *Luke*'s narrative, for reasons to be discussed below, is much longer than *Matthew*'s. The genealogies given for Jesus (*Matthew* 1:1–17 and *Luke* 3:23–43) neither conform nor do they encompass the same stretches of history, since each author seeks to register his own important point about time and its coming to "fullness" with the appearance of Christ. According to *Matthew*, the record of male progenitors runs from Abraham to Joseph, "the husband of Mary, of whom Jesus was born, who is called Christ" (1:16). There is no apparent worry on the author's part that Joseph is the husband who, as he will soon report, is a nonparticipant in the virgin's pregnancy. *Matthew*'s observation (in 1:17) that the genealogical record may be counted by three periods of fourteen generations seems more crucial to him: the birth of Jesus occurs at an auspicious time, a turning point in history.

The two-volume work by the author of *Luke* and *The Acts of the Apostles* has as a dominant theme the spread of the message of and about Jesus to "the nations," and his universalist perspective prompts him to record a genealogy from Jesus to Adam, who, having no human father, is (also) referred to as "the son of God" (*Luke* 3:38). At the outset of *Luke*'s geneal-ogy, which comes *after* the birth narrative, we see him exercising artful finesse in language about Jesus's parenthood: "Jesus, when he began his ministry, was about thirty years of age, being the son (as was supposed) of Joseph, son of Heli" (*Luke* 2:23).

The two evangelists' genealogies present us with something other than straightforward historical reportage. Here, and elsewhere in the two Gospels' birth stories, clues and clear affirmations point to who Jesus *is to be*—or, rather, attributes of him as messiah and Lord are being written back into his early life. Jesus's birth and childhood must be shown to have already revealed his promise and glory. This is a sample of what historians of religion think of as retrospective "founder elevation."

The Nativity Account in *Matthew*: Themes and Objectives

Finding what is distinctive in the Matthean nativity story's presentation of Mary calls, first, for a review of its contents. Its opening (*Matthew* 1:18–25) recounts the discovery of Mary's pregnancy by Joseph, to whom she is betrothed, Joseph's education by the angel about how this occurred and what the boy-child shall be named, Joseph's marriage to Mary, the birth itself (in a single sentence), and the naming of Jesus. The narrative next tells (2:1 12) of the magi searching for a newly born "king of the Jews" and of King Herod's efforts to learn from them this child's where-abouts, so that he might, not "pay him homage," as he says, but eliminate a potential threat to his royal house. Chapter 2:13–23 contains the angel's directive that Joseph flee with Mary and Jesus to Egypt for safety from Herod, and a three-verse segment (2:16–18) recounting Herod's response to the failure of the magi to inform him of infant Jesus's location—the "slaughter of the innocents." *Matthew*'s record of the birth and first years of Jesus concludes (in 2:19–23) with Joseph's return of Jesus and his mother to their homeland—not to Bethlehem, but, to avoid notice by Archelaus, Herod's son ruling in Judea, to a Galilean town named Nazareth.

Traits of *Matthew*'s nativity account—its points of special interest and emphasis as well as its specific strategies—deserve our attention as com-parativists. The author is concerned from the beginning and throughout to establish and secure the reality of Mary's virginity. She found herself to be "with child by the Holy Spirit" prior to the time she lived with Joseph, her husband to be (1:18). The "angel of the Lord" urges him to take Mary as his wife and to name the child Jesus (a form of Joshua, its root being *yasha*, which means "he saves"), for Jesus will deliver "his people from their sins." Then the angel announces:

> Look, the virgin shall conceive
> and bear a son,
> and they shall name him
> Emmanuel,
> which [*Matthew* adds] means, "God is with us"
> (*Matthew* 1:23).

The notice at 1:25 that Joseph, after marrying Mary, "had no marital relations with her until she had borne a son" (other ancient texts of *Matthew* read "her firstborn son") reinforced Mary's virginal status—most likely in response to some who some were suspicious of the claim.

A detail within this part of the narrative is noteworthy: in the angel's reference to Joseph as "son of David" and in having Joseph take Mary into his house, *Matthew*, as biblical scholar John Meier observed, presents the once wary husband as a man "confer[ring] Davidic paternity on her child and so insert[ing] her child into its proper place in salvation history."[5] (The Gospel's introductory phrase had already pinpointed the chief figures in Jesus's heritage, calling him "Jesus the Messiah, the son of David, the son of Abraham.")

Intriguingly, here, and at all other critical points in *Matthew*'s story of the birth of Jesus, Joseph is the recipient of news and important commands relating to the birth of Jesus to Mary. Though without Mary there would be no story to tell, in this Gospel the angel does not communicate with her, nor does she speak. In *Matthew*, the angel's "annunciation" of the birth of the child Jesus is not addressed to the girl who is to bear him, but to Joseph—soon to be her husband, but not the child's father. The same holds true in the episode that only *Matthew* reports. Mary is not involved in Joseph's responses to the angel of the Lord when (in 2:13–14) he is urged to "take up the child and his mother, and flee to Egypt"—removing them from Herod's threatening reach. The angel's summons to Joseph also prompts the family's return to their home country.

A strong feature of the *Gospel of Matthew* is its repeated employment of words from Hebrew prophets to demonstrate the foreordained character of all that happened to, and all that was accomplished by, Jesus. Just prior to his telling of Mary's conception, the consternation of Joseph, and the angel's dream-messages to him about the son's name and mission, with it's quotation of *Isaiah* 7:14 ("Look, the virgin shall conceive and bear a son, and they shall name him Emmanuel"), the evangelist inserted his "formula" explanation: "All this took place to fulfill what had been spoken by the Lord, through the prophet."

The practice of proof-texting by writers of the Gospels lent authority to their representations of Jesus—and, importantly, enabled them to create new events in his life. *Matthew*'s account of the escape to Egypt of Joseph, Mary, and the endangered Jesus is a provocative case in point. Noting that Jesus remained in Egypt until Herod died, the evangelist added:

> This was to fulfill what had been spoken by the Lord through the prophet, "Out of Egypt I have called my son" (*Hosea* 11.14).

Though for the prophet Hosea the word "son" designated Israel itself, Matthew turns the quotation to another purpose: it was Moses *in Egypt* and the oppression of the Pharaoh that the evangelist had in mind. Herod's pursuit and slaughter of young Hebrew males was a replay of what the Pharaoh had ordered Egypian midwives to do (*Exodus* 1:15–22). It is this threat, murder, which Jesus must escape. But the Gospel writer has a strategic point to make: Jesus must leave the realm of Herod so that he may in time be "called. . . . out of Egypt" by the Lord's angel. Transparently *Matthew* invokes and promises, on the infant Jesus's behalf, future power of the sort that accomplished the liberation, the redemption, of Moses and his people.

The Moses-Jesus linkage is important to *Matthew*'s understanding of the gospel message he composes. Later, in chapter 5, when *Matthew* presents the mature Jesus as the teacher-prophet who comes, not to abolish, but to fulfill the Law (*Matthew* 5:17), he pictures him delivering his new and more stringent version of law-obedience from a mountain top (while in *Luke* Jesus delivers his sermon "standing on a level place" in *Luke* 6:17ff.). *Matthew* is seen to be employing Moses at Sinai as a prefigurement, a prototype, of Jesus. His theologizing moves beyond the broad claim that all that took place in Jesus was ordained by God to put forward a specific Christian claim: Moses's exodus from the Pharaoh's oppression and Moses's reception of divine law anticipated and pointed to the day when Jesus the messiah would bring to true and ultimate fulfillment God's salvation of his people.

Matthew is distinguished by its interpretive strategy, which is at work throughout the Gospel narrative. The quotation of *Isaiah* 7:4 in support of the truth of Mary's virgin birth-giving to the one who is "God with us," is not at all different, functionally, from the explanation late in the Gospel of why Jesus's disciples abandoned him at the time of his arrest. In this instance the proof-text, *Zechariah* 13:7, comes from Jesus's lips at the "Last Supper":

> You will all become deserters because of me this night, for it is written:
> "I will strike the shepherd,
> and the sheep of the flock will
> be scattered."

Scholars call this mode of argument "apologetic," seeing it as a literary extension from ancient legal briefs in which a person defends himself against accusations, providing some form of authoritative evidence to the contrary. But whose accusations required scripture-based rebuttal from the Gospel writer? What kinds of attacks were being made concerning Mary's virgin birth, or the number of her children, or, for that matter, Jesus's unreliable disciples? The next chapter will investigate just this question. It would be wrong to suggest, however, that defense against critics was the sole purpose and benefit of bolstering claims about Jesus's life and actions through ancient scriptural prophecies. The presentation of a new revelation from God as a series of happenings long-awaited, certain to come, God-approved, and *now* fulfilled, held strong appeal for those already convinced of Jesus's identity as the promised messiah and God's son, and certainly also for those contemplating acceptance of this savior and association with the new community formed in his name.

The Nativity Account in *Luke*: Themes and Objectives

Centuries of Christian festivals celebrating the birth of Jesus homogenized the New Testament's two nativity stories, obscuring significant differences between the Matthean and Lukan versions. *Luke* is unique in several ways. Structurally, it is volume one of its author's longer history, which continues in the Holy-Spirit empowered *acta* (deeds) of the apostles—especially Peter and Paul. *Luke*'s nativity story weaves together two miraculous births—that of John (who will become the baptizer) to the priest Zechariah and his long-barren wife, Elizabeth, and that of Jesus to Mary, "a virgin engaged to a man whose name was Joseph, of the house of David" (1:27).[6] The careers of John and Jesus are linked from the beginning, a fact that *Luke* has important reasons for emphasizing, as we shall see.

Whereas *Matthew* employed biblical prophecies to advance and explain his narrative, *Luke* sustains his nativity story's momentum (and authority) by means of versified speeches declared to be inspired by the Holy Spirit.

Elizabeth exclaims "with a loud cry" to Mary: "Blessed are you among women, and blessed is the fruit of your womb" (1:42). Mary's response opens with these words:

> My soul magnifies the Lord,
> and my spirit rejoices in God
> my Savior,
> for he has looked with favor on
> the lowliness of his servant.
> Surely, from now on all
> generations will call
> me blessed;
> for the Mighty One has done
> great things for me,
> and holy is his name (*Luke* 1:46–49).

Zechariah hymns his praise to God for providing him and Elizabeth with their child John, "who will be called the prophet of the Most High" (1:76), and a "heavenly host" sings to the shepherds, who travel on to Bethlehem to find "Mary and Joseph, and the child lying in the manger" (2:16). (The description of Jesus's birth a few verses earlier [2:7] was brief, but its reference to him as Mary's "firstborn"—which intimated later children—would spark controversy.) In Jerusalem when Jesus was brought there to be circumcized, Simeon (promised by the Holy Spirit that he would not die before he had seen "the Lord's Messiah") praised God in verse, while the nearby propetess, Anna, spoke of the child "to all who were looking for the redemption of Israel" (2:21–28).

No more famous moment exists in Christian nativity traditions than the passage telling of Mary's being surprised:

Luke 1:26 [The angel Gabriel] came to her and said, "Greetings [or: Hail], favored one! The Lord is with you." 29 But she was much perplexed by his words and wondered what sort of greeting this might be. 30 The angel said to her, "do not be afraid, Mary, for you have found favor with God. 31 And now you will conceive in your womb and bear a son, and you will name him Jesus. 32 He will be great, and will be called the Son of the Most High, and the Lord God will give to him the throne of his ancestor David. 33 He will reign over the house of Jacob forever, and of his kingdom there will be no end." 34 Mary said to the angel, "How can this be, since I am a virgin?" 35 The angel said to her, "The Holy Spirit will come upon you, and the power of the Most High will overshadow you; therefore the child to be born will be holy; he will be called Son of God. 36 And now, your relative Elizabeth in her old age has also conceived a son; and this is the sixth month for her who was said to be barren. 37 For nothing will be impossible with God." 38 Then Mary said, "Here am I, the servant of the Lord; let it be with me according to your word." Then the angel departed from her.

Mary has a voice in *Luke*'s nativity story. Spoken to, she ponders what is said, answers with questions, and then makes and declares her decision. To have the young virgin speak and act on her own terms alters the story of Jesus's birth: it now is about Mary and child, with Mary's personality and personhood taking a more central place—and affecting the narrative's content, plot, and tone. A daughter of Israel, Mary submits to servanthood, giving herself over in obedience to God and to God's purposes. In *Luke* she appears as a woman who possesses agency in participating in the salvific purposes of the "Most High."

Portrayed by *Luke* forty-two verses later, in 2:1–20, the nativity of Jesus is told in a single verse: "And she gave birth to her firstborn son and wrapped him in bands of cloth, and laid him in a manger, because there was no place for them in the inn" (2:7). The report is plain enough, though the term *prototokon* (firstborn) will later spark discussion in connection with questions about Jesus's siblings and about Mary's "perpetual virginity"—before, during, and after the birth of Jesus—that believers will soon claim for her. Other and different interests are in play for the Gospel-writer, however. Like Matthew, *Luke* is concerned to have the pregnant Mary in Bethlehem at the propitious time, and the census ordered by Caesar Augustus and enacted by Quirinius, governor of the Syrian province, causes Joseph, accompanied by Mary, to travel there. The one who will be messiah/king, should be born in David's city. The "good tidings" of the "sign" the shepherds will see there—a child lying in a manger—is accompanied by a display of the Lord's glory, and by a large chorus of "the heavenly host" whose song gives glory to God "in the highest heaven" and beckons or pledges peace on earth for those whom God favors (2:14). While the shepherds are pictured praising God for this revelation as they return home to their labors, *Luke* inserts a glimpse of Mary, and of her interior self. All the words being spoken about the birth of her son she "treasured … and pondered in her heart" (2:19). A reservation or foreboding seems to be suggested, and the theme surfaces shortly thereafter, when Simeon the holy man tells Mary (2:34–35):

> This child is destined for the falling and rising of many in Israel, and to be a sign that will be opposed so that the inner thoughts of many will be revealed—and a sword will pierce your own soul too.

Simeon's words, of course, anticipate Jesus's arrest and execution—but their attention to these events' impact upon his mother is explicit. It adds to what the reader or hearer of this portion of *Luke* knows about Mary's experiences.

What immediately follows in this version of Jesus's birth story affords yet another glimpse. Before introducing the adult Jesus, who will be pictured approaching John the Baptist at the Jordan river, *Luke* has the tale of Joseph's and Mary's discovery of their "lost" twelve-year-old son in the Temple. The boy Jesus had not joined them in their journey homeward at Passover's conclusion, choosing rather to speak with, and to question, the Jerusalem sages: "And all who heard him were amazed at his understanding and his answers" (2:47). There is sharpness in Jesus's response to Mary's agitation over his staying behind in the city. He asks an authoritative and telling question: Where else would he have been but in his "Father's house"? On this occasion too "his mother treasured all these things in her heart" (2:51). Here again *Luke* has unveiled Jesus's mother as someone embodied, a person whose actions can be seen, whose thoughts can be guessed at—sensed. The development of the profile and identity of Mary in this Gospel has come quite a distance from the first reference to her in a Christian document, Paul's spare description of her as a young Jewish maiden. Mary's *presence* in *Luke*'s Gospel, then, is stronger than in *Matthew*'s narrative. In her encounter with Gabriel she has negotiated, coming to discernment of the divine event in which she is caught up. In response to Elizabeth's acclamation, she has "magnified" God for finding her, in her "lowliness," worthy of favor and blessing. Mary has been spoken to by the inspired Simeon, and she speaks to and is answered by her young son, whom she knows to be God's Son. Further, we learn that she ponders what may transpire in the story she shares with Jesus. In no other New Testament writing is Mary given so prominent a place and so suggestive a characterization. Mary becomes imaginable as a human being, a person responsive to a mysterious and daunting invitation, and a mother with her own ideas, feelings, and will.

Because *Luke*'s author, too, had specific strategic interests, one of his major concerns deserves closer scrutiny. He wanted the relationship of John the Baptist and Jesus firmly clarified, and invented a way to accomplish this. Noticeably, all the New Testament Gospel writers spent considerable—and effective—energy building the case for the superior powers and the greater importance of Jesus in comparison to John. At the Jordan River John suggests that Jesus should be baptizing *him*, and at several points John talks about the one more worthy, whom he precedes. The Gospel portraits of John identify him, then, as the prophet-forerunner preparing the way for Jesus, who is God's messiah, and (as the voice from the heavens declares while Jesus is baptized) God's "beloved son, with whom [God] is well pleased."[7] Interestingly, however, the followers of the two men—two discrete groups of disciples—appear in the Gospel texts, asking searching questions about their respective leaders. Writing in the latter part of the first century, the evangelists make it clear that some confusion or competition swirled around the two men's authority and "credentials." In the course of settling the question, *Luke* 3:15–16 conveys what was involved in the two parties' exchanges:

> As the people were filled with expectation, and all were questioning in their hearts whether he might be the messiah, John answered all of them by saying, "I baptized you with water; but one who is more powerful than I is coming; I am not worthy to untie the thong of his sandals. He will baptize you with the Holy Spirit and fire."

Unique to *Luke* is its retrojection of the issues concerning the adult roles of John and Jesus into the story of their orgins—into his dual nativity stories. We see the author's creativity at work. The angel's appearance to Zechariah, with the promise of a child to be named John comes before Gabriel's visitation of Mary. Elizabeth's conception of John in her old age is a divine gift, but not an unprecedented one—Sarah (and Hannah, as we shall see) had been similarly blessed.

Mary's virginal conception of Jesus is represented as a miracle infinitely more glorious. But the chronology of things needed reassertion: both the narrator and Gabriel make note of the fact that Elizabeth became pregnant six months before Mary. What followed was the briefly described, but all-important, event at the home of Elizabeth, whose greeting of her kinswoman caused her baby to leap in her womb (in joy, we learn a few verses later). This is a recognition scene—of Jesus by John—both in utero. This is how long, the writer asserts, the superiority of Jesus was known to John.

Those aware of the events of the two nativities would never have harbored any doubts about the male children's identities or their relationship with one another, however. Even before John was conceived, Zechariah learned from the angel that his son would be an ascetic, spirit-filled from his mother's womb, and that he would "turn many of the sons of Israel to the Lord their God . . . in the spirit and power of Elijah . . . to make ready for the Lord a people prepared" (1:15–17). Mary's son, by contrast, is clearly marked for *his* mission by being called, as Gabriel informs Mary (1:32, 35), "the Son of the Most High," "the Son of God." Jesus will assume the throne of David his ancestor in his powerful capacity as the messiah-king announced by God's angel.

Desiring to put to rest any further debate or discussion of the matter—and adding the earliest possible authoritative evidence bearing upon it—the writer of *Luke* secures, from his Gospel's onset, the truth about the Baptizer's greatness as Jesus's forerunner, and the truth about Jesus's messiahship and divine sonship. The reader or hearer of the parallel birth and infancy stories in *Luke* could not fail to register the message that as Jesus is greater than John, so too is Mary's submission to the miraculous conception and birth more worthy of praise and celebration than Elizabeth's still fully wondrous conception and birth of John. Both sets of mother and child are blessed, but Jesus and Mary are especially and distinctively God-favored. *Luke* the interpreter shows, therefore, how their presence elicits joy and worshipful wonder from Elizabeth and John. In all of this, by constructing a narrative apologia against any claims that John had authority equal to, or greater than that of Jesus, the evangelist closely links the two who will be contemporary prophet-teachers while more definitely describing who each one will be, and what role each will play in the drama of God's inbreaking reign.

The comprehensive theological vision of the author of *Luke* and *The Acts of the Apostles* can only be touched upon here, and mostly in reference to Mary's place in it. The writer's universalism emerged first in the tracing of Jesus's lineage beyond Abraham back to Adam, and in his being celebrated by Simeon as "a light for revelation to the Gentiles" as well as the Jews.

The opening chapters of the author's second volume display his conviction that the Holy Spirit, operative in the events surrounding Mary's conception and birth of Jesus, is *now*, after Christ's death and resurrection, extending its sway. Jesus, in his last words to his followers before ascending to heaven, promises that the Holy Spirit will come upon them and that they will be his witnesses (proclaimers) "in Jerusalem, and in Judea and Samaria, and to the ends of the earth" (*Acts* 1:8). The group returned to Jerusalem, and among them as they prayed were "certain women, including Mary the mother of Jesus, as well as his brothers" (*Acts* 1:14). The signal event of *Acts* is the descent of the Holy Spirit upon Jesus's devotees on the Pentecost (the Jewish festival held fifty days after Passover). A painting in the sixth-century Rabbula Gospels imagines Mary centrally positioned among those upon whom "tongues of fire" came to rest.[8]

Immediately, the languages that his apostles speak are intelligible to those present from other nations and cultures who hear them. The list is long, naming peoples from near and far—Mesopotamians, Cappadocians, Asians, Egyptians, Libyans, and visitors to Jerusalem from Rome. The future of the proclamation of and about Jesus as God's Son is the work, now, of the Holy Spirit—in the endeavors of apostles and other missionaries, and within the many who will receive and accept it. The careers of Peter and Paul provide the framework for this movement of the Spirit.

Easy to recall is young Mary's dialogue with Gabriel, and her recognition of what God has done for her:

> My soul magnifies the Lord,
> and my spirit rejoices in God my Savior,
> for he has looked with favor
> on the lowliness of his servant.
> Surely from now on all
> generations will call
> me blessed (*Luke* 1:46–48).

Before and after the event at Pentecost, the powers of the Holy Spirit spread to the many. According to *Luke*, the tidings about Jesus are for "all nations." Universal recognition of Mary is, of course, part of this revelation's dissemination. She spoke inspired prophecy about her reputation. It comes true, and soon, in another early, and very influential, Christian story of Mary.

Mary the Pure: *The Protevangelium of James*

"The apocryphal wellspring of Marian legends," a second-century writing awkwardly titled *Protevangelium of James* (*PJ*) is devoted to the life of Mary—from her miraculous conception to the time in which she conceives and gives birth to Jesus.[9] Its closing passages concern Herod's slaughter of the innocents, and the fates of John the Baptist and his parents—only some of the evidence that its author was familiar with *Matthew* and *Luke*, in addition to other Christian writings. In fashioning the story of Mary's birth and girlhood—events that preceded what the already circulating Gospel nativity stories told— *PJ* reveals a prevailing interest in Mary's virginity, its celebration, and its defense. This prestory serves to justify and fortify her worthiness for the miraculous "servanthood" she accepts, at Gabriel's coaxing. "Mary's purity," as Ronald Hock wrote, is the text's "unifying theme."[10] Again, we are able to sense issues in the mind of the author, an apologist who upholds a primary Christian claim of Jesus's birth from a virgin—against skeptics and detractors. A result of his focused attention on Mary is that her role as mother of Jesus is greatly enhanced. She, as well as her son, is to be admired—and held in honor. Many of the foundations upon which the churches' veneration of Mary would be built are in this narrative, a writing as prominent in Christianity's early centuries as any other.

A combination of summary and highlighting of this entertaining text will have to suffice, even though I shall interject my own interpretations of *PJ*'s highly interpreted story of Mary. The opening scenes introduce Mary's parents-to-be: the wealthy and pious Joachim, who is prevented from making the initial offering on a Temple feast day of the Lord because he has not "produced an Israelite child," and his wife Anna, who laments her childlessness (*PJ* 1–2).[11] Joachim takes up a forty-day fast in the wilderness, vowing to himself that he will not eat or drink until he receives a visit from God. Anna, stung by her servant's charge that God has punished her with sterility, adopts another style of protest, casting off the clothes of a mourner and donning her wedding dress. Under a laurel tree she prays: "O God of my ancestors, bless me and hear my prayer, just as you blessed our mother Sarah and gave her a son, Isaac." (Joachim also had recalled the patriach Abraham, whose son was born "in his last days.") Her several lamentations, rhythmically triggered by a "Poor me!," speak of being cursed by her people and banished from the temple, and of her barrenness as something making her inferior to animals, waters, and the earth—all of which replenish their kind.

In language very similar to *Luke* 2's "annunciation" to Mary, the distressed woman is spoken to and then responds to the Lord's angel:

> "Anna, Anna, the Lord God has heard your prayer. You shall conceive and bear, and your offspring will be spoken of in the whole world." And Anna said, "As the Lord my God lives, if I bear a child, whether male or female, I will bring it as a gift to the Lord my God, and it will serve him all the days of its life" (*PJ* 4.1–2).

The declaration that Anna's child will have world-renown (as Mary had said of herself in *Luke* 1:48b) and Anna's pledge of her offspring to God together signal what will characterize the early years of Mary.

Anna and Joachim are informed separately by an angel (later identified as Gabriel) that their prayers have been heard. Joachim started toward home, on the way laying plans for a grand feast, and Anna, seeing him, "rushed out and threw her arms around his neck," exulting, "I, who was childless, shall conceive." The next line reports that "Joachim rested the first day in his house," seeming to hint at seized sexual opportunity in consequence of the Lord's promise. But a certain ambiguity surrounds the means and timing of Mary's conception, since some variant readings in the manuscript of *PJ* suggest that the pregnancy has already occurred prior to the couple's reunion. The "kiss" or embrace of Joachim and Anna won a firm place in Christian art treating the story of Mary's parents. This figure or icon encouraged the belief that the conception of Mary was effected through her parents' embrace of greeting in itself.[12]

This episode contributed a new dimension to the purity attributed to Mary—namely, the view that even before her holy childhood, she was sinless by virtue of the *unique* conception of her by her parents. It is worth pausing momentarily to distinguish the ways Christians in the eastern Mediterranean (Greek, Syriac, Armenian, etc.) and Roman Catholics in the Latin-speaking West understood, and over the centuries, came to articulate, their teaching. The Roman Catholic teaching of the "immaculate conception" of Mary (*not* of Jesus, though this misunderstanding is widespread), came under the influence of Augustine's doctrine of original sin, with the result that ecclesial doctrine in the Latin churches held that Mary's own conception was immaculate—that is, that she was conceived and born free of the stain (*macula*, Latin) of sin which all other humans had inherited in consequence of the Fall of Adam and Eve. This teaching was accorded the status of dogma under Pope Pius IX in 1854. In its early centuries unaware of, and later resistant to, Augustine's view that the stain occurring in Eden made humans incapable of *not* sinning, the Christian East celebrated Mary's purity in other terms, in some cases exploiting the familiar Eve-Mary associations by attributing to Mary the sinless character of the first mother *before* the sin in the Garden, and in others laying emphasis upon the obedience and holy deeds of Mary throughout her childhood, in the time of her conception of Jesus, and beyond.

While the understanding of Mary's miraculous conception by means of a kiss of greeting was to gain many adherents, the alternate opinion that Mary was wonderously but naturally begotten of Joachim and Anna remained strong. Readers and hearers of this portion of *PJ* (and those exposed to its later retellings in Christian contexts) knew the story for which this nativity story is now an extended preview: Anna is not, like Mary, a virgin, but a self-described "widow" (her reaction to having been abandoned by her fasting husband, and the reason for the mourning clothes that she put aside). Whether the text allows one to imagine that Joachim is the actual or biological father of Anna's child or not, the pregnancy is the miraculous result of God-answered prayer, and is extraordinary in the manner of other such late and divinely enabled begettings and child-bearings—for example, that experienced by Abraham and Sarah, but more especially that featuring Elkanah's wife, Hannah, whose son Samuel was also an answer to prayers. Hannah, dedicating her son to God, leaves him as a child in the Israelite sanctuary in Shiloh, proceeding to sing her song—in which "[her] strength is exalted in [her] God" (*1 Samuel* 1–2).

The birth, the learning of the baby's gender from the midwife, and the purification ritual of Anna are briefly told. She nurses her daughter and names her Mary. The next several chapters (6–10) chronicle Mary's parents' concern for preserving the sanctity that her God-enabled existence warrants. She is not to tread on ordinary ground until she is taken to the Temple to reside there (Joachim and Anna are pictured pondering how long this might be delayed) while in the meantime, they make Mary's room into a sanctuary, keeping her diet pure, and arranging visits to her from "undefiled daughters of the Hebrews" (6.1). When, as a three-year-old, Mary is greeted and received at the Temple, the priest enunciates again her fame—no longer a prediction, but a reality—as one whose name the Lord "has magnified . . . among all generations," adding, "because of you the Lord at the end of the days will reveal his redemption to the sons of Israel." Dramatically,

> he [the priest] placed her on the third step of the altar, and the Lord put grace upon her and she danced with her feet, and the whole house of Israel loved her (7.3).

The "gracing" of the child is consonant with something else the author has reported: both of her parents have gained assurance—Joachim by seeing his own image, apparently undistorted, in the mirror-headpiece worn by the Temple priest at the time of sacrifice (5.1–3), and Anna, in the removal of her curse of childlessness, and being blessed (4.9)—that their sins have been forgiven. The parents of the holy child are themselves holy, no longer captives of evil.

Of Mary's years of residence in the Jerusalem temple, overseen by Zachariah (the *PJ*'s spelling of Zechariah) the priest, we learn only that she was fed there "like a dove," angels delivering her food. At twelve years old, the onset of her menses becomes a worry to keepers of the sanctuary. Before she might pollute it, a place (and husband or keeper) must be found for her. Righteous widowers are summoned by "the trumpet of the Lord" to the temple, and asked to bring their staffs. Joseph's rod, returned to him after it had been prayed over by the high priest, signaled that he was to "receive the virgin of the Lord as [his] ward." Only his staff, one among many, had given a sign; from it a dove came forth and settled on the carpenter's head. Joseph expresses his trepidations. He already has sons from an earlier marriage (a narrative element that can give an explanation of Jesus's siblings, and also make Mary's virginity, before and after the birth of Jesus, possible, given a God with whom nothing is impossible). Further, Joseph says, trying to avert his selection, he is old. He will be laughable as young Mary's guardian. But a warning about the punishments awaiting rebels against God's will silences Joseph. After taking his new charge to his home, Joseph immediately (the author presumes his readers' understanding of this) leaves Mary, departing to do construction work elsewhere. God will protect you, he tells her.

A new theme is introduced into the lore accumulating around "the Lord's virgin" for whom Joseph now is responsible. When the priests decide to make a veil for the Temple, and are in the process of seeking out "pure virgins of the tribe of David" to accomplish the weaving, they recall that Mary qualifies—also, that she "was pure before God"—as if to say that she was especially sanctified. (Modern commentators, noting that there was no such tribe, assume that the intent of the fiction was to deepen the connection to the Davidic monarchic line of Jesus'mother.) Of the seven colors to be woven into the curtain, Mary was assigned the last two, those designated for her spinning—"the scarlet and the pure purple." Returning to Joseph's house to begin her labors, she started with the scarlet yarn. It was at this time, the narrator interjects, that Zachariah the priest became dumb, and was replaced by Samuel until he was able to speak once more. We note the compression of attention given to the father of John the Baptist.

The annunciation scene in *PJ* 11 conforms closely to that in Luke 1:28, but adds details which are important to the author's reformulation, through symbols, of the story's meanings. Confused by the invisible voice that hailed her while she was drawing water outdoors, Mary, "trembling . . . went to her house and put down the pitcher . . . and sat down on her seat and drew out the purple thread." Then "the angel of the Lord" appeared before her, saying, "Do not fear, Mary; for you have found grace before the Lord of all things and shall conceive by his Word."

Though the angel continues with a version of the Lukan formula in 1:35 ("the power of God will overshadow you"), new language emerges. Mary will become pregnant "by his [the Lord's] Word" or "through his *Logos*." God acts in history "by his Word," the writer asserts. He is tapping early Christian Logos-theology, according to which the Word/Son who is Creator—that is, God's agent of creation—will be active in his own creation within Mary. The role of God's Word in Mary's conception of the child to be named Jesus prompts intriguing understandings of Mary's impregnation among later interpreters, both Christian and Muslim, as we shall see.

The picture of Mary as spinner of thread, likewise, opens new exegetical possibilities—both in the *PJ* itself, and in later retellings of her story. Following the angel's visit, the text reads, Mary "made ready the purple and scarlet and brought them to the priest" (12.1), once more receiving with the priest's blessing the proclamation, "Mary, the Lord God has magnified your name, and you shall be blessed among all generations of the earth." Subtly introduced, perhaps, up to this point in the *PJ*'s telling of the births of Mary and Jesus, is the significance attaching to the scarlet and pure purple threads that have been assigned to Mary. They are shorthand statements about the issue that caused *Luke* to intertwine the nativities of Jesus and John the Baptist. What the reader may have inferred about the symbolism of scarlet as blood, and of pure purple (*porphyry*) as indicative of kingship, comes clearer when it is revealed that Elizabeth (not named earlier in connection with the young virgins selected for the task of weaving the Temple curtain), upon hearing the visiting Mary's approach, "tossed aside the scarlet thread [she was spinning], ran to the door, and opened it." The child within Elizabeth is destined to be a prophet who pays with his life, while Mary's baby, the true anointed one, will both die and be raised in majesty. Colors of thread convey the conclusion that *Luke* spent many lines of narrative working out.

New events involving John the Baptist and his parents appear in the *Protevangelium*'s closing chapters, as if added to an earlier version of the text. In flight from Herod's "murderers," Elizabeth asked a mountain to offer refuge, and the rock fantastically obliged by splitting open and taking (sealing?) her and her child inside, while an angel protected them (22.1–3). Zachariah, harassed for information about the whereabouts of his son, responded to the threat by exclaiming that he was a "witness of God" (23.3). The translation might just as well be "martyr," since this writer lives at the beginnings of Roman persecutions of Christians, and would have been aware of the assignment of that title to both Jews and Christians who died in defense of their communities' beliefs. The *PJ* then tells of the secret slaying of Zachariah, the discovery in the Temple sanctuary, not of his body, but of "his blood, now turned to stone," and the mourning of "all the tribes of the people."[13] Symeon—he who would not die "until he had seen the Christ in the flesh"—is selected high priest by lot (23.3–24.1).

The most novel portion of the latter half of the *PJ*—that concerning the birth of Jesus—gives to Christian tradition a vivid alternative story. Crises abound. Returning home from his business trip, Joseph is perplexed and appalled to find Mary pregnant (six months so), and in the midst of his wailings of self-blame and fear of God's reaction to his failure to protect "the virgin out of the temple of the Lord," we find him invoking the Eden tragedy: "For as Adam was absent in the hour of his prayer and the serpent came and found Eve alone and deceived her, so also has it happened to me" (13.1).

Mary, said to be sixteen at the time (other manuscript variants say "fourteen" or "fifteen"), then hears Joseph's accusation:[14]

> You who are cared for by God, why have you done this and forgotten the Lord your God? Why have you humiliated your soul, you who were brought up in the Holy of Holies and received food from the hand of an angel? (13.2).

Weeping, Mary responds, "I am pure, and know not a man." Unlike *Luke* 1:34, here Mary's assertion of her virginity is not made to Gabriel, but to the shaming Joseph. She is not defiant in response, but in tears she utters the word "pure" (*kathara*). It is this attribute that defines her in *this* nativity story.

When Joseph decides (in keeping with *Matthew*'s storyline) to "put Mary away quietly"—that is, divorce her—he is reassured in a dream that he is not to be afraid of the child, which was "of the Holy Spirit." Awakening, he thanks God and commits himself to Mary's protection.

But new trouble arose after the scribe Annas paid a call to inquire why Joseph had not been seen at Temple prayers. Seeing and reporting to the priest that Mary was pregnant, "defiled" by Joseph, Annas precipitated a trial of Joseph and Mary. The charge against them was not that the two had had illicit sex, but that they had married, and yet had not served public notice of this. The religious and social implications of their crime are spelled out in the accusation put to Joseph: "You have consummated your marriage in secret and have not disclosed it to the children of Israel, and have not bowed your head under the mighty hand in order that your seed might be blessed."

A truth test is ordered, the priest compelling them "to drink the water of the conviction of the Lord" in order that they will own their crime—and if guilty, die. But returning from the separate places they had been sent in the surrounding hills, Mary and Joseph amaze the people, "because sin did not appear in them." The priest promptly releases them, considering them adjudged innocent by the Lord God. A rejoicing Joseph returns Mary, the pregnant virgin still under his care, to his house.

We turn now to the strange and wonder-filled nativity story contained in the *PJ*. We can linger only over its most dramatic features—those that quickly and enduringly contributed to the amplification of legend about Mary and her birth-giving.

Noticing that Mary seems uncomfortable astride the she-ass she rides toward Bethlehem (enrollment of Joseph and his family in the Imperial census necessitates the journey, as in *Luke* 2:1–5), he asks why she is sometimes sad in expression, and then laughing.[15] She reports that she visualizes "two peoples, one weeping and lamenting and one rejoicing and exulting" (17:2). Hers is a premonition of judgments, human and divine, that will follow as consequences from the birth of her son. Short of their destination, Mary asks to be taken down from her mount "for the child within me presses to come forth" (17.3). In a barren spot Joseph succeeds in finding a cave, and, leaving her with his sons, he sets out in search of a Hebrew midwife in the territory near Bethlehem. The reader is unprepared for what follows in the text. Joseph gives a first-person account of an extraordinary experience: he walks but does not walk, sees people eating and not eating, a shepherd about to strike a sheep and then not. Events are frozen in what J. K. Elliott describes as "the catalepsy of all creation."[16] The cosmos is attuned to the momentous thing transpiring in the cave— the birth of the Son of God. A midwife presents herself, and is told that Mary (Joseph reveals that she is *that* Mary who was raised in the temple, and conceived her child by the holy Spirit) is delivering her child nearby. At the cave, a bright overshadowing cloud gives way to light, as Joseph says, ending his monologue, "so that our eyes could not bear it" (19.2). The brightness withdraws until the baby Jesus appears. He is immediately nursed. No purification needs or requirements are in view. Mary is *kathara*—pure and God-consecrated. She has, with no damaging or sullying effects to her, borne the messiah.

At this point another, soon to be famous, test—of Mary's purity—is described.

> The midwife came out of the cave, and Salome met her. And she said to her, "Salome, Salome, I have a new sight to tell you about; a virgin has brought forth, a thing which her condition does not allow." And Salome said, "As the Lord my God lives, unless I insert my finger and test her condition, I will not believe that a virgin has given birth." And the midwife went in and said to Mary, "Make yourself ready, for there is no small contention concerning you." And Salome inserted her finger to test her condition. And she cried out, saying, "Woe for my wickedness and my unbelief; for I have tempted the living God; and behold, my hand falls away from me, consumed by fire!". . . . And behold an angel of the Lord appeared and said to her, "Salome, Salome, the Lord God has heard your prayer. Bring your hand to the child and touch him and salvation and joy will be yours." And Salome came near and touched him, saying, "I will worship him, for a great king has been born to Israel." And Salome was healed as she had requested, and she went out of the cave ["justified," as a variant reading adds] (*PJ* 19.3–20.4).

The stage set for its dramatized teaching by a doubting Salome, this interpretive retelling of the birth of Jesus brings into sharp relief a new claim about Mary—namely, that she maintained before, during, and after the birth of Jesus her inviolate virginity. It stands alongside the document's claim, put on the widower Joseph's lips earlier in the narrative (9.2), that his sons were born to his previous wife, a "fact" that removes the possibility that Mary and Joseph together had other children—that is, that Jesus's siblings were actual siblings. The *PJ* makes possible and intentionally promotes a new facet of Mariology; it presents Salome's vaginal inspection of Mary as another "fact," a narrative proof that Mary's virginity was "perpetual." However graphically described, there is more than physical examination being invoked by the teller of this new nativity story. Divine powers are at work, as is evident from the ignition into flames of Salome's probing finger—portrayed as proper penalty for her dubiety, her failure to trust in the miraculous actions of God—and from her healing.

Does the text's omission of any reported labor pains hint at their absence? Was Mary, the pure one, free of the burden of the "pain of childbirth" which all (other) women after the fallen Eve were to endure? The *Gospel of Pseudo-Matthew*, an eighth-century writing well familiar with the *PJ*, removes doubts, adding more to the legend. The first midwife, here named Zelomi, examined Mary after Jesus's birth, and exclaimed:

> Lord, Lord God Almighty, mercy on us! It has never been heard or thought of that any one should have her breasts full of milk and that the birth of a son should show his mother to be a virgin. But there has been no spilling of blood in his birth, no pain in bringing him forth. A virgin has conceived, a virgin has brought forth, and a virgin she remains.[17]

So captivating is the *PJ* version of Mary's delivery of Jesus, with its testing by Salome, that we might fail to recognize another, and important, feature in the story: Jesus's healing of Salome's hand is his first miracle. He only has to be touched, so strong is the power within him. Other apocryphal Gospels such as the popular *Infancy Gospel of Thomas* will continue the theme, producing more biography of the youthful years of Jesus in which he confounded teachers with wisdom not available to them, performed acts of creation, and manifested the might to both condemn and save those he encountered. For the author of the *Protevangelium of James* this powerful cure by the minutes-old savior born to Mary will suffice. The conclusion of his treatment of Jesus and his parents consists in a borrowing of *Matthew's* account of Herod and the visit of the Magi.

The goals of the *PJ* in its encouragement of devotion to Mary, with her purity and holiness on display in her miraculous virginity, are sufficiently transparent to enable us to infer from the writing itself what kinds of questions or suspicions its author thought it crucial to address. By the second century, disputes about her origins and her sexual history were in the air—needing to be confronted and answered. Defense of Mary's virginity now necessitated a more detailed story than the two evangelists had needed to compose some several decades earlier. We are aware that Origen in the third century knew and approved of the report that Jesus's "brothers and sisters" were products of Joseph's former marriage, posing no challenge to Christians' celebration of the virgin, whom he was among the first to call *theotokos*—mother of God.[18] From Origen's lengthy answer to the philosopher Celsus's attack on Christianity (written around 175 CE), we learn what kind of ridicule was in circulation among educated pagans near the time of the *PJ*'s composition. About Mary and the purported "actual" father of Jesus named Pandera we shall learn more in the next chapter. The field of religious apologists and polemicists was well-populated. From the viewpoint of Jewish writers, the Christian claims about their messiah and his mother required strong response. Proponents of Roman piety for the Gods and the societies they sustained, like Celsus, were eager to ridicule the "superstition" called Christianity, and took pleasure in puncturing their sacred myths. Christian writers also were enthusiastic participants in the warfare of competing truth claims, and the *Protevangelium* owns a place in that conflictual context.[19] Equally important to its author, however, is the strengthened testimony about Mary, the subject of his work, that he is offering to those within his own community of belief.

Those elements in the *PJ* that can be read as responses to skeptical critiques of Mary—the provision of her Davidic roots, and of noble and righteous (not impoverished, as some had suggested) parents—form parts of a story starting with the birth of Mary. They were intended as much to nourish the faithful as to rebuke critics. How splendidly blessed and exalted by God was Jesus's mother. The regular reminders that she grew up in the Temple, receiving as a "dedicated" and blessed child her nourishment from an angel's hand, taken together with Mary's words and actions in the drama, form positive, honor-evoking lore. Ronald Hock's argument that the genre of the *Protevangelium* is "an *historia* which has the structure and purpose of an *encomium*" is both convincing and enlightening.[20] One of the author's most urgent objectives was to celebrate Mary and to place her life and works at the heart of the gospel of salvation that was taking shape among Christians of his era.

Increasingly in Christianity's first two centuries Mary's story is enhanced—her characterization given more detail in her words and actions, and also in the testimonies (collected in the *PJ* and elsewhere) of her parents and admirers during her childhood. What Mary's virginity signifies in *Matthew* and *Luke*, while they strive to undergird belief in the uniqueness of the son born to her, is far outstripped by efforts in the *PJ* to explain the initial purity of the young girl and then to build a narrative contending that her only child was Jesus, and that her virginity was, by God's miraculous power, preserved. To further magnify Mary this writing came into being. But there was more to be done, and the most informative signs of this development can be found in sermons delivered as new Feast Days were dedicated to the Virgin. To a sampling of these we turn now.

A NEW "GREAT EVENT" IN MARY'S STORY

In the Gospels, the *PJ*, and, we surmise, in early Christian preaching and teaching, the life of Mary had no conclusion.[21] Surprisingly, we find evidence only in the late fourth and early fifth centuries of Christian writers creating a proper climax for the saga of the one they honored as the ever-Virgin Mother of God. Narrating the conclusion of Mary's earthly life necessitated *more story*, and it promoted a more ambitious understanding of Mary as a key actor in the "divine economy"—God's salvific plan for humankind.

Bishop Epiphanius of Salamis, writing in the 370s, reported and puzzled over several different and incompatible Christian understandings of the climax of Mary's life that he had learned of: the belief that Mary died ("slept") and was buried, or that she suffered a martyr's death (a fulfillment of Simeon's prophecy in *Luke* 2:35 that her soul would be pierced by a sword), or that Mary remains alive, an immortal being.[22] Clergy and theologians selected and developed for themselves particular strands among emerging traditions about Mary's departure from earth, and some explained in their homilies how their decisions were made.

In a sermon on the Feast of Mary's "falling asleep" (called in Greek, *koimesis* and in Latin, *dormitio*), John, a bishop of Thessalonica in the early seventh century, told his congregation how many contending narratives existed to choose from, and the care needed to justify his discriminations between them. Before launching into his exposition of Mary's rise to heaven, he notes that he counts as reliable

not everything we have found written, in different ways in different books, about that event, but only what truly happened, what is remembered as having taken place, and what is witnessed until today by the existence of actual sites. We have gathered these testimonies together in love of truth and fear of God, taking no account of fabricated stories. . . . But having listened with beneficial compunction to the truly awe-inspiring and great wonders that took place, in a way really worthy of God's mother, at the time of her entering into divine rest, we shall offer to that spotless Lady, Mary Mother of God, thanks second only to God, and the praise that befits her.[23]

Within John's account of "what truly happened" there stands an episode in which an angel appears before Mary bearing both an announcement from the Lord, and a gift. The latter is a palm branch sent from the one "who planted Paradise." She is told to hand the palm to the Apostles, "so that they may carry it as they sing before you, for after three days you will lay aside your body."[24] Mary is quick to interrogate the angel: why not palm branches for each of the apostles? What is your name? Gently reprimanded (his name is "too wonderful for human ears"), Mary obeys the angel's bidding and goes, preceded by the angel's light and with the palm branch in hand, to the Mount of Olives. The mountain shakes and trees bow in veneration as she ascends it. Again, Mary queries the one accompanying her:

> Are you not the Lord? For such a great sign has come to pass through you: so many trees bowing before you! I say that no one can cause such a sign except the Lord of glory, who entrusted himself to me.

By her last phrase, Mary pays due tribute to the Lord as the actor of wonders, but the wonder she has witnessed trumpets also her own worthiness: she it was whom the Lord chose for his incarnation, his becoming God in flesh. The hearers of the sermon are led to understand that it was Mary's walking by that induced Nature's gesture of adoration.

A certain ambiguity about Mary's interlocutor continues as he agrees with her remark about miracles as the province of the Lord, and then says:

> But I am the one who receives the souls of those who humble themselves before God; I bring them to the place of the just, on that day when they depart from the body. And when you, too, lay aside your body, I will come to you in person ... [adding after another of Mary's questions] When God sends a mission to you, I will not come alone, but all the armies of angels will come and sing before you. Hold fast then, to the palm branch.[25]

Reminiscent of her reaction to Gabriel's announcement in *Luke*, Mary in this instance, too, is an intense interrogator. On the other hand, a feature of her personality seems to appear for the first time: we see her apprehensions about what will befall her. This glimpse of Mary's fearfulness nonetheless has ambiguity about it, since she who experiences trepidation is portrayed as a divine or near-divine self, blessed and supported by earthly and heavenly holy ones, and by God her Son, who oversees her death and its aftermath.

Both ordinary and extraordinary aspects of Mary are portrayed in the next scene. She has returned to her home in Jerusalem, now illuminated by the palm branch's radiance—a sign of protection and purpose. There, identifying herself to Christ as his mother, she prays in earnest for his help and reassurance. Protect me, she asks, from any "power [that might] come against me in that hour," and fulfill your earlier promise, when you said "Do not weep—neither angels nor archangels will come against you, nor cherubim nor seraphim, nor any other power, but I myself will come to meet your soul."[26]

John the preacher proceeds to tell of Mary's gathering of friends and relatives, whom she dissuades from mourning, of the prayer she is leading when the first of the apostles (John, Jesus's most-loved disciple), and then of the arrival of the rest (including Paul) on clouds, to be in attendance at her death and burial. The reunion of Christ's first followers and their conversations with each other are concluded by their common prayer blessing Mary, "mother of all the saved."[27] Again, Mary has questions to ask: why have you come here? Who informed you that I am about to die, and how have you traveled to this place? Upon hearing their testimonies, Mary blesses the Lord, making clear that she had learned from him that they would come to her, and that he himself had promised that she would be able to see him at the time she left her body. Peter commences a sermon that lasts through the night, at one point addressing especially "the virgins with Mary." He concludes with declarations about death as a moment—a time in which the righteous (those who maintain virginity are the chief example) will look forward to being taken to a place of repose in the company of "the immortal bridegroom."

This time has arrived for Mary, who, having prepared her burial garment, lays down on her bed, where she is surrounded by the apostles, Peter at her head and John at her feet.

And about the third hour of the day, there was a great clap of thunder from the heavens, and a sweet fragrance, which caused all those present to be overpowered by sleep, except for the Apostles alone, and three virgins, whom the Lord appointed to stay awake so that they might be witnesses of Mary's funeral rites and her glory. And behold, the Lord came on the clouds, with a multitude of angels beyond number. And Jesus himself and Michael entered the inner chamber where Mary was . . . and as soon as the Savior entered, he found the Apostles with holy Mary, and he embraced them all. After this, he embraced his own mother. And Mary opened her mouth and blessed him, saying, "I bless you . . . You foretold that you would not allow angels to come again to seek my soul, but that you would come for it yourself. It has happened, Lord, according to your word. Who am I, lowly one [that I am], that I have been counted worthy of such glory?" And having said this, she brought the course of her life to its fulfill-ment, her face turned smilingly towards the Lord. And the Lord took her soul and placed it in the hands of Michael, after wrapping it in veils of some kind, whose splendor it is impossible to describe.[28]

The final phase of the "great event" has yet to occur, as the dialogue that follows indicates. All the people present hear "the very body of the Holy Mother" call out, powerfully urging her son to remember her—to remem-ber that she is his creation, that she guarded him, "the treasure entrusted [to her]." Again, there is a pledge from the savior before he disappears: he will not abandon her—that is, her body.

John continues, telling of an attempt by Jewish leaders to disrupt the procession of Mary's body toward her tomb near Gethsemane—a piece of narrative anti-Judaism we shall encounter in fuller form shortly. The account of Mary's last days is brought to its proper denouement in its telling of her burial by the Apostles. The climax of the Virgin's earthly life contains another miracle—one that ties her life course even more closely to that of her Son.

> And after the third day, they opened the sarcophagus to venerate the precious tabernacle [i.e., the mortal body] of her who deserves all praise, but found only her grave-garments; for she had been taken away by Christ, the God who became flesh from her, to the place of her eternal, living inheritance.[29]

The bishop of Thessalonica's festal sermon ends with the teaching he is most eager to communicate: those who glorify the "immaculate Mother Mary Theotokos" will be glorified by her Son, for "he will save [them] from every danger and he will fill their households with good things. . . . and they will receive forgiveness of their sins, both here and in the age to come." This prom-ise is made to all who call upon her, "celebrating her memorial every year."[30]

The commemoration of Mary's death and resurrection that John is establishing in his church as a major observance raises the Virgin to a height greater than her formerly incomplete story allowed, and then, with new enthusiasm for her blessings and works, the bishop's words valorize the mediatorial powers of the holy and pure one who serves the people of faith. The Mother of God is an agent of help, an advocate who dwells in the highest of heaven's realms.

A complement to John's Dormition sermon is a contemporaneous work, Theoteknos's *Encomium on the Assumption of the Holy Mother of God.*[31] Of particular interest in this text is the manner in which, on the way to further enhancement of the person and role of Mary, the preacher builds his new story of the conclusion of Mary's earthly life upon elements familiar to us from the *PJ.* The *Encomium* is the only notice and trace we possess of Theoteknos, who presided over an episcopal see east of the Jordan river, in Livias, near Mount Nebo. His sermon's opening words hold more clues about the circulating traditions concerning the "great event, " some familiar from John's homily and others Theoteknos himself deemed most authentic:

> After his resurrection from the dead and his assumption into heaven, after he had taken his throne at the right hand of his God and Father—even though he is inseparable from his heart—in the immaculate flesh which he had taken from Mary, the holy Mother of God, [Christ] summoned all his holy disciples and apostles to come through the clouds and gather by that spotless, holy one who never knew marital union; he gathered them for a great event, for she who had become wider than the heavens and higher than the cherubim was to receive the palm of reward to which she had been called, and to be taken up into heaven. For if he has blessed his saints with the whole kingdom of heaven, if he opened Paradise to a thief with a single word, how much more [would he have been eager to welcome] the one who made him a home in her womb—the one whom he had created, whom he had formed, from whom he became flesh, as [he willed].[32]

Theoteknos's initial words and images were more easily taken in by his hearers than they can be by most modern readers, Christian or otherwise. Particular significance attaches to the "immaculate flesh" Jesus has from his mother, and to the vast "width" and "height" attributed to Mary. The affirmation that Christ, as preincarnate Logos of God, had formed the one in whom he was formed (i.e., enfleshed) was, for the faithful of Theoteknos's era, not a riddle, but a familiar theological commonplace. The name "Mother of God" (*theotokos*), though long in use as an honorific title by those honoring the virgin, had become a contested title in the churches' Christological controversies of the fourth and fifth centuries. Some Christian leaders protested that the term was misleading and erroneous because it so underlined Christ's divinity that it all but effaced his humanness. Would not *anthropotokos*, "man-bearer," they argued, better describe Mary, since she bore the human (i.e., the fully human being possessed of mind, soul, and body) in whom the divine Logos was incarnate? The church councils of Ephesus (431) and Chalcedon (451) labored to find the language adequate for describing the joining of both the divine and human natures of the Son of God in a single unified being, and preserved the controversial *theotokos* in their doctrinal formulae. Many churches did not concur, but Theoteknos and his church in Livias obviously ascribed to these councils' title for Mary.[33]

According to Theoteknos, the great event has to do with Christ's (fulfilled) desire to see the Mother of God rewarded for faithfulness and merits—and especially because through her obedient servanthood she undid and reversed the crime of Eve and its burden. Thus she is now positioned above the cherubim, and welcomed in the "communion of saints" residing in the kingdom of heaven.

While reporting and extolling Mary's being "taken up," Theoteknos revisits his earlier doctrine, which has become both Mariological and Christological: Mary "was found worthy to bear as her own son, without human seed, her own creator."[34] Then, elaborating upon the testimony given in the *PJ*, the bishop-orator reminds his audience that "while [Mary] was still in the loins of her father Joachim, her mother Anna received a message from a holy angel, who said to her, 'Your seed shall be spoken of throughout all the world.'" Yes, the miracle of Mary's birth was not that she was born of virgin, having no human father, but that God provided for her to be born of an extraordinary, righteous couple: "she was begotten like the cherubim, from pure and spotless [clay]. (The sense of the sentence is not entirely clear, though it seems to be attributing an immaculateness—a sin-free condition—either to Anna, or to both parents.) Mary's life in the temple, where, Theoteknos asserts, "the maiden stood alongside Christ the king" (he imagines and refers to the presence of the preincarnate Word), maintained and increased that purity which made her worthy of being the *theotokos*, the God-bearer. In the manner of classical orations of praise, the subject's pedigree is held up for admiration. The worthiness (rewarded by the angel visitations) of her parents are part of the explanation of Mary's unusual attributes as a child and young woman—her virtues, now reformulated as Christianity's highest values (especially for a female), are purity, holiness, stainlessness.

Mary's penetration by the sword (her experience of sorrow when she considered the course of her son's life, especially that he "stood before Pilate like a slave and was nailed to a cross and sealed in a tomb") was no match for her subsequent joy—at Christ's resurrection and ascension, and in imagining him sitting, enthroned, with God the Father, "and this joy is great, and gladness has taken hold of the blameless one."

Theoteknos, recalling aloud the course of Mary's life, has been preparing the way for proclaiming what the feast day celebrates. It was only right, he submits, that his mother should see her Son reigning from on high, hear angelic and human voices proclaim and praise him. Right, also, that the apostles would come to surround her, and

> right that her most holy body, which bore God, which had received God and was made like God, that spotless body radiant with divine light and full of glory, would be borne in procession by them and by the angels and confined for a short time to the earth, and then to be taken up in glory to heaven along with her soul, which was so pleasing to God.[35]

And so did it happen that Mary's "immaculate body and her pure soul," escorted by angels, were taken up to heaven. In his remark that Mary's body "was made like God," becoming radiant, Theoteknos uses a doctrine of deification (in Greek: *theosis,* "becoming divine") popular among Christians of the eastern Mediterranean. Mary is an example, par excellence, of the divinization of a holy person or saint effected by Christ's incarnation—in which the divine Word became human. In this way, also, and for this reason, did Mary warrant the new honor being bestowed upon her. Theoteknos uses another supporting testimony from the *PJ* to strengthen his Mariology: "For if she had received nourishment from angels in the Lord's temple, while she was still a child, how much more should she be served by the powers on high after she had become herself the Lord's temple!"[36]

Absent from Theoteknos's completion of Mary's story is an element we met in John of Thessalonica's sermon—the descent of Christ as Mary's death approaches, to receive her soul. According to that scenario, to Mary's soul in heaven her body will be reunited (sooner or later, and by different means, depending on the writers' views), and she will be in the company of her son, reigning in heaven as a "Queen."[37]

Theoteknos pictures instead a single action in which the Virgin, body and soul together, is "taken up"—(he uses the word *analepsis,* which translates as "assumption"). The preacher's thinking and choice of language is in all likelihood modeled on that of *Luke* 9:51, where Christ's ascension is described by the same term.[38] Certainly the bishop has other biblical personalities in mind, as a second *a fortiori* (from lesser to greater) argument makes clear:

> If Enoch, who pleased God, was taken up "that he may never see death" (*Genesis* 5:24; *Hebrews* 11:15), how much more would God have taken up the soul of her whom he had made one body with divine grace, to the paradise of delight where the divine light shines without end! And if he commanded that Elijah, who was a prophet, should mount to heaven in a chariot of fire (*1 Kings* 2:11),

how much more she who is foretold and called blessed in the prophets' writings, who shines in an outstanding way among the prophets and apostles like the moon in the midst of stars.[39]

Mary's fate was different from these, for she *did* die. Yet the "God-bearing body of that holy one . . . was kept incorrupt and free of decay . . . [together] with her pure and spotless soul," and was carried by the archangels to that place "where it remains, exalted above Enoch and Elijah and all the prophets and apostles, above all the heavens, below God alone." We see in Theoteknos's simple declaration of Mary's death an upholding of both aspects of the incarnation and its ramifications: she is the source of Jesus's human existence, and she shares with him, who truly lived and died, the debt that mortals must pay; Mary also lives again (and forever) her life that has been made like God's, taking her place on high. Theoteknos's imaging of Mary's assumption, though atypical, has in common with John of Thessalonica's narrative the chief purpose of making Mary of Bethlehem, Nazareth, and Jerusalem still visible as Mary in heaven, and of enabling her to be regarded as both human (therefore accessible) and maximally glorious (with might to serve those who call upon her).

Theoteknos includes in his narrative an altercation with Jews during the apostle's procession, with Mary's body, from Mount Sion to Gethsemane. According to this legend (which John of Thessalonica also told), while angels' songs of praise sounded above the procession,

the unbelieving Jews, who had killed the Lord, looking down the valley, saw her remains lying on the bier and went towards it, intending to do violence in that very spot to the body which God had honored. . . . All those who meant to attack her and burn her body were struck with blindness; and one of them, who touched her bier with his own hands, was deprived of them—they were cut off![40]

By this show of powerful judgment the "immaculate flesh was glorified," and all of these unbelievers were converted—to *this* belief: "they confessed her Mother of God, and the one whom they had vilified as a seductress they now praised in their song as God's own Mother."[41] The subsequent miraculous healings of those Jews who had been intent upon putting the torch to Mary's body, and the reconnection of the hands to the most audacious man (known, from other sources, as Jephonias), are attributed to Christ, but Theoteknos immediately reverts to his earlier theme by arguing that no one should consider impossible "the miracle worked by the all-holy Mother of God ... for she had remained a virgin incorrupt."[42] These are more than simple resonances with the *Protevangelium*; the assertion that the power of Mary's body stemmed from her perpetual virginity can be seen as a product derived from that early text, and the tale of the restoration of Jephonias's hands owes much to the episode involving Salome, whose treatment (with offending hands) of Mary's body brought physical punishment upon her.

Consistent with other dormition sermon accounts of the procession of Mary's body to her burial place, Theoteknos reports the apostolic prayers and speeches (Peter and Paul offer the most compelling) preceding her burial. In his telling, the prayerful watch is interrupted by thunder and an earthquake:

> And they saw the holy virgin being taken up into heaven, so that there, where a place had been prepared for her by her Son, she might abide in free access to him, joining the choirs of angels and the company of prophets and angels. [Theoteknos adds:] She is teacher and prophet, the boast of the virgins.[43]

The sermon is not quite complete. The preacher returns to a stock theme in writings and songs celebrating the Virgin he had mentioned earlier—namely, the correction of Eve's sin. In this updated form of Irenaeus's "recapitulation" theology, there are colorful and evocative additions, thanks to themes in *Song of Songs* 3 and 4. Mary, having "sought her beloved and found him," has obtained what Eve (and Adam), through disobedience, lost. Mary, saying "Breathe on my garden" (*Song of Songs* 4:10), refers to the opening of Paradise that the Word who dwelt within her has accomplished.

Theoteknos works into his closing minutes further castigations of these "unbelieving ones" for failing to recognize Mary, the Messiah's mother. They did not "glorify her as a member of their people." What, then, will transpire on the great day of judgment?

> They will see and be amazed, when they look at [Christ] coming in glory on the clouds of heaven (*Matthew* 24:30). Then they will be converted, and will beat their breasts and will call her blessed, along with Anna, the bosom that nursed her. Then they will give glory to her who is descended from David, and will say to her, "You are of our race and flesh. Now we know that you are higher than the heavens, and the bride of the heavenly King. Now we know that all the prophets spoke on your account."[44]

Most striking in this passage is its insistence that the Mother of God must receive the same kind of faith and approbation as had in earlier centuries been accorded to her son. This comes about through Theoteknos's interpretive strategy of shifting the subject from Jesus to Mary in his *contra Iudaeos* argument: it is because you Jews refused to learn of *Mary* from passages in your own scriptures that you merit punishment from God.[45] Theoteknos's charge is based upon exegetical arguments that Jews would have found debatable, if not wholly specious.

> "O mountain, from you a holy stone is cut out, and the place of its cutting cannot be found" (*Daniel* 2:34), and another [prophecy], "The sun has risen, and the moon remains in its course" (*Habakkuk* 3:11).

Addressing Mary—and his congregation—Theoteknos states these passages' true sense: "Christ has come forth from you and your virginity remains in place."[46] The Jews have not understood and believed their own scripture, he contends.

In the sermon's expected benediction addressed to the Trinity, we are reminded a final time of what Theoteknos, celebrant of the ever-virgin Mother of God's assumption into heaven, believes the import of this great event to be:

> While she lived on earth, she watched over us all, and was a kind of universal providence for her subjects. Now that she has been taken up into heaven, she is an unassailable fortification for the human race, and intercedes for us with God the Son, with whom and through whom be glory to the Father with the all-holy Spirit, now and always and for the ages of ages. Amen.[47]

The Dormition sermon of John of Thessalonica and the Assumption Day sermon of Theotokos are windows on the development of the cult of Mary, revealing—or discovering—lore about the "great event" that opened the way for believers to imagine both the end of the Virgin's earthly life and her eternal presence above. Already held aloft in believers' praise and honor for having given birth to the Son of God and being present at the time of his death, and of his own ascension into heaven, Mary's role and status were enhanced by theologians and preachers in the fifth through eighth centuries. She was exalted by ecclesiastics like Andrew of Crete, Proclus of Constantinople, and by John of Damascus, who spoke of the Virgin's transport "to the royal dwelling place of heaven as queen."[48] The celebrated Byzantine *Akathistos Hymn* hailed and invoked Mary as "the supreme Mother and protrectress of all who call upon her."[49] Displacer of other divine mothers long honored in Greek and Roman history, the Christians' ever-virgin Mother of God and heavenly advocate for the faithful was accorded her own distinctive status as human mother, divinized saint above all saints, and a participant in the redemptive work enacted by God through Christ.

Mary's full exaltation was effected not only in sermons and liturgies, but also in art. It is a thought-provoking fact that in the several centuries prior to the eighth century outbreak of inner-Christian controversy about the use of religious pictures or icons, "images of the Virgin and Child greatly outnumber[ed] surviving or known images of Christ alone."[50]

ARTISTS' IMAGES OF MARY AT THE BIRTH OF CHRIST AND AT HER DORMITION OR ASSUMPTION

A shift in emphasis is easy to detect between the time in the third through fourth centuries when Mary was shown welcoming the magi in fresco paintings on catacomb walls and ceilings, and sculpted scenes on sarcophagi, and a later period (fifth through eighth centuries) which featured in its array of portrayals of the Virgin the icons of Mary that stood in churches or were portable (for use in urban public processions).[51] Not surprisingly, the legends that came from apocryphal writings and from newly created narratives about her dormition or assumption play a major role in the artists' contributions to the cult of Mary, giving to the Mary known from New Testament a plenary "magnifying" narrative. Initially, one could argue, Mary was recognized principally as the one "full of grace" whose place in the gospel-presentation of Jesus gave explanation of, and justification for, his identification as "Son of God." In stages over the succeeding centuries, even though praise of Mary was intimately connected to worship of Christ, the Virgin's story took on a life of its own. It was *her* glorication that was taking place.

Here at the end of our exploration of Christian literary and sermonic tellings and amplifications of Mary's saga, I have selected only a few pieces of art—ones enabling us to follow in visual representations some by-now-familiar themes and storylines. Each work presents interpretation of happenings in the sacred biography of the Mother of God—graphic exegeses to be seen in tandem with the texts we have surveyed. Each also shares the texts' main purpose: setting forth an episode in the Virgin's expanding hagiography in a way that bestows on her the highest honor and adoration. The first example (Figure 13.1) is rich in its iconography.

The main subject in this early sixth-century ivory plaque is obvious enough.[52] The viewer's eye is drawn to Mary, where it is met by her steady and direct gaze. There is a frozen-in-time aspect to Mary, with her wide eyes, simple clothing (gown and cowl, with no halo), and her symmetrically

Figure 13.1 Ivory plaque depicting Adoration of the Magi, and, below, the Nativity. Early Byzantine period. Ivory: 21.5 x 12.3 cm. © The Trustees of the British Museum, London. British Museum M&ME1904, 7-2, 1.

placed hands. The same can be said for the Christ-child, sitting in her lap in a fixed and erect posture—even while he extends his one hand in bless-ing, holding a scroll in the other. Mother and child are here presented in their powerful stability, suggesting that the proper response to them is reverence, perhaps reverent prayer.[53] Surrounding Mary, and smaller in size, as this hieratic image requires, are the three Persian magi. They are slightly more mobile in posture, even though the manner in which they stand and regard Mary seems to fix them in place, like remembered venera-tors who now have become types. "They all cover their hands in deference to the sanctity before them," Antony Eastmond writes.[54] The angel holding a cross-topped standard, with eyes turned toward the head of Mary, also raises a hand in salutation. The ivory's central feature, then, is a portrait free of narrative movement (in which we would see Mary, as depicted else-where and earlier, turned toward the approaching wise men, or face to face with an angel to whom she listens or speaks). "All eyes on Mary, the Mother of God, and on her divine child!" the imagery urges. Portrayal of the Virgin as presence more than actor, visible to her beholders frontally and majesti-cally, was increasingly seen in this period's church mosaics and in painted and carved icons, such as this one. They do not so much "tell a story" as they signal the grandeur of Mother and Child. Those who lay eyes on them, as pictured, are beckoned to respond as the magi and angel do.

Of particular interest to us is a carved narrative scene that stands out-side the frame of the major image. Its placement below, in a smaller and secondary space, is intriguing on several grounds. We should ask first what the scene itself tells and conveys. Immediately we recognize an extrabibli-cal event which has become a part of Christian artists' repertoire of images. To the left Mary reclines in a curious flower-blossom shaped chair, her right hand raised to her face as she turns toward the kneeling Salome. We know why the midwife is reaching to touch Jesus in his swaddling clothes. The artist presumes that those who see his work will know why the ox and ass are also attentive to what is happening. Their appearance is not surprising, since, according to another apocryphal text, the *Gospel of Pseudo-Matthew*, the two animals adore the child, fulfilling prophecies: "The ox knows his owner and the ass his master's crib," and "Between two animals you are made manifest" (*Isaiah* 1:3 and *Habakkuk* 3:2, respectively).[55]

Salome, her hand quickly withering as a consequence of her audacious examination of Mary to test the claim that she remained a virgin *postpar-tum*, is following the directions of the (unpictured) angel. She raises her right arm to touch the newborn Jesus, and we, like the ancient viewer, know what results from this. The narrative scene is, above all else, a dem-onstration of the miracle of Mary's virginity, but also, and colorfully so, a miracle of healing for the doubting Salome, who is converted to belief, and (in *Ps.-Matthew*'s account) becomes a converter of others by proclaiming the wonders she has witnessed.[56]

We must return to the most distinctive aspect of our ivory—namely, the coupling of the iconic presentation of Mary and Child in majesty with the visual narrative, below, of Salome's punishment and healing. In what way does this juxtaposition create and contribute to a view of Mary that is new, further ennobling her? Antony Eastmond writes about the small scene in the lower register:

> It provides evidence of a shift in emphasis in the meaning of the Nativity over this period (the sixth century). The story of Salome acts as a testament to the power of the Mother of God, since it concerns the fate of those who doubt the truth of the virgin birth. Although the miracle cure is performed by the Christ-Child, the emphasis in the story is on the power of Mary. Salome, skeptical witness, is shown the veracity of the virgin birth. This iconography can be seen as the culmination of the pre-Iconoclastic cult of the Virgin, which had grown through the 5th century, when the Ecumenical Council of Ephesus in 431 declared Mary to be the Theotokos.[57]

Here, as in the dormition sermons' invocations of apocryphal Mary-legends during her festivals, the Mary story at *this* stage in the history of her increasing veneration concentrates upon the glory and powers that her virginity bestows upon her and represents in her, making her the companion of her Son in heaven, the model for those living lives of asceticism, and the merciful one who will speak for sinners, seeking forgiveness for them. Salome is a dramatic and useful case in point: her forgiveness and restoration came as a result of her turn around regarding Mary's divinely ordained—and perpetual—virginal purity.

A fascinating subsequent twist in this story of Salome, a character whose actions interpret Mary, is that she soon takes up another role in artists' repertories of Nativity imagery. This transition is seen clearly in the following early Byzantine painting (Figure 13.2).[58]

Now shown doing the expected and usual work of a midwife, rather than illustrating her "test" and her recovery, Salome, with her unidentified companion (Zelomi, as she is named in *Ps.-Matthew* 13), washes the infant Jesus in a scene beneath Mary and the Christ-child in his crib. This visual restatement about Salome displaces her as an instance of miracle—the miracle testifying to Mary's perpetual virginity. Salome's new place and role in the nativity has its own interpretive purposes, as historians of Christian art have observed.[59] The woman (or usually two women), pictured as bathing

Figure 13.2 The Nativity. Eighth–ninth centuries CE. Sinai. Monastery of St. Catherine. Painting: 32.6 x 19.7 cm. Reproduced through the courtesy of the Michigan-Princeton-Alexandria Expedition to Mount Sinai.

the newborn Jesus, Son of God, can be understood to lend support to one of the contesting parties in the inner-Christian dispute beginning in the eighth century about icons, or holy pictures. Was it permissible to show deference to material images, as if they themselves could receive worship? Was a form of idolatry being practiced in the veneration of representations that sought to capture in perishable matter (the creations of artists) the God who cannot, by definition, be circumscribed or contained—and his Son, who is of the same divine essence?

The defensive (and offensive) argument of iconophile (image-favoring) Christians against the iconoclasts proposed that the incarnation of the Son of God not only allowed but invited depictions—images in and through which the faithful could recall the life and actions of their Lord and also lift their eyes and imaginations to him, the ascended Christ. Artists were, in this situation, keen to produce images that emphasized Christ's humanness, which was of course gained from the miraculously "graced" but completely fleshly and human ever-Virgin Theotokos. In the heat of the battle over icons, to have in artistic representations of the Nativity the naked Jesus, human enough to require being washed after his birth, was to underline (and further interpret) belief in the Word's taking on bodily humanity, and to honor Mary, from whose flesh he was formed. Against those who claimed that holy pictures and their veneration were inspired by Satan, John of Damascus in his *On Divine Images* 1.16 aimed this rebuttal:

> Of old, God the incorporeal and formless was never depicted, but now that God
> has been seen in the flesh and has associated with human kind, I depict what
> I have seen of God. I do not venerate matter, I venerate the fashioner of matter,
> who became matter for my sake and accepted to dwell in matter and through
> matter worked my salvation, and I will not cease from reverencing matter,
> through which my salvation was worked.[60]

So too, John asserts, is Mary is worthy of unqualified veneration, for in her conception and in her providing "the existence of the flesh in the Word Himself," a union of the two wrought salvation—that is, divinization—of humankind:

> In this the Mother of God, in a manner surpassing the course of nature, made
> it possible for the Fashioner to be fashioned and for the God and Creator of the
> universe to become man and deify the human nature which he had assumed.[61]

To look back at the icon is to see in the child being bathed, and in his mother, fully recognizable humanity. The little man-boy being sprinkled with water is an enfleshed being—while simultaneously being seen and understood as the Son who is "of the same essence" as God, his Father. Salome's character and name (with a cross surmounting it—this she has in common with Joseph) now signifies her as "a devoted witness of the Incarnation."[62] She has become, as a midwife washing the newborn Jesus (who is the Word of God), an emblem of eighth-century claims about Jesus, Mary, and of the important and theologically justified use of "material" images in the faith and by the faithful.

In the Orthodox Christian East, Salome's name, and her earlier claim to fame, are in the process of slipping away. This Sinai icon does not feature her, but the one who was born and his mother. So it is that in the smaller scene, positioned beneath the reclining Mary, though Salome is present, the subject is the haloed, *washable* Christ.

Our tracing of the Christian story of Mary has taken us well beyond the religion's earliest centuries precisely because work was required of post-fourth-century interpreters—writers and artists—to compose an ending—the Virgin Mother of God's dormition and assumption into heaven. In the realm of monumental art, one of the most glorious renditions of Mary's life is preserved in the Kariye Camii (or Chora church) in Istanbul, whose early fourteenth-century mosaics and paintings feature an exquisite image of Jesus's reception of Mary's soul as she dies, and (in addition to a program of depictions of the life of Christ) pictorial presentations of the many great moments of Mary's life, most of these owing their inspiration to the *PJ*.[63]

Our third piece of art in this chapter, Figure 13.3, is a tenth-century ivory, probably from Constantinople. It is among the earliest representations of what Theoteknos had called the "great event."[64]

The artist locates the event beneath an elaborate baldachin or canopy whose columns are topped with acanthus leaves "blown" upward. Detail is given to the characters' faces—both those of the principals and those who lament in the background. The angels are carved in relief deep enough to suggest that they *are* hovering, and below Christ's head and beneath the angels' outstretched and covered hands, the Greek inscription reads *he koimesis*. The dormition sermons considered above help us to recognize in this well-wrought ivory the haloed Christ who, while gazing upon his (haloed) mother in death, lifts her soul (child-like in form, robed, and itself haloed) toward the awaiting angels. (Other versions of this dormition scene identify the angels as Michael and/or Gabriel, and often portray Mary's soul as a child partially or totally wrapped in a garment suggestive of a tightly wound shroud—not nearly so vital in appearance as here.) The onlookers gaze upon the body of Mary, as Christ does, and the two foregrounded figures have been identified, on the basis of similar dormition iconography,

Figure 13.3 The Koimesis of Mary. Byzantine ivory, late tenth century. Ivory: 18.7 x 14.9 cm. © Metropolitan Museum of Art, New York. Metropolitan Museum 17.190.132.

as Peter, close behind Mary's head (the censer once in his hand now broken off and lost), and Paul at the foot of the bier. Viewers of this image of Mary's "sleeping" saw not simply a visual narration of an ancient and holy happening, but the insignia of one of the church's "Twelve Great Feasts" (*dodekaorton*). Believers' attitudes toward such an image, both on the occasion of this public ceremonial veneration of Mary held on August 15, and at other times, are indicated in a similar ivory—apparently more accessible to devotees—which shows the wear from touches and kisses on the breasts and face of the Theotokos.[65]

The rise of the veneration of Mary from the first to the tenth century and beyond owes a very great deal to the steady devotion to Mary as God's mother *and* to Mary herself—for her obedience, her humility, her manifested powers, for her human accessibility, and for her continuing presence as the hearer of the fears and hopes of the people of God. The icon—an exquisite work of art to modern eyes—belongs to a family of artifacts, like Bethlehem pilgrims' oil-containing flasks decorated with pictures of Mary's life; and stamps, seals, and jewelry pieces, all of which are invested in hopes for the holy Virgin's protection and help.

Inscribed on such tokens and household items, as well as on grand pieces of art fashioned for churches, clergy, and for the wealthy and powerful (including emperors and empresses), we repeatedly meet the formula, "Mother of God, help [name]"—"Theophila," owner of a seal lock, or "thy servant Philip the Bishop," named on gilt copper depicting Mary pointing to Jesus, or "the Christ-loving lord Nikephoros Botaneiates" during whose reign (1078–1081) a beautiful serpentine roundel was created, bearing the image of the Virgin praying.[66] In earlier years it was the Lord, nearly exclusively, whose help was beckoned in Christian inscriptions (*Kyrie boethei*, "Lord help"). The eruption of adoration of Mary beginning in the fifth century and increasingly expressed in writings and in pieces of art leads to petitions for her *boetheia,* her assistance, every bit as much as her son's.

Phrases in John of Damascus's celebrated *Homily I on the Dormition* trumpet the power and importance of Mary's story—her acts and God's acts in and through her.

> The angels and archangels carried you there. . . . Heaven received your soul with joy. . . . You have not simply gone up to heavens like Elijah, nor have you simply been transported, like Paul, to the third heaven. You have gone on to the very royal throne of your Son, where you see him with your own eyes and rejoice; you stand beside him in great indescribable freedom. . . . You are a blessing for the world, sanctification for all things, rest for the weary, consolation for the grieving, healing for the sick, a harbor for the storm-tossed, forgiveness for sinners, friendly encouragement for the sorrowing, ready help [*boetheia*] for all who call upon you.[67]

CONCLUSION

Beginning with the New Testament Gospels—specifically with the Lukan and Matthean nativity accounts, and then turning to a work dependent upon these, but with its own new narratives to add, the *PJ*, we traced an early development of narrative-supported teaching about Mary. Its trajectory was an ascending one that portrayed Mary increasingly as a person of purity, of obedience, and of action. She was a God-selected virgin when she gave birth to the Son of God, the messiah. In giving birth she did not lose her virginal purity. Indeed, through the wondrous circumstances of her own conception, and the God-dedicated character of her life as a Temple-cloistered girl and a young woman given over to Joseph's care, Mary demonstrated her unique holiness, and its accompanying status and power. The role of the *PJ* in this historical dynamic was pivotal. Though we did not pause to consider them directly, proposals about Mary's continuing virginity in the years after Jesus's birth, with explict disavowals that his reported siblings were products of the marriage of Joseph and Mary, came into play from the fourth century on, energized by inner-Church debates over the relative values of the lives lived in virginity (ascetically) or in marriage. By the end of the fifth century Christians understood and revered Mary as the ever-Virgin Mother of God, and they came to know this through the ongoing and creative postbiblical interpretations of Mary's story we have surveyed—interpretations that nourished the faithful, but were in some measure also apologetic rebuffs aimed at doubters and disbelievers.

In art and texts (sermons in particular) from the sixth century on, we met the other highly significant phase in the Christian development of Mary's story—this one compelled by the need for an ending unprovided by the New Testament. Interpreters expanded the scriptural narrative in order to retell Mary's conception, birth, and calling to become the *theotokos*, and the same kind of elaboration was used by those who fashioned accounts of her "sleep," attended by friends, saints, angels, and her descending Son, as well as of her elevation to heaven, and her service there. These additions provided the full story supporting the glory and devotion attributed to Mary by Christian believers.

In attending to the evolution of the cult of Mary within the churches, I have postponed discussion of Jewish questions, criticisms, and counter-narratives about Jesus and his mother, and their influence upon Christians. Jewish writers (though no artists, as far as we know) possessed their own story (or stories) of Mary. To this interesting piece of history—again, of textual exegesis and interpretation—we now turn.

CHAPTER 14

◦◇◦

Miriam, Mother of Yeshu
the False Messiah

Jewish Counterstories

A shameless person is, according to R. Eliezer, a bastard; according to R. Joshua, a son of a woman in her separation [the period of time in which sexual intercourse is prohibited]; according to R. Akiba, a bastard *and* a son of a woman in her separation. Once, elders sat at the gate when two boys passed by; one had his head covered, the other bare. Of him who had his head uncovered, R. Eliezer said, "A bastard!" R. Joshua said, "A son of a woman in her separation." R. Akiba said, "A bastard *and* a son of a woman in her separation." They said to R. Akiba, "How has your heart impelled you to the audacity of contradicting your colleagues' words?" He said to them, "I am about to prove my point." Immediately he went to the boy's mother, and found her sitting in the market and selling pulse. He said to her, "My daughter, if you tell the answer to what I ask you, I will bring you to eternal life." She said to him, "Swear this to me!" Then R. Akiba took the oath with his lips, while he cancelled it in his heart. He said to her, "Of what sort is your son?" She said to him, "When I went to my bridal chamber, I was in my separation, and my husband stayed away from me. But the best man (Hebrew: *shushbini*) came to me, and by him I have this son." So the boy was discovered to be both a bastard and the son of a woman in her separation. At that point they said, "Great is R. Akiba, in that he as put to shame his teachers." In the same hour they said, "Blessed be the Lord God of Israel, Who has revealed His secret to R. Akiba ben Joseph" (*Talmud Tractate Kallah* 18 b).[1]

We find in this passage from a Jewish tractate titled "Bride" several points of interest. Its teaching about how a shameless boy was "engendered" is as striking as the competition between three sages, and the attribution of great power to victorious Rabbi Akiba, who (with the help of a justified deceit) received from the Lord a clear revelation. The picture of a bridegroom who is Torah-observant (in not approaching his bride during the period of time in which sex is disallowed (see *Leviticus* 15:16ff.)), but does not keep an eye on his best-man, smacks of low comedy. *Not* made explicit in the narrative, which dates from the eighth century CE, is the identity of the woman and her boy, but we shall see in a more complete and earlier Jewish account with a similar storyline that they are identifiable as Miriam and Yeshu, Mary and Jesus.

What most required correction and debunking by those seeking to overturn the claim of Jesus's messiahship were his reputed miracles and his resurrection from the dead. It was through Mary's association with Jesus that she—and particularly the belief in her virgin pregnancy and birth-giving—also became a contested topic between those who did, and those who did not believe that in Jesus a new revelation from God had come to Israel and to the nations.

In the course of framing their presentations of Jesus and Mary, the Gospel writers were compelled to answer certain questions circulating among critics and skeptics. By whose power did Jesus heal people—God's or Be-elzebub's? Was he a magician? *Matthew*, sensitive to the issue, left out of his Gospel a description of one of Jesus's cures—that of a deaf man with a speech impediment. In *Mark*'s account of the story, which the author of *Matthew* knew, by putting his fingers in the man's ears, spitting and touching his ears, and speaking a single word (the Aramaic *ephphatha*, that is, "Be opened"), Jesus healed the man like a wonder-worker.[2]

Aware that some were denying Jesus's resurrection, *Matthew* (and he alone) expanded upon the report of Jesus's burial (*Matthew* 27:62–66). The "chief priests and Pharisees," he relates, visited Pontius Pilate and urged him to "order the tomb to be made secure until the third day, lest his disciples go and steal him away, and tell the people, 'He is risen from the dead.'" The text concludes:

> Pilate said to them, "You have a guard of soldiers; go, make it as secure as you can." So they went with the guard and made the tomb secure by sealing the stone.

Not only does the evangelist frustrate what he regards as an insidious rumor by protecting the burial place from tampering, he administers a counterthrust by making the Jewish leaders themselves the guarantors of the tomb's remaining closed.[3]

Did the Christian Gospel writers leave in their compositions traces of their awareness that some doubted stories of Mary's purity—particularly that she conceived and gave birth to Jesus as a virgin? We notice that in both *Matthew* and *Luke* it is related that Mary was pregnant before she came to live with Joseph, and bore her son quite soon thereafter. In *Matthew* 1:18–25, Joseph is represented as believing that Mary became pregnant by someone other than him—that is, that she has been unfaithful during their betrothal—so he ponders whether to "divorce her quietly." The angel then tells him to take Mary for his wife. We should not rule out the possibility, New Testament scholar Raymond Brown suggested, that in this angelic command in *Matthew* 1:20–21 the evangelist had an apologetic motif in his presentation. . . . *If* that charge [that Jesus was fathered by an unnamed man] were already in circulation when Matthew was writing, this narrative could be read as an effective response to it, even as the peculiarly Matthean narrative of the guard at the tomb (27:62–66; 28:11–15) constituted an effective response to the Jewish charge that Jesus's disciples had stolen his body from the tomb.[4]

Another passage in the New Testament has prompted inquiry about the presence of anti-Jesus and anti-Mary criticisms known to the evangelists. John 8:31ff., which contains Jesus's denial that he "has a demon," contains a debate about fatherhood—of the Jews, and of Jesus. Set in the wider context of Jesus's claim that he is "from above"—that is, from the (heavenly) Father who sent him into the world—Jesus challenges his interlocutors' claim of being descendents of Abraham. Since they are attempting to kill him, he argues, their actual father is the devil, who "was a murderer from the beginning, and does not stand in the truth, because there is no truth in him" (*John* 8:37–44a). There crops up in the midst of this sharp exchange an interesting comment by Jesus's opponents (whom John names "the Jews"): "They said to him, 'We are not illegitimate children; we have one father, God himself.'" Raymond Brown noted: "He [Jesus] has been talking about his heavenly Father and about their real father, but were there not rumors about his own birth? The Jews may be saying, '*We* were not born illegitimate, but you were.' The emphatic use of the Greek pronoun '*We*' allows that interpretation."[5]

Clear, if only a few, signs reveal the Gospel writers' awareness of slights and suspicions about Jesus's miracles and the aftermath of his execution.

More difficult to assess is evidence that opponents of the Jesus-movement at the time of the Gospels' writing engaged in anti-Mary ridicule—particularly the charge that she bore an illegitimate son.[6] We are left to ponder whether *that* element in first-century Jewish suspicions—that Yeshu was a bastard—had a life of its own among critics of Jesus's messianic claims, or whether their only echoes stem from the two Gospel infancy accounts themselves.

This chapter examines four writings from the period between the second and seventh centuries in which appear a variety of Jewish criticisms of Miriam, the mother of Yeshu. Two of these sources present Jewish critics of Christian belief in the virgin birth of Jesus, but their authors are not Jews. The other two are Jewish writings: a history of Jesus that is a parody of a Christian Gospel, and an apocalypse that describes the true mother of the messiah Menahem, who in the 600s CE is eagerly awaited.

TRYPHO THE JEW: "A 'VIRGIN'? YOU'VE MISREAD ISAIAH'S PROPHECY!"

Sometime between 155 and 160 CE the Christian philosopher Justin composed his *Dialogue with Trypho the Jew,* a reconstruction of two days of debate that had occurred some twenty years earlier. The work would, as expected, demonstrate the superiority of Justin's reasoning, biblical knowledge, and theologizing over that of his opponent, a learned Jewish teacher. Trypho is, of course, under Justin's authorial management, and therefore has often been regarded as no more than a foil for the assertions Justin advanced. However, Trypho's presentations of Jewish ideas, especially his biblical exegeses and his arguments from history—as Justin has allowed him to possess and represent these—have undergone critical reassessment. Trypho's opinions, historian Judith Lieu has maintained, are *not* plausible as a group of ideas and points entirely constructed by Justin.[7] Lieu comments further:

> Justin's Judaism is a near-monolithic entity of unbelief. . . . the Jews occupy a special place. They alone are or possess potentially the true philosophy, a potential never fulfilled by them; they alone are culpable for that failure. Trypho's Judaism is something very different: a viable religious alternative, pursuing its own piety in obedience to God's Law. Both [Judaisms] are still visible, something that was not to last long in the "Adversus Iudaeos" literature.[8]

There is no mistaking the major point of contention between the two men. Trypho states:

> If the Messiah has been born and exists anywhere, he is not known, nor is he conscious of his own existence, nor has he any power until Elijah comes to anoint him and to make him manifest to all. But you [Christians] have believed this foolish rumor, and you have invented for yourselves a Christ for whom you blindly give up your lives.[9]

Justin Replies

> My friend, I pardon you, and may the Lord forgive you, for you don't know what you say; you have been instructed by teachers who are ignorant of the meaning of the scriptures, and, like a fortune-teller, you blurt out whatever comes into your mind. . . . We have been led to God through this crucified Christ, and we are the true spiritual Israel, and the descendants of Judah, Jacob, Isaac, and Abraham, who, though uncircumcised, was approved and blessed by God because of his faith and was called the father of many nations.[10]

All of the issues raised and implied in these two antagonists' brief statements—and more—fill the *Dialogue.* Our focus is necessarily narrower: we want to discover and analyze the character of Trypho's response to Christian teaching concerning the mother of Jesus.

In the first part of his argument Trypho asserts that believers in Jesus misunderstand and falsely apply one of *their* favorite scriptural passages, *Isaiah* 7:14. According to Justin,

> Trypho objected, "The quotation is not 'Behold, a virgin shall conceive and bear a son,' but 'Behold, a young woman shall conceive and bear a son,' and so forth, as you quoted it. Furthermore, the prophecy as a whole refers to Hezekiah, and it can be shown that the events described in the prophecy were fulfilled in him."[11]

The Hebrew term that appears in the Isaiah passage, *almah,* is the pivot in Trypho's correction. His objection to Justin has to do with the difference in their respective Greek translations of the Tanakh. Trypho insists that the Greek translation he and other Jews use reads *neanis* (young girl, or maiden), a term closer in meaning to the Hebrew *almah* (young woman), while Justin's translation erroneously renders *parthenos* (virgin). Trypho is fully aware that it was in *this* word that Christians found a prophetic foretelling of the birth of Jesus.

A double foolishness resides in this understanding of Isaiah's prophecy, Trypho argues, ignoring the biological improbability and moving directly to the theological absurdity of the Christians' claim: "You are attempting to prove what is incredible and practically impossible, namely, that God deigned to be born and to become man."[12]

Trypho then levels his second critique:

> In Greek mythology there is a story of how Perseus was born of Danae, while she was a virgin, when the one whom they call Zeus descended upon her in the form of a golden shower. You Christians should be ashamed of yourselves, therefore, to repeat the same kind of stories as these men, and you should, on the contrary, acknowledge this Jesus to be a man of mere human origin. If you can prove from the scriptures that he is the Christ, confess that he was considered worthy to be chosen as such because of his perfect observance of the Law, but do not dare to speak of miracles, lest you be accused of talking nonsense, like the Greeks.[13]

Though his likening of Christian Mary beliefs to the "nonsense" of Greek myths has rhetorical-polemical flare, Trypho's attack centers in the language and content of *Isaiah* 7:14. He charges that Justin and his fellow-believers have embraced a flawed translation of this text predicting that the Lord will give a sign in the birth of a child. Firmly and confidently, Trypho corrects Justin: not *parthenos*, but *neanis*. The Greek text of the Bible in his possession refers to a maiden, not a virgin.

Justin's response is intriguing. He defends the Septuagint as *the* authoritative Greek translation of Hebrew scripture, his remarks being polemical in strategy and intonation. Feigning surprise and alarm at Trypho's correction, he chides him by asking if he is rejecting the Greek text that *his* Jewish forebears produced more than four centuries earlier.

> I certainly do not trust your teachers when they refuse to admit that the translation of the scriptures made by the seventy elders at the court of King Ptolemy of Egypt is a correct one, and attempt to make their own translation.[14]

Justin's comment, which faults the Jews for abandoning a work by their elders, acknowledges a more recent Greek translation that Trypho and other Jews use in synagogues of the diaspora.[15] He was not ignorant of the fact that, to use the historian Marcel Simon's phrase, "from the moment when the Christians began to draw their arguments from [the Septuagint], and appropriate it in order to confound the Jews, the latter [were] seen gradually to turn away from it."[16] Indeed, Justin complains that Trypho's current Greek Bible omits a number of phrases in the writings of the prophets and in the psalms which Christians have used as crucial proof-texts from the Septuagint.[17] The immediate point of contention concerns their differing translations of the Hebrew *almah* in *Isaiah* 7:14, but this dispute over the correct rendering of a single word contains a much wider significance; the production of other Greek translations used by Jews was caused, at least in part, by competition with Christians who had coopted the Septuagint through their interpretations. Jewish avoidance of the text used by Christians can only be seen as a significant social interaction between opponents. It is historically significant that the word *neanis*—not *parthenos*—appeared in the three second-century CE post-Septuagint Greek translations by Aquila, Symmachus, and Theodotian that were included in Origen's third-century comparison of texts, his *Hexapla*.[18]

A second line of argument against Christianity's misguided interpretation of Isaiah's prophecy Trypho delivers with caustic bluntness: are Justin and his fellow believers blind to the fact that this passage, read in its entirety (i.e., from *Isaiah* 7:1–8:4), "refers to Hezekiah, and [that] it can be shown that the events described in the prophecy were fulfilled in him"?[19] Trypho points to the historical context of Isaiah's testimony in the Lord's name. Verses 15–16 of *Isaiah* 7 read:

> He [the child to be born] shall eat curds and honey by the time he knows how to refuse the evil and choose the good. For before the child knows how to refuse the evil and choose the good, the land before whose two kings you are in dread will be deserted.

Noting that before the described child is weaned—that is, in the near future—this prophecy about Samaria and Damascus being carried away by the king of Assyria (8:1–4) was to be fulfilled, Trypho (and many others, he implies) had long recognized that the prophecy pointed to Hezekiah, king of Judah in the eighth century BCE. *This* righteous ruler's birth the prophet foretold—the ruler from the lineage of David who had removed the idolatry insinuated into the Temple cult by his father Ahaz, and had been a steadfast defender of Israel, withstanding the siege by Sennacherib, king of the Assyrians. It is wrongheaded and an absurd case of special pleading, Trypho asserts, to apply Isaiah's promise to the recent messiah-pretender named Jesus.

Justin, in response, denies that the prediction in *Isaiah* 8:4 ("Before he had known how to call father or mother, he received the power of Damascus and the spoils of Samaria in the presence of the king of Assyria") was ever fulfilled in the history of Israel. But, he asserts (his exegesis here pressurized by his commitment to happenings under the "new covenant"), such an event *did* occur, and recently, when the Magi came from Arabia, and they encountered Herod, "then king of your country, whom scripture calls the king of Assyria."[20]

It becomes apparent, in this instance and others, that in the face of Justin's presentations of numerous scriptural passages which he regards as fulfilled by Jesus, Trypho has in his biblical interpreter's repertoire several counterinterpretations that celebrate Hezekiah, King of Judah. Where Justin and his community ardently sought foretellings of Jesus in ancient Jewish prophecies, Trypho insisted that more sober and history-conscious judgments would make clear that these predictions referred to recognized heroes in the era of the prophets themselves—men like Hezekiah, or Solomon.

If, as I and others suspect, Trypho's interpretation of *Isaiah* 7:14ff. was consciously constructed to refute the Christians' understanding of the verses, his identification of Hezekiah as the predicted figure was by no means novel and arbitrary, given the biblical books' characterizations of this king as righteous, associated with Isaiah, and a champion of reform, eliminating false worship.[21] We do know that themes consonant with Trypho's exegetically generated high estimation of the eighth-century king were continued and confirmed in other Jewish sources, for we find at several points in the *Talmud* the lionizing of Hezekiah as the Davidic ruler who was destined to become messiah.[22]

The topics, scriptural texts, and the manner of debate between Trypho and Justin in their capacities as philosopher-exegetes do not exhaust what the *Dialogue* reveals to us about relations between Jews and Greeks in their day. Interspersed between their quarrels over biblical interpretations, each discloses his resentments about the other group's actions—in the past, and presently. At several points Justin takes issue with the defamatory propaganda of Jewish "truth squads"—selected emissaries from Jerusalem who appeared soon after the news of Jesus's resurrection was publicly broadcast. These men, Justin says, reported far and wide "the outbreak of the godless heresy of the Christians and . . . spread those ugly rumors about us which are repeated by those who do not know us."[23] And the same teams of anti-Christian missionaries, Justin complains, "accuse [Jesus] of having taught . . . irreverent, riotous and wicked things of which you everywhere accuse all of who look up to and acknowledge him as their Christ, their teacher, and the Son of God."[24] He continues:

> And now, to top your folly, even now, after your city has been seized and your whole country ravaged, you not only refuse to repent, but you defiantly curse [Jesus] and his followers.[25]

Justin's sharpest grievance is sounded repeatedly in the *Dialogue*.

> To the utmost of your power you dishonor and curse in your synagogues all
> those who believe in Christ.[26]
>
> Agree with us, therefore, and do not insult the Son of God; ignoring your
> Pharisaic teachers, do not scorn the King of Israel, as the chiefs of your syna-
> gogue instruct you to do after prayer.[27]
>
> . . . in your synagogues you curse all those who through him have become
> Christians—and the Gentiles put into effect your curse by killing all those who
> merely admit they are Christians. To all of our persecutors we say: "You are our
> brothers; apprehend, then, the truth of God." But when neither they nor you
> will listen to us, but you do all in your power to force us to deny Christ, we resist
> you and prefer to endure death, confident that God will give us all the blessings
> which he promised us through Christ. Furthermore, we pray for you that you
> might experience the mercy of Christ; for he instructed us to pray even for our
> enemies.[28]

The synagogue cursing of Christ and Christians moves Justin both to
condemn Jews of his day for this ritualized deprecation, and to invite them
to desist—and to convert.

Are we able to trust Justin's report of Jewish cursing of Christ and
Christians in second-century synagogues known to him? Confidence rings
in his several claims that leaders of synagogue worship conduct this ritual,
and that it takes place "after prayer." William Horbury writes:

> Justin, the first non-Jewish witness who directly alleges a synagogue curse, was
> right in supposing that Christians, both Jewish and gentile, were cursed in syna-
> gogue. The curse, one of a number of measures against emergent Christianity,
> was a form of the Benediction of the *minim*. This malediction on heretics was
> approved at Jamnia under Gamaliel II and incorporated in the Tefillah [a prayer
> form], which at this time was gaining an importance as a bond of Jewish unity.
> The wording of the benediction was variable, and no surviving text can be
> assumed to reproduce a specimen form of the Jamnian prayer. As has often been
> noted, it could apply to heretics other than Christians; but the impression of
> Jewish opposition given by Christian sources from Paul to Justin, confirmed by
> the scattered but hostile references to Christianity in early rabbinic literature,
> suggests that Christians were prominently in view at the time of the benedic-
> tion's approval.[29]

The use (sometime in the late first or early second century) of the *Birkath
ha-minim*, which was a blessing *against* those of errant belief and practice

(*minim* translates as "heretics"), stands at one chronological side of Justin's writings, while at the other we have evidence that accords with the synagogue curse to which Justin referred several centuries earlier. *Talmud Tractate Sanhedrin* 43a, reads:

> On the eve of Passover they hung Jeshu. And the crier went forth before him forty days, saying, "He goes forth to be stoned because he has practiced magic and deceived, and let Israel astray. Anyone who knows anything in his favor let him come and declare concerning him." And they found nothing in his favor. And they hung him on the eve of Passover.[30]

In this rabbinic recollection of Jesus, which gives in brief the grounds for cursing him and his devotees, we notice not only that he is damned on account of the absence or silence of any of his disciples when he needed witnesses, but also the suggestion of a close causal connection between his being a deceiver (in his healings and teaching), and his condemnation. Curiously, a note about a sentence of stoning remains in a declaration about his hanging/crucifixion. Questions about Yeshu's origins—that is, his birth from a virginal Miriam—do not figure in this brief account of him; indeed, there is no reference here to his or others' claims that he was God's royal messiah. According to this formula, Yeshu was an unsupported charlatan who met his end during the feast of Passover.

Justin's Trypho makes no response to his opponent's outcry about the cursing, or damning, of the Christian's savior. The charge, at least as it is presented in the *Dialogue*, stands—stands, that is, as a notice of Jewish denunciation of Christianity that has become institutionalized: in their gatherings for prayer, Jesus and his followers are cursed as heretics.

The *Dialogue* also records Trypho's criticisms of the Christians, and we should pause over several of them, since they reveal what constituted distance and dislike between Jews and Christians who were by then, at least in the social world described by Justin and Trypho, two distinct and oppositional groups. The Christians' unwillingness or inability to set themselves apart—that is, to tighten their group identity in the manner that Jews do—is seen by Trypho to be a sign of weakness. Do they, he asks, actually constitute a "people," for all their talk about being the blessed members of a "new covenant" with the God of Israel? Why do they fail to adhere fully to Jewish law and call upon only selected portions of scripture when they argue for their current standing with God, claiming themselves to be, as Justin put it, "the true spiritual Israel"? Trypho finds these features of Christian belief and behavior reprehensible.

For Trypho the most repulsive aspect of Christian teaching—born of the church's (and certainly Justin's) eschatology—is the arrogant picture they draw of their messiah's "second coming." Justin himself articulates this doctrine's background in insisting, first, that the lamb offered at the Jewish Passover "was truly a type of Christ, with whose blood the believers, in proportion to the strength of their faith, were anointing their homes, that is themselves," and, second, that God foresaw that the Jews' Temple worship would be temporary, since "there would come a time, after Christ's passion, when the place in Jerusalem (where you sacrificed the paschal lamb) would be taken from you by your enemies, and then all sacrifices would be stopped."[31]

Trypho challenges Justin's eschatology and its purpose:

> Tell me truthfully, do you really believe that this place Jerusalem shall be rebuilt, and do you actually expect that you Christians will one day congregate there to live joyfully with Christ, together with the patriarchs, the prophets, the saints of our people, and those who became proselytes before your Christ arrived? Or do you put this forth only to win the argument?[32]

The Christians' bold picture of the triumph believers will enjoy in the imminent future (a vision which Justin admits he and many, but not all, members of the churches share) bluntly declares the defeat and the passing from God's care of the Jews, and could only have been heard by Jews as inflamatory, injurious, and hateful. The irreconcilable soteriologies underlying and informing the dialogue in Ephesus come into view—who are God's redeemed? Trypho's reaction to the insulting Christian doctrine of the "last days" is so definite that Justin promises to record his comments faithfully when he commits the record of their debate to writing.

It is important to conclude this consideration of selected passages in Justin's *Dialogue* by pointing once again to the contest over the meaning of *Isaiah* 7:14ff. Trypho, we recall, attacks the ignorance and special interest involved in the Christians' attachment to the word *parthenos* found in the older Greek translation, the Septuagint, and also faults them for their unwillingness to recognize that Isaiah's words foretold a king—Hezekiah—to be born in the *prophet's* era, not in the era in which he and Justin live. Of particular interest to us is the fact that throughout this discussion Trypho neither mentions Mary by name nor offers any comments, disparaging or otherwise, about her. While declaring Jesus to be simply a human, Justin's Trypho does *not* suggest that from his infancy—because of his mother's actions—he was a "shameful" child.

Negative characterization of Mary, this one, too, attributed to a Jew, is our next subject.

CELSUS'S EXPOSÉ OF MARY'S DISGRACEFUL PAST, WITH ITS TALMUDIC PARALLELS

Celsus, the late second-century critic of Christianity we have met in earlier chapters, wrote his *On True Doctrine* only twenty years after the death of Justin—whose presentation of Christianity was his chief target. To read Celsus's criticisms of the Christian movement is to become aware of the combative humor he waged on his opponents and of his seriousness in defending ancient truth, the Roman empire, and its supporting deities.

Celsus will, in the course of his treatise, honor the Jews because they long ago became a nation, and developed, as all peoples do, customs, laws, and religion: they "observe a worship which may be very peculiar, but is at least traditional."[33] On the other hand, he casts doubt on their belief "that they are in favor with God and are loved ... more than other folk," and at one point argues that their leader (Moses) was a sorcerer.[34] Celsus adjudges nations and cultures authentic on the basis of their antiquity, and the presence among them of the original truths from which the wisdom of the Greeks flowed forth and which the laws and religion of the Roman empire enshrine and perpetuate. Despite their lengthy history and traditions, the Jews are not bearers of "true doctrine." Rebels against Egypt and its religious customs, the Jews (as the Christians later did to them) broke away from their original people, and their "revolt led to the introduction of new ideas."[35]

A Jewish spokesperson is of great value to Celsus, however, as he attacks what he regards as the utterly novel and ungrounded teachings of nascent, but, by the late second century, burgeoning, Christianity. Celsus's Jew, made a contemporary of Jesus, is well-placed to open the polemics against the Jesus story and the Mary story.

Aware of details from the Gospels and other circulating Christian teachings, Celsus and his Jew are eager to put forth incriminating questions. Why did Jesus, a God, need to be spirited away to Egypt under Herod's threat of death? Certainly a true deity would not have had any fear. Why could Jesus not maintain the loyalty of his small group of followers, who fled from him when conflict arose? In this he compares unfavorably with a leader of a band of robbers, who do not abandon their chief. If there were so many doubts about his status as God's son during his public ministry, with the result that a great many did not believe in him, should he not have revealed his powers to everyone after his resurrection, making a convincing public show of himself? These are only a few in a barrage of queries Celsus sets forth in *On True Doctrine*. There is no mistaking the glee of an effective satirist, which no doubt contributed to the writing's popularity.

Mary is not spared. She comes under attack just after a charge that during his time in Egypt, and on the basis of his acquisition of magical powers, Jesus called himself God—a divine being. But, Celsus/the Jew wonders, if he was God, what kind of birth was he claiming for himself?[36]

> Then was the mother of Jesus beautiful? And because she was beautiful did God have sexual intercourse with her, although by nature He cannot love a corruptible body? It is not likely that God would have fallen in love with her since she was neither wealthy nor of royal birth; for nobody knew her, not even her neighbors. . . . When she was hated by the carpenter and turned out, neither divine power nor the gift of persuasion saved her. Therefore, these things have nothing to do with the kingdom of God.[37]

Fantasizing a divine impregnation of a human female, Celsus exercises the cultural standard that being well-born trumps beauty, and that Mary was a nobody, a disgraced person bereft of any trace of the divine, and unable (due to her lack of education?) to be compellingly intelligent. And, he concludes disparagingly, you Christians claim that she gave birth to the son who would introduce the reign of God?

Another mocking comment about Mary is interesting in what it reveals about the critic's familiarity with Christian writings.

> The men who composed the genealogy boldly said that Jesus was descended from the first man and the kings of the Jews. . . . the carpenter's wife would not have been ignorant of it if she had had such a distinguished ancestry.[38]

Celsus is aware of Luke's list of ancestors (back to Adam), presumes that the lineage is hers, not Joseph's, and zeroes in on what he considers a laughable implausibility: how could she not have known who she was?

Two other passages assault the character of the mother of Jesus, marking an intensification in the anti-Mary polemic of Celsus's treatise. In the first of these, Celsus's Jew conducts an exposé of Christian falsehoods about Jesus's origins:

> He fabricated the story of his birth from a virgin. . . . he came from a Jewish village and from a poor country woman who earned her living by spinning. . . . she was driven out by her husband, who was a carpenter by trade, as she was

convicted of adultery. . . . after she had been driven out by her husband and while she was wandering about in a disgraceful way she secretly gave birth to Jesus.[39]

Ridiculed in this counternativity story, of course, are the claims of Jesus's royal lineage and traditions of "the holy family" already prized among believers in Jesus's messiahship. Joseph's reactions to Mary's pregnancy, and his consideration of divorce (*Matthew* 1:18–19), are taken in a new direction: the charge of adultery against her, Celsus's Jew declares, was made and upheld. A notice connecting Mary with spinning (familiar to us from the *Protevangelium of James*) seems here to be "spun" in order to indicate her social lowliness. An unexpected element is introduced—the picture of Mary's nefarious secrecy as she gives birth to her son in isolation. This motif serves to debunk the two Gospels' reports not only of Joseph's presumed solicitude at the time of the child's delivery (in Bethlehem, according to *Luke* 2:17, and a few miles short of the city, in the *Protevangelium*), but also of the drama surrounding the event—its recognition and celebration by congregating angels, sages from the east, and star-led shepherds.

The second passage adds more dramatic—and damning—information:

> the mother of Jesus [was] turned out by the carpenter who was betrothed to her, as she had been convicted of adultery and had a child by a certain soldier named Panthera.[40]

The charge of adultery (Joseph understood to be Mary's cuckolded husband) at this point includes the corollary: Mary produced an illegitimate son. Here in Celsus's late-second-century critique, then, are some of the basic elements of what we met at the chapter's beginning in the eighth-century text relating Rabbi Akiba's pursuit and questioning of the mother with the brash son. And the shame, as made plain in the identification of Jesus's father by Celsus's Jew, has a dimension that runs beyond sexual immorality. Not only is the ancestry attributed by Christians to Miriam/Mary (and to Jesus) a sheer fabrication, she bore the child of a non-Jew.

The adulterous father's name has been the subject of considerable discussion among scholars of Judaism and Christianity. Panthera was a known Roman name, one sometimes found in use as a surname among soldiers. Nearly a century ago it was suggested that Celsus's Jew gave to Jesus's father the name Panthera as a scornful pun on Parthenos.[41] It might have been possible to pin the blame for the Panthera-as-father rumor directly on Celsus the anti-Christian Hellenistic philosopher if not for the name's appearance, linked to Jesus, in certain passages in the *Babylonian Talmud*.

In *Shabbat* 104b we read of an action attributed to Jesus, and of the rabbis' confusion about Jesus's name, and Mary's:

> It is taught that Rabbi Eliezer said to the Wise, "Did not Ben Stada bring spells from Egypt in a cut in his flesh?" They said to him, "He was a fool, and they do not bring evidence from a fool." Ben Stada is Ben Pantera. Rabbi Hisda said, "The husband was Stada, the lover was Pantera." The husband was [actually] Pappos ben Judah, the mother was Stada. The mother was Miriam the dresser of women's hair. As we say in Pumbeditha, "She has been false to [*satah da*] her husband."[42]

The legal context framing this discussion has to do with whether writing (more than two letters) on the Sabbath is permitted, and the case under discussion seems to center in a scratching or writing of spells committed by (as the discussants take for granted) the "fool" Yeshu/Jesus. Our passage, however, is most concerned with sorting out two names that are associated with Yeshu. Is it correct, the rabbis seek to determine, to call the fool who brought magic from Egypt "in a cut in his flesh" Ben Stada (son of Stada) or Ben Pantera (son of Pantera)? First comes a point meant to clarify: the son of Stada and the son of Pantera are the same person. Whence the two names? Rabbi Hisda proposes that Yeshu's putative father, the husband of Miriam, was Stada, while Pantera, Miriam's lover, was his actual father. But his assertion is challenged. The husband was named Pappos ben Judah. Stada was, then, the name of Miriam, here identified (in another menial vocation) as a womens' hair dresser. The argument stands, but needs more work, since Mary's known name and title derives from her work-name, "dresser" or "plaiter" of hair. Stada must be given another sense or placement. So the discussion, concerned entirely with sorting out which of the two names attributed to Jesus, son of Pantera or son of Stada, was most accurate, concludes by invoking a saying from a Babylonian center of rabbinic study: the name "Stada" is a scurrilous nickname, punned as indicating that Miriam cheated on her husband, and bore an illegitimate son.[43]

The text identifies Pantera as the lover of Miriam who impregnated her, authenticating Jesus's name as "son of Pantera."[44] Taken together with the testimony of Celsus's Jew, *Talmud Shabbat* 104b testifies to the existence of what Daniel Boyarin terms "the Jewish slander tradition ... that Jesus was the bastard son of a Roman soldier named Panthera."[45] Of course the object of this anti-Mary polemic was to undermine the Christian story of her virginal conception of Jesus by the Holy Spirit of God and to demolish the trumped-up genealogy which tied both her and her son to the Davidic and Aaronic lines.

In another text, *Babylonian Talmud Sanhedrin* 106a, it is surely Mary who is singled out and condemned, not for a single act of adultery, but for her vocation, more shameful than mere spinning or hairdressing: "Rabbi Papa said, 'This is what they say: She was the descendant of princes and governors, but played the harlot with carpenters.'"[46]

These assaults on Mary and the Christian story of her holiness accompanied a greater number of Talmudic denunciations of Jesus as a magician whose teachings misled Jews, and who deserved the punishment of death he received.

A comment by Robert Van Voorst enables us to take stock of the content and forms of Jewish anti-Christianity surveyed so far in this chapter and at the same time anticipate what lies ahead:

> All Jewish sources treated Jesus as a fully historical person. Like classical opponents of Christianity, the rabbis and the later Toledoth Yeshu used the real events of Jesus's life against him. They believed that Jesus had an unusual conception (the product of some sin), worked amazing deeds (by evil magic), taught his disciples and the Jewish people (heresy), was executed (justly, for his own sins), and was proclaimed by his disciples as risen from the dead (conspiratorially).[47]

TOLEDOTH YESHU: MIRIAM'S PART IN ISRAEL'S "GREAT MISFORTUNE"

A boisterous and fast-moving Jewish *Toledoth Yeshu* ("Life of Jesus") is a stinging parody of the Jesus portrayed in the Christian Gospels. The *TY* emerged sometime in the sixth century as a written text, collecting Jewish and Christian lore about Jesus from earlier times. As it was copied and further elaborated well into the Middle Ages, later materials were added as well. Morris Goldstein referred to the *TY*'s content as "garbled," noting not only that there are occasional repetitions of events and many variants in its several renditions, but also that the narrative itself is chronologically loose.[48] Events surrounding the birth of Jesus are placed in 90 BCE, during the reign of King Jannaeus. Unexpected characters take their place on stage, with Queen Helene succeeding her husband in power (displacing Herod and others as she becomes Israel's ruling authority and judge), and the fourth-century CE Rabbi Tanhuma appears in a minor role in the time of Yeshu's death.[49] Modern commentators have noted that while this Jewish version of Jesus's life is too late to be of use in historical Jesus studies, it does, as a keen-edged polemic, shed instructive light on Jewish-Christian relations.[50] It may have Emperor Justinian's sixth-century crack down on Jews as its chief backdrop, but the continuing existence of the text itself spurred tensions—indeed, Martin Luther translated the work into German in 1566 in order to expose and excoriate its portrayal of Jesus.[51]

This Jewish lampoon of Jesus was dedicated to demonstrating in vivid episodes how false—and ludicrous—were the churches' cherished understandings of their savior's holy origins, his teachings, his powers and miracles, and his resurrection. In short, all bases upon which Christians founded and propagated the belief that Yeshu/Jesus was the Messiah and Son of God—were erroneous, and legitimately open to ridicule. Such was the *TY*'s brief as a counterhistory and an "anti-Gospel."[52]

Toledoth Yeshu opens by announcing that a "great misfortune befell Israel" with the appearance of Joseph Pandera, a resident of Bethlehem who was "a disreputable man of the tribe of Judah." The author knows of other tales circulating among Jews about Jesus and his birth, but gives his own report:

> Near [Joseph Pandera's] house dwelt a widow and her lovely and chaste daughter named Miriam. Miriam was betrothed to Yohanan, of the royal house of David, a man learned in the Torah and God-fearing. At the close of a certain Sabbath, Joseph Pandera, attractive and like a warrior in appearance, having gazed lustfully upon Miriam, knocked upon the door of her room and betrayed her by pretending that he was her betrothed husband, Yohanan. Even so, she was amazed at his improper conduct and submitted [to his advances] only against her will. Thereafter, when Johanan came to her, Miriam expressed astonishment at behavior so foreign to his character. It was thus that they both came to know the crime of Joseph Pandera and the terrible mistake on the part of Miriam. Whereupon Yohanan went to Rabban Shimeon ben Shetah and related to him the tragic seduction. Lacking witnesses required for the punishment of Joseph Pandera, and Miriam being with child, Yohanan left for Babylonia. Miriam gave birth to a son and named him Yehoshua, after her brother. This name later deteriorated to Yeshu. On the eighth day he was circumcised. When he was old enough the lad was taken by Miriam to the house of study to be instructed in the Jewish tradition.[53]

What are this narrative's main assertions (and assumptions), and how do they stand in relation to other pieces of Jewish anti-Jesus and anti-Mary propaganda with which we are now familiar? We discover new names for Yeshu's actual father (Joseph Pandera) and for his mother's betrothed husband (Yohanan). The writer may well be poking fun at the Christian genealogies when he (too) highlights the Davidic lineage of the man who did *not* impregnate Miriam. Both men are Jews, one ignoble and the other Torah-enlightened and pious. The pagan (idolator) soldier is gone.

Miriam's sexual assault by Pandera and the resulting pregnancy constitute her "terrible mistake," but not her crime. If the incident were being acted out on a stage, its ambiguities (and its humor, for some in the audience) would be plain to see. Miriam resists the roughness of the sexual encounter she supposes she is having with her betrothed, but is forced to submit. That all of this happens in a darkness so deep that she gains no glimpse or impression of her "lover" is, not accidentally, hard to believe. The scene in which Miriam and Johanan discover exactly who had earlier engaged in sex with Miriam is a "revelation" worthy of a comic play (or a television soap opera), yet it is at the same time a serious and cleverly wrought exposé of the Christians' Mary.

Within *this* nativity story the two scenes quash the beliefs in Mary's virginal conception *and* in her nonsexual relationship with Joseph (who here is Johanan). Yet it is also true that Miriam, as characterized in this episode, is not an immoral woman. She has been duped by a conniving adulterer, and now pays the price. The Gospel notice in *Matthew* 2:18–19 which treats Joseph's concern about what to do with Mary, who became pregnant "before they came together," undergoes revision (and narrative expansion) here: Johanan entreats his rabbi Shimeon ben Shetah, but the effort to bring a conviction of Joseph Pandera fails for lack of witnesses. Yohanan (unlike Joseph in the Christian account) abandons the pregnant Miriam, moving to Babylonia (or in some versions of the text, to Egypt). Miriam delivers Yehoshua, whose name she takes from her brother, without benefit of an angelic message. The mention of Miriam's sibling seeks, I suspect, to undermine traditions from the *Protevangelium of James* about the extraordinary birth of Mary herself, the unique answer to the prayers of her parents, Zechariah and Anna. More explicit is the argument that the names Jehoshua and Yeshua are not equivalent (contra *Matthew* 1:21), but that the name associated with Jesus, Yeshu, is a degraded form of its noble precedent (as in the naming of Joshua), with its sense that "he (God) will save."

In signaling Miriam's attention to Yeshu's circumcision, and her enrollment of him in the nearby *beth midrash*, this portion of TY indicates her loyalty and commitment to Jewish practice. Her betrothed, we recall, was notable for his knowledge of the Torah and his respectful fear of God. Miriam and her son are Jews. The "great misfortune that befell Israel" had nothing to do with a Gentile soldier or the action of a foreign intruder, but rather resulted from the deed of a sexual predator from the tribe of Judah.

Yet the "Life of Jesus" is only beginning to be told, and this anti-Gospel's account of Yeshu's conception and birth is a calculated prologue—the introduction of the drama's main conflict. The scandalizing disclosure of

Yeshu's true father only goes so far in explaining Yeshu's waywardness. *TY* moves quickly to seek a further cause, and we recognize the tale.

> One day Jeshu walked in front of the Sages with his head uncovered, showing shameful disrespect. At this the discussion arose as to whether this behavior did not truly indicate that Yeshu was an illegitimate child and the son of a *niddah*.[54]

We note that Rabbi Akiba's detection of the double-crime that causes a mother to give birth to a shameless and willful child appears here in a different guise. Is it being intimated that Miriam's impurity as a *niddah*—as much as, or more significantly than, the deceitful immorality of his father—accounts for Yeshu's brash inclination toward evil? The text of *Toledoth Yeshu* has Miriam admit only to the fact that Yeshu is the bastard son of the notorious Joseph Pandera, *not* that she conceived him in a time of her separation. Miriam is spared *this* ridicule even while she is being exposed as no God-visited virgin, but the victim of a rapist.

The boy Yeshu's impudence and transgression quickly surpass "shameless" bare-headedness. In a discussion with rabbis he argues against the view that Moses was the greatest of prophets, since he required advice from his father-in-law Jethro (*Exodus* 18:13–23). It is this audacity that impels the elders to seek and then discover (from Shimeon ben Shetah) the actual circumstances of Yeshu's conception and his birth—her assault by Joseph Pandera. The narrative adds more about the rogue behavior of Yeshu, which necessitates his flight, under pressure from his critics, to "the upper Galilee."

According to *TY*, the public career of its protagonist was that of a wonder-working messianic pretender. Not in Egypt, however, did he gain his skills as a worker of miracles, but in his own people's great sanctuary. In the reign of Queen Helene, we are informed, precautions were taken to protect the "secret of the Name," the knowledge of which would allow a person to be "able to do whatever he wished."[55] Its letters (the Tetragrammaton, or *YHWH*) were inscribed on the Temple-guarded Foundation Stone—that upon which, according to tradition, God originally established the world. *TY* provides colorful description both of the challenge facing opportunistic Yeshu *and* of his successful trickery.

> The Sages took measures so that no one should gain this knowledge. Lions of brass were bound to two iron pillars at the gate of the place of burnt offerings. Should anyone enter and learn the Name, when he left the lions would roar at him and immediately the valuable secret would be forgotten.

Our antihero had devised a plan.

> Yeshu came and learned the letters of the Name; he wrote them upon the parchment which he placed in an open cut on his thigh and then drew the flesh over the parchment. As he left, the lions roared and he forgot the secret. But when he came to his house he reopened the cut in his flesh with a knife and lifted out the writing. Then he remembered and obtained the use of the letters.[56]

The Talmudic charge in *Tractate Shabbat* 104b against Ben Stada, the fool who brought spells from Egypt "in a cut in his flesh," takes on a different life in *TY*, exchanging for the alien source of magic Israel's own holy place—from which Yeshu surreptitiously captures powers deriving from the Name of the Most High. His crime is not, in this case, set in the context of violating the Sabbath rest by writing; it consists, rather, in taking for himself what belongs to God alone—a sheer act of blasphemy. *Toledoth Yeshu* is elaborating and intensifying the son of Miriam's shameless presumption. A robber of what is most holy and pure, Yeshu is no longer a rude and harmless fool, but a threat to God and God's people.

We read that, having gathered three hundred and ten Jewish young men as disciples, Yeshu commenced his mission among his people. Given what has been told of his origins, Yeshu's initial proclamation is designed for comic effect. He accuses all who had disbelieved in and ridiculed his *birth* of being corrupt, which he defines as seeking after greatness and power. Also meant to generate mirth is the scene in which Yeshu teaches his heretical doctrines, all of which concern the revelation of his identity, with scriptural evidence provided:

> Yeshu proclaimed, "I am the Messiah; and concerning me Isaiah prophesied and said, 'Behold, a virgin shall conceive, and bear a son, and shall call his name Immanuel.'" He quoted other messianic texts, insisting, "David my ancestor prophesied concerning me: 'The Lord said to me, thou art my son, this day have I begotten thee.'"[57]

The greater portion of this "Life of Jesus" relates a series of clashes and confrontations. The deeds of Yeshu trouble the sages, who several times capture him and bring him before Queen Helene (not Pilate).[58] Having granted the sign of power that his followers requested of him—the healing of a lame man by speaking the divine name over him, and then the cure of a leper—the insurgents surrounded and worshipped Yeshu, acclaiming him "Messiah, Son of the Highest." Hearing of these things, the Sanhedrin set about capturing Yeshu, under the guise of an invitation to visit them in Jerusalem. Yeshu requires that he be greeted "as a Lord" and, to fulfill the prophecy of Zechariah, enters the city riding an ass.[59] What follows, and the terms in which charges are leveled, are important to notice:

> The Sages bound him and led him before Queen Helene, with the accusation: "This man is a sorcerer and entices everyone." Yeshu replied, "The prophets long ago prophesied my coming: 'And there shall come forth a rod out of the stem of Jesse,' and I am he; but as for them [his accusers], Scripture says, 'Blessed is the man that walketh not in the counsel of the ungodly.'" Queen Helene asked the Sages: "What he says, is it in your Torah?" They replied: "It is in our Torah, but it is not applicable to him; for it is in Scripture: 'And that prophet which shall presume to speak a word in my name, which I have not commanded him to speak or that shall speak in the name of other gods, even that prophet shall die.' He has not fulfilled the signs and conditions of the Messiah."[60]

Though introduced to Helene as a sorcerer, the debate that takes place before her has to do with prophecy, false prophecy, and "ungodly" enemies of prophets. From this arrest Yeshu was granted freedom by Helene when, after claiming messiahship and the power to revive the dead, he accomplished that feat (pronouncing of the Ineffable Name) when "a dead body was brought in." The queen, judging Yeshu's deed to be "a true sign," chastised and then dismissed his antagonists—the Sanhedrin and the sages.[61]

Pursued at another time in the upper Galilee by the Temple sages, Yeshu urged pacifism upon his followers—"Wage no battle!"—when they were resisting another attempt to arrest him. Then,

> He spoke the ineffable Name over the birds of clay and they flew into the air. He spoke the same letters over a millstone that had been placed upon the waters. He sat in it and it floated like a boat.[62]

The crowds thrilled at the sight, and Yeshu ordered his opponents to report these dazzling acts to Helene. Upon hearing them, she "trembled with astonishment."[63]

A new strategy required seeking a person who would be equal in strength to Yeshu. Selecting a man named Judah Iskarioto, they equipped him for battle by giving him access to the Temple, where he too, like Yeshu, gained knowledge of the letters of the sacred Name.

Yeshu's first meeting with this newly appointed nemesis is one of the most entertaining scenes in the *Toledoth Yeshu* and, for that matter, in all of Jewish anti-Christian polemical writing:

> When Yeshu was summoned before the Queen, this time there were present also the Sages and Judah Iskarioto. Yeshu said: "It is spoken of me, 'I will ascend into heaven.'" He lifted his arms like the wings of an eagle and he flew between heaven and earth, to the amazement of everyone. The elders asked Iskarioto to do likewise. He did, and flew toward heaven. Iskarioto attempted to force Yeshu to the earth but neither one of the two could prevail against the other for both had the use of the Ineffable Name. However, Iskarioto defiled Yeshu, so that they both lost their power and fell down to earth, and in their condition of defilement the letters of the Ineffable Name escaped from them. Because of this deed of Judah they [Yeshu's followers] weep on the eve of the birth of Yeshu.[64]

Though he too is a victim of his own action, Iskarioto's "defilement" of Yeshu succeeds in polluting and disempowering him. We are left to wonder what Iskarioto's act was, and the manuscript tradition of *TY* offers variant explanations. Though some versions of this incident employ the Hebrew term *hishtin* in connection with the result (*ve-nitma,* or "defiled"), as if to suggest that Iskarioto urinated on Yeshu, this action would not, by Hebrew purity laws, have constituted a defilement. More reasonable is the phrase found in other manuscripts, which describe what transpired as Iskarioto's aerial wrestling with Yeshu as *metame be-mishkav dakhar*, an act of sex or attempted sex between two males which involved ejaculation of semen—that is, a polluting act bringing about *tum'ah*, impurity.[65] Passages in *Leviticus* (18:22 and 20:13) which prohibit lying "with a male as with a woman"—*mishkevei ishah*—stand in the background. Again, the scene's activity is, by all standards of parody and comic theater, successfully hilarious in its damning exposure of Yeshu.

Can we know what might have inspired the author in his creation of this episode? Stories of Simon Magus's air-borne antics entertained with displays of magical powers, and their cessation (Simon crashes, sustains injuries, and dies).[66] But another well-known story, this from rabbinic lore, the *Recall of Rabbi Nehuniah Ben Ha-Qanah,* was more relevant to his theme. It is from his heavenward mystical journey through the heavens, as Nehuniah approaches the seventh, that his colleagues seek to recall him from his ecstatic state and flight. A problem has arisen in his attempt to describe the sixth heaven's guardians, and the rabbi's students ask their superiors—Rabbi Ishmael in particular—to bring their teacher back to consciousness in order that he might speak clearly. Only an impurity associated with Nehuniah can bring him safely from his close proximity to the divine throne. A cloth used by a woman for internal examination after her second immersion in the ritual bath—which might carry the smallest trace of blood—is obtained by Ishmael. Then the cloth, wrapped around a bough of myrtle, was placed on the lap of Nehuniah as he sat for his mystical vision. This resulted in his "dismissal from before the throne of glory"—a descent required by a "minute possibility of ritual impurity."[67]

The dynamic of the "recall of Rabbi Nehuniah" corresponds to that in the aerial battle of Yeshu and Iskarioto—the fall from the heavens because of impurity—and each of the tales, while holding a lesson, is amusingly extravagant. But an important piece of holy geography and its inaccessibility to the unworthy is also in play: as in the forms of mysticism in which approach to the *merkavah* (the chariot throne on which God sits) is sought, the seven heavenly realms (the *hekhalot*—that is, the "chambers," "palaces," or "temples" through which the rabbis attempt to ascend) have guardians at their gates. These angelic protectors of the holy repel those who are impure. This feature of mystical ascent mirrors biblical thought concerning the Temple, which defends itself against the unclean. Similarly, even though the scene is comic, the two men doing battle in the air in *Toledoth Yeshu* are cast from the skies upon becoming ritually impure.[68] The story is fantastic and playful, but its application to Yeshu and his messianic claims is in earnest. Yeshu's brazen imposture is repelled by the God of Israel. In terms of the plot line, this plummeting from the skies signals the beginning of the end of Yeshu's career—of his "mission."

Toledoth Yeshu presents Judas Iscariot as being, from the beginning, an agent of the rabbis with a role to play, not an eleventh-hour defector from Jesus's band of disciples. Iskarioto is a carefully reimagined player in this anti-Gospel's drama.

We should pause over the report in *TY* that because Judah Iskarioto defiled Yeshu, "they [his devotees] weep on the eve of the birth of Yeshu." A reference to such a ritual does appear in the diary of Egeria, the later fourth-century Christian pilgrim. This ritual weeping occurred, however, not at the time of the celebration of Jesus's nativity, but on the Wednesday of Holy Week, just before the commemoration of Jesus's arrest. In that day of scriptural readings, prayers, and singing within the Church of the Resurrection, when the worshippers arrive at the entrance of the cave revered as Jesus's place of burial (the "Holy Sepulcher"), Egeria writes,

> A presbyter stands in front of the railing and he takes the Gospel book, and reads the passage about Judas Iscariot going to the Jews and fixing what they

must pay him to betray the Lord. The people groan and lament at this reading in a way that would make you weep to hear them.[69]

If the author of *TY* knew of that Christian practice, he had good reasons for framing the story otherwise, having the Christian cries of sorrow relate, not to Iscarioto's betrayal, but to his frustration of Yeshu's ascent to his Father in heaven.

In all of this, *Toledot Yeshu* proposes that Yeshu's fall to the earth and his loss of the memory of the secret Name was the unmasking of a fraud—an unimpeachable reproof of all claims Christians made for the uniqueness of Jesus's birth, the sanctity of his mother, his distinguished ancestors, the genesis of his might and his deeds, and, finally, of his standing and relationship with Israel's God.

Even though Miriam does not reappear in the narrative, a survey of later parts of this Jewish "Life of Jesus" is warranted: its alterations and subversions of early Christian accounts of Jesus hold further clues about the text's argument and viewpoint—especially as the fate of Yeshu is narrated. The sequence of events, and their locations, are unexpected.

Part of Yeshu's "passion"—the binding of him to the pillar, the vinegar offered for him to drink, and the imposition of his crown of thorns—takes place at the synagogue in Tiberias (where these torments were apparently meted out by Jews rather than Roman soldiers), but his death is postponed.[70] In the course of conflict and struggle between the elders and Yeshu's followers, he (with his disciples) escapes to Antioch. Returning to Jerusalem (again "riding upon an ass") on the day before Passover, Yeshu is said to be intent upon restoring his powers—by regaining the secret of the Name. At this point Iskarioto's role, familiar from the Gospels, is played out: as Yeshu enters the city with his large company of supporters, "one of them, Iscarioto, apprised the Sages that Yeshu was to be found in the Temple," and there identified him by bowing toward him, enabling his capture. The disciples, we are told, had sworn on the Ten Commandments not to reveal Yeshu's identity, and an exchange takes place in which Yeshu will not give his name, but offers four others (Mattai, Nakki, Buni, and Netzer), each one touching off a duel of verse-quotations between Yeshu and the sages. The names, some of those given to Yeshu's disciples in *Talmud Tractate Sanhedrin* 45a, here are part of the ruse intended to foil the captors at the point of arrest.[71]

Yeshu is put to death at the "sixth hour on the eve of the Passover and of the Sabbath," but only with difficulty. Having earlier proclaimed that "no tree would hold him," he was only able to be suspended on a "carob-stalk, for it was a plant more than a tree, and on it he was hanged until the hour for the afternoon prayer." In order that his body might not "remain all night on the tree," in violation of the law, Yeshu was buried quickly outside the city.[72]

Queen Helene comes to center-stage a final and decisive time, where she must adjudicate again between disputants. From Yeshu's disciples and from the Sages she demands evidence. What has become of Yeshu's corpse? The "bold followers" of Yeshu testify to her that their leader's body is absent from his grave—that, as he foretold, he has ascended, alive, into heaven. We learn otherwise from the narrator, who reports that a man had taken Yeshu's corpse from the grave and "brought him into his garden and buried him in the sand over which the waters flowed into the garden."[73] Consternation follows the queen's demand that within three days the body of Yeshu must be shown to her. Aware of the crisis, the gardener reveals his deed to Rabbi Tanhuma, confessing that he took his action in order to prevent Yeshu's followers from stealing his corpse. Recovered from the garden by the Sages, Yeshu's body is dragged to the queen "tied to the tail of a horse," and is identified to her: "This is Yeshu who is said to have ascended to heaven." Satisfied by the proof presented to her, Helene declares Yeshu a false prophet "who enticed the people and led them astray, [and] she mocked [his followers] but praised the Sages."[74]

The "Life of Jesus" would seem to have reached its properly inglorious end, but a continuation tells of the "acts of [Yeshu's] apostles"—and the role of Simeon Kepha (a figure who seems to combine both Paul and Peter) in separating, on Jesus's counsel, the Christian holy days from those of the Jews. We must pass over these fascinating latter pages of the text in order to return to this counter-Gospel's representations of Yeshu—and Miriam.

Jesus's messiahship is steadily denied in *Toledoth Yeshu*, rebuking the notion that he is "son of God," and eliminating him from the ranks of God's true teachers and prophets. In content, tone, and rhetorical strategies, *Toledoth Yeshu*, in comparison with briefer texts so-far considered, enthusiastically scandalizes—collecting polemics into a story for popular Jewish (we presume) consumption. Throughout *TY*, alongside the satire proper to a counterhistorical "Life of Jesus," we meet an interpretation of happenings which creates and promotes an affirmation of Judaism. We see this especially clearly in the text's developed view of a Yeshu who does *not* belong in the category of an agent of "foreign" magic, but rather is presented as a false prophet.

At the first presentation of Yeshu to the queen, the sages announce, "This man is a sorcerer and entices everyone." The debate and contest that ensues, however, has to do with whether or not Yeshu is the messiah he claims to be. Do his prophetic warrants (he is a "rod out of the stem of Jesse") or do his opponents' denials of them ("a prophet which shall presume to speak a word in my name, which I have not commanded him to speak" will die) seem to have greater sway? The matter is initially clarified—to the queen's satisfaction—by a miracle, Yeshu's raising of a man from the dead. Is his action "sorcery" or a demonstration of messianic (and "prophetic") authority?

Yeshu heals, creates birds from clay, and retrieves a person from death by a method associated with magicians—the pronouncing of a verbal formula. And yet the *TY* foregoes a known Jewish and Talmudic commonplace about the origin of Yeshu's powers. His ability to work wonders is not a product of training with practitioners of *mageia* in Egypt. Rather, he gains his extraordinary potencies through a bold raid on the reservoir of holiness located in the Temple. From the letters on God's "foundation stone" he purloins the power needed to display his messiahship and gain his following. His raid on the divine Name is direct, not oblique. He grasps after and gains what belongs to God, and that is *not* an unholy power, even if it is one illicitly obtained. Yeshu is an interloper, but not an alien one; nor is his capacity for miracle-working "deviant" either in the sense that it stems from a foreign (extra-Jewish, and thus idolatrous) divine source, or in the sense that it is from Satan.[75]

While critical of the stealth by which its protagonist stole the power of the Ineffable Name, *Toledoth Yeshu* does not and of course cannot regard this power as polluted or evil. This much is clear from the story's testimony to the Tetragrammaton's effective use when the sages arrange for it to be made available to their selected "allies," Judah Iscarioto and Simeon Kepha. So it is not in its essence wicked or sullied power by which Yeshu does his extraordinary feats. Though he did so furtively and shamefully, Yeshu has tapped the powers of the Most High.

To what end, according to the story itself? Yeshu *aspired to*, or arrogantly *seized* the role of messiah. This the *TY* conveys through presenting his words and deeds, and even in depicting his final "triumphal entry" to Jerusalem (to regain knowledge of the Name). If Yeshu's teaching is erroneous or heretical, and dangerously "entices everyone," as the sages initially report to Helene, the reader has evidence only of his statements concerning the king who will appear as "a rod out of the stem of Jesse" (*Isaiah* 11:1). "I am he," Yeshu answers, or *instructs*, those who accuse him of magic. The debate over his identity must be settled, Yeshu insists, on biblical and eschatological terms. So it is that his healings, and especially his flight, authorized by *Isaiah* 14:13 ("I will ascend to heaven") are performances in keeping with his status: he is the promised one. Interestingly, the "Life of Jesus" spends no effort trying to prove that his miracles were sham-events or tricks. Yeshu is portrayed as having actually done these miracles, equipped as he was with might deriving from God. His ability to fly (reminiscent of rabbinic legends about Satan, Balaam, and Simon Magus taking wing), was, as the narrative frames reality, "real" enough to require the enlisted Judah Iscarioto's equal capacity, gained through his (this time approved) knowledge of the holy name of God. From the *TY*'s angle of vision Yeshu is God's challenger, and Jewish narratives, biblical and otherwise, know of God's patience—to a point—with rebels.

The sages' charge that Jesus was a sorcerer does not actually win the day in the narrative; Queen Helene, when the corpse of Yeshu was presented to her, reached her final judgment, "realizing that Yeshu was a false prophet who enticed people and led them astray."

The *Toledoth Yeshu* strives to show Yeshu as part of a thoroughly Jewish story—making its antihero a rebel within Judaism, a messianic pretender, not an alien intruder nor an agent of Satan. It was to this end that the *TY* maintained that Yeshu's crime was that of being a "false (Jewish) prophet"—an unholy pretender capable of misleading the folk, a resister of God—rather than branding him a wizard or sorcerer. Sustaining that categorization of Yeshu (and the frame and orientation of his biography) required that in the *TY* Yeshu speak his opponents' language, share with them the scriptures they debate, and participate in their cultus—even to the point that both he and the sages resort to the same holy armory and its weapon, the Ineffable Name. Indeed, it is striking that in this anti-Jesus novella Yeshu is portrayed defending his messianic claims with just those prophecies that we know from the New Testament and from Justin and Trypho were Christian favorites. Yeshu and the rabbis battle over the meaning of scriptures actually at the root of earliest friction and disagreement about Jesus, while the polemical instincts of this writing might have taken the liberty to put on Yeshu's lips more dubious, vulnerable, and comical prophecies by which he ventured to proclaim himself the fulfillment of messianic expectations.

Significantly, then, many of the basic elements of the Christian teachings of and about Jesus are being respected in the *TY*, even while he and the traditions about him are under strong attack, being debunked. In the end, Yeshu's life is framed and defined by the category of messiah, the role he steadily claimed but never possessed, and the role to which his defeat and death gave the lie. As portrayed in this writing, the life of Jesus the would-be messiah took place entirely within, and only rendered sense and meaning as a "great misfortune [that] befell Israel"—i.e, as an episode in the communal narrative which the *TY* understands to be its own.

Yeshu's biography cannot quite be said to be "restrained" in its defamation of him, but there exists a purposive measure, or calculation, in the way his portrait is drawn. Yeshu was the clever and overreaching young man gone wrong. Was his fault due to genetics—to duplicitous Joseph Pandera? Is Yeshu, as *TY* sees things, thoroughly "his father's son," set out on a larger stage? These questions return us to our chapter's key interest, as we look once more at *Toledoth Yeshu's* characterization of Miriam.

The "mistake" described as terrible is Miriam's, even though she was an unwilling participant. This heretofore unfamiliar account of how Miriam conceived her child excludes from its portrayal of her any of the salacious accusations already in circulation. It was *not* because she was an unreliable and untrustworthy fiancée or wife, nor because she was a licentious profligate, nor because she was the local guild of carpenters' prostitute, that she became pregnant. Israel's "great misfortune" (which finally must be understood to consist in the appearance of Yeshu) is not due to Miriam's own incentives. She was a victim overpowered. Even the insertion of the rabbinic tradition that Yeshu's youthful brashness derived from the fact that he was a bastard *and* that Miriam was a *niddah* undergoes revision in our version of the *TY*, the latter charge being denied. Her "mistake" was due to her having been assaulted "against her will," and later giving birth to the illegitimate son of Joseph Pandera, a "disreputable man of the tribe of Judah." This single charge against Miriam, therefore, does not damn or disapprove her in terms so harsh as those found elsewhere (Celsus's Jew, for example, would have had no interest in arguing that Mary was an *unwilling* partner in her liaison with her Roman soldier, Panthera). And we recall that the *TY* depicts Miriam as a dutiful Jewish mother tending to her son's circumcision and his early schooling in their religion.

David Biale asked, "Why should a text intent upon pillorying Christianity resort to such a detail [the seduction of innocent Miriam by her neighbor] that softens the inversion of the Gospel account?"[76] The basic charge against her stands, of course: Miriam was not a virgin selected by God to conceive through God's spirit and she did not give birth to the promised messiah, but to an illegitimate son *not* of Davidic lineage. And yet, more pronouncedly than in the case of Yeshu, the *TY's* rendering of Miriam is measured and moderated—clearly unwilling to disparage and malign her in virulent terms already popular in other Jewish critiques of the Christian Mary story. The Miriam of *TY* is less than a villain. She can even be seen as a directed participant in a biography that illuminates, in the end, the ways (to quote one of Biale's phrases) "that Jews really control Christian history after all."

That the *Toledoth Yeshu* might employ Miriam as an unfortunate actor whose role supports the larger story of Israel's posterity—especially as this pertains to the defeat of Yeshu and his followers—may be thought a subtle possibility, except for the fact that the events involving her and her son are the central display in the thesis that Jews can and do manage the Christianity they confront. What *is* undeniable is that the *TY* works to produce "versions" of Yeshu and Miriam that are easily distinguishable from both (positive) Christian and earlier and current (negative) Jewish portraits and valuations of the two. The work may well have sought to produce figures that were not so outlandish—and laughable—as to distract its readers and hearers from taking in the narrative's more determined teaching, one meant to defend and embolden Jews in their dealings with aggressive Christians, and to solidify Jews' confidence in their faith and their communal identity.

There is yet another line of interpretation to be considered, I believe, in considering the Miriam of the *Toledoth Yeshu*. Keeping Yeshu within recognizable Jewish categories and context in order to name his crime and offense in its particular way—acknowledging that he exercises magic but branding him, finally and definitively, a false prophet and deceiver of people—is a paramount goal in this writing. Christian theologians and exegetes of the same period took the Jewishness of their messiah with profound seriousness—in order to deflect as nonsense the claim that Jesus's powers were exotic and foreign, disconnected from the powers bequeathed upon Israel's kings, priests, and prophets. It was in Christianity's vital supersessionist interests to celebrate their messiah as one bearing in himself all the promises received by the race of Abraham, Moses, and David. And for Jews protesting Jesus's messiahship, to dismiss the troublesome Yeshua as a magician, as a sheer outlier from Judaism, would have been inadequate to the writing's purpose, for Yeshua had to be shown to be false and inauthentic in terms consistent with Jewish messianic hopes.

In the *Toledoth Jeshu* the disrespect and deceit in Yeshu's proclamation of his own messiahship is forecast in his father, and then acted out by Yeshu himself. Joseph Pandera's modus operandi entails illicit desire, stealth, trickery, and determination to possess the one he longs for. By the standards of Jewish law and accustomed civil behavior he is dishonorable. His gaze of lust fixes on the "lovely and chaste daughter" of a widow, one he has no right to approach and violate. She is Miriam, betrothed to "Yohanan, of the royal house of David, a man learned in the Torah and God-fearing." This proper young woman Joseph Pandera violates, casting her into a life of misfortunes. The portrayal and action of Pandera in the writing's opening lines are the storyteller's give away, a preview of what will now be told. Yeshu, whose biography this is, will take his father's traits, appetites, and conspicuous skills in self-interested deception to dangerous lengths. He will outwit the Temple's system for protecting the "Secret Name," stage marvelous feats to win decisions before the queen, and perform signs to gain loyalty from his followers, or as they are called, "insurgents."

It is not from Miriam that Yeshu inherits his yearning for power and his genius for cunning strategies. If, as we have seen, genetic causes are sought for a person's character—for his being a God-fearer, or for being callous in his disregard for the holy (of which a bare head is a symbol), Yeshu owes his rebellion and his grasping after God's powers to Joseph Pandera. By comparison and by necessity—in order for this portrayal of Yeshu to be maintained—Miriam is unfortunate and "only against her will" a sinner—an adulteress; she is not impure by her own intention, nor is she an evil mother.

We must conclude that while denying her any of the lofty attributes Christian veneration had accorded her, the *TY* renders Miriam a sympathetic and also a pathetic figure. This is her characterization, and though it does not spare her dishonor, it patently avoids the condemnations of those passages in the *Talmud* which defame her as a wanton, promiscuous low-life.

Because, then, *Toledoth Yeshu* interprets Christian traditions from a Jewish viewpoint that has not only polemical, but also its own constructive, goals, Miriam is, even while being decisively dethroned as the Christian Mariologists' virgin queen, a person treated with (again, measured) respect. The pinpointed source of her son's character, imprinted with stealth and chicanery, is Joseph Pandera, the opposite of Miriam's Johanan, and the cause of Miriam's "mistake." These are among the narrative intentions within the *TY* that produced an unexpected Miriam—a tragic Jewish mother of a shameless and failed pretender to a God-ordained royal throne.

SEFER ZERUBBABEL: HEPHZIBAH AND THE BEAUTIFUL STATUE—TWO MOTHERS

"What will be the form of the eternal house?" Interrupted in his prayer by a vision, Zerubbabel shouted out a question to God, whose voice he heard, though he "did not see his form."[77] The biblical hero's other queries were linked with this issue, with its presumption of a new and lasting Temple of God in Jerusalem. So Zerubbabel was not asking about something else when he said: "When will the Light [i.e., the redemption] of Israel come?"[78]

Toward the conclusion of this writing, the answers are given by the angel Michael (sometimes identified as Metatron). The day approaches when two messiahs, Nehemiah of Ephraimitic lineage, and Menahem of Davidic, accompanied by Elijah, will come to Jerusalem, and all the people of Israel, including the resurrected dead, will rejoice. God "will bring down to earth the Temple that was built above," and the people's sacrifices offered there will be accepted. When God stands on the Mount of Olives, the "exiles"— scattered Israel, and those who have died—will be brought "home."[79] And the time or season when this "eternal house" will descend and "light" of Israel will shine? "When 990 years from the destruction of Jerusalem have been completed," Michael informs Zerubbabel.[80]

Like other apocalypses (the biblical book of *Daniel*, for example) which are replete with angelic messengers and divine disclosures of what the future holds, *Sefer Zerubbabel* employs in its vision several of this genre's standard literary devices. One involves telling of the many woes and wars which must take place before the end of this (evil) age and the beginning of the messianic age, when God's justice will prevail. Such histories of the future make the readers aware of where things stand chronologically by making obvious which of these convulsions have already occurred, or are unfolding at the time of the author's writing. But time's compressibility and extension are accordian-like in a visionary text like *Sefer Zerubbabel*, and are put to good purpose. By pretending to be an account of divine revelations to a Jewish hero of the sixth century BCE, but addressing contemporary history and its turmoils in the seventh century CE, the authority and credibility of this apocalypse's predictions are helped by the accepted model of prophecy and fulfillment. Further, the author's choice of Zerubbabel as recipient of revelations is immediately salient, for his renown derives from his leadership in the reconstruction of the Jerusalem temple in the aftermath of Israel's defeat by Babylonia and that nation's "captivity" of Israel's sages and leaders. Now, by the time of *Sefer Zerubbabel*'s composition, Jews had for centuries visited the despoiled site on the date, the 9th of Av, to lament the catastrophe of the Temple's burning. In this document, Zerubbabel, restorer of the earlier temple, receives divine information about the "form" and the time of the anticipated eternal house of God.

The text's present is indicated by reference to the conflicts from 604– 630 CE in which the Byzantine Christian empire fought and eventually triumphed over Persia. In *Sefer Zerubbabel*'s list of the ten rulers who must suffer defeat when the expected Davidic messiah appears, "the ninth is Shiroi, king of Persia."[81] Further, the tenth king, who is described as "Armilos, son of Satan, who came from the stone statue of a woman," is identified as the ruler of all these kingdoms, as it is revealed to Zerubbabel that "He (Armilos) will ascend in his strength and conquer the whole world."[82] Armilos, whose name has led some commentators to wonder if it is a play on Romulus, was transparent to readers of this apocalypse as Heraclius, who ruled as the Byzantine emperor from 610 to 641. Heraclius effectively ended Sassanian rule in Persia by defeating Chosroes II in 628, and regained the relic of the Cross which Persian forces had taken after gaining control of Jerusalem in 614. Shiroi, murderer and successor of his father, Chosroes II, was in power only in 628, when he sought a peace treaty with Heraclius (*SZ*'s Armilos). The events of the first three decades of the seventh century had considerable impact on Palestine and the lives of Jews, whose attitudes toward conquest of Christian Jerusalem by the Persians were enthusiastically positive—at least according to Christian reporters.[83]

Two imaginary female actors appear alongside the thoroughly historical figures of Armilos/Heraclius and Shiroi in *Sefer Zerubbabel*'s foreseen drama. They hold importance for us in that each derives from and is related to Miriam—or, rather, to Mary, as she was called and celebrated by Byzantine Christians. The first, Hephzibah (her name means "my delight is in her"), is the prodigious mother of the coming Davidic messiah; her role in ushering in God's rule and the redemption of Israel is pivotal—comparable to that of her soon-to-be-triumphant son, Menahem.[84] The second female character is the beautiful statue—unnamed, but obviously a representation of the Virgin—who gives birth (by Satan, the father) to the ruler, Armilos. The Virgin's son, the world's sovereign, is an obstacle in the Jewish messiah's way—hence Armilos (Heraclius) is at one point portrayed as the anti-Messiah, or anti-Christ (the final enemy of the one to be anointed):

> The hair of his head is colored like gold. He is green to the soles of his feet. The width of his face is a span. His eyes are deep. He has two heads. He will rise and rule the province with terror. Satan is the father of Belial. All who see him will tremble.[85]

We are in the world of apocalyptic vision, where historical and transhistorical forces gain personification as monstrous actors in a cosmic war between good and evil—a war that spins toward its climax. (Christians, for their part, are celebrating Heraclius's victory over Shiroi in grandiose terms, likening his "rest" after six years of war to that taken by the Lord of creation.[86])

Early in Zerubbabel's account of the revelations to him, he is spirited away on a journey to Nineveh (the damned kingdom which stands for "Rome the Great"—i.e., Constantinople). There he meets a lowly and "despised" man who is Hephzibah's son. Menahem tells his time-traveling inquirer, "I am the Lord's anointed, the son of Hezekiah, and I am imprisoned until the time of the end." The angel Michael confirms this, telling Zerubbabel that the person standing before him *is* Menahem, the messiah born in the time of king David, and hidden now in the enemy's capital until the time of his manifestation. When Zerubbabel asks what signs Menahem will perform, Metraton, commander of God's angelic armies, describes first the actions of his mother:

> The Lord will give Hephzibah . . . a staff for these acts of salvation. A great star will shine before her. All the stars will swerve from their paths. Hephzibah, mother of Menahem son of Amiel . . . will go out and kill two kings [the rulers of Yemen and Antioch]. . . . This war and these signs will take place on the festival of weeks in the third month.[87]

Hephzibah's weapon, the staff made of almond wood, is of course extraordinary; it had been possessed by Moses, Aaron (in whose possession it sprouted), Joshua, and David. The staff serves her well in her war with the king of Persia, and she bequeaths it to Menahem's co-messiah, Nehemiah, son of Hushiel, from the line of Ephraim, when he goes to battle. The weapon does not, in that instance, protect Nehemiah from being killed by the forces of the mighty Armilos, but he is raised from the dead, and positioned at the gates of Jerusalem, ready to fight again, when he joins with Menahem and Elijah the prophet, in the ultimate battle with their foe Armilos/Heraclius.

Sefer Zerubbabel's portrayals of the stone mother of Armilos are equally intriguing, with Zerubbabel's first glimpse of her taking place when his angel-escort takes him to "the house of disgrace and merrymaking"—that is, a church: "[Michael] showed me a marble stone in the shape of a virgin. The beauty of her appearance was wonderful to behold," says Zerubbabel.[88] This marble figure is the center of attention in the apocalypse's description of the last outrageous deeds of Armilos, Menahem's soon-to-be vanquished arch-enemy:

> This Armilos will then take his mother, the stone from which he was born, out of the house of disgrace of the scoffers. From all over, the nations will come to worship that stone, burn incense, and pour libations to her. No one will be able to look upon her face because of her beauty. Whoever does not bow down to her will die, suffering like an animal.[89]

There are things not to be missed in the passage—obvious, familiar comments about Christian defamers of Judaism ("scoffers") and a complaint concerning the absence of solemnity, or sanctity, in their meeting places. We find also the not-at-all enigmatic reference to the power (and threat) resident in an icon of the Virgin Mary. The author of *Sefer Zerubbabel* and

his readers know of military uses to which the Virgin's portraits and stat-
ues had been put in defense of Constantinople, and as a means of offense
in battles—including several waged by Heraclius's forces.[90] The rise of
Mary to the status of a "general" (*strategos*) who defends and wages war
for Christian emperors and their people is expertly chronicled in Bissera
Pentcheva's study of Byzantine icons of the Virgin.[91]

How, at the conclusion of a study of Jewish treatments of Mary, do we
place and evaluate Hephzibah, the mother of the triumphant Jewish messiah on the one hand, and on the other, Mary, the stone image of a beautiful virgin who is revealed to be, with Satan, the parent of the anti-Messiah,
Armilos, or the king of the Christian empire? How do these female representations, made active characters in a prophetic drama of the day of Israel's
salvation, stand in relation to the Mary being celebrated by Christians in
the seventh century in "Nineveh," and among its kings and queens?

Martha Himmelfarb and David Biale, recent analysts of *Sefer Zerubbabel*,
have pointed to the writing's shrewdly transgressive, but also somewhat
ambivalent, reversals of Christian lore in the course of creating a Jewish
vision of end-time triumph—one that gives focal attention to the two
female players in the drama. As a Jewish response to Christianity's Mary
(that is, to the Mary envisioned in the seventh century as the empowered
bearer of God, now enthroned in heaven), each woman, or better, each
mother portrayed in *Sefer Zerubbabel,* has been carefully wrought and
artfully set forth. Hephzibah is an alternative and *competitive* messiah's
mother, and the nonvirginal beautiful statue is a sardonic vilification of
Mary and, simultaneously, of the deity-blessed royalty of Byzantium.

Both Hephzibah and Mary the beautiful statue, as portrayed, reverse and
disrupt Christian claims about God's salvific plan, and about which people
will rejoice on the day God gathers those dearest to him, commencing the
messianic age. The fashioning of the roles and characters of Hephzibah
and of the living statue fascinates us also because the articulation of the
two mothers' anti-Christian meanings borrows and in distinctive ways
depends significantly upon the very Mary tradition being undermined. We
meet this interpretive stratagem elsewhere in *SZ*, perhaps most conspicu-
ously in its representation of the messiah Menahem, who while hidden in
the enemy's camp before his victorious epiphany, takes on the form (as
Christians believed Jesus had) of scripture's "suffering servant" passages in
Isaiah 53. Menahem, when first met by Zerubbabel, was "a man, despised
and wounded, lowly and in pain."[92]

Hephzibah is mighty in ways bearing no resemblance whatever to the
humble and servant-obedient Mary of the New Testament and other
early Christian writings. However, when her militancy is considered in

Figure 14.1 Virgin Mary enthroned, ninth-century ivory plaque, Aachen, Germany. Metropolitan Museum Medieval collection 17.190.49. Plaque: 22 x 14.5 x 0.8 cm. © Metropolitan Museum of Art, New York.

parallel with a certain understanding and iconology of Mary emergent in the Byzantine and in the Latin Christian world, the differences are very nearly obliterated, as the imagery of the warlike Virgin in this ninth-century Carolingian ivory (Figure 14.1) shows.[93]

Under the pressure that comes from informed and conscious religious rivalry, Hephzibah, the Jewish good and fierce mother of Menahem, manifests divine might, her staff of Aaron a counterpart to the cross that Mary holds (or brandishes) in the icon.[94] Hephzibah is the fearsome force understood to hold her station next to the messianic throne. She is Menahem's God-approved and God-enabled co-redeemer—for the "Light of Israel" comes as much through her victorious actions as through his. In this respect, though she corresponds to Mary, and is an "answer" to the Virgin's eminent role in Christian theology and piety. Hephzibah is the anti-Mary, for she is mother of the *true* messiah. This Jewish Madonna is a martial mother of single purpose, protecting and promoting her son, the Davidic champion, and guarantor of Israel's future. She is not Mary, but it is fair to say that she is what the *Sefer Zerubbabel* regards as a requisite counterpart—a "great mother" for the coming messiah of God. To put this point more forcefully, Hephzibah owes not only her existence to the prominence of the mother of the Christians' messiah, Jesus, but also draws from certain established aspects of the Byzantine Christian Mary (ones consonant with the fierce heroines Deborah and Yael in the *Book of Judges*)—namely her attributes as a militant woman of strength, stamped as a warrior for God.[95]

Here the "rod of Aaron" that she wields demands closer consideration, since there appears to have been much at stake in reclaiming or regaining this symbol for Judaism, and for its messianic hopes. Was the view held by some rabbis that the staff would be the Messiah's scepter, the sign of his sovereignty, the chief influence on this important feature in the portrayal of Hephzibah? I think we must recognize as a strong factor in *SZ*'s counter-Marian thinking the much-used and probably widely known Christian appropriation of the budding rod of Aaron described in *Numbers* 17.

As early as the writing of the *Protevangelium of James*, the image of the sprouting staff was employed to dramatize the extraordinary choice of Joseph to be Mary's guardian. This narratological use of Aaron's staff, however, soon gave way to allegorical and typological motifs: declarations hailing Mary herself as rod of Aaron in Christian festivals, and in liturgies and poetry. Within a collection of prayers and songs used in Syrian liturgies, we find in *Panqita* 45:

> Hail Mary, pure and sacred young woman, O residence of the heavenly king! Hail Mary, Rod of Aaron! Hail Mary, closed gate that is not opened! Hail Mary, breathing temple of the exalted God! Hail Mary, rod of strength and lamp of ample light! Hail Mary, who received the greeting of Gabriel and gave life to the House of Adam![96]
>
> While the rod which here *is* Mary betokens strength, its prevailing sense as metaphor pointed towards fruitfulness, towards Mary's identity as *Theotokos*, as we see in one of Ephrem's fourth-century hymns dedicated to showing what biblical signs were fulfilled in Christ's birth:
> ... worthy of faith is the daugher of Eve [mother of the living]
> who without a man bore a child!
> The virgin earth gave birth to that Adam, head of the earth;
> The Virgin today gave birth to [second] Adam, head of heaven.
> The staff of Aaron sprouted, and the dry wood brought forth;

> his symbol has been explained today—it is the virgin womb
> that gave birth.
> Put to shame is the people [the Jews] that holds the prophets
> to be true,
> for if our Savior had not come, their words would have become lies.[97]

The sharp conflict between Jews and Christians over what certain scriptural motifs and passages *must* mean is revealed once more in Ephrem's bristling and caustic last verse, which can be rephrased: without fulfillment of your biblical prophecies in the revelation of Christ, they would be empty, and false.[98] "Of course," wrote Kathleen McVey, "Ephrem ignores the possibility that the messianic prophecies would be fulfilled at a later date," and this possibility is, more than two centuries after his writing, being set forth in a Jewish writing as a divinely revealed certainty. The *Sefer Zerubbabel* is a *confident* apocalypse. Its writer cannot have been unfamiliar with this popular motif of Aaron's rod as it had been adopted by Christians and in several ways interpreted. Given the growth of the Mary cult, and the broad publicity of the Virgin Mary's powers and attributes, Hephzibah was virtually compelled to be allied and equipped with the staff of Aaron. Regnant Christianity, with its regal "virgin of God" whose blossom was Jesus, is being challenged and answered.

About the inspiration of "the heroic Hephzibah" and of the statue-mother of Armilos by Satan, Himmelfarb wrote:

> The author of Sefer Zerubbabel was clearly of two minds about the figure of the Virgin Mary. Even as he used some aspects of the figure of Mary as a model for Hephzibah, he conferred other aspects on the statue that gives birth to Armilos. This statue is a sort of demonic counterpart to Hephzibah, a reflection of the author's perception of the Virgin Mary as idol and mother of the antichrist. . . . While Sefer Zerubbabel repeatedly identifies [Hephzibah] as the mother of the Davidic messiah, it never shows her acting as a mother toward her son. Nor is she given any recognizably feminine functions. Her primary activity is warfare, about as masculine a pursuit as possible, although . . . one the author might well have associated with the Virgin Mary. Hephzibah is never shown in the company of her husband, whose identity is not even clear. . . . The anxieties of the author of Sefer Zerubbabel about the figure of the Virgin Mary run so deep that when he adapts her for Jewish use, he all but eliminates her feminine aspects, including maternal ones.[99]

Hostile Jewish attitudes toward the Christian Mary and her story are evident also in *SZ*'s demeaning depiction of her as animated statue. The assertion that she, the representative and also the iconic presence of Mary in the Church, was sexually active, producing a son, is a polemical commonplace already familiar to us, but the branding of Armilos (who is representative of the Christian empire, but also of Christ) as the son of Satan is new, and a sharply insulting element of parody. As Peter Schäfer comments:

> Not only is Mary *not* a virgin, but she even has intercourse with Belial/Satan, obviously the counterimage of God! It is difficult to imagine a nastier and more obscene counternarrative to the New Testament birth story.[100]

To those Jews who first read *Sefer Zerubbabel*, what did the statue of the virgin signify—she who "was wonderful to behold," but on the other hand, unable to be gazed upon "because of her beauty"? As political and theological commentary, the image seen in and outside the "house of disgrace and merrymaking" is a double mother: the bearer of a Christian world-conqueror, Heraclius, in whose reign and society Jews cannot yet find the light or salvation for which they long, and also the genatrix of a fraudulent "anointed one." In and "behind" Heraclius, Jesus himself is to be seen—child of the devil destined to torment his foes, but also to be vanquished. *This* Mary of the *SZ* is the villain mother, whose son can be nothing other than demonic. She, the statue spouse of Satan, is mother of Heraclius, head of Constantinople and of its churches—a far cry from the *theotokos* of Christian veneration. The marble figure bore no God, but had intercourse with the Devil, and gave birth to an opponent of God's will.

Although the author of the apocalypse may be ambivalent, as has been suggested, finding in the Mary he disdains (Armilos's mother) a certain attraction, this ambiguity about her cannot turn or depend upon the steady references to the statue's beauty. To the time-traveling and vision-endowed Zerubbabel she is glorious, "wonderful to behold," but to others she possesses a beauty too dangerous to gaze upon. The figure's beauty threatens and bewitches, its powers wholly in keeping with her evil character. Armilos's statuesque mother is presented as powerful and dangerous in a mode and with a purpose different from Hephzibah's; anyone who will not bow down to her, in the time of Armilos's fateful encounter with Menahem, we recall, "will die, suffering like an animal."

By turning the Christian mother of God into the partner of Satan whose offspring fills the role of anti-Christ—he whom the true messiah, Menahem, will slay by the "breath [of] his nostrils"—*SZ* sets the eschatological program straight for Jews, and subverts Christian understandings and beliefs about her, and her eternal reign in heaven.

Sefer Zerubbabel inventively transforms and then deploys aspects of Miriam in a revelation designed, above all else, to sustain Israel (or Judaism) in eschatological confidence. A counter-Mary—Hephzibah—and a demonized Mary help to tell the future's story. Due in no small measure to the power in warfare of Menahem's mother, and to the picture of the ultimate defeat of the beguiling statue's imposter son, this benighted age will end, the "eternal house" will descend from above, and "the time of salvation" will be accomplished.

CONCLUSION

Jewish anti-Mary and anti-Jesus critiques and attacks—especially those contained in Jewish writings like *Toledoth Yeshu* and *Sefer Zerubbabel*—stood alongside and responded to polemics developed in Christianity. Our study of Jewish, Christian, and Muslim disputations over their scriptures and their theologies has regularly displayed the separate communities' efforts at defense and attack—often vehement. It is a historical given that religious attitudes and biases toward the "other" are picked up and interiorized within a group or person in subtle and unconscious ways, becoming ingrained as elements in a worldview.

Michael Wex's *Born to Kvetch,* written in 2005, is a provocative study of the development of Yiddish as, among other things, a code language enabling criticism of those who are not initiated to it.[101] Though invented in a medieval society in which Jewish life and language had to respond to a dominating Christianity, today's Jews may, and often do, use determinedly pointed phrases without knowledge of their original context or sense. Invoking *Toledoth Yeshu*'s medieval description of Jesus in Hebrew—"*a mamzer ben ha-nidoh*, the bastard son of an unclean woman"—Wex proceeds to explore the anti-Christian meaning of several Yiddish phrases: for example, *a mamoshes vi der goyisher got*, which describes an argument or excuse that has about as much substance or truth as the God of the *goyim* (i.e., none). The phrase, Wex notes, further translates into this response to the Christian ritual in which the consecrated bread is elevated while the priest intones Jesus's words, "This is my body": to the Yiddish speaker, the sense of *a mamoshes vi der goyischer got* amounts to "it's as close to the real truth as the notion that the blood of Jesus has set us free"—that is, not at all.[102]

A similar oppositional Yiddish formulation is *nisht geshtoygen un nisht gefloygen*—that is, "it didn't climb up and it didn't fly." Its conveyed sense is: "Preposterous!" or "Nonsense!"[103] Many accustomed to the phrase, however, are unaware of its basis, which is a response to the Christian depiction of Jesus's resurrection and ascension. The phrase owes a debt to *Toledoth*

Yeshu, which was intent to reveal about these preachments: "Untrue—it did not happen!" "It didn't climb up and it didn't fly" refers to Jesus and his body, which could not possibly have climbed to heaven nor ascended there by flight.[104]

Wex's comments about the rootedness of Yiddish in denial and ridicule of Christian truth-claims are a fitting postscipt for this chapter's subject. They also remind us of the manner in which bias and slander can and do become part of any religious community's vocabulary—even becoming so ingrained as to be heedless. Here the example is one in Judaism. The phenomenon is of course equally present in Christianity and Islam, and in other living religious traditions. This instinct or drive toward denigration is the dangerous and destructive shadow side of a faith community's assertion and celebration of its special truth and peoplehood, which is believed to be owned exclusively. Whether in quips or in sustained efforts to defame, such negative judgments against the beliefs of the "other"—the exchangeable infidel—perdure.

To bring this chapter to a close, and to anticipate an important element in the next—Islam's understandings of Mary/Maryam—a brief ammendment is required. It will have been noticed that in the four texts surveyed we met no efforts to associate Miriam the mother of Yeshu with her venerable predecessor, Miriam of the Tanakh, the honored "prophetess, sister of Aaron" (*Exodus* 15:20) who celebrated the victorious liberation from Pharaoh with song and with dancing with timbrels. Characterized by polemic writings either in harsh or in more sympathetic terms, the mother of Yeshua was not to be regarded a descendant of the heroine who stood side by side with Moses and Aaron as those whom God sent before the people of God when he redeemed them from slavery (*Micah* 6:4). Though the Miriam of Hebrew scripture was not an idealized figure (for joining Aaron in challenging Moses's marriage of a Cushite woman, she receives a sharp divine punishment in *Numbers* 12), the combination of her role in the Moses infancy story (managing to persuade the Pharaoh's daughter to bring Moses to a proper wet-nurse, his own mother) and her role as coleader, with her brothers, in the exodus triumph, yielded for her a place of deep respect in Jewish lore. The Miriam tradition was embellished in the course of rabbinic discussions. Prophetic powers attributed to her were rooted primarily in Miriam's prediction of a son to be born in her family who would be savior of the Israelites—one whose powers would be evident at his birth, and played out in time, when he would make waters dry up.[105] During Moses's birth, Jochebed, his mother, was pain-free, "for pious women are not included in the curse pronounced upon Eve, decreeing sorrow in conception and childbearing."[106] *Exodus Rabbah* provides a scene in which the presence of the newborn Moses floods the family dwelling with light—at which point Amram kisses his gifted prophetess daughter on the head—and also tells of the chagrin of Moses's mother when she must set her son afloat in the bulrushes; she, with her special son's life at risk, rewards Miriam with a blow to the head.[107] There is the story of a traveling well, named after Miriam, that accompanied and sustained the Hebrews in their forty-year journey and, finally, an explanation of her death, like the deaths of Moses and Aaron, while still in the wilderness, "because she was a leader of the people along with [them], a woman who "occupied a place as high as that of her brothers."[108] The description of Miriam as "sister of Aaron" needed some clarification. Why not "of Moses"?: "She was named such because in reality, she made this prophesy when she was only the sister of Aaron, Moses not having been yet born." (This description is used in reference to Mary, mother of Jesus, in a charged scene in the Qu'ran's Surah *Maryam*, as will be seen below.)

The prophetess Miriam had only a name in common with Miriam the mother of Yeshua, for the latter, in the eyes of Jewish narrators of her sorry story, was utterly bereft of the better attributes of the daughter of Amran, "sister of Aaron." She was, after all, the dishonored mother of an exposed messiah-pretender. Determined, of course, by the need to defend against and to refute the Mary of the Christians, this viewpoint denied Miriam, mother of Yeshua, an honorable ancestry.

It now remains to examine how the early Muslim representation of Mary—in which her son *was* expressly declared to be both "messiah" and "prophet"—correlates to these two competing visions. Who, in the Qur'an, and in the understandings of Islam's scripture interpreters, was Maryam, mother of ʿIsa?

CHAPTER 15

✧

Maryam, Mother of `Isa

"Chosen . . . Over the Women of All Peoples"

When Muhammad began receiving revelations, the discussion between Christians and Jews over Mary and her son became a trialogue. Numerous qur'anic passages give evidence of the immediately more complex debate over Mary's identity, nature, and character. Surah 4:156, in the course of faulting the Jews for violating their convenant with God, reprimands them for "their monstrous slander of Mary." The chief source of this accusation is an event vividly described elsewhere in the Qur'an—a scene that will occupy us more than once in this chapter. Another confrontative passage was among the verses placed within the entry of the Dome of the Rock, completed in 691 in Jerusalem. Turned toward the city's most important Christian monument, the Church of the Holy Sepulcher, some 400 meters away, this inscription's words put forth a strong challenge:

> People of scripture,
> do not go to excess in your religion,
> and do not say anything about God but the
> truth. The Messiah Jesus son of Mary
> was only a messenger, a word, from God,
> which God sent down to Mary,
> a spirit from God.
> So believe in God
> and God's messengers.
> And do not speak of a trinity;

it is best for you to refrain.

God is one sole divinity,

too transcendent to have a son,

in possession of all in the heavens and on earth.

And God is a good enough patron (Surah 4:171).

Jewish low opinions of Mary and Christian exaggeration about her and her son are both false, but very differently blasphemous. Jews dishonor a prophet's mother especially honored by God, and the Christians' titles for both Jesus and Mary offend—he is not the "Son of God" nor is she "mother of God." The corrections of their opponents' errant beliefs are already present in the phrase seen in the quotation above, and regularly used by Muslims: `Isa ibn Maryam, or, Jesus son of Mary. To explore and spell out the implications of the three words is to become aware of Muslim Mariology—that is, those vital understandings and presentations of Mary/Maryam which increased the honor and reverence accorded her as one of God's specially elect.

Traces of Muslims' experiences involving Mary appear in surprising places. The destination for pilgrims journeying to Jerusalem's *Haram al-Sharif*, or "Noble Sanctuary," was the Dome which celebrated Muhammad's miraculous *miraj*, or "Night Journey." While circling within the structure and offering their prayers, they were able to see the footprint left upon the rock by the Prophet when he commenced his ascent to heaven. Afterward pilgrims visited other locations devoted to sacred events or people, and then descended to the al-Aksa mosque. What next followed was a circuit taking them to numerous other gates, domes, and prayer niches on the platform and along the compound's walls.

As early as the eighth century, perhaps—and certainly by the tenth century—`Isa and Maryam were among those recognized: visible near the point of juncture of the southern and eastern walls of the sacred precinct was the *mihrab*, or prayer chamber, which Mary had once occupied, and (nearby) the cradle of Jesus.[1] The positive force of these two stations for Muslims was based in scripture—the Qur'an's own disclosures concerning Mary's residence in the temple as a child dedicated to God (Surah 3:37) and her son's declaration of his prophethood just after his birth (Surah 19:29–30). From its beginnings, Islam viewed Jesus and his mother as favorites of God.

Jesus was a servant (`abd Allah) and a prophet of God (*rasulullah*) who had been given the Gospel to be preached to the Jews, and empowered to fortify his mission by the signs that began with his birth and continued powerfully in his teachings and miracles.[2] One of the wonders of Jesus (denied by those Christians who worshipped near his sepulcher) was that

Jesus had not died. God rescued him from his execution (while allowing a seeming crucifixion), in order that he might perform his specific duties at the End-time, when the great Resurrection occurs.[3]

The following pages will consider the various forms of attention paid in the Qur'an and early Muslim tradition to Maryam herself, for though much of her glory derives from her son, 'Isa the prophet, whose role in the unfolding of God's purposes for humankind is nothing less than essential, she possesses an eminence that is decidedly her own.

MARY IN THE QUR'AN: HERESIES CONFRONTED, AND HER TRUE STORY TOLD

There is no question that Mary is the female figure to whom the greatest attention is given in the Qur'an. There are 70 verses that refer to her, and she is named specifically in 34 of these (24 in relation to Jesus, son of Mary). Only three other persons—Moses, Abraham, and Noah ... are mentioned by name more frequently than is Mary. She is, in fact, the only woman who is identified by name in the Qur'an and she enjoys the special honor of having one of its 114 chapters titled after her (*Maryam*, Sura 19).

—Jane Smith and Yvonne Haddad[4]

Competing Doctrines

Formal or categorical differences between Muslim and Christian beliefs about Jesus and Mary are theological, for at root Islam's monotheism—its commitment to the unicity (*tawhid*) of God—excludes certain ways of thinking about this mother and son, who, however unique and extraordinary, remain what they are: creatures. There is God, the only God, and there are all those whom God has called into being: angels, houris, demons, rulers, prophets—every man, woman, and child who exists or once existed in the world. Having no associates, no coexisting divine partners, God alone is "Lord." All beings are to acknowledge that reality, turning in obedience to the single source and guardian of life.

The Christians are faulted for bestowing a species of honor upon Mary and her son that is theologically impermissible—and heretical. Surah 5:116–117 imagines a dialogue meant to silence their claims:

116 And God will say,
"O Jesus, Son of Mary, did you tell the people,

'Take to me and my mother as deities
rather than God'"?
He will say, "Glory to You!
It is not for me to say what I have no right to.
If I used to say that, You would have known it.
You know what is in my essence,
while I do not know what is in Your essence.
For You are the one
Who knows all hidden secrets.
117 I never told them anything
but what You instructed me—'Worship God,
my Lord and your Lord.'
And I was a witness to them
While I sojourned among them.
And when You took me,
It was You who were watching over them.
And You are witness to all things."

In these terms the qur'anic Jesus sets the record straight about his self-understanding, resolutely denying that he claimed divinity for himself or for Mary. He is God's worshipful servant—not himself a God "besides" (or distinct from) God. Jesus's plain testimony comes down to this: I never did and never could have declared myself or my mother a deity—an associate or a partner to You.

Most intriguing in this qur'anic passage, from a historical standpoint, is the suspicion attributed to God: that Christians believed that Mary, like her son, was a divine being—perhaps one of the persons in the "three," the Trinity. The idea seems strange and far-fetched, scriptural though it is, but we must weigh the strong possibility that it arises from observations of the church's systematic promulgation, from the late fourth century on, of the cult of the Virgin. Knowledge of Christian feasts celebrating events in the life of Mary would have sufficed to raise alarm that in their glorification of Mary the people of the churches had gone too far in the direction of treating her as a goddess.

That these qur'anic passages have the effect of teaching and reassuring Muslims should not obscure to us their potential impact on other audiences—Jews, Christians, and others who might be either opponents or potential converts. These texts and others we shall consider frequently possess adversarial force and intent. They contain warnings to heretics which, read or heard by Muslims, reinforce their own religious commitments—and identity.

MARY IN THE QUR'AN
The Narratives

Believed to have come from the earlier period of revelations to Muhammad when (some scholars believe) he struggled to convince his fellow Meccans of his divine commission, a substantial account of Mary's story appears in the surah which bears her name.

Surah *Maryam* 19:16–33 relates in sequence the angel-visitation to Mary, the birth of Jesus, the encounter between Mary and her own people when she returns to them with Jesus in her arms, and the infant Jesus's self-introduction.

16 And mention Mary in the Book:
when she withdrew from her people
to a place in the East.
17 and secluded herself from them,
We sent her Our spirit,
Which appeared to her just like a man.
18 She said,
"I take refuge from you
with the Benevolent One,
if you are conscientious."
19 He said, "I am only
a messenger from your Lord,
to give you a sinless son."
20 She said, "How will I have a son,
when no man has touched me
and I have not been unchaste?"
21 He said, "It will be so."
He said, "Your Lord says,
'It is easy for Me; and We intend
to make him a sign for humankind,
and a mercy from us.'
So the matter is decided."
22 So she carried him,
secluding herself with him
in a far away place.
23 Then labor pains impelled her
to the trunk of a palm tree.
She said, "Would that I had

died before this
and been completely forgotten!"
24 Then he called to her from below,
saying, "Do not grieve;
your Lord has put a stream beneath you,
25 and shake the trunk of the palm toward you
to let fresh ripe dates fall by you.
26 Then eat and drink and be of good cheer:
but if you see any man, say, 'I have dedicated
a fast to the Benevolent One, so I shall not
talk to any human being today.'"
27 Finally she carried him
to her people: they said, "Mary,
you sure have done
an unheard-of thing!
28 O sister of Aaron,
your father was not a bad man,
and your mother was not a whore."
29 Now she pointed to him.
They said, "How can we talk to one
Who is an infant in the cradle?"
30 He said, "I am indeed the servant of God,
who has given me scripture
and made me a prophet,
31 and he made me blessed wherever I am;
and has prescribed prayer and charity
for me as long as I live,
32 and kindness to my mother as well;
and did not make me an arrogant malcontent.
33 And peace is upon me
the day I was born,
and the day I died,
and the day I am resurrected,
alive."

Each of these scenes is charged with emotion and surprise. Mary, self-isolated, is alarmed when she sees the human form in which God's angel appears. Requiring him to declare his identity and his purpose, she learns that he is one sent by God, not a being from whom Mary needs divine protection. The tidings of a son Mary will conceive and bear prompt a dialogue—and the angel's assurance that she, a virgin, can conceive and give birth. But Mary's issue, or offspring, is no ordinary creation. Her conception of Jesus is a happening decreed by God. She will produce a son who is an *aya*, a "sign," of God's creative power in the universe.

Pregnant, Mary further withdraws from the zone of human dealings, and when her labor (to which she has the response of a fully human woman) commences, she stands near a palm tree. Someone "below" her (who? an angelic voice? Jesus in utero, or just emerged?) consoles her, giving instruction about the water and fruit that will sustain her. The provision of food and drink—the stream in particular—is marked as a significant revelation elsewhere in the Qur'an, where it is not part of a narrative, but a formula-like statement about God's revealing of Jesus and Mary. Surah 23:49–50 reads:

> 49 But We had given Moses scripture
> that they might be guided.
> 50 And we made a sign
> of the son of Mary and his mother,
> and We sheltered them both
> on the high ground
> with security and flowing springs.

That a compressed account of God's revealing of Jesus and Mary is concentrated on his birth from her, rather than on other events and actions in Jesus's life, contains, as we shall see below, an important and emphatic Muslim teaching about the two together, and about Mary herself.

Mary's vow to fast and to be silent allows a scene change—to a tense and all-important confrontation. Seeing Mary with what they believe to be a bastard child in her arms, her people—the Jews—revile her for her terrible sin, measuring her against the unimpeachable sexual behavior of her forebears. The language of Surah 19:28 deserves close consideration. In scathingly addressing Mary as "sister of Aaron," her distraught kinsfolk level their accusations by invoking not one, but two ancestors—her namesake Maryam/Miriam who celebrated with her brothers the Hebrews' deliverance from Egypt, and Aaron, the originator and personification of the priestly tradition.[5] The force of her people's criticism draws, however, from what Aaron (more than his sister) directly represents: how could you, a woman in the priestly lineage and, further, one possessing the purity required for those dedicated to serve and reside in the Temple, have committed so grave a transgression? The ancient Miriam signifies for Mary's detractors not the champion prophetess who shared in the exodus victory, but rather a paragon of moral uprightness who is in that way, too, akin to her brother. The reference to Mary's father as "not a bad man" and her mother, who "was not a whore," are not Mary's ancient ancestors Imran and his wife, whose children were Miriam, Moses, and Aaron, but rather those parents of Mary who go unnamed in the Qur'an, even while it is clear who they are. Christian lore, in particular the *Protevangelium of James*, had extolled the virtues of Joachim and Anna, and these figures form part of the Qur'an's Mary story, as we notice here. The condemnation of Mary for betrayal of her family's righteousness in 19:28 intensifies the disapproval being registered against the virgin and her miraculously created child.

In the midst of her interrogation, however, the "sign" of Mary's son is manifest. `Isa the cradled infant is his mute mother's defender and advocate. In a testimony of fully mature authority, he informs those shaming Mary who he is—the son of Mary through God's gracious election of her. He is guardian of God's message, prophet, blessed, under obligation throughout his life to offer his *salah* and *zakat* (his prayer and almsgiving), and to treat his mother kindly. God, the newborn `Isa/Jesus proclaims, has not made him arrogant or disgruntled. He is an envoy of the Almighty.

A Christian Latin text from the eighth to ninth centuries, *The Gospel of Pseudo-Matthew*, contains a tradition concerning a palm tree that nourishes Mary with fruit and water—not while she is in the throes of childbirth, but as she journeys to Egypt after Jesus's birth. A vocal Christ-child, Jesus is the chief actor in these events. He commands the palm to bow downward—even to Mary's feet—so that its fruit may be gotten and yield a "vein of water" to quench the thirst of the holy family and their cattle.[6] On Jesus's order, a branch from the tree is transported by angels to paradise, where it is prepared for all the saints there—a motif we encountered in the writings treating Mary's dormition and assumption into heaven. (We recall from Chapter 13 that John, bishop of Thessalonica, told in his sermon of Mary's carrying a palm branch while ascending the Mount of Olives, and of trees bending down in acknowledgment of her triumphal procession.) That early Islam was familiar with a Christian tale along these lines is clear enough. What captures our attention, however, is its presentation and function in the Qur'an, and its particular features: the motif of the palm-tree is tied to Mary's labor-pangs, and the infant Jesus's words to her, if indeed his, rather than the angel's voice, can be understood to sound from beneath her. In the clash with Mary's people the infant's words constitute an apologetic—a defense of his mother against their hostile damnation of her—wrapped in a pronouncement on his own behalf.

Surah *Maryam*'s narrative account concludes with verses ensuring that any hearer of Mary's qur'anic story would comprehend the ways it contrasts with erroneous Jewish and Christian teachings.

19:34 That was Jesus, son of Mary,

a word of truth about which they doubt.

35 Having a son

is not attributable to God,

who is beyond that,

and when having determined something

merely says to it "Be,"

and it is.

36 [Jesus said:] "And God is in fact

my Lord and your Lord—

so serve God:

this is a straight path."

37 But the sects differ among themselves;

and woe to those who have refused to believe,

for the meeting of a distressing day

38 when they will hear better and see better,

the day they come to Us.

But those who do wrong

are in evident error today.

39 So warn them of a day of sorrow,

when the matter will be decided,

as they are heedless

and do not believe.

40 It is We who will inherit

the earth and everyone on it,

as it is to Us

that they will be returned.

The argument of Surah 19:35—that a son cannot be attributed to God—defends the revelation against doubters and is remonstrative—indeed, it sounds an alarm for those who hope to be accepted by God as believers. Jesus's first statement to Mary's kinsfolk, "I am indeed the servant of God (*inni `abd Allah*)," at 19:30, is fully consonant with his words in 19:36: "And God is in fact my Lord and your Lord—so serve God." Both are strong, positive theological and prophetological claims.

Christological disagreements among Christians themselves (questions surrounding whether Christ possessed one divine nature, or two natures—divine and human), still hotly contested in many seventh-century churches, are cited in 19:36, giving evidence of qur'anic awareness of the church's unsettled beliefs and ecclesial divisions. Similar knowledge of Jewish and Christian doctrines of "the last days" enable their confrontation by the Qur'an's own visions of the events of the end-time.[7] The combination of proper understanding of Jesus with the manner in which the fates and fortunes of God's creatures would be determined at the time of judgment surfaces again later in the surah, giving a consistency to two important and interwoven threads running through the chapter:

19:85 One day We will gather the conscientious
to the Benevolent One, like an embassy
to a royal court.
86 And We will herd the sinners into hell,
like animals to water.
87 No one has the power to intercede,
except someone who has an agreement
with the Benevolent One.
88 And yet they say,
"The Benevolent One
has begotten a son."
89 You have certainly come up
with a terrible thing!
90 The skies are nearly
rent asunder from it,
the earth nearly splits,
and the mountains nearly crumble,
91 that they should assign a son
to the Benevolent One:
92 it is only as a servant
that every being
in the heavens and on earth,
without exception,
comes to the Benevolent One,
94 who has counted and numbered them;
95 and to whom each of them
will come alone on the day of resurrection.

In Surah 3 (*The Family of Imran*), a revelation from Muhammad's Medinan period, there appears another piece of narrative concerning Mary—this one extending back to her own birth and childhood.

3:35 A woman of Imran said,
"My Lord, I devote what is in my womb
exclusively to the service of God;

so accept this from me,
for You are the all-hearing, the all-knowing."
36 Then when she gave birth to her,
she said, "My Lord,
I have given birth to a girl,"
though God knows better what she bore—
"and the male is not like the female.
And I have named her Mary;
and I commend her
and her progeny
to Your protection
from Satan the accursed."
37 Her Lord accepted her
with a gracious reception,
and caused her to grow up beautifully,
and entrusted her to Zacharias.
Whenever Zacharias went to her
in her private chamber,
he found supplies with her.
He said, "Mary, where did you get this?"
She said, "It is from God;
for God provides
for whomever God will,
beyond all accounting."
38 There Zacharias prayed to his Lord.
He said, "My Lord, grant me
good progeny from You;
for you hear prayer."
39 Then the angels called him
while he was standing there
praying in the room,
saying, "God gives you glad tidings of John,
verifying a word from God, noble, chaste;
a prophet, one of the righteous."
40 He said, "My Lord, how can I have a son,
as I am already old, and my wife is barren?"
"Thus does God do what God wills."
41 He said, "My Lord,
give me a sign."
"Your sign is that you shall not speak
to anyone for three days,

except by signals.
And remember your Lord a lot,
and glorify God
In the evening and the morning."
42 And the angels said, "O Mary,
God has chosen you and purified you,
chosen you over the women of all peoples."

The opening verses, as noted earlier, contain unmistakable echoes from the traditions contained in *Protevangelium of James*, which told of Mary's birth to Joachim and Anna and of her childhood in the temple, under the protective care of angels and the priest Zachariah. The narrative, however, everywhere bears definite Muslim imprints. Imran's wife (i.e., Mary's own mother in the lineage of Imran—Hanna, as Muslim commentators will call her) addresses the all-hearing and all-knowing God, and in her request that she herself and her progeny be protected, she speaks of Satan the accursed, or as one translator has it, evoking pilgrims' practice at Mina during the Hajj, the one "ever deserving to be stoned."[8]

A spotlight is shone upon Zachariah's role as Mary's guardian. Not only her relative and one among the ranks of Temple priests, Zachariah was selected to be her special guardian through a form of lots involving the casting of quills or reeds. In the course of his visitations of Mary in her Temple prayer chamber, Zachariah learns that she is the recipient of food from angels (3:37). No reference is made to the need to find another guardian for Mary when, approaching puberty, she must be removed from the holy building in which she was sequestered. This was a pivotal moment in the *Protevangelium of James*, introducing Joseph—himself chosen by lottery, we recall—a contests of staffs, during which he wondrously produced a dove.

Notably, the *PJ*, whose traditions are self-evidently present in Surah 3's presentation of Mary, did not weigh and compare the attributes of John and Jesus (as *Matthew* and *Luke* had), but concerned itself with the dedication of Mary to God by Anna, drawing attention to the conditions of purity in which the child was born, raised, dedicated to service in the Temple, and given over to the protection of Zachariah. All but displacing that element in the *Gospel of Luke*'s portrait of Mary as a Miriam *rediviva*, a prophetic visionary who sings in the *Magnificat* of the wonder that God "has looked with favor on the lowliness of his servant" and that "from now on all generations will call [her] blessed," the *PJ* reoriented Mary's portrayal, concentrating it on her innocence and virginal purity.[9] In this respect, The qur'anic Maryam has significantly more in common with the Mary of the *PJ* than the Gospel writers' Mary—with telling consequences.

The Angelic Tidings

What the angels proclaim in Surah 3:42 has been called by Jane McAuliffe "the acme of Qur'anic exaltation of Mary."[10]

> And the angels said, "O Mary,
> God has chosen you and purified you,
> chosen you above the women of all peoples."

The passage's meaning seems plain enough: God chose Mary (the one dedicated to him) and God accomplished her purification (*tahharaki* equals "purified you"), at which point he selected her above all other women—to give birth to the Messiah `Isa/Jesus.

Muslim exegetes, recognizing the strength of this assertion and spying a double-election in it (forms of "chosen," `*stafaki,* occurring twice in the sentence) offered several different interpretive opinions. Some associated the initial choosing with divine assent to Mary's mother's dedication of her child to God. This event they saw as initiating the holy childhood in which young Mary manifested her obedience to God's will, until the time when the second choosing resulted in God's gift to her of the child Jesus, conceived without a human father. This was a reading quite like the plain-sense one I suggested just above.[11] But the claim that God "purified" Mary elicited varied questions and understandings: was the suggestion (a) that she had been saved from "impure actions and . . . and the disparagements of the Jews," as the twelfth-century scholar al-Zamakhshari contended, or rather (b) that her purification involved being spared from unbelief and shameful behavior, freed from the conditions of menstruation, and also protected from contact with men, and as al-Razi, al-Zamakhshari's contemporary, posited?[12] Further, did God's choosing of Mary signify that she was the worthiest, or most "elect" of all women everywhere and throughout all time, or only in the age in which she lived? Were not other women in Muslim tradition accorded the highest place in God's favor, not least the prophet Muhammad's daughter Fatima, also said to have been blessed by freedom from menstruation?[13]

A capsulization of the angelic message falls in 3:45–46. The "word" (*kalimah*) from God given to Mary will bear her name: `*Isa ibn Maryam.* It is he, identified as her son, who will speak with authority both as a babe and as a mature man, meriting the honor due to him in this world, and also in the hereafter, as one of God's intimates. When Mary queries her visitors from heaven about how she, a virgin, can give birth, she hears the firm response about God's ability to create as and when he wishes: "God simply says to [something] 'Be!' and it is." Surah 3 continues:

48 [The angels said,] "And God will teach him scripture
and wisdom, and the Torah and the Gospel,
49 and to be an emissary
to the children of Israel;
'I have come to you with a sign from your Lord.
I will make you a figure of a bird out of clay,
and breathe into it,
whereat it will become a bird,
with God's permission.
And I heal the blind and the leprous,
and revive the dead,
with God's permission.
And I tell you what to consume
and what you keep in your homes.
Surely there is a sign in that for you,
if you are believers.
50 And verifying the Torah before me,
and to legitimize for you
some of what had been forbidden you,
I have come to you with a sign
from your Lord.
So be conscious of God and obey me.'"

Here is one of the Qur'an's most extensive descriptions of Jesus's deeds and words. The earlier and brief designation of Jesus as messiah is elaborated: his training by God in wisdom and in scriptures, "Torah and the Gospel," prepares him for his mission to Israel, during which the demonstrations of power Jesus himself pronounces will be manifest—an act of creation, healings and raisings of the dead, and the display of his clear knowledge of private practices of those to whom he speaks (48–49).

Jesus's promise that he will fashion a living bird from clay is interesting not only in that it echoes a motif known from early Christian apocryphal texts (e.g., the creation of twelve sparrows reported in the *Infancy Gospel of Thomas* 2.1), but also because this particular miracle might be suspected of impinging upon, or even transgressing, God's singular existence as Lord and Creator. How is it that God is willing to cede an act of creation to the creaturely Jesus? The deed highlights a significant honor granted to

Jesus, of course, but his power in this case is carefully qualified, for it will be accomplished, like the resurrections he performs, with God's permission. Whether the role of the Word and Son of God as creator "of all that is, seen and unseen" (as declared in Christian creeds of the time) is being intentionally whittled down to appropriate size and corrected in this episode cannot be inferred from the qur'anic text itself. A later Muslim commentator named Wahb, however, was alert to the theological ramification of Jesus's miracle. His retelling of the narrative removed any suggestion that Jesus's bird-creation encroached upon God's power and province.

> Jesus' bird flew only as long as people were looking at it. When it passed out of sight it fell dead, to distinguish the work of mortal man from the work of God, and to teach that perfection belongs only to God.[14]

Mary's conception of Jesus—God's Spirit and breath and word

Neither of the two narratives we have considered provides a description of how Mary's pregnancy occurred; that is, the precise nature of her conceiving. Elsewhere, however, the Qur'an tells of Mary's being blown upon by God's Spirit—in an act of creation analogous to that performed by God which brought Adam's clay form to life (Surah 15:26–29).[15]

That the several qur'anic descriptions of Mary's conception of Jesus present God's spirit in differing forms and actions did not escape commentators' attention. Barbara Stowasser wrote:

> In Mary's story, the spirit is life-creating force of, or from, God. To this day, however, Islamic exegesis has differentiated between "Our [God's] spirit" sent to Mary in the form of a man (19:17) and "Our [God's] spirit (of) which we breathed into Mary" (21:91; 66:12). While the former has been "personalized" by way of identification with Gabriel, the latter is understood as the life substance with which God (directly) awakened Adam to life from clay, just as it (directly) awakened Jesus to life in Mary's womb. Classical exegesis established that Gabriel was the means, or instrument, of God's creative power. But contemporary thinkers perpetuate the notion that "somehow," God's spirit in the form of a well-shaped human" *qua* Gabriel in human form was a different "entity" than the spirit which God breathed directly into Mary.[16]

Surah al-Anbiya, "The Prophets," places notices of Zachariah and Mary (together and in sequence) at the end of a series of reports of God's favored ones: Abraham, Lot, Noah, David and Solomon, Job, Ishmael, Idris, Dhu'l Kifl, and finally Jonah.[17] How did the birth of sons destined to be envoys of God happen to a man whose wife was infertile and to an unmarried woman who was a virgin?

> 21:89 And there was Zacharias;
> when he cried to his Lord,
> "My Lord, do not leave me alone [with no heir],
> even though You are the best of heirs,"
> 90 We answered him,
> giving him John,
> having made his wife fertile.
> For they would hasten to good works,
> and call on Us with love and awe.
> And they were humble to us.
> 91 Then there was the one
> who kept her virginity,
> and We breathed of Our spirit into her,
> and We made her and her son a sign for all peoples.

From this very brief account, the hearer or reader of Surah 21:89–91 learns of two very differently remarkable births—of John to Zachariah's wife, made fertile by God in response to his prayer, and of Jesus to Mary, whose virginity is saluted in the course of disclosing the manner by which she became pregnant. Within the two conception and birth narratives (and, of course, in many other qur'anic treatments of God's interactions with humans), we see at work the calculus in theistic religions which must wrestle with the interplay between divine purpose and human agency. It may be inferred from Surah 21:89–91 that, along with their privileged genealogy, the practiced holiness and righteous character of Zachariah and Mary constitute virtues that elicit God's favor and actions toward them, and on their behalf. But doesn't 21:91 also attest to the truth that the birth to Mary is decidedly *God's* act—his communication in and by the lives of Mary and Jesus of a "sign" which will benefit all people who acknowledge and accept it?

"We Blew into Her Through Our Angel"

Pregnancy accomplished through a breathing into or upon Mary is attested also in Surah 66, *Prohibition*. It appears, interestingly, at the end of a presentation in 66:10–12 of bad and good examples of female obedience. The wives of Noah and Lot ignored their obligations to their righteous men and the divine will, both deservedly "being told to enter hell along with the damned." The wife of the Pharoah, by contrast, was faithful when she asked to be rescued from her tyrant husband.[18] In 66:12 we read:

> And Mary, the daughter of Imran,
> who defended her chastity,
> so We breathed some of Our spirit into her,
> and she confirmed the pronouncements
> and the scriptures of her Lord,
> and she was among the devout.

In this statement extolling Mary's virtue the Qur'an speaks again of the manner in which God's Spirit conceived in her the Messiah Jesus—even suggesting that her wondrous impregnation strengthened her belief, or indeed initiated her full submission to God.

Postqur'anic Muslim commentators will quickly begin mulling over these testimonies, asking questions quite similar to those considered by Christian Mariologists who both ante-dated and were also contemporaneous with Islam's beginnings: how exactly did this Spirit's breath enter the virgin, and through which bodily orifice? After prolonged discussions, Christians by the fifth century came to a consensus that Mary had conceived "through the ear."[19] Muslim commentators, beyond asking which part of her garment the breath of God's spirit entered, speculated that it entered through Mary's mouth.[20] Concerns for having Mary's virginal condition maintained were more important for both religions' apologists than desires to fend off crude picturings of Mary's conceiving, though these latter sensitivities were not absent.

Mary as Unique "Sign"

In qur'anic tellings of Mary's being visited by God's Spirit, and of Mary's being chosen, twice, by God (3:42), significant pieces of Islamic theology are deeply set. These passages articulate not only why her selection to be Jesus's mother indicates that she enjoys in God's eyes the highest favor among all women, but also how Islam's reasons for honoring and exalting her differ from those of the Christians.

The second issue should be taken up first. It has an obvious starting and ending point: Jesus is not *a* or *the* son of God. God in His transcendence does not need nor have an associate in ruling all that is. St. Paul and other Christians had spoken figuratively of their divine Christ as the "second Adam," but the qur'anic assertion—"Jesus was to God like Adam was: God created Him from dust"—carries its own strong and *restrictive* sense: Jesus is, like Adam, another human being. We return to a declaration in Surah 4, *Women*.

> 4:171 The Messiah Jesus Son of Mary
> was only a messenger, a word from God,
> which God sent down to Mary,
> a spirit from God.

Inspection of the language employed here pays dividends—especially the Arabic word *ruh*. One Qur'an translator renders the sentence this way: "The Messiah Jesus, son of Mary, was but God's Apostle—[the fulfillment of] His promise which he had conveyed unto Mary—and a soul (*ruh*) created by Him," noting that *ruh* can be rendered "breath of life" and "soul."[21] Jesus is created, given the breath of life, ensouled, in the same manner as God has called into being all other human creatures. The wonder—the miracle in Jesus's creation, then—derives from a dramatic uniqueness having to do entirely with Mary. Mary's chastity, her virgin state, can be considered the basis for her being chosen for Jesus's conception. In Surah 21:91, as in Surah 66:12, Mary's protected virginity appears to be a cause of her selection by God, and for the blowing (the word *ruh* is again in play) into her.

It cannot be claimed, of course, that God in any corporeal manner *engendered* Jesus in Mary. She, being selected to become the mother of Jesus, received the soul or breath of God via the angel. The utterance "Be!" was that action of God which resulted in Jesus's animation within Mary. The sign to be known throughout the world is the miraculous conception and birth by which Maryam, with no male partner, produced `Isa. And what sturdy theological "given" frames and sustains this claim? Her son was not a divine being but a messenger—`Isa, this man, God included in the company of his most loved prophets.

Who, then, is Mary, and how is it that she was chosen above all other women? I noted earlier that the title, "Jesus, son of Mary," stood in obvious opposition to the churches' labeling of Mary as *theotokos*, mother of God (or God-bearer). This much is true, but the point falls short of capturing Islam's stronger and more positive investment in the phrase `*Isa bin Maryam*. Two recent scholarly theses wonderfully illuminate the singularity of Mary in Muslim thought and devotion. The first comes from Tarif

Khalidi, who in his *The Muslim Jesus*, makes a keen observation about a particular qur'anic perspective on the life of the messiah Jesus:

> Unlike the canonical Gospels, the Qur'an tilts backward to [Jesus's] miraculous birth rather than forward to his Passion. This is why he is often referred to as "the son of Mary" and why he and his mother frequently appear together. At his side, she confirms his miraculous pure birth.[22]

Khalidi's point holds for the classical commentators as well, who dwell centrally on the angelic visitation, the birth of her son, and Mary's encounter with her accusatory kinfolk, even though these writers also recount the later deeds of Jesus, with Mary in his company. Jesus's escape from execution—his ascension—and his future return—all are taken up by the exegetes, while Mary's death is treated very sparely.[23]

Mustansir Mir has illuminated important meanings within Surah 3:45–51. The "word" or *kalimah* that Mary will bear corresponds not at all to a divine being (as in the Logos-theology of the Christians), but points directly to God's statement, "Be!"—and its result. So Jesus is honored in being God's utterance, *kalimah,* while God's power to create is simultaneously emphasized. No human male partner, fiancé or husband, is in view; Jesus will exist because of God's "word" or utterance that creates. What special honor, then, accrues to Mary? Mir's insights take us to the heart of the matter:

> Since the angels are talking to Mary, one would expect them to tell her that her son will be called simply Jesus. Instead, they say that he will be known as "Jesus son of Mary." This naming of Jesus in the verse has fourfold significance:
>
> (a) It asserts categorically that Jesus will be born of one parent only.
>
> (b) It implies that, for a child to be known after its mother rather than after its father may, in ordinary circumstances, be considered a matter of shame, but in the case of Jesus, whose birth was brought about by the *kalimah* of "Be!" the matronymic constitutes a distinction.
>
> (c) It signifies that Jesus being known after his mother is a distinction for his mother as well.
>
> (d) Above all, it signifies that Jesus neither was the son of God nor had a human father, but was a human being born of a female human being.[24]

The revelation in Surah 21:19, in light of Mir's final two observations, emphatically asserts, first, that when God "made [Mary] and her son a sign for the worlds," they together constituted a display of his power and

purpose, and, second, that Jesus is *her* son, not the Lord's. Maryam therefore stands at the center of this wondrous event, being celebrated for the
purity and the obedience on account of which God honors her above all
other women. Beyond simply countering Christianity's thinking and naming of Mary as mother of the God, Jesus Christ, the Qur'an encloses and
articulates its own understanding of the messiah's birth in the distinctive
name given to him, "ʿIsa ibn Maryam." Its force is: "Jesus, messiah and
prophet of God, born of *Mary!*"

Thus will Mary, Jesus's sole parent, be distinguished and revered in the
early and developing faith and piety of Islam.

AL-TARAFI OF CORDOBA, COMMENTATOR
ON MARYAM'S STORY

Four centuries after Muhammad's death, Ibn Mutarrif al-Tarafi (997–
1062) penned his "Stories of the Prophets."[25] The story of Mary is still
being sorted out in al-Tarafi's *Qisas al-anbiya,* the author obviously making
interpretive decisions. He knows quite well what other scholars have done
to fill in narrative gaps and to clarify obscure or mysterious items in the
qur'anic text. Quickly we learn what kinds of emendations he believes are
necessary, and how he supplies these:

> *The angels said, 'O Mary, God has selected you',* that is, chosen you, *and purified
> you,* that is, from menstruation and the blemishes which are part of the nature
> of all women, *and chosen you above all women of the world* (3:42), that is, chosen
> you for Jesus. No other woman in the world carried the like of Jesus. It is said,
> [God] has chosen you over all women in the world during your time because of
> your obedience to Him.[26]

Al-Tarafi does not elaborate on the initial reference to God's choice of
her, but only reiterates it. The view that God's purification involved not
only the exemption of Mary from menstrual bleeding but also the absence
of "blemishes" needs clarification. The commentator does not refer to the
kinds of (mostly physical) defects of the sort that allowed annulment of
marriages, but rather insists that in the purity surrounding Mary's wondrous pregnancy, she had been protected from contact with men and
potential "impure actions," or from religious doubt or improper forms of
piety thought to be practiced by women.[27]

Affirmative judgment follows with regard to the second claim concerning why Mary was chosen: only she was elected to be mother of Jesus, and

thus hers was a unique pregnancy and motherhood. Al-Tarafi suggests that it was not, however, in all of history, but only "during [her] time," that Mary's obedience marked her as a woman above all others. The Qur'an's apparent exclusive honor attributed to Mary was challenged in the name of other claimants, later being overcome, as noted above, by the Muslim community's reverence for Muhammad's daughter. The exegete of Cordova dutifully reports, neither giving nor withholding assent, that "it is related" that the prophet distinguished between Mary as the best of women and his first wife, Khadija, as the best of the women in paradise, and also (via the testimony of Anas ibn Malik) that he had called a quartet the best women of the world: Mary, daughter of 'Imram, Asiya (the Pharaoh's wife), daughter of Muzahim, Khadija, daughter of Khuwaylid, and Fatima, his daughter.

A dramatic gloss is given to Surah 3:43, in which the divine command to Mary that she prostrate and bow in prayer in the company of others is transformed into testimony to her laudable excess: "She did not cease being in her state of dedication until her feet became swollen and pus began to flow from them because of the length of time she had been standing."[28] Such descriptions of endurance in prayer and its effects on the body appear frequently in Christian writings celebrating pillar-standing ascetics, but early Islam has its own stories of pious rigor to relate.[29] Al-Tha'labi tells of the prophet John's boyhood attraction to the Temple to watch rabbis and monks in their garments of hair and wool—ascetics who had attached themselves to the building's walls by chains extending from their collar bones.[30] Whatever might have been the source of Al Tarafi's association of Mary with the rigors of devoted religious observance, he wants it included in his admiring record of her life.

Reference in Surah 19:16 to Mary's withdrawal from her people "to a place in the East" recalls to al-Tarafi the assertion of Ibn Abbas's about the Christians' preference of their *qibla* to the east—specifically toward Jesus's birthplace. The object that set Mary apart from the people—"a veil"— needs clarification: it was "a screen of palm-leaf stalks . . . to protect her from the sun."[31]

Mary's encounter with the Spirit in the form of "a perfect man" (19:17) elicits several interesting bits of commentary. We learn that this is Gabriel, even if Mary remains convinced that her visitor, or intruder, is a threat to her and her virginity. Here the suggestion that Mary, at the end of a menstrual cycle, has "purified herself," and believes herself vulnerable, expands upon the statement in 19:18: "She said, 'I take refuge from you with the Benevolent One, if you are conscientious.'" Al-Tarafi adds: "During this time she thought she was with a male human being."[32]

Being informed by Gabriel that he is a messenger from her Lord, sent to give her a pure boy, Mary poses her questions about how this could happen, in view of her chastity, to which the angel responds with a bit more elaboration about an act that is "easy" for God: "It is not difficult for Him to create him and grant him to you without a man to impregnate you." This is a sign, "that is, a symbol and proof of My creating him, *and a mercy from us . . . a thing decreed* (19:21) given to you [Mary] and to those who believe in her son and declare the truth of his breath in you."[33] An act decreed in God's judgment and foresight, "God blew into her with his Spirit and she became pregnant with Jesus." Two different understandings of how the angel of God caused the conception to occur are offered. One has it that

> Gabriel blew into the opening of her cloak such that the breath went into her womb, [but] Al-Suddhi said that Mary went out wearing a robe, so Gabriel took her by her sleeves and breathed into the opening of her cloak so that it opened in the front and his breath entered her chest. So she became pregnant.[34]

Both explanations, while trying to suggest (or answer) how the Spirit entered her body, use her clothing as a means of maintaining Mary's modesty by obviating a tactile encounter. In the first example the breath is said simply to have gone to her womb, and we notice in the second that the woman never before touched by a man still has not been, since it is Gabriel, no man, who handles not her, but the sleeve of her cloak, opening it for the *ruh*'s entry. The breath's penetration is treated even more cautiously in another commentator's description of the scene: "Then he blew into the pocket of her loose outer garment that she had removed, and when he had left her, she put on this garment and conceived Jesus."[35]

Yet another intriguing explanation of the manner in which the conception was accomplished came from the Andalusion scholar al-Qurtubi (d. 1273):

> Some say that it is not possible for creation to come out of the blowing of Gabriel because the infant would be part angel and part human. The truth is that when God created Adam and took the covenant with his progeny, He made some of the liquid in the backs of the fathers and some in the uterus of their mothers. When the waters join, a child is formed. God made both waters in Mary, part in her uterus and part in her back. Gabriel blew in order to arouse her desire. The woman cannot conceive unless her desire is aroused. When her desire was aroused with the blowing of Gabriel, the water in her back descended to the uterus, and became mixed and then became fertilized.[36]

Elemental biological mechanics of Mary's impregnation do, then, occupy some of the exegetes' thoughts.

Al-Tarafi's emendations to the earlier exchange between Mary and Gabriel, however, deserve special scrutiny, emphasizing as they do what is remarkable about the sign God has given: *He*, God, is the creator and *she* (with no human father involved) is the woman whose election by God to "carr[y] the like of Jesus" elevates her to the highest rank among women. While al-Tarafi repeats the events of Mary's youth in a manner that corresponds fully with the Qur'an's testimony, he presents Mary as a participant in these things. As a child she manifested obedience, in her dialogue with the announcing angel she asked *her* questions, and she embraced the rigors of constancy in prayer. Acted upon by God, Mary acted in response, according to al-Tarafi's retelling of her life. As had happened earlier, when Christian preachers and writers caused their Mary tradition to build upon itself, a developing portrait of Mary and her personhood emerged in which distinctive Muslim teachings lent their contours to the ways that she was extolled and celebrated; Mary's place in Islamic tradition took on greater significance.

From Christian sources, as already adopted and adapted by his predecessors, Al Tarafi found more grist for his mill. We met in earlier chapters the only Joseph/Yusuf named or referred to in the Qu'ran—son of Yaqub, the handsome young man sold by his brothers into slavery in Egypt, where he withstood the sexual enticements of his master's wife. Muslim commentators on Mary's story, however, were well aware of the Joseph who was prominent in Christian nativity accounts, and welcomed him into their narratives. Designated a nephew of Mary, Joseph is presented by al-Tarafi (and by many of his predecessors, including al-Tabari) neither as a carpenter nor as Mary's espoused husband, but rather as a devout man who, like Mary, rendered service in the temple.

> Some of the exegetes say that Mary's nephew, Joseph by name, was with her in the temple. He used to serve her and speak to her from behind a veil. He was the first to learn about her pregnancy. He was disturbed by that, not understanding how it came about.[37]

Over time, Joseph grew more confused, since he "remembered the merits which God had bestowed upon her and that Zechariah had protected her in the temple." So, although

> Satan had no way in which to reach her, [Joseph] was unsettled. He thought of him [Satan] with her while her belly grew and he feared that sin had occurred.[38]

One day Joseph was emboldened to put to her three questions: "Mary, does a plant grow without a seed?" "Does a tree grow without rain falling on it?" "Can there be a child without a man involved?" The virgin met these with counterquestions, one of which challenged Joseph's understanding of God's omnipotence. Joseph knew that God needed only to say to something "Be!" and it was created. But seeing through to his real concern,

> Mary said to him, "Do you know that God created Adam and his wife, Eve, without a man and a woman?" "Certainly," Joseph replied. When she said that to him, he realized for himself that her child was something from God and it was inappropriate for him to question her about it. That was when he realized that she was concealing her situation.[39]

The young virgin, in al-Tarafi's presentation of her, proves to be a teacher-theologian in the Socratic style. The attitude of reverence for, rather than close questioning of, God's omnipotence pervades their dialogue: submission, not querulousness, is marked as a value for believers. In this portion of the exegete's filling out of the Mary narrative, Joseph has played his part, and having been accounted for, he departs from the stage.

More evidence of al-Tarafi's concern to elide some Christian (and, now, Muslim) traditions with those of the Qur'an itself appears in the telling of the onset of Mary's labor, which is presumed to have begun while she was still in the Temple. Going far away from the "sacred house. . . . she took refuge in a donkey's manger built around a palm-tree, which she hugged."[40] Her flight and her outcry while in labor (19:23) are recounted: "I felt ashamed before the people," she claims, and her wish that she had died before going into her birth pangs is rephrased, yielding "I am like something forgotten whose request and memory has been forgotten."[41]

The voice that came from below Mary in her emergency is identified by al-Tarafi as Gabriel's. Other exegetes claimed it was the speech of Jesus, and al-Tha'labi left the question to his readers, saying that choice and placement of vowels could yield either name, Gabriel or Jesus.[42] The ambiguity of the text gives an opening to multiple perspectives. We notice the desire of commentators to determine which angel is being described in a given qur'anic passage, on the one hand, and on the other, their curiosity having to do with the length of Mary's pregnancy, and the time when the infant Jesus commenced to speak. Estimates on the first ranged from one hour to nine months, and on the second, speech in utero to speech just after birth.[43]

According to al-Tarafi, the stream that erupts and flows toward Mary gives life to a "dry tree stump" among the nearby palms, making it productive of succulent fruit. The flourishing of the moribund plant for Mary is a continuation of the theme of miraculous happenings around her, for some commentators had said that the food brought to her by angels when she was in her Temple prayer cell was from another season than the one in which she received it. An additional flourish to the narrative about the sustaining stream that issued from the tree Mary grasped is found in al-Tha'labi's commentary on the incident. Mary's plight is seen as similar to that of another woman in a desert place, and similarly given miraculous assistance:

> Ibn ʿAbbas said that either Jesus or Gabriel struck the ground with his foot, and the water appeared; and that the palm tree came to life after having been desiccated. Its branches hung down, and it put forth leaves and fruit and bore fresh dates.[44]

The verbal play involves the well at Mecca: Zamzam and Mary's spring were opened by the foot of an angel or a prophet: Ishmael or Gabriel, and Jesus or Gabriel.

Hostility to Mary's Pregnancy and Her Child
Within the House of Imran

Addition of details allows the commentator to heighten the drama surrounding Mary's encounter with her people. They are searching her out, having failed to find her in the Temple. It is the cry of a magpie atop the palm which Mary grasps that draws the crowd toward her, only a part of the elaboration of 19:27 ("Finally she carried him to her people") that al-Tarafi provides. Mary went out to meet them

> because she was not suspicious of them. One of her nephews, whom she had named, came to her and they said to him, "Mary has become pregnant as a result of fornication! Now the king will kill her!" So he went to her and took her and escaped with her. When he had traveled some distance, he intended to kill her but Gabriel told him that the child was from the holy spirit, so he held back from doing that and stayed with her.[45]

The nephew trying to perform the honor killing is Joseph, once again in Mary's presence. In al-Tarafi's exposition Joseph seems to be late reaching Mary and her interrogators, but he hears (without demurring) her (and his) own family members protest that her child she presents to them is illegitimate. Though we had last seen him making a decision to be silent about Mary's pregnancy, troubling as it had been to him, here his actions are contradictory—he is an ominous rescuer. Most striking in this episode is Joseph's journey with Mary "some distance" (an apparent echo of the *Gospel of Matthew*'s story of the "flight into Egypt" by the holy family). Joseph's plan to dispatch Mary, put aside only when he gains reassurance from Gabriel that Jesus was "from the holy spirit," is more drastic by far than what was told in *Matthew* 1:19–20, where Joseph's plan to "dismiss . . . quietly" the dishonorably pregnant Mary is subverted on the counsel of the angel who appears to him in his dreams.

Returned to the scene of the encounter of Mary and "her people," al-Tarafi has comments to make about the passage, Surah 19:27–29, which contains the excoriation of Mary's commission of "a monstrous act" and the shaming address of her as "sister of Aaron."[46] The anguish of Imran, here named by al-Tarafi as Mary's father, is expressed in his tearing of his cloak and covering his head in dust. The sense of the people's accusation is given: "you have done a strange thing and provoked a great occurrence."[47] Mary's presumed surrender of her virginity—the abandonment of that purity of life that was sustained and prized through the years within her community—appears to be the catastrophe, rather than the action of the vengeful king that her fornication will incur.

The long-lasting conversation and debate among qur'anic interpreters about Mary's genealogy, and how she is related to al-Imran, is al-Tarafi's next topic. He wants his readers to know who is the Imran and who is the Aaron her behavior purportedly has betrayed, and what is the reputation of her parents.

> This Aaron, to whom Mary was compared, was a righteous man; they used to name every righteous man Aaron. It is mentioned in the works of exegesis regarding this Aaron that 40,000 people escorted his funeral procession, all of them named Aaron. The family of Mary said to her, "O resembler of Aaron in righteousness that we used to see from him in you, *Your father*, that is, `Imran, *was not an impure man*, committing impure acts, *nor was your mother an unchaste woman*, that is, a fornicator who should be censured; that is, your parents were righteous and you desire righteousness in such a way that you are excellent like Aaron the righteous man. So how can you be involved in this severe matter?"[48]

The biblical forebears themselves are of course not on the scene, but their histories and their reputations for virtue are represented as living on in others from that lineage—namely, Mary's more immediate predecessors. Thus Mary's supposed fornication constituted a violation of her family's commitment to excellence "like Aaron['s]." Mary's silent gesture toward her infant son indicates her unwillingness to bear yet more insults from her scolders, who, according to al-Tarafi, say to her, "you were making fun of us when you suggested that we speak to this child; that makes your fornication even more significant a matter to us."[49]

The exposition of the story's dénoument by Al-Tarafi advances a special claim:

> Then, at that moment, Jesus leaned over on to his left side and pointed with his finger, speaking about his mother and making clear his status, saying *"Lo, I am God's servant; God has given me the book, and has made me a prophet. He has made me blessed wherever I may be* (19:30–31), that is, He ordained it for me when I was in the belly of my mother.[50]

Adding the explicit note that Jesus's speech is "about his mother," and putting on the child's lips the concluding remark that his mission and blessedness were ordained when he was in his mother's womb, al-Tarafi goes beyond what is in the cited qur'anic text. His interpretive additions bring more emphasis to the declaration by the child Jesus about his "calling" by God, and to his speech that silences the suspicions brought down on Mary, vindicating her. A need beyond narrative coherence, however, is at work through these small emendations. The exegete gives us another example of the Muslim tradition's penchant for thinking of Jesus more in relation to his birth from Mary than in terms of his future—a dynamic that stands in contradistinction to Christianity's focus on subsequent events—most particularly his suffering, his death and resurrection, and then his ascension into heaven.

Al-Tarafi has taken care to restate and reinforce the major Muslim tenet about Mary: that, as Mir put it, "Jesus neither was the son of God nor had a human father, but was a human being born of a female human being."[51] For the single parenthood of this prophet of God *she* was chosen above "the women of the worlds."

The Frustration of Iblis and the Sinlessness of Mary and Jesus

Al-Tarafi reported that Joseph, perceiving that Mary was pregnant, wondered how this evil could have occurred in God's sanctuary, where she was safeguarded by angels and Zachariah the priest. In that holy place, as we read, "Satan had no way in which to reach her, yet [Joseph's] mind was unsettled."[52] Iblis, the agent of evil ever seeking to gain power over God's creatures, had a very good chance of being envisioned by retellers of Mary's story as one of the principal actors in the drama. Certain questions presented themselves: if Mary's pregnancy was "something from God" and not an instance of Satan's success in tempting her, how were his malevolent actions forestalled? Further, if Mary and her son were somehow exempted from, or proved themselves stronger than, Satan's wiles, how did it happen that they were spared the test that all creatures face? How and why were they exceptions?

In al-Tha'labi's telling of the birth of Jesus, predating al-Tarafi's, light is shed on these matters, thanks to a backstory attributed to Wahb b. Munabbih, an eighth-century Yemenite collector of prophets' legends. When, on the morning after Jesus's birth, all idols toppled, being turned on their heads, the devils were alarmed, for

> there was nothing more useful in destroying the children of Adam than the idols. The devils used to enter their [the images'] insides, speak to the people, and decide their affairs; and people thought that it was the idol that spoke to them.[53]

Traveling to their leader, "Iblis, the accursed," to discover what had happened, they found him ignorant of what they reported. Promptly undertaking his own fact-finding mission,

> Iblis flew away, and remained away for three hours, during which he came to the place where Jesus had been born. When he saw the angels surrounding it, he knew that there was where the event had occurred. Iblis tried to get at Jesus from above; but lo, the heads and shoulders of the angels reached the sky. He tried to get at him from under the earth; but lo, the feet of the angels were anchored firmly. He tried to enter between them, but they prevented him. Proof of this is the *hadith* of the Prophet: "Satan stabs every son of Adam between his shoulders with his finger, except for Jesus son of Mary, whom God had shielded from him. He came to stab him, but he stabbed the shield [instead]."[54]

Returning a great distance to his waiting demon-servants, Iblis informed them that Jesus's birth had indeed been the cause of the idols' collapse, a happening that discredited and demeaned the demons in people's eyes. Iblis testified:

> Before him, no womb ever enclosed a child without my knowledge, or gave birth to one unless I was present with her. I certainly hope that more people will be led astray by him than will be led to the right path; but there has never been a

prophet who was more powerful against me and you, than this one who has just been born.[55]

In Iblis's words, which disclose the crisis in the demonic realm, al-Tha'labi is able to discover and propound a two-fold tribute to Mary's son. First, Jesus was chosen by God—above all children, we could say—for protection at birth from the presence and harmful influence of Iblis, his finger-stab. Second, in Iblis's later contests with him, Jesus proved to be the mightiest among God's prophets—at least in the realm of resistance to Satan. Iblis's comments about Mary's son have the weight of a Muslim equivalent to what among Christians would count as a "high Christology," since it gives Jesus, though a human and not a divinity, the highest standing among God's favored envoys (up to that point in history, it must be presumed). In the form it is reported as a teaching from the commentator Wahb, the fanciful narrative, with its concluding estimate of the prophet Jesus, is not, however, without a precedent.

The seed of the ideas we've just met in Wahb's picture of how Jesus's birth affected Iblis and his minions was present in another form of the *hadith* quoted by al-Tha'labi:

> Abu Huraira said, "I heard Allah's Apostle saying, 'There is none born among the off-spring of Adam, but Satan touches it. A child therefore, cries loudly at the time of birth because of the touch of Satan, except Mary and her child.'" Then Abu Huraira recited: "And I seek refuge with You for her and for her offspring from the outcast Satan" (Surah 3.36).[56]

Though Islam held no doctrine of Adam's and Eve's original sin infecting and affecting all of their progeny, this notion of Satan's continuing zeal and power in making his damaging mark on each newborn—opening the way to temptations and sins—was, as this *hadith* shows, an early and popular belief. Drawing support from Surah 3:36, in which the wife from the lineage of Imran tells the Lord that she has given birth to a female child, naming her Mary, Abu Huraira contended that Jesus's extraordinary condition of remaining untouched by Satan at birth belonged also to Mary. The saying attributed to Muhammad amounts to a confirmation of God's action on behalf of Jesus *and* Mary, and in itself is a brief narrative expansion not unlike that of our commentator's scenes, for it, too, seeks to tell how Iblis's usual practice was frustrated. The tradition that the infant Mary also was spared a finger-stab from Iblis tends in the direction of an attribution of sinlessness or impeccability accorded to prophets: the 'isma that is distinctive to God's envoys (even if they remain vulnerable to faults, or *dhunub*, of the sort Jonah committed).

All of these extended narratives contribute to the honoring—the exaltation—of Mary in her faithful purity. God, as selector of Mary, is the agent in this matter—the source and guide of her faith and actions. At the same time, the story is Mary's, for her spotlessness is in great measure her "work"—her living in uncompromised obedience and devotion. She became to all women an exemplar of the virtue of safeguarding chastity (66:12); from the time of her birth and impeccable childhood to that season in which God gave to her a "word," a pure son, and then, shortly thereafter, when the sign provided a vindication of her righteous virginity against her family's abusive calumny, and finally, in her continued presence with Jesus as he began his work as miracle-worker and messenger of God.

The qur'anic veneration of Maryam gives an outline of her saga that exegetes and commentators, as we have seen, took pleasure in amplifying. Even this very selective sampling of the growth of traditions that Mary inspired among Muslim interpreters provides preliminary answers to questions posed at this chapter's outset: we have come to know who she became in early Islam's religious consciousness, and for what reasons she gained such honored status and popular esteem.

Upon these considerations David Marshall opens another intriguing perspective, one born of his efforts to explore correspondence between certain qur'anic topics and themes with events in the life of Muhammad. Taking note of the fact that in revelations to Muhammad in the Meccan period (612–622 CE) many passages are devoted to the prophets who are battlers for monotheism (Noah, Abraham, Lot, and Moses) but only one treatment (19:16–33) of Jesus, Marshall proposes that the Jesus-narrative was not of such great relevance to Muhammad's challenging situation there, at the seat of the polytheistic culture of the Quraysh. Marshall continues:

> This point gathers strength as we look more closely at that narrative [i.e., 19:16ff] and notice that it in fact focuses more attention on Mary than on Jesus. . . . Despite the great significance of speech by the infant Jesus, it is at least arguable that the main interest in the narrative, and certainly its main relevance to Muhammad in Mecca, is in Mary's drama. Like Muhammad, Mary receives a divine message brought to her personally by an angelic being; Muhammad might therefore naturally have seen in Mary someone whose experience was similar to his own. Furthermore, like Muhammad, Mary experiences rejection and vilification by her own people because of this divine initiative singling her out for a special task. Then she is miraculously vindicated by God in the face of

those who scoff at her—the dénouement for which the rejected Muhammad waited and hoped. Thus at least part of the significance of this narrative is that it contains the pervasive Meccan motif of the rejection and vindication of God's chosen servant, a theme which was highly relevant to Muhammad's experience and his expectations. It may seem strange to think of Mary functioning as a type of Muhammad in this way, and indeed it may well be that the obvious dissimilarities between Mary and Muhammad account for the fact that, unlike a number of Meccan narratives, this Mary-narrative is not repeated. This analysis of the story of Mary indicates that despite the fact that there is comparatively little Meccan material on Jesus and Mary, such material as there is should be interpreted in the light of the basic observation that the Qur'anic Mary and Jesus have their significance and their coherence in their relatedness to the experience of Muhammad. They are part of the religious pre-history which culminates in the coming of Muhammad and the revelation of the Qur'an.[57]

Marshall's thesis contributes to our understanding of how the story of Maryam gained so important a place in the Qur'an, and thereafter compelled the attention of interpreters and story tellers.

EVIDENCES FOR PROPHETHOOD: THE CASES OF ZACHARIAH AND MARY COMPARED

While the Quran's parallel annunciation stories make plain that the son John/Yahya born to Zachariah and the son Jesus/'Isa born to Mary will be prophets, they do not make the same claim for the parents, despite their commonalities. Both the temple priest and the virgin dedicated by her mother to temple dwelling had been privileged to receive God's angel visitors and to converse with them—a privilege often said to belong, distinctively, to God's messengers. Loren Lybarger noted that despite the many elements in the qur'anic treatment of Mary underscoring that she belongs "in the ranks of the truly devout"; nevertheless, "Maryam ... is never explicitly established as a prophet through formal annunciation."[58]

An ambiguity in this matter pivots around which aspect of Miriam, sister of Aaron and Moses, Muslim tradition associates with Mary, mother of Jesus. We noted in chapter 13 that the developing Mariology of the Christians left behind *Luke*'s presentation of Mary singing prophetic songs (on the model of her Hebrew namesake in *Exodus*) in favor of the *Protevangelium of James*'s elaborate depiction of the unusual child pledged to God by her mother, the pure and temple-protected female whose virginity was not compromised in her delivery of Jesus. The Qur'an's portrait of Mary in Surah 3, we have seen, shares that dominant image of the pure virgin, and does not emphasize her tie to Miriam in her capacity as the woman understood to be the first female prophet in the history of the peoples of the Book. Neither does Miriam's character as prophetess and prototype of Mary register in Al-Tha`labi's commentary, even though he valorizes her, along with the Pharaoh's wife, in quoting a *hadith* about paradise-in-preparation: "This Rock of the Temple rests on a palm tree by a river in Paradise, and by this river Asiyah bt. Muzahim and Miriam, the daughter of Amran, arrange the ornaments of the people of Paradise for the Resurrection Day."[59]

In the qur'anic story in which Mary's people see that she has given birth to a child, we noticed that Mary *is* linked to Miriam—and indeed chastened by the criteria set by her honored ancestry. Surah 19: 28 reads "O sister of Aaron, your father was not a bad man, and your mother was not a whore." It is not prophecy, however, that defines Miriam in this accusation, but her chastity—Mary is believed to have violated the high moral standard of her ancestress—and her ancestral line, running to her own mother and father. We should recognize that the invocation of brother Aaron, rather than Moses, evokes themes already at work in the qur'anic representation of Mary—those aspects of temple sanctity and priestly care for God-dedicated children that give shape to *Surah* 3's portrait of her. In this focused commitment to Mary's purity and her virginity we note that a particular perception of Mary as prophetess does not control the qur'anic presentation of her. Nonetheless, Hosn Abboud asserted that "signs of Maryam's prophethood (`alamat nubuwwat Maryam*) were well established in the Qur'anic vision," and these were what gave rise to vigorous debate on the topic by Islam's classical exegetes.[60]

In the days of al-Tarafi and in the same city of Cordova, a jurist of the Zaharite ("literalist") school, Ibn Hazm (d. 1064), stirred controversy by claiming that women visited, spoken to, and inspired by God's angels, like Mary, Sarah, and the mother of Moses, were to be counted as prophets. Ibn Hazm cut a distinction between *nubuwwa* and *risala*—that is, "prophethood" and "messengerhood," respectively—holding that while men comprised the second category, "the knowledge the mothers of Isaac, Jesus, and Moses received from God (through word or inspiration) was as true as the knowledge received by male prophets by revelation."[61] Among his support-texts was *Surah* 5:75, which calls Mary "a woman of truth" in the same way it terms the prophet Joseph, son of Jacob and dream-analyst, "man of truth" in *Surah* 12:46. Ibn Hazm proceeded to rank Mary and Asiyah (wife of the pharaoh) as "the two perfect women" above all other female prophets, just as Muhammad and Abraham outranked God's other male messengers.[62]

The same Al Qurtubi we met earlier, who entertained a biological picture of how Mary possessed both the male and female "liquids" needed for Jesus's conception, was another proponent of the view that she was a prophet. He based his argument on the by-now familiar passage in Surah 3:42, in which the angel announces that God has "chosen" (`stafaki), "purified" (tahharaki), and "chosen" (again, `stafaki) her: "truly Maryam is a prophetess because God (may He be praised) inspired her through the angel in the same way He inspired the rest of the male prophets."[63] Advocacy for Mary's ranking as a prophet was a minority view, believed by its opponents unsupportable on the grounds that Mary was a female. The text they invoked stands in Surah 12, "Thunder": "And We only sent before you men, from people of communities, men whom We inspired" (12:109). Other oppositional kinds of arguments were offered up as well—for example, those of the late twelfth- to early thirteenth-century commentator Fahkr al-Din al-Razi. Jane McAuliffe summarizes them:

> Al-Razi ... begins his treatment of this verse [3:42] by connecting Mary's divine
> selection to her mother's prenatal dedication of her to God's service. He is par-
> ticularly careful to insist that Mary's being the recipient of the angels' announce-
> ment in no way implies that she is a prophet. The status of prophet is reserved
> for men alone as al-Razi carefully documents on the basis of 12:109. Al-Razi
> takes the pains to establish this because it means the divine favor evidenced by
> the sending of Gabriel must be attributed either to Jesus or Zachary and only
> secondarily to Mary.[64]

For al-Razi, Zachariah, in contrast to Mary, is "lifted" to the prophethood he shares with Jesus. Although the Qur'an calls Zachariah neither a nabi nor a rasul, he appears to be counted in 19:1–58 (in the same way Mary might have been, given her similar introduction in the text at 19:16) as one of the many prophets whose names and stories are to be "recited" by Muhammad. In Surah 6:83–86, a fairly comprehensive qur'anic roll-call of those God sent and guided includes: Abraham, Isaac, Jacob, Noah, David, Solomon, Joseph, Moses, Aaron, Zachariah, John, Jesus, Elias, Ishmael, Elisha, Jonah, and Lot. The verses that follow leave little question what rank is accorded to Zachariah, for 6:86–89 describes these male individuals as "blessed over all people," chosen and "guided ... to a straight path," and recipients of "scripture, and law, and prophethood."[65] The statement in 19:30—[Jesus] said, "I am indeed the servant of God, who has given me the Scripture and made me a prophet (*wa-ja`alani nabi-yyan*), and made me blessed wherever I am"—applies, of course, to Mary's son, but not to her.

Zachariah's place among the prophets of God is secure. Al-Tabari reported Ibn Ishaq's teaching that when the Israelites fell into sin after their return to Jerusalem from Babylonia,

> God sent again messengers to them. Some of them were rejected, some slain, until the last prophets sent to them were Zechariah, John, the son of Zechariah, and Jesus, son of Mary.[66]

There is no reason to doubt, given nearly identical formal aspects of God's approach and speech to them through his agents, that to all except a minority of exegetes and students of the law like Ibn Hazm and al-Qurtubi, Zachariah's maleness was a positive factor in certifying his prophecy, while Mary's femaleness was a disqualifier.

If not a prophet, then by what term or language could Mary's exalted role and status be named? Jane McAuliffe located in the Qur'an commentary of Mahmud b. `Umar al-Zamakhshari (d. 1144) what must be counted the early exegetes' most laudatory title. His own exposition of 3:42 holds that God accepted Mary as the one dedicated to him by her mother, "and selected [her] for an exalted mark of esteem" (*karama*); and "He chose [her] by giving her `Isa without a father; that hasn't happened to any other woman."[67]

This *karama* and its origination in God's action is the glory and blessing particular to Mary. That Jesus, or `Isa, cannot be God's son, but is God's creature, called into existence to join the ranks of the Lord's messengers, is a positive and fundamental piece in the Qur'an's understanding of who God is, and how God's will is revealed and realized in "this world and the next." Mary, too, is not divine but creaturely—one who, like her son, eats the food which humans eat.[68] Nor, as the prevailing tradition will have it, is she counted among the prophets. Her claim to fame, and to the high regard and devotion of Muslims, is grounded in three distinct perceptions of her: she is (1) *siddiqah*, "a veracious woman" (5:75); (2) a person God selected for special esteem (*karama*); and (3) most centrally, so dedicatedly a chaste woman that she is blessed in the miracle of her motherhood of Jesus. Even if with the passage of time she shared with other noble women from the scriptural past or from the Prophet's life history her qur'anic preeminence among all women, and even ultimately surrendered that to Fatima, yet in her uniqueness as the sole parent of Jesus, and with him, a sign from God (21:91, 23:50), she stood grandly alone.[69]

MARYAM DEPICTED: TWO PAINTINGS
OF VIRGIN AND CHILD

A report tells of Muhammad entering Mecca and encountering images of
Mary and Jesus.

> When the apostle prayed the noon prayer on the day of the conquest he ordered
> that all the idols which were around the Ka'ba should be collected and burned
> with fire and broken up. Fadala b. al-Mulawwih al-Laythi said, commemorating
> the day of the conquest.
>> Had you seen Muhammad and his troops
>> the day the idols were smashed when he entered,
>> you would have seen God's light become manifest
>> and darkness covering the face of idolatry.
>> From Hahim b. 'Adda b. Hanif and other traditionists: Quraysh had put pic-
> tures in the Ka'ba including two of Jesus and Mary (on both of whom be peace!).
> . . . The apostle ordered that the pictures should be erased except those of Jesus
> and Mary.[70]

This *hadith* has a variant form—one in which the prophet relents, and has
these pictures also washed away—yet the images were known to be present by a celebrated transmitter of *hadith*, 'Ata b. Abi Rabath, who died in
732.[71] Gülru Necipoğlu argues that the prominence of Jesus in the Dome of
the Rock's inscriptions should not be surprising, given the report "that the
Prophet reverently preserved only the images of Jesus and his mother within
the Ka'ba, effacing other painted representations, which depicted Abraham
holding divination arrows, as well as prophets, angels, and trees."[72] What did
later painters—those standing within or familiar with the Muslim tradition—
choose to depict in their images of Mary and Jesus, and for what reasons? We
cannot devote a chapter to Islam's Mary story without giving this question
the consideration it warrants. The artists had their own viewpoints to convey.

Figural depictions of personalities of the Qur'an came into full flower
when artists began portraying human beings and historical and scriptural
events in works of various genres—for example, a thirteenth-century
copy of the *Maqamat* by al-Hariri, which features a painting of a Ramadan
procession, a fourteenth-century painting of Muhammad and Gabriel at
the time of the first revelation (among other scenes) in Rashid al Din's
Jami al-Tawarikh, or "Universal History," sixteenth-century versions of
the *Falnama* (writings containing divinations) which were replete with
images drawn from qur'anic lore, and, as we've seen earlier, in illuminations supplied for Muslim books devoted to stories of the prophets.[73] The

two sixteenth-century paintings now to be discussed were inspired by passages in Surah 19: one a splendid image of Mary gaining refreshment at the palm tree (19:23–26), and the other a depiction of the confrontation during which her infant son spoke, to silence her agitated kinsfolk (19:27–33). The pictorial contents of both images impel us to ask once again in what ways the artists' iconographies perform interpretation. Are the two paintings analogous in purpose to the narrative expansions by means of which al-Tarafi in his *Lives of the Prophets* retold—and, he presumed, clarified—the story of Mary and Jesus? We consider first Figure 15.1.

Mary at the Palm Tree

Originating in Iran in the decade 1570–1580, this miniature painting appears in a copy of Abu Ishaq Ibrahim Nisaburi's Persian volume of "Stories of the Prophets," composed in the eleventh century.[74] The viewer's eyes fix first upon Mary, who shakes the date palm tree for its fruit, while at her feet, the promised stream flows from the tree's base. Next seen is the small figure of the bundled Jesus, a flame nimbus surrounding most of his body. Whether or not the other elements in the qur'anic passage (19:23–26) are implied or assumed to be known—that is, Mary's birth pangs and her expressed wish that she'd not lived to experience them—the scene itself shows Mary postpartum, now intent upon obtaining the fresh dates that will feed her and her newborn son. Pale purple in hue, the dates are visible—especially the small object just beginning to drop from the branches, and the more detailed, though dimly painted, date that is descending upon her, and another that flies out toward the right edge of the illustration.

The painter's interest centers both in her actions (the movement of her arms and upturned face) and in her clothing (the outer cloak cinctured at the waist, bright red with gold patterns, and her head-covering held in place by a gold band across her forehead). As in all efforts to give graphic form to figures familiar from a narrative read or recited, the artist has made choices, even if in depicting Maryam and `Isa as he does, he depends upon known precedents—other images.[75] In its style the work bears strong correspondence to Safavid paintings of the late sixteenth and early seventeenth century, especially in its depiction of the woman's body, with her belt and the sway of her dress, and her elongated torso.[76]

Though the representation of this episode in Mary's life might be taken as a reasonable approximation of what the Qur'an describes, with no noticeable additions or twists, several art historians have spied artistic commentary in the presentation of what shares Mary's space—the palm tree. The growth of leaves and production of fruit appears on only one side

Figure 15.1 Maryam and the newborn 'Isa. © The Chester Beatty Library, Dublin. Chester Beatty Library Persian Ms. 231, Fol. 227a.

of the top of the tree, as if blossoming is half-begun.[77] This graphic interpreter's pictorial expansion of a newly fructifying palm matches several classical commentators' assertions that the tree sprang to life in its dormant season. I suspect that the plain language (with its final adjectives) of *Surah* 19:25—"and shake the trunk of the palm toward you to let ripe, fresh dates fall by you"—easily sparked suppositions among early hearers that these dates for Mary were something out of the ordinary. Though al-Tarafi had interpreted the seclusion sought by Mary to be a "screen of palm-leaf stalks" to shelter her from the sun, some commentators who preceded him had sensed that the qur'anic palm tree and its fruit signified more.[78] "When her days were accomplished, she went out into the wilderness by night and sat under a dry tree, which became verdant for her time, [and] God also brought forth for her a spring of clear, running water," wrote al-Kisa'i.[79] Al-Tha`labi's report is more expansive:

> The story goes that when the pangs of childbirth came upon her violently, she took shelter under a palm tree. It was a withered palm-tree, having no boughs, or stumps of branches or roots, but the angels surrounded it, and rank upon rank they encompassed it. That palm-tree was at a place called Bethlehem. . . . They say that when she gave birth to Jesus, God made a river flow for her: its water was sweet and cold when she drank of it, and warm when she used it for washing."[80]

The story al-Tha`labi employs has its eyes on Mary—on *her* need of the tree's shelter and *her* need of the water of changeable temperatures. Though Jesus is in the narrative and the painting (could he have just spoken to Mary about the dates and the water?), the event being presented features Maryam the virgin—her actions at the time of her birth-giving to the promised messiah-prophet.

What significance for Muslim interpreters rests in this, the ripe fruit flourishing either from a dead tree or one that produces out of season? Both the commentary-writers and the artist of the painting seem to be pushing their readers and viewers to this insight: why would such an extraordinary thing *not* occur—in the time of Mary's doing what no other woman has done? A piece of theology is being advanced: nature itself is a servant to what God now discloses in Mary's conceiving and giving birth to Jesus. In other words, everything in Mary's story is preternatural; she is one chosen by God to "carr[y] the likes of Jesus," a prophet of God. The same motif carries over to Figure 15.2.

Another sixteenth-century miniature painting in a copy of Nisaburi's "Stories of the Prophets," this one treats the content of the lines, already

Figure 15.2 Maryam presents ʿIsa to her people. © Topkapi Palace Museum Archives, Istanbul. Topkapi Palace Museum Ms. H. 1225, Folio 209b.

familiar to us, that immediately succeed the Qur'an's narrative of Mary and the palm tree:

> 19: 27 Finally she carried him
> to her people: they said, "Mary,
> you sure have done
> an unheard-of thing!
> 28 O sister of Aaron,
> your father was not a bad man,
> and your mother was not a whore."
> 29 Now she pointed to him.
> They said, "How can we talk to one
> who is an infant in the cradle?"
> 30 He said, " I am indeed the servant of God,
> who has given me scripture
> and made me a prophet."

The painting's composition reveals how much more the artist wished to communicate about the incident than the text actually tells. The most striking clue is the inclusion of Zachariah in the scene; as noted earlier, he is not mentioned in the qur'anic account of this event.

The two lines of Persian atop and beneath the image contain a mixture of plain description and clues about a broader framing of this altercation. The writing begins with a reference to Zachariah, who is identified as being a descendant from the children of David, "peace be upon them," and then describes the action of Mary, who is "from the children of Aaron":

> Mary pointed to Jesus, peace be upon him, [saying] "Speak with him." "How can we speak with a baby?" they said. God Almighty made Jesus Speak.

The last sentence concludes the writing in the lower band of Persian on the folio.

Certain actions and attitudes of the persons seated in the foreground, within the green and pink bands, are recognizable. With one exception the eight persons kneeling or sitting are turned toward Mary and Jesus, and many of them are finger-pointing—registering their disapproval of her and the child in her arms. The male figure dressed in gray-green is doubly occupied: one among the accusers of Mary, he signals hostile questioning with his left hand, while his face tilts upward toward Zachariah. The message of his upturned right hand is ambiguous.

Mary and Jesus, turned toward each other, are adorned with rounded flame halos, and Jesus, not in a cradle, is nearly erect in her arms. He is a bit too large and well-formed for a very newly born child, but imaginable as an infant who, we know, will soon address the assembled group. The episode's action is frozen in the moments of Mary's condemnation. Elements in the iconography are striking. Jesus, noticeably, does not face in the direction of his mother's taunters. Does his posture simultaneously hint of his concentrated devotion to her, and that he has not yet begun his defense of Mary and his self-proclamation?

An attempt to read the image of the mother and child too much in terms of the actions and responses in the scene of contestation probably misses an important clue. While involved in a highly charged drama within their history, the representation of Mary and Jesus is strongly iconic—that is, posed, fixed, and formulaic in a way not unlike Christian paintings of the Virgin and child, and for that matter, of Egyptian paintings of Isis and Horus. Maryam and 'Isa are positioned in relation to each other as they should be, given who they are. They seem impervious to those who gesticulate around them—those whom we know to be heaping shame upon Mary and disparaging her son. Their representations suggest graphically that the virgin and her child are unaffected by the angry commotion around them.

Zachariah is similarly presented; he does not turn his gaze downward, as if participating in the drama surrounding Mary and Jesus, nor does he seem to engage others who populate the scene. The artist, however, has information to convey about the revered priest and prophet, and his role in this scene.

The painting captures a theme present in the Qur'an and attractive to the exegetes. After her mother dedicated the child Mary to God, "her Lord accepted her with a gracious reception, and caused her to grow up beautifully, and entrusted her to Zacharias" (Surah 3:37). During the years she lived in her prayer chamber in the sanctuary, Zachariah tended her and monitored her condition, guarding her from any assault on her innocence and purity. This linkage and relationship between Zachariah and Mary is plainly signified in the painting, with divinely appointed Zachariah positioned protectively above his charge—and her controversial offspring. Zachariah, understood in this way, is not to be counted as one among those committing "their monstrous slander against Mary" (4:156). He knows the truth—indeed, one of God's elect, Zachariah represents steady justice in the face of human error, and in this case, slander. The artist has placed him in the midst of a scene of controversy, and yet the prophet is shown to be above the fray, one who witnesses to Mary's righteousness, which shortly will be confirmed before the doubters by the infant in her arms.

The portrayal of Mary's confrontation with "her people" sets the haloed triad apart from all other figures shown. Zachariah's fiery nimbus is grand, leaving no doubt about his hallowed status. The rounded but still flame-like haloes surrounding the faces of Mary and Jesus are proportional to their sizes. These three are among God's most favored: Zachariah because God heard and granted his wish for "a good offspring," and because God blessed him with responsibility for Mary; Mary because the Spirit of God made her the virgin mother of a son to be known in this world and the next by her name; and Jesus, because God made him able to declare, as he does to Mary's angry interrogators, "I am the servant of God. He has given me the scripture and made me a prophet."

ZACHARIAH'S MARTYRDOM

There is in Zachariah's story another celebrated chapter—one that many exegetes saw in terms of continuing suspicions about the priest's relationship with young Mary. According to this strain of tradition, Zachariah's presence at the scene of Mary's interrogation and shaming is necessary precisely because he, too, is accused. Nisaburi's *Qesas-ol-Anbiya* recounts this part of the Mary story.[81] Becoming aware of Mary's pregnancy, the crowd (of "pious people") was surprised and rushed to Zachariah with this insinuating comment: "You were alone with her when she did this." Zachariah's response—"She does not do this"—fails to satisfy the people. Pressing their suspicion, they reframe the question, asking, "Where did she get this?" "Ask her!" Zachariah retorts.[82]

Even after the infant Jesus spoke to them, the enraged group was not through with Zachariah, according to al-Tabari.[83] He and other early commentators consistently and explicitly identify Mary's people as the Jews, rather than simply as members of the family of Imran. An old and familiar interreligious recrimination is coming to the fore. Al-Tha`labi's colorful account of the destiny of Zachariah is one of most detailed:

> It has been said that the cause of Zachariah's murder was that Iblis came to the Israelites' council and charged Zachariah with having violated Mary, saying that it was none other than he who had made her pregnant, for it was he who used to go to her. So they sought Zachariah, and he fled, and the foolish and evil ones among them followed him. While he was passing through a valley full of trees, Satan appeared to him disguised as a herdsman, and said, "Zachariah, they have overtaken you; pray to God to open this tree for you." He did so, and it split open for him, and he entered it, but Iblis pulled out the fringe of [Zachariah's]

cloak. Then the Israelites came upon Satan and said, "Herdsman, have you seen a man here of such-and-such description?" He said, "Yes, he bewitched this tree, it opened for him and he entered it. This is the fringe of his cloak." So they cut down the tree with Zachariah in it, and cut it in half lengthwise with a saw. Then God sent the angels, and they washed Zachariah, prayed over him, and buried him.[84]

The tale of a prophet being "sawn asunder" while enclosed in a tree derived from Jewish precedents, especially rabbinic accounts of Isaiah's being murdered for declaring, "I dwell in the midst of a people of unclean lips" (*Isaiah* 6:1).[85] A rabbinic targum on the *Book of Lamentations* discusses the death of *a* Zechariah—not the sixth-century BCE author of the biblical book, but the son of Jehoida whose stoning is recounted in *2 Chronicles* 24:20–22.[86] Qur'anic commentators consistently identified the righteous victim as Zachariah, father of John, tailoring this drama to their own purposes. Nisaburi's narration of the scene, to which the painter would or could have had access, has slightly different twists than al-Tha'labi's:

> They [the Israelites] came to Zachariah and told him: "O Zachariah, Mary committed adultery and when you realized that the people became aware of it, you sent her to Sham [Aleppo]." And they attempted to kill him. Zachariah escaped from them and went out of town towards Sham . . . and there was a tree with an opening inside. Zachariah, seeing the pursuing crowd, entered inside the tree and by the order of the Almighty the opening closed over him. Once the crowd reached the place, they did not see him and wanted to return. [But] Iblis, damnation be upon him, came and told them that Zachariah entered the tree. They said, "This would never happen." Iblis replied, "You cut this tree. If he were there he would be killed, and if not, what would you lose?" They came with a saw and cut the tree in half with Zechariah. And the blood of Zachariah did not rest until seventy thousand of the Israelites were killed.[87]

Figure 15.3 is an example of this scene, more popular than any other episode of a prophet's life among illuminators of manuscripts of the "Lives of the Prophets."[88]

I opened this chapter with a brief demonstration of how the earliest qur'anic community stepped immediately and squarely into the realm of competitive discourse already productive of the Jews' and Christians' adversarial counterteachings and polemics. In these final pages, and in this third painting, we meet again expressions of the rhetoric and art of religious difference and conflict. Making "the Israelites" collaborators with Satan in the martyrdom of Zachariah, the writers, and later, the artists,

Figure 15.3 The martyrdom of Zakariya. From a 1577 CE copy of Nisaburi's *Qisas al-Anbiya*. Painting: 10.5 x 7.7 cm. © The New York Public Library, Astor, Lenox, and Tilden Foundations. Spencer Collection, Pers. Ms. 1, 163a.

were sustaining and sharpening anti-Judaism ideas present in the Qur'an. The faults and crimes of the "People of the Book" (in this case, the reference is to the Jews) are listed in *Surah* 4:153–161: the audacious demand to see God's face, the creation of the golden calf, violation of the covenant, slandering of Mary, the false claim of having crucified and killed Christ, blocking people from God's path, the practice of usury, and the unfair pro curement of the wealth of others.

In the midst of these there is the pronounced curse against "their murder of prophets unjustly" (4.155). Though the Hebrew scriptures as well as the Christian New Testament had similarly excoriated those who murdered their prophets,[89] the Qur'an and its interpreters leveled this charge at the Israelites in particular (enforced in this by Christianity's long-standing accusations not only concerning the "ancient" prophets, but also John the Baptist and Jesus). From the vantage point of al-Tabari and al-Tha'labi, their successor Nisaburi, Persian chronicler of the prophets' lives, *and* of artists fashioning illuminations for Qisas books, the martyrdom of Zachariah—priest, prophet, and guardian of Mary—was a prime example of Israelite violation of the divine will. Zachariah, like his son, suffered persecution by his own people. In this Zachariah and John were securely conjoined with the "messiah Jesus, son of Mary," all three being servants of the Lord. Not surprisingly, scenes depicting the frustrations of the Jews in their attempt to crucify Jesus—showing a substitute for him on the gallows, or Jesus ascending beyond the reach of his captors—also secured places as illuminations in many manuscripts.

The ending of the prophet Zachariah's life was honorable—made more so by yet another addition to the saga by exegetes. As the men with the saw approached the tree enclosing him, a voice from heaven announced:

"This event was ordered by me, to test your endurance. If you utter a cry, your name will be erased from the list of prophets." Zachariah replied, "My Lord, since my blood is shed for your sake, even if they cut out my tongue, I shall try to say nothing else but thanks to you."[90]

These words from the tree conclude a distinctly Muslim passion story. The narrative and image informed and bolstered the several martyrologies—that is, teachings concerning dying for the faith—which Sunnis and Shi'is developed over time.

As told and painted, the Muslim presentations of the killing of Zachariah demonized the Jews, who in this act collaborated with Iblis. At the same time, the last chapter of Zachariah's life alluded to the tests that he, John, and Jesus withstood in their clashes with the very people, their own, to whom they were sent as prophets. Eclipsing both of these interests, however, is what the exegetes steadily registered: it was for the honor of Mary, mother of Jesus, no less than for his own, that Zachariah defied the Israelites' calumny, fell prey to their persecution, and finally suffered a death ultimately signaling the victory of a servant of God. The painting does not fall under the same heading as the two just considered—for Mary does not appear in it. And yet, because of its focused perspective on Zachariah as the protector of the young virgin's life of purity, his martyrdom does not gain full independence as a story of *this* prophet. It is, instead, integral to the Muslim story of Maryam.

Conscious and critical of Judaism's disparagement of the mother of Jesus as a wanton woman, and of Christianity's "go[ing] to excess in [their] religion," Islam fashioned its own story of Mary in accord with its theology, specific qur'anic notices concerning her, and the exegetes' explorations of the levels of meaning borne in her life events. The resulting presentations of Mary made clear who she was—namely, the one elected by God to give birth to the prophet Jesus—and how, through her actions as *siddiqah*, one among the truly committed and worshipful ones, she became a female paragon.

Two bedrock Muslim convictions—in God's oneness, and in the all-important role of prophets in the revelation and workings of God's purposes—directly affected the content and contours of Muslim understandings of Mary. The human mother of the human *rasulullah* Jesus, she did not pretend to be divine, but lived to serve and worship her Lord. Mary enjoyed the honor of being a sign to the world, a miraculous disclosure, with her son, of the Almighty's merciful dominion over all things.

Discernible within the Qur'an and in classical commentary are three interrelated but different registers of a Muslim Mariology. First, language both descriptive and categorical was employed to establish her special role and standing in the larger history of God's revealed plan. Her *karama*, the mark of esteem lifting her above the women of the worlds, consisted in her being doubly chosen by God—as one having been dedicated to his service, and as the one honored with the angelic tidings of her virginal conception and birth of so great a son as "the likes of Jesus."

A second projection of Mary played out in her narrative, and did so in such a way that alongside the story's recording of God's agency in making her Jesus's parent, full tribute was paid to her response, her own actions. To cite the central moments, Mary maintains the vocation of being pure and holy as a girl, and then a young woman; she heeds God's angels and trusts in the promise they announce; she commences her life of prayer (in prostration and bowing); she produces her son, registering only the usual lamentations in her labor, and she withstands in her silent obedience her relatives' accusations of fornication. Through the commentators' and painters' retellings, new dimensions are added to Mary's personhood, all attesting to her admirable strength of character. The portrait, finally, is of a resolute and faithful woman, tested—and blessed—by her Lord.

A third presentation of Mary is in the qur'anic mode of capturing succinctly what religious-moral significance for Muslims resides in her story and her example. In *Surah* 66:12 God acclaims her who "defended her chastity"—a virtue in itself for those who have not married, and in her case, a requisite for the special exercise of God's will. Equally important is Mary's submission to the command to "obey [her] Lord, devoutly worship, and bow in prayer with those bowing in prayer" (3:43), for in this she is visible as a steadfast and exemplary member of that community which in its particular form and frequency of *salat* seeks and receives God's guidance and mercy. Finally, the tradition holding that Mary and her son escaped, with the assistance of God's angels, the harm done to all creatures by Satan is a reminder of dangers and temptations, and the kind of life that is needed in order to combat and frustrate Iblis's assaults. These were the lessons from Mary's story which were embraced by all who heard of her, for each has to do with that faithfulness to God which defines the Muslim.

Maryam's significance in early and continuing Islam, a phenomenon underestimated even today outside of Muslim societies, was multifaceted and rich. Perhaps this chapter has focused so steadily on Islam's narrative and teachings about Maryam that it has created the impression that she figures as centrally in Islam's broader vision and theology as she does in the scheme of salvation advanced by Christians. Perspective is easily maintained, however, by recognizing that for Muslims Maryam is the blessed virgin mother of a prophet who is a forerunner to Muhammad, the women of whose household will ultimately command preeminence.

Nonetheless, the myriad ways in which Maryam continued and continues to exercise her presence among Muslims are fascinating and diverse. Some of the forms of devotion directed toward her can serve as this chapter's closing notices: for centuries Muslim women (like Christian) have visited Mary shrines, offering their prayers (for a child, or for milk for nursing) and offering baked cakes;[91] the *mihrabs* of mosques not infrequently bear the inscription from *Surah Maryam* 3:37 in which the term appears, denoting Mary's prayer chamber in the temple;[92] pilgrims to the *Haram al-Sharif* continue to this day to see and commemorate Mary's *mihrab* and the cradle that held her son; Sufi mystics still see in Mary an instance, par excellence, of mystical intimacy—her soul raised to divine illumination;[93] a popular

Egyptian *wali*, or saint, recounted in 1971 his surprising dream encounter with Mary—one that brought him "peace in daily life" and a longing for her, since, as he wrote in one of his diaries, "every expression of her personality fills me with wonder and reverence."[94] Venerable and beloved was (and is) Maryam in her God-bestowed *karama*.

Comparative Summary

Mary, Miriam, Maryam

Unlike the other four narratives taken up in this book, Mary's story, in its earliest form, did not come from Jewish scripture, but from the initial writings of Jesus-followers. The nativity accounts in *Luke* and *Matthew* supported believers' confidence that Jesus was God's Messiah and Son from the beginning. This conviction was in no small measure inspired and confirmed for Christians by a prophecy from the *Book of Isaiah*, which foretold a virgin's bearing of a son who would be called Emmanuel (*Isaiah* 7:14, quoted in *Matthew* 1:23). Much was added to the lore surrounding Mary in the 2nd century Christian writing named the *Protevangelium of James*, which contributed significantly to the churches' enthusiasm for her. It told of the wondrous circumstances of her birth, and of the protection of her purity and holiness in her home and in the Temple precinct, where she resided, having been dedicated to God by her mother, Anna. The *PJ* also provided a more elaborate nativity story than those in the New Testament—including the testimony that Mary remained a virgin *after* the birth of her son, Jesus.

Ridicule of the churches' claims about Mary and the birth of Jesus was quick in coming. We observed that Christians were faulted for not using the correct Greek translation of the prophecy in *Isaiah*, which spoke, the critics insisted, not of a virgin, but simply of a young woman. Rumors and reports of Mary's being cast out by Joseph, of her adultery, and of the name of Jesus's actual father, circulated in the writings of the pagan philosopher Celsus and in certain Talmudic texts. Evidence for thorough Jewish knowledge of Christian traditions about Mary and Jesus appeared in the sixth century Jewish *Toledoth Yeshu*, which mimicked the Gospels, and in the course of portraying Jesus as a would-be king of Israel—messiah—related the incident of Mary's impregnation by a lustful neighbor.

Increasing Christian reverence for the virgin Mary, we saw, met steady resistance in Judaism of the late antique and early Medieval periods. Jewish counterstories about Mary depended upon, exploited, and subverted well-studied Christian tellings and retellings of her narrative. One form of this response we met in the seventh-century Jewish apocalyptic *Sefer Zerubbabel*, which featured the mother of the coming *true* Messiah, Hephzibah, whose powers far exceeded those of Mary.

The stakes in this Christian-Jewish opposition—this contest—were high, and measures of its hostility surfaced in fifth-century Christian sermons concerning the end of Mary's life. We recall that a bishop named Theoteknos pointedly denounced the "unbelieving Jews who had killed the Lord," and he delighted in telling of the divine wrath visited upon some Jews who attempted to attack Mary's body as it was carried on a bier to her funeral.

The clash between Jews and Christians over Mary was of course rooted in their basic and profound disagreement about Jesus's identity. For Judaism the mother of a trickster claiming to be God's anointed one deserved no honor at all, while Christianity steadily built its festival celebrations upon Mary's virginal purity and virtue, and especially her role as *theotokos*—god-bearer.

The Qur'an's presentation of Maryam, mother of `Isa, proved to be intriguing both in its declarations about who she was, and in its details about her experiences. It contained the account of the angelic announcement that she, a virgin, would give birth to a "sinless son," and described the event itself, in the vicinity of a nourishing palm tree. In *Surah* 19 (*Maryam*) we learned of Mary's appearance before her people, who scorned her for holding in her arms a son presumed to be a bastard child. When the infant `Isa spoke, he declared himself to be a prophet of God.

Later Muslim commentators and several painters elaborated and added further drama to the story by having Mary's protector, Zachariah the Temple priest (and father of Yahyah, John the Baptist) become the suspected father of her child. Members of the house of Imran—that is, Jews—were pictured as pursuing Zachariah, and with Satan's assistance, killing him. These anti-Jewish motifs seemed less pronounced, however, in the Qur'an and in Muslim commentary, than Muslim criticism of the Christians, who blasphemously misidentified `Isa/Jesus and erred in believing Maryam/Mary was a god-bearer. They should have recognized and honored her as the woman chosen by God above all others—to be the single parent of her prophet son.

The argument made by several scholars that Maryam belonged in the rank of the prophets (had she not spoken with Jibril, and submitted to God's will for her?) did not ultimately succeed, though Muslim veneration of her was, from the seventh century on, firm and fervent: she was the virgin whom God had selected for *karama*—for special esteem.

In its adoption and adaptations of Christian Mary-traditions Muslim teaching reflects full consciousness of its competitor. Major elements from the *Protevangelium of James* live on in the Surah named *Family of Imran*, but the virgin's son will not be Emmanuel—"God with us." `Isa is to be an emmisary of the Most High. The representation of Jewish hostility to Zachariah, on the grounds that he is Jesus's father and therefore must be killed, owes much to Christianity's well-worn assertions that Israelites were murderers of the prophets God sent to them.

We garnered our information about the contentions among Muslims, Jews, and Christians from surviving literature and art—especially those sources that revealed rival tellings of shared stories. It is interesting to read two episodes in Ibn Ishaq's biography of Muhammad. One concerned a very physical altercation in a mosque, where Jews came to hear Muslim stories, and then made the mistake of scoffing at them. The other tells of more civil contact, but a still intense conflict of ideas; Christians from Najran came to meet with Muhammad, and among the important topics that needed sorting out was this: what could *correctly* be said about Jesus and his mother!

Epilogue

Before summarizing in thesis form what I believe this study has brought to light, I want to reiterate a distinction made at the book's outset, and throughout its chapters. Interpreters of the Bible and Qur'an whose writings and art we surveyed had two central goals. First, they sought to build and sustain their own religious society's identity, purpose, and confidence in their uniqueness—as God's special people. Telling, retelling, and refashioning sacred narratives were intentional efforts at reinforcing each community's core beliefs, codes of behavior, and modes of worship.

The rabbis' considerations of Jonah and the fish were often in this vein. The disobedience, anger, and continuing resentment on the part of God's prophet was arresting drama, but built into it were warnings for those obligated to obey the Torah. Even though one rabbinic text attempted to repair Jonah's image by portraying him as God's future warrior and the slayer of the Leviathan, the stronger force of Jonah's story became institutionalized in Judaism's Yom Kippur liturgy, where the model of penitence came not from him, but from the Ninevites. The tale of Jonah and the fish spoke to Jews of God's demand for righteousness—and capacity for forgiveness.

Muslim commentators, treating the Qur'an's revelation about Yusuf in Egypt and the tempting of him by his master's wife, added more narrative: in her old age confessing her faults and converting to Islam, Zulaykha presented herself to Yusuf as a woman of purified love, and the two married. Zulaykha's repentance reminded believers of the qur'anic assurance that submission to God, however late in life, brings divine acceptance and care. In yet another way this expansion of the story of Yusuf and Zulaykha benefited its readers and hearers; when its allegorical sense was taught, the pair's ardor symbolized (and encouraged) the longing of souls for the divine Beloved.

Another community-directed trajectory of scriptural interpretation appeared in the development of Christian devotion to Mary. We visited that era, commencing at the end of the fourth century, when church leaders (theologians and preachers) began to imagine and describe the last days of the Mother of God—the end of her earthly life and her transport to heaven. The building of these Marian doctrines did not have debate with adversaries as their reason for being, but rather served to buoy the hopes of the faithful: Mary, glorified in heaven, was portrayed as one dedicated to interceding with her Son on behalf of sinners, and for those in all kinds of need and trouble.

The second focus or objective of Qur'an and Bible interpreters was to defend their respective faiths' belief systems against attacks and, whenever possible, to score victories over their opponents' arguments. Three examples, replaceable with many other such conflictual interpretations, cast clear light on the frequently contentious character of early and continuing culture contact between the three religious communities.

Within the oldest preserved verses of the Qur'an—those inscribed at the Dome of the Rock—were firm challenges to the Christians' teachings about Mary and Jesus. The verses' messages were: Desist from thinking that God had need of a partner, or, given his exalted nature, would have a son. Do not call Maryam God's mother. She is, rather, the mother of the prophet 'Isa. And cease your talk of a trinity. Unambiguously confrontative statements, these propositions were strategically placed at the Muslim pilgrimage site in Jerusalem whose entrance faced the celebrated basilica which was alternately named for Jesus's burial place or the site of his resurrection. The followers of Muhammad, we learned, revered Maryam and 'Isa greatly, but vehemently opposed the Christians' understandings of who this mother and son were.

To stay with the same subject, we recall that two postbiblical Jewish writings were counteroffensives against Christian teachings about Jesus and Mary. The parody of Jesus's life, *Toledoth Yeshu*, was comedic in content but earnest in its attack, representing Jesus as a trickster and messianic pretender who stole from the Temple the magical power by which he did wonders. His fantastic sky-battle with Judah Iscarioto, however, revealed the weakness that would bring his career to an end. Mary's miraculous virgin birth was, at the text's opening, debunked with a darkly humorous account of her impregnation by a lecherous neighbor. This boisterous "Life of Jesus" no doubt entertained Jews who learned *this* history of Jesus's mother, but its insults consisted in sharp-edged repudiations of Christians' foundational convictions. The Jewish apocalypse titled *Sefer Zerubbabel* was certainly a response to the powerful success of the Christians' veneration ot a Mary possessed of great powers. It envisioned the militant Hephzibah, mother of the soon-to-reign true messiah, Menahem. Mary appeared in the drama as a statue, or idol. Both of these Jewish writings—revealing impressive knowledge of the literature, thought, and practices of their Christian opponents—gave evidence of sharply oppositional relations between the two communities.

The Christian writer Irenaeus contrasted Abel's and Cain's offerings to God with anti-Jewish polemic in mind. He argued that Jews were unable to make a pure sacrifice or to offer true worship, having re-enacted Cain's murder of his righteous brother in crucifying Jesus. Because the Jews' hands were "full of blood," Irenaeus insisted, the blessing of God now belonged to followers of Jesus, not to the people of the synagogues. This argument can be assumed to have bolstered Christians' assurance about who they were in the eyes of God, but its more fervent intention was to accuse and abuse Jews with the charge that in killing Jesus of Nazareth, they had committed deicide.

Several scriptural commentaries that we encountered came close to combining the two objectives of community upbuilding and confrontation of competitors. We could point to the painting in Nisaburi's *Stories of the Prophets* which depicted Ibrahim's family gathered near the Ka'ba in Mecca to receive the angel Jibril's announcement of the birth of Ishaq. This story is ours, the painting asserts, making Islam's most sacred place its location. By doing so, the artist's interpretation commandeered this crucial moment—and revelation—in the sacred histories of Jews and Christians.

The two mosaic portraits of Sarah gazing upon Abraham's angelic visitors—one in the Sepphoris synagogue, the other in Rome's Sta. Maria Maggiore—have strong similarities but also an intriguing difference, in that the Christian image shows a simple cross on the structure from which Sarah peeked. The symbol invoked, in the church setting, Sarah as the prototype of Mary (and the victory of her son), addressing Christians' convictions and hopes. At the same time, this decoration consciously coopted the event's meaning in relation to Jews' understanding of the promise of the birth of Isaac, in whom their covenant was guaranteed.

From data like these emerged this exploratory book's findings. They can be framed, at its conclusion, as a two-part argument, or thesis.

First, Jewish, Christian, and Muslim interpreters of the scriptural stories of the Bible and the Qur'an were crucial tradition-shapers; they continuously explained narratives, probed their layers of meaning, and adapted their retellings to different times and circumstances. The oxygen for the perdurance and viability of each community's treasury of memory and tradition came from these imaginative commentators, whose preservation *and* fine-tunings of biblical and qur'anic lore enabled them to broadcast afresh God's self-revelations, enunciate moral teachings, ensure gainful worship practices, and, not least, assert a politics of belief—one confident in God's exclusive bond with their own particular and exclusive religious society. Scriptures and their meanings were not fixed or static, but always unfold-ing—vital and current precisely because they were creatively renewed and refreshed.

Second, competitive scripture interpretation was a singularly powerful force in the early divergence between Christians, Jews, and Muslims, and in their separation into discrete, independent religious cultures. The com-petitions over scriptural interpretations did not consist merely in reflex-ive responses—that is, quick rebuffs of unwelcome criticisms. Rather, we have learned that being questioned and engaged by their competitors had profound results. Each faith community, so challenged, was compelled to penetrate more deeply a familiar story—and to create new tellings of it that sharpened and bolstered its own sense of being Jewish, or Christian, or Muslim.

These two conclusions respond directly to perennial questions that his-torians of cultures and religions pose concerning the dates, character, and content of initial and ongoing encounters among the Jews, Christians, and Muslims. We have in these chapters gleaned important information about how much, and in what detail, the interpreters knew of each others' scriptures, beliefs, teachings, and religious observances. Further, within the more transparently adversarial interpretations of the shared sacred stories, we discerned patterns of religious-ideological distancing and insti-tutional boundary-setting that were historically decisive. In the hands of Jewish, Christian, and Muslim interpreters the sagas of Adam's sons, of Abraham's women (and Abraham himself), of Joseph in Egypt, of Jonah, and of Mary proved most noteworthy for their carefully wrought distinc-tions from one another. Working from shared stories, the three religions recast these in order to advance their own specific purposes.

The historical data in this study compelled us to look carefully at this dynamic in the work of the scripture commentators—the distinction-drawing and attention to particularities that made Islam Islam, Judaism Judaism, and Christianity Christianity. In many modern efforts to gen-erate cooperation among religions, the phrase "Abrahamic religions" is employed to suggest a fundamental kinship, original unity, and a set of basically congruent beliefs and ethics. We recall, however, that two differ-ent Abrahams and an Ibrahim appeared in the earliest interactions among Jews, Christians, and Muslims. Perhaps interreligious conversations in our era would more honestly proceed by taking up difficult and irreconcilable variances in belief and practices, working toward understanding—even appreciation—of these. Notions of an essential and unbreakable familial closeness and concord that enwraps Jews, Christians, and Muslims are romantic, and also historically false.[1]

Often heard in contemporary public and private discourse is the claim that Jews, Christians, and Muslims believe in, and pray to, the same God. Our comparative investigations of the five biblical-qur'anic narratives compelled us to ask how similar were the theologies, or the pictures and understandings, of God, in the three religions? Alongside the attention we gave to distinctions between Jewish, Christian, and Muslim formal doctrines of God, we pondered the ways in which the exegetes and commentators, imagining God at work—hearing, speaking, responding to, acting on behalf of the characters in the five stories—presumed "their" God to be present. As the Muslim Yunus was distinguishable from the Jonah of Jews and the Christians' Jonah, so too seemed to be the God with whom the prophet had his dealings, depending upon the religion of the commentator. We found substantial evidence in our sources that exegetes and storytellers were aware of particular ways in which *their* God would address a person or a people, or would mediate judgment and bestow mercy. With regard to the centuries featured in this book, the supposition that Jews, Christians, and Muslims meant the same thing by the word God is very difficult to maintain. It would also face a difficult test, I am sure, if carefully examined today in the three religions *and* (to make the test as complex as it should be) in their various branches and parties. Interestingly, contemporary theologians ponder this old question with more subtle care and sharpness: do Jews, Christians, and Muslims pray to same God?[2]

All stories that persist, being significant for a human group's memory and collective identity, undergo change. I made this assertion in the Prologue as a *preparatio* for what readers would immediately encounter: the purposeful adaptations Jews, Christians, and Muslims would make in telling and retelling five sacred stories—each community tending carefully to its own vital interests.

The intrinsic openness of the interpretative process, with its fluid powers to search out new meanings fit for diverse times and circumstances, was highlighted in the works of "our" writers and artists. Unsurprisingly, though, the findings of these exegetes in the literature and art of the first through sixteenth centuries became platforms for further interpretive pursuits. This would be the conclusion drawn from a similar study of progressive reinterpretations of holy writings in the sphere of interactions between Jews, Christians, and Muslims from the seventeenth to the twenty-first centuries. So long as their sponsoring communities exist, understandings of sacred stories continue to extend themselves. Without too much difficulty, we detect in the language of today's political and religious leaders adaptations of passages in sacred literatures that may gain privilege or protection for particular religious communities, or stake a claim to certain territories and holy sites. (A parallel invocation of foundational figures and documents can be heard from advocates for particular economic philosophies, nationalisms, forms of government, and political ideologies.)

In this study of peoples who shared sacred stories, but lived by rival interpretations of them, I have sought only the historical yield of their culture contacts. The exploratory drive of communities contemplating their histories with their present and future prospects in mind, when inspected comparatively, reveals something unusual and significant. Even with their communities' particular hopes and goals in mind, Jews, Christians, and Muslims were (and are now) neither compelled to agree nor compelled always to disagree on interpretations of their shared scriptural stories. Interpreters are entirely occupied, that is to say, in using their sacred stories and traditions as resources for the continuing articulation and rearticulation of their people's view of the world—of its difficulties and promises.

This endeavor on the part of Jews, Christians, and Muslims (and also of Hindus, Buddhists, and other communities equipped with authoritative writings and lore) preserves and renovates the stories of their sacred histories—the narratives upon which their most profound loyalties and commitments are based.

ABBREVIATIONS

ANF	Ante-Nicene Fathers
ACW	Ancient Christian Writers
CCQ	*The Cambridge Companion to the Qur'an*
CEI	*Concise Encyclopedia of Islam*
CS	Cistercian Studies
EQ	*Encyclopedia of the Qur'an*
FOC	Fathers of the Church
JECS	*Journal of Early Christian Studies*
JQR	*Jewish Quarterly Review*
JR	*Journal of Religion*
JRA	*Journal of Roman Archaeology*
LCL	Loeb Classical Library
NEJ	*The New Encyclopedia of Judaism*
NPNF	Nicene and Post-Nicene Fathers
ODJR	*The Oxford Dictionary of the Jewish Religion*
SI	*Studia Islamica*
WUNT	*Wissenschaftliche Untersuchungen zum Neuen Testament*

NOTES

PROLOGUE

1. See Bruce Lawrence, *The Qur'an: A Biography*, [62]–82; John Burton, "Collection of the Qur'an," in Jane McAuliffe, ed., *Encyclopedia of the Qur'an* (EQ) I, 351–361; Fred M. Donner, "The Historical Context," and Claude Gilliot, "Creation of a Fixed Text," in Jane McAuliffe, ed., *The Cambridge Companion to the Qur'an*, 23–39, 41–57, resp.
2. Carmel McCarthy, tr., "Saint Ephrem's Commentary on Tatian's Diatessaron," *Journal of Semitic Studies*, Supplement 2, 139.

PREVIEW, CHAPTERS 1–3

1. Jan Brenner, "Brothers and Fratricide in the Ancient Mediterranean," 77–92.

CHAPTER 1

1. A review of debates about the character and dating of the Torah, or Pentateuch, with clear and compelling "provisional conclusions," is provided in Joseph Blenkinsopp, *The Pentateuch* (with quoted phrase, 51). Blenkinsopp's treatment of "chronological markers" within the writings of the Pentateuch led him to the view that the five book collection was created in connection with the building of the Second Temple, ca. 530 BCE after the Exile, when Israelite society and cultus were reformed in Judah during the period of Persian rule in the region.
2. Daniel Boyarin, *Intertextuality and the Reading of Midrash*, 41.
3. Notable advocates for the notion that images in the Ashburnham Pentateuch owe much to Jewish sources have been J. Stryzgowzki, *Orient oder Rom*; Joseph Gutmann, "The Jewish Origin of the Ashburnham Pentateuch Miniatures," 53–72; K. Schubert, "Die Miniaturen des Asburnham Pentateuch im Lichte der rabbinischen Tradition," 191–212 and "Jewish Traditions in Christian Painting Cycles," 208–260. Eighteen of an estimated sixty-nine original illuminations in the codex survive. See Bezalel Narkiss, "Reconstruction of Some of the Original Quires of the Ashburnham Pentateuch," 19–38. Dorothy Hoogland Verkerk, "Moral Structure in the Ashburnham Pentateuch," 71, observed that the majority of scholars date the manuscript to a period between the late sixth to the early eighth centuries, and gives its provenance as the Latin West—either Gaul or northern Italy. The first edition and description of the illuminations in the manuscript was that of Oscar von Gebhardt, *The Miniatures of the Ashburnham Pentateuch*. This manuscript is one of the several illustrated biblical books treated in Kurt Weitzmann, *Late Antique and Early Christian Book Illumination*,

17, 118–125. In a decorated frontispiece the transliterated Hebrew names for the first five books of the Bible are reported, with translations given of their Latin titles—e.g., *"bresith quam nos genesi decimus, hellesmoth qui exodus appelatur."* The book reveals its Christian liturgical uses by indicating, for example, that one lection is assigned for Easter, while another is to be read on the occasion of the ordination of deacons.

4. *The Life of Adam and Eve* 1. The *Vita* is translated and given an introduction by M. D. Johnson, "Life of Adam and Eve," in James H. Charlesworth, *The Old Testament Pseudepigrapha*, 249–295. It is not clear whether this writing is of Jewish or Christian authorship. The connection between the Ashburnham Pentateuch's portrayal of Adam and Eve and the *Vita* is made by J. Gutmann, "Jewish Origin," 64, whose footnote cites Louis Ginzberg's attention to the Latin *Vita* (which he regarded as "essentially Jewish") in *Die Haggada bei den Kirchenvaetern und in der apokryphischen Literatur*, published in 1900. See also the comments in Kurt Schubert, "Jewish Traditions," 249.

5. Schubert, "Jewish Traditions," 251.

6. Ibid.

7. See Weitzman, *Late Antique and Early Christian Book Illumination*, 32–[33], Plate 1, Vergilius Vaticanus fol. 5v, *Georgics*.

8. My view differs from that of Dorothy Verkerk, who argued in "Moral Structure," 79–80, that the virtue of Abel is a prominent interest or message of the artist. Verkerk's opinion appears also in her fuller study, *Early Medieval Bible Illumination and the Ashburnham Pentateuch*, 112–117.

9. Verkerk, *Early Medieval Bible Illumination and the Ashburnham Pentateuch*, 113–114, draws attention to other Christianity-specific signals in folio 6r—specifically the reference to Christian eucharistic liturgy in the scenes of the offerings made by the brothers, who bring a loaf, a lamb, and a chalice. The artist's association of the Christian ritual with the Cain and Abel offerings is ultimately confused and confusing, however, in that it does not take into account the divine rejection of Cain's gift of grain, the loaf.

10. On the spread of Aramaic—and also Greek—within multilingual Judaism both within Palestine and in the Diaspora, see John Bowker, *The Targums and Rabbinic Literature*, 3–8. While the special status of Hebrew as the language of revelation and of law was secure, translations were necessary "for two reasons, first so that the Jews themselves could understand their own scriptures, and second so that non-Jews could understand them as well. It follows that since the emphasis in translation was on understanding, there was a tendency right from the start to express meaning rather than to be scrupulously literal" (4–5).

11. On the dating (and naming) of *Pseudo-Jonathan*, see Bowker, *Targums*, 26–27. Also, James Kugel, *Traditions of the Bible*, 944, in his helpful section on "Terms and Sources," where Targums, generally, and the important Targums Onqelos and Neophyti are discussed alongside *Pseudo-Jonathan*. Geza Vermes's important article "The Targumic Versions of Genesis 4:3–16," 92–126, in the course of comparing the several targums on the Cain and Abel story, stresses the need to work toward dating elements within targums individually. He finds within this section of *Ps-Jon* (he prefers to call the targum 1J, for Targum Yerusalmi 1) materials that, on the basis of comparison with themes found in Josephus and the New Testament, belong to the 1st century CE, having "probably originated in pre-Christian times" (116).

12. Bowker, *Targums*, 13. Bowker, 12–15, draws upon a passage in *Pesiqta Rabbati* (14b) in noting the distinction between the Torah reading and the interspersed translation. He further notes that our evidence makes clear that "there was no such thing as a single Aramaic translation: there was a continuous process of exegesis which produced traditions of interpretation in different areas of Judaism, and the synagogue targums undoubtedly reflected that process" (15).

13. Ibid., 132. Bowker's translation and printing of the text in two kinds of type is used throughout our inspection of *Ps-Jon.*

14. See Vermes, "Targumic Versions," 111–112, in which he invokes and builds upon the work of Guilding, *The Fourth Gospel and Jewish Worship*, 34. The rabbis did, however, debate the date of offerings made by Cain and Abel, as we shall see shortly in the commentary in *Genesis Rabbah.*

15. Vermes, "Targumic Versions," 112. It is worth noting the ways the New Testament writers emphasize the death of Jesus within the events of Passover. This appears to be a reliable historical report, but it also serves theological and ritual purposes important to the evangelists, as we see in various details—e.g., that Jesus, described early in John's Gospel as the "lamb who takes away the sins of the world," does not, at the time of his crucifixion, have his legs broken, thus remaining a pure/whole victim. (On the relative silence of the Gospel writers about typical Passover activities Jesus and his disciples would have engaged in, see the remarks of E. P. Sanders, *The Historical Figure of Jesus*, 249–252.)

16. Vermes, "Targumic Versions," 112. Other opinions were held, as we shall observe. *Exodus* 21:19 falls within a set of rules conveyed to Moses concerning violence, while the handmaid with two disputing sons in *2 Samuel.* 14:6 is the woman from Tekoa who visits King David at Joab's instigation. The verses' references to dispute between two men/two brothers come to the targumist's mind, and he selects from the first text the stone as the murder weapon (though the regulation also speaks of the "fist").

17. Vermes, "Targumic Versions," 113–116. At the conclusion of his essay (124–125), Vermes explores the combination of justice and love as a double characterization of God's action, and interestingly moves from St. Paul's formulation of justice and grace (in successive ages) to appearances of "the joint action of Justice and Love" as themes under discussion in rabbinical writings, and in Philo, who wrote just prior to New Testament times. In connection with the human *yetzer hara* and what interpreters saw as its implication in *Genesis* 4:7, Bowker cites the teaching found in *Aboth de Rabbi Nathan* 16: R. Reuben said: "How can anyone escape the evil inclination when the first drop put by a man into a woman is the evil inclination? It lies at the beginning (or 'opening') of the heart, as it is written,... *sin coucheth at the door*." R. Judah haNasi said: "Let me give you a parable: to what may this be likened? The evil impulse is like two men entering a place of lodging where one of them is arrested as a thief. He was asked, 'Is there anyone with you?' He might have said, 'No one,' but in fact he thought, 'If I am going to be executed, let my companion be executed with me.' Likewise the evil inclination says: 'Since there is no hope for me in the world to come, I will destroy the whole body as well' " (*Targums*, 138).

18. The phrase *nasa ʾawon* can mean either "to bear (i.e., to be burdened with) sin or to forgive (i.e., take away) sin." Another *targum*, Onqelos, takes the second sense, having Cain say, "My guilt is too great to forgive," which Vermes construes to "reflect Cain's despair, even in God's mercy, and show that he remained impenitent." Vermes, "Targumic Versions," 117–118, argues that Targum Onqelos's

exegesis (and viewpoint on this issue) is also that of the Septuagint and the Vulgate translations, and "is indirectly supported by Josephus (in *Jewish Antiquities* 1.2.2 [60]): 'He did not take his punishment as a warning, but as an incentive to increase vice.'" Vermes adds that the Palestinian *targums*, including *Ps-Jon*, take Cain's words as a prayer for forgiveness, and he finds in Josephus this tradition as well. Bowker, *Targums*, 140, notes the passage in *Jewish Ant.* 1.2.1 (58): "God . . . exempted him from the penalty merited by the murder, Cain having offered a sacrifice and therewith supplicated him not to visit him too severely in his wrath."

19. See Vermes, "Targumic Versions," 103, 118–119; in the latter pages Vermes treats the two attempts undertaken by early Jewish interpreters to explain the delay in Cain's death and judgment by God—i.e., that Cain required the duration of seven generations in order to repent of his crime, or that this amount of time was needed in order for the integrity of his confession (of repentance) to be tested. Kugel, *Traditions*, 155, comments: "Strange to tell, Cain's protest to God, 'My punishment is too great to bear' (*Genesis* 4:13), might also be translated 'My sin is too great to forgive.' Now, this is clearly *not* what Cain was saying. But ancient interpreters, who were fond of preaching the virtues of repentance, seized on this opportunity to claim that the world's first murderer was overcome with his own guilt after the deed was done. Even after God had pronounced a severe sentence upon him, Cain still cried out: 'My sin is too great [for You] to forgive.' (If, as just seen, Cain's sentence was suspended for seven generations, was it not in consideration of these heartfelt words?)."

20. On the long and painful history of diverse interpretations of the mark put on Cain, see the intriguing and influential study by Ruth Mellinkoff, *The Mark of Cain*, and in particular reference to this biblical moment, her comment: "According to Jewish tradition the tetragrammaton (YHWH) was a most holy sign conveying divine protection. It was generally thought to be reserved for only the just. It is certainly noteworthy that it is the Pseudo-Jonathan targum that provided such a positive interpretation of the mark of Cain, for it dramatically focuses on the linking of a positive sign toward Cain's repentance with a mark or sign for Cain that is an emblem of honor and protection" (28). Christian interpretations of Cain's mark will come to light in the next chapter; this narrative element is absent from the Qur'an, and is only briefly referred to by a Muslim historian who notes its presence in Jewish tradition.

21. Boyarin, *Midrash*, 41.

22. See the following entries for *Genesis Rabbah*: Paul Mandel in *The Oxford Dictionary of the Jewish Religion*, 268; Moshe David Herr in *Encyclopaedia Judaica* 7, 400–401. In H. Freedman and Maurice Simon, trs. and eds., *Midrash Rabbah*, vol. 1, xxvii, Freedman notes that *GR* differs from "Tannaitic Midrashim which are fragmentary in character, chiefly in that the parashiyyoth (sections, chapters) of Genesis Rabbah begin with proems, such as always characterize the beginnings of homilies collected in the homiletic Midrashim. Each chapter of the work is headed by the verse which is to be explained, and prefaced by a number of comments on a different verse of the Bible, the last of which always leads back directly to the verse of Genesis under discussion."

23. Neusner, *The Components of Rabbinic Documents IX Genesis Rabbah*, Part 1, xlv. These themes are not in clear evidence in the section of *GR* 22 under discussion here, but one can imagine the debate treated below about the meaning of the Revelation and of acceptable sacrifice in relation to these ideas.

24. The translation used here and throughout this volume, unless otherwise noted, is that of H. Freedman and Maurice Simon, *Midrash Rabbah*. See also Jacob Neusner, *Genesis Rabbah*. The view that Adam was the first creature of sexual experience is attributed to R. Huna and R. Jacob in R. Abba's name, in *GR* 22.2.

25. Freedman and Simon, *Midrash Rabbah*, Genesis 1 (22.5), 182, n. 8, citing Theodore Albeck, remark that R. Jose's restriction was "because before the Revelation people were unworthy of enjoying any part of an animal consecrated to God."

26. Freedman the translator comments that the sense is "blackened"—the result of being burnt up. Melinkoff, *Mark of Cain*, 76–80, points to traditions that attribute blackness—Negroid attributes—to Cain and his progeny, particularly as Cainites are linked to African races in medieval Europe and in some modern religious doctrines.

27. From several midrashic accounts, including *GR* 22.7, Ginzberg composes a variant of this in *Legends* 1, 108–109: "One day a sheep belonging to Abel tramped over a field that had been planted by Cain. In a rage, the latter called out, 'What right hast thou to live upon my land and let thy sheep pasture yonder?' Abel retorted: 'What right hast thou to use the products of my sheep, to make garments for thyself from their wool? If thou wilt take the wool of my sheep wherein thou art arrayed, and wilt pay me for the flesh of the flocks of which thou has eaten, then I will quit thy land as thou desirest, and fly into the air, if I can do it.'"

28. See Ginzberg, *Legends*, 1, 65–66. A brief overview of the topic (with bibliography) is found in Joseph Dan, "Lilith," in *The Oxford Dictionary of the Jewish Religion*, 421–422. See also Judith Baskin, "Rabbinic Judaism and the Creation of Woman," 125–130.

29. This is one of several accounts of Adam's sons competing for one of the sisters—in some cases a twin of Abel, but in others the twin of Cain. Kugel, *Traditions*, 148–149, cites texts telling of the twin sisters and their names.

30. See Ginzberg, *Legends* 1, 116–117, a synthesizing of several legendary accounts, and also Cassuto, *Book of Genesis*, 189–190, where the link of the passage to Cain is noted (v. 24), and the author observes that a "thematic connection consists in the fact that Lamech follows in the steps of his forefather and also slays a person, boasting of his cruel deed with a brazenness reminiscent of Cain, who did not hesitate to say to the Lord's face: Am I my brother's keeper? . . . [The Torah's] aim appears to have been to introduce at this early stage a subject that would serve as preparatory proof of what was to be stated later (vi 5): that the wickedness of man was great in the earth, and that every imagination of the thoughts of his heart was only evil continually, and thereafter (vi 13): and the earth was filled with violence."

31. Kugel, *Traditions*, 153, cites another interpretation, one found in *Midrash Tanhuma, Bereshit* 9, which specifies the murder weapon: "How did he kill him? He made many wounds and bruises with a stone on his arms and legs, because he did not know whence his soul would go forth, until he got to his neck." The killer, of course, has no precedents for his action.

32. R. Huna cites the use of the plural in *2 Kings* 9:26 in reference to Naboth and his sons, and "the Rabbis" point to "the bloods [*deme*] of the sons of Johoiada in *2 Chronicles* 24:25 (*GR* 22.9).

33. Simeon has read the Hebrew term `alay ("against Me," i.e., against God) in place of *elay* ("from the ground"), and on this basis pictures Abel asking God for an explanation of his nonintervention.

34. Others explain God's meaning differently: The earth will yield its fruits to others, but not to Cain (R. Eleazar). No, it will be productive for no one (R. Jose b. Hanina). *Deuteronomy* 28:38 speaks of sowing "much seed out into the field" but harvesting only a little. How much is a little? A *se'ah* (measure) of seed will bring in an equal measure of produce, says one rabbi, while another asserts that production, in the aftermath of Cain's crime, will be halved. Or does the verse really concern itself with who will benefit from "the ground" after Cain's staining of it with his brother's blood, or with the quantity of its future yields? No, one voice maintains. The text states that henceforth the earth's "strength" will not bring in the crops; the ground will give its yield through the strength of human toil (*GR* 22.10).

35. The translation in Freedman and Simon, *Midrash Rabbah*, vol. 1, 190, has here been slightly adapted. As Freedman and Simon make clear, it is "Thou hast driven" that inspires the reference in *GR* 22.11 to Adam's expulsion from Eden in the past, while Cain is understood to comment that "Now Thou drivest me out" (Freedman and Simon, *Midrash Rabbah*, vol. 1, 190, and n. 6).

36. Mellinkoff, *The Mark of Cain*, 19ff. Mellinkoff suggests that the "varied and contradictory interpretations [within *GR* 22.12] demonstrate the different attitudes towards Cain" relating to the issue of his penitence (or the absence of it). Is he pitiable or a damnable archetype of perversity?

37. See Mellinkoff, *Mark of Cain*, figures 15, 19, 20, and comments on pp. 59ff. about possible meanings attaching to the "horn": a weapon for self-protection? A "concrete manifestation of his bestial nature"?

38. Freedman and Simon, *Midrash Rabbah* 1, 191, n. 6.

39. Marcus, *Philo, Questions and Answers on Genesis*. Noted on the title page is the fact that Marcus translated *Questions and Answers on Genesis* (hereafter, *QG*) "from the ancient Armenian version of the original Greek." Marcus comments on this in his introduction, ix–xiii. Papers dealing with various aspects of Philo's *QG* are collected in David Hays, ed., *Both Literal and Allegorical*.

40. Goodenough, *Philo Judaeus*, 48–49, referred to *Questions and Answers on Genesis* as one of Philo's great writings, and notes that we have "only a few scattered fragments of it in Greek, and large sections, but only sections in Armenian.... The Questions was originally quite as important a work as any of Philo. The method is again commentary, but this time Philo discusses the text verse by verse, and usually under two heads, the literal meaning and the intellectual meaning. Each section is introduced by the 'question': 'What does it mean when it says'—and then a verse is quoted."

41. Dawson, *Allegorical Readers and Cultural Revision in Ancient Alexandria*, 98.

42. The long history of allegorical interpretation as it pertains to Philo's setting is treated, among other places, in Louis Ginzberg, *On Jewish Law and Lore*, 127–150, and Dawson, *Allegorical Readers*, 23–72. See also Irmgard Christiansen, *Die Technik der allegorischen Auslegungswissenschaft bei Philon vom Alexandrien*.

43. *The Sacrifices of Abel and Cain* 13, 53. LCL Philo series, vol. II, 134–135. (Numbers following the titles of the treatises denote sections, then lines in the text.)

44. Ibid., 13, 54.

45. *On the Posterity and Exile of Cain* 12, 42. LCL Philo series, vol. II, 350–351.

46. For a solid account (with complexities confronted) of Philo's understanding of the hierarchy of souls, the fortunes of the virtuous one, and the question of whether evil souls pass out of being, see David Winston, *Logos and Mystical Theology in Philo of Alexandria*, 27–42. The chapter is titled "The Psyche and Its Extra-Terrestrial Life in Philo's Anthropology."

47. *The Worse Attacks the Better* 14–15, 47–49. LCL Philo series, vol. II, 232–235.

48. *Philo, Questions and Answers on Genesis* 76. LCL, Philo series, supplement 1, 44–45. Philo supports his point by noting what Homer, in *Odyssey* 12.118, said about Scylla, "She is not a mortal but an immortal evil, [and this] was said more appropriately about him who lives evilly and enjoys many years of life"–i.e., Cain.

49. *Genesis Rabbah* registered the opinion that the "mark" was a horn. On the history of the horned Cain, see Melinkoff, *Mark of Cain*, 59–75.

50. See Wolfson, *Philo* I, 395–413, and esp. 404–405.

51. See *2 Maccabees* 6:12–7:42, which dates from the second century BCE, and *4 Maccabees* 5:1–18:24, the more philosophically "framed" and explicated version of the martyrdoms of Eleazar and the seven brothers and their mother, composed probably ca. mid-first century to early second century CE. In *4 Maccabees* 18:9–19, the mother recounts the heroes' stories her husband read to the family, listing "Abel slain by Cain, and Isaac who was offered as a burnt offering, and . . . Joseph in prison" among many who, in maintaining their faithfulness in adversity, gave "witness" (*martys*).

52. *The Posterity and Exile of Cain* 12, 42–43. LCL Philo series, vol. II, 352–353.

53. The story of Cain and Abel does not figure prominently in Philo's explicitly political works, but in the sense in which Dawson understands Philo's work as "cultural revision," all of Philo's interpretive writings—indeed, all of his exegetical efforts—are both social and political in their intentions and effects. In referring to the corpus of explicitly political writings of "Philo the politicus," I have in mind those treatises identified and described by Goodenough, in *Philo Judaeus*, 52–74, and Goodenough's interesting judgments (64) about the relationship of "his life of thought" and "of action."

54. *The Worse Attacks the Better* 45, 164–166. LCL Philo series, vol. II, 310–313.

55. Ibid., 45, 166. LCL Philo series, vol. II, 312–313.

56. Ibid., 48, 175. LCL Philo series, vol. II, 316–317.

57. Ibid., 58, 178. LCL Philo series, vol. II, 318–319.

58. *The Posterity and Exile of Cain* 54, 184–185. LCL Philo series, vol. II, 438–439.

CHAPTER 2

1. The stories of Balaam's becoming a prophet for hire (*Numbers* 22–24) and of Korah's role in attempting to overthrow Moses and Aaron as leaders of the Israelites in the wilderness are intended to further underline the avarice and the illegitimate effort to usurp that characterize the troublers of Jude's community. Cain, for his part, is easily identifiable as the rebel who does violence to his God-approved brother.

2. The passage can be understood in two different historical settings—that of Jesus's public mission ca. 30 CE, and that of the Christian community in possession of this Gospel some 50 to 60 years after the death of Jesus. *Matthew* may well preserve memory of Jesus echoing the words of the prophet Elijah (in *1 Kings* 19:14: "the Israelites have forsaken your covenant, torn down your altars, and have put Your prophets to the sword. I alone am left, and they are out to take my life"). By the time of *Matthew*'s composition, Jesus's crucifixion at the

hands of the Romans (Jesus, according to tradition, having been "handed over" by Jewish leaders) was, of course, secure history for members of the churches. Interestingly, though put in the form of a forecast of future killings and crucifixions of those sent by Jesus, the language of these Matthean verses reflects knowledge of conflicts subsequent to Jesus's death, and perhaps familiarity with accounts of the deaths of Stephen and Peter (who according to the apocryphal *Acts of St. Peter* 38, was crucified upside down).

3. Among the several studies of the catacomb's architecture, decorations, and painting programs (diverse in style and content), see especially Antonio Ferrua, *Catacombe Sconoscuite*, and William Tronzo, *The Via Latina Catacomb*.

4. Ulrika Schubert, *Spätantikes Judentum und frühchristliche Kunst*, 14–15, argues, on the basis of passages in several targums (*Nephyti, Ps. Jonathan*), that the bearded old man ushering Adam and Eve out of the garden is a representation of the *shekinah*, the divine presence, but the image as painted does not require this interpretation. It shows what the verses in *Genesis* describe, with the Lord as the actor. The Vulgate reads, at 3:23–24: *Et emisit eum Dominus Deus de paradiso voluptatis, ut operaretur terram de qua sumptus est. Eiecitque Adam: et collocavit ante paradisum voluptatis cherubim, et flammeum gladium, atque versatilem, ad custodiendam viam ligni vitae.*

5. See 1.1 in the *Vita Adae et Evae*, and Ashburnham Pentateuch, fol. 6r.

6. Tronzo, *Via Latina,* 24.

7. Ibid., 13.

8. James Stevenson, *The Catacombs*, 65.

9. In an interpolation to Ignatius of Antioch's early second-century *Epistle to the Magnesians* which is thought to date to the fourth century, we read a summary of the assault by Joab and his band described in *2 Samuel* 18:14: "Absalom . . . who had slain his brother, became suspended on a tree, and had his evil-designing heart thrust through with darts." For summary comments on the several recensions of Ignatius's letters and the history of scholarly discussion of the critical questions involved, see William R. Schoedel, *Ignatius of Antioch*, 3–7, and Cyril C. Richardson, *Early Christian Fathers*, 81–83.

10. Eusebius is aware of Irenaeus's *Proof of the Apostolic Preaching*, but the work survives only in an Armenian translation. See the remarks in Joseph P. Smith, *St. Irenaeus*, 3–12, concerning the history of the text. Translations of the *Proof* used here are from Smith's volume.

11. It is from Irenaeus's writings and those of his companion in championing "right doctrine," the North African churchman, Tertullian, that we learn most of what we know about Marcion's theology—and about his interpretations of scripture.

12. Michael Allen Williams, *Rethinking "Gnosticism,"* 23–28. According to Williams, the Christianity of Marcion presents "a problematic case" when it is considered a form of gnosticism, but Williams proceeds in his book to question and clarify the category of gnosticism itself.

13. On the various forms of this idea (with its roots in the texts cited) and the inclusion of the phrase "he descended to hell" in "the Apostle's Creed," see J. N. D. Kelly, *Early Christian Creeds*, 378–383.

14. Williams, *Rethinking*, 25–26, took note of this motif in Marcion's teaching.

15. The excerpts are from Adolf von Harnack, *Marcion*, translated in Wayne Meeks, ed., *The Writings of St. Paul*. See the English translation of Harnack's study by John E. Steely and Lyle Bierma, Adolf von Harnack, *Marcion*, with the "antitheses" on pp. 60–62.

16. Harnack theorized that Marcion's idea of two Gods—one of the Hebrew Scripture, the Creator, and the other the Good God who "belongs to" Christ—was inspired by Jesus's parables of good and evil trees, and especially by Pauline ideas (in *Galatians* and *Romans*) about the contrast between law and grace, between judgment and pardon. Harnack supposed that these oppositions, stretched to a breaking point, rather than other kinds of Gnostic speculations about upper and lower realms and their rulers, provided the decisive energy in Marcion's theology.

17. Meeks, *Writings of St. Paul*, 188 (antithesis 3).

18. Ibid., 188 (antithesis 5).

19. Ibid., 189 (antithesis 15).

20. Irenaeus asserts that Marcion says salvation belongs to souls which had learned his doctrine.

21. See *Romans* 16:16, and *1 Peter* 5.14, Justin, *Apology* 45, etc.

22. God's comment to Cain in *Genesis* 4:7 ("Sin couches at the door; its urge is toward you, yet you can be its master") stands behind, and clarifies this translation: "To you shall be his desire, and you shall rule over him."

23. In *Against Heresies* (*Adv. Haer.*) 1.10.1 Irenaeus proposes that "the church, although scattered over the whole civilized world to the end of the earth, received from the apostles and their disciples its faith in one God, the Father Almighty, who made the heaven and the earth, and the seas, and all that is in them, and in one Christ Jesus, the Son of God, who was made flesh for our salvation, and in the Holy Spirit, who through the prophets proclaimed the dispensations of God—the comings, the birth of a virgin, the suffering, the resurrection from the dead, and the bodily reception into the heavens of the beloved, Christ Jesus our Lord, and his coming from the heavens in the glory of the Father to restore all things, and to raise up all flesh, that is, the whole human race, so that every knee may bow, of things in heaven and on earth and under the earth, to Christ Jesus our Lord and God and Savior and King, according to the pleasure of the invisible Father, and every tongue may confess him, that he may execute righteous judgment on all. The spiritual powers of wickedness, and the angels who transgressed and fell into apostasy, and the godless and wicked and lawless and blasphemous among men, he will send into the eternal fire. But to the righteous and holy, and those who have kept his commandments and have remained in his love, some from the beginning [of life] and some since their repentance, he will by his grace give life incorrupt, and will clothe them with eternal glory" (tr. from Richardson, *Fathers*, 360). We should notice particularly in this anti-Gnostic "rule of faith" the propositions that there is no God superior to the Creator, that there was only one Son of that one God, that the Son became incarnate—enfleshed—in Jesus the Christ in order to work salvation, actually died, was raised from the dead, and ascended, still enfleshed, into heaven. Further, the attention given to the judgment (by Christ) of the unrighteous and righteous, and their ultimate fates, bears directly upon our topic.

24. Erich Dinkler, "Abbreviated Representations," 400.

25. André Grabar, *Early Christian Art From the Rise of Christianity to the Death of Theodosius*, 265.

26. See the keen argument concerning the reasons and circumstances influencing the emergence of early Christian art and its various strategies for depicting God's acts in Paul Corby Finney, *The Invisible God*, esp. 146–297.

27. Robin Jensen, "The Economy of the Trinity at the Creation of Adam and Eve," 533. A variation of the scene occurs on another of the Trinity sarcophagi, one sometimes referred to as the Dogmatic Sarcophagus, in the Vatican's Museo Pio Cristiano. Jensen has presented persuasive ideas about the identity and importance of this same figure or person as he appears there.

28. See Jenson, "Trinity," 529–532, for her careful analysis of this image in the Arles sarcophagus.

29. Robert C. Hill, *Chrysostom, Homilies on Genesis 18–45*, 24.

30. Ibid., with translation slightly adapted.

31. Translation is from Edward G. Mathews, *St Ephrem the Syrian*, 126–127.

32. S. P. Brock, "A Syriac Life of Abel," 467–492. For Brock's helpful introduction to the text, the basis of his view that the work was composed in Syriac (not translated from Greek), and the rationale for its dating, see pp. 467–471. Translations used in what follows here are Brock's.

33. Brock, *Abel*, 468–469; the first part of the quotation from p. 469.

34. Brock, *Abel*, 470, notes that in *Abel* "there are but few links with Jewish traditions, and that Symmachus has most in common with the Christian writers of the fourth, and especially the fifth and sixth centuries, though, compared with them, his treatment, especially in the second half of the Life—takes on a highly original form that is by no means devoid of real literary quality." Clear evidence of the writer's familiarity with Ephrem's *Commentary on Genesis* appears at several points: *Abel* 8, 11–12, 14.

35. The reference is to the date of Jesus's crucifixion, of course, but we shall meet in succeeding chapters other associations of important biblical events and ceremonies with the month of Nisan.

36. Brock, *Abel*, 488, n.6, comments: "Symmachus deliberately has only Abel speak here, in order to heighten the dramatic effect."

37. Brock, *Abel*, 489, in reference to *Abel* 11, notes that Symmachus here is reliant upon Ephrem, *Comm. Gen.* 3.5. He also mentions the view of Victor Aptowitzer, *Kain und Abel*, 25, that Symmachus is criticizing the teaching in *Asc. Isaiah* 9:7–10 that Abel was, like Enoch, translated to Paradise.

38. Cf. Ephrem, *Comm. Gen.* 3:7; the derivation is noted in Brock, *Abel*, 490. We met the idea of Cain's desire to be sole possessor of the earth in *Genesis Rabbah* 22.7 and also in the arguments of Philo that Cain's name signals acquisitiveness. The point was registered by Aptowitzer in *Kain und Abel*, 15ff.

39. Eve's description of Cain as a son she "acquired" resonates, as noted above, with Jewish traditions seen in the previous chapter about etymologies given to Cain as a dedicated acquisitor. Is it possible or likely that in Eve's comment here in *Abel* 17—"Cain, whom I acquired"—we hear echoes of Jewish interpretations of Eve's comment in *Genesis* 4.1, like that which prompted *Targum Pseudo-Jonathan* to suggest that Sammael was Cain's father?

40. Brock observes that Cain's repentance is represented in Jewish interpretations (*Pesikta Rabbati* 47.1; 50.5 and Josephus, *Antiq.* 1.58), but not in Ephrem's *Commentary on Genesis*—the source from which Symmachus gains some of his ideas and themes. See Brock, *Abel*, 491, on *Abel* 19, and in n. 44.

41. A phrase in God's words to Moses in *Exodus* 32:9ff. Irenaeus enlisted here in service of polemic against Jews and Judaism, as it had similarly been applied in *Acts* 7:51, in Stephen's speech to the council of priests in Jerusalem which resulted in his martyrdom.

CHAPTER 3

1. Tarif Khalidi, *The Qur'an*, 87.
2. Muhammad M. Pickthall, *Glorious Qur'an*, 106.
3. A. J. Arberry, *The Koran Interpreted*, 132.
4. Ebrahim Moosa's note to me about this passage clarified the ritual and ethical requirement that human genitalia be covered, noting the two scholars' commentaries on this point.
5. Norman A. Stillman, "The Story of Cain and Abel in the Qur'an and the Muslim Commentators," 236ff., notes earlier scholars' tracing of this episode to *Pirke de Rabbi Eliezer* (Friedlander edition and translation, p. 156), in which Adam and Eve deal with Abel's body, and to *Midrash Tanhuma* (*Tan. Bereshit* 10), where it is Cain's burden to bury his brother. Al-Baydawi's account (in his *Anwar al-Tanzil* 1.255) is described as "an almost verbatim translation of the original midrash." Ginzberg, *Legends* 1, 113 summarizes the *PRE* account of the disposal of Abel's body: "For a long time it lay there exposed, above ground, because Adam and Eve knew not what to do with it. They sat beside it and wept, while the faithful dog of Abel kept guard that birds and beasts did it no harm. On a sudden, the mourning parents observed how a raven scratched the earth away in one spot, and then hid a dead bird of his own kind in the ground. Adam, following the example of the raven, buried the body of Abel, and the raven was rewarded by God."
6. See parallels at 17:15 and 29:12.
7. See Heribert Busse, "Cain and Abel," EQ I. 271. Greater elaboration is provided by Asad, *Message of the Qur'an,* 147, n. 36, who writes concerning "my sin as well as your sin": "It is evident from several well-authenticated *ahadith* that if a person dies a violent death not caused, directly or indirectly, by his own sinful actions, his previous sins will be forgiven (the reason being, evidently, that he had no time to repent, as he might have done had he been allowed to live). In cases of unprovoked murder, the murderer is burdened—in addition to the sin of murder—with the sins which his innocent victim might have committed in the past and of which he (the victim) is now absolved: this convincing interpretation of the above verse has been advanced by Mujahid (as quoted by Tabari)."
8. Busse, "Cain and Abel," EQ I, 271.
9. Ibid.
10. M. Muhsin Khan, *Sahih Bukhari*, 4.54.54.
11. See Tarif Khalidi, *The Muslim Jesus*, 32–33.
12. See Mohammad Fadel, "Murder," EQ III, 459–460.
13. Stillman, "Cain and Abel in the Qur'an and Muslim Commentators," 237: "The concluding verse [5:32] seems to establish an overall Jewish origin for this qur'anic narrative. This last verse harks back to the mishnaic moral to the biblical story [i.e., *Mishna Sanhedrin* 4.5: 'Whoever destroys one life in Israel is regarded by Scripture as if he had destroyed an entire world. Whoever saves one life in Israel is regarded by Scripture as if he had saved an entire world']. . . .Although this moral is carried over into the Qur'an, the word-play upon which it is based [the plural 'bloods' in *Genesis* 4:11] is not. Nor is it taken up by the Muslim exegetes. Al-Baydawi, for example, explains that this moral is stated at the end of the qur'anic narrative because Cain 'violated the sanctity of blood, initiated the custom of killing (*sanna 'l-qatl*), and thereby encouraged men to the practice.'"
14. Khan, *Sahih Bukhari*, 9.83.6. http://hadithcollection.com/sahihbukhari.

15. Muhammad Qasim Zaman, "Sin, Major and Minor," EQ V, 20.
16. Khan, *Sahih Bukhari*, 9.83.11. http://hadithcollection.com/sahihbukhari.
17. Franz Rosenthal, *The History of al-Tabari*, Volume I, includes a fine essay on the "Life and Works" of al-Tabari, 5–134. The quotation about al-Tabari's *History* is from William M. Brinner, *The History of al-Tabari,* Volume II, vii.
18. All translations of al-Tabari used herein, unless noted otherwise, are from Rosenthal, *al-Tabari*, cited by text section and by page number, e.g., [137], 307.
19. Rosenthal, *Al-Tabari* I, [137], 307.
20. We saw in the preceding chapters that the question of how Adam's line was to continue produced varying solutions in Jewish and Christian commentary— for example, in *Genesis Rabbah* 2.7, as we noted above, and in other writings earlier and later than that midrash. Exegetes' musings over the appearance of women among the children of Adam and Eve, for propagation's sake, and more specifically, the sisters who were meant to be mates for Cain and Abel, crop up repeatedly in Jewish and Christian writings—e.g., in pseudepigraphical works like the second-century BCE *Book of Jubilees* (in 4.2 there is reference to Awan, apparently Abel's sister) and *Testament of Adam*, dated to the second to fifth century CE, which reports (in 3.5) that it was passion for Lebuda (not Qalima, as in many other legends) that motivated Cain to murder Abel. In several places, Louis Ginzberg treats this tradition in its variant forms—e.g., the sixth-century CE Christian Syriac writing, *The Treasure Cave* (or, in the E. A. Wallis Budge translation, *The Book of the Cave of Treasures*), which presents Cain and Lebuda as twins, and Abel and Qalimath as the succeeding set; see L. Ginzberg, *Legends*, Vol. 5, 138–138, n. 17, and L. Ginzberg, *Die Haggada bei den Kirchenvätern und in der aprokryphischen Literatur*, 60. *Pirke de Rabbi Eliezer* 21, which presents Abel's unnamed twin as the woman prompting the brothers' dispute, has been thought the source of this and other materials in the Qur'an (a theme in Abraham Geiger's 1833 *Was hat Mohammed aus dem Judenthum aufgenommen?*), but "would seem to have been finally redacted after the advent of Islam," according to Stillman, "Cain and Abel in the Qur'an and Muslim Commentators," 231.
21. Rosenthal, *Al-Tabari* I, [138], 308.
22. Ibid.
23. Pickthall rendered the Arabic: And man assumed it. Lo! he hath proved a tyrant and a fool.
24. Rosenthal, *Al-Tabari* I, [139], 309.
25. Ibid.
26. Ibid.
27. Ibid., [138], 309.
28. Ibid., [140], 310.
29. Ibid.
30. Ibid., [140], 310–311.
31. Ibid., [140–141], 311.
32. Ibid., [141], 311.
33. Ibid.
34. Ibid., [143], 312, n. 877.
35. See Rosenthal, *Al-Tabari* I, 312, nn. 878–883, on the several interesting translation issues in this presentation of the verses from *Genesis*.
36. Rosenthal, *Al-Tabari* I, [143], 313.
37. Ibid.

38. Rosenthal, *Al-Tabari* I, 313, n. 887, comments that in his *Commentary* (*Tafsir*, VI, 120), al-Tabari notes at this point that Cain's offering was "the most odious of" his crops.

39. Ibid.

40. Ibid., [143], 314.

41. Ibid., [144], 314, and [146], 317.

42. Cyril Glassé, *The Concise Encyclopedia of Islam*, 157–158. Cain is said to have descended from the mountain holding Qalima by the hand, as he fled to `Adan in the Yemen. Rosenthal, *Al-Tabari* I, 314, n. 894: "The name of the town of Aden in South Arabia and the identical Biblical Eden suggested the Yemenite location here."

43. Rosenthal, *Al-Tabari* I, [144–145], 314–315.

44. Ibid., [145], 315.

45. Ibid.

46. Ibid., [145], 316.

47. Ibid., [146], 316. See 316, n. 901.

48. Franz Rosenthal, "*Sweeter Than Hope*," 29, n. 121. He cites the use of these verses in numerous writings, in which they came "to enjoy considerable popularity," and also mentions the denial, by Jubayr b. Mut`im (d. 678/679), that these were genuine Adamic verses.

49. Rosenthal discusses some of the confusions and contradictions involved (Labhada is the name given to Cain's twin, and Iqlima that of Abel's twin, in Ya`qubi's *History*) in the tradition of names, noting that al-Tabari, with more confidence in his source than other writers of *tafsir*, quoted from Ibn Ishaq's *Mubtada'*. Rosenthal, *Al-Tabari* I, ([146–147], 317, nn. 903–905).

50. Rosenthal, *Al-Tabari* I, [139], 310.

51. William M. Brinner, `*Ara'is Al-Majalis Fi Qisas Al-Anbiya' or Lives of the Prophets*, 75. Hereafter, this Brinner work is abbreviated as *Lives*.

52. Brinner, *Lives*, 74.

53. Ibid.

54. Ibid., 75.

55. See the comments on `*ismat al-anbiya*, "protection of the prophets" in chapter 12 415, and n. 7.

56. Ibid. Emphasis added.

57. Ibid., 75.

58. Ibid., 76.

59. Ibid., 77.

60. Ibid.

61. Ibid., 78.

62. Ibid. The poetic form of the lament of Adam, and of the verse responses of both Eve and Iblis which accompany it, are attributed to the labors of Ya`rab b. Qahtan b. Hud, competent in both Syriac and Arabic, and extolled as "the first to ride a horse, to speak Arabic, and to compose poetry."

63. Ibid.

64. Ibid., 80.

65. Ibid.

66. Ibid., 79.

67. Rosenthal, *Al-Tabari* II, [350], 130.

68. Wheeler Thackston, Jr., ed., *Muhammad ibn `Abd Allah al-Kisa'i, Tales of the Prophets (Qisas al-anbiya)*, 79.

69. Thackston, *Tales*, at 347, n. 64, explains the dark mole as "a foreshadowing of the sign of prophecy detected in the Prophet Muhammad by the Syrian monk Bahira."
70. Brinner, *Lives*, 82.
71. Al-Biruni, *The Chronology of Ancient Nations*. Biruni spent most of his life in a silk route city called Khwarizm—known today as Khiva, in western Uzbekistan.
72. Sachau, *Chronology* IX.225, 210–211.
73. See Priscilla Soucek, "An Illustrated Manuscript of al-Biruni's Chronology of Ancient nations," 134. Soucek's close study of the paintings in the 1307 copy of Chronology is incorporated within a fine treatment of the entire work's interests and purposes.
74. Soucek, "Manuscript of al-Biruni's Chronology," 103, [132].
75. Ibid., 134.
76. See Sarwat Okasha, *The Muslim Painter and the Divine*, 40–106, and Rachel Milstein, Karin Rührdanz, Barbara Schmitz, *Stories of the Prophets*, which treats a group of twenty-one sixteenth-century manuscripts in Persian which preserve the *Qisas* ("Stories of the Prophets") compositions of three authors: Ibrahim b. Khalaf Naysaburi (or as he is called in this book, Nisaburi), Muhammad Juwayri, and Muhammad b. al-Hasan al-Dayduzami.
77. The text is found in Habib Yaghmai, ed., *Qesas-ol-Anbiya by Abu Ishaq Ibrahim ibn Mansur Nisaburi*.
78. See comments about the fifteenth-century painting of Habil with a sheep, and Adam standing with the two brothers, in Milstein et al., *Stories*, 111.
79. Milstein et al., *Stories*, 110–111.
80. Ibid., 110: "This story was rarely chosen by later artists as worth painting, perhaps because it has neither heroes nor saints, and the moral lesson it transmits is rather enigmatic. The episode reappears, however, in the illustrative cycle of the *Qisas* group, where it constitutes one of the most repeated and conventional iconographies. The basic formula represents Qabil carrying his brother's dead body on his back in a rural landscape . . . etc."

CHAPTER 4

1. Anat Gilboa, *Images of the Feminine in Rembrandt's Work*, 30–31.
2. We notice the echo, or replay, of the theme in 12:17: "But the Lord afflicted Pharaoh and his house with great plagues because of Sarai, Abram's wife," causing the Pharaoh to summon Abraham and ask him why he has deceived (and punished) him.
3. Jon D. Levenson, *The Death and Resurrection of the Beloved Son*, 173–174.
4. See, for example, *1 Chronicles* 29:18 and *Exodus* 33:1, where God speaks of the land he "swore to Abraham, Isaac, and Jacob"; also *Leviticus* 26:42, and *Jeremiah* 33:26.
5. H. Freedman and M. Simon, eds., *Midrash Rabbah: Genesis*, volumes 1–2.
6. Reflecting on the child-bearing of the matriarchs—Sarah and Rebekah, notably—we read a passage from the *Jerusalem Talmud* in H. Freedman and M. Simon, *Midrash Rabbah*, vol. 1, p. 378, n. 1: "Y.T.: Righteous women, as in the case of Sarah, find pregnancy more difficult of attainment than rubies."
7. In this instance, and in the one involving Abimelech, the rulers gave their daughters to Sarah. The reasoning: "Better let my daughter be a handmaid in this house [i.e., the house of woman of Sarah's character and God-protected power] than a

mistress in another house." See Freedman, Simon, *Midrash Rabbah: Genesis, GR* XLV.1, 380.

8. *GR* XLV.4, 381.
9. Ibid. Freedman, at 381, n. 6, gives the literal translation of "by an effort of will power" as "they mastered themselves."
10. *GR* XLV.4, 381.
11. *GR* XLV.4, 382.
12. Ibid.
13. *GR* XLV.5, 383. Explanatory additions in brackets are my own.
14. *GR* XLV.6, 384.
15. *GR* XLV.6, 384.
16. *GR* XLV.7, 385.
17. *GR* XLV.9, 386.
18. An interpretation of 16:12 (NRSV: "And he shall live at odds with all his kin") tends in the same direction, likening Ishmael to an enemy of Israel who "fell" (suggested in place of "dwell" on the basis of the account of Ishmael's death in *Genesis* 25:17) before an attempt to "stretch out his hand against the Temple" (*GR* XLV. 9). But which enemy of Israel is in view—Nabatea, and their king, Aretes? The armies of Rome? See Freedman, Simon, *Midrash Rabbah: Genesis*, 387, n. 1.
19. See *1 Chronicles* 5:19: "they went to war with the Hagarites," and also *1 Chronicles* 5:10, 5:20.
20. Gerald Friedlander, *Pirke de Rabbi Eliezer*. Kugel, *Traditions*, 933, writes of the work: "Its allusions to Islamic culture and to Arab rule over the land of Israel certainly suggest that this work was put into its final form after the Arab conquest—according to some, as late as the eighth or ninth century CE. At the same time, the text preserves many ancient traditions, including quite a few known only from the biblical Apocrypha and Pseudepigrapha."
21. *PRE* 32, 231.
22. Ibid.
23. *PRE* 30, 221–221.
24. *GR* XLV.10, 387.
25. Ibid.
26. *GR* LII.3, 462–463.
27. *GR* LIII.6, 466.
28. *GR* LIII.9, 468.
29. *GR* LIII.8, 467.
30. Ibid.
31. At *GR* LII.10, 468–69, we see the rabbis elaborating upon the great feast in colorful terms. The conquest element is strongly projected. Og is there, dressed down by "the Great One of the world" for his impudence in calling Isaac scrawny. God proceeds to warn him that he will see myriads of Isaac's descendants, and be done in by them. Reference is made to *Numbers* 21:34: "And the Lord said unto Moses: Fear him not; for I have delivered him into thy hand." The celebratory meal was ominous. Thirty-one (or more) of the kings slain by Joshua were all there. The passage's message is clear: the fates of Israel's (later) foes were sealed already in the days of the first patriarch.
32. *GR* LIII.11, 470.
33. Ibid.
34. *GR* LIII.12, 471, n. 1.

35. *GR* LIII.13, 472. Ishmael was born fourteen years before Isaac. See *Genesis* 16:14 and 21:5.
36. *GR* LIII.13, 472.
37. *GR* LIII.13, 473.
38. *GR* LIII.14, 474.
39. *GR* LIII.15, 474.
40. Many tomes have been devoted to the topic, but see the brief essay, "Representational Art," 366–371. Rachel Hachlili's "Synagogues in the Land of Israel," 113, quotes "an Aramaic paraphrase in *Targum Pseudo-Jonathan* of *Leviticus* 26:1, which modifies the Bible's stern prohibition against making and bowing down to 'carved stone':

    > . . . nor shall you place a figured stone in your land to bow down upon it. But a pavement figured with images and likenesses you may make on the floor of your synagogue[s]. And do not bow down [idolatrously] to it, for I am the Lord your God.

41. Ze'ev Weiss and Ehud Netzer, *Promise and Redemption*. See also Ze'ev Weiss, *The Sepphoris Synagogue*, 360 pages + 211 illustrations.
42. See Seth Schwartz, *Imperialism and Jewish Society*, 142–145, [203]–206. Christian buildings in Sepphoris are described in Ze'ev Weiss and Ehud Netzer, "Sepphoris in the Byzantine Period," 81–89. The authors comment (85): "The proximity of private and public buildings, both on the acropolis and in lower Sepphoris is rather surprising, as this phenomenon has not been encountered elsewhere in Palestine. In both Roman and Byzantine Sepphoris large and ornate mansions were built close to simple homes, a feature noted throughout the city. Moreover, a clear and rigid division into neighborhoods according to social, religious, or economic status cannot be discerned."
43. The quotation is from Ze'ev Weiss, "The Sepphoris Synagogue Mosaic and the Role of Talmudic Literature in Its Iconographical Study," 20–21.
44. Essays in Levine and Weiss, eds., *From Dura to Sepphoris*, engage in various ways the interpretation advanced by Weiss and Netzer in *Promise and Redemption*. A challenging critique and re-evaluation appears in Schartz, *Imperialism*, 248–259.
45. Ze'ev Weiss, "The Sepphoris Synagogue Mosaic," 3–24.
46. Robin M. Jensen, *Face to Face*, 120: "The equality of the three [visitors] and their function as symbols of the three distinct persons [of God] with one shared nature may be intentionally expressed by the composition. Here, however, the iconography also points to the importance of the eucharistic offering made directly below, at the altar in the center of the presbyterium."
47. Weiss, "The Sepphoris Synagogue Mosaic," 23.
48. See Edward Kessler, "Art Leading the Story," 67–68.
49. The hand of God first appears in Jewish art in just this scene painted next to the Dura Europos synagogue's Torah shrine, though in that instance, the ram's horns, entangled in a tree, hold him in place; there is no rope tether.
50. *Mishnah Yoma* 5.6.2–6, and *Talmud Yoma* 39a, b.
51. See the provocative treatment of this question of the ram tied to, rather than caught up in the tree's branches, in Kessler, "Art Leading the Story," 73–81, esp. 78–81. Kessler's concluding sentences are these: "Artists also expanded the role of the ram. The ram in the Biblical story is on the mountain in the land of

Moriah by chance and plays a minor role in Rabbinic literature, whereas in artistic midrash the ram is quite different through its significant size and prominent placement."

52. *GR* LVI.5, 495.
53. *GR* LVI.9, 498.
54. *GR* LVI.9, 499.
55. See Levenson, *Death and Resurrection*, [173]–199.
56. The translation is from Samuel A. Berman, *Midrash Tanhuma-Yelammedenu*, 148–149. For the history of the text, see Marc Bregman, *The Tanhuma-Yelammedenu Literature*.
57. Levine and Weiss, *From Dura to Sepphoris*, 27.
58. See Joseph Yahalom, "The Sepphoris Synagogue Mosaic and Its Story," 84, for his comments about "barefoot worship and the sanctuary."
59. See Clement of Alexandria, *The Instructor* (*Paedagogus*) 1.5.23, and Origen, *Genesis Homily VIII*. 6. Origen, while interpreting themes from *Hebrews* 5–10 for his third-century congregation, proclaimed: "That Isaac himself carries on himself 'the wood for the holocaust' is a figure because Christ also 'himself carried his own cross,' [cf. *John* 19:17] and yet to carry 'the wood for the holocaust' is the duty of a priest. He himself, therefore, becomes both victim and priest." The translation is from Ronald E. Heine, *Origen*, 140–41.
60. Hebert Kessler, "The Sepphoris Mosaic and Christian Art," 66, 70. Kessler adds (70): "the text accompanying the miniatures depicting the sacrifice of Isaac in the manuscripts of the *Christian topography* provides a typological reading of the Hebrew Bible; Isaac carrying the fire wood on his shoulders on the way to his sacrificial death is taken as a type of Jesus carrying the cross to Golgotha, 'Abraham leading his son to sacrifice on one of the mountains symbolizes the mystery of the passion and resurrection of Christ'. Any such interpretation is, of course, precluded in a synagogue floor mosaic."
61. Edward Kessler, *Bound by the Bible*.
62. Edward Kessler, *Bound by the Bible*, 29.
63. Ibid., 113.
64. Ibid., 115, 116. It is because of attention to the question of Isaac's willingness that rabbinical texts (unlike Jewish artistic representations) point to his maturity (thirty-seven years of age, twice in *GR*). Kessler, 110–113, proposes that this emphasis serves as a counter against some Christian arguments (like that of Melito of Sardis) that Isaac, as antetype, was preparatory and "young" in relation to Christ crucified, who actualized what Isaac had only typified. This competitive interplay between interpretations is, Kessler insists, another case of "exegetical encounter" between Jewish and Christian interpreters of *Genesis* 22:1–19.
65. *PRE* 31, 224, trans. slightly altered. Joseph Yahalom, "The Sepphoris synagogue mosaic and its story," in Levine and Weiss, eds., *From Dura to Sepphoris*, 87, calls attention to this exchange between Eliezer and Ishmael in its several versions in *Pirke d'Rabbi Eliezer* and in the later *Midrash Hagadol* and *Midrash VaYosha*, and offers his own commentary on the two as they appear in the Sepphoris mosaic: "The picture in the mosaic ... which shows Eliezer holding, or waving, the rope that is tied to the ass, seems to support his claim to Abraham's possessions. (He was, in other words, a loyal servant.) On the other hand, Ishmael's spear, the weapon of war used in the desert, indicates a clear threat to the faithful servant."
66. See Avigdor Shinan, "Synagogues in the Land of Israel," 130–152.

67. *PRE* 32, 233–234.
68. Kessler, "The Sepphoris Mosaic and Christian Art," 72.

CHAPTER 5

1. Elizabeth Clark's essay "Interpretive Fate amid the Church Fathers" appears in Phyllis Trible and Letty Russell, eds., *Hagar, Sarah, and Their Children*; this quotation at 143.
2. The making of Sarah into a virtue is akin to Philo's treatment of her in his *On Abraham* 42: "Everywhere and always she was at his side, no place or occasion omitted, his true partner in life and life's events, resolved to share alike the good and the ill. She did not, like some other women, run away from mishaps and lie ready to pounce on pieces of good luck, but accepted her portion of both with all alacrity as the fit and proper test of a wedded wife." I find convincing the argument advanced in Hugh Montefiore, *A Commentary on the Epistle to the Hebrews*, 194, that Sarah, not Abraham, is the subject of the sentence in *Hebrews* 11:11, yielding: "By faith Sarah herself, though barren, received power to conceive, even when she was too old, because she considered him faithful who had promised."
3. Sanders, E. P., *Paul and Palestinian Judaism*. See treatment of Sanders, and others in John G. Gager, *Reinventing Paul*.
4. It remains a matter of scholarly debate whether these "agitators" (5:12), with their "Judaizing" agenda were Jews who had become followers of Jesus ("Jewish-Christians," as they are sometimes labeled), insisting upon a mode of belief and behavior that continued in observance of Judaism's precepts, or, rather, that they were Gentile converts who were intent upon incorporating in their new faith one of the central "traditions of the ancestors," as Paul identifies Judaism in a phrase.
5. Sanders, *Paul*, [431]–556.
6. See *Galatians* 3:6–29, and *Romans* 4. *Genesis* 15:6 is cited by Paul in *Galatians* 3:6 and *Romans* 4:3.
7. Hans Dieter Betz's analysis of this passage, to which I am much indebted in what follows, is found in his commentary, *Galatians*, 238–252. On the passage in *Galatians* 4:21–31, Betz comments: "Paul's method of interpretation is stated clearly in v 24a. What he calls 'allegory' is really a mixture of what we would call allegory and typology. It should be admitted that both methods are closely related. Typology interprets historical material commonly used in primitive Christianity. Persons, events, and institutions of Scripture and tradition are taken as prototypes of present persons, events, and institutions, which are explained as their fulfillment, repetition, or completion within a framework of salvation history. In distinction to typology, allegory takes concrete matters mentioned in Scripture and tradition (mythology) to be the surface appearance or vestige of underlying deeper truths which the method claims to bring to light. Thereby concrete matters in the text are transported into general notions of philosophical or theological truth. Paul's text consists of quotations of LXX and Jewish haggadic material in Greek translation; he does not make any distinction between the two. In a general sense Paul's interpretation of the Abraham tradition and of the figures of Hagar and Sarah is part of a history of such interpretations. Paul, however, does not simply take over this interpretation, but at the same time he gives it his own imprint" (239).

8. Jerusalem as a heavenly place is spoken of only here in Paul's letters, but is imagined in various ways in Jewish apocalyptic and early Christian writings like *4 Ezra* 7:26; 10:40ff, *Jubilees* 4:26, *2 Apoc. Baruch* 4:207; 32:2–3, *1 Enoch* 90:28ff., *Hebrews* 12:22–24, and *Revelation* 21:1–22:5. See notes 81–85 in Betz, *Galatians*.

9. Ernest De Witt Burton, *Galatians*, 226.

10. Betz, *Galatians*, 249.

11. See G. Walter Hansen, *Abraham in Galatians*, 162.

12. Leander Keck, in his introduction to *Romans* in Wayne Meeks, ed., *The HarperCollins Study Bible*, 2115, drew attention to the fact that the discussion in Romans is framed in a situation quite unlike that in which Paul defended his "gospel to the uncircumcised" when meeting with James, Peter, and John in Jerusalem (the event Paul recounts in *Galatians* 1–2): "in Rome he needed to defend the continuing validity of Israel in God's purpose. His letter, therefore, insists that there is one gospel for all humanity, albeit 'to the Jew first'" (1:16).

13. Ronald E. Heine, *Origen: Homilies on Genesis and Exodus*, 127–135. In quotations of Heine's translation, slight changes and adaptations are made in spellings of names ("Hagar" for "Agar," for example). These sermons of Origen, preached in Caesarea Maritima ca. 238–244, survive in Latin translations—or better, paraphrases—by the scholar-monastic Rufinus of Aquileia (ca. 340–410), a supporter of Origen's when controversy swirled around his work and thought, tending in the direction of branding "Origenism" a heresy. Heine, *Origen*, 1–43, provides a concise and helpful introduction to the life of Origen and to the history of these sermons, including treatment of Rufinus as translator.

14. Gerhard von Rad, *Genesis*, 225.

15. Butterworth, *On First Principles*, 4.2.4.

16. Origen, *Homily VII*, 127.

17. Ibid.

18. Ibid., 128–129.

19. Origen, *First Principles* 4.3.5, 297.

20. Origen, *Homily VII*, 129.

21. Ibid., 130.

22. Ibid., 131. Here, Origen's debt to Paul is surpassed by his debt to Philo, who in the course of working out via allegory a lesson about the training of the mind (Abraham), and its need for "preliminary studies" (Hagar) to which knowledge, philosophy, the virtues (Sarah) gives assent, represents Hagar's flight "from the face of Sarah" (*Genesis* 16:6–8) in these terms: "the soul was found fleeing from virtue, not being able to receive discipline." See Philo, *Questions and Answers on Genesis* 3:27, 47. In *The Posterity and Exile of Cain* 33:130, the idea is connected to another segment of the story of the two women: "[God], [i.e., scripture] shows us Hagar filling a water-skin and giving the child drink. Hagar represents imperfect training, being handmaid of Sarah who represents perfect virtue."

23. Origen, *Homily VII*, 131.

24. John L. Thompson, *Writing the Wrongs*, 31.

25. Origen, *Homily VII*, 131–132.

26. Origen, *Homily VII*, 133.

27. In its own context in the Hebrew text of *Proverbs* the advice invokes metaphors of water/liquids in relation to male-female relations, sexual enjoyment, and warnings against a man's intoxication with another woman, and "embrac[ing]

the bosom of an adulteress" (v.20). Further, it clearly warns *against* letting waters spill out into the streets and flow away.

28. Origen, *Homily VII*, 133.

29. Rufinus has added *vivae* to the old Latin text of the Bible that he quotes, which refers simply to *puteum aquae* (a well of water), but his adaptation no doubt reflects the Greek of Origen, who has drawn "living" water from *John 4:10–11* into his treatment of *Genesis 21:19*.

30. Origen, *Homily VII*, 133.

31. Thompson's assessment of Origen's treatment of Hagar is incisive. In his *Writing the Wrongs*, 31, we read: "What makes Origen's image of Hagar truly enigmatic . . . is that, having drawn such a potentially toxic connection between Hagar and the unspiritual 'letter,' he shows no interest in vilifying Hagar. Paul may think that Hagar symbolizes the old covenant, but Origen sidesteps any such conclusion. Instead of faulting Hagar, whether the historical concubine or the allegorical one, Origen allegorically disparages the *bottle* (of water) that Abraham gave to Hagar as she left. In this way Origen does not brand Hagar with the stigma of the law and the letter, but actually frees her from both: 'The bottle of Law is the letter, from which that carnal people drinks . . . This letter frequently fails them, . . . for the historical understanding is defective in many things.' The Church on the other hand, drinks from the fountain of spiritual interpretation—as does Hagar, it would suddenly seem. She thus emerges not as a scapegoat but as an exemplar of sorts. Like the Samaritan woman . . . Hagar has had her eyes opened to see the true well of living water, which is Jesus Christ. Apparently, she is no longer to be counted among the 'carnal' Jews."

32. Origen, *Homily VII*, 134.

33. Ibid.

34. Ibid., 134–135.

35. See in particular Daniel Boyarin, *A Radical Jew* and John David Dawson, *Christian Figural Reading*.

36. Oscar von Gebhardt, *The Miniatures of the Ashburnham Pentateuch*, 14.

37. In another Sta. Maria Maggiore mosaic scene, the haloed Christ oversees the blessing that Melchizedek bestows upon Abraham from the clouds above, his hand extended downward toward Melchizedek and the basket of loaves he lifts up toward the patriarch, who is a mounted warrior at the head of his army.

38. See in Robin Jensen, *Face to Face*, 191–194, a helpful summarization of the development of early iconographic traditions of Mary. The theology and supersessionist ideology of Christian power in the fifth century was aggressive, with typology its forceful medium. The strong theme of Jas' Elsner's *Imperial Rome and Christian Triumph* is summarized in his comments, 228, on Sta. Maria Maggiore's art:

> It comprehensively reinterprets a detailed Old Testament cycle (on the nave walls) in terms of its fulfillment in the triumph of Christianity. It is not just that specific Old Testament themes prefigure the life of Christ, but that the whole narrative of Jewish history is presented as subservient to, completed in, the Incarnation. . . . Such visual programmes in the major churches transposed the relatively small-scale typological images of catacombs and sarcophagi, as well as the still tinier Christian imagery of gems, glassware, and ivory to a monumental grandeur. In doing so, they transformed a sectarian imagery of cult identity into a canonical

iconography of state religion where the only place for pagans (such as the Magi) or Jews (the figures in Old Testament cycles) was as a stage to be surpassed in Christianity's teleology of triumphalism.

CHAPTER 6

1. The motif figures prominently in the encounter between angelic announcers and both Sarah, here, and Mary in Surah 19:45, as we shall see in chapter 15.
2. Al-Tha'labi, *Lives*, 139; he looks back on the Meccan valley from the 11th c. CE.
3. Reuven Firestone, *Journeys in Holy Lands*, 65.
4. See Firestone, "Abraham," EQ I, 7–8, who comments on the inconsistency of references to Abraham's sons and progeny, including the suggestion in some places that Jacob is also born of Sarah, and thus is Isaac's brother, as well as the occasional listing of Ishmael as if he were not part of Abraham's family.
5. See, for example, 2:136; 3:48; 4:163; 6:48; 19:49; 21:72; 37:112–113.
6. In the preceding verses, 6:84–85, we find a listing that has no concern whatever for chronology, following mention of Abraham, Ishmael, Isaac, Jacob and the tribes with Jesus, Job, Jonah, Aaron, Solomon, and David. Though the combination of names in a string is sometimes presented with some attention to chronology (e.g., from Noah, onward, as in 3:33, or in 7:59–64, which moves from Noah to Hud, Shu'aib, Saleh and Moses), different kinds of orderings are common. There is supposed to be no ranking of God's messengers (2:136). More important is the assertion that no generation of humankind, no people in the creation, was left without an apostle sent to warn and to exhort (10:47).
7. Firestone, *Journeys*, 45.
8. Ibid., 47.
9. Barbara Freyer Stowasser, *Women in the Qur'an, Traditions, and Interpretation*, 49.
10. Brinner, *History* II, 61–62.
11. Ibid., 63. The isnad gives Abu Kurayb, Abu Usamah, Hisham, Muhammad, Abu Hurayrah, the Messenger of God.
12. Ibid., 63–64. Brinner comments, in note 178 on p. 64, that his translation, "Arabs" in the quotation from Abu Hurayrah represents the Arabic *yâ banî mâ´ al-sam â'*, "O sons of the water of heaven."
13. Ibid., 65.
14. Ibid.
15. Thackston, *Tales*, 151.
16. Brinner, *History* II, 67.
17. Firestone, *Journeys*, 58.
18. Ibid., 63–71, which surveys the variety in different scholars' and storytellers' treatments of the "The Transfer to Mecca." The quoted phrase appears on p. 63.
19. Brinner, *History* II, 72. Brinner, in a note on the same page, comments that the commentaries reveal a range of assumptions about chronology: that when Sarah demanded the expulsion of Hagar and Ishmael, Isaac had not yet been born (al-Kisai), that both sons of Abraham were alive when he took Hagar and Ishmael to Mecca for the building of the Ka'ba (as here, in al-Tabari), and that among differing accounts in al-Tha'labi, one notes that conflicts between the boys, a motif found in Jewish legends, as we saw earlier, led Sarah to demand the ouster.
20. Ibid.

21. Ibid., n. 204. Brinner notes that al-Tha'labi mentions only the piercing of Hagar's ear by Sarah—another tale of the origin of a culturally established practice. Stowasser, *Women*, 47, and 147, n. 55, comments upon the report in Ibn Kathir's *Qisas* I, 202 that in response to Sarah's vow to cut three of Hagar's limbs, Abraham urges the piercing of her ears and circumcision, and says: "This and similar traditions must be read as religious legitimization of female circumcision. The scripturalist context is important in that Abraham's circumcision, sign of God's covenant, plays a prominent role in the Islamic Hadith."
22. Brinner, *Lives*, 139.
23. Ibid.
24. Gordon D. Newby, *The Making of the Last Prophet*, 74. Newby's recovery of materials from Ibn Ishaq included interesting additional traditions concerning Abraham's two women. It was Hagar who roasted the calf served to the messengers visiting Abraham "to announce the glad tidings of Isaac and Jacob to him and to Sarah" (p. 7); she had been dead twenty years when Abraham "came from Armenia on Buraq, along with the Shechinah" to build the House, "and she was buried in al-Hijr" (p. 74). Sarah and Isaac are said to have made the pilgrimage from Syria, while Abraham, transported by Buraq, performed the Hajj annually (p. 76).
25. Newby, *Last Prophet*, 75.
26. Brinner, *History* II, 69. Ibn Kathir related that "Adam had previously pitched a tent [qubbah] over the spot, that Noah's Ark circumambulated it for about 40 days, but this is all based on reports from the Israelites," and cannot be verified, true or not. See Wheeler, *Prophets*, 101.
27. Brinner, *History* II., 70.
28. Ibid., 73, slightly altered.
29. Ibid., 76.
30. Ibid. In *Pirke de Rabbi Eliezer* 216 we learn of a rabbinic tale about Hagar's dress as she was expelled: "He sent her away with a bill of divorcement, and he took the veil, and he bound it around her waist, so that it should drag behind her to disclose (the fact) that she was a bondwoman."
31. Ibid., 74.
32. Ibid.
33. Brinner, *Lives*, 140.
34. Michael Wolfe, ed., *One Thousand Roads to Mecca*, xxii. See William A. Graham, "Islam in the Mirror of Ritual," 53–72 (quotations from 66, 68, 69) for an illuminating essay on how Islamic ritual is to be assessed as "commemorative."
35. See *PRE* 216, and Ginzberg, *Legends* V, 247, n. 216, where a passage in *Targum Yerushalmi* is cited that attributes Ishmael's fear in his dire circumstances that he and his mother were undergoing punishment for their idolatry.
36. Stowasser, *Women*, 44.
37. Brinner *History* II, 80.
38. Ibid., 80–81.
39. Firestone, *Journeys*, 135: "When all the traditions are collated we find a surprisingly close count. One hundred thirty authoritative statements consider Isaac to be the intended victim; one hundred thirty-three consider it to have been Ishmael."
40. Ibid., 135–137, which describe al-Tabari's exegetical answers to the issues raised by the "backers" of Ishmael.

41. See Ginzberg, *Legends* I, 278, and V, 250, n. 235.
42. Brinner, *History* II, 84–85.
43. Ibid., 92–93.
44. Ibid., 93.
45. The legend that the horns of the ram sacrificed in Ishmael's place could be seen in the Ka`ba is found, among other places, in the writings of al-Tabari. ("According to Ibn al-Muthanna—`Abd al-A`la—Dawud—`Amir: This verse, 'Then we ransomed him with a tremendous victim,' refers to Ishmael, and the two horns of the ram are hanging in the Ka`ba.'") See Brinner, *History* II, 87, and also al-Tha`labi's report in Brinner, *Lives*, 158.
46. Brinner, *Lives*, 164.
47. Rachel Milstein (Milstein, et al., *Stories*, 122) writes that this episode, "central as it is to Islamic theology and historiography, has not been popular in Islamic painting, probably because it does not contain an astounding miracle or a serious conflict between good and evil, and it lacks dramatic elements that would suggest pictorial narrative."
48. Our text bears a specific date: 18 Shawwal 984 (January 8, 1577).
49. A modern edition of the *Qisas* of Nisaburi (it should be noted that the same author Nisaburi is identified in Milstein, et al., *Stories*, as Ibrahim b. Khalaf al-Naysaburi) was produced in 1961 by Habib Yaghmai, who based its text on two of the work's earliest surviving manuscripts from the thirteenth and fourteenth centuries CE. Yaghmai declared Abu Ishaq Ibrahim Nisaburi's *Qisas* to be the most ancient and intriguing Persian rendition of the lives of the prophets, pointing to its inclusion of installments on Shith (Seth) and Ya`qub (Jacob) not found in the *Qisas* writings of al-Tha`labi and al-Kisa'i. Al-Nisaburi's text follows that of al-Tabari's *History*, or rather, that edition of al-Tabari made about forty years after his death by Bal`ami, who himself is said to have translated this work into Persian in 963 CE. Distinctive features of the *Qisas al-anbiya'* of Nisaburi include variations in the chronology of episodes in Moses's life, a series of accounts of lesser figures after the treatment of Jesus's/`Isa's life, and a very full narrative of Muhammad's story. A comparison of the text recounting the life of Abraham and his family in Yaghmai's edition with that of our sixteenth-century illuminated manuscript reveals that editors and copyists in the intervening three hundred years were faithful; only minor changes occur—usually in forms of altered wording and vocabulary, or the occasional deletion or addition of phrases. See Habib Yaghmai, ed., *Qesas-ol-Anbiya*.
50. While finishing these lines, which mark the end of this story concerning the establishment of the Ka`ba, the copyist apparently ran out of room and was prevented from adding the anticipated further words of the *labbayka*—"Here I am!" In this passage, the section that runs from "People! . . . forgive you" is in Arabic, rather than Persian, for a reason hard to uncover. It is not a quotation from the Qur'an, but may be an element preserved from a *hadith*.
51. Yaghmai, *Nisaburi*, 72–73.
52. Yaghmai, *Nisaburi*, 66.
53. Ibid., 72.
54. Ibid., 70.
55. Ibid., 72.
56. Ibid., 71.

PREVIEW, CHAPTERS 7–9

1. The phenomenon of the "narrative expansion," already mentioned several times, is described and extensively explored by James L. Kugel, *In Potiphar's House*, 6, and throughout.

2. Ambrose's *On Joseph* is presented as hagiography; see esp. 1.1–4.

CHAPTER 7

1. Nahum Sarna, *Understanding Genesis*, 227, writing about the ending of an era with the deaths of Joseph and his father, notes: "Both Jacob and Joseph die with the divine promise of redemption on their lips. The patriarchal period thus opens [in *Genesis* 12:2ff] and closes on the same note. The formative period in Israel's history is over and the real national drama is about to unfold."

2. James B. Pritchard, *Ancient Near Eastern Texts*, 23. Papyrus D'Orbiney, British Museum ms. 10183, is dated to around 1225 BCE.

3. Pritchard, *Ancient Near Eastern Texts*, 24. See, for example, Claus Westermann, *Genesis 37–50*, 64–65, with its summary of the tale from the thirteenth century BCE, and comments on some scholars' rejections of any connection or dependence of *Genesis* 39 with it, and on other scholars' varied understandings of how elements of "The Two Brothers" were adapted for this part of Joseph's story.

4. Sarna, *Understanding Genesis*, 217, suggests that the "Two Brothers" story was written for sheer entertainment, thus standing in contrast to the ways in which the narration of his encounter with his master's wife gives particular attention to "Joseph's reaction and upon the incident as a causative link in the chain of events leading to Joseph's subsequent rise to power, his reconciliation with his brothers and their settlement in Egypt." See also the comments of Victor P. Hamilton, *The Book of Genesis*, 472, who more sharply distances the two writings from one another, even while granting a limited parallelism.

5. Westermann, *Genesis 37–50*, 64–65. Westermann draws upon J. Skinner's running summary of the already abridged version of the story published in Pritchard, *Ancient Near Eastern Texts*, 23–25. The full text is given in M. Lichtheim, *Ancient Egyptian Literature*, 2:203–211.

6. Nahum Sarna, *The JPS Torah Commentary, Genesis*, 271.

7. Ibid.

8. Ibid.

9. Ibid., 273.

10. Ibid.

11. See Eric Lowenthal, *The Joseph Narrative in Genesis*, 34–35. Westermann, *Genesis 37–50*, 63–64, regards the phrase "but the food he ate" not as a euphemism for sex relations, but, following Ruppert, "as a fixed expression, a *pars pro toto*, to indicate his private affairs."

12. Hamilton, *Book of Genesis*, 461. Hamilton mentions the view, found in rabbinic texts we shall treat below, that Joseph's master's "food" is a euphemism referring to his wife.

13. Lowenthal, *Joseph Narrative*, 34.

14. Westermann, *Genesis 37–50*, 63–64, casts vv. 5–6a as a statement about the Lord's prospering [the term is *salah*] of Joseph that overflows in the form of blessing [*barak*] upon his master and all of his holdings, thus winning for Joseph his confidence; this attention of the Lord continues the effects of the Lord's presence with Joseph, accounting for his good appearance (akin to the same motif in relation to David in *1 Samuel* 16:18).

15. Hamilton, *Book of Genesis*, 462–463.

16. Ibid., 463. Hamilton notes that "Prov. 7:23 comes the closest—perhaps—to connecting adultery and the death penalty: 'he does not know that it will cost him his life.' In short, the sanctions are not historical but rational. Proverbs does not warn against adultery because God's Torah forbids it, but because the adulterer can expect that vengeance will be sought by the husband, leaving the adulterer in a disgraced, humiliated condition. Avoid adultery lest you arouse the passion of the husband." Do we hear both self-protective urgency *and* advocacy of behavior worthy of God's respect in Joseph's response to his eager and frustrated listener?

17. Lowenthal, *Joseph Narrative*, 37. See also Sarna, *Genesis*, 274, who notes in reference to the word "Hebrew" in the speech of Potiphar's wife: "there seems to be no doubt of a derogatory intent here. In contrast to her report to her husband (v. 17), the woman does not term Joseph a slave. She artfully knows how to adjust her language to the needs of the situation. In addressing her domestics, probably Egyptians, she appeals to their suspicion of foreigners and flatteringly employs the plural 'us' (contrast v. 17), as though to imply that Joseph is threatening their common values and that she and they have mutual interests to defend that erase differences in class and status."

18. The repetition, at this point, of the idea of having something "in (someone's) hand"—i.e., having responsibility for or power over it—is a sample of the narrator's art. The seductress holds power over Joseph's future, she believes, retaining his coat.

19. Lowenthal, *The Joseph Narrative*, 38.

20. Sarna, *Genesis*, 275–276.

21. Westermann, *Genesis 37–50*, 68. Lowenthal, *Joseph Narrative*, 38, mentions not only the correspondence of the two disrobings of Joseph, but proceeds to argue that the theme of Divine retribution is in play in these: "As Joseph had humiliated his brothers by wearing his 'coat' of distinction, so will he now be humiliated through a 'coat.' And as the brothers used his coat as circumstantial evidence for his death [to Jacob], so the woman is about to use it to 'prove' his crime."

22. Erich S. Gruen, *Heritage and Hellenism*. To those who know these splendid books by Kugel and Gruen, my indebtedness to their work will be quite apparent in the pages that follow.

23. *Talmud Tractate Yoma* 35b. Translated in Ben Zion Bokser, *The Talmud*, 103–104.

24. Jubilees 39.6–9. Translation (slightly adapted) is from R. H. Charles, *The Apocrypha and Pseudepigrapha of the Old Testament in English*, 70.

25. See the comments of Gruen, *Heritage and Hellenism*, 85.

26. *Genesis Rabbah* 86.3, 801. The bracket encloses the editors' explanatory footnote, # 4, on the page.

27. Ibid., 802. A critical note on this page comments, in reference to the quotation of *Ps.* 38.28, that the Masoretic text gives "saints" in the plural, and wonders if the text cited in the *GR* differed. I think it more likely that this was an adjustment made for the interpreter's/interpreters' purpose of linking the passage specifically to Joseph.

28. *Genesis Rabbah* 87.5, 810. The final bracketed comment is an explanatory gloss on the last sentence from Jacob Neusner, *The Components of the Rabbinic Documents IX*, 109.

29. *Genesis Rabbah* 87.6, 811.

30. Is it implied that Joseph shunned the performed dramas, avoiding their representation of deities at play—even "dallying" with each other?
31. *Genesis Rabbah* 87.7, 811–812. The graphic description of what befell Joseph at the moment of his attempted sex with Potiphar's wife seems to suggest either drastic clumsiness on his part, or perhaps a very premature ejaculation.
32. Kugel, *Potiphar's House*, 98.
33. Ibid., 21. Kugel cites this passage, *4 Maccabees* 2:1–4. The translation used here is that of Hugh Anderson, found in James Charlesworth, *The Old Testament Pseudepigrapha*, 2, 546. Anderson's introduction and critical translation of *4 Maccabees* appear in [531]–564. Attention to the thesis of this philosophical representation of the torture and deaths visited by Antiochus Epiphanes upon the martyrs occurs at 1.1–9, and is repeated. The Greek term translated as "rational faculty" is *logismos*, and *sophron* equals "temperate." *Hedupatheias* equals "sensuality" (or "licentiousness," in another translation).
34. This is the translation of Philo's title given in the volume to be quoted frequently below: F. H. Colson, *"On Joseph" in Philo*, 141. The Greek allows the alternative: "Life of a Politician."
35. Colson, *Philo* 6:160–161.
36. Colson, *Philo* 6:154–155. After recounting Joseph's betrayal by his brothers and Jacob's sorrowing at news of his son's death, Philo plainly states his own interpretive approach to biblical writings: "After this literal account of the story, it will be well to explain the underlying meaning, for broadly speaking, all or most of the law-book is an allegory."
37. Colson, *Philo* 6, 162–163.
38. Ibid.
39. Ibid., 6, 166–167.
40. Ibid., 6, 168–169.
41. Ibid.
42. Ibid., 6, 164–167.
43. Ibid., 11, 170–171.
44. Ibid., 12, 170–171.
45. Ibid., 14, 174–175.
46. Gruen, *Heritage*, 77.
47. Gruen, *Heritage*, 79 and Kugel, *Potiphar's House*, 98.
48. Gruen, *Heritage*, 109.
49. Herbert L. Kessler, "Vienna Genesis," 458.
50. Kurt Weitzmann, *Late Antique and Early Christian Book Illumination*, 83. See also Weitzmann's comments on Jewish commentary in relation to the two other "Vienna Genesis" Joseph-scenes: Plate 26, "Joseph's Departure," and Plate 27, "Joseph in Prison," 80, 85, respectively.
51. Ginzberg, *Legends*, vol. 2, 5, 44–59, 76, 126–127. In recent years, Ginzberg's enterprise has been joined by numerous others, as this chapter's text and notes make plain.
52. Kugel, *Potiphar's House*, 57. Kugel's acknowledgment of the dangers of speculating about the subjects and possible meanings of the nonbiblical elements of iconography in the Vienna Genesis is born of his consciousness of the work and different conclusions reached by other scholars. In this particular matter of the identification of the baby, it is instructive to see how others make the connection to Asenath, speculate about the role of exegesis in placing an astrologer (male or female?) on the scene, and address questions about the scenes in the

lower register of the this painting, page 31. See Michael Levin, "Some Jewish Sources for the Vienna Genesis," 241–244, and Kurt Schubert's comments in his "Jewish Traditions in Christian Painting Cycles," 225–227.

53. Joseph Gutmann, "Joseph Legends in the Vienna Genesis," 182–183.

54. Victor Aptowitzer, "Asenath, the Wife of Joseph," 257 and 257, n. 44.

55. Kugel, *Potiphar's House*, 57; See also Levin, "Jewish Sources," 244, who speculates that borrowing from classical representations may have influenced the composition of the scene in the lower register.

56. Schubert, "Jewish Traditions in Christian Painting Cycles," 230. The midrash tradition to which Schubert refers is the thirteenth-century rabbinical work *Midrash Gadol Genesis* (ed. Margulies), on *Genesis* 39:14.

57. Ibid.

58. Kugel, *Potiphar's House*, 64, n. 47.

59. Ginzberg, *Legends* 2, 57, 76.

60. Ibid., 57.

61. David H. Wright's sharp-edged cautionary comments in his review of Katrin Kogman-Appel's contribution "Bible Illustration and the Jewish Tradition" in John W. Williams, ed., *Imaging the Early Medieval Bible*, [61]–96, which appear in *The Medieval Review* 00.07.08, are these: "The search for comparable rabbinic details in Christian art has too often led to special pleading. Do we really need rabbinical learning to lead the painter of the Vienna Genesis to show Potiphar's wife in bed when trying to seduce Joseph? We must reject the infamous proposition that nothing is ever invented, but always derived from an earlier archetype; we must admit that coincidence is always possible, especially when common sense might suggest independent invention. We must also be a little cautious in interpreting minor details that have no labels; is the modestly draped and veiled woman outside Joseph's prison in the Vienna Genesis necessarily Potiphar's wife still trying to seduce him? Identifying such motifs has become a major industry, especially in Israel, but we still have no unquestionable instance of copying from an ancient illustrated Jewish manuscript."

62. *Testament of Joseph* 9.1. See Charleworth, ed., *The Old Testament Pseudepigrapha*, vol. 1, 821.

63. Kogman-Appel, Katrin, "Bible Illustration and the Jewish Tradition," [61]–96.

CHAPTER 8

1. *Clement of Alexandria, The Instructor* 3.11. Translation by A. Cleveland Coxe in ANF II, 297.

2. *Clement of Alex., Miscellanies* 7.11. Translation by A. Cleveland Coxe in ANF II, 540.

3. Ibid., 541 (Coxe's translation is altered slightly).

4. Ibid.

5. Origen, *Gen. Hom.* 15.2, translated by Heine, *Origen*, 204–205.

6. Eusebius of Caesarea, *Preparation for the Gospel* 7.8, translated by Edwin H. Gifford.

7. Ibid., 336.

8. Ibid.

9. Ibid.

10. Ibid.

11. Ibid., 204–205.

12. Ibid., 206.

13. Ibid., 207.
14. Ibid., 208.
15. Ibid.
16. Ibid., 209–210.
17. Jerome, *Dialogue against the Pelagians* 3.8. The controversy prompted by this late work of Jerome apparently led to eastern Pelagians wreaking havoc upon his Bethlehem monasteries. See the remarks in John N. Hritzu, *Saint Jerome*, 226–229.
18. John Chrysostom, *Homily 62*, Hill, *Chrysostom*, 211.
19. See the comments of Michael P. McHugh, *Saint Ambrose*, 4–5.
20. Ambrose, *On Joseph* 5.23, McHugh, *Saint Ambrose*, 204.
21. McHugh, *Saint Ambrose*, 204.
22. Ibid., 206.
23. Ibid., 207.
24. Again, Kugel, *Potiphar's House*, 98.
25. Ambrose, *On Joseph* 2.7–8, McHugh, *Ambrose*, 191–192.
26. Ambrose., *On Joseph* 3.14, McHugh, *Ambrose*, l96.
27. Ambrose, *On Joseph* 6.31, McHugh, *Ambrose*, 210.
28. Ibid.
29. Ambrose, *On Joseph* 10.56, McHugh, *Ambrose*, 222–227.
30. Ambrose, *On Joseph* 14.82, McHugh, *Ambrose*, 235.
31. *Epistle of Barnabas* 13. Translation in Francis X. Glimm, Joseph M.-F. Marique, and George G. Walsh, *The Apostolic Fathers*, 213. Cyprian, *To Quirinius* 1 ("Heads" 21). Elsewhere, Cyprian refers to the Joseph story in order to elaborate the dangers of envy (*Jealousy and Envy* 5), asserting that persecution has forever befallen the righteous (*Exhortation to Martyrdom, to Fortunatus* 9), and to use Joseph's forgiveness of his brothers as an example of patience (*The Good of Patience* 10). See these treatises in Roy J. Deferarri, tr., in *Saint Cyprian: Treatises*, FOC 36.
32. Epiphanius, *On the Twelve Gems* 11. Edited and translated by Robert P. Blake, *Epiphanius*, 161. Jews were not the only targets upon which Epiphanius could turn the Joseph story.
33. Epiphanius, *Panarion* 1.2.17.4–7. The translation is from Frank Williams, *The Panarion of Epiphanius of Salamis, Book 1*, 97–98. The "archon" is the demiurge—from the Barbelites' viewpoint, the Hebrew Bible's benighted creator God.
34. Augustine, *Expositions on the Psalms* (Ps. 80); see NPNF (First Series), vol. 4, 392.
35. Benedicta Ward, *The Sayings of the Fathers*, (Agathon 22), 23.
36. Ward, *Sayings* (Poemen 102), 181.
37. Ward, *Sayings* (Orsisius 1), 161. Joseph's courage in times of trial is often associated with the test met by the three Hebrews—Shadrach, Meshach, and Abednego—whom Nebuchadnezzar had cast into a fiery furnace (*Daniel* 3). See Chrysostom, *Homilies on Genesis*, Hill, 207–208, where the "three children on account of their virtue enjoyed grace from on high and were seen to prove superior to the fire," as did Joseph prove superior to the grasp of Potiphar's wife.
38. Ward, *Sayings* (John the Dwarf 20), *90*.
39. R. M. Price and John Binns, *Cyril of Scythopolis*, 265.
40. Jerome, *Ep.* 145; *Hymns on Paradise* 7.7, as translated by Sebastian Brock, *St. Ephrem the Syrian*, 121; Theodoret of Cyrus, *Ecclesiastical History* 21.25.

41. Theodoret of Cyrrhus, A *History of the Monks of Syria*, M. Price, tr., 202.

42. Paulinus, *Poem* 27; P. G. Walsh, tr., *The Poems of St. Paulinus of Nola*, 293.

43. The two ideas—virtue and its dangers—were easily linked by Ambrose: "what about the holy Joseph, and the chastity and justice he displayed? . . . As for his chastity—he rejected the seductive advances of his master's wife, and turned down all its rewards. As for his justice—he showed a contempt for death, banished his fears, and opted for a life in prison." Ambrose, *On Duties* 2.12.59. Translation is by Ivor J. Davidson, *Ambrose, De officiis*, vol. 1, 300–301.

44. Blake, *Epiphanius De Gemmis* 161.

45. See Deborah Mauskopf Deliyannis, *Ravenna in Late Antiquity*, especially ch. 6, "Ravenna's Early Byzantine Period, AD 540–600," 201–[276]. Also, her translation of the ninth-century history written by Agnellos, *The Book of the Pontiffs of the Church of Ravenna*, in which the rise to popularity and the accomplishments of Maximianus are chronicled.

46. Guiseppe Bovini, *Ravenna*, 201.

47. Otto G. von Simson, *Sacred Fortress*, 64.

48. Meyer Schapiro, "The Joseph Scenes on the Maximianus Throne in Ravenna," 35. (The piece first appeared in 1952 in *Gazette des Beaux Arts*, vol. XL, Series 6, 27–38.)

49. Bovini, *Ravenna*, 202, states that of the four "hands" detected as the carvers of the throne's ivories, "one of high artistic talents and possessing a marked feeling for plastic relief, must have done the ten plaques with episodes from the life of Joseph."

50. See and compare the identifications of the scenes in Volbach, *Early Christian Art*, 356, and Bovini, *Ravenna*, 205–206. On (8)—Bovini: "Joseph interrogates his brothers, who have come from Canaan, now in the throes of famine, to buy food. Joseph consents to their request but insists on holding the young Simeon as hostage." (42:18–26); Volbach: "Judah's entreaty to Joseph" (44:18ff.) that he not require that they return with Jacob's youngest son, Benjamin. Deliyannis, *Ravenna*, 216, describes the ivory's depiction as "Benjamin before Joseph," which is recorded in *Genesis* 43:15–34.

51. Bovini, *Ravenna*, 206.

52. John Beckwith, *Early Christian and Byzantine Art*, 116.

53. See Peter Brown's incisive account of the purposes of Ambrose in redoing Cicero's *De Officiis* in his *Through the Eye of the Needle*, 126–134.

54. Ambrose, *On Duties* 1.18.66, Davidson, *Ambrose*, vol. 1, 137.

55. Ambrose, *On Duties* 1.18.76, Davidson, 163.

56. Ambrose, *On Duties* 1.19.88, Davidson, 169.

57. Ambrose, *On Duties* 2.8.41, 54; Davidson, 291, 299, Not surprisingly, the section begins with Solomon's judgment concerning the two women's claims to be mother of a baby boy.

58. Ambrose, *On Duties* 3.6.39, Davidson, 379.

59. Bovini, *Ravenna*, 206.

60. Ambrose, *On Duties* 3.3.42, Davidson, 381.

61. Davidson, in the introduction of his translation of Ambrose, *De Officiis*, 91, comments: "The direction of fourth-century society was more and more being determined by episcopal power-brokers like Ambrose, who in many respects had emerged as a new class of imperial administrators, functioning as arbiters in civil disputes, counselors on practical affairs covering everything from marriage arrangements to financial dealings, intermediaries between government

and people, and spokesmen for whatever ad hoc range of interests might be perceived to be of value to their local churches' social cause."

62. Ambrose, *On Patriarchs* 11:54. Michael McHugh, tr., *Saint Ambrose, Seven Exegetical Works*, 271.

63. Ambrose, *On Duties* 1.24.112, Davidson, 183.

64. Schapiro, "Joseph Scenes on the Maximianus Throne," 37–38.

65. Note that Schapiro, 36–37, wondered whether "[in] his vision of the "saintly" Joseph as a perfect administrator and statesman, Ambrose was perhaps inspired by the treatise of Philo on Joseph."

66. Erich Gruen sharpened this point for me in a helpful discussion.

67. Gruen, *Heritage*, 108.

CHAPTER 9

1. Al-Nisaburi, the fourteenth-century Sufi writer producer of a text, *Stories of the Prophets*, gave the wife of the Aziz the name Zulaykha, indicating that she had earlier been called Ra'il. See Gayane Karen Merguerian and Afsaneh Najmabadi, "Zulaykha and Yusuf," 490, and n. 25; also Stowasser, *Women*, 52–56 and 194, n. 12.

2. Surah 12.1–3. On the important and perplexing questions of how Arabic terms referring to recitation, writing, and book should be understood, see Daniel A. Madigan, *The Qur'an's Self-Image*.

3. See Leah Kinberg, "Dreams and Sleep," in McAuliffe, ed., EQ I, 546–553. Kinberg notes that early Islamic traditions, a combination of *hadiths* and the opinions of the producers of *tafsir*, put the prophets' dreams (*ru'ya*) at the same level and authority as revelations to them. In Surah 12 the dreams attributed to Yusuf himself, and those brought to him, are symbolic in nature, requiring interpretation. Each is predictive of future happenings: Joseph's dominion over those in his family, the positive and negative fates of his two fellow prisoners, and Pharaoh's dreams of the healthy and unhealthy cows and stalks of corn. The thirteenth-century commentator Qurtubi contributed to evaluations of the power of dreams and interpretations (in relation to revelations—which did not continue after Muhammad's death). Kinberg describes his argument that dreams were "truth holders" in that they were akin to prophecies that were borne out in time. Qurtubi declared Yusuf to be "a prophet and the best dream-interpreter on earth" (Kinberg, 549).

4. Stowasser, *Women*, 51.

5. We met earlier, in chapter 7, Kugel's location of the background for several of the qur'anic elements in the Yusuf story—particularly the elaboration of the gathering of the women—in a Jewish text originating in Yemen, the *Midrash ha-Gadol*.

6. To Cleary's translation I have made an insertion noting that Yusuf is now speaking, after Zulaykha's admission of guilt.

7. Stowasser, *Women*, 52.

8. This "well known saying of the Prophet, recorded on the authority of Abu Huraira, by Bukhari and Muslim," is quoted in Asad, *Message of the Qur'an*, 340, in connection with 12:23.

9. Zamakhshari's view is paraphrased by Asad, *Message*, 340, n. 23.

10. Brinner, *Al-Tabari, History* 2.155.

11. Ibid., 155–156.

12. Ibid., 156.

13. Ibid.
14. Brinner, Al-Tha`labi, *Lives of the Prophets*, 200. See 3.1, n. 14.
15. Ibid., Al-Tha`labi, *Lives of the Prophets*, 198–199. See a version of this dialogue in Brinner, *Al-Tabari, History* 2.155.
16. Thackston, Al-Kisa'i, *Tales of the Prophets*, 175.
17. Brinner, Al-Tha`labi, *Lives of the Prophets*, 199.
18. Brinner, *Al-Tabari, History* 2, 159–160.
19. Ibid., 165.
20. Ibid.
21. Brinner, Al-Tha`labi, *Lives of the Prophets*, 199.
22. Ibid., 199–200. Al-Tha`labi records the same teaching again, this time from Gabriel, who represents the hand-biting Jacob: "Joseph, are you doing what fools do, you whom God destined to be one of the prophets?"
23. Ibid., 158.
24. Ibid., 157–158. One of these four infant witnesses, as we shall see in chapter 15, was `Isa/Jesus, making his declaration in another situation involving accusations of sexual misconduct. Tradition (the teaching with its *isnad* is included in al-Tabari's report, 158) held that the other two were the son of Mashatah, daughter of the Pharaoh, and a child who overturned his mother's charge that she was made pregnant by the revered hermit, Jurayj.
25. Ibid., 203: An intriguing comment about Yusuf's prison sentence—this one with a theological component—is attributed to al-Suddi: "So he [the Aziz] imprisoned him although he knew of his innocence, in order to avert suspicion of his wife. All this came about because God had devised Joseph's imprisonment so as to cleanse him from his desire and make him atone for his lapse." Here the fault of Joseph and its continuing taint is acknowledged and addressed.
26. Ibid., 202.
27. Merguerian and Najmabadi, "Zulaykha," 489, and 505, n. 24. The authors' first reference to "later commentaries" in which the idea of the women's spontaneous menstrual bleeding appears does not refer to modern writers; cited as a chief contributor to this interpretation is Al-Baydawi, a late thirteenth-century writer (whose works included a commentary on Surah 12).
28. Brinner, *Al-Tabari, History* 2, 167. While Asenath, daughter of Potiphera the Egyptian priest, is named as the mother of Manasseh and Ephraim in *Genesis* (46:20), here Zulaykha takes her place, certainly in the interest of this story-elaboration's focus on the "reunion" of Joseph with his former temptress.
29. The passage is cited (and translated) in Merguerian and Najmabadi, "Zulaykha," 496.
30. Ibid.
31. David Pendlebury, ed., tr. of *Yusuf and Zulaikha*, 14. Pendlebury renders Jami's verse in prose.
32. Pendlebury, *Yusuf and Zulaikha* by Jami, 15.
33. Ibid., 15.
34. Annemarie Schimmel, *My Soul Is a Woman*, 22. Schimmel writes (65): "Zulaikha thus becomes the woman-soul who lives out her life in harsh repentance and endless longing. 'If you are not Zulaikha and are not ground on the mill of love, do not waste time talking of Yusuf of Canaan' is the warning Sana`i, the mystic poet of Ghazna (d. 1131), gives. To his way of thinking, only the one acquainted with the pain of loving Yusuf has any right to speak of love. The poets know that 'love tore Zulaikha from the veil of chastity,' as Hafiz put it, and she became the

symbol for all who suffer the pangs of unrequitable love and longing. She thus
became the courageous, strong heroine willing to bear anything for the sake
of her Beloved." For Yusuf and Yulaykha themes elsewhere in the volume, see
also, 34–53 ("Women in Sufism"), 60–68 (in "Women in the Quran and in the
Tradition"), 107–117 ("Brides of God").

35. Pendlebury, *Yusuf and Zulaikha* by Jami, 82–83.
36. One meaning of "zone" is girdle or belt, stemming from the Greek word *zona*.
    Seventeenth-century poet Robert Herrick invoked this archaic sense in his "An
    Epithalamy to Sir Thomas Southwell And His Lady":

    > O Venus! thou to whom is known
    > The best way how to loose the zone
    > Of virgins, tell the maid
    > She need not be afraid,
    > And bid the youth apply
    > Close kisses if she cry

37. Ralph T. H. Griffith, tr., *Yusuf and Zulaikha*, 211–212.
38. See Stowasser, *Women*, 51. Again (and also just below) I use her rendering of
    Surah 12.24.
39. Pendlebury, *Yusuf and Zulaikha* by Jami, 129.
40. Ibid.
41. Ibid.
42. Ibid., 130.
43. Ibid., 128.
44. Schimmel, *My Soul Is a Woman*, 65.
45. One among hundreds of modern Muslim acknowledgments of Zulaykha as
    admirable lover and the beloved is found in a 2008 music video featuring the
    renowned singer Nashenas's melody "Tonight I Have Zulaykha." Excerpts from
    a film version of Zulaykha's "entire" life provide the visual effects. See www.you-
    tube.com/watch?v=rgcfNcpZVS4.
46. Stowasser, *Women*, 55–56: "It is noteworthy that Zulaykha's story is not a
    prominent feature in exhortations of contemporary Muslim literature on
    women. Certainly, the themes of 'women's cunning is enormous' and 'women
    are *fitna* [sources of social anarchy]' continue to echo in the contemporary con-
    servative insistence on, for example, the duties of veiling and segregation; but
    such is in general moral and legal terms without reference to the female pro-
    tagonist of the Joseph story with whom these themes appear in Qur'an and
    medieval Tafsir. . . . More important now may be [the story's] ongoing popular-
    ity in the contemporary pious storytelling traditions. . . . With contemporary
    Muslim audiences, the old themes of true love and deliverance continue to
    sound their echo as the star-crossed lovers live as symbols of human devotion
    and its reward. Not unlike Majnun in 'Majnun and Layla,' the woman Zulaykha
    in the popular tales of 'Joseph and Zulaykha' stands for the power of human
    love. This, however, can rob her story of the moralistic punch that contempo-
    rary Muslim preachers and writers would need to construct of this tale a warn-
    ing example of what happens to 'a cunning woman.'"
47. Annemarie Schimmel, *Mystical Dimensions of Islam*, 429, in Appendix 2, "The
    Feminine Element in Sufism," wrote: "The Sufis were well aware of the posi-
    tive aspects of womanhood. Some of the Koranic tales could serve as beautiful
    illustrations of the role of women in religious life. The most famous example

is that of Potiphar's wife as told in Sura 12. the woman completely lost in her love of Joseph is a fine symbol for the enrapturing power of love, expressed by the mystic in the contemplation of divine beauty revealed in human form. The ecstasy of love leads everyone who experiences it into the same state as the women at Zulaykha's table who cut their hands, rather than the fruit they hold, upon seeing the overwhelming beauty of her beloved. Thus, Zulaykha has become, in Sufi poetry, the symbol of the soul, purified by ceaseless longing in the path of poverty and love. Her story was given its classical poetic form by Mami; a very fine example in the Turkish-speaking world is the epic written by Hamdi (d. 1503), in which Zulaykha sings her longing in profoundly moving verses, having lost every trace of self-will in the hands of this primordial and eternal love."

PREVIEW, CHAPTERS 10–12

1. Ray Gambell and Sidney G. Brown, "James Bartley—A Modern Jonah or Joke?" appeared in *Investigations on Cetacea*, 325–337. The zoological category of *cetacea*, which includes whales, dolphins, and porpoises, draws its name from the Latin *cetus*, and the Greek *kêtos* ("whale"). I am indebted to Alan Baldridge, long of the faculty of Stanford University's Hopkins Marine Station, for this delightful reference.
2. Ibid., 330. Wilson's article "The Sign of the Prophet Jonah and its Modern Confirmations" appeared in the *Princeton Theological Review*, 630–642.
3. Ibid., 330.
4. Gambell and Brown, "James Bartley," 330, 327, resp.

CHAPTER 10

1. Uriel Simon, *Jonah*, v.
2. Jack M. Sasson, *Jonah*, 144–146, and 327–328, where Sasson comments provocatively about the too-unsubtle distinction between history and fiction in relation to ancient stories.
3. Ibid., 160–215, delves into all of these issues surrounding Jonah's "Canticle from the Depths," offering not only his critical judgments but also giving a comprehensive account of other scholars' views. See also Simon, *Jonah*, 15–24, and the penetrating approach to the psalm/prayer in Phyllis Trible, *Rhetorical Criticism*, 160–171.
4. Simon, *Jonah*, v. Compare Sasson's discrimination of separable elements in the four chapters in his *Jonah*, viii.
5. *Talmud Tractate Sanhedrin* 89b. See I. Epstein ed., *The Babylonian Talmud*, 593–594.
6. A related motif has Jonah sharply at odds with his Lord about what prophecy is, and how it functions. Jonah's complaint that God does *not* judge and punish the Ninevites as he, the prophet, had foretold, is in tension with a view of prophecy in which God maintains the power to effect change—in this case, to bring to repentance and reform a "great city." The latter understanding regards the prophets' words as divine tools or instruments, rather than (strictly) as predictions that providence *will* support.
7. Cited in Meir Zlotowitz and Nosson Scherman, *The Twelve Prophets*, xxiii.
8. D. R. A. Hare, *Lives of the Prophets*, chapter 10, 392–393. This piece of Jonah lore appears also in the later work, *PRE* (see Friedlander, *Pirke de Rabbi Eliezer*, 239–240).

9. The passage appears in Simon, *Jonah*, viii, and is part of the author's critical interrogation of the view that themes of "universalism vs. particularism" constitute the book's chief message, concluding at p. x: "Jonah does not symbolize Israel, and Nineveh does not symbolize the gentile world. What is more, the people of Israel and the kingdom of Assyria are not even mentioned in the book. Nineveh is described as a wicked city like Sodom, whose inhabitants deal unjustly with one another, and not as the capital of an empire enriched by plunder. The narrator makes no mention of its citizens' worship of idols, neither in the description of their sin nor in the account of their repentance."

10. Ibid.

11. Josephus, *Jewish Antiquities* 9.208–214; see Ralph Marcus, ed. and trans., *Josephus*, 109–113.

12. Louis H. Feldman's "Josephus' Interpretation of Jonah," 1–29, concludes with these words: "The biblical version [of Jonah] is more an unfulfilled prophecy than a book about a prophet, whereas Josephus' is about a prophet and, via Nahum, of a fulfilled prophecy. In an effort to appeal to his non-Jewish audience, he has emphasized the qualities of character of Jonah and muted the role of God. He has avoided taking responsibility for the central miracle of the book, the episode of Jonah in the big fish. Above all, in order not to offend his Roman hosts, who were very sensitive about proselytizing by Jews, he avoids subscribing to the biblical indications that the inhabitants of Nineveh had repented and had turned to Judaism, in whole or, at any rate, in part."

13. The phrase "three days and three nights" was not an exact measure, but an idiomatic expression connoting "for a while, but not too long." See Simon, *Jonah*, 19.

14. Uriel Simon writes: "Jonah does indeed sin, but his prayer from the belly of the fish is quite devoid of contrition, while his silence at the end of the book leaves the extent of his change outside the narrative." Simon, *Jonah*, viii (see also 15–25).

15. The passage is from L. Ginzberg, *Legends of the Jews* 4, 249–250, and represents what Ginzberg has joined and condensed from passages from *PRE* 10 and *Midrash Jonah* 96–97 in order to further elaborate the narrative. A parasang equals 5.6 kilometers, so the great fish's expectoration of Jonah projected him through the air over 4,800 kilometers.

16. The trigger for this version of what happened while Jonah was in the deep is the appearance of in the Hebrew text of chapter 2 of the word *dag* ("fish," masculine, at 2:1,11) and then its feminine form, *daga* (2:2). Believing that the slightest textual issues or irregularities are divine invitations to look more deeply between the lines, the rabbis have here generated *midrash*, fanciful as it may be, that helps to explain Jonah's turning back toward the God he wanted to escape.

17. *Zohar, Vayaquel* (*Exodus*) 199a. The translation, slightly revised, is from Maurice Simon and Paul Levertoff, *The Zohar*, 173.

18. Several allusions to resurrection occur in the *Zohar*: when Jonah was cast into the water, his soul departed and ascended to the throne of God, where it was judged and sent back to his body; as for the great fish, it died when Jonah entered it, but was revived three days later. In the succeeding section (199b) to what is quoted above, we read this vision: "That [day] will come to pass when the Angel of Death will depart from the world, as it is written: (*Isaiah* 25:8) 'He will destroy death forever, and the Lord God will wipe away tears from all faces; and the reproach of his people will he take away from off all the earth.' It is of that occasion that it is written: 'And the Lord spoke to the fish, and it vomited

out Jonah upon the dry land,' for as soon as that voice will resound among the graves they will all cast out the dead bodies that they contain. . . . The truth is that all the dead will be restored to their former state while in the graves, but some of them will rise and others not. Happy is the portion of Israel, of whom it is written: (*Isaiah* 27:19) 'My dead bodies shall rise.' Thus in the narrative of that fish we find words for the healing of the whole world. As soon as it swallowed Jonah it died, but after three days was restored to life and vomited him forth. In a similar way the Land of Israel will in the future first be stirred to new life, and afterwards 'the earth will cast forth the dead'" (Simon and Levertov, *Zohar*, 175–176.) On the *Zohar*'s resurrection teaching, see Ariyeh Wineman, *Mystic Tales from the Zohar*, 103–115, and especially the comments about the *Zohar*'s knowledge of *PRE*, 111–112.

19. Friedlander, *Pirke de Rabbi Eliezer*, xiii–lvii. For the convenience of those who wish to see what surrounds the texts being cited in *PRE*, page numbers in Friedlander's translation, rather than textual divisions, are given.

20. The "fifth day" motif recurs, for the Leviathan was presumed to have been among the "great sea monsters" formed on that day (*Genesis* 1:21).

21. Similarities between *Jonah* and *Job* are often noted—e.g., in Simon, *Jonah*, xix–xxi. Job's questioning of God far outweighs in number of verses and dramatic weight Jonah's angered complaint to God in 4:1–4. Jonah's audacity in arguing with God, though, is like Job's, and is similarly chastened and "put in place" by a teaching concerning that power and grandeur of the Lord, over against which all human accomplishments and claims must be weighed . . . and silenced. In this sense, Jonah's grievances are presented from the perspective of the Hebrew Bible's wisdom literature: God's superiority discloses human occupations as vanity—all for naught, arrogant and prideful. In the *PRE*'s presentation of Jonah, however, all of these connotations are trumped because the prophet is there a participant in his God's saving actions.

22. Though the Leviathan is seen as a good creature of the good God in *Psalm* 104:26, later tradition turned Leviathan into a malevolent and sinister monster. The conquest of the monster, often considered the work of Gabriel, here falls to the prophet.

23. See *Talmud Tractate Bavra Batra* 74b–75a for R. Johanan's teachings about the death of the Leviathan, the "banquet for the righteous," and the use of the monster's skin to adorn the tabernacle and the walls of Jerusalem.

24. Friedlander's translation has been slightly modified here, as elsewhere, to modernize its language and to turn certain phrases into sentences. The bracketed explanation of the "day of salvation" as the time of "Messianic judgment" is taken from n. 3 on Friedlander, *Pirke de Rabbi Eliezer*, 72.

25. Ginzburg, *Legends*, 5, 253. Having prophets ascend, rather than die, or be raised from the dead precisely in order that they may be present to play their parts in eschatological happenings is not unusual, as we shall see in Muslim teachings about the Day of Judgment in chapter 15.

26. Friedlander, *Pirke de Rabbi Eliezer*, 72–73, n. 12, tells of editions of the text which read: "They vowed and performed (it) that each one would bring his wife and all his household to the *fear* of the God of Jonah." Friedlander adds: "The 'Phoboumenoi' [those who fear] and 'Seboumenoi' [those who worship] correspond to these proselytes who fear God."

27. Friedlander, *Pirke de Rabbi Eliezer*, 342, n. 6: "The first editions read: 'and all who did *not* do these things.'"

28. Simon, *Jonah*, 19: "The designation [in 2:2] of the Lord as Jonah's God links this verse with the captain's speech (1:6) and with Jonah's own self-description as one who fears the Lord (1:9). This echo is probably intended to tell us that, when he prays, Jonah has at long last submitted to the authority of his God (cf. *Deuteronomy* 17:19). This expression also appears in the body of the psalm (v. 7), but there it expresses the intimacy of gratitude."

29. This summary of *Midrash Jonah* 2, a medieval work, comes from Ginzberg, *Legends* 5, 252. A later section in this *midrash* (34–35) features a lengthy prayer in which Jonah asks that his sins be forgiven (Ginzberg, *Legends* 6, 351, n. 37).

30. On the public recitation of the *haftarot* in early synagogue worship, see Michael Fishbane, *Haftarot*. The JPS Bible Commentary, xxiii–xxvi.

31. Fishbane, *Haftarot*, xxix.

32. See *Talmud Tractate Yoma* 85b: "Death and the Day of Atonement, if one is penitent, atone. Penitence atones for slight breaches of positive or negative commandments; for grave sins, it effects a suspension, till the Day of Atonement completes the atonement. To him who says: 'I will sin, repent, sin again, and repent again,' is not given the opportunity to repent. For him who thinks, 'I will sin; the Day of Atonement will atone for my sins,' the Day of Atonement does not atone. A sin towards God, the Day of Atonement atones for; but a sin towards his fellowman is not atoned for by the Day of Atonement so long as the wronged fellowman is not righted." Here the English translation is from Michael L. Rodkinson, tr., *Babylonian Talmud, Book 3: Tracts Pesachim, Yomah and Hagiga*, 132.

33. *Talmud Tractate Yoma* 87b. Relaxation of the rule is supported by *Jeremiah* 1:5, which tells of God's knowledge and care of children while still in the womb.

34. Ps.-Philo, *De Jona* 18–19. Folker Siegert, *Drei hellenistisch-jüdische Predigten*. The quotation is from Daniel Stökl Ben Ezra, *The Impact of Yom Kippur on Early Christianity*, 57. Folker's edition and translation is of an Armenian version of what was originally a Greek writing by a Hellenistic Jew sometime between the second and fourth centuries. I am grateful to my friend and colleague Stephen Hinton for his translation help with Siegert's German, here and below. See Adam Kamesar's fine review of Siegert's work in *Journal of Biblical Literature* 113.3 (Autumn, 1994), 527–529. See also Michael E. Stone, *Jewish Writings of the Second Temple Period*, 246, who notes that Ps.-Philo's "On Jonah" emphasizes God's compassion both for the Ninevites and for Jonah. Günter Stemberger criticizes the view that Ps.-Philo's *De Jona* was a Yom Kippur sermon in Alexander Deeg, et al., *Preaching in Judaism and Christianity*, 46–48.

35. We recall that the phrase belongs to the self-justifying Jonah ("This is why I fled to Tarshish at the beginning, for I knew that you were a gracious God") in *Jonah* 4:2, See also *Psalm* 103:8, *Exodus* 34:6, and *Psalm* 145:8.

36. See Trible, *Rhetorical Criticism*, 183–191. Throughout my survey of these verses in *Jonah* 3:8-4:3 and their employment of repentance language, I am much indebted to Trible's analyses in 180–205.

37. Trible, *Rhetorical Criticism*, 187–188.

38. Ps.-Philo, *De Jonah*, 18–19. The tension still exists in Pseudo-Philo's portrait of Jonah, however, since the ending of the episode quoted just above does not skirt the issue of his continuing resentment of God's actions, even his final accusation that God is too soft, too easily moved by human wailings and tears (Ps-Philo, *De Jonah*, 40–41).

39. The homilist's desire to depict a repentant Jonah stands on the early end of a centuries-long persistence in addressing the problem. Sasson, *Jonah*, 275, n. 9: "The Jewish Renaissance rabbi Sforno (sixteenth century CE) actually suggests that Jonah's prayer [of repentance] is lost. . . . [while] Calvin finds here a Jonah who, "carried away by a blind and vicious impulse, is nevertheless prepared to submit himself to God.""

40. Geoffrey Wigoder, ed., *The New Encyclopedia of Judaism*, 754–755: "Tashlikh: Ceremony performed on the first afternoon of Rosh Ha-Shanah (the New Year) unless it falls on a Saturday, in which case it is postponed to the next day. The ritual consists of going to a body of water and throwing a few crumbs of bread while reciting verses from the prophets Micah and Isaiah. The verse in *Micah* 7:19 reads, 'You will cast [*taschlikh*] all their sins into the depths of the sea': hence the name of the ceremony. The earliest reference to the custom is found in the fifteenth-century *Sefer ha-Maharil* by R. Jacob of Mölln of Germany. Although he forbade the use of breadcrumbs in the ceremony, his prohibition was not heeded." Abraham Millgram, *Jewish Worship*, 469, wrote: "The famous sixteenth century rabbi Moses Isserles gives this ceremony a highly rationalistic explanation. When the Jew goes for tashlik, he sees the waters and contemplates God, who created the mighty seas. These thoughts tend to awaken feelings of penitence, which lead to God's forgiveness of his sins. According to this interpretation it is the repentance that rids people of their sins; the casting of the sins into the depths of the sea is a mere dramatization of the central theme of the Rosh Hashanah service."

41. Again, an entry in Wigoder, *New Encyclopedia of Judaism*, 440–441, gives a succinct description of the rite, albeit in its more modern form: "Kapparot ('expiation'). The custom whereby, during the night or early morning of the day preceding the Day of Atonement, an adult Jew takes a live fowl (male for a man, female for a woman) and, holding it by the neck, swings it around his/her head three times, saying, "This is my atonement, this is my ransom, this is my substitute. This cock/hen shall meet its death but I shall enjoy a long and pleasant life.' The fowl is then slaughtered and either given to the poor directly or its monetary value donated to charity; the innards are thrown to the birds, also deemed an act of charity. The sins of the penitent person (an adult may also make separate expiation for his children) are thus symbolically transferred to the fowl, rescuing the individual from a possible negative judgment on the Day of Atonement. In modern times, 18 coins are often substituted for the fowl. Prior to the ceremony it is customary to recite verses from *Psalm* 107 (10, 14, 17–21) and *Job* 33 (23–24) which relate to God's readiness to forgive those who sit in gloom and darkness. The ceremony of *kapparot* is not mentioned in the *Talmud* and apparently originated in Babylonia in the geonic period (9th cent.)."

42. We note the grounds or assumptions upon which the art agency, Ward and Company, designated the Jonah scenes on this gem "early Christian": "The most popular of all narrative scenes in early Christian art was the story of Jonah, usually depicted as a compact cycle of episodes, which include Jonah cast from a ship to the waiting "great fish," who takes the form of the classical sea monster, or *ketos*; spit out by the *ketos*; and asleep under the gourds. The Old Testament story of Jonah was reinterpreted as a reference to Salvation, Baptism, and to the Resurrection of Jesus." The figure of a bull incised on the other side is explained as a first-century BCE carving—but one that did not hinder its later

redecoration for Christian use. This Jonah iconography is unusual in that it displays the full range of the most commonly represented moments—Jonah being cast from the ship toward the waiting great fish, his disgorgement (at the lower right), his greeting by an angel who offers him clothing, and his reclining under the gourd plant.

43. See Rachel Hachlili, "Synagogues in the Land of Israel," 120, pl. XIa, and for a photo of the Daniel found in En Samsun. See also Stephen Fine, *Art and Judaism in the Greco-Roman World*, 95, where the large carved stone is described as a "Torah Shrine base." Robert C. Gregg and Dan Urman, *Jews, Pagans, and Christians in the Golan Heights*, 103–106, presented a cautious identification of the image as Daniel and the lions, and also a reserved assessment of this artifact and its relation to a synagogue.

44. See the provocative article by Jessica Dello Russo, "The Monteverde Jewish Catacombs on the via Portuense," 1–37.

45. *Talmud Tractate Berakhot*, Gemara on IX, I (cited in Goodenough, *Jewish Symbols*, 2, 223). In the first-century CE writing which gained the title *3 Maccabees*, the priest Eleazar in his prayer (chapter 6) that God show his power again, as in the past—against the Pharaoh and Sennacherib—includes these examples of divine protection: "The three companions in Babylon who had voluntarily surrendered their lives to the flames so as not to serve vain things, you rescued unharmed, even to a hair, moistening the fiery furnace with dew and turning the flame against all their enemies. Daniel who through envious slanders was thrown down into the ground to lions as food for wild animals, you brought up to the light unharmed. And Jonah, wasting away in the belly of a huge, sea-born monster, you, Father, watched over and restored, unharmed, to all his family" (*3 Maccabees* 6:6–9).

46. See Robert Milburn, *Early Christian Art and Architecture*, 269. The so-called Boulonge dish, thought to date from the fourth century, was discovered in Homblières, France. On both the Boulonge glass dish, and the other found in Trier, each bearing the image of the *akedah*, a form of the prayer for life ("in God," or "forever") is inscribed, inspired by the miracle of God's intervention, and Isaac's deliverance. No writing appears in the Hermitage Museum's gold glass scene, the image of which is shown as plate 25 in Blank, *L'Art Byzantine*.

47. Jensen, *Understanding Early Christian Art*, 90: "Moses in the rock-striking scene was transformed into Peter, possibly inspired by a legend that told of Peter baptizing his Roman jailers with water that sprung forth when he struck the walls of his cell." Jensen cites C. O. Nordström, "The Water Miracles of Moses in Jewish Legend and Byzantine Art," an article reprinted in J. Gutmann, ed., *No Graven Images*, 277–308, and refers also to her own "Moses Imagery in Jewish and Christian Art," 395–398.

48. Spier, *Picturing the Bible,* 9. Spier has recently highlighted the correspondence between phrases in the Podgoritza Cup's inscriptions to language in the *ordo commendationis animae*, a fourth-century Christian prayer commending souls of the dead to God.

49. Ibid., 8–10. In *citing Talmud Tractate Ta`anith* 15a, Spier is referring to "remembrances" earlier than those contained in the Jewish text *"Prayer for the recommendation of the soul,"* which dates from the ninth century. See Jensen, *Understanding Early Christian Art*, 71. Levi, "Podgoritza Cup," 56, suggests that the origins of such prayers naming heroes can be found in *Psalm* 105, and in

1 *Maccabees.* 4:30 (where deeds of God through David, and then Jonathan are strung together).

CHAPTER 11

1. The image of the risen Christ, rather than Jonah and the whale, within the loop of the R appears in a sixteenth-century French text, a Gradual, as the Easter introit. It is held in the Denison Library of Scripps College, Claremont, CA., and is catalogued as Perkins 4, folio 78, recto.
2. See, for example, *Jeremiah* 2:20–23; 3:8–11; 5:7–9 and *Hosea* 4:12–15.
3. Obviously the writer is not concerned about the difference between the three complete days noted here and his own description of Jesus's being raised on the third day, "after the Sabbath, as the first day of the week was dawning" (*Matthew* 28:1). See John P. Meier, *Matthew*, 138.
4. The lives of all three actually bridged centuries: Tertullian, ca. 160–ca. 220; Origen, ca. 185–254; Aphrahat, ca. 270–ca. 345. Tertullian's writings, though, are thought to bridge the second and third centuries.
5. Tertullian, *On Prayer* 17. The translation, slightly altered, is from ANF vol. 3, 686.
6. Sebastian Brock, *The Syriac Fathers on Prayer and the Spiritual Life,* 12. Brock suggested (27, n. 7) that the idea of Gabriel playing this role derived from the biblical book of *Daniel,* where the archangel serves as interpreter of the prophet Daniel's visions (8:15–27), and then, as a divine intermediary when he speaks his prayers:

   > While I was uttering my prayer, the man Gabriel, whom I had seen earlier in a vision, came to me in swift flight at the time of the evening sacrifice. He came and said to me, "Daniel, I have now come out to give you wisdom and understanding. At the beginning of your supplications a word went out, and I have come to declare it, for you are greatly beloved" (*Daniel* 9:21–23).

   Aphrahat contributes to a tradition that closely associates Gabriel with Jonah, a theme we shall see below in considering Christian images of Jonah, and in the next chapter, where Muslim tradition steadily features the relationship between Yunus and Jibril.
7. Translations from Origen's *On Prayer (de Oratione)* are by Rowan Greer, ed. and tr., *Origen,* 107.
8. Ibid., 106–107.
9. Ibid., 108.
10. G. W. Butterworth, *Origen,* 263.
11. Rufinus of Aquileia (ca. 400) was an early proponent of this theory (later argued over because of it's notion of divine trickery). Alister McGrath, *The Christian Theology Reader,* 348, translates Rufinus's argument: "[The purpose of the incarnation] was that the divine virtue of the Son of God might be like a kind of hook hidden beneath the form of human flesh [. . .] and to lure on the prince of this world to a contest: that the Son might offer him his human flesh as a bait and that the divinity which lay underneath might catch him and hold him fast with its hook. [. . .] Then, just as a fish when it seizes a baited hook not only fails to drag off the bait but is itself dragged out of the water to serve as food for others; so he that had the power of death seized the body of Jesus in death, unaware of

the hook of divinity which lay hidden inside. Having swallowed it, he was immediately caught. The gates of hell were broken, and he was, as it were, drawn up from the pit, to become food for others."

12. Robin McGregor, tr., *Ancient Bible Commentaries in English: Jonah: Commentary by St. Jerome,* 7.

13. Cyril of Jerusalem, Catechetical *Lecture* 14.18, Edward H. Gifford, tr., *Cyril,* 99.

14. Henry Chadwick, tr., *Origen,* 440, 443. Because of his sense that Celsus's tract, *On True Doctrine,* written ca. 175 CE, continued to trouble Christians (and perhaps potential converts), one of Origen's sponsors, Ambrosius, convinced Origen to interrupt his work in composing biblical commentaries and to write a refutation of Celsus's views. Origen did so, some seventy-five years after Celsus's book was first in circulation. The result was a lengthy treatise which preserves some (how much, we cannot know) of Celsus's text.

15. Sister Wilfrid Parsons, tr., *Saint Augustine, Letters,* vol. 2, 170. The letter's title is: "One book in explanation of six questions raised by the pagans."

16. Ibid.

17. Ibid.

18. Ibid., 171.

19. Ibid., 171–172.

20. Ibid., 173.

21. Ibid., 174-177.

22. An excellent description of this context and its dynamics appears in Sidney Griffith, "Christianity in Edessa and the Syriac-Speaking World," 5–20.

23. See Kathleen McVey, "Ephrem," 427–428. On Ephrem's programmatic polemical references to the Jews, see the careful study by Christine Shepherdson, *Anti-Judaism and Christian Orthodoxy.*

24. Kathleen E. McVey, *Ephrem the Syrian,* 15.

25. A tenth-century icon at St. Catharine's Monastery at Mt. Sinai shows King Abgar with the image of Jesus, the *mandylion,* in his lap. See the image, and a succinct description of the history of this gift (which in the tradition takes different forms), in Robert S. Nelson and Kristen M. Collins, eds., in *Holy Image,* [134]–135. St. Thaddeus is pictured as having handed the object to Abgar, and four saints are pictured in two panels beneath the main scene: Paul of Thebes, Antony of Egypt, Basil of Caesarea, and Ephrem.

26. McVey, *Ephrem,* 261, n. 3.

27. Ibid., 40.

28. Ibid., 443.

29. Ibid., 453.

30. Ibid., 460.

31. Ibid., 457.

32. I should describe, if only parenthetically, a related but different form of this motif that occurs in one of Ephrem's *Nisibene Hymns.* Ambivalence about Jonah's character is absent from *Hymn* 55 in this collection, where the poet weaves together one of Jesus's more sensational healing miracles with events in the prophet's life. In *Mark* 5:1–20, Jesus encounters a man possessed with "an unclean spirit" who names himself "Legion," saying that there are many like him who are devil-tormented. Jesus's exorcism sends the man's evil spirit into a large herd of swine, who rush to the sea and drown. Following a refrain in Ephrem's hymn—"To You be glory, because the Evil One saw you and was troubled!"—Satan berates Jesus, complaining that he wasn't satisfied simply with

defeating Legion—the demons and devils—but was also redressing Satan's capture of Jonah son of Amittai.

"On Legion therefore He was avenging [Jonah] when he seized and cast him into the sea. Jonah emerged after three days and came up; but Legion stayed for a long time, for the depth of the sea closed upon him at the command" (Ephrem, *Nisibene Hymns* 13.3).

The translation is by John Gwynn in NPNF (second series) vol. 13, 193. Again, the evangelist Matthew's linkage of Jonah and the Son of man informs Ephrem's thinking: their being raised up after the three days and three nights is evidence of God's power to defeat death. Jonah's deliverance from the sea monster simultaneously signifies Jesus's resurrection.

33. See Sebastian Brock, *The Luminous Eye*, 20–21.
34. McVey, *Ephrem*, 444–445.
35. *Jeremiah* 4:4:

> "Circumcise yourselves to the Lord,
> remove the foreskins of your hearts,
> O people of Judah and inhabitants of Jerusalem
> or else my wrath will go forth like fire
> and burn with no one to quench it,
> because of the evil of your doings"
> (NRSV translation).

36. McVey, *Ephrem*, 454–455.
37. Ibid., 455.
38. Sebastian Brock, introduction and translation, *Saint Ephrem*, 26. Robert Murray, *Symbols of Church and Kingdom*, 15, writes of another's teaching about the practice of chastity, and draws out its implications: "Aphrahat himself refers to the possible choice of marrying 'before baptism,' though in the ethos of early Syriac Christianity it is not unlikely that there, as in the west, lay people often put off baptism till late in life for fear of falling from the ideal of chastity held up to them; earlier, they will have put it off till an age when *qaddisuta* (abstinence) became less difficult." In an accompanying note (note 5), Murray points to hints of resistance by people of more advanced years to taking the abstinence pledge: the fifth-century writer Isaac calls upon "older people" to repent and come to baptism.
39. Ibid., 450 (and n. 680).
40. *Hymn* 46.17 does not, as some have hoped, refer to nor correspond with the incident in the *Gospel of John*, 13:4–17, in which Jesus washes the apostles' feet. It seems to refer to some practice on behalf of special "saints" in the life of Syriac churches.
41. McVey, *Ephrem*, 450.
42. Ephrem notes dangers to virgins: *Hymn* 1.9: "If a robber seizes you and you are raped in the field/the unclean man's force will be persuasive evidence that you are chaste/just as Sarah in the bosom of Pharaoh was chaste/for she did not commit adultery by her own will;" 11: "Wine accomplished difficult things [when Noah's daughters caused his drunkenness] so that by it women stole conception./How much more will it accomplish this easy thing:/that men by it steal the signs of virginity./The girls pillaged the treasure of the old man [their father];/You keep your treasury from the young [men]./One drunk on wine is more tolerable than

one drunk on hateful love." And on a virgin's weakness in 3.15: "Will you lose your Betrothed and acquire instead of Him a false betrothed/that you may console yourself, saying, 'Even if I lost [one] still I found another.'/Because his love lies and is deceitful and dwells upon all,/he is not able to be your companion./ Then your remorse will increase" (McVey, *Ephrem*, 263, 265, 274, respectively).

43. McVey, *Ephrem*, 450.

44. Jensen, *Understanding*, 172. A similar observation is made by David Balch, "From Endymion in Roman *Domus* to Jonah in Christian Catacombs," [273], who specifies the frequency of *particular* scenes of Jonah in this time period: "Jonah-cast-into-the-sea appears 38 times, Jonah-and-the-*ketos* twenty-eight times, and Jonah-at-rest 42 times in various media, including mosaics, wall-paintings and sarcophagi."

45. Erich Dinkler, "Abbreviated Representations," 398.

46. For an interesting treatment of the Selene myth, see Michael Koortbojian, *Myth, Meaning, and Memory on Roman Sarcophagi*.

47. The range of opinion about the Christian adaptations of Endymion's pose to Christian Jonah representations is wide, indeed. See Grabar, *Christian Iconography*, 31–33, Jensen, *Understanding Early Christian Art*, 172–173, L. V. Rutgers, *Subterranean Rome*, 92–96, and Jas' Elsner, *Imperial Rome and Christian Triumph,* 152–156.

48. Tertullian, *On the Soul* 55 (trans. from ANF vol. 3, 231). This reference to the pagan notions of resting places occurs within a striking passage in which Tertullian, expanding upon Paul's vision (in *1 Thessalonians* 4:13–17) of Christ's coming on clouds at the end of the age to retrieve the dead and those still alive, challenges a popular view that upon being raised up to paradise, the saved will meet the already present "patriarchs and prophets . . . removed from Hades in the retinue of the Lord's resurrection." Tertullian argues that martyrs who have shed their blood as witnesses to Christ populate paradise. His proof-text is from the Latin martyrology of Perpetua, noting that "on the day of her passion, she saw only her fellow-martyrs there, in the revelation which she received of Paradise." Others awaited Christ's trumpet call on the Day of Resurrection.

49. The epitaph, dated to the second and third centuries, and found in Claudiopolis (Bithynia) appears as inscription #29, "Awaiting the Trumpet of God," in *New Documents Illustrating Early Christianity,* vol. 9, [102]–105. The fuller description of the volume is in S. R. Llewelyn, ed., *New Documents Illustrating Early Christianity*. This inscription's translator and commentator is J. W. Pryor. The "trumpet" refers to the phrase in *1 Thessalonians*, and the epitaph's concluding warning about not disturbing "the work [of God] the begetter" speaks of the creature—the entombed person—one made, or produced, by God.

50. In *John*, John the Baptist's reference to Jesus as "lamb of God" (Greek: *amnos tou Theou*) accompanies the Gospel writer's own descriptions of the Word or Jesus as "the one who comes from above" or "from heaven" (e.g., 3:31). In Latin translations the Baptist proclaims Jesus in these words: *Ecce agnus dei, ecce qui tollit peccatum mundi* (Vulgate, *John* 1.29). *1 Peter* 1:18–19 gives another New Testament elaboration on sacrifice, writing of the ransom from their ancestors' errant ways by means of "the precious blood of Christ, like that of a lamb without defect or blemish." The *Book of Revelation* also refers frequently to Christ as lamb, sometimes (especially at 12:8, 11) in terms of his/its sacrificial death.

51. Other notable examples of the image of the *agnus dei* are these: a sarcophagus in Ravenna's mausoleum for Galla Placidia (the lamb stands in front of
a cross), which is a sixth-century work, despite a traditional association of it
with Valentinian III (d. 445); the band of an apse mosaic in the church of Saints
Damian and Cosmas in Rome, where "he" stands upon a rock from which the four
rivers of paradise flow, encircled by the flock of the twelve apostles. The image of
the lamb standing on the rock from which the rivers issue, with the lambs encir-
cling him, must depend in some measure upon passages like *Revelation* 22:1 and
7:17 about the source of "living water," and 21:14, where a vision of the holy city
Jerusalem descending from heaven also describes the city walls' foundations,
on which appear "the twelve names of the apostles of the Lamb." Interestingly,
a canon (82) of the Council of Trullo in Constantinople in 692 CE called for the
discontinuation of using the image of the lamb to represent Christ, urging that
he be depicted in icons in his human form.
52. But recall the angel bringing clothing to naked Jonah, depicted on the carved
carnelian gem, in the preceding chapter.
53. See Volbach, *Early Christian Art*, plate 225; the angel (Gabriel?) stands behind
the Virgin's left shoulder, holding the orb. See also Weitzmann's comment on
the orb's decoration with a cross below, in n. 65.
54. See *1 Corinthians* 15:24–28.
55. I am grateful to Bissera Pentcheva for her counsel on this symbolism. For the
angel-held X-marked orb in a panel of a sixth-century ivory diptych depicting
Virgin and child, see Volbach, *Early Christian Art*, plate 225. An instructive
representation of Michael holding an orb (this one decorated with a cross)
is found in a thirteenth-century Christian ivory (two leaves of a triptych
survive); see Helen C. Evans and William D. Wixom, *The Glory of Byzantium*,
45–46, #12.
56. Again, the mosaics of Ravenna illuminate our subject: in the apse mosaic of San
Vitale, a theophany of Christ shows him seated on a blue orb; on one side an
angel presents the church to Ecclesius, the archbishop (521–532) who requested
the basilica's building, while on the other the angel receives from Christ, to be
given to the early martyr-saint of the city, Vitalis, the gold wreath, a crown of
glory of the kind that saints in Ravenna's art programs (see especially the two
baptisteries) carry in procession to Christ or to his throne.

CHAPTER 12

1. Thomas W. Arnold, *Painting in Islam*, 110.
2. See Sheila S. Blair, *A Compendium of Chronicles*, 86–87, figs. 52, 53. Blair juxta-
poses images of illuminations treating Jonah from the two Arabic fragments
of Rashid al-Din's history. One, showing Jonah being vomited forth from the
fish, is in the Khalili Collection (K 34, folio 299a), while the painting above is in
the collection of the Edinburgh University Library (E 25, folio 25b). Blair writes
(87): "This illustration apparently combines two moments in the text, the episode with the whale and the later moment of Jonah recovering his strength
beneath the gourd that God caused to grow to provide him with food and shelter. The whale, seen from a different angle than in the later illustration in the
history of the Jews, also swirls dramatically and has scales shaded with pink."
3. Andrew Rippin, *Muslims*, 25.

4. The renderings of *al-musabbihin*, "exalt" in our translation, vary: "extol God's limitless glory" (Muhammad Asad), "struggled hard" (Ahmed Ali), "glorified" (Marmaduke Pickthall).

5. Abdullah Usuf Ali, *The Meaning of the Holy Qur'an*, 1154.

6. Asad, *Message of the Qur'an*, 887, n. 27.

7. See the clear treatment of `ismah` in Shahab Ahmed, "Ibn Taymiyyah and the Satanic verses," *Studia Islamica*, 1998/2 (mars) 87, 70–71. In connection with his topic Ahmed comments: "With the spread of the concept that Muhammad constituted the model personality whose normative conduct (sunnah), as recorded in the Hadith, was to be imitated by every Muslim, the idea that he should not sin must have appeared both logical and persuasive" (70).

8. Gordon Newby, *The Making of the Last Prophet*, 1–28.

9. Ibid., 2.

10. Newby reconstructed this once-excised part of the work through retrieval of sayings of Ibn Ishaq preserved by other Muslim writers—dominantly, the exegetical and historical works of al-Tabari.

11. Ibid., 224. (This and the following translations of Ibn Ishaq, including the quotations of the Qur'an, are Newby's.)

12. Ibid., 225.

13. Ibid.

14. Ibid.

15. Ibid.

16. Ibid., 224–225.

17. See Gisela Webb, "Angel," 84–92, and especially 89–92.

18. Kathleen McVey, *Ephrem*, 439–440.

19. Brinner, *Al-Tha`labi*, [681].

20. In this section on al-Tha`labi's commentary, Brinner's translations of qur'anic passages are used.

21. Brinner, *Al-Tha`labi*, [681].

22. Ibid., 682.

23. Ibid., 682.

24. Ibid.

25. Ibid., 683.

26. Ibid.

27. Ibid., 684.

28. Ibid.

29. Ibid.

30. See A. J. Wensink, "`Ashura," 705. The Arabic term derives from the Hebrew word *asor*, which appears in *Leviticus* 16:29 in reference to the Day of Atonement. As a voluntary rather than obligatory fast day, `Ashura was (and is) honored by Sunni and Shia Muslims, the latter marking on that day the martyrdom of Husayn ibn Ali at Karbala in 680 CE.

31. Brinner, *Al-Tha`labi*, 684.

32. Ibid., 685.

33. Brinner, *Al-Tha`labi,* 685.

34. See Michael Schwarz, "The Letter of al-Hasan al-Basri," 15–30.

35. The Qur'an translation here is Schwarz's.

36. Again, the translation is by Schwarz.

37. Schwarz, "Letter of al-Hasan," 19.

38. Brinner, *Al-Tha`labi*, 685.
39. I owe much to Behnam Sadeghi in this summary of al-Hasan's viewpoint, and it is he who directed me to the splendid piece by Schwarz, "The Letter of al-Hasan al-Basri."
40. *Sahih Bukhari*, 4.55.627 (emphasis added).
41. Brinner, *Al-Tha`labi*, 686.
42. Brinner, *Al-Tha`labi*, 687.
43. Ibid.
44. Ibid., 688.
45. Wheeler M. Thackston, Jr., *Tales of the Prophets*, 322.
46. Al-Kisa`i, *Tales*, 322.
47. Ibid., 323.
48. Ibid., 324.
49. Ibid., 325.
50. See Al-Tabari, *History* II, 61–61, and *Genesis* 12:10–20 and ch. 20.
51. Al-Kisa`i, *Tales*, 326.
52. Wheeler, *Prophets*, 172. Emphasis added. The full name of the commentator was Abu al-Qasim Sulayman b. Ahmad b. Ayyub al-Tabarani.
53. For this, and for the translation of the Persian verses that follow, I am indebted to my colleague, Shahzad Bashir. See also the translation in Farhad and Bagci, *Falnama*, 278.
54. Shahzad Bashir pointed out to me that the two smaller texts in Arabic that run vertically on the outer edges of the bottom verse are interesting in themselves, since they give several names and titles of Ali, indicating a Shi'i affiliation of the calligrapher or his patron.
55. The translation of the *falnama* text is from Farhad and Bagci, *Falnama*, 278. The attribution of a forty-day fast to Daniel (in the Hebrew Bible—*Daniel* 10:2–3— the fast is of three weeks' duration) is a tradition probably influenced by Moses/ Musa's "forty days," and it obviously fits well with, and supports, the augur's primary reference here to the number of days Yunus was thought to have spent in the fish. The final phrase is, of course, the English translation of *Inshallah*.
56. The *Masnawi,* or *Masnavi* (both spellings appear here, in accordance with several translators' choices) was a work of Rumi's later years composed of poems giving voice to Sufi spiritual teachings.
57. Jawid Mojaddedi, tr., *Rumi*, 184.
58. Reynold Nicholson, *The Mathnawi of Rumi Jalálu'ddín Rúmí.* Nicholson's translation is altered slightly, and the pronouns modernized.
59. See Rachel Milstein et al., *Stories*, 140.
60. Annemarie Schimmel, *The Mystical Dimensions of Islam*, 218–219.
61. Shahzad Bashir, *Sufi Bodies*, 128.
62. Mirkhwand, or Mirkhond, was the name by which Muhammad bin Khavendshah bin Mahmud (1432–1498) was commonly known. His work, one of the great Persian histories, was composed in Hirat. See F. F. Arbuthnot, ed., and Edward Rehatsek, intro. and trans., *The Rauzat-Us-Safa*, x–xi.
63. Behnam Sadeghi identified for me the portion of Mirkhwand's text that frames the illumination. See Arbuthnot and Rehatsek, *Rauzat-Us-Safa* 1.2, 116–117, where this passage occurs. The scene described, though particular in its own details of what happened, is reminiscent of rabbinic *midrashim* reporting that men on the ship lowered Jonah over the side three times, to different depths,

to see if the raging waters would subside, before they despaired of saving him, whereupon he either jumped or was thrown into the sea.

64. Mirkhwand, *Rauzat-Us-Safa*, 1.2, 116.

PREVIEW, CHAPTERS 13–15

1. G. Langmuir, "Anti-Judaism as the Necessary Preparation for Anti-Semitism," *Viator* 2 (1971), 383.

CHAPTER 13

1. See Averil Cameron's admirable survey, "The Early Cult of the Virgin," and also Cyril Mango's "Constantinople as Theotokoupolis."

2. Germanus of Constantinople, *Dormition of the Holy Mother of God, Homily* I, 1.10, in Brian J. Daley, tr. and ed., *On the Dormition of Mary*, 163.

3. *John* 2:1–11, *Mark* 3:31–35 (and parallels, *Matthew* 12:46–50, *Luke* 8:19–21), and *John* 19:25–26, resp.

4. A concise review of various scholars' approaches to *Revelation* 12 can be found in Grant R. Osborne, *Revelation*, 454–507. For an excellent survey of the cautious, then enthused, treatment by early Christian writers of *Revelation* 12 as a Marian text, see Stephen Benko, *The Virgin Goddess*, 130–136.

5. John P. Meier, *Matthew*, 7. Meier's heading for his treatment of the nativity in *Matthew* 1:18–25 reads: "Jesus, Virginally Conceived Yet Son of David." Meier comments (9): the "main concern for [Matthew] at the end of the story is not the virginity of Mary, but the function of Joseph, who places Jesus in the Davidic line by adoption."

6. See Raymond Brown, *The Birth of the Messiah*, 92, and 116, n. 45, which notes that "Luke's Mary, who is betrothed to Joseph of the House of David (1:27) has a relative, Elizabeth, who is of the House of Levi, descended from Aaron (1:5, 36)." Often overlooked in the genealogy of *Luke*'s Gospel are the Levite tribe's names (Levi and Mattatha/Mattathias/Matthat) which occur frequently in a list of ancestors including people from David's line. *This* nativitiy story shows interest in revealing that Jesus stands in the tradition of priests as well as kings. See also the treatment of this theme in James D. Tabor, *The Jesus Dynasty*, 51–56.

7. *Mark* 1:9–11; *Matthew* 3:16–17; *Luke* 3:21–22, with only slight variations between them.

8. See Kurt Weitzmann, *Late Antique and Early Christian Book Illumination*, plate 38. (Mary in the company of Jesus followers at the ascension is seen on plate 36.)

9. The phrase comes from Nicholas Constas, *Proclus of Constantinople and the Cult of the Virgin in Late Antiquity*, 325. The title given to the text in the sixteenth century is misleading, as J. K. Elliott points out in *The Apocryphal New Testament*, [48]–49: "The title by which the book is now known originated with Postel's Latin translation *Protevangelion sive de natalibus Jesu Christi et epsius Matris virginis Mariae, sermo historicus divi Jacobi minoris* (Basle, 1552; Strasbourg, 1570) because he wished to imply that the contents of *PJ* were older than those in the canonical Gospels. The title in the Bodmer Papyrus V text is 'The Birth of Mary: Revelation of James.' The second half of the title is patently unsuitable, as *PJ* is in no sense apocalyptic. Even the first half is not entirely accurate because much more is related than Mary's birth. Variations of this title occur in other manuscripts. Origen refers to the book as 'that of James.'"

10. Ronald F. Hock, *The Infancy Gospels of James and Thomas*, 14–15.

11. Translations from the *PJ* are from Elliott, *Apocryphal New Testament*, Introduction and text from [46]–67.

12. Numerous examples from church paintings and mosaics, as well as icons, of the stand-alone scene depicting the embrace of Joachim and Anna are displayed in Jacqueline Lafontaine-Dosogne's *Iconographie de L'Enfance de la Vierge dans l'Empire Byzantine et en Occident*, vol. I, figures 14, 20, 31, 42, and vol. II, figure 1. In the narthex of the monastery church of Daphni a well-preserved eleventh- to twelfth-century mosaic portrays in a single image the two annunciations of the birth of a daughter to Anna and Joachim, shown in the settings described in the *PJ*, with Anna near a tree filled with birds, and Joachim in a place of isolation. In Istanbul's fourteenth-century Kariye Camii (Chora Church), one is able to see the two "moments" under discussion here quite close to each other: Joachim in the wilderness, being approached by the angel, and below and to the right, a mosaic portrait of the embrace of Mary's parents-to-be, reunited in the city.

13. *PJ* is engaging in narrative expansion, probably taking up an already confused reference in *Matthew* 23:35 to the death of a certain Zechariah, son of Barachia, whom, Jesus tells the scribes and Pharisees, "you murdered between the sanctuary and the altar." See Hock, *Infancy Gospels*, 73, 75, note on *PJ* 23.1–9.

14. In *Matthew* 1:19, Joseph does not address Mary, but resolves to divorce her.

15. In *PJ* 17:1–2 (Elliott, *Apocryphal New Testament*, 63) we learn of Joseph's quandary about how to enroll Mary: "Now there went out a decree from the king Augustus that all those in Bethlehem in Judaea should be enrolled (*Luke* 2:1; *Matthew* 2.1). And Joseph said, 'I shall enroll my sons, but what shall I do with this child? How shall I enroll her? As my wife? I am ashamed to do that. Or as my daughter? But all the children of Israel know that she is not my daughter. On this day of the Lord the Lord will do as he wills.'"

16. Elliott, *Apocryphal New Testament*, 51.

17. Elliott, *Apocryphal New Testament*, 93. In this narrative, Mary gives birth without assistance, and Jesus stands up, while angels sing "Glory to God in the highest, etc." (*Luke* 2:14). Elliott comments, in introducing *Pseudo-Matthew*, that it "used to be known as *Liber de Infantia* (sc. of both Mary and Jesus,) or the *Historia de Nativitate Mariae et de Infantia Salvatoris*. He continues: "It was very influential in the Middle Ages and was the main vehicle for popularizing *Protevangelium Jacobi* . . . and the Infancy Gospel of Thomas," 84.

18. Origen, *Comm. in Matth.* 9.2. Elliott, *Apocryphal New Testament*, 49, also calls attention to the earliest reference to *PJ* in the same work by Origen, at 10.17, and of his knowledge of the birth of Jesus in a cave (in *Against Celsus* 1.51.). Hock, *Infancy Gospels*, 11, points to the knowledge of the text by Origen's predecessor: "Clement of Alexandria (d. before 212) even more clearly [than Origen] knows this gospel, as he speaks of a midwife who attended Mary and proclaimed her to be a virgin (*Stromateis* 7.16.93), precisely what is said in the Infancy Gospel of James (19:16–18)."

19. Particularly interesting, in view of the criticisms *PJ* is answering, is the treatise penned in 383 CE by St. Jerome *Against Helvidius*. The controversy at hand was about marriage and how it ranked as a manner of Christian living in comparison with the vocation of voluntary virginity. The Christian teacher Helvidius's argument for the superiority of marriage was in large part built from elements within the New Testament birth and nativity stories, closely examined—e.g., his contention that the phrase in *Matthew* 1:18 that speaks of a time "before [Joseph's

and Mary's] living together" presumes that they later *did* "come together" (have a sexual relationship). Within this Christian debate, Jerome was an advocate for the view that Mary remained a virgin after Jesus's birth, and for what in this context was presented as a corollary preference for a Christian life of sexual continence over marriage. Many of his assertions follow from, or present alternative but similar, claims familiar to us from Mary's story as retold in *PJ*. Jesus's designation as "first born son" signified, in this case, *only* rather than *eldest*; Jesus's "brothers and sisters" were not the offspring of Joseph and Mary, but of Clopas and his wife Mary (who, according to *John* 19:25, accompanied Mary, Jesus's mother, and Mary Magdalene at the foot of the cross). But an unusual twist in Jerome's attack on Helvidius consists in his belief about Joseph—that he too practiced virginity, influenced by Mary, making himself worthy of the dignity of being called the Lord's father. See John R. Hritzu, tr., *Saint Jerome*, 20–23 (Jerome, *On The Perpetual Virginity of Mary. Against Helvidius* 6–8a).

20. Hock, *Infancy Gospels*, 18.
21. It is from the sermon in praise of the Virgin by Theoteknos that we have the phrase "great event"; other phrases descriptive of events at the end of Mary's earthly life abound—e.g., "this new wonder [worked by the Ascended Christ] in his Mother," "a new spectacle" (St. Andrew of Crete), and "O wonder truly above nature! O amazing event!" (John of Damascus).
22. Epiphanius, *Against Heresies* (*Panarion*) 7.23.9. See Stephen J. Shoemaker, *Ancient Traditions of the Virgin Mary's Dormition and Assumption*, 14.
23. John of Thessalonica, *The Dormition of Our Lady, the Mother of God and Ever-Virgin Mary* 3, in the translation by Daley, *Dormition*, 48–49.
24. Ibid., 49.
25. Ibid., 50.
26. Ibid., 51.
27. Ibid., 56–57.
28. Ibid., 62–63.
29. Ibid., 67.
30. Ibid.
31. Theoteknos's sermon makes use of more than one of the three distinguishable early dormition traditions which modern scholarship has identified and analyzed, so in that sense is "atypical" in its mixing and not matching. See Shoemaker, *Mary's Dormition and Assumption*, 65.
32. Theoteknos, *An Encomium on the Assumption of the Holy Mother of God*, 1, in Brian E. Daley, S. J., *On the Dormition of Mary: Early Patristic Homilies*, 71. Daley's translation is given here and in other excerpts of this work that follow.
33. Daley, *Dormition*, 13–14, summarizes what can be known of the Theoteknos's sermon for a Feast of the Dormition (which he dates to the early seventh century), and of his Palestinian diocese, Livias, which "disappears from the extant lists of Christian sees after the Muslim invasions of the 630s." Shoemaker, *Mary's Dormition and Assumption*, 65, dates the sermon to "around the turn of the seventh century, if not slightly earlier."
34. Daley, *Dormition*, 72.
35. Daley, *Dormition*, 73.
36. Daley, *Dormition*, 73.
37. Luigi Gambero, *Mary and the Fathers of the Church*, 397–398, points especially to Andrew of Crete, who, supported by *Psalm* 45:9 ("The queen stands at your right hand, arrayed in gold"), accords royal attributes to Mary in his Nativity and

Dormition homilies, calling her "Queen of the Human race," and saying of the Feast of the Nativity that it is "royal . . . a banquet of the Queen."

38. Daley, *Dormition*, 14.
39. Theoteknos, *Encomium* 4, Daley, *Dormition*, 73. Daley notes that the text is uncertain at the point which he translates "the soul of her whom he had made one body with divine grace." Some idea of Mary's being *united* with God's grace or blessing is intended.
40. Theoteknos, *Encomium* 6, Daley, *Dormition*, 76. A fascinating treatment of both literary and artistic representations of the legend of the Jews' disturbance of Mary's funeral—and of the plight of the man (Jephonias) whose arms were lopped off–is provided in ch. 9, "Counter-evidence: Mary and the Jews," of Peter Schäfer's *Mirror of His Beauty*, [172]–197.
41. Theoteknos, *Encomium* 6, Daley, *Dormition*, 75–76.
42. Daley, *Dormition*, 76.
43. Theoteknos, *Encomium* 7, Daley, *Dormition*, 76–77.
44. Theoteknos, *Encomium* 8, Daley, *Dormition*, 77–78.
45. Theoteknos has in his armory of proof-texts *Psalm* 71.6, *Psalm* 44:2, *Ezekiel* 44:10, *Daniel* 2:34, and *Habakkuk* 3:11. His typological reasoning is well displayed in his explanation of the last passage.
46. Theoteknos, *Encomium* 8, Daley, *Dormition*, 78. The explanation applies strictly to the last quotation, but its sense covers the former as well.
47. Theoteknos, *Encomium* 10, Daley, *Dormition*, 80.
48. John of Damascus, *On the Dormition I*, 13, Daley, *Dormition,* 198.
49. See Cameron, "Early Cult of the Virgin," 13, in reference to the final stanza of the hymn, which calls upon Mary in these phrases, among others: "O unshakable tower of the Church. . . . O impregnable wall of the kingdom . . . you, through whom trophies of victory are assured . . . you, through whom enemies are vanquished . . . you, who are the healing of my body . . . you, who are the salvation of my soul." The translation here is from Vasiliki Limberis, *Divine Heiress*, 158.
50. Averil Cameron, "Early Cult of the Virgin," 3.
51. See Annemarie Weyl Carr, "The Mother of God in Public," 325–337. Two major studies, with different and intriguing results, investigate the rise of the cult of Mary, including the role of the Akathistos Hymn, in the Byzantine capital. Vasiliki Limberis, *Divine Heiress*, highlights the elevation of Mary and her cult in Constantinople as "civil religion" through the strong agency of Pulcheria, daughter of the emperor Arcadius, and sister of Theodosius II. Iconography and ideology of both the regal Pulcheria and the city's protective goddesses were strong factors in the construction of the "divine heiress." Bissera V. Pentcheva, *Icons and Power*, argues that it was during the rule of Leo I in the latter half of the sixth century that the Theotokos cult greatly expanded, and only after iconoclasm, in the tenth century, and in the Isaurian and Macedonian dynasties, that public representation of Mary—e.g., processions of her image—became important in Constantinopolitan civic life. See also Averil Cameron, "The Theotokos in Sixth-Century Constantinople," 79–108.
52. See Antony Eastmond's fine description of this ivory (Catalogue no. 1), which he entitles "Plaque of the Adoration of the Magi and the Miracle of Salome," Maria Vassilaki, ed., *Mother of God*, 266. The object may have been one panel in a multipaneled piece. Its provenance is uncertain, though educated guesses include Syria, Constantinople, and Bethlehem. The breakage and damage (loss of two

crosses that once stood atop the columns supporting the arch, and chipped bottom) do little to distract from the excellent craftsmanship of the artist.

53. The linear representation of the magi approaching Mary and child (who look toward them) was displayed in Figure 8.2 in chapter 8. It is also familiar in sarcophagi—e.g., two in the Vatican and two at the Musée Réattu in Arles: Weitzmann, *Age of Spirituality* #375 (418–419), Fig. 53 (398), and Figs. 55–56 (400–401).

54. Eastmond, "Plaque of the Adoration of the Magi and the Miracle of Salome," in Maria Vassilaki, ed., *Mother of God*, 266.

55. Elliott, *Apocryphal New Testament*, 94.

56. Ibid., "And she went to the child with haste and worshipped him and touched the fringe of the clothes in which he was wrapped, and instantly her hand was cured. And going out she began to cry aloud and to tell the wonderful things she had seen and which she had suffered and how she had been cured, so that many believed through her preaching." The legend of Salome was more than four centuries old when the carver of the ivory placed it at the bottom of his plaque. Beginning sometime in the late fifth to early sixth centuries the story was pictured in a number of various other objects—e.g., in an ivory carving decorating the seat-back of the throne of Maximianus of Ravenna; in nearly exactly the same design, though smaller, on an ivory pyxis from sixth-century Syria; on a gold medallion, where the representation of Salome preparing to test Mary's virgin-status stands, like our ivory, in miniature beneath the main scene above, the annunciation by Gabriel to Mary (the text of *Luke* 1:30 is inscribed in a curve around the top of the disk); and in a textile from sixth- to eighth-century Coptic Egypt, which portrays Salome approaching Mary with her disproportionately large hand.

57. Eastmond, "Plaque of the Adoration of the Magi and the Miracle of Salome," 266.

58. George Galavaris, "Early Icons (from the 6th to the 11th Century)," 91–101, with plate on 140, #6. The piece is the center plaque of a tryptic, and measures 32.6 x 19.7 cm.

59. Eastmond, "Plaque of the Adoration of the Magi and the Miracle of Salome," 266: "However, soon after this ivory was carved Christian interest in the Nativity shifted. As the validity of Christian art came under pressure from Iconoclasts, theologians sought to promote the Nativity as evidence of the dual nature of Christ, of his incarnation as man. . . . Emphasis in the story and interpretation of the Nativity moved away from the fact of the virgin birth to that of the Incarnation of Christ as man. This was then used to support arguments in favor of the efficacy of painting images of Christ, since it was his human form that was being depicted. In this, Salome was transformed from the skeptical tester of the virginity of Mary to the devoted witness of the incarnation."

60. The translation is from Andrew Louth, *St. John of Damascus*, 29. The translation has been altered slightly in capitalizing "Fashioner" as did the translator of the following quotation. In this passage John proceeds to name many "material" things he bows down to, or honors: the wood of the cross, Golgotha, the tomb, the "all holy book of the Gospel" and the eucharistic table and its offering: "is not the body and blood of my Lord matter?"

61. John of Damascus, *Orthodox Faith* 3.12. Translation is from Frederic H. Chase, Jr., *Saint John of Damasus*, 295.

62. See n. 59 above.

63. In the late eleventh- to early twelfth-centuries mosaics of the monastery church of Daphne we find another splendid series of scenes from the life of Mary. See Henry Maguire, "The Cycle of Images in the Church," 147–150.

64. The icon shows in its color the effect of both some burning and later application of coating. In the Metropolitan Museum of Art's collection, it is described (catalogue # 101, "Icon with the Koimesis") by Charles T. Little in Helen C. Evans and William D. Wixom, eds., *The Glory of Byzantium*, 154–155.

65. Evans and Wixom, eds., *Glory of Byzantium*, 150 (catalogue # 95). The icon, housed in the Museum of Fine Arts in Houston (Laurence H. Favrot Bequest (71.6)) is in another way "tactile"—in its original imagery. As Annemarie Weyl Carr notes in her description of this ivory, "Peter bends over the bier from behind, laying his hand in a gesture of remarkable intimacy on the Virgin's womb beneath her prominent breasts, as if to recall the recurrent theological invocations of the Virgin as the womb that bore God. Paul too stretches his hands over the Virgin's body, for accounts of the Koimesis often quote him as exclaiming that in seeing the one who gave flesh to God, he had seen God's flesh, though he did not see Jesus himself."

66. Examples of the inscriptional formula ΘΕΟΤΟΚΕ ΒΟΗΘΕΙ (Mother of God, help) abound. For the three noted above, see Eunice Dauterman Maguire, Henry P. Maguire, and Maggie J. Duncan Flowers, *Art and Holy Powers in the Early Christian House*, 86, 97 (#33, Cone seal, eighth–tenth centuries); Evans and Wixom, eds., *The Glory of Byzantium*, 495–496 (#331, Plaque with the Virgin Hodegetria: description by Rebecca W. Corrie), and 176–177 (#130, Roundel with the Virgin Orans, described by Robert C. Ousterhout). Related blessings and amulet-like implorings of Mary, Theotokos, are found in Grabar, *Ampoules de Terre Sainte*, 33 (Pl. XXXI, a medallion decorated with an Annunciation scene, with inscription), in Vikan, "Byzantine Pilgrims' Art," in Safran, *Heaven on Earth*, 35–46, where the "help" plea is addressed to the Lord, and to the Cross, as it is elsewhere to Mary and to other saints. Also noteworthy are the two enameled finger rings in the Dumbarton Oaks collection, both with the formula ΘΕΟΤΟΚΕ ΒΟΗΘΙ on the band, and bearing the names of a prominent jurist and admiral of the eleventh and twelfth centuries (treated by Aimilia Yeroulanou, "The Mother of God in Jewelry," 233–234, who comments at the end of her entry that the jewelry she discusses, including the rings, "point to the conclusion that the intimate and personal nature of the relationship between the believer and the amulet-ornament is a special aspect of the veneration of the Theotokos. Even iconographic elements like the prayer and supplication of the Virgin, whose intervention was invoked by the faithful for man's salvation, and scenes such as the blessing of marriage and the Annunciation, clearly reveal the more human dimension of the Virgin and the hopes that were placed in her protection"). The abbreviated form of the phrase asking Mary's help appears also on numerous Byzantine coins, of which the gold Tetarteon of Nikephoros Phokas (963–969), and the Histamenon of John I Tsimiskes (969–976) are splendid examples, the first picturing the Virgin and Nikephoros as partners in ruling, and the second showing her crowning the emperor, the hand of God extending toward his cross-topped crown from above. See Vasso Penna, "The Mother of God on Coins and Lead Seals," 209–217, with these two coins described at 365–366 (#45b, #46b).

67. Daley, *Dormition*, 196.

CHAPTER 14

1. See Heinrich Laible, "Jesus Christ in the Talmud," 33–34. The translation is from Laible and Steane, but adapted. About the writing, *Kallah* ("Bride), see Günter Stemberger, *Introduction to the Talmud and Midrash*, 229, where the text is classified as an "extracanonical tractate" represented in the *Babylonian Talmud*. It treats "engagement, marriage and conjugal relations," and is in several other texts recommended as important for rabbinic scholarly study. The date is eighth century CE, if it is, as supposed, a work of Yehudah Gaon. Otherwise, it belongs generally to the early Gaonic period, ca. 620–800.

2. See E. P. Sanders, *The Historical Figure of Jesus*, 144–149.

3. John P. Meier, *Matthew*, 356–357, writes: "This story, unique to Mt, reflects the arguments over the resurrection which raged between Jews and Christians in the first century. Apparently the Jews explained the resurrection of Jesus by charging that the disciples had stolen Jesus's body from the tomb... . Mt's church—the core of the story probably existed before Mt—replied with a charge of its own: that Jewish and Roman military might have conspired to prevent any resurrection and *a fortiori*, any grave-robbery, but God's might defeated mens' arms by raising Jesus anyway. The story is therefore a product of Jewish polemics and Christian apologetics that should not be taken as an eyewitness report of what happened in A.D. 30."

4. Raymond E. Brown, *The Birth of the Messiah*, 142. See also pp. 526–527, in which Brown treats the possibility of "public knowledge of the early birth," with this result: "the opponents of Jesus would deem him illegitimate and Mary unfaithful... ."

5. Brown, *Birth*, 541–542. Yet another controverted text, *Mark* 6:3, is taken up by Brown on pp. 537–541. In most manuscripts of *Mark*, Jesus is identified (by people in Nazareth) as "the carpenter, the son of Mary," raising at least the possibility that this reference *not* to a father may be "an expression of contempt for him (and her)" (p. 539). That the phrasing is changed (or "corrected") in other Markan mss. ("the son of the carpenter and of Mary") and also elsewhere (*Matthew* 13:55: "the son of the carpenter"; *Luke* 4:22: "the son of Joseph"; *John* 6:42: "the son of Joseph") suggests that a concern exists either to deflect a slur on Mary and her son, or to clarify the *two* "parents" of Jesus, or both.

6. Brown, *Birth*, 542. About Mary's reputation Brown concludes that "we simply do not know whether the Jewish charge of illegitimacy, which appears clearly in the second century, had a source independent of the infancy narrative tradition."

7. Judith M. Lieu, *Image and Reality*, 104.

8. Lieu, *Image and Reality*, 148. Lieu has in mind Christian writings that have no interest in discussion, but only denunciation and damning—for example, the brand of anti-Jewish formulations found in Cyprian's *Testimonia* (or *Ad Quirinium*), written in 248. Flat and punitive declarations, bearing no sign of interest in "open" discourse, since the Jews' fate has been sealed, are given by Cyprian as "headings" in his three books—e.g., "That the Jews have fallen under the heavy wrath of God, because they have departed from the Lord, and have followed idols," "Also because they did not believe the prophets, and put them to death," "That the Jews could understand nothing of the Scriptures unless they first believed in Christ," "That two peoples were foretold, the elder and the younger; that is, the ancient people of the Jews, and the new one which should be [constituted] of us." See the translation by Ernest Wallis, "*Three Books of Testimonies Against the Jews*," 507–508 (for the statements quoted), and 507–557.

9. Justin, *Dialogue* 8, Falls, *Justin Martyr*, 161. Trypho refers to the current Roman government's intermittent persecutions of loyalists to Jesus—the purge to which Justin himself fell victim ca. 165, hence his honorific naming as "the martyr," or "witness." See the account of the trial and death of Justin and his companions in Herbert Musurillo, ed. and tr., *The Acts of the Christian Martyrs*, [42]–61.

10. Justin, *Dialogue*, 9, 11, Falls, *Justin Martyr*, 161, 165. The last of Justin's sentences quoted, with its assertion that Christians are now the covenant people, comes a bit later in the initial exchange between the two men.

11. Justin, *Dialogue* 67, Falls, *Justin Martyr*, 254

12. Justin, *Dialogue* 68, Falls, *Justin Martyr*, 256.

13. Justin, *Dialogue* 67, Falls, *Justin Martyr*, 254. See Justin's response in *Dialogue* 84, Falls, Justin Martyr, 282.

14. Justin, *Dialogue* 67, Falls, *Justin Martyr*, 254. We recall that the Septuagint (LXX) was, according to a favored tradition, a third-century BCE work sponsored by Ptolemy II Philadelphus which was given an accompanying myth of authority: seventy/LXX translators, working independently, produced identical translations from the Hebrew.

15. Lieu, *Image and Reality*, 127, comments: "Justin knows the Greek version of the scriptures used, probably not just from debates but from actually having had the opportunity to study them. While some of his difficulties seem to arise from the fact that this version [Trypho's] apparently was a more 'Hebraising' version compared with the Septuagintal texts which have come down to us, rather more [of Justin's difficulties] go back to discrepancies between the Christian collection of Testimonies [i.e., passages from the Tanakh/Hebrew Bible used as 'proof texts' to build and support Christian beliefs] from which he drew and the copies of the whole Bible, or of continuous biblical text."

16. See Marcel Simon, *Verus Israel*, 299. Also, 298–301, 498, n. 145, in regard to the new translations, particularly that of Apion, which (299) "by comparison with the Septuagint . . . reflects a manifest recoil from Hellenism," and Simon's suggestion that the condemnation of the Greek language at the time "is as much anti-Christian as it is anti-Greek."

17. Justin, *Dialogue* 71–74, 137, Falls, *Justin Martyr*, 262–267, 359–360.

18. See Frederick Field, *Origenis Hexaplorum* II, 463.

19. Justin, *Dialogue* 67, Falls, *Justin Martyr*, 254.

20. Justin, *Dialogue* 77, Falls, *Justin Martyr*, 270–271.

21. Lieu, *Image & Reality*, 124, writes: "Not all of this 'Jewish' exegesis [that Justin presents, or has Trypho present] can be authenticated, and some seems unlikely, but enough does have parallels that lead to the conviction that Justin did have immediate knowledge of postbiblical Judaism. Indeed, his setting of the exegesis in a polemical context may accurately reflect the origin of Jewish interpretations which now survive independently of this context. For example, the historicizing interpretation of the royal psalms, applying them in most cases to Hezekiah, *may have developed as a reaction against their messianic interpretation by Christians or others*" (emphasis added). Lieu's comment concludes with a parenthesis giving examples of these texts: *Psalm* 110.4, treated in *Dial.* 33, and also *Psalm* 24.10 ("Lift up your gates, O princes, and be lifted up, O eternal gates, that the king of glory may appear"), which Justin says Trypho and his fellow-Jews refer to Hezekiah, or to Solomon.

22. Several references to Hezekiah as the messiah appear in rabbinic writings, and are listed in Schäfer, *Mirror*, 212, n. 113. See the article "Hezekiah" by David A. Glatt-Gilad, 320–321.
23. Justin, *Dialogue* 17, Falls, *Justin Martyr*, 173.
24. Justin, *Dialogue* 108, Falls, *Justin Martyr*, 316.
25. Justin, *Dialogue* 108, Falls, *Justin Martyr*, 316.
26. Justin, *Dialogue* 16, Falls, *Justin Martyr*, 172.
27. Justin, *Dialogue* 137, Falls, *Justin Martyr*, 359.
28. Justin, *Dialogue* 96, Falls, *Justin Martyr*, 299–300. Cf. Justin, *First Apology* 31, in which his brief history of the Jews includes the charge that they, the Jews, counting Christians their enemies, have killed and persecuted them, just as now the Roman authorities do.
29. William Horbury, *Jews and Christians*, 108. See all of Horbury's chapter, "The Benediction of the *Minim*," 67–110.
30. The translation is from Stephen G. Wilson, *Related Strangers*, 185 (which is set within his careful assessment of "Jewish Reactions to Christianity," his chapter 6).
31. Justin, *Dialogue* 40, Falls, *Justin Martyr*, 208.
32. Justin, *Dialogue* 80, Falls, *Justin Martyr*, 275–276.
33. Origen, *Against Celsus* 5.25, Chadwick, *c. Celsum*, 283.
34. Origen, *Against Celsus* 5.42, 1.26–25, Chadwick, *c. Celsum*, 297, 26.
35. Origen, *Against Celsus* 3.5, Chadwick, *c. Celsum*, 131.
36. Origen, *Against Celsus* 1.39, Chadwick, *c. Celsum*, 37–38.
37. Origen, *Against Celsus* 1.39, Chadwick, *c. Celsum*, 37–38.
38. Origen, *Against Celsus* 2.32, Chadwick, *c. Celsum*, 93.
39. Origen, *Against Celsus* 1.28, Chadwick, *c. Celsum*, 28.
40. Origen, *Against Celsus* 1.32, Chadwick, *c. Celsum*, 31.
41. Chadwick, *c. Celsum*, 31, n. 3. Chadwick notes that the author of a 1917 article, L. Patterson, "thinks that some Jewish controversialist seized on the name perhaps because of its similarity to *parthenos*."
42. The translations here and of the next text, *Talmud Tractate Sanhedrin* 106a, are from Robert E. Van Voorst, *Jesus Outside the New Testament*, 109, 113. For a careful assessment of those Talmudic texts in which some scholars have seen references to Jesus, while others have not, and also for Van Voorst's interpretative comments on those in which he thinks reference to Jesus is assured, see pp. 104–122, his section on "The Rabbinic Tradition: Jesus the Magician and Deceiver." Provocative (and divergent) views of Talmudic references to Jesus and Mary, including analyses of the passage in question here, are found in Peter Schäfer, *Jesus in the Talmud*, [15]–24, and in Daniel Boyarin's review of Schäfer's book titled "Nostalgia for Christianity," 49–76.
43. The origin and association of the name ben Stada with Yeshu remains unclear, though the possibility has been advanced that such a person once identified with the spread of false teaching was "attached" to Jesus and charges against Jesus sometime before the time of this text, that is, in the late fifth to early sixth centuries.
44. According to Van Voorst, *Jesus Outside the New Testament*, 117, Ben Pantera "is a certain mention of Jesus by pseudonym in the *Talmud*." What about Pappos the son of Jehudah? His introduction as the husband of Miriam is creatively ironic, and humorous. Peter Schäfer writes: "That Poppos b. Yehuda is identified as the husband originates from another story in the Bavli, transmitted in the name of

R. Meir, that Pappos v. Yehuda, when he went out, used to lock his wife in their house—obviously because he had reason to doubt her fidelity (b Git 90a). This behavior on the part of Pappos b. Yehuda is quite drastically compared to that of a man who, if a fly falls in his cup, puts the cup aside and does not drink from it anymore—meaning that Pappos b. Yehuda not only locks away his wife so that she cannot go astray, but that he also refrains from intercourse with her because she has become doubtful [i.e., not trustworthy]."

45. Daniel Boyarin, "Nostalgia for Christianity," 66.
46. Van Voorst, *Jesus Outside the New Testament*, 113.
47. Van Voorst, *Jesus Outside the New Testament*, 134.
48. See Morris Goldstein, *Jesus in the Jewish Tradition*, 148–154, for his English translation of *Toledoth Yeshu*. Goldstein's translation is used here. See, now, the studies of *TY* gathered in Peter Schäfer, Michael Meerson, Yaacov Deutsch, eds., *Toledot Yeshu* ("The Life Story of Jesus") Revisited.
49. Goldstein, *Jesus*, 149ff. (where the text's date 3671 is transposed to 90 BCE) and 302, n. 41, referring to Tanhuma. Shimeon ben Shetah, another figure referred to in the work, lived in the second and first century BCE. Recall the placement of an out-of-century Poppos ben Jehuda, "a Palestinian scholar (not portrayed as a sage and without the title 'Rabbi') of the first half of the second century C.E." in b Shab 104b's reference to Jesus's days, as noted in Schäfer, *Jesus in the Talmud*, 16.
50. Goldstein, *Jesus*, 165; David Biale, "Counter-History and Jewish Polemics Against Christianity," 130–137; Van Voorst, *Jesus Outside the New Testament*, 133–134; Schäfer, *Mirror*, 209–212.
51. Goldstein, *Jesus*, 147, 162–163.
52. Biale, "Counter-History," 130–145, gracefully but forcefully re-examines Amos Funkenstein's description of the workings of counter-history on the way to his own assessment of the two works with which we conclude our survey of Jewish anti-Christian traditions, this and *Sefer Zerubbabel*.
53. Goldstein, *Jesus*, 148–49.
54. Ibid., 149.
55. Ibid., 149.
56. Ibid., 149–150.
57. Ibid., 150. (Goldstein has for good reasons translated *almah* in the seventeenth-century Wagenseil Hebrew/Aramaic text of *TY* as "virgin.")
58. Biale comments, in "Counter-History," 135: "There are no Romans in the Sefer toldot yeshu; Pilate is replaced by a Jewish queen, named Helene, who converted to Judaism but was attracted to Christianity, a figure Krauss showed to be an amalgam of the wife of the Hasmonean Alexander Yannai, Salome, who was also known as Helene, the proselyte Helene of Adiabene and the mother of Constantine. There is no trial in front of the high priest but instead a hearing in front of the queen with the rabbis leading the attack against Jesus."
59. *Zechariah* 9:9; see *John* 12:15, and *Matthew* 21:5.
60. Goldstein, *Jesus*, 150–151.
61. Ibid., 151.
62. Ibid. Jesus fashions twelve sparrows from clay and has them fly away chirping in the *Infancy Gospel of Thomas* 2:1–4; Elliott, *The Apocryphal New Testament*, 75–76.
63. Goldstein, *Jesus*, 151.
64. Ibid., 151–152.

65. Biale, "Counter-History," 133–134, comments: "When he [Yeshu] sees that he is surrounded, he announces that he wants to go up to his father in heaven, and employing the divine name, takes off in flight, reminiscent of the aeronautical tricks of Simon Magus. Judah lifts off after him and, in a dramatic aerial combat, brings Jesus crashing down to earth by ejaculating on him, thus rendering him and the magical name of God impure. Some of the versions more prudishly have Judah urinate on Jesus, but urine does not cause cultic impurity."

66. See Biale, "Counter-History," 134. Simon Magus's flight, and his collapse to the earth, at Peter's bidding of God, is found in *The Acts of Peter* 32. See Elliott, *The Apocryphal New Testament*, 422–423: [Peter, under pressure to perform a miracle as grand as Simon Magus's flying, (believers in the great crowd in Rome look toward him) prays:] "'Make haste, O Lord, show your mercy and let him fall down and become crippled but not die; let him be disabled and break his leg in three places.' And he fell down and broke his leg in three places. And they cast stones on him, and each went to his home having faith in Peter. . . . And Simon, being in misery, found some helpers who carried him by night on a stretcher from Rome to Aricia. There he remained and stayed with a man named Castor who on account of sorcery had been driven from Rome to Terracina. Following an operation Simon, the messenger of the devil, ended his life."

67. I am indebted to Charlotte Fonrobert for the insight that the two stories have significant themes in common. For a splendid treatment of the story of Rabbi Nehuniah, see Lawrence H. Schiffman, "The Recall of Rabbi Nehuniah ben Ha-Qanah from Ecstasy in the *Hekhalot Rabbati*," 269–281.

68. I owe also to Charlotte Fonrobert the observation of the connections that link the journeys of Nehuniah, the purity requirements of the Temple, and the impurity which tumbles Yeshu and Iscarioto from the skies. See Michael D. Swartz, "Jewish Visionary Tradition in Rabbinic Literature," 198–221.

69. John Wilkinson, *Egeria's Travels*, 153.

70. Even though the New Testament Gospels do not specifically mention it (*John* 19:1 and *Mark* 14:65 may, however, presume its existence), and vary in their reports of the flogging, the pillar or column believed to have been the place of Jesus's flagellation by Roman soldiers was well-known to Christian pilgrims. Paula, whose pious travels in the late fourth century Jerome recounts, "was shown [in Jerusalem] the pillar . . . stained with the Lord's blood," and a certain Theodosius, writing in the sixth century, tells of seeing the column in the Church of Holy Sion: "it has on it a miraculous mark. When he [Jesus] clasped it, his chest clove to the stone, and you can see the marks of both his hands, his fingers and his palms. They are so clear that you can use them to take "measures" for any kinds of disease, and people can wear them round their neck and be cured." See Wilkinson, *Jerusalem Pilgrims Before the Crusades*, 49, 84, for the texts quoted. (Wilkinson, *Pilgrims*, 84, n. 33, points to a passage from Gregory of Tours to illuminate what the measures most likely were: "Gregory of Tours, writing in 585 A.D. (1.7–712) says that many people 'go to the column (of scourging), make ribbons of cloth and put them around it' . . . They take them away as 'blessings to help them in sicknesses.'")

71. See Gustaf Dalman, *Jesus Christ in the Talmud*, 71–79.

72. Goldstein, *Jesus*, 152–153. The relevant biblical passages are *Deuteronomy* 22:23; 27:15–26; 28:15–28.

73. Ibid., 153.

Notes (659)

74. Ibid.
75. Biale, "Counter-History," 136: "The Sefer toldot yeshu does not turn the son of God into the son of Satan, as we might expect from a counter-history, but rather into an audacious trickster operating within the rabbinic elite."
76. Ibid., 134–135.
77. Martha Himmelfarb, "Sefer Zerubbabel," 71. Himmelfarb's English translation is used in what follows, and her introduction, 67–70, informs comments made below about the dating of *Sefer Zerrubabel* and some of its main themes. In seeking to understand why this text gives such prominent attention to the messiah's mother (a novelty in Jewish messianic thinking), and what understanding of Mary, as statue, is being put forward, I, like others, am indebted to Himmelfarb's fine interpretive comments regarding *SZ* in her "The Mother of the Messiah in the Talmud Yerushalmi and Sefer Zerubbabel," [368]–389.
78. Ibid., 72.
79. Ibid., 79. The theme of exiles restored, with the question "Who bore us these?" is drawn (and then adapted) from *Isaiah* 49:14–21, in which Zion's lamentation that God has forsaken and forgotten her is refuted: "The children born you thought you had lost shall yet say in your hearing, 'The place is too crowded for me; make room for me to settle.' And you will say to yourself, 'Who bore these for me when I was bereaved and barren, exiled and disdained—by whom, then, were these reared? I was left all alone—and where have these been?'" On the correspondence between *SZ*'s projections for the future and those Jewish hopes described by the Christian theologian and biblical exegete Jerome in several of his writings, see Robert L. Wilken, "The Restoration of Israel in Biblical Prophecy," 455–457.
80. Himmelfarb, "Sefer Zerubbabel," 71.
81. Ibid., 78. The anonymous *Chronicon Paschale* preserves a copy of the "memorandum" in which "Shiroi" (or Shiroe, or Kavadh II Seroe) acknowledged Persia's defeat by Heraclius, addressing him as "Heraclius, our most pious and god-protected emperor. . . . the most clement emperor of the Romans, our brother" while also declaring his intention "to live in peace and love with you, the emperor of the Romans, our brother, and the Roman state and the other nations and other princes around us." See Michael Whitby and Mary Whitby, trans. with notes and introduction, *Chronicon Paschale 248–628 AD*, 188; also, the text, with brief historical contextualization, in Dignas and Winter, *Rome and Persia*, 148–151.
82. Himmelfarb, "Sefer Zerubbabel," 80.
83. See Jan Willem Drijvers, "Heraclius and the *Restitutio Crucis*: Notes on Symbolism and Ideology," 176–177: "The Byzantine defeat by the Persians [i.e., at Jerusalem] could not have been better expressed than by the removal of the Cross, which had given Byzantine emperors since Constantine the Great so many victories over their enemies, [and] was for Christians in the Mediterranean world and beyond the ultimate Christian symbol, and had given Jerusalem its special status as the unique city of Christendom. While the Christians lamented, the Jews rejoiced. The latter had, if we believe the Christian sources, supported the Persians in their conquest of Palestine and its major cities, including Jerusalem. The details about the taking of Jerusalem are obscure and the (Christian) sources are biased and contradictory, but it does seem that the Jews played a role in its capture. They may even have ruled, or at least had dominance over, Jerusalem for some years, and attempted to

transform it into a Jewish city again. Furthermore, the Jews may have made efforts to resume the Temple services. However, this was temporary and by 617 the Persians seem to have returned the city to the Christians, then led by Modestus, replacing the patriarch Zachariah who had been exiled to Persia. Modestus began restoring the demolished churches and it seems that the life of the Christian community gradually went back to normal."

84. See Himmelfarb, "Sefer Zerubbabel," 67, and "The Mother of the Messiah," 383.

85. Himmelfarb, "Sefer Zerubbabel," 80–81.

86. Mary Whitby points to the extent of Christians' glorification of Heraclius as the God-blessed conqueror of the Persians. A piece of writing done by his "personal spin-doctor, the Poet George of Pisidia, celebrated the beginning of a new cosmic era of peace. A fragment from his poetry, embedded in the chronicle of Theophanes, celebrates Heraclius's return to Constantinople after campaigning in the East in terms of the biblical Creation story: 'Now the emperor, having defeated Persia in the course of six years, made peace in the seventh and returned with great joy to Constantinople, thereby fulfilling a certain mystical allegory: for God completed all of Creation in six days and called the seventh a day of rest. So the emperor also, after undergoing many toils for six years, returned to the City amid peace and joy and took his rest.'" Mary Whitby, "The Biblical Past in John Malalas and the *Paschal Chronicle*," 292–293 (with translation of Theophanes AM 6119 by Cyril Mango and Roger Scott, *The Chronicle of Theophanes Confessor*, 457).

87. Himmelfarb, "Sefer Zerubbabel," 73.

88. Ibid., 74–75.

89. Ibid., 80.

90. Himmelfarb, "The Mother of the Messiah," 384: "Hephzibah appears to be the Jewish answer to the new role the Virgin Mary had come to play in the Byzantine empire. As early as 586 the general Philippikos used an image of Christ to encourage his troops in the battle of the Arzamon River. Not long after the Virgin Mary started to appear alongside her son as protector and rallying point in battle. In 610 Heraklios used images of the Virgin in his naval campaigns as he attempted, successfully, to wrest the empire from his predecessor Phokas. During Heraklios' reign, when the Avars besieged Constantinople in 626, the patriarch Sergios had pictures of the Virgin and Christ child painted on the gates of the west side of the city. When the Arabs besieged Constantinople in 717, a procession circled the walls of the city with an image of the Virgin and relics of the 'true cross.'" Himmelfarb notes that earlier works by Lévi (1920) and Kitzinger (1954) cited these incidents.

91. Bissera V. Pentcheva, *Icons and Power*, [60]–103.

92. See the comments in Himmelfarb, "Sefer Zerubbabel," 83, n. 29. and also Biale, "Counter-History," 139, where he adds the comment that "the midrashic topos [that places a suffering Messiah "waiting like a beggar a the gates of Rome"] is sharpened: the suffering Messiah [Menahem] is imprisoned in a Christian Church!"

93. This ivory was created in Aachen sometime between 800–825. In the Metropolitan Museum's description of the piece, we read: "The spindles in Mary's left hand often appear in depictions of the Annunciation, as she receives the news that she is to be the mother of Jesus. The military appearance of her dress and the cross-topped scepter she holds suggest that she could also have been understood here to represent the triumph of the Church."

94. Biale, "Counter-History," 139, comments that "the rabbis believed [Aaron's staff] would become the Messiah's scepter," and we note that in the text Hephzibah puts it in the hand of Nehemiah ben Hushiel.

95. Ibid., 139. Biale points to the influence of the combined figures of Deborah and Yael, who wage war and kill the enemy (*Judges* 4 and 5), in the *SZ*'s creation of Hephzibah.

96. *Panqita* 45. See Whitby, "The Biblical Past in John Malalas and the *Paschal Chronicle*," 292–293. Himmelfarb, "Sefer Zerubbabel," 73.

97. Ephrem, *Hymns on the Nativity* 1, in the translation of Kathleen McVey, *Ephrem the Syrian: Hymns*, 65. I have added the bracketed [mother of the living] on the basis of McVey's note 16, and the phrase [the Jews] to reflect the sense of McVey's comments, 65–66, n. 18, on Ephrem's use of the term `mm, "the people," to denote "the Jewish people over against "the peoples," the Gentiles.

98. Ephrem, *Hymn of the Nativity* 1.15b–18. McVey, *Ephrem*, 65–66, n. 18: "Ephrem clearly states here the polemical aspect of Christian typological interpretation of the Jewish scripture: if Jews do not accept Christian interpretation of the prophets (and typological interpretation of even the Torah), their own scripture is invalidated." The linkage or identification of Mary and "the rod of Aaron" (or, sometimes, the rod of Jesse) is a frequent theme in patristic exegesis; see Thomas Livius, *The Blessed Virgin in the Fathers of the First Six Centuries*, 107–108, 155, 413, 424, etc. Like Ephrem in his challenge to Jewish interpreters of "the rod of Aaron," Proclus the archbishop of Constantinople in the next century had Mary speak for herself in one of his sermons: "For the sake of the unbelieving Jews, I ask the Virgin this: Tell me, O Virgin, who made you a mother before marriage? How did you become a mother and remain a virgin? Tell the Jews. Silence the mouths of unbelievers. She answers me with power and says: 'Why are the Jews amazed that a virgin gave birth, and yet express no surprise that, contrary to the laws of nature, the dry rod (of Aaron) blossomed and bloomed? They see a staff without root blooming indoor, and ask neither how nor why, but about me they do not cease from their disputations.' 'Behold a virgin shall conceive in the womb and shall bring forth a son.'" Translation is from Nicholas Constas, *Proclus of Constantinople*, 233.

99. Himmelfarb, "Mother of the Messiah," 384–385.

100. Schäfer, *Mirror*, 213.

101. Michael Wex, *Born to Kvetch*.

102. Wex, *Kvetch*, 18–20.

103. See Wex, *Kvetch*, 21, where he submits a more colloquial interpretation: "Each individual word of *nisht geshtogyn un nisht gefloygn* would be comprehensible to a German-speaker, but it's unlikely that the German would ever guess what it really refers to, even if he or she caught the meaning of 'bullshit.'"

104. Wex, *Kvetch*, 20.

105. Ginzberg, *Legends*, vol. 2, 264. Philo's version of this story is in *Biblical Antiquities* 9:9. "Now he [Amran] had one son and one daughter, and their names were Aaron and Maria, 10. And the spirit of God came upon Maria by night, and she saw a dream, 2 and told her parents in the morning saying: 'I saw this night, and behold a man in a linen garment stood and said to me: "Go and tell thy parents: behold, that which shall be born of you shall be cast into the water, for by him water shall be dried up, and by him will I do signs, and I will save my people, and he shall have the captaincy thereof alway."' And when Maria had told her dream her parents believed her not."

106. Ibid.
107. *Exodus Rabbah* 1, 22. Maurice Mergui, tr., *Le Midrash Rabba sur l'Exode*, 34. Additional discussion, 38, expands upon Miriam's volunteering to find a Hebrew wet-nurse for the child now belonging to the Pharaoh's daughter—but rejecting the breasts of "idolatrous" women—displays rabbinic reasoning about the ethnic "rules" for the nursing of Hebrew children.
108. See Ginzberg, *Legends,* vol. 3, 52, and vol. 4, 306.

CHAPTER 15

1. See the rich and carefully documented study of two periods of the Dome of the Rock in Gülru Necipoğlu, "The Dome of the Rock as Palimpsest," [17]–105, and especially 20–35 for early testimonies to the "Mihrab of Mary" and the "Cradle of Jesus" (*mahd `Isa*), and 70–73 for documentary evidence of the presence of these in the Suleyman's sixteenth-century restoration of the holy site.
2. Surah 4:171.
3. Daniel A. Madigan, "Themes and Topics," 89, comments: "the complexity of the statements about the death of Jesus (Q 3:55; 4:157–159) has opened the way to a variety of opinions in the commentary literature. The most widely held opinion is that the Qur'an denies Jesus's death and that, therefore, he is alive and will return, undergoing death before being raised alive with the rest of creation on the day of judgment. Others hold that it is only the reality of the crucifixion that is denied, leaving open the possibility that Jesus died another kind of death, perhaps natural. Others still would interpret the verses in Q 4 as denying neither Jesus's death itself, nor the reality of the crucifixion. They see there only an assertion that, even though Jesus died, the end result was that the Jews did not succeed in doing away with him, since God raised him up. Though they boasted of having done so 'it was only made to seem so to them' (Q 4:157)."
4. Jane I. Smith and Yvonne Y. Haddad, "The Virgin Mary in Islamic Tradition and Commentary," 162. Many are surprised to learn that although many women are referred to in the Qur'an (e.g., "your spouse"—Adam's [2:35]; "his wife" laughing, when the angels visit Abraham [11:71], and "his wife"—the Egyptian's— in the Joseph story [12:21]), Mary alone is privileged in being named. (Mary is named nineteen times in the New Testament.)
5. The designation "sister of Aaron" seems to denote simply that Mary stands in the line of Aaron the priest. Al-Tabari, *The History of Al-Tabari* vol. 4, 120, is an early witness to such an understanding of names spoken by Mary's accusers to shame her: "They came angrily and called out to her. Then she brought the child to her folk, carrying him, and they said, 'Mary, you have surely committed a monstrous [that is, grave] thing! Sister of Aaron, thy father was not a wicked man, nor was thy mother a woman unchaste. What is it with you, sister of Aaron?' [Al-Tabari explains:] She was descended from Aaron, the brother of Moses, so that this expression is the equivalent of saying, 'Oh, brother of tribe such and such;' it indicates a family relationship."
6. See Elliott, *Apocryphal New Testament*, [84]–99, and especially *The Gospel of Pseudo-Matthew* 20–21, where we read: "And it came to pass on the third day of their journey, while they were walking, that Mary was fatigued by the excessive heat of the sun in the desert; and seeing a palm-tree she said to Joseph, 'I should like to rest a little in the shade of this tree.' Joseph therefore led her quickly to the palm and made her dismount from her beast. And as Mary was sitting there, she looked up to the foliage of the palm and saw it full of fruit and said to

Joseph, 'I wish it were possible to get some of the fruit of this palm.' And Joseph said to her, 'I am surprised that you say so, for you see how high the palm-tree is, and that you think of eating its fruit. I am thinking more of the want of water because the skins are now empty, and we have nothing with which to refresh ourselves and our cattle.' Then the child Jesus, reposing with a joyful countenance in the lap of his mother, said to the palm, 'O tree, bend your branches and refresh my mother with your fruit.' And immediately at these words the palm bent its top down to the very feet of Mary; and they gathered from it fruit with which they all refreshed themselves. And after they had gathered all its fruit it remained bent down, awaiting the order to rise from him who had commanded it to bow down. Then Jesus said, 'Raise yourself, O palm, and be strong and be the companion of my trees which are in the paradise of my Father; and open from your roots a vein of water which is hidden in the earth and let the waters flow, so that we might quench our thirst.' And it rose up immediately, and at its root there began to gush out a spring of water exceedingly clear and cool and sparkling. And when they saw the spring of water, they rejoiced greatly and were all satisfied, including their cattle and their beasts and they gave thanks to God. [21] And on the day after, when they were setting out from there, and at the hour in which they began their journey, Jesus turned to the palm and said, 'This privilege I give you, O palm-tree, that one of your branches be carried away by my angels, and planted in the paradise of my Father.'"

7. Islam's classical teachings about the final things, which speak variously of "the day of judgment" (*yawm al-din*), "the day of resurrection" (*yawm al-qiyama*), and "the hour" (*al-sa`a*) are well-treated in Jane Idleman Smith and Yvonne Yazbeck Haddad, *The Islamic Understanding of Death and Resurrection*, 1–97. See also Arzina R. Lalani's entry, "Judgment," in EQ III, 64–68.

8. Tarif Khalidi, *The Qur'an*, 45.

9. *Luke* 1:48. See Mary F. Foskett, "Miriam/Mariam/Maria," 63–74.

10. Jane Dammen McAuliffe, "Chosen of All Women," 20.

11. See the careful exposition of different interpretations in McAuliffe, "Chosen of All Women," 19–28. Early debate about whether Mary's election "among" or "above" all women subordinates other celebrated women in the scriptural tradition and beyond—most notably, Fatima, whose profile in *hadith* literature makes her a contender with Mary for the most worthy among women—and about whether Mary should be counted a prophet, is masterfully exposed here.

12. Ibid., 21.

13. Ibid., 22–28, where the challenges to Mary's preeminence and advocacy for Fatima is a steady theme in commentary on this verse by the Shi'i. McAuliffe's concluding sentences are: "The transference of characteristics between Mary and Fatima that may be traced in the works examined ineluctably binds the two figures together so that the shadow of one crosses backstage while the other is before the footlights. Yet in absolute terms, Fatima's status as the first female of Islam is unchallenged both among the Shi'i where it is so heavily stressed, and among the majority of Sunnis. Mary may stand as her counterpoint in an earlier epoch, but little more than that."

14. Al-Tha`labi, *Lives of the Prophets*, 656. Wahb b. Munabbih, regarded as a reliable transmitter of *hadith*, lived from 656–736.

15. Surah 15:26: "We created the human being from clay, from formed mud. 27 As for the sprites, we created them earlier, from the fire of a penetrating wind. 28 Your Lord said to the angels, 'I am going to create a human being from clay, from

formed mud. 29 Now when I have put him in order and breathed some of My spirit into him, then bow down to him.'" (See also 38:72, on Adam's creation.) The Qur'an's manner of likening Adam and Jesus as two humans brought into being by God's breath entails, of course, a similarity in unusual genealogy or parentage, Adam having neither a father nor mother, and Jesus having only a mother.

16. Stowasser, *Women in the Qur'an*, 76.

17. Though early Muslim commentators debate which figures from Jewish tradition are to be identified as Idris and Dhu'l Kifl, Enoch, and Ezekiel (respectively) are supposed by some to be the surest candidates, while others regard these associations as quite uncertain. See Brannon Wheeler, *Prophets in the Quran*, 45–48, 161–163, on the range of opinions among commentators, and Andrew Rippin, *Muslims*, 25–25, on some difficulties in identifying Islamic prophets with biblical ones.

18. *Surah* 66: 10–11.

19. Nicholas Constas, chapter 5, "'The Ear of the Virginal Body': The Poetics of Sound in the School of Proclus," in *Proclus of Constantinople and the Cult of the Virgin in Late Antiquity*, [273]–313. See in Constas, 201, a series of sentences at the conclusion of Proclus's *Homily 3 On the Incarnation* that capture the preacher's rising rhetorical flair: "And when was human flesh ever essentially united without change to God, if not yesterday? When the Virgin was heavy with child, (when) the Word entered in through her sense of hearing, (when) the Holy Spirit fashioned the living temple of the body, (when) the Most High emptied himself into the form of a servant, (when) the womb of a virgin contained the mystery of the divine dispensation." Constas, 278, describes some competing views maintaining that Mary had conceived through her nostrils (sense of smell), or through her mouth, one text having Mary report, "Gabriel came . . . he opened my mouth, he went down into my womb . . . and ministered unto that which was inside my innermost part."

20. See Stowasser, *Women in the Qur'an*, 74, and 160, n. 63.

21. Muhammad Asad, *The Message of the Qur'an*, 137, and note 181.

22. Tarif Khalidi, *The Muslim Jesus*, 14. He continues: "But his 'death' is equally miraculous: he is lifted up to God, where according to later Islamic tradition he remained alive and waiting to fulfill his appointed role at the end of time, a role merely hinted at in the Qur'an (43:61)."

23. Al-Tha`labi, *Lives*, 674, contains a report from Wahb of the killing of Jesus's disciples, and the flight of Mary and John, who was ordered to "stay close" to her. As a pursuer closed upon the two, "the earth split open for them and they disappeared into it."

24. Mustansir Mir, *Understanding the Islamic Scripture*, chapter 12: "Jesus: Birth, Miracles and Mission," 81–89, and especially 82–83.

25. Roberto Totolli, *Biblical Prophets in the Qur'an and Muslim Literature*, 155ff. A brief account of al-Tarafi's work, and the translation used here of that section of his *Qisas al-Anbiya* treating Mary and Jesus appears in Norman Calder, Jawid Mojaddedi, Andrew Rippen, eds. and trs., *Classical Islam*, [59]–63.

26. Calder, Mojaddedi, Rippen, eds. and trs., *Classical Islam*, 60. Note that the Qur'an quotations appear in italics in the translation.

27. Al-Tarafi was surely aware of the marriage laws concerning such things as skin diseases, malformed or dysfunctional sex organs, and signs of insanity—but these obviously were not "part of the nature of all women." See the opinions

of al-Tabari and al-Zamakhshari about the nature of Mary's purification that are recounted in McAuliffe, "Mary and Fatima," 20-21. The "blemishes," or defects, are listed in the work by Ibn Rushd (Averroes), *The Distinguished Jurist's Primer*, under the rubric of the *Book of Nikah* (Marriage). Ibn Rushd, linked also to Cordova and living in the century following al-Tarafi, relates: "Malik and al-Shafi`i agreed that revocation [of marriage] is on the basis of four defects: insanity, leprosy, *baras* (skin disease like leprosy, and disease of the sex organ that prevents intercourse—*qarn* or *ratq* (birth defect in which the vulva is blocked, or the sides of the vulva are joined together) in a woman, and impotence or castration in a man." Other defects were also proposed and debated: "black colour, baldness, excessive vaginal odour, and foul breath." The quotations are from Rushd, *The Distinguished Jurist's Prime*, Vol. 2, 59. Similar "blemishes" (Hebrew: *mumim*) were subjects of concern in rabbinic teachings on marriage, and a succinct description of this set of issues is found in Hagith Sivan, *Palestine in Late Antiquity*, 279–296, and especially 286–289. The identifications and descriptions of physical blemishes in a marriage partner—defects capable of annulling a marriage—stem from earlier purity traditions in which such "imperfections" disqualify a person from being a priest, or render an animal unfit for religious sacrifice. Interestingly, the Qur'an, in Surah 2:71, records Moses's teaching that a sacrificed animal be without blemish (*shiyah*).

28. Calder, Mojaddedi, Rippen, eds. and trs., *Classical Islam*, 61.

29. Similar, but more dramatic, versions of the damaging effects of prayer on the feet appear in acccounts of Simeon Stylites (d. 459 CE). In Robert Doran, ed. and tr., *The Lives of Simeon Stylites*, 129, we read: "For he outwardly bound his feet upon a stone, while clothed inwardly with the true faith. In open view the flesh of his feet ruptured from much standing, but his steadfast mind was on fire for his Lord, a contest in secret"; and on p. 131: "Who then would see this and not marvel, who hear and not be amazed at the man whose feet were worn away and yet stood day and night." See the study by Patricia Cox Miller in her "Desert Monasticism and 'the Body from Nowhere,'" 137–153. To Rabi`a al-`Adawiyya, the famous eighth-century CE Muslim female ascetic and saint, similar prayerful ardency is also ascribed. In John Renard, ed., *Windows on the House of Islam*, 133–134, the author translates of a portion in Munawi's *Life of Rabi`a*: "She used to perform a thousand ritual prostrations both day and night; so someone asked, 'What is your goal in this?' She said, 'I desire no reward for it; I do it so that the Messenger of God, may God bless him and give him peace, will delight in it on the day of Resurrection and say to the prophets, "Take note of what a woman of my Community has accomplished.'"" It is a fair assumption that an inspiration for Rabi`a's strenuous discipline of prayer was Mary, who was enjoined (in 3:43) to bow and prostrate herself in *salat*."

30. Al-Tha`labi, *Lives*, 631–633, records John's successful persuasion of his parents to allow him to don the hair coat and cowl in which he joined the ascetics: "Then he went to the Temple and began to worship God with the rabbis and monks, till the long hair ate into his flesh. One day John looked at his emaciated body and wept. Then God revealed Himself to him, saying, 'John, do you weep because you are emaciated? By my glory and power, if I had given vent to My fire you would certainly have put on long garments of iron, rather than sackcloth!' Then John wept until the tears consumed the flesh of his cheeks and his molar teeth appeared to all who beheld him." A saying by his father spurred John's ardor,

and the episode concludes with Zachariah's acknowledgment of the virtue in his son's tears, giving thanks to "the most Merciful of the merciful ones."

31. Calder, Mojaddedi, Rippen, eds. and trs., *Classical Islam*, 61.
32. Ibid.
33. Ibid.
34. Ibid.
35. Al-Tha'labi, *Lives,* 639.
36. The translation is from Smith and Hadad, "The Virgin Mary in Islamic Tradition," 167. Loren Lybarger, "Gender and Prophetic Authority in the Qur'anic Story of Maryam," 265, writes concerning the exegetes' treatments of Maryam's pregnancy, including that of al-Qurtubi: "Desiring to preserve the deity from any implication of biological paternity (a point crucial in the differentiation of the Qur'anic version of events from those of opposing communities), Muslim commentators have struggled with understanding the mechanics of Maryam's miraculous conception. Most allow for a degree of ambiguity, stating simply that the angel blew his breath/spirit into Maryam through her sleeve opening, under her blouse's neckline, or into her mouth. Al-Qurtubi goes into greater detail: he actually posits a unique biological apparatus within Maryam's body that combines male and female sexual capabilities. This apparatus conceives almost hermaphroditically when the shock of the spirit's appearance jolts it into operation." Lyberger's last sentence does not give full attention to the fact that it is not, for al-Qurtubi, the appearance of Gabriel, but "the blowing" and its arousal of desire in Mary, that results in her fertilization.
37. Calder, Mojaddedi, Rippen, eds. and trs., *Classical Islam*, 62.
38. Ibid., 62.
39. Ibid., 62.
40. Ibid.
41. Ibid.
42. Al-Tha'labi, *Lives,* 642–643.
43. Al Tha'labi, *Lives,* 645, wrote: "Mujahid related that Mary said, 'When I was alone with Jesus, he conversed with me and I with him; and when someone distracted me from him, he glorified God in my womb, and I heard it.' And God is All-Knowing." (On the teaching that Fatima spoke while within the womb of Khadija, and its parallels to notions of Jesus's early speech, see McAuliffe, "Mary and Fatima," 26.)
44. Ibid., 643.
45. Calder, Mojaddedi, Rippen, eds. and trs., *Classical Islam*, 63.
46. The translation here is from Khalidi, *The Qur'an*, 243.
47. Calder, Mojaddedi, Rippen, eds. and trs., *Classical Islam*, 63.
48. Ibid. Al-Tarafi maintains that Mary's father is `Imran, not Joachim, but see 3:35, where the reference to "`Imran's wife" reveals that it is the story with the characters Joachim and Anna that is in view. The unnamed wife tells God that the child she dedicates to him is a female.
49. Ibid.
50. Ibid.
51. Mir, *Understanding the Islamic Scripture*, 83.
52. Calder, Mojaddedi, Rippen, eds. and trs., *Classical Islam*, 62.
53. Al-Tha'labi, *Lives,* 643–644.
54. Ibid., 644.
55. Ibid.

56. The *hadith* is found in Khan, *Sahih Bukhari*, 4.55.641. In a Muslim child-birth ritual practice called *talqîn* the *shahadah* ("There is no God but God") is spoken into the newborn's ear, a prophylactic against Iblis's approach.

57. David Marshall, "Christianity in the Qur'an," 3–29. The succeeding lines in this argument read: "The miraculous speech of the infant Jesus (19:30–33) further illustrates this point. The self-description of Jesus in vv. 30–31 (as with so much of the speech of the Qur'anic prophets) could be put into Muhammad's mouth without any alteration: "I am God's servant; God has given me the Book, and made me a Prophet . . . and he has commanded me to pray and give alms as long as I live."

58. Lybarger, "Gender and Prophetic Authority in the Qur'anic Story of Maryam," 260.

59. Al-Tha`labi, *Lives*, 513.

60. Hosn Abboud's "Idhan Maryam Nabiyya," 183. Abboud, 186, offers her own contribution to the question by pointing to matters of genealogy: "My contention that Mary is a prophetess in Islam relies on the matrilineal naming of Jesus: Jesus the son of Maryam. Though certainly given to the fatherless Jesus to emphasize his human nature and avoid attributing any paternity to God, Jesus's matrilineal name does, if Qur'anic tradition is to be adhered to, suggest the prophethood of both mother and son. For, if the prophets Zachariah and his son John, Maryam and her son Jesus, Abraham and his sons Isaac and Jacob *are from the offspring* (the same genealogical line as Q 19:58 indicates) of Adam, Noah, Abraham and Israel, *then* for Jesus to be a prophet, being the son only of a mother, that mother must be a prophetess. In other words, if Jesus is to remain firmly embedded in the line of prophets, Maryam must also be considered a prophetess."

61. Stowasser, *Women in the Qur'an*, 77.

62. Ibid.

63. Abboud's "Idhan Maryam Nabiyya" is the source of my comments about this debate, and one of my several guides as I try to trace this affirmation's sources back through relevant passages in the Qur'an to themes we have met in the Christian Mary-narratives, themselves influenced by the Hebrew Bible's depiction of Miriam, especially in *Exodus* 15:20. In light of this Muslim discussion, Ephrem the Syrian's proposal in the late fourth century that Mary received prophethood is intriguing to read. Her prophetic gift is transmitted through prophets past, especially Simeon and her own son, Jesus. See Ephrem's *Homily on Our Lord* (de Dom. Nos. 53–54) as it is treated in Christina Shepherdson, *Anti-Judaism and Christian Orthodoxy*, 100.

64. McAuliffe, "Mary and Fatima," 21.

65. See David Marshall, "Zechariah," in EQ IV, 574–576, who treats the different emphases that appear in Meccan and Medinan references to Zechariah—the thematic presence of mercy in the face of trials in the former, and of contestation with the Jews in the latter—and their correspondence to Muhammad's circumstances in the two locations.

66. Al-Tabari, *The History of Al-Tabari* IV, 108. Ibn Ishaq provides a line of descent for the three from David.

67. McAuliffe, "Mary and Fatima," 21, citing Mahmud b. `Umar al-Zamakhshari, *Al-Kassaf `an haqa'iq gawamid al-tanzil wa `uyun al-aqawil fi wuguh al-ta'wil* (Beirut: D'ar al-Kitab al-`Arabi, n.d.,), vol. 1, 362.

68. *Surah* 5:75.

69. McAuliffe, "Mary and Fatima," 26–28, in which McAuliffe traces the development, especially in Shi'i circles, of an enhancement of Fatima's story, a process that used and surpassed several Marian themes in telling of a dream-prophecy of Fatima's birth, her speech while in her mother, Khadija's, womb, and her virginal freedom from menstruation, "as befits a prophet's daughter."

70. The quotation, from al-Izraqi's *al-M'usharrafa* (*Chronicles of Mecca the Glorious*), 1.70 and 1:107, is in Guillaume, tr., *The Life of Muhammad*, 552.

71. The differing accounts show evidence of editorial changes, since they are from same source, al-Azraqi's ninth-century treatment of Mecca. See Martin Lings, *Muhammad*, 300, and n. 2. Also, Guillaume, tr., *The Life of Muhammad*, 552, n. 3. The reference to `Ata b. Abi Rabah is taken from Necipoğlu, "The Dome of the Rock as Palimpsest," at the conclusion of 96, n. 155.

72. Necipoğlu, "The Dome of the Rock as Palimpsest," 52, and 95, n. 155.

73. See Sheila R. Canby, *Islamic Art in Detail*, 32–[44], on "The Human Figure." Also, Oleg Grabar, *Masterpieces of Islamic Art*, esp. 14–49, 60–121, 142–[147], and 200–207 ("Islam and the visual expression of faith"). On the Falnama paintings as "models for *Qisas al-Anbiya* miniatures," see Barbara Schmitz, "A Royal Persian Prototype?" 65–74, and the list of scenes, 83–86.

74. The text is found in Habib Yaghmai, ed., *Abu Ishaq Ibrahim Nisaburi, Qesas-ol-Anbiya*.

75. See Rachel Milstein, "The Iconography and the Ideological Program," in Milstein, et al., *Stories*, 25–40.

76. I am indebted to Emine Fetvaci for this observation. See Sheila R. Canby, *Persian Painting*, 76–88, and the similar representations not only of female figures (Shirin in Fig. 48, and one of the lovers in Fig. 57), but also of several males—particularly the "prince" in red in Fig. 53).

77. Wright, *Islam*, 213, observes that the palm Mary shakes is shown to be a "half-dead, fruit-bearing tree," and mentions, in connection with this painting, the tradition present in some *Qisas* texts that "it was Jesus who, immediately after his birth, told his mother to shake a dead palm tree, which, the instant she touched it, sprang to life, spouting leaves and dates for her to eat." It is a bit puzzling that other vegetation in the foreground and background appear to be verdant and in season.

78. Calder, Mojaddedi, Rippen, eds. and trs., *Classical Islam*, 61. Al-Tabari, *History IV*, 119, contains an early narrative expansion of the qur'anic account: "When the time arrived for Mary to give birth, she went out to the eastern side of the prayer niche. She reached the edge, 'and the birthpangs surprised her by the trunk of the palm tree.' As she was suffering the delivery, ashamed before the people, she exclaimed, 'Would that I had died before this, and become a thing forgotten [that is, the memory of me should be forgotten, as well as any trace of me, and no eye would see me].' But Gabriel called unto her from below, 'No, do not sorrow; see, your Lord has set below you a rivulet [that is, a watercourse]. Shake also yourself the palm trunk [it was a broken-off trunk].' She shook it and, lo and behold, it was a palm tree; he produced for her a stream in the prayer niche, and dates fresh and ripe came tumbling down. He then said to her, 'Eat, therefore, and drink, and be comforted.'"

79. Al-Kisa'i, *Tales of the Prophets*, 329.

80. Al-Tha`labi, *Lives*, 642–643.

81. Yaghmai, *Nisaburi, Qesas-ol-Anbiya*, 268.

82. Ibid. The translations of parts of Nisaburi's Persian text in this chapter are by my Stanford colleague, Kavous Barghi. The final episode concerning Zachariah is sometimes linked, not with Mary's condemnation by her people, but with John's death at the hands of king Hiradus (Herod), after which the prophet flees. This is one of the "placements" suggested in Al-Tha'labi, *Lives*, 637–638.

83. Al-Tabari, *History* vol. IV, 120: "Then the Israelites said, 'Only Zechariah made her pregnant; he used to have relations with her.' So they sought him, but he had fled from them."

84. Al-Tha'labi, *Lives*, 637–638.

85. Varying accounts of Isaiah's death include the elements of being pursued (by King Manasseh), hiding in a cedar tree, being discovered because of extruding garment fringe, and dying from the sawblade—e.g., *Palestinian Talmud Sanhedrin* 10. The execution of Isaiah by saw (but not as he is enclosed in a tree) appears also in *The Martyrdom of Isaiah* 4:6–5:14.5.

86. See Christian M. M. Brady, *The Rabbinic Targum of Lamentations*, 56–58.

87. Yaghmai, *Nisaburi, Qesas-ol-Anbiya*, 372.

88. Milstein, "The Stories and their Illustrations," in Milstein, et al., *Stories*, 154.

89. See, for example, *Zechariah* 9:26, *Luke* 13:34, and Paul's *1 Thessalonians* 2:14–16.

90. Milstein, "The Stories and their Illustrations," in Milstein, et al., *Stories*, 155.

91. See, e.g., Alexandra Cuffel, "From Practice to Polemic," 408: "The sixteenth century author Greffin Affagart described women from the 'Turks, Moors, and Christians' traveling to the Milk Grotto, a place where the nursing Mary dripped milk while she and her family hid from Herod. According to him, barren women or those who could not produce milk, cured themselves by pulverizing the scrapings from the cave wall and drinking them in water. According to a late medieval emigrant to the Holy Land, Friar Francesco Suriano, at the place where Mary gave birth, Muslim women baked bread to distribute to expectant mothers to ease their pains."

92. Renard, *Windows*, 43–45.

93. See Kristin Z. Sands, *Sufi Commentaries on the Qur'an in Classical Islam*, 97–109, and especially 107, with its treatment and quotation of Ruzbihan al-Baqli's commentary on Surah Maryam 19:22.

94. See Anthony H. Johns, "Ahmad Wahib's Dream," 352–353.

EPILOGUE

1. Jon Levenson has questioned assumptions surrounding the adjective "Abrahamic" with new force. See his *Inheriting Abraham*, and his pungent editorial in the *Wall Street Journal*, "Enlisting the Biblical Abraham as Peace Broker."

2. Considerations of these issues from the perspective of modern theology and philosophy, with a view to constructive dialogue between the religions, are found in Miroslav Volf, *Allah*, and in his edited volume that collects numerous contributions: *Do We Worship the Same God?*

BIBLIOGRAPHY

Abboud, Hosn. "Idhan Maryam Nabiyya" ('*Hence Maryam Is a Prophetess'*): *Muslim Classical Exegetes and Women's Receptiveness to God's Verbal Inspiration.*" Pages 183–196 in *Mariam, the Magdalen, and the Mother.* Edited by Deirdre Good. Bloomington: Indiana University Press, 2005.

Abboud, Hosn. *Mary in the Qur'an: A Literary Reading.* Routledge Studies in the Qur'an Series. New York: Routledge, Taylor & Francis, 2014. (Published earlier in Arabic: *Al-Sayyida Maryam fi al-Qur'an al-Karim: Qira'a Adabiyya.* Beirut: Dar al-Saqi, 2010.)

Ahmed, Shahab. "Ibn Taymiyyah and the Satanic verses." *SI* 2 (1998): 64–124.

Al-Biruni. *The Chronology of Ancient Nations.* Edited and translated by C. Edward Sachau. Frankfurt: Minerva GMBH, 1969.

Al-Bukhari, Muhammad ibn Isma'il. *Sahih al-Bukhari: The Translations of the Meanings of Sahih al-Bukhari Arabic-English.* 9 vols. Trans. Muhammad Muhsin Khan. Al-Nabawiya: Dar Ahya Us-Sunnah, 1976.

Al-Nisaburi, Abu Ishaq Ibrahim ibn Mansur. *Qisas al-anbiya.* Title variation: *Qesos-ol-Anbiya.* Persian Texts Series, 8. Edited by Habib Yaghmai. Tehran: B.T.N.K., 1961.

Al-Tabari. *The History of Al-Tabari,* vol. IV. The Ancient Kingdoms. Translated by Moshe Perlmann. Albany: State University of New York Press, 1987.

Ali, Abdullah Usuf. *The Meaning of the Holy Qur'an.* Brentwood, MD: Amana Corp., 1993.

Aptowitzer, Victor. "Asenath, the Wife of Joseph: A Haggadic Literary-Historical Study." *Hebrew Union College Annual* 1 (1924): 239–306.

Arberry, A. J. *The Koran Interpreted.* New York: Simon and Schuster, 1955.

Arbuthnot, F. F., and Rehatsek Edward. *The Rauzat-Us-Safa; or Garden of Purity, by Muhammad bin Khavendshah bin Mahmoud.* Oriental Translation Fund, New Series, 2 volumes. London: Royal Asiatic Society, 1891.

Arnold, Thomas W. *Painting in Islam: A Study of the Place of Pictorial Art in Muslim Culture.* New York: Dover Publications, 1965 edition, with new introduction by B. W. Robinson (original publication by Oxford University Press in 1928).

Asad, Muhammad. *The Message of the Qur'an.* Gibraltar: Dar Al-Andalus, 1980.

Augustine. *Expositions on the Book of Psalms.* NPNF (First Series), Vol. 8. Edited by A. Cleveland Cox. Grand Rapids, MI: Eerdmans, 1974.

Ayoub, Mahmoud M. *The Qur'an and its Interpreters.* Vol. 1. Albany: State University of New York Press, 1984.

Ayoub, Mahmoud M. *The Qur'an and its Interpreters.* Vol. 2. *The House of Imran.* Albany: State University of New York Press, 1992.

Balch, David. "From Endymion in Roman *domus* to Jonah in Christian Catacombs: From Houses of the Living to Houses for the Dead. Iconography and Religion in Transition." Pages 273–302 in *Commemorating the Dead: Text and Artifacts in Context. Studies of Roman, Jewish and Christian Burials.* Edited by Laurie Brink and Deborah Green. New York: De Gruyter, 2008.

Bashir, Shahzad. *Sufi Bodies: Religion and Society in Medieval Islam.* New York: Columbia University Press, 2011.

Baskin, Judith. "Rabbinic Judaism and the Creation of Woman." Pages 125–130 in *Judaism Since Gender.* Edited by M. Peskowitz and L. Levitt. New York: Routledge, 1996.

Beckwith, John. *Early Christian and Byzantine Art.* New York: Penguin Books, 1979.

Ben Ezra, Daniel Stökl. *The Impact of Yom Kippur on Early Christianity: The Day of Atonement from Second Temple Judaism to the Fifth Century. WUNT* 163. Tübingen: Mohr-Siebeck, 2003.

Benko, Stephen. *The Virgin Goddess: Studies in Pagan and Christian Roots of Mariology.* Leiden: Brill, 1993.

Berman, Samuel A. *Midrash Tanhuma-Yelammedenu.* Hoboken, NJ: KTAV Publishing House, 1996.

Betz, Hans Dieter. *Galatians.* Hermeneia-A Critical and Historical Commentary on the Bible. Philadelphia: Fortress Press, 1979.

Biale, David. "Counter-History and Jewish Polemics Against Christianity: The Sefer toldot yeshu and the Sefer zerubavel." *Jewish Social Studies* 6.1 (1999): 130–145.

Blair, Sheila S. *A Compendium of Chronicles: Rashid al Din's Illustrated History of the World.* The Nasser D. Khalili Collection of Islamic Art, vol. 27. London: The Nour Foundation, in assoc. with Azimuth Editions and Oxford University Press, 1995.

Blake, Robert P. *Epiphanius De Gemmis: The Old Georgian Version and the Fragments of the Armenian Version.* Studies and Documents 2. London: Christophers, 1934.

Blank, Alice. *L'Art Byzantine dans les musées de l'Union Soviétique.* Hungary: Èditions d'art Aurora, Leningrad, 1985.

Blenkinsopp, Joseph. *The Pentateuch.* New York: Doubleday, 1992.

Bokser, Ben Zion. *The Talmud.* Classics of Western Spirituality. New York: Paulist Press, 1989.

Borg, Malies ter. *Sharing Mary. Bible and Qur'an Side by Side.* Charleston, SC: Create Space, 2010.

Boss, Sarah Jane. *Mary: The Complete Resource.* London: Continuum, 2007.

Böttrich, C., Ego, Beate, and Eissler, Friedman. *Abraham in Judentum, Christentum und Islam.* Göttingen: Vandenhoeck & Ruprecht GmbH & Co., 2009.

Böttrich, C., Ego, Beate, and Eissler, Friedman. *Jesus und Maria in Judentum, Christentum und Islam.* Göttingen: Vandenhoeck & Ruprecht GmbH & Co., 2009.

Bovini, Guiseppe. *Ravenna.* Translated by Robert Erich Wolf; photographs by Leonard von Matt. New York: Harry N. Abrams, Inc., 1971.

Böwering, Gerhard. "The Scriptural 'Senses' in Medieval Sufi Qur'an Exegesis." Pages 346–365 in *With Reverence for the Word: Medieval Scriptural Exegesis in Judaism, Christianity, and Islam.* Edited by Jane Dammen McAuliffe, Barry D. Walfish, and Joseph W. Goering. New York: Oxford University Press, 2003.

Bowersock, G. W., Brown, Peter, and Grabar, Oleg. *Late Antiquity: A Guide to the Postclassical World.* Cambridge, Mass.: The Belknap Press of Harvard University Press, 1999.

Bowker, John. *The Targums and Rabbinic Literature.* Cambridge: Cambridge University Press, 1969.

Boyarin, Daniel. *Intertextuality and the Reading of Midrash*. Bloomington: Indiana University Press, 1990.

Boyarin, Daniel. *A Radical Jew: Paul and the Politics of Identity*. Berkeley: University of California Press, 1994.

Boyarin, Daniel. "Nostalgia for Christianity: Getting Medieval Again." *Religion and Literature* 42 (2010): 49–76.

Brady, Christian M. M. *The Rabbinic Targum of Lamentations*. Studies in Aramaic Interpretations of Scripture 3. Leiden: Brill, 2003.

Bregman, Marc. *The Tanhuma-Yelammedenu Literature: Studies in the Evolution of the Versions*. Piscataway, NJ: Gorgias Press, 2003.

Brenner, Jan. "Brothers and Fratricide in the Ancient Mediterranean: Israel, Greece and Rome." Pages 77–92 in *Eve's Children: The Biblical Stories Retold and Interpreted in Jewish and Christian Traditions*. Edited by Gerard P. Luttikhuizen. Leiden: Brill, 2003.

Brinner, William M. `Ara'is Al-Majalis Fi Qisas Al-Anbiya' or Lives of the Prophets*. Studies in Arabic Literature vol. 24. Boston: Brill, 2002.

Brinner, William M. *The History of al-Tabari,* vol. II, *Prophets and Patriarchs*. Bibiotheca Persica. Edited by Ehsan Yar Shater. Albany: State University of New York Press, 1987.

Brock, Sebastian P. "A Syriac Life of Abel." *Le Museon* 87 (1974): 467–492.

Brock, Sebastian P. *St. Ephrem the Syrian, Hymns on Paradise*. New York: St. Vladimir's Seminary Press, 1990.

Brock, Sebastian P. *The Syriac Fathers on Prayer and the Spiritual Life*. CS Series 101. Collegeville, MN: Cistercian Publications, Inc., 1987.

Brock, Sebastian P. *The Luminous Eye: The Spiritual World Vision of Saint Ephrem*. CS Series 124. Kalamazoo, MI: Cistercian Publications, 1985.

Brown, Peter. *Through the Eye of a Needle: Wealth, the Fall of Rome, and the Making of Christianity in the West, 350–550 AD*. Princeton, NJ: Princeton University Press, 2012.

Brown, Raymond. *The Birth of the Messiah*. New Haven, CT: Yale University Press, 1999.

Burton, Ernest De Witt. *Galatians*. International Critical Commentary. Edinburgh: T. & T. Clark Publishers, 1921.

Burton, John. "Collection of the Qur'an." Pages 351–361 in EQ I. Edited by Jane McAuliffe. Leiden: Brill, 2005.

Busse, Heribert. "Cain and Abel." Pages 270–272 in EQ I. Edited by Jane McAuliffe. Leiden: Brill, 2005.

Butterworth, G. W. *Origen: On First Principles*. New York: Harper & Row Publishers, 1966.

Byron, John. *Cain and Abel in Text and Tradition: Jewish and Christian Interpretations of the First Sibling Rivalry*. Leiden: Brill, 2011.

Calder, Norman, Mojaddedi, Jawid, and Rippen, Andrew. *Classical Islam: A Sourcebook of Religious Literature*. New York: Routledge, 2003.

Cameron, Averil. "The Early Cult of the Virgin." Pages 5–15 in *Mother of God: Representations of the Virgin in Byzantine Art*. Edited by Maria Vassilaki. Milan: Skira Editori, 2000.

Cameron, Averil. "The Theotokos in Sixth-Century Constantinople." *Journal of Theological Studies* NS 29 (1978): 79–108.

Canby, Sheila R. *Persian Painting*. London: British Museum Press, 1993.

Canby, Sheila R. "The Human Figure." Pages 32–44 in *Islamic Art in Detail*. London: British Museum Press, 2005.

Carr, Annemarie Weyl. "The Mother of God in Public." Pages 325–337 in *Mother of God: Representations of the Virgin in Byzantine Art*. Edited by Maria Vassilaki. Milan: Skira Editori, 2000.

Chadwick, Henry. *Origen: Contra Celsum*. Cambridge: Cambridge University Press, 1965.

Charles, R. H. *The Apocrypha and Pseudepigrapha of the Old Testament in English*, Vol. II. *Pseudepigrapha*. Oxford: Clarendon Press, 1913.

Christiansen, Irmgard. *Die Technik der allegorischen Auslegungswissenschaft bei Philon vom Alexandrien*. Tübingen: J.C.B. Mohr, 1969.

Clark, Elizabeth. "Interpretive Fate amid the Church Fathers." Pages 127–147 in *Hagar, Sarah, and Their Children*. Edited by Phyllis Trible and Letty Russell. Louisville, KY: Westminster John Knox Press, 2006.

Colson, F. H. *Philo, "On Joseph."* LCL, Philo, vol. VI. Cambridge, MA: Harvard University Press, 1935.

Colson, F. H., and Whitaker, G. H. *Philo, "On the Cherubim," "The Sacrifices of Abel and Cain," "The Worse Attacks the Better," "The Posterity and Exile of Cain."* LCL, Philo, vol. II. Cambridge, MA: Harvard University Press, 1929.

Constas, Nicholas. *Proclus of Constantinople and the Cult of the Virgin in Late Antiquity*. Supplements of Vigiliae Christianae, Vol. 66. Leiden: Brill, 2003.

Cox, A. Cleveland. *Clement of Alexandria, "The Instructor," "Miscellanies."* ANF II.I, Grand Rapids, MI: Eerdmans Publishing Company, 1967.

Cuffel, Alexandra. "From Practice to Polemic: Shared Saints and Festivals as 'Women's Religion' in the Medieval Mediterranean." *Bulletin of the School of Oriental and African Studies* 68.3 (2003): 401–419.

Daley, Brian J. *On the Dormition of Mary: Early Patristic Homilies*. Crestwood, NY: St. Vladimir's Seminary Press, 1997.

Dalman, Gustaf. *Jesus Christ in the Talmud, Midrash, Zohar, and the Liturgy of the Synagogue*. New York: Arno Press, 1973.

Dan, Joseph. "Lilith." Pages 421–422 in *ODJR*. Edited by R. J. Zwi Werblowsky and Geoffrey Wigoder. New York: Oxford University Press, 1997.

Danby, Herbert. *The Mishnah*. Oxford: Oxford University Press, 1931.

Davidson, Ivor J. *Ambrose, De officiis*. Oxford Early Christian Studies vol. 1. Oxford: Oxford University Press, 2001.

Dawson, David. *Allegorical Readers and Cultural Revision in Ancient Alexandria*. Berkeley: University of California Press, 1992.

Dawson, David. *Christian Figural Reading* and the Fashioning of Identity. Berkeley: University of California Press, 2002.

Deferarri, Roy J. *Saint Cyprian: Treatises*, FOC 36. New York: Catholic University Press, 1958.

Deliyannis, Deborah Mauskopf. *Ravenna in Late Antiquity*. Cambridge: Cambridge University Press, 2010.

Deliyannis, Deborah Mauskopf. *Agnellos of Ravenna, The Book of the Pontiffs of the Church of Ravenna*. Medieval Texts in Translation. Translated by Deborah Mauskopf Deliyannis. Washington, DC: The Catholic University of America Press, 2004.

Dignas, Beate, and Winter, Engelbert. *Rome and Persia in Late Antiquity: Neighbors and Rivals*. Cambridge: Cambridge University Press, 2007.

Dinkler, Erich. "Abbreviated Representations." Pages 396–448 in Kurt Weitzmann, *Age of Spirituality*. New York: Metropolitan Museum of Art, in association with Princeton University Press, Princeton, NJ, 1979.

Donner, Fred M. *Narratives of Islamic Origins: The Beginnings of Islamic Historical Writing.* Studies in Late Antiquity and Early Islam, No. 14. Princeton, NJ: Darwin Press Inc., 1998.

Donner, Fred M. "The Historical Context." Pages 23–39 in *CCQ.* Edited by Jane McAuliffe. Cambridge: Cambridge University Press, 2006.

Doran, Robert. *The Lives of Simeon Stylites,* CS Series 112. Kalamazoo, MI: Cistercian Publications Inc., 1992.

Drijvers, Jan Willem. "Heraclius and the *Restitutio Crucis*: Notes on Symbolism and Ideology." Pages 175–190 in *The Reign of Heraclius (610–614)—Crisis and Confrontation.* Edited by G. J. Reinink and B. H. Stolte. Louvain: Peeters Publishers, 2002.

Eastmond, Antony. "Plaque of the Adoration of the Magi and the Miracle of Salome." Page 266 in *Mother of God: Representations of the Virgin in Byzantine Art.* Edited by Maria Vassilaki. Milan: Skira Editori, 2000.

Elliott, J. K. *The Apocryphal New Testament: A Collection of Apocryphal Christian Literature in an English Translation.* Oxford: Clarendon Press, 1993.

Elsner, Jaś. *Art and the Roman Viewer: The Transformation of Art from the Pagan World to Christianity.* Cambridge Studies in New Art History and Criticism. Cambridge: Cambridge University Press, 1995.

Elsner, Jaś. *Imperial Rome and Christian Triumph: The Art of the Roman Empire* AD *100–450.* Oxford History of Art. Oxford: Oxford University Press, 1998.

Epstein, Isidore. *The Babylonian Talmud.* London: The Soncino Press, 1935.

Eusebius of Caesarea. *Praeparatio Evangelica.* Edwin H. Gifford, tr. *Eusebius: Preparation for the Gospel* II. Grand Rapids, MI: Baker Book House, 1981.

Evans, Helen C., and Wixom, William D. *The Glory of Byzantium.* New York: The Metropolitan Museum of Art, 1997.

Fadel, Mohammad. "Murder." Pages 459–460 in EQ III. Edited by Jane McAuliffe. Leiden: Brill, 2005.

Farhad, Massumeh with Bagci, Serpil. *Falnama: The Book of Omens.* London: Thames & Hudson, 2009. (A publication by the Freer Gallery of Art and the Arthur Sackler Gallery, Smithsonian Institution.)

Feldman, Louis H. "Josephus' Interpretation of Jonah." *American Journal for Jewish Studies* 17.1 (1992): 1–29.

Ferrua, Antonio. *Catacombe Sconoscuite: Una Pinacoteca del IV secolo sotto la Via Latina.* Florence: Nardini Editore, 1990.

Field, Frederick. *Origenis Hexaplorum* II. Hildesheim: Georg Olms Verlagsbuchhandlung, 1964.

Fine, Steven. *Art and Judaism in the Greco-Roman World.* New York: Cambridge University Press, 2005.

Finney, Paul Corby. *The Invisible God.* New York: Oxford University Press, 1994.

Firestone, Reuven. "Abraham." Pages 7–8 in EQ I. Edited by Jane McAuliffe. Leiden: Brill, 2005.

Firestone, Reuven. *Journeys in Holy Lands. The Evolution of the Abraham-Ishmael Legends in Islamic Exegesis.* Albany: State University of New York Press, 1990.

Fishbane, Michael. *Haftarot.* The JPS Bible Commentary. Philadelphia: Jewish Publication Society, 2002.

Foskett, Mary F. "Miriam/Mariam/Maria." Pages 63–74 in *Miriam, the Magdalen, and the Mother.* Edited by Dierdre Good. Bloomington: University of Indiana Press, 2005.

Freedman, Harry, and Simon, Maurice. *Midrash Rabbah*, 10 vols. London: Soncino Press, 1939.

Friedlander, Gerald. *Pirke de Rabbi Eliezer*. New York: Hermon Press, 1965.

Gager, John G. *Reinventing Paul*. New York: Oxford University Press, 2000.

Galavaris, George. "Early Icons (from the 6th to the 11th Century)." Pages 91–101 in *Sinai: Treasures of the Monastery of Saint Catherine*. Edited by Konstantinos A. Manafis. Athens: Ekdotike Athanon S.A., 1990.

Gambell, Ray, and Brown, Sidney G. "James Bartley—A Modern Jonah or Joke?" *Investigations on Cetacea* 24 (1993): 325–337.

Gambero, Luigi. *Mary and the Fathers of the Church: The Blessed Virgin Mary in Patristic Thought*. San Francisco: Ignatius Press, 1999.

Gätje, Helmut. *The Qur'an and its Exegesis*. Translated by Alford T. Welch. Oxford: Oneworld Publications, 1996.

Gaventa, Beverly Roberts. "'All Generations Will Call Me Blessed': Mary in Biblical and Ecumenical Perspective." *The Princeton Seminary Bulletin* 18.3 (New Series) (1997): 250–261.

Gaventa, Beverly Roberts. *Mary: Glimpses of the Mother of Jesus*. Personalities of the New Testament. Philadelphia: Fortress Press, 1999.

Gebhardt, Oscar von. *The Miniatures of the Ashburnham Pentateuch*. London: Asher & Co., 1883.

Geiger, Abraham. *Was hat Mohammed aus dem Judenthum aufgenommen?* Leipzig: Verlag M. W. Kaufmann, 1832.

Geissinger, Aisha. "Mary in the Qur'an: Rereading Subversive Births." Pages 379–392 in *Sacred Tropes: Tanakh, New Testament, and Qur'an as Literature and Culture*. Edited by Roberta Sterman Sabbath. Leiden: Brill, 2009.

Gifford, Edwin H. tr., *Cyril, Archbishop of Jerusalem: Catechetical Lectures*. NPNF (Second Series) 7. Grand Rapids, MI: Eerdmans, 1969.

Gifford, Edwin H. tr., *Eusebius of Caesarea, Preparation for the Gospel*. Grand Rapids, MI: Eerdman, 1981 reprint of 1903 Clarendon House publication.

Gilboa, Anat. *Images of the Feminine in Rembrandt's Work*. Delft: Eburon Publishers, 2003.

Gilliot, Claude. "Creation of a Fixed Text." Pages 41–57 in *CCQ*. Edited by Jane McAuliffe. Cambridge: Cambridge University Press, 2006.

Ginzberg, Louis. *Die Haggada bei den Kirchenvätern und in der aprokryphischen Literatur*. Berlin: S. Calvary, 1900.

Ginzberg, Louis. *The Legends of the Jews*, 6 vols. Philadelphia: Jewish Publication Society, 1909–1928.

Ginzberg, Louis. *On Jewish Law and Lore*. Philadelphia: Jewish Publication Society, 1955.

Glassé, Cyril. *The Concise Encyclopedia of Islam*. New York: Harper & Row, 1989.

Glatt-Gilad David A. "Hezekiah." Pages 320–321 in *ODJR*. Edited by R. J. Zwi Werblowsky and Geoffrey Wigoder. New York: Oxford University Press, 1997.

Glimm, Francis X., Marique, Joseph M.-F., and Walsh, George G. *The Apostolic Fathers*. FOC. New York: CIMA Publishing Co., 1947.

Goldstein, Morris. *Jesus in the Jewish Tradition*. New York: Macmillan, 1950.

Goodenough, Erwin R. *An Introduction to Philo Judaeus*. Oxford: Blackwell, 1962.

Goodenough, Erwin R. *Jewish Symbols in the Greco-Roman Period*. 12 vols. Bollingen Series 37. New York: Pantheon Books, 1953–1965.

Grabar, André. *Ampoules de Terre Sainte*. Pages 35–46 in "Byzantine Pilgrims' Art" in *Heaven on Earth*. Edited by Linda Safran. University Park: Pennsylvania State University Press, 1998.

Grabar, André. *Christian Iconography: A Study of Its Origins*. A. W. Mellon Lectures in the Fine Arts, Bollingen Series, 35, 15, 10. Princeton, NJ: Princeton University Press, 1968.

Grabar, André. *Early Christian Art From the Rise of Christianity to the Death of Theodosius*. Translated by Stuart Gilbert and James Emmons in the series edited by André Malraux and Georges Salles, *The Arts of Mankind*. New York: Odyssey Press, 1968.

Grabar, Oleg. *Masterpieces of Islamic Art: The Decorated Page from the 8th to the 17th Century*. New York: Prestel, 2009.

Graham, William A. "Islam in the Mirror of Ritual." Pages 63–73 in *Islam's Understanding of Itself*. Edited by Richard G. Hovannisian and Speros Vryonis, Jr. Malibu, CA: Undena Publications, 1983.

Greer, Rowan. *Origen*. Classics of Western Spirituality. New York: Paulist Press, 1979.

Gregg, Robert C., and Urman, Dan. *Jews, Pagans, and Christians in the Golan Heights: Greek and Other Inscriptions of the Roman and Byzantine Eras*. Atlanta, GA: Scholars Press, 1996.

Griffith, Ralph T. H. *Yusuf and Zulaikha*. London: Trübner & Co., 1882.

Griffith, Sidney. "Christianity in Edessa and the Syriac-Speaking World: Mani, Bar Daysan, and Ephraem; the Struggle for Allegiance on the Aramaean Frontier." *Journal of the Canadian Society for Syriac Studies* 2 (2002): 5–20.

Gruen, Erich S. *Heritage and Hellenism: The Reinvention of Jewish Tradition*. Hellenistic Culture and Society, vol. 30. Berkeley: University of California Press, 1998.

Guilding, Aileen. *The Fourth Gospel and Jewish Worship*. Oxford, 1960.

Guillaume, A. *The Life of Muhammad. A Translation of Ishaq's Sirat Rasul Allah*. Oxford: Oxford University Press, 2007.

Gutmann, Joseph. "Cain's Burial of Abel: A Jewish Legendary Motif in Christian and Islamic Art." *Eretz Israel* 16 (1982): 92–98.

Gutmann, Joseph. "Joseph Legends in the Vienna Genesis." *Proceedings of the Fifth World Congress of Jewish Studies* 5.4 (1973): 181–184.

Gutmann, Joseph. "The Jewish Origin of the Ashburnham Pentateuch Miniatures." *JQR* 44 (1953–54): 53–72.

Gutmann, Joseph, ed. *No Graven Images*. New York: KTAV, 1971.

Hachlili, Rachel. "Synagogues in the Land of Israel: The Art and Architecture of the Late Antique Synagogues." Pages 96–129 in *Sacred Realm*. Edited by Steven Fine. New York: Oxford University Press and Yeshiva University Museum, 1996.

Hamilton, Victor P. *The Book of Genesis: Chapters 18–50*. Grand Rapids, MI: Eerdmans Publishing Company, 1995.

Hansen, G. Walter. *Abraham in Galatians: Epistolary and Rhetorical Contents*. Journal for the Study of the New Testament, Supplement Series 29. Sheffield: Sheffield Academic Press, 1989.

Hare, D. R. A. *Lives of the Prophets*. Pages 379–400 in *The Old Testament Pseudepigrapha* 2. Edited by James H. Charlesworth; translated by D. R. A. Hare. Garden City, NY: Doubleday & Co., 1985.

Harnack, Adolf von. *Marcion: Das Evangelium vom fremden Gott*. Leipzig: J. C. Hinrichs, 1924.

Hays, David. *Both Literal and Allegorical—Studies in Philo of Alexandria's Questions and Answers on Genesis and Exodus*. Brown Judaic Studies 232. Atlanta, GA: Scholars Press, 1991.

Heine, Ronald E. *Origen: Homilies on Genesis and Exodus*, FOC 71. Washington, DC: Catholic University of America Press, 1982.

Herr, Moshe David. "Genesis Rabbah." Pages 400–401 in *Encyclopaedia Judaica* 7. Jerusalem: Keter Publishing House, 1982.

Herrick, Robert. "An Epithalamy to Sir Thomas Southwell And His Lady." Pages 189–192 in *Poetica Erotica: Rare and Amatory Verse*, vol. 1. Edited by T. R. Smith. New York: Boni and Liveright, 1921.

Hill, Robert C. *Chrysostom, Homilies on Genesis 18–45*. FOC 82. Washington, DC: Catholic University of America, 1990.

Hill, Robert C. *Saint John Chrysostom: Homilies on Genesis 46–67*. FOC 87. Washington, DC: Catholic University of America Press, 1992.

Himmelfarb, Martha. "Sefer Zerubbabel." Pages 67–90 in *Rabbinic Fantasies: Imaginative Narratives from Classical Hebrew Literature*. Edited by David Stern and Mark Jay Minsky. New York: Jewish Publication Society, 1990.

Himmelfarb, Martha. "The Mother of the Messiah in the Talmud Yerushalmi and Sefer Zerubbabel." Pages 369–389 in *The Talmud Yerushalmi and Graeco-Roman Culture* III, Texts and Studies in Ancient Judaism 93. Edited by Peter Schäfer. Tübingen: Mohr Siebeck, 2002.

Hirshman, Marc. *A Rivalry of Genius. Jewish and Christian Biblical Interpretation in Late Antiquity*. Translated biy Batya Stein. Albany: State University of New York Press, 1996.

Hock, Ronald F. *The Infancy Gospels of James and Thomas*. The Scholars Bible, Vol. 2. Santa Rosa, CA: Poleridge Press, 1995.

Hodgson, Marshall G. S. *The Venture of Islam*, vol. 1. Chicago: University of Chicago Press, 1974.

Horbury, William. *Jews and Christians*. Edinburgh: T&T Clark, 2006.

Hourihane, Colum. *Abraham in Medieval Christian, Islamic, and Jewish Art*. University Park: Pennsylvania State University, 2013.

Hoyland, Robert G. *Arabia and the Arabs*. London: Routledge, 2001.

Hoyland, Robert G. *Seeing Islam as Others Saw It: A Survey and Evaluation of Christian, Jewish and Zoroastrian Writings on Early Islam*. Princeton, NJ: Darwin Press, Inc., 1998.

Hritzu, John N. *Saint Jerome: Dogmatic and Polemical Works*. FOC 53. Washington, DC: Catholic University of America, 1965.

Hurwitz, Siegmund. *Lilith—The First Eve: Historical and Psychological Aspects of the Dark Feminine*. 3rd revised edition. Einsiedeln, Switzerland: Daimon Verlag, 2009.

Ibn Rushd. *The Distinguished Jurist's Prime: A Translation of Bidayat Al-Mujtahid*. Vol. 2. Center for Muslim Contribution to Civilization. Translated by Imran Ahsan Khan Yyazee. Reading, UK: Garnet Publishing Ltd., 2000.

Jensen, Robin M. "Exegesis and the Earliest Christian Images." Pages 65–86 in *Picturing the Bible: The Earliest Christian Art*. Edited by Jeffrey Spier. New Haven, CT: Yale University Press in conjunction with the Kimbell Art Museum, Fort Worth, Texas, 2007.

Jensen, Robin M. *Face to Face: Portraits of the Divine in Early Christianity*. Minneapolis: Fortress Press, 2005.

Jensen, Robin M. "The Economy of the Trinity at the Creation of Adam and Eve." *JECS* 7:4 (1999): 527–546.

Jensen, Robin M. "Moses Imagery in Jewish and Christian Art." *SBL Seminar Papers* (1992): 395–398.

Jensen, Robin M. *Understanding Early Christian Art*. New York: Routledge, 2000.

John of Damascus. *Orthodox Faith*. Pages 165–406 in *Saint John of Damascus. Writings*. FOC 37. Edited and translated by Frederic H Chase, Jr. New York: Fathers of the Church, Inc., 1958.

John of Thessalonica. *The Dormition of Our Lady, the Mother of God and Ever-Virgin Mary*. Pages 47–70 in *On the Dormition of Mary: Early Patristic Homilies*. Edited and translated by Brian E. Daley and S. J. Crestwood. New York: St. Vladimir's Seminary Press, 1997.

Johns, Anthony H. "Ahmad Wahib's Dream." Pages 352–353 in *Windows on the House of Islam: Muslim Sources on Spirituality and Religious Life*. Edited by John Renard. Berkeley: University of California Press, 1998.

Johnson, M. D. "The Life of Adam and Eve." Pages 249–295 in *The Old Testament Pseudepigrapha*, vol. 2. Edited by James H. Charlesworth. Garden City, NY: Doubleday, 1985.

Josephus. *Jewish Antiquities*. Translated by Ralph Marcus. LCL *Josephus*, 6. Cambridge, MA: Harvard University Press, 1987.

Kamesar, Adam. "Review of Folker Siegert, Drei hellenistisch-jüdische Predigten: Ps.-Philon, "Über Jona", "Über Jona" (Fragment) und "Über Simson," II, Kommentar nebst Beobachtungen zur hellenistischen Vorgeschichte der Bibelhermeneutik." *Journal of Biblical Literature* 113.3 (Autumn, 1994): 527–529.

Keck, Leander. Introduction to *Romans*. Pages 2114–2116 in *The HarperCollins Study Bible*. Edited by Wayne Meeks. New York: Harper Collins, 1993.

Kelly, J. N. D. *Early Christian Creeds*. New York: David McKay Company, 1960.

Kessler, Edward. "Art Leading the Story: The *Aqedah* in Early Synagogue Art." Pages 73–81 in *From Dura to Sepphoris: Studies in Jewish Art and Society in Late Antiquity*. JRA Supplementary Series 40 (2000). Edited by Lee I. Levine and Ze'ev Weiss. Portsmouth, RI: Journal of Roman Archaeology, 2000.

Kessler, Edward. *Bound by the Bible: Jews, Christians and the Sacrifice of Isaac*. Cambridge: Cambridge University Press, 2004.

Kessler, Herbert L. "The Sepphoris Mosaic and Christian Art." Pages 65–71 in *From Dura to Sepphoris Studies in Jewish Art and Society in Late Antiquity*. Edited by Lee I. Levine and Ze'ev Weiss. JRA Supplementary Series 40 (2001). Portsmouth, RI: Journal of Roman Archaeology, 2000.

Kessler, Herbert L. "Vienna Genesis." Pages 458–459 in *Age of Spirituality*. Edited by Kurt Weitzmann. New York: The Metropolitan Museum of Art, in association with Princeton University Press, Princeton, NJ, 1979.

Khalidi, Tarif. *The Qur'an*. New York: Penguin Books, 2008.

Khalidi, Tarif. *The Muslim Jesus: Sayings and Stories in Islamic Literature*. Cambridge, MA: Harvard University Press, 2001.

Khan, Muhammad Muhsin. *Sahih al-Bukhari: The Translations of the Meanings of Sahih al-Bukhari Arabic-English*. 9 vols. Translated by Khan, Muhammad Muhsin. Al-Nabawiya: Dar Ahya Us-Sunnah, 1976.

Khan, Muhammad Muhsin. *Sahih al-Bukhari*. http://hadithcollection.com/sahihbukhari.

Khan, M. Muhsin. *Translation of Sahih Bukhari*. Chicago: Kazi Publications Inc, 1995.

Kinberg, Leah. "Dreams and Sleep." Pages 546–553 in EQ 1. Edited by Jane McAuliffe. Leiden: Brill, 2005.

Klar, Marianna O. *Interpreting al-Tha`labi's Tales of the Prophets: Temptation, Responsibility and Loss*. New York: Routledge, 2009.

Kogman-Appel, Katrin. "Bible Illustration and the Jewish Tradition." Pages 61–96 in *Imaging the Early Medieval Bible*. Edited by John W. Williams. University Park: Pennsylvania State University Press, 2002.

Koortbojian, Michael. *Myth, Meaning, and Memory on Roman Sarcophagi.* Berkeley: University of California Press, 1995.

Kraus, Samuel. *Das Leben Jesu nach jüdischen Quellen.* New York: Georg Olms Verlag: 1977.

Kugel, James. *In Potiphar's House.* Cambridge, MA: Harvard University Press, 1990.

Kugel, James. *Traditions of the Bible.* Cambridge, MA: Harvard University Press, 1998.

Lafontaine-Dosogne, Jacqueline. *Iconographie de L'Enfance de la Vierge dans l'Empire Byzantine et en Occident*, vol. I. Bussels: Palais des Académies, 1964.

Laible, Heinrich. "Jesus Christ in the Talmud." Pages 1–108 in *Jesus Christ in the Talmud, Midrash, Zohar, and the Liturgy of the Synagogue.* Edited by Gustav Dalman, translated by A. W. Steane. New York: Arno Press, 1973 edition.

Langmuir, Gavin. "Anti-Judaism as the Necessary Preparation for Anti-Semitism." *Viator* 2 (1971): 383–389.

Lawrence, Bruce. *The Qur'an: A Biography.* London: Atlantic Books, 2006.

Levenson, Jon D. "Enlisting the Biblical Abraham as Peace Broker." Page 11 in *The Wall Street Journal*, November 9, 2012.

Levenson, Jon D. *Inheriting Abraham: The Legacy of the Patriarch in Judaism, Christianity, and Islam.* Princeton, NJ: Princeton University Press, 2012.

Levenson, Jon D. *The Death and Resurrection of the Beloved Son: The Transformation of Child Sacrifice in Judaism and Christianity.* New Haven, CT: Yale University Press, 1993.

Levi, Peter. "The Podgoritza Cup." *The Heythrop Journal* 4.1 (1963): 54–60.

Levin, Michael. "Some Jewish Sources for the Vienna Genesis." *Art Bulletin* 54.3 (1972): 241–244.

Lichtheim, Miriam. *Ancient Egyptian Literature*, 3 vols. Berkeley: University of California, 1973–1980.

Lieu, Judith M. *Image and Reality—The Jews in the World of the Christians in the Second Century.* Edinburgh: T&T Clark, 1996.

Limberis, Vasiliki. *Divine Heiress: The Virgin Mary and the Creation of Christian Constantinople.* New York: Routledge, 1994.

Lings, Martin. *Muhammad.* Rochester, VT: Inner Traditions, 1983.

Livius, Thomas. *The Blessed Virgin in the Fathers of the First Six Centuries.* London: Burns & Oates, Ltd., 1893.

Llewelyn, S. R. *New Documents Illustrating Early Christianity*, vol. 9, A Review of the Greek Inscriptions and Papyri Published in 1986–87. Grand Rapids, MI: Eerdmans Publishing Company, 2002.

Lodahl, Michael. *Claiming Abraham. Reading the Bible and the Qur'an Side by Side.* Grand Rapids, MI: Brazos Press, 2010.

Louth, Andrew. *St. John of Damascus, Three Treatises on the Divine Images.* Crestwood, NY: St. Vladimir's Seminary Press, 2003.

Lowenthal, Eric. *The Joseph Narrative in Genesis: An Interpretation.* New York: Ktav Publishing House, 1973.

Lybarger, Loren. "Gender and Prophetic Authority in the Qur'anic Story of Maryam: A Literary Approach." *JR* 80.2 (2000): 240–270.

Madigan, Daniel A. *The Qur'an's Self-Image. Writing and Authority in Islam's Scripture.* Princeton, NJ: Princeton University Press, 2001.

Madigan, Daniel A. "Themes and Topics." Pages 79–95 in *CCQ*. Edited by Jane McAuliffe. Cambridge: Cambridge University Press, 2006.

Maguire, Eunice Dauterman, Maguire, Henry P., and Flowers, Maggie J. Duncan. *Art and Holy Powers in the Early Christian House*. Illinois Byzantine Studies II. Urbana: University of Illinois Press, 1989.

Maguire, Henry. "The Cycle of Images in the Church." Pages 121–151 in *Heaven on Earth: Art and the Church in Byzantium*. Edited by Linda Safran. University Park, PA: Pennsylvania State University Press, 1998.

Mandel, Paul. "Genesis Rabbah." Page 268 in *ODJR*. Edited by R. J. Zwi Werblowsky and Geoffrey Wigoder. New York: Oxford University Press, 1997.

Mango, Cyril, and Scott, Roger. *The Chronicle of Theophanes Confessor*. Oxford: Oxford University Press, 1997.

Mango, Cyril. "Constantinople as Theotokoupolis." Pages 17–26 in *Mother of God: Representations of the Virgin in Byzantine Art*. Edited by Maria Vassilaki. Milan: Skira Editori, 2000.

Marcus, Ralph, tr. and ed., *Philo, Questions and Answers on Genesis*. LCL, Philo series, supplement 1. Cambridge, MA: Harvard University Press, 1961.

Marshall, David. "Christianity in the Qur'an." Pages 3–26 in *Islamic Interpretations of Christianity*. Edited by Lloyd Ridgeon. Richmond, Surrey, UK: Curzon, 2001.

Marshall, David. "Zechariah." Pages 574–576 in EQ IV. Edited by Jane McAuliffe. Leiden: Brill, 2005.

Marx, Michael. "Glimpses of a Mariology in the Qur'an: From Hagiography to Theology via Religious-Political Debate." Pages 532–563 in *The Quran in Context*. Texts and Studies on the Qur'an. Edited by Angelica Neuwirth, Nicolai Sinai, and Michael Marx. Leiden: Brill, 2010.

Mathews, Edward G. *St Ephrem the Syrian: Selected Prose Works*. FOC 91. Edited by Kathleen McVey. Washington, DC: Catholic University of America Press, 1994.

McAuliffe, Jane. "An Introduction to Medieval Interpretation of the Qu'ran." Pages 311–319 in *With Reverence for the Word: Medieval Scriptural Exegesis in Judaism, Christianity, and Islam*. Edited by Jane Dammen McAuliffe, Barry D. Walfish, and Joseph W. Goering. New York: Oxford University Press, 2003.

McAuliffe, Jane. "Chosen of All Women: Mary and Fatima in Qur'anic Exegesis." *Islamochristiana* 7 (1982): 19–28.

McAuliffe, Jane. "Christians in the Qur'an and Tafsir." Pages 105–121 in *Muslim Perceptions of Other Religions Throughout History*. Edited by J. Waardenburg. New York: Oxford University Press, 1999.

McAuliffe, Jane. *Qur'anic Christians: An Analysis of Classical and Modern Exegesis*. New York: Cambridge University Press, 1991.

McAuliffe, Jane. "Qur'anic Hermeneutics: The Views of al-Tabari and Ibn Kathir." Pages 46–62 in *Approaches to the History of the Interpretation of the Qur'an*. Edited by A. Rippin. Oxford: Clarendon Press, 1988.

McAuliffe, Jane. "The Genre Boundaries of Qur'anic Commentary." Pages 445–461 in *With Reverence for the Word: Medieval Scriptural Exegesis in Judaism, Christianity, and Islam*. Edited by Jane Dammen McAuliffe, Barry D. Walfish, and Joseph W. Goering. New York: Oxford University Press, 2003.

McAuliffe, Jane Dammen, Walfish, Barry D., and Goering, Joseph W. *With Reverence for the Word: Medieval Scriptural Exegesis in Judaism, Christianity, and Islam*. New York: Oxford University Press, 2003.

McGrath, Alister. *The Christian Theology Reader*. Oxford: Wiley-Blackwell, 2011.

McGregor, Robin. *Ancient Bible Commentaries in English: Jonah: Commentary on by St. Jerome*. Edited by John Litteral, translated by Robert McGregor. Ashland, KY: Litteral's Christian Library Publications, 2014.

McHugh, Michael P. *Saint Ambrose: Seven Exegetical Works*. FOC 65. Washington, DC: Catholic University Press, 1971.

McVey, Kathleen. "Ephrem." Pages 427–428 in *Late Antiquity: A Guide to the Postclassical World*. Edited by G. W. Bowersock, Peter Brown, and Oleg Grabar. Cambridge, MA: The Belknap Press of Harvard University Press, 1999.

McVey, Kathleen E. *Ephrem the Syrian—Hymns*. Classics of Western Spirituality. New York: Paulist Press, 1989.

Meeks, Wayne. *The Writings of St. Paul*. New York: W. W. Norton, 1972.

Meier, John P. *Matthew*. Collegeville, MN: A Michael Glazier Book, The Liturgical Press, 1980.

Mellinkoff, Ruth. *The Mark of Cain*. Berkeley: University of California Press, 1981.

Merguerian, Gayane Karen, and Najmabadi, Afsaneh. "Zulaykha and Yusuf: Whose 'Best Story'?" *International Journal of Middle Eastern Studies* 29 (1997): 485–508.

Mergui, Maurice. *Le Midrash Rabba sur l'Exode*. Tome 1, Textes fondateurs de la tradition juive/Paris: Objectif transmission, 2007.

Milburn, Robert. *Early Christian Art and Architecture*. London: Wildwood House, 1989.

Miller, Patricia Cox. "Desert Monasticism and 'the Body from Nowhere'." *JECS* 2.2 (1994): 137–153.

Millgram, Abraham. *Jewish Worship*. Philadelphia: Jewish Publication Society, 1971.

Milstein, Rachel, Rührdanz, Karin, and Schmitz, Barbara. *Stories of the Prophets: Illustrated Manuscripts of Qisas al-Anbiya'*. Islamic Art and Architecture Series No. 8. Costa Mesa, CA: Mazda Publishers, 1999.

Mir, Mustansir. *Understanding the Islamic Scripture: A Study of Selected Passages from the Qur'an*. London: Pearson Longman, 2008.

Mojaddedi, Jawid. *Rumi: The Masnavi, Book Two*. Oxford: Oxford University Press, 2007.

Montefiore, Hugh. *A Commentary on the Epistle to the Hebrews*. New York: Harper & Row, 1964.

Murray, Robert. *Symbols of Church and Kingdom: A Study in Early Syriac Tradition*. New York: Cambridge University Press, 1975.

Musurillo, Herbert. *The Acts of the Christian Martyrs*. Oxford: Clarendon Press, 1972.

Narkiss, Bezalel. "Reconstruction of Some of the Original Quires of the Ashburnham Pentateuch." *Cahiers Archeologiques* 22 (1972): 19–38.

Narkiss, Bezalel. "Representational Art." Pages 366–371 in *Age of Spirituality*. Edited by Kurt Weitzmann. New York: The Metropolitan Museum of Art, 1979.

Necipoğlu, Gülru. "The Dome of the Rock as Palimpsest: `Abd al-Malik's Grand Narrative and Sultan Süleyman's Glosses." Pages 17–105 in *Muqarnas, Vol. 25. Frontiers of Islamic Art and Architecture: Essays in Celebration of Oleg Grabar's Eightieth Birthday*. Edited by Gülru Necipoğlu and Julia Bailey. Leiden: Brill, 2008.

Nelson, Robert S., and Collins, Kristen M. *Holy Image—Hallowed Ground: Icons from Sinai*. Los Angeles: Getty Publications, 2006.

Neusner, Jacob. *The Components of the Rabbinic Documents IX. Genesis Rabbah*. South Florida Academic Commentary Series, 92. Atlanta, GA: Scholars Press, 1997.

Neusner, Jacob. *Genesis Rabbah: The Judaic Commentary to the Book of Genesis, A New American Translation*, 3 volumes. Atlanta, GA: Scholars Press, 1985.

Neusner, Jacob, and Frerichs, Ernest S. *"To See Ourselves as Others See Us": Christians, Jews, "Others" in Late Antiquity*. Chico, CA: Scholars Press, 1985.

Neuwirth, Angelica, Sinai, Nicolai, and Marx, Michael. *The Quran in Context. Historical and Literary Investigations into the Qur'anic Milieu*. Texts and Studies on the Qur'an. Leiden: Brill, 2010.

Neuwirth, Angelica. "The House of Abraham and the House of Amram: Genealogy, Patriarchal Authority, and Exegetical Professionalism." Pages 499–531 in *The Qurun in Context*. Texts and Studies on the Qur'an. Edited by Angelica Neuwirth, Nicolai Sinai, and Michael Marx. Leiden: Brill, 2010.

Newby, Gordon D. *The Making of the Last Prophet: A Reconstruction of the Earliest Biography of Muhammad*. Columbia, SC: University of South Carolina Press, 1989.

Nicholson, Reynold. A. *The Mathnawi of Rumi Jalálu'ddín Rúmí*. 6 vols. Istanbul: Konya Metropolitan Municipality, 2004.

Nirenberg, David, *Anti-Judaism: The Western Tradition*. New York: W. W. Norton, 2013.

Okasha, Sarwat. *The Muslim Painter and the Divine. The Persian Impact on Islamic Religious Painting*. London: Park Lane Press, 1981.

Osborne, Grant R. *Revelation*. Grand Rapids, MI: Baker Academic, 2002.

Parsons, Sister Wilfrid. *Saint Augustine, Letters*, vol. 2 *(83–130)*. FOC 18. New York: Fathers of the Church, Inc., 1953.

Pelikan, Jaroslav. "Heroine of the Qur'an and the Black Madonna." Pages 67–80 in *Mary Through the Centuries: Her Place in the History of Culture*. New Haven, CT: Yale University Press, 1996.

Penna, Vasso. "The Mother of God on Coins and Lead Seals." Pages 209–217 in *Mother of God*. Edited by Maria Vassilaki. Milan: Skira Editori, 2000.

Pendlebury, David. *Yusuf and Zulaikha—An Allegorical Romance by Hakim Nuruddin Abdurrahman Jami*. London: Octagon Press, 1980.

Pentcheva, Bissera B. *Icons and Power: The Mother of God in Byzantium*. University Park, PA: Pennsylvania State University Press, 2006.

Pickthall, Muhammad M. *The Glorious Qur'an*. 3rd edition. Elmhurst, NY: Tahrike Tasile Qur'an, Inc.

Porton, Gary G. *Understanding Rabbinic Midrash*. Hoboken, NJ: Ktav Publishing Co., 1985.

Price, R. M. *Theodoret of Cyrrhus, A History of the Monks of Syria*. Kalamazoo, MI: Cistercian Publications, 1985.

Price R. M., and Binns, John. *Cyril of Scythopolis: The Lives of the Monks of Palestine*. Kalamazoo, MI: Cistercian Publications, 1991.

Pritchard, James B. "The Two Brothers." Page 23 in *Ancient Near Eastern Texts*. Edited by James B. Pritchard. Princeton, NJ: Princeton University Press, 1969.

Reinink, G. J., and Stolte, B. H. *The Reign of Heraclius (610–614)—Crisis and Confrontation*. Louvain: Peeters Publishers, 2002.

Renard, John. *Windows on the House of Islam: Muslim Sources on Spirituality and Religious Life*. Berkeley: University of California Press, 1998.

Reynolds, Gabriel S. *The Qur'an and Its Biblical Subtext*. New York: Routledge, 2010.

Richardson, Cyril C. *Early Christian Fathers*. New York: Macmillan, 1979.

Rippin, Andrew. *Muslims: Their Religious Beliefs and Practices*. New York: Routledge, 2005.

Robinson, Neal. *Discovering the Qur'an: A Contemporary Approach to a Veiled Text*. Washington, DC: Georgetown University Press, 2003.

Rodkinson, Michael L. *Babylonian Talmud, Book 3: Tracts Pesachim, Yomah and Hagiga*. New York: New Talmud Publishing Company, 1918.

Rosenthal, Franz. *"Sweeter Than Hope": Complaint and Hope in Medieval Islam*. Leiden: Brill, 1983.

Rosenthal, Franz. *The History of al-Tabari*, vol. I, *General Introduction and From the Creation to the Flood*. Bibliotheca Persica. Edited by Ehsan Yar Shater. Albany: State University of New York Press, 1989.

Russo, Jessica Dello. "The Monteverde Jewish Catacombs on the via Portuense." *Roma Subterranea Judaica* 4 (2010): 1–37. Publication of the International Catacomb Society.

Rutgers, L. V. *Subterranean Rome*. Leuven: Peeters, 2000.

Safran, Linda. *Heaven on Earth: Art and the Church in Byzantium*. University Park, PA: Pennsylvania State University Press, 1998.

Saleh, W. A. *The Formation of the Classical Tafsir Tradition: The Qur'an Commentary of al-Tha`labi (d. 427/1035)*. Texts and Studies on the Qur'an, vol. I. Leiden: Brill, 2004.

Sanders, E. P. *The Historical Figure of Jesus*. New York: Penguin Books, 1993.

Sanders, E. P. *Paul and Palestinian Judaism*. Philadelphia: Fortress Press, 1977.

Sands, Kristin Z. *Sufi Commentaries on the Qur'an in Classical Islam*. Routledge Studies in the Quran. New York: Routledge, 2006.

Sarna, Nahum. *The JPS Torah Commentary: Genesis*. Philadelphia: Jewish Publication Society, 1989.

Sarna, Nahum. *Understanding Genesis*. New York: Schocken Books, 1970.

Sasson, Jack M. *Jonah*. The Anchor Bible, vol. 24B. New York: Doubleday, 1990.

Schäfer, Peter, Meerson, Michael, and Deutsch, Yaacov. *Toledot Yeshu* ("The Life Story of Jesus") Revisited. Texts and Studies in Ancient Judaism 143. Tübingen: Mohr Sievack, 2001.

Schäfer, Peter. *Jesus in the Talmud*. Princeton, NJ: Princeton University Press, 2007.

Schäfer, Peter. *Mirror of His Beauty: Feminine Images of God from the Bible to the Early Kabbalah*. Princeton, NJ: Princeton University Press, 2004.

Schäfer, Peter. *The Talmud Yerushalmi and Graeco-Roman Culture* III, Texts and Studies in Ancient Judaism 93. Tübingen: Mohr Siebeck, 2002 and Princeton University Press, Princeton, NJ, 2002.

Schapiro, Meyer. "The Joseph Scenes on the Maximianus Throne in Ravenna." Pages 34–47 in *Late Antique, Early Christian and Medieval Art: Selected Papers*. Edited by Meyer Schapiro. New York: George Braziller, Inc., 1979.

Schiffman, Lawrence H. "The Recall of Rabbi Nehuniah ben Ha-Qanah from Ecstasy in the *Hekhalot Rabbati*." *Association for Jewish Studies Review* 1 (1976): 269–281.

Schimmel, Annemarie. *My Soul Is a Woman—The Feminine in Islam*. New York: Continuum, 1997.

Schimmel, Annemarie. *Mystical Dimensions of Islam*. Chapel Hill: University of North Carolina Press, 1975.

Schleifer, Alia. *Mary: The Blessed Virgin of Islam*. Louisville, KY: Fons Vitae, 1997.

Schmitz, Barbara. "A Royal Persian Prototype?" Pages 65–91 in *Stories of the Prophets*. Edited by Rachel Milstein, Karin Rührdanz, and Barbara Schmitz. Costa Mesa, CA: Mazda Publishers, 1999.

Schoedel, William R. *Ignatius of Antioch: A Commentary on the Letters of Ignatius of Antioch*. Hermeneia—A Critical and Historical Commentary on the Bible. Philadelphia: Fortress Press, 1985.

Schubert, K. "Die Miniaturen des Asburnham Pentateuch im Lichte der rabbinischen Tradition." *Kairos* 18 (1976): 191–212.

Schubert, K. "Jewish Traditions in Christian Painting Cycles: The Vienna Genesis and the Ashburnham Pentateuch." Pages 208–260 in *Jewish Historiography and Iconography in Early and Medieval Christianity*. Edited by Heinz Schreckenberg and Kurt Schubert. Minneapolis: Van Gorcum & Company BV/Fortress Press, 1992.

Schubert, Ursula. *Spätantikes Judentum und frühchristliche Kunst*. Studia Judaica Austriaca, vol. 2. Vienna: Herold, 1974.

Schwartz, Seth. *Imperialism and Jewish Society, 200 B.C.E to 640 C.E.* Princeton, NJ: Princeton University Press, 2001.

Schwarz, Michael. "The Letter of al-Hasan al-Basri." *Oriens* 20 (1967): 15–30.

Scourfield, J. H. D. *Consoling Heliodorus: A Commentary on Jerome Letter 60.* Oxford Classical Monographs. Oxford: Clarendon Press, 1993.

Segal, Alan F. *Rebecca's Children: Judaism and Christianity in the Roman World.* Cambridge, MA: Harvard University Press, 1986.

Sells, Michael. *Early Islamic Mysticism: Sufi, Qur'an, Mi'raj, Poetic and Theological Writings.* Classics of Western Spirituality 86. New York: Paulist Press, 1996.

Serfass, Abigail Wadsworth. *Inherent Ambiguity in the Book of Jonah: An Invitation to Ancient Readers.* M.T.S. thesis, Church Divinity School of the Pacific, 2008.

Shepherdson, Christine. *Anti-Judaism and Christian Orthodoxy: Ephrem's Hymns in Fourth-Century Syria.* North American Patristics Society. Patristic Monograph Series 20. Washington, DC: Catholic University of America Press, 2008.

Shinan, Avigdor. "Synagogues in the Land of Israel: The Literature of the Ancient Synagogue and Synagogue Archaeology." Pages 130–152 in *Sacred Realm: The Emergence of the Synagogue in the Ancient World.* Edited by Steven Fine. Oxford: Oxford University Press, 1996.

Shoemaker, Stephen J. *Ancient Traditions of the Virgin Mary's Dormition and Assumption.* Oxford Early Christian Studies. New York: Oxford University Press, 2002.

Siegert, Folker. *Drei hellenistisch-jüdische Predigten. Ps.-Philon, "Über Jona," "Über Simson" und "Über die Gottesbezeichnung "wohltätig verzehrendes Feuer."* Bd. 1: Übersetzung aus dem Armenischen und sprachliche Erläuterungen. *WUNT* 20. Tübingen: Mohr-Siebeck, 1980.

Simon, Marcel. *Verus Israel—A Study of the Relations Between Christians and Jews in the Roman Empire (AD 135–425).* Oxford: Oxford University Press, for the Littman Library, 1986.

Simon, Maurice, and Levertoff, Paul. *The Zohar*, vol. 4. New York: Soncino Press, 1984.

Simon, Uriel. *Jonah.* The JPS Bible Commentary. Philadelphia: Jewish Publication Society, 1999.

Simson, Otto G. von. *Sacred Fortress: Byzantine Art and Statecraft in Ravena.* Princeton, NJ: Princeton University Press, 1987.

Sirat, R-S., Berranger, Olivier de, Seddik, Youssef. *Juifs, chrétiens, musulmans: Lectures qui rassemblent, lectures qui séparent.* Paris: Bayard, 2007.

Sivan, Hagith. *Palestine in Late Antiquity.* Oxford: Oxford University Press, 2008.

Smith, Jane I., and Haddad, Yvonne Yazbeck. *The Islamic Understanding of Death and Resurrection.* New York: Oxford University Press, 2002.

Smith, Jane I., and Haddad, Yvonne Yazbeck. "The Virgin Mary in Islamic Tradition and Commentary." *The Muslim World* 79 (1989): 161–187.

Smith, Joseph P. *St. Irenaeus, Proof of the Apostolic Preaching.* ACW 16. New York: Newman Press, 1952.

Soucek, Priscilla. "An Illustrated Manuscript of al-Biruni's Chronology of Ancient Nations." Pages 103–168 in *The Scholar and Saint: Studies in Commemoration of Abu'l-Rayhan al-Biruni and Jalal al-Din al-Rumi.* Edited by Peter Chelkowski. New York: New York University Press, 1975.

Stemberger, Günter. *Introduction to the Talmud and Midrash.* Translated by Markus Bockmuehl. 2nd edition. Edinburgh: T&T Clark, 1996.

Stemberger, Günter. "The Deresah in Rabbinic Times." Pages 7–21 in *Preaching in Judaism and Christianity: Encounters and Developments from Biblical Times to*

Modernity. Edited by Alexander Deeg, Walter Homolka, and Heinz-Günther Schöttler. Berlin: Walter de Gruyter, 2008.

Stern, David, and Minsky, Mark Jay. *Rabbinic Fantasies: Imaginative Narratives from Classical Hebrew Literature.* Yale Judaica Series. New Haven: Yale University Press, 1998.

Stillman, Norman A. "The Story of Cain and Abel in the Qur'an and the Muslim Commentators: Some Observations." *Journal of Semitic Studies* 19 (1974): 231–239.

Stone, Michael E. *Jewish Writings of the Second Temple Period.* Minneapolis: Augsburg Fortress Press, 1984.

Storey, C. A. *Persian Literature.* London: Luzac & Company, 1970.

Stowasser, Barbara Freyer. *Women in the Qur'an, Traditions, and Interpretation.* New York: Oxford University Press, 1996.

Stryzgowzki, J. *Orient oder Rom: Beiträge zur Geschichte der Spätantiken und Frühchristlichen Kunst.* Leipzig: J. C. Hinrichs'sche Buchhandlung, 1901.

Swartz, Michael D. "Jewish Visionary Tradition in Rabbinic Literature." Pages 198–221 in *The Cambridge Companion to the Talmud and Rabbinic Literature.* Edited by C. E. Fonrobert and M. S. Jaffee. Cambridge: Cambridge, 2007.

Tabor, James D. *The Jesus Dynasty.* New York: Simon & Schuster, 2006.

Thackston, Wheeler. *Muhammad ibn ʾAbd Allah al-Kisaʾi, Tales of the Prophets (Qisas al-anbiya).* Chicago: Great Books of the Islamic World, Inc., 1997.

Theodoret, *Church History, Dialogues and Letters.* Translated by Jackson, Blomfield. NPNF (Second Series) 3. Grand Rapids, MI: Eerdmans, 1969.

Theoteknos, *An Encomium on the Assumption of the Holy Mother of God.* Pages 71–81 in *On the Dormition of Mary: Early Patristic Homilies.* Edited and translated by Brian E. Daley and S. J. Crestwood. New York: St. Vladimir's Seminary Press, 1997.

Thomas, David. *Early Muslim Polemic against Christianity: Abur ʾIsa al-Warraq's "Against the Incarnation."* Cambridge: Cambridge University Press, 2002.

Thompson, John L. *Writing the Wrongs: Women of the Old Testament among Biblical Commentators from Philo through the Reformation.* Oxford: Oxford University Press, 2001.

Totolli, Roberto. *Biblical Prophets in the Qur'an and Muslim Literature.* Curzon Studies in the Qur'an. Translated by Michael Robertson. Richmond, Surrey: Curzon Press: 2002.

Thurlkill, Mary. *Chosen Among Women: Mary and Fatima in Medieval Christianity and Shi'ite Islam.* South Bend, IN: University of Notre Dame Press, 2007.

Trible, Phyllis. *Rhetorical Criticism: Context, Method, and the Book of Jonah.* Philadelphia: Augsburg Fortress, 1994.

Tronzo, William. *The Via Latina Catacomb: Imitation and Discontinuity in Fourth-Century Roman Painting.* University Park, PA: Pennsylvania State University Press, 1986.

Van Voorst, Robert E. *Jesus Outside the New Testament.* Grand Rapids, MI: Eerdmans, 2000.

Verkerk, Dorothy Hoogland. "Moral Structure in the Ashburnham Pentateuch," 71–87, in *Image and Belief.* Edited by Colum Hourihane. Princeton, NJ: Princeton University Press, 1999.

Verkerk, Dorothy Hoogland. *Early Medieval Bible Illumination and the Ashburnham Pentateuch.* Cambridge: Cambridge University Press, 2004.

Vermes, Geza. "The Targumic Versions of Genesis 4:3–16." *The Annual of Leeds University Oriental Society,* Volume 3 (1961): 81–114.

Volbach, Wolfgang F. *Early Christian Art.* New York: Harry N. Abrams, Inc., 1961.

Volf, Miroslav. *Allah: A Christian Response*. New York: HarperOne, 2012.

Volf, Miroslav. *Do We Worship the Same God?: Jews, Christians, and Muslims in Dialogue*. Edited by Miroslav Volf. Grand Rapids, MI: Eerdmans, 2012.

Von Rad, Gerhard. *Genesis: A Commentary*. Philadelphia: Westminster Press, 1961.

Wallis, Ernest. "*Three Books of Testimonies Against the Jews*." Pages 507–557 in "The treatises of Cyprian. " Edited by Alexander Roberts and James Donaldson. ANF 5. Grand Rapids, MI: Eerdmans, 1965.

Walsh, P. G. *The Poems of St. Paulinus of Nola*. ACW 40. New York: Newman Press, 1975.

Ward, Benedicta. *The Sayings of the Fathers*. Revised ed. Kalamazoo, MI: Cistercian Publications, 1984.

Webb, Gisela. "Angel." Pages 84–92 in EQ I. Edited by Jane McAuliffe. Leiden: Brill, 2005.

Weiss, Ze'ev. "The Sepphoris Synagogue Mosaic and the Role of Talmudic Literature in Its Iconographical Study." Pages 15–30 in *From Dura to Sepphoris: Studies in Jewish Art and Society in Late Antiquity*. JRA Supplementary Series 40 (2001). Edited by Lee I. Levine and Ze'ev Weiss. Portsmouth, RI: Journal of Roman Archaeology, 2000.

Weiss, Ze'ev. *The Sepphoris Synagogue: Deciphering an Ancient Message through Its Archaeological and Socio-Historical Contexts*. Jerusalem: Israel Exploration Society, 2005.

Weiss, Ze'ev, and Netzer, Ehud. *Promise and Redemption: A Synagogue Mosaic from Sepphoris*. 2nd edition. Jerusalem: The Israel Museum, 1998.

Weiss, Ze'ev, and Netzer, Ehud. "Sepphoris in the Byzantine Period." Pages 81–89 in *Sepphoris in Galilee. Crosscurrents of Culture*. Edited by Rebecca Martin Nagy, Carol L. Meyers, Eric M. Meyers, and Ze'ev Weiss. Raleigh: North Carolina Museum of Art, 1966.

Weitzmann, Kurt. *Late Antique and Early Christian Book Illumination*. New York: George Braziller, 1997.

Wensink, A. J. "'Ashura." Page 705 in *The Encyclopedia of Islam, New Edition*, vol. 1. Edited by H.A.R. Gibb, et al. Leiden: Brill, 1960.

Westermann, Claus. *Genesis 37–50: A Commentary*. Tr. By John J. Scullion. Minneapolis: Augsberg Publishing House, 1982.

Wex, Michael. *Born to Kvetch: Yiddish Language and Culture in All its Moods*. New York: St. Martin's Press: 2005.

Wheeler, Brannon. *Prophets in the Quran*. New York: Continuum, 2002.

Whitby, Michael, and Whitby, Mary. *Chronicon Paschale 248–628 AD*. Translated Texts for Historians 7. Liverpool: Liverpool University Press, 1989.

Whitby, Mary. "The Biblical Past in John Malalas and the *Paschal Chronicle*." Pages 279–302 in *From Rome to Constantinople: Studies in Honour of Averil Cameron*. Edited by Hagit Amirav and Bas ter Haar Romeny. Leuven: Peeters, 2007.

Wigoder, Geoffrey. "Kapparot ('expiation')." Pages 440–441 in *NEJ*. Edited by Geoffrey Wigoder. Jerusalem: Jerusalem Publishing House, 2002.

Wigoder, Geoffrey. "Tashlikh." Pages 754–755 in *NEJ*. Edited by Geoffrey Wigoder. Jerusalem: Jerusalem Publishing House, 2002.

Wilken, Robert L. "The Restoration of Israel in Biblical Prophecy: Christian and Jewish Responses in the Early Byzantine Period." Pages 443–471 in *"To See Ourselves as Others See Us": Christians, Jews, "Others" in Late Antiquity*. Edited by Jacob Neusner and Ernest S. Frerichs. Chico, CA: Scholars Press, 1985.

Wilkinson, John. *Egeria's Travels*. Warminster: Aris & Phillips Ltd., 1999.

Wilkinson, John. *Jerusalem Pilgrims Before the Crusades*. Warminster: Aris & Phillips, 1977.

Williams, Frank. *The Panarion of Epiphanius of Salamis, Book 1 (Sects 1–46)*. Leiden: Brill, 1987.

Williams, Michael Allen. *Rethinking "Gnosticism"—An Argument for Dismantling a Dubious Category*. Princeton, NJ: Princeton University Press, 1996.

Wilson, A. J. "The Sign of the Prophet Jonah and Its Modern Confirmations." *Princeton Theological Review* 25.4 (1927): 630–642.

Wilson, Stephen G. *Related Strangers: Jews and Christians 7—170 C.E.* Minneapolis: Fortress Press, 1995.

Wineman, Ariyeh. *Mystic Tales from the Zohar*. Princeton, NJ: Princeton University Press, 1998.

Winston, David. *Logos and Mystical Theology in Philo of Alexandria*. Cincinnati: Hebrew Union College Press, 1985.

Winter, Timothy. "Mary in Islam." Pages 479–502 in *Mary: The Complete Resource*. Edited by Sarah Jane Boss. London: Continuum, 2007.

Winter, Timothy. "Pulchra Ut Luna: Some Reflections on the Marian Theme in Muslim-Catholic Dialogue." *Journal of Ecumenical Studies* 36.3 (1999): 439–469.

Wolfe, Michael. *One Thousand Roads to Mecca: Ten Centuries of Travelers Writing about the Muslim Pilgrimage*. New York: Grove Press, 1997.

Wolfson, H. A. *Philo: Foundations of Religious Philosophy in Judaism, Christianity, and Islam*, 2 vols. Cambridge, MA: Harvard University Press, 1962.

Wright, David H. Review of John Williams, ed., *Imaging the Early Medieval Bible*. *The Medieval Review*. 7.8 (2000–2007).

Wright, Elaine. *Islam: Faith-Art-Culture: Manuscripts of the Chester Beatty Library*. London: Scala Publishers Ltd., 2009.

Yaghmai, Habib. *Qesas-ol-Anbiya by Abu Ishaq Ibrahim ibn Mansur Nishaburi*. Persian Texts Series, 8. Tehran: B.T.N.K, 1961.

Yahalom, Joseph. "The Sepphoris Synagogue Mosaic and Its Story." Pages 83–92 *From Dura to Sepphoris: Studies in Jewish Art and Society in Late Antiquity. Journal of Roman Archaeology*. Supplementary Series 40. Edited by Lee I. Levine and Ze'ev Weiss. Portsmouth, RI: Journal of Roman Archaeology, 2000.

Yeroulanou, Aimilia. "The Mother of God in Jewelry." Pages 227–235 in *Mother of God*. Edited by Maria Vassilaki. Milan: Skira Editori, 2000.

Zaman, Muhammad Qasim. "Sin, Major and Minor." Pages 19–28 in EQ V. Edited by Jane McAuliffe. Leiden: Brill, 2006.

Zlotowitz, Meir, and Scherman, Nosson. *The Twelve Prophets: Jonah*. Brooklyn: Mesorah Publications, 1980.

ART CREDITS

Fig. 1.1   Cain and Abel. Ashburnham Pentateuch. Bibliothèque nationale de France, Paris.

Fig. 2.1   The offerings of Abel and Cain (with Adam and Eve). Via Latina Catacomb. Pontifical Commission for Sacred Archeology, Rome.

Fig. 2.2   The expulsion of Adam and Eve from Eden. Via Latina Catacomb. Pontifical Commission for Sacred Archeology, Rome.

Fig. 2.3   Passion sarcophagus. Vatican, Lateran Museum, Rome. © Genevra Kornbluth.

Fig. 2.4   Passion sarcophagus. Detail. © Genevra Kornbluth.

Fig. 2.5   Trinitarian God interacting with Abel and Cain. Detail. Museo Pio Christiano, the Vatican. © Vanni Archive/Art Resource, New York.

Fig. 3.1   Deceased Habil visits his parents. From a copy of Al-Biruni's the *Chronology of Ancient Nations*. Edinburgh University Library, Edinburgh. Special Collections Department.

Fig. 3.2   The raven teaches Qabil how to bury Habil's body. From a copy of a ms. of Nisaburi. Topkapi Palace Museum Archives, Istanbul.

Fig. 4.1   Abraham casting out Hagar and Ishmael. Rembrandt van Rijn, etching, 1637. The Metropolitan Museum of Art, New York. Art Resource, New York.

Fig. 4.2   Sarah depicted in a mosaic panel of the Sepphoris synagogue. Photo courtesy of Prof. Zeev Weiss, The Sepphoris Excavations, The Hebrew University of Jerusalem.

Fig. 4.3   Drawing courtesy of Prof. Zeev Weiss, The Sepphoris Excavations, The Hebrew University of Jerusalem.

Fig. 4.4   Abraham welcomes strangers, prepares to sacrifice Isaac. San Vitale, Ravenna. Art History Images.

Fig. 4.5   Abraham's attendants and the aqedah. Photo courtesy of Prof. Zeev Weiss, The Sepphoris Excavations, The Hebrew University of Jerusalem.

Fig. 4.6   Drawing courtesy of Zeev Weiss, The Sepphoris Excavations, The Hebrew University of Jerusalem.

Fig. 4.7   Aqedah scene from the Beth Alpha synagogue. Photo courtesy of the Center for Jewish Art at the Hebrew University of Jerusalem.

Fig. 5.1   Sarah makes her case to Abraham. Detail. Ashburnham Pentateuch. Bibliothéque nationale de France, Paris.

Fig. 5.2   Sarah's encounter with Abimelech. Detail. Ashburnham Pentateuch. Bibliothéque nationale de France, Paris.

Fig. 5.3   The hospitality of Abraham. Santa Maria Maggiore, Rome. Art History Images.

Fig. 5.4   The Annunciation. Sta. Maria Maggiore, Rome. Art History Images.

Fig. 6.1 The angel Jabril visits Ibrahim's family. From a copy of Nisaburi's *Qisas al-Anbiya*. The New York Public Library, Astor, Lenox, and Tilden Foundations.

Fig. 7.1   Marc Chagall, *Potiphar's Wife* (1958). The Haggerty Museum, Marquette University, Milwaukee, Wisconsin. [2014] Artists Rights Society, New York/ADAGP, Paris.

Fig. 7.2   Joseph runs from Potiphar's wife, and other scenes. The Vienna Genesis, Österreichische Nationalbibliothek Bildarchiv und Grafiksammlung, Vienna.

Fig. 7.3   Potiphar's wife displays Joseph's garment. The Vienna Genesis. Österreichische Nationalbibliothek Bildarchiv und Grafiksammlung, Vienna.

Fig. 7.4   Joseph in prison. The Vienna Genesis. Österreichische Nationalbibliothek Bildarchiv und Grafiksammlung, Vienna.

Fig. 8.1   Joseph scenes on a fragmentary sarcophagus. Detail. Vatican collection. Biblioteca Hertziana, Rome.

Fig. 8.2   Adoration of the Magi, sarcophagus. Detail. Vatican collection. Biblioteca Hertziana, Rome.

Fig. 8.3   Episcopal chair of Maximianus. Museo Arcivescovile, Ravenna. Art History Images.

Fig. 8.4   Joseph's sale to Potiphar and his punishment after accusations by Potiphar's wife. Maximian's cathedra, Ravenna. Photo: Alfredo Dagli Orti/Art Resource, New York.

Fig. 8.5   Joseph oversees provision of grain to his brothers. Maximian's cathedra, Ravenna. Photo: Alfredo Dagli Orti/Art Resource, New York.

Fig. 9.1   Yusuf appearing at Zulaykha's gathering of Egyptian ladies. From a Nisaburi *Qisas* ms. The New York Public Library, Astor, Lenox, and Tilden Foundations.

Fig. 9.2   Zulaykha reaches for the fleeing Yusuf. The National Library of Israel, Jerusalem.

Fig. 9.3   Yusuf grabs Zulaykha from behind. The National Library of Israel, Jerusalem.

Fig. 10.1   The opening column of *Jonah*, Xanten Bible, Germany, 1294. The New York Public Library, Astor, Lenox, and Tilden Foundations.

Fig. 10.2   Jonah and great fish. Durand collection, the Louvre. Art Resource, New York.

Fig. 10.3   Gem incised with cycle of Jonah scenes. Courtesy of Jeffrey Spier and Christian Schmidt.

Fig. 10.4   The Podgoritza Cup. The State Hermitage Museum, St. Petersburg. Photograph © State Hermitage Museum; photo by Svetlana Suetova, Konstantin Sinyavsky.

Fig. 11.1   Jonah and the whale, The Melk Missal. The Walters Art Museum, Baltimore.

Fig. 11.2   Marble sarcophagus with Jonah scenes. The Trustees of the British Museum, London.

Fig. 11.3   Marble sarcophagus with Jonah scenes. The Trustees of the British Museum, London.

Fig. 11.4   Sarcophagus depicting Selene and Endymion. Courtesy of the Getty Museum.

Fig. 11.5   Lamb reclining on cloud. Detail, Jonah sarcophagus. The Trustees of the British Museum, London.

Fig. 11.6   Jonah scenes on the Murano Diptych. Detail. Museo Nazionale, Ravenna. Art Resource, New York.

Fig. 11.7   Christ enthroned. Murano Diptych. Museo Nazionale, Ravenna. Art Research, New York.

Fig. 12.1   Yunus beneath the vine, and the fish. Illumination in Rashid al-Din's *Jami al-Tawarikh* (*Compendium of Chronicles*). Edinburgh University Library, Edinburgh.

Fig. 12.2   The angel Jibril flies toward Yunus. Painting from a Persian ms. of Rashid al-Din's *Compendium of Chronicles*. The Metropolitan Museum of Art, New York. Art Resource, New York.

Fig. 12.3   Jibril flies to Yunus, who emerges from the fish. From a Persian Falnama. Topkapi Palace Museum Archives, Istanbul. Topkapi Palace Museum Ms. H. 1702, f. 27b.

Fig. 12.4   Yunus emerging from the fish. An illumination in Juwayri's *Qisas al-anbiya*. Columbia University, Smith collection, MS X892.9 Q1/Q, New York.

Fig. 12.5   Dervishes. Painting from Kamal al-Din Husayn Gasurgahi's *Majalis al-ʿushshaq* ("*The Assemblies of the Lovers*"). The British Library Board, London.

Fig. 12.6   Yunus's ordeal. Illumination in a copy of Mirkhwand's *Rauzat-us-Safa' (Garden of Purity)*. The Israel Museum, Jerusalem.

Fig. 13.1   Ivory plaque depicting Adoration of the Magi, and nativity. The British Museum.

Fig. 13.2   The Nativity. Monastery of St. Catherine. Reproduced through the courtesy of the Michigan-Princeton-Alexandria Expedition to Mount Sinai.

Fig. 13.3   The Koimesis of Mary. The Metropolitan Museum of Art, New York. Art Resource, New York.

Fig. 14.1   Virgin Mary enthroned. The Metropolitan Museum of Art, New York.

Fig. 15.1   Maryam and the newborn ʿIsa. The Chester Beatty Library, Dublin.

Fig. 15.2   Maryam presents ʿIsa to her people. Topkapi Palace Museum Archives, Istanbul.

Fig. 15.3   The martyrdom of Zakariya. The New York Public Library, Astor, Lenox, and Tilden Foundations.

MODERN AUTHORS CITED

INDEX

SUBJECT INDEX

Illustrations are indicated by italic page numbers.

*Names of modern scholars and titles of primary sources are found in separate
indexes: Modern Authors Cited and Index of Primary Sources.*